THE EUROPEAN COMPANY LAW ACTION PLAN REVISITED

The European Company Law Action Plan Revisited

Reassessment of the 2003 priorities
of the European Commission

Edited by

Koen Geens
(Jan Ronse Institute K.U.Leuven)

and

Klaus J. Hopt
(Max Planck Institute for Comparative and International Private Law)

Leuven University Press

ISBN 978 90 5867 805 8
D / 2010 / 1869 / 3
NUR: 827

Design & cover: Friedemann BVBA

Table of Content

Preface

The harmonisation of company law has been constantly on the agenda of the European Union. With a view to protecting the interests of third parties and of participants in legal persons, Article 44(2)(g) of the Treaty of Rome prescribed the coordination of the guarantees required from such legal persons. Although third party and shareholder protection was certainly the main rationale underlying the Company Law Directives in the sixties, seventies and eighties of the last century, the Berkhouwer Report (1966) revealed two other objectives the founding fathers had in mind while conceiving the idea of company law harmonisation: first, promoting freedom of establishment and second, preventing the abuse of such freedom. In fact, it was most of all the latter, i.e. the fear of the Netherlands becoming the Delaware of Europe, that inspired Article 44(2)(g). At that time the Netherlands was the only one of the six original Member States where the real seat theory had, shortly after World War II, been replaced by the more Anglo-Saxon incorporation doctrine.

Ironically, at the beginning of the 21st Century, it was the privilege of the Danish and the Dutch States, both "incorporation" countries, to fail in successfully making the abuse argument before the European Court of Justice: in the famous Centros (1999) and Inspire Art (2003) cases, the legislation these states had designed to protect their (third party) citizens against companies which were first artificially incorporated in other countries before really being established in theirs was held to be contrary to the freedom of establishment.

The Court was apparently at ease with its reasoning since comparative law research had shown that the US model of state competition was more fruitful than harmful: Delaware was not so much the bottom state, but on the contrary one of the states with the most highly developed corporate law, and moreover with very experienced company law judges.

Since then, the European Commission seemed convinced that the Court itself needed no further guidelines for shaping its policy on the freedom of establishment of companies. Therefore the Commission felt ready to refocus its company law strategy. The Commission instructed the Winter Group to prepare a comprehensive report on the subject, and on the basis of that report wrote its Company Law Action Plan which was issued on 21 May 2003.

Reading the Plan, one cannot help having the impression that, from now on, European company law policy will focus on listed companies and will try to enhance their efficiency by way of state competition if possible, and by harmonisation only if need be. Even more than on substance – such as the "one share one vote" principle – the plan insists on methods to be used, both by the EU and the companies themselves: in the aftermath of the Lamfalussy process, the use of secondary legislation is strongly recommended, e.g. in the field of corporate governance; moreover, companies should be forced to focus on disclosure and new technologies in building up their relationship with the market and the shareholders. Immediately after the launching of the Plan, at the beginning of 2004, the IFRS rules became everyday practice. The "one share one vote" principle was given a lot of praise and attention, but after thorough study did not, for the time being, survive the impact assessment phase (December 2007).

With regard to non-listed companies, freedom of establishment should, according to the Plan, be additionally furthered by new types of European companies: after the Societas Europaea (Regulation 2001/2157) came the Societas Cooperativa Europaea (Regulation 2003/1435). Europe is still awaiting the light vehicle, the European Private Company. Other freedom of establishment priorities which were put forward in the Plan have meanwhile been realised, such as the Cross Border Merger Directive (2005/56) and Directive 2006/68 which modified the Capital Directive (1977/91). On the other hand, the Draft Directive on transfer of the registered office did not make it through the impact assessment at the end of 2007.

Six years have passed since the Company Law Action Plan was launched. Thus the appropriate time has come to revisit it, in the light of the most recent developments (including the Cartesio decision of the European Court of Justice of 16 December 2008). Such is precisely the purpose of this book. Five papers on the main topics of company law reform were prepared by the Jan Ronse Institute of KULeuven for a conference held on 9 January 2009, and it had the honour and the pleasure of the participation of many among the most reputed European Company Law experts. The papers, together with these experts' responses and the ensuing discussions, have been carefully edited and give an accurate overview of the latest state of affairs of European company law.

The editors warmly thank the authors, the respondents and the chairmen, as well as the colleagues and the staff members of the Jan Ronse Institute and Graham Buik who carefully proofread this book.

Koen Geens
(Jan Ronse Institute K.U.Leuven)

Klaus J. Hopt
(Hamburg Max Planck Institute)

The European Company Law Action Plan Revisited: An Introduction

Klaus J. Hopt[1]

"The European Company Law Action Plan 2003 Revisited" is an excellent topic for celebrating the 20th anniversary of the Jan Ronse Institute at the Catholic University of Leuven. The Institute was founded in 1988 by the late Professor Jan Ronse, a highly renowned authority on Belgian and Dutch company law, with the goal of undertaking education and research in the field of company, association, and financial law. In doing so, Professor Ronse was a pioneer and a visionary.[2] We must remember that in the early 1980s the slogan of "Eurosclerosis" was circulating, the Delors Commission with its White Book on the Completion of the Internal Market of 1985 was far from completing its turnaround, and on 20 September 1988, Margaret Thatcher gave her widely noted speech in Bruges declaring Europe to be a mere "family of nations." At that time European company law was in its infancy, and it did not seem to be a promising child. But Professor Ronse's vision came true, and the Ronse Institute accompanied this growth with its activities. The cumulative list of publications from the company law group at KULeuven and its Ronse Institute is truly impressive.[3] The title of one of the last publications by Professor Koen Geens, our host today, asks "Quo vadis ius societatum?"[4]

The topic of this conference has much in common with what has just been recalled. On 4 July 2001, the unheard of happened: the European Parliament voted down the draft Thirteenth Directive by 273 to 273 votes, thereby provoking an institutional crisis. It was Commissioner Bolkestein who pointed

---

1 Professor of Law and former Director of the Max Planck Institute for Comparative and International Private Law in Hamburg, member of the High Level Group of Company Law Experts of the European Commission. This introduction is based on the introductory speech delivered at the conference on "The European Company Law Action Plan 2003 Revisited" on 9 January 2009 in Leuven on the occasion of the 20th anniversary of the Jan Ronse Institute. The introductory character of the speech has been maintained, and references to the contributions made to this conference and reprinted in an updated version in this book have been added, as well as some footnotes for further reading.

2 Cf. *Gebruykt dese mynen arbeit tot uwen besten - Miscellanea Jan Ronse*, Biblo, Kalmthout, 2009, 670 pp. and the academic session commemorating Professor JAN RONSE (1921-1988) / Academische zitting in herinnering aan Professor Jan Ronse (1921-1988), chair: WALTER VAN GERVEN, lectures by JAAP WINTER on "Moving forward EU Corporate Governance and Company Law" / "Voortgang maken met Corporate Governance en het Vennootschapsrecht in Europa" and by JO VANDEURZEN on "The message of Professor Jan Ronse for the lawyers of tomorrow" / "De boodschap van Professor Jan Ronse voor de juristen van morgen", at KULeuven on 9 January 2009. Cf. also J. WINTER, "Jus Audacibus. The future of EU company law", in M. Tison/H. de Wulf/C. van der Elst/R. Steennot, eds., *Perspectives in Company Law and Financial Regulation. Essays in Honour of Eddy Wymeersch*, Cambridge (Cambridge University Press) 2009, p. 43.

3 www.law.kuleuven.be/jri

4 K. GEENS, "200 jaar vennootschapsrecht in perspectief: quo vadis ius societatum?", *Tijdschrift voor Privaatrecht*, 2007, 73.

the way ahead by convening the High Level Group of Company Law Experts as his first step towards the Company Law Action Plan 2003.[5] I shall resist the temptation to dwell on the history, content, and aftermath of the Action Plan,[6] though I myself and other friends who are present today were members of the High Level Group. Instead, I want to approach the key question of today: What are the chances for the Action Plan to be as successful in the long run as the Ronse Institute has been within its sphere of action? This is by no means certain. It is true that the two Group reports on the Takeover Directive and the Action Plan received unusually wide attention throughout the Union and beyond. The first stage with the short-term actions has been completed, with the notable exception of the Fourteenth Directive on cross-border transfer of seat. But the medium-term stage has been halted by Commissioner McCreevy, and the only long-term action of the plan, the possible introduction into the Second Directive of an alternative regime, has been called off. It is a rough time, and not only for European company law. While the Commission puts on the brakes, the European Parliament wants to go ahead. The mood in the Member States tends towards subsidiarity instead of thinking federally; within a number of Member States, national egoism is even more popular than ever and there is a great wave of protectionism. On top of this, the financial markets crisis marks a historic division between the pre-subprime and post-subprime eras.

In view of all this, the question posed by Koen Geens for this conference – "Quo vadis ius societatum?" – is more than just academic; it concerns fundamental issues of European integration. How to tackle this? Let me try to prepare the ground by considering five reform areas of the program, and some perspectives for reform beyond the financial markets crisis.

---

5 A Modern Regulatory Framework for Company Law in Europe, Report of the High Level Group of Company Law Experts, European Commission, Brussels, 4 November 2002, 161 p., reprinted in: G. FERRARINI/K.J. HOPT/J. WINTER/E. WYMEERSCH, eds., *Reforming Company and Takeover Law in Europe,* Oxford (Oxford University Press) 2004, Annex 3, pp. 925-1086. See also the related Report of the High Level Group on Issues Related to Takeover Bids, European Commission, Brussels, 10 January 2002, 96 p., idem at Annex 2, pp. 825-924. Cf. K.J. HOPT, "Modern Company and Capital Market Problems: Improving European Corporate Governance After Enron", in: *Journal of Corporate Law Studies* 3 (2003) 221-268, available also at ssrn, and K.J. HOPT/ E. WYMEERSCH, eds., "Company Law and Corporate Governance in Europe – Interim Report and Reflections on the Ongoing Reforms in the European Union and in Selected Member States – ", *RabelsZ* 69 (2005) issue 4, pp. 611-795. Members of the High Level Group have written a further report for the Commission: see "European Corporate Governance in company law and codes, Report of the High Level Group of Company Law Experts," *Rivista delle società* 2005, 534-587.

6 Communication from the Commission to the Council and the European Parliament, Modernising Company Law and Enhancing Corporate Governance in the European Union – A Plan to Move Forward, Brussels, 21.5.2003, COM (2003) 284 final. As to this Action Plan, see the contributions in FERRARINI et al. (note 5) and K.J. HOPT, "European Company Law and Corporate Governance: Where Does the Action Plan of the European Commission Lead?" in: K.J. Hopt/E. Wymeersch/ H. Kanda/H. Baum, eds., *Corporate Governance in Context – Corporations, States, and Markets in Europe, Japan, and the US –,* Oxford (Oxford University Press) 2005, p. 119, available also at ssrn.

Stock-taking

As to stock-taking I can be very brief, since the various contributions give an excellent basis. The three more general questions regarding European company law are the following: What has been achieved? Where have we failed? And why are we where we are with European company law and not further?

As to the first question, some believe that European company law is trivial. I think that this is a superficial observation. Of course, we all know that there are many shortcomings in what we have, and major areas of company law are not harmonized at all as the fate of the draft Fifth Directive and the pre-draft of the Ninth Directive illustrate. On the other hand, the sheer number of directives and ECJ cases dealing with company law is already impressive.[7] So are some of the changes brought about by them – without taking a stand on whether the decisions were right or wrong, or whether the changes they bring are good or bad.[8] Just have a look at the Accounting and Auditing Directives. In some countries, including my own, they have changed national law and practice profoundly. Or take the Statute for a European Company. One may discuss how important this new legal form is for practice, but in such prominent cases as the German *Allianz* or the *Porsche Corporation*, it was very important indeed. As to the relevance of the ECJ cases, one cannot even argue. *Centros* and its successor decisions have profoundly changed the European company law landscape and have launched a whole new era of competition among company law legislators throughout the Union. The success of the British private limited company on the Continent and the German limited liability company law reform by the so-called MoMiG of October 2008 are just two examples.

This is not to say that there are not many loopholes, and the Takeover Directive gives examples of the many different types. Take the option and reciprocity regime of Art. 12 of the Directive, or the varieties of transformation and even straightforward evasions, as described in a Commission staff report of February 2007.[9] There is a strong reluctance among Member States to lift takeover barriers, a popular fear of globalization, and a general trend towards political protectionism.[10] Germany is unfortunately no exception. But on the other side, one should look carefully at each single case. Options may also have a positive effect,[11] in particular if they are not just given to the Member State,

[7] See K.J. HOPT/E. WYMEERSCH, eds., *European Company and Financial Law, Texts and Leading Cases,* 4th ed., Oxford (Oxford University Press) 2007.

[8] Cf. S. GRUNDMANN, *European Company Law,* Antwerp/Oxford (Intersentia) 2007; as to the Member State company laws, cf. M. ANDENAS/F. WOOLDRIDGE, *European Comparative Company Law,* Cambridge (Cambridge University Press) 2009.

[9] Report on the implementation of the Directive on Takeover Bids, Commission Staff Working Document, Brussels, 21.02.2007, SEC(2007) 268.

[10] K.J. HOPT, "Obstacles to corporate restructuring: observations from a European and German perspective" in: *Essays in Honour of Eddy Wymeersch, supra* note 2, p. 373.

[11] G. HERTIG/J. A. McCAHERY, "A Legal Options Approach to EC Company Law", in G. Ferrarini/E. Wymeersch, eds., *Investor Protection in Europe,* Oxford (Oxford University Press), 2006, p. 119;

as has been the case traditionally, but to the market participants themselves as in Art. 12 para. 2, precited. The same could be pointed out for reciprocity. It is true that it departs from the general anti-frustration principle, but it may also facilitate the decision of companies to opt in to the regime of Art. 9 and 11.

Why are we where we are and not further with European company law? The answer is politics and lies primarily in the European Council and the Member States. While the European Commission and particularly the Court have moved European company law forward considerably, the Member States have slowed down the process in many instances, sometimes engaging in real horse trading as with the Takeover Directive. But after all, as Bismarck said, politics is the art of the possible. When seen in this perspective, the stock of European company law is not so bad at all.

Reform problems

The reform problems that the Action Plan has identified and that are in the public eye are many, too many for a one-day conference. But the most critical of these reform problems will be dealt with in the workshops this morning and this afternoon. Therefore I can confine myself to some words on each of them from a European and comparative law perspective. These are, of course, personal observations and I certainly do not purport to preempt in any way the presentation of the reports and the workshop discussions. But one or the other question might be taken up in the workshops and might even be brought back this afternoon into the panel discussion with possible answers and recommendations for action.

1. Capital[12]

One of the most controversial problems in today's European company law debate is legal capital. When we discussed it in the High Level Group, we were influenced by the common view of economists on legal capital and the experiences of jurisdictions like the US under the Revised Model Business Corporation Act 1984, New Zealand, and with the private limited company also the UK.[13] Other schemes of creditor protection had proven to work well there, in particular a solvency test bolstered with a certificate checked by an auditor like in New Zealand and by serious liability rules. We were well

cf. also S. B. BARTMAN, "The Impact of Optional EU Law Making on National Company Law", *European Company Law* 5 (2008) 271-276 and G. BACHMANN, "Optionsmodelle im Privatrecht", *Juristen-Zeitung* 2008, 11.

[12] Part 1 of this book; see the report by J. M. NELISSEN GRADE/M. WAUTERS, *infra* p. 25, the response by J. RICKFORD, *infra* p. 62, the discussion, *infra* p. 70, and the summary, *infra* p. 61.

[13] Cf. the comparative work by P. MARX, *Der Solvenztest als Alternative zur Kapitalerhaltung in der Aktiengesellschaft*, Baden-Baden (Nomos) 2006.

aware that deregulating the Second Directive with its mandatory legal capital protection would not be welcomed by all Member States. We therefore proposed a very cautious way forward. The European Commission followed this careful approach in its Action Plan and committed itself only to launching a feasibility study.[14] But the inclusion of long-term action on capital maintenance, i.e., the possible introduction into the Second Directive of an alternative regime (depending on the outcome of the feasibility study), showed sympathy with the proposal.

What we underestimated was the fierce resistance to change in some Member States, in particular Germany. The strong commitment to reform by practice and academia in some other countries like the UK was less surprising. In Germany, legal capital has been a venerable creditor protection device for both the stock corporation and the limited liability company since the early days of German corporate law, and ever since it has been refined by a great number of court decisions and voluminous legal commentary work. The resistance did not so much come from the legislators, but from an alliance of academics and judges as well as from legal practitioners in general, who were accustomed to what they had always had. The reaction proved how strong path dependencies can be, in particular if certain rules have been embedded in extensive case law and mountains of doctrine.

The battle lines of today are marked out by the two eminent reports in the UK and in Germany, and two persons and friends: Jonathan Rickford, who has an intimate knowledge of the practices in the City and Marcus Lutter, who many years ago wrote his professor thesis on comparative legal capital in the European Community.[15] My task here is not to take sides in the dispute, though as a member of the High Level Group with its unanimous recommendation to the Commission I have been singled out in Germany as a dangerous modernist on this issue. The only point I would like to make is one that seems to me to be important well beyond the legal capital discussion. It concerns the approach European company law should take if such strong path dependencies exist. In the legal capital discussion, there are good points on both sides; in particular, much depends on empirical data that we do not yet have. But if this is so, why should all Member States be forced to use the same legal capital standard? If there is reasonable disagreement on the pros and cons, why should a country not be allowed to have its own way and to experiment with it? The argument that the European landscape would become too complicated does not hold. With sufficient disclosure, the market participants would certainly be able to distinguish and to value the presence or absence of legal capital for what it means for them. Legal homogeneity within the Common Market is not an aim in itself. What counts is a well-functioning internal market. And we see that it functions: A number of Member States including Germany have reacted to the

[14] As to this study made by KPMG see NELISSEN GRADE/WAUTERS, *infra* p. 30 < no. 6 >.
[15] NELISSEN GRADE/WAUTERS, *infra* p. 40 et seq. < nos. 21, 22 >.

market pressures from abroad and have introduced a lighter form of limited liability company, as in Germany with the MoMiG statute of October 2008.

The legislative developments related to legal capital problems prove still another point that is important to our discussion, though it may lead beyond: company law is closely linked to other sectors of the law. European company law should not be seen and reformed in isolation. This is well known for the relationship between company law and capital market law[16], but it is no less true for company law and insolvency law. The German MoMiG statute proves the point. The long-standing company law rules on shareholders' loans to the company have been replaced by rules on voidability in insolvency, and have been moved from the German GmbH statute to the Insolvency Statute. Of course, one reason for this might also have been the hope to escape the consequences of the company case law of the European Court of Justice, a hope which, however, might very well prove to be fallacious. What is really needed is a certain degree of European harmonization of insolvency law. This harmonization should include *inter alia* directors' liability in the proximity of insolvency[17] and, as the financial crisis[18] has shown, a better system for early rescue of failing companies. After all, company law is not only about the birth and the growth of the company, but also about its decline and rescue.

2. Corporate governance[19]

As many of you know, corporate governance is one of my favorite research fields, but this is exactly why I shall be very brief here. Corporate governance comprises internal and external mechanisms like takeovers. The building blocks of a good corporate governance system are the board, labor (in particular if there is codetermination in the board), banks and creditors, independent auditing and of course the markets, primarily the stock market and the market for corporate control.[20] These building blocks can be found in all industrialized societies, even though in very different path-dependent combinations and shapes. The board is certainly a key issue,[21] but so are the very different shareholder structures[22] in the United States and the United Kingdom on the one side and in continental

---

16 Cf. N. MOLONEY, *EC Securities Regulation,* 2nd ed., Oxford (Oxford University Press) 2008.

17 See NELISSEN GRADE/WAUTERS, *infra* p. 49, 55 < nos. 34, 41 >.

18 See *infra* p. 22-23.

19 Part II of this book; see the report by H. LAGA/F. PARREIN, *infra* p. 79, the response by E. WYMEERSCH, *infra* p. 126, the discussion, *infra* p. 129, and the summary, *infra* p. 125.

20 Cf. K.J. HOPT, "Die internationalen und europarechtlichen Rahmenbedingungen der Corporate Governance", in: P. Hommelhoff/K. J. Hopt/A. v. Werder, eds., *Handbuch Corporate Governance, Leitung und Überwachung börsennotierter Unternehmen in der Rechts- und Wirtschaftspraxis,* Stuttgart (Schäffer-Poeschel) 2nd ed. 2009, p. 39. See also most recently C. B. BÜHLER, *Regulierung im Bereich der Corporate Governance,* Zurich/St. Gallen (Dike) 2009.

21 LAGA/PARREIN, *infra* p. 101 et seq. < nos. 18 et seq. >.

22 GEENS/CLOTTENS, *infra* p. 149, et seq. < nos. 6 et seq. > and LAGA/PARREIN, *infra* p. 84 et seq. < no. 4 >. See also K.J. HOPT, "American Corporate Governance Indices as Seen from a European Perspective", UNIVERSITY OF PENNSYLVANIA LAW REVIEW PENNUMBRA 158 (2009) 27.

Europe on the other. As far as regulatory measures are concerned, the most prominent is certainly mandatory disclosure which under the influence of American law[23] has come to Europe and is now at the center of European company law. More recently the corporate governance discussion has reached out to the non-listed companies[24] and even to the nonprofit sector[25]. Yet all this is a wide field, not only for lawyers and economists, but also for other historical and social science disciplines.[26] At this stage one could be tempted to say a word about the notorious La Porta debate[27], but I shall refrain. Let me just say that I am convinced that good corporate governance is a major asset for the companies in our countries and in the European Union, both as it relates to competition with each other and with the multinational companies and foreign states.[28] The crux and the intellectual challenge of corporate governance is finding the right mix of instruments, determining whether and to what degree mandatory or fall-back law is needed and, if it is needed, what the role of the European Union should be. As with the other topics, I distrust the easy answers here, i.e., letting everything be ordered by the market or by self-regulation or by requiring more state action and stringent national and European legal rules. But I am well aware that middle solutions are much more difficult than the extremes. What we need are European framework rules. But what they should look like is the Hamletesque question for our discussions. This is even more true today under the shadow of the financial crisis.[29]

3. One share/one vote[30]

Here again we have a battle of creeds. The Action Plan placed the one share/ one vote issue or, as it is commonly called, "1S1V", under the medium-term action concerning corporate governance and announced an "examination of the consequences of an approach aimed at achieving a full shareholder democracy

[23] LAGA/PARREIN, *infra* p. 86 et seq., 118 et seq. < nos. 5, 31 >; J. VON HEIN, *Die Rezeption US-amerikanischen Gesellschaftsrechts in Deutschland,* Tübingen (Mohr Siebeck) 2008; K.J. HOPT, "Company Law Modernization: Transatlantic Perspectives", *Rivista delle società* 51 (2006) 906.

[24] J. A. MCCAHERY/E. P. M. VERMEULEN, eds., *Corporate Governance of Non-Listed Companies,* Oxford (Oxford University Press) 2008.

[25] K.J. HOPT/T. VON HIPPEL, eds., *Comparative Corporate Governance of Non-Profit Organizations,* Cambridge (Cambridge University Press) 2010.

[26] Cf. e.g. P. FRENTROP, *History of Corporate Governance 1602-2002,* Amsterdam (Deminor) 2002; C. J. MILHAUPT/K. PISTOR, *Law & Capitalism,* Chicago/London (The University of Chicago Press) 2008.

[27] Cf. e.g. R. LA PORTA/F. LOPEZ-DE-SILANES/A. SHLEIFER, "The Economic Consequences of Legal Origins", JOURNAL OF ECONOMIC LITERATURE 46 (2008) 285; M. J. ROE/J. I. SIEGEL, "Finance and Politics: A Review Essay Based on Kenneth Dam's Analysis of Legal Traditions in *The Law-Growth Nexus*", JOURNAL OF ECONOMIC LITERATURE 47 (2009) 781.

[28] Cf. also the mixed evidence found by S. BHAGAT/B. BOLTON, "Corporate Governance and Firm Performance", *Journal of Corporate Finance* 14 (2008) 257.

[29] See *infra* p. 22 et seq. and EDDY WYMEERSCH in his response, *infra* p. 126: "boards have been utterly ineffective".

[30] Part III of this book, see the report by K. GEENS/C. CLOTTENS, *infra* p. 145, the response by J. M. GARRIDO, *infra* p. 192, the discussion, *infra* p. 197, and the summary, *infra* p. 191.

(one share/one vote), at least for listed companies." The High Level Group dealt with the issue in its first report on takeover bids of 10 January 2002. It pleaded for a level playing field for takeover bids, proposed the new breakthrough rule, and stated as the two guiding principles shareholder decision making and proportionality between risk bearing and control. The Group was aware that the logic of these two principles reaches well into general company law. But it shied away from making proposals beyond takeover regulation. This was not only because of our limited mandate as to the first report, but also and more so because we knew that going all the way would be a major operation, fundamentally affecting the ways listed companies in many parts of the Union are controlled, financed, and operated.

We were all the more surprised that Commissioner McCreevy named this issue as the top company law priority on his agenda. He underestimated the fierce political resistance from interest groups, but also the vast economic varieties of control-enhancing measures in the various Member States and their economic pros and cons as described in the two reports by ISS Europe, the ECGI, and Shearman & Sterling.[31] In a 180-degree turn, the Commissioner decided to refrain from any action in this context, even concerning more transparency. In my opinion this may be a political answer for the outgoing Commission, but it cannot be the long-term answer. In view of the many open questions found by the two studies, the European Corporate Governance Forum Working Group on Proportionality of June 2007[32], to which several of the High Level Group members belonged, showed a way to approach the problem step by step, by starting with more disclosure. In the view of the Group, full board entrenchment is just unacceptable from a corporate governance perspective. But so is the freedom of the controlling shareholder to reap personal advantages from the company to the detriment of his fellow shareholders. Our Group has been well aware of the pros and cons of the one share/one vote rule as well as of the less far-reaching rules on the mandatory bid and the breakthrough.[33] But in the end we think that in the interest of the internal market things cannot stay as they are. Without denying a certain convergence, I personally doubt that in the long run continental Europe will gradually converge towards the UK model.[34] Unlike in the UK, industry is still important on the Continent and institutional

[31] See GEENS/CLOTTENS, *infra* p. 147 et seq. < no. 3 >. Two of the most recent contributions are by R. ADAMS/D. FERREIRA, "One Share – One Vote: The Empirical Evidence", *Review of Finance* 12 (2008) 51-91, and M. BURKART/S. LEE, "One Share – One Vote: The Theory", *Review of Finance* 12 (2008) 1.

[32] For more details on the report, see K.J. HOPT in *Essays in Honour of Eddy Wymeersch, supra* note 2, at 392 et seq.

[33] See the excellent and exhaustive treatment by GEENS/CLOTTENS, *infra* p. 147 et seq., 149 et seq. < nos. 3 et seq., 6 et seq. >. See also the response by J. M. GARRIDO, *infra* p. 192. Cf. more generally P. DAVIES/K.J. HOPT, "Control Transactions" in: R. Kraakman/J. Armour/P. Davies/L. Enriques/H. Hansmann/G. Hertig/K.J. Hopt/H. Kanda/E. Rock, The Anatomy of Corporate Law, A Comparative and Functional Approach, 2nd ed., Oxford (Oxford University Press) 2009, p. 225.

[34] But see GEENS/CLOTTENS, *infra* p. 184 < no. 50 >.

investors are not playing the same role,[35] *inter alia* due to different old-age provision systems. But I do hope that the incoming European Commission and the new Commissioner in charge will be less indolent than the old one or, if not, that the European Court of Justice will continue to play its role as a promoter of Europe and its internal market.[36] Of course and as always, the problem with the one share/one vote rule is where to draw the right balance between fairness and efficiency.

4. Financial reporting[37]

Here we are in the middle of a revolution. I am not just talking about the numerous technical details of financial reporting, nor about the timely and heated fair value debate. There are more fundamental questions to be asked and decisions to be made: How do we Europeans with our specific legal tradition deal with the mass of materials embodied in the IAS and the IFRS? At least on the Continent, we are used to general principles and bodies of legal rules that are kept within reasonable limits. Is the difference between listed companies and non-listed companies the only right divide for financial reporting, or are size and economic significance more important criteria? How do we avoid overly burdensome requirements for SMEs without sacrificing adequate disclosure to the creditors and the market?[38] What should be done with consolidated accounts, and how shall we reconcile financial reporting with fiscal reporting? The IAS/IFRS are privately set bodies of rules. In Germany, some constitutionalists have taken the view that the legislator cannot blindly accept such rules and impose them as mandatory rules. So did the EU when establishing the endorsement requirement. But is the EU endorsement process a sufficient guarantee in view of the mass of highly technical standards,[39] or does it just amount to a sampling of major politically or economically important issues? In a long-range perspective, the need for convergence between IFRS and US GAAP is irrefutable, and indeed some progress has already been made in this respect. But will this go on under the new US administration,[40] and are we possibly sacrificing too many of our own principles? Last but not least: What will be the lasting impact of the financial markets crisis on financial reporting?[41] Mitigating the procyclical effects of financial reporting is of course an important

---

35 Institutional investors are much more important in the UK than even in the US.

36 I agree with GEENS/CLOTTENS, *infra* p. 184 < no. 50 > that the role of the court is inherently a limited one.

37 Part IV of this book; see the report by K. VAN HULLE/F. HELLEMANS, *infra* p. 209, the response by H. BECKMAN /P. VAN DER ZANDEN, *infra* p. 272, the discussion, *infra* p. 278, and the abstract, *infra* p. 271.

38 VAN HULLE/HELLEMANS, *infra* p. 255 et seq. < nos. 54 et seq. >.

39 See the frightfully long lists in VAN HULLE/HELLEMANS, *infra* p. 228 et seq. < no. 21 >.

40 After long negotiations, foreign companies in the US have been allowed to use IFRS for their financial reports, but the process of opening this option to US companies has come to a halt. How flexible the new SEC will be is still open to speculation.

41 VAN HULLE/HELLEMANS, *infra* p. 262 et seq., 266 < nos. 64 et seq., 70 >.

problem, but hidden reserves as in the old days in Germany and other countries are not the answer and financial reporting was only one of many issues which have come up in the financial crisis and need reform.

5. Corporate mobility[42]

Corporate mobility is the very essence of the internal market. We should do everything to promote it for the sake of entrepreneurial freedom as well as for the healthy effects of competition. Much has been achieved already by the European legislators and the European Court of Justice. But there are many scenarios not yet dealt with by the Commission and the Court.[43] Much still needs to be done.

As far as the Commission is concerned, the about-face of Commissioner McCreevy dropping the plan for a Fourteenth Directive on cross-border transfer of seat is deplorable, and it has rightly been criticized by the European Parliament and by practitioners and academics in the Member States. I am aware of the difficulties created by German labor codetermination and other obstacles. But in the end, similar problems have been mastered. Examples are the Statute for a European Company, the Tenth Directive on cross-border mergers, and the Takeover Directive. We can only hope that the new Commission will reassess the problem.[44]

As to the ECJ, one has to acknowledge that the Court has handed down many courageous decisions. But will the Court be courageous enough to continue this line of judgments? Is *Cartesio* the last word?[45] At one point the Court says, "(a)s community law now stands," and adds that the Member State of incorporation cannot, "by requiring the winding-up or liquidation of the company, ... prevent ... that company from converting itself into a company governed by the law of the other Member State, to the extent that it is permitted under that law to do so." This might lead the way to future decisions. But even if the ECJ goes further ahead, it cannot do the job alone. German practitioners tell me that *Sevic* is a great decision that opens the route to more corporate mobility, but to base a concrete cross-border merger that is outside the Tenth

---

42 Part V of this book; see the report by M. WYCKAERT/F. JENNÉ, *infra* p. 287, the response by L. TIMMERMAN, *infra* p. 332, the discussion, *infra* p. 334, and the abstract, *infra* p. 331.

43 WYCKAERT/JENNÉ, *infra* p. 290 et seq., 294 et seq., 300 et seq. < nos. 2, 5, 10 et seq. >, have tried to set out all possible scenarios.

44 This seems to be the majority view in practice and theory, cf. also WYCKAERT/JENNÉ, *infra* p. 318 et seq. < no. 27 >.

45 I am among those who had hoped that the ECJ would decide along the lines proposed by Advocate General Maduro on 22 May 2008. But WYCKAERT/JENNÉ, *infra* p. 317 < no.25 >, are right to ask that the concept and the foundations of unfettered corporate mobility should be looked into in more detail. See also the response by L. TIMMERMAN, *infra* p. 333 < no. 4 >, who argues that there is an inherent tension in company law between its facilitating role and its goal of shareholder protection and that as to the latter there is a deficit in the jurisprudence of the ECJ. In my opinion, an interesting route for European company law could be to impose a fiduciary duty on the controlling shareholder like in German law.

Directive on *Sevic* alone is a risky affair since a court decision simply cannot provide all the details needed for such a transaction.

There are many additional questions concerning corporate mobility and the actors involved in the transactions and the complicated contracts needed for performing them. One is the role of the notary public. The reasons for not dealing with this topic in more detail in the Action Plan, and indeed in the High Level Group report,[46] are simple. The function of the notary public reaches far beyond company law into commercial law (in particular the commercial and enterprise register), estate law, and even procedural law, if we look at the modern mediation movement. By the same token, the notary public systems in the Member States differ considerably. If the European Commission or indeed the European Court of Justice were to take up this area, questions like the following would be asked by both the general public and the legislators in the different countries: What are the experiences with the Latin system and others in those countries where they coexist? Is there cross-border competition between the notaries of the different Member States, apart of course from the public status of the notary public in some countries? What about competition between, for example, German or other Member States' notaries and Swiss notaries? Should European company law enlarge the mandatory role of the notaries in order to protect the shareholders and the general public? Is this what the profession wants? Is it compatible with this protection to offer company contract models and other forms as can be found in the new British company code and in the draft European Private Company Statute? Finally: If the services of the notary to entrepreneurs are to be expanded, what does this mean for the professional association between notaries and the big international law and auditing firms and, in particular, would that be compatible with the particular independence of the notary public? In sum: What should be recommended to the European Commission for the future of European law?

Perspectives

What is the conclusion of this stock-taking and the look at some of the reform problems of European company law? Some answers will be found in the reports, the responses, the discussions and the summaries mentioned above. But without anticipating them, let me present some preliminary thoughts of my own.

One timely answer is "better regulation" as propagated by Commissioner McCreevy. But this is a truism, and views on what constitutes better regulation differ widely. Another offer is far-reaching deregulation of the existing directives as mentioned among other options by the Commission under the same Commissioner. But the European Parliament as well as industry and practice,

46 This is why it was finally decided not to include in this book the section on the role of the notary public in company law from the Leuven conference (cf. note 1).

at least in Germany, are far from supporting this route. A third answer is this: European company law as well as some European law in general should confine itself to cross-border issues. In the Statute for a European Company there is such a prerequisite. Yet the dividing line between internal and cross-border trade and national and multinational companies is becoming more and more blurred. As we know from antitrust law, even transactions fully outside the EU may affect competition within, and many medium-sized and even small companies are nowadays living off export and sometimes are leaders in their segment in the world market. The draft European Private Company Statute rightly refrains from such trans-border requisites, though this is politically controversial. Let us hope that the drafters will end up being successful with this and not give in to Member State pressures.

My own personal conclusions from what we have seen are different. Let me quickly sum them up in three theses at the end of my opening remarks. They concern 1) the need in European company law for flexible mixed system solutions, 2) adequate enforcement, and 3) the financial market crisis and beyond.

Flexible mixed system solutions

As I said before, I distrust pure solutions. They are academically challenging and often conceptually easy, but down at the grassroots of the economy and society they are seldom right. What is needed is usually a flexible solution in a mixed system, though of course finding the right mix is controversial and difficult. This right mix must be found on two levels: between market and regulation and between national regulation and European rules.

As to the first level: The presumption should be for the market and personal freedom of the market participants. To take an example from my own country, I would prefer a system of private bargaining on labor codetermination. The German system is too inflexible and therefore has not been an export success. The European solution found in the SE Directive is, of course, a political compromise. Germany has blocked European company law harmonization on this issue for decades. Still, the compromise found starts with the right idea, namely bargaining between capital and labor on codetermination.[47] The *Allianz* case proves that this can lead to decent solutions like a smaller board and representation of foreign labor. I also see a role for private law-making in the shadow of company law, such as more freedom for corporate by-laws than we have under mandatory German stock corporation law. In a more international example, this would include more room for experimentation

[47] Unfortunately, for political reasons Chancellor Angela Merkel has promised that the new government also will neither touch German labor codetermination nor deregulate to a certain degree labor dismissal rules, though the first measure could help to attract foreign capital and the second would help unemployed workers.

and bonding by voluntary codes of conduct, as in the international corporate governance code movement. But free markets fail where they do not deal adequately with entrenchment of managers in public companies as well as with misappropriation or tunneling[48] by controlling shareholders. Therefore, we need anti-frustration rules like those contained in the Takeover Directive and beyond, and fiduciary duties of controlling shareholders towards the company and their fellow shareholders, with such duties possibly extending beyond the individual company in the group.[49]

As to the second level, we need a mixed system in which the body of company law may remain with the Member States, but where competition of rule-makers and legislators as well as European framework rules set limits. Of course, we can hold different opinions on where these limits should be drawn, what can be left up to legislative competition, and what should be set up by European company law. My own choice would be in dubio pro competition. Issuer choice is an important factor. But sometimes issuer choice needs legal backing against Member State egoism, as *Centros* and the successor decisions of the ECJ amply demonstrate.[50] As to the Capital Directive, I tend to advocate more freedom to choose from different, non-legal capital-based systems, provided they give equivalent or even better creditor protection. As to one share/one vote, the difficulty lies in striking the balance between fairness and efficiency. Cross-border mobility certainly needs mandatory European rules for opening the frontiers since this is the very essence of an internal market. In the takeover field, I think that if options are granted, they should not just be granted to the Member States, but passed on to the market participants who bear the financial consequences of such choices. To this extent, I feel that Art. 12 is progressive. By the same token, I have long been a fervent advocate of free choice between the one-tier and the two-tier board system[51].

Adequate enforcement

When we talk about European company law, we usually talk about substantive company law rules and tend to forget that enforcement is vital.[52] There is a

---

[48] S. JOHNSON/R. LA PORTA/F. LOPEZ-DE-SILANES/A. SHLEIFER, "Tunneling", 90(2) American Economic Review 22 (2000); L. ENRIQUES/G. HERTIG/H. KANDA, "Related-Party Transactions" in: Kraakman et al., *supra* note 34, p. 153 et seq.

[49] Cf. *supra* note 45.

[50] See *supra* note 45.

[51] Cf. K.J. HOPT/P. C. LEYENS, "Board Models in Europe - Recent Developments of Internal Corporate Governance Structures in Germany, the United Kingdom, France, and Italy", *European Company and Financial Law Review* 2004, 135 at 163 et seq., available also at ssrn; reprinted in E. Gepken-Jager/G. van Solinge/L. Timmerman, eds., *VOC 1602-2002, 400 Years of Company Law,* Deventer (Kluwer) 2005, p. 281. See also A. B. GILLETTE/T. H. NOE/M. J. REBELLO, "Board Structures Around the World: An Experimental Investigation", *Review of Finance* 12 (2008) 93.

[52] J. ARMOUR/H. HANSMANN/R. KRAAKMAN, "Agency Problems and Legal Strategies" in: Kraakman et al. (*supra* note 34), p. 45 et seq.; M. B. FOX, "Civil Liability and Mandatory Disclosure", 109 *Colum L. Rev.* 237 (2009).

fundamental reciprocity between substantive and procedural company law. Giving rights to shareholders without giving them the standing to enforce these rights against the management or the controlling shareholders is pointless. This opens up the discussion on derivative suits, minority rights, and finally maybe even association actions and class actions, as presently discussed in the antitrust field and in consumer regulation.[53] Again I see here a case for an adequate mix between state supervision and private enforcement. In capital market-related company law areas, supervision and enforcement by capital market authorities is more important than private enforcement. But the latter may supplement the former. To do this it may need more disclosure and special inquiries by experts, possibly with a carefully drafted group-wide dimension. In the end, enforcement needs courts, good courts. Yet as we know from certain accession candidates, adapting national company law verbatim to the acquis communautaire may be easier than installing a competent and incorruptible court system. If a country does not yet have such courts, *ex post* rules do not work and bright line *ex ante* rules may also be needed in company law.

The financial markets crisis and beyond

Let me end with a word on the financial markets crisis. In a January 2008 statement from a respected and experienced observer of European company law developments in Brussels, I read this about the plans of the Commission: "In spite of the relatively small number of new initiatives, there is nevertheless no danger of 2008 being overly quiet." One year later we are wiser. The financial markets crisis has opened a new era, not only of financial law, but of rule-making more generally[54]. The problem is twofold: to find the adequate rules, including European company law rules, for crisis situations, and to have them confined to those exceptional situations. From case law we know that "hard cases make bad law." This is also a danger for the present-day crisis legislation in all our Member States. True, the state must intervene in such crises, but it must also step back when the crisis is over. There is a real danger that the progress we have made in curtailing golden shares, subsidies, protectionist measures, and other ways and means not compatible with the internal market may stay on. But sooner or later the economy will recover, and the market will continue to be the better regulator than the state. For normal times we need less state and more

[53] P. MATTILL/V. DESOUTTER, "Die europäische Sammelklage – Rechtsvergleichende und EU-rechtliche Betrachtungen, Wertpapier-Mitteilungen 2008, 521.

[54] See e.g. the analysis and reform proposals of the DE LAROSIÈRE group which have been followed by the European Commission in its proposals on 23 September 2009 on a new European financial architecture: The High-Level Group on Financial Supervision in the EU, Report, Brussels, 25 February 2009. Cf. also M. HELLWIG, *Systemic Risk in the Financial Sector, an Analysis of the Subprime-Mortgage Financial Crisis,* Jelle Zijlstra Lecture, Wassenar 2008. The German Lawyers Association (Deutscher Juristentag) will deal with the reform problems at its 150th anniversary session in Berlin in September 2010 (chair: K.J. Hopt and T. Mayen, reporters: M. Hellwig, W. Höfling and D. Zimmer).

market, and in the market we need less entrenchment of management and less tunneling by controlling shareholders. The role of company law academia and practice is not to forget this and to work together with the national and European legislators on the future of European company law.

Let me conclude with a word of thanks to Professor Koen Geens for calling us together to this challenging conference and for choosing such a timely topic. We certainly can look forward to stimulating ideas and animated discussions on the five topics in the workshops (from which we expect brief reports back to the plenary session)[55] and in the final panel debate.[56] But we also look forward beyond this day to a consistent joint publication with the aim of presenting the state of the art of European company law at the beginning of the second decade of the 21st century.

[55] The responses to the five reports can be found in the book behind the reports. As to the reports of the five workshops, see the summaries at the end of each chapter.

[56] Cf. *infra* p. 345 et seq.

Reforming Legal Capital: Harmonisation or Fragmentation of Creditor Protection?

Jean-Marie Nelissen Grade[1] *and Matthias Wauters*[2]
Jan Ronse Institute – K.U.Leuven

Abstract

Legal capital once was the cornerstone of creditor protection in European limited liability companies but has been strongly criticised over the last decade. The European Action Plan 2003 announced a feasibility study to examine possible alternatives. This paper provides an overview of the current debate on legal capital and of the most important alternative regimes that were proposed by company law experts, in particular with respect to distribution restrictions. It emphasises the importance of insolvency law to creditor protection. The authors conclude that the current situation will cause a diversity which is detrimental to a European level playing field. They advocate that the European Union should provide for a harmonisation of distribution restrictions, based on solvency and liquidity tests which may, in the long run, replace the Second Company Law Directive. A minimal harmonisation of insolvency law, in particular by introducing a uniform concept of wrongful trading and fraudulent conveyance, would also largely benefit creditor protection in a cross-border context.

Table of Contents

---

1 Professor K.U.Leuven, Attorney Belgian Supreme Court Bar (Linklaters).
2 Research Fellow K.U.Leuven, Attorney Brussels Bar (Eubelius).

1. Introduction: the European path to reforming legal capital requirements to date

1. ***Capital requirements under debate.*** The capital formation and maintenance rules are considered to be one of the cornerstones of European company law. The minimum capital requirement for public limited liability companies and the detailed rules on capital formation, shareholder distributions, acquisition of own shares and the alteration of capital, set out in the Second Company Law Directive (hereinafter referred to as the "Second Directive"), express a continental – and in particular, a German[3] – approach to shareholder and creditor protection, but are not part of the Anglo-American tradition. It is therefore not surprising that, unlike other Member States, the United Kingdom and Ireland did not extend the scope of the Second Directive to private companies and continued to offer limited liability to corporate forms without minimum capital requirement.[4]

Given the divergence between the Anglo-American reality and the European legislative framework, the capital requirement has fostered a continuing debate between legal scholars on the pros and cons of such a stringent regime for its aspired beneficiaries, i.e. the shareholders and creditors of a limited liability company.[5]

---

[3] A direct source of inspiration for the Second Directive was M. Lutter's doctoral thesis *Kapital, Sicherung der Kapitalaufbringung und Kapitalerhaltung in den Aktien- and GmbH-Rechten der EWG*, Karlsruhe, Verlag C.F. Müller, 1964. The provision on financial assistance, however, has a UK origin.

[4] J. FREEDMAN, "Limited Liability: Large Company Theory and Small Firms", *Modern Law Review* 2000, 335.

[5] E.g. H. EIDENMÜLLER and W. SCHÖN (eds.), *The Law and Economics of Creditor Protection. A Transatlantic Perspective*, The Hague, Asser, 2008, 489p.; M. LUTTER (ed.), *Legal Capital in Europe, ECFR* 2006, special volume 1, Berlin, De Gruyter, 2006, 701p.; L. ENRIQUES and J. MACEY,

2. ***Capital regime under pressure.*** Since the second half of the 1990s, several elements have added particular relevance to this debate.

First, in 1996 the European Commission initiated a process to simplify the European legislation on the Single Market (SLIM, "*Simpler Legislation for the Internal Market*"), in the framework of the general tendency towards deregulation. Part of this project was dedicated to company law, and in 1999 several recommendations to simplify the Second Directive were proposed in order to allow greater flexibility to companies and their shareholders.[6]

Secondly, the European Court of Justice was invited on several occasions to interpret and clarify the application of the freedom of establishment, proclaimed by the Treaty of Rome, to companies established within the European Union. The exact consequences of the well-known milestone decisions (Segers, Daily Mail, Centros, Überseering, Inspire Art and, recently, Cartesio) are not always self-evident. They are discussed in the contribution of M. Wyckaert and F. Jenné. What is certain is that, *de facto*, these Court rulings significantly increased the possibilities for European companies to transfer their entire business to another Member State without the need to form a new company in the host Member State or to comply with the stricter rules, if any, applicable to the companies incorporated and located in that host state. Or, to put it differently, this created a true regulatory choice for private companies and made state competition an undeniable reality.[7]

The corporate mobility enabled by this case law resulted in the presence of "Limiteds" governed by the law of England and Wales in Belgium as well as in other Member States. Commercial websites offer off-the-shelf "Limiteds" and provide all administrative services for the acquirer of such a company to open a branch in its own Member State, as an alternative to the incorporation of a private limited liability company under the law of the resident's state.[8] In order to avoid an "invasion of Limiteds", several Member States have introduced

---

"Creditors versus Capital Formation: the Case against the European Legal Capital Rules", *Cornell Law Review* 2000-01, 1165; E. FERRAN, "Legal Capital Rules and Modern Securities Markets – the Case for Reform, as Illustrated by the U.K. Equity Markets", in K.J. HOPT and E. WYMEERSCH (eds.), *Capital Markets and Company Law*, Oxford University Press, 2003, 115; E. FERRAN, "The Place for Creditor Protection on the Agenda for Modernisation of Company Law in the European Union", *ECFR* 2006, 178; F. KÜBLER, "The Rules of Capital Under Pressure of the Securities Markets", in K.J. HOPT and E. WYMEERSCH (eds.), *Capital Markets and Company Law, o.c.*, 95; H. MERKT, "Der Kapitalschutz in Europa – ein rocher de bronze?", *Z.G.R.* 2004, 305; P. MÜLBERT and M. BIRKE, "Legal Capital – Is There a Case against the European Legal Capital Rules?", *EBOR* 2002, 695; W. SCHÖN, "The future of legal capital", *EBOR* 2004, 429.

6 *Report from the Commission. Results of the Fourth Phase of SLIM*, COM (2000) 56.

7 See also, *ex multos*: C. TIMMERMANS, *Company Law as Ius Commune*, Antwerp, Intersentia, 2002, 13; H.J. DE KLUIVER, "Inspiring a New European Company Law? Observations on the ECJ's Decision in *Inspire Art* from a Dutch Perspective and the Imminent Competition for Corporate Charters between EC Member States", *ECFR* 2004, 123. From a *law & economics* perspective: S. GRUNDMANN, "Regulatory Competition in European Company Law – Some Different Genius?", in G. FERRARINI, K.J. HOPT and E. WYMEERSCH (eds.), *Capital Markets in the Age of the Euro. Cross-Border Transactions, Listed Companies and Regulation*, The Hague, Kluwer Law International, 2002, 561.

8 Described by Kübler as the "erosion of capital law". F. KÜBLER, "The Rules of Capital Under Pressure of the Securities Markets", *l.c.*, 114.

– or are considering the introduction of – a simpler and more flexible legal framework for private limited liability companies, reducing or even completely abolishing capital requirements.[9]

3. *High Level Group considers alternative to Second Directive regime.* The High Level Group of Company Law Experts, initially set up by the European Commission to prepare a compromise for the rejected draft Takeover Bid Directive, was entrusted with an extended mandate to provide recommendations for a modern regulatory European company law framework.

The High Level Group aimed at a fundamental review of European company law, which it considered to contain still too many impediments to the creation of a true internal market. Many of its recommendations related to corporate governance issues,[10] but its final report also addressed, amongst other things, capital formation and maintenance rules. The High Level Group proposed a simplification of the Second Directive, along the lines recommended by the SLIM group. It also advised the Commission to review the feasibility of an alternative to the capital formation and maintenance rules. This entirely new system of creditor and shareholder protection could become optional for Member States as an alternative to the existing Second Directive regime. Key elements of such a system would be the abolition of the concept of legal capital and allowing distributions to shareholders on the basis of solvency tests rather than the availability of distributable reserves.[11]

4. *Company Law Action Plan 2003.* In its Company Law Action Plan of 2003,[12] the Commission supported the proposals made by the SLIM group as supplemented by the High Level Group to simplify the Second Directive.

---

[9] In France, the Law of 1 August 2003 abolished the minimum capital requirement for an SARL, which can be incorporated with a capital of EUR 1. Since 1 January 2009, this is also the case for the SAS (art. 227-2 Code de commerce). As of 1 November 2008, Germany also offers limited liability without a real capital contribution with the introduction of a new corporate form, the *Unternehmers-gesellschaft* (UG), with a minimum capital requirement of EUR 1. However, the UG must constitute a legal reserve of 25% of the profits of the financial year which can only be used to increase the share capital. Once the capital and the legal reserve amount to EUR 25,000, the UG can be converted into a GmbH with a legal capital of at least EUR 25,000. This conversion is not mandatory but a UG that maintains its status will have to continue complying with the stringent reserve requirement. In the Netherlands, a draft bill was submitted to the Dutch Parliament on 31 May 2007 ("*Wet vereenvoudiging en flexibilisering bv-recht*"), abolishing the obligation to raise a minimum capital at incorporation. In Belgium also, the government intends to lower the capital requirement for newly incorporated SMEs to EUR 1. It recently adopted a bill in that respect which will be submitted to Parliament shortly. Like the German UG, the so-called "starters-BVBA" will have to comply with strict reserve requirements, and the company will no longer qualify for the favourable tax regime for SMEs if there are significant profit distributions.

[10] See the contribution of H. Laga and F. Parrein.

[11] Report of the Group of Company Law Experts on a Modern Regulatory Framework for Company Law in Europe, 4 November 2002, 78-93.

[12] Communication from the Commission to the Council and the European Parliament - Modernising Company Law and Enhancing Corporate Governance in the European Union - A Plan to Move Forward, COM (2003) 284 final, Brussels, 21 May 2003, 17-18, no. 3.2.

Except for the partial reduction of the scope of the prohibition on financial assistance, the recommendations are of a rather technical nature and do not fundamentally depart from the policy orientations expressed in the Second Directive. The proposals can therefore be considered as refinements of the Second Directive, with a view to limiting legal requirements and restrictions in those cases where they did not really contribute to the effective protection of shareholders and third parties. The amendments do not, however, represent a fundamental reform.

As to the alternative regime for creditor and shareholder protection, potentially replacing the concept of legal capital, as advanced and briefly outlined by the High Level Group, the Commission took the view that a feasibility study was required to elaborate on the exact characteristics of such an alternative regime, to examine its ability to offer equivalent safeguards in comparison with the Second Directive and to identify its practical benefits for the promotion of business efficiency and competitiveness.

The intention of launching a study was largely welcomed by the respondents to the consultation organised by the Commission, but the introduction of the alternative regime itself was heavily questioned. Some respondents argued that it would reduce both creditor protection and the level of harmonisation that had already been achieved within the European Union and that it was therefore not advisable to introduce an entirely new system mainly inspired by non-European jurisdictions.[13]

5. *Amendments to the Second Directive.* In October 2004, the Commission submitted a proposal to amend the Second Directive in order to simplify and improve some capital protection rules, implementing the proposals of the SLIM group and the High Level Group in this respect. The slightly amended draft directive was adopted on 6 September 2006.[14] It mainly addresses (i) the reduced need for expert valuation of contributions in kind in some well-defined circumstances, (ii) the expanded right for a company to acquire its own shares up to the limits of distributable reserves, (iii) a partial relaxation of the prohibition against the company providing financial assistance for the acquisition of its shares by third parties and (iv) changes to the legal procedures for creditors in case of capital reduction.[15]

Transposition of these amendments to the Second Directive was required by 15 April 2008, but since most of the provisions authorise Member States to introduce additional flexibility into their national legislation, the implementa-

[13] Synthesis of the responses to the Communication of the Commission to the Council and the European Parliament, A Working Document of DG Internal Market, 15 November 2003, 19.

[14] Directive 2006/68/EC of the European Parliament and of the Council of 6 September 2006 amending Council Directive 77/91/EEC as regards the formation of public limited liability companies and the maintenance and alteration of their capital, *OJ* L 264, 25.09.2006, 32.

[15] For a critical analysis, see e.g. E. WYMEERSCH, "Reforming the Second Company Law Directive", available at http://papers.ssrn.com/sol3/papers.cfm?abstract_id=957981.

tion of these amendments is not really an issue. By the end of May 2009, only Luxembourg still had to notify the European Commission on the status of the transposition into its national legislation.

6. ***European feasibility study on alternative to the legal capital regime.*** As announced in May 2003, the Commission called for a feasibility study that eventually not only covered the analysis of an alternative to the capital maintenance regime but also included an examination of the implications of IFRS on profit distribution, since the IAS Regulation (EC) 1606/2002 allowed Member States to accept IFRS also as an accounting framework for individual accounts, which has a direct effect on the application of the profit distribution rules established by the Second Directive.

In January 2008, KPMG, which had been commissioned to carry out the study, published its report, concluding that the compliance costs related to capital regimes are generally not overly burdensome. The transition to an alternative system should therefore not be motivated by the objective of reducing costs.[16] This conclusion corroborates the intuitive findings of the respondents to the consultation launched by the High Level Group, indicating that the particularities of the European legal capital regime do not put European companies at a competitive disadvantage, although it is not considered as a strategic advantage either.[17] Indeed, the Second Directive only requires a limited amount of legal capital (EUR 25,000), which appears to be rather symbolic in practice.[18]

7. ***No immediate action to be expected at European regulatory level.*** Based on this study, the Commission concluded that "*the current capital maintenance regime under the Second Company Law Directive does not seem to cause significant operational problems for companies. Therefore no follow-up measures or changes to the Second Company Law Directive are foreseen in the immediate future.*"[19]

---

[16] KPMG, *Feasibility study on an alternative to the capital maintenance regime established by the Second Company Law Directive 77/91/EEC of 13 December 1976 and an examination of the impact on profit distribution of the new EU-accounting regime*, January 2008, 1. Study available at: http://ec.europa.eu/internal_market/company/docs/capital/feasbility/study_en.pdf.

[17] Report of the High Level Group of Company Law Experts on a Modern Regulatory Framework for Company Law in Europe, 4 November 2002, 78-79.

[18] See Article 6(1) of the Second Directive. Note, however, that the *Societas Europaea* (SE) requires a share capital of at least EUR 120,000 (Article 4(2) of Regulation (EC) 2001/2157 of 8 October 2001 on the Statute for a European company (SE), *OJ* L 294, 10 November 2001, 1).

[19] Position of DG Internal Market and Services, *Results of the external study on the feasibility of an alternative to the Capital Maintenance Regime of the Second Company Law Directive and the impact of the adoption of IFRS on profit distribution*, 2, available at: http://ec.europa.eu/internal_market/company/docs/capital/feasbility/markt-position_en.pdf.

2. Overview

8. ***Pressure on capital regime: bottom-up approach.*** The absence of a coordinated initiative at the European level to reform legal capital requirements does not imply that such reform is no longer of current interest. On the contrary, at present many Member States are examining the introduction of a more flexible legal framework, at least for private limited liability companies (see 2 above).

Likewise, the European Commission has recently presented a proposal for a Statute on a European Private Company setting the minimum capital requirement at EUR 1,[20] thereby admitting indirectly that the rules on capital established by the Second Directive are no longer the preferential way to deal with the issue of creditor protection in a limited liability context.

9. ***Overview.*** Hereinafter, we briefly recall the double function of the legal capital (section 3 below) and summarise the main arguments made in favour and against the legal capital regime (section 4 below). Section 5 gives an overview of the alternative regimes with a view to ensuring creditor protection, such as mandatory disclosure and insurance and the different solvency and liquidity tests that have been advanced by company law experts as an alternative to the distribution restrictions set out in the Second Directive. Specific attention is paid to the proposal for a Statute for a European Private Company since this may be particularly relevant for the future orientation at the European level. Based on this overview, we cannot but conclude that the debate on legal capital is not only a matter of legal and efficiency issues but also reflects historical, socio-economic and contextual preferences (section 6 below). Sections 7 and 8 elaborate on alternative techniques of creditor protection that are situated on the borderline of corporate and insolvency law. The question whether insolvency law may be the better place to ensure creditor protection and, therefore, whether Europe should aim at a harmonisation of insolvency law is addressed in section 9. We conclude that the current situation is detrimental to a European level playing field and suggest that the European Union provides for a harmonisation of distribution restrictions, based on solvency and liquidity tests. A minimal harmonisation of insolvency law, in particular by introducing uniform concepts of wrongful trading and fraudulent conveyance, would also largely benefit creditor protection in a cross-border context (section 10 below).

[20] Proposal for a Council Regulation on the Statute for a European Private Company, COM (2008) 396 final, 26 June 2008, 7-8.

3. Functions attributed to the legal capital

10. ***Internal organisational function of legal capital.*** It is generally accepted that the purpose of the legal capital rules is twofold.

On the one hand, the legal capital has an organisational function, because it forms the basis of the respective rights of the shareholders.[21] However, it should be pointed out that this "internal" role of the capital concept is linked to the existence of a share capital but does not relate to the capital amount, which in turn would not have any logical relation to the company's activities. Indeed, the organisational function of legal capital can be achieved with a merely symbolic amount or even without the legal capital regime.[22]

That the relationship between the capital contribution and the internal governance rights is still predominantly present in the current corporate governance debate is evidenced by the increased tendency to favour proportionality between *capital* and control, culminating in the basic "one share one vote" rule: voting rights should be proportional to the equity stake.[23]

Also worth mentioning is the European requirement to offer preferential subscription rights to existing shareholders if new shares are issued for a cash consideration. This rule is intended to protect existing shareholders against a value transfer to new investors and allows existing shareholders to prevent a dilution of their voting power. This individual shareholder's right can be limited or cancelled, provided that such a decision is in the corporate interest and the relevant procedures are complied with. The same applies to the issue of shares below par value. Such a decision is not prohibited but triggers specific information obligations. Although it is often mentioned in this context, we believe that the authority of the board to issue new shares is a matter of corporate governance rather than an issue directly linked to the concept of legal capital.

11. ***Legal capital as a technique of creditor protection.*** On the other hand, legal capital is intended to provide a "cushion" that absorbs losses before the risk thereof is shifted to the company's creditors. From a traditional continental perspective, this is seen as the counterbalance for limited liability. An important – if not the core – function of this technique of creditor protection lies in its preventive effect. It is intended to avoid the distribution to shareholders of the net asset value up to the amount of the share capital (and other equity items that are treated in the same way by virtue of the law or the articles of

[21] See the second recital of the preamble to the Second Directive; see also Article 54 of the Belgian Companies Code ("*when the shares have equal value, each share confers one vote*"); H. FLEISCHER, "Legal Capital: A Navigation System for Corporate Law Scholarship", in H. EIDENMÜLLER and W. SCHÖN (eds.), *The Law and Economics of Creditor Protection. A Transatlantic Perspective*, *o.c.*, 30.

[22] M. MIOLA, "Legal Capital and Limited Liability Companies: the European Perspective" *ECFR* 2005, 419.

[23] Reference is made to the contribution of K. Geens and C. Clottens, no. 3, raising the issue of shares that are not fully paid up and shares that are deliberately created as non-voting securities.

association) and serves as an alarm when liabilities threaten to exceed assets, i.e. when the company is in the vicinity of insolvency.[24]

Therefore, the Second Directive imposes capital formation, maintenance and alteration rules, combined with strict distribution rules with a view to safeguarding the interests of creditors. The minimum capital requirement constitutes a seriousness test, reducing the risk of completely unrealistic projects being set up,[25] while the essence of the capital regime lies in the distribution restrictions, requiring that distributions to shareholders are paid only when there is a sufficient surplus of net assets over the legal capital and non-distributable reserves. Many technical provisions are intended to safeguard the reality of the latter terms of the equation and protect the creditors against a voluntary reduction thereof.

The net asset calculation is based on a balance sheet test and mandatory rules apply to the presentation and disclosure of the financial statements that form the basis for the test. Fiduciary duties of directors are not nonexistent, especially when the company enters a pre-insolvency zone, but the rules or standards in that respect have not been harmonised at the European level.

12. ***Are both functions to be linked?*** Although at first sight the link between the internal and external function of legal capital may seem efficient from a legislative viewpoint, we agree, with Schön, that this link is neither self-evident nor required and that it is therefore rather detrimental to the case for legal capital. The technique of legal capital may gain clarity if the two functions are disconnected, using separate concepts when, on the one hand, the equal treatment of shareholders is at stake and, on the other hand, creditor protection is envisaged.[26] This is in fact what is done when the concept of legal capital is maintained but its amount is set at a merely symbolic level.

4. Legal capital: a merely transitional phase or a powerful regulatory tool?

13. ***The legal capital debate: introduction.*** The animated debate on the added value of capital requirements has reached a point where passionate believers oppose strong non-believers.

It has been argued that the legal capital rules are the most efficient way of limiting distributions prior to a company's insolvency, providing less room for manipulation than the *ad hoc* solvency tests used in Anglo-American systems. In

---

[24] M. MIOLA, *l.c.*, 421.

[25] H. EIDENMÜLLER, B. GRUNEWALD and U. NOACK, "Minimum Capital in the System of Legal Capital", in M. LUTTER (ed.), *Legal Capital in Europe*, *o.c.*, 25.

[26] W. SCHÖN, *l.c.*, 447; also: M. KAHAN, "Legal Capital Rules and the Structure of Corporate Law: Some Observations on the Differences Between European and U.S. Approaches", in K.J. HOPT and E. WYMEERSCH (eds.), *Capital Markets and Company Law*, *o.c.*, 148.

support of legal capital, it was also pointed out that many European companies have a legal capital exceeding by far the required minimum, which evidences that there is no general reluctance to voluntarily offer additional safeguards to creditors.[27] At the same time, the main argument made against the concept of legal capital is that it is not effective or, at least, that it is not (sufficiently) achieving the aspired objectives: the one-size-fits-all approach would not be adapted to the specific situation of a particular company, and compliance with the highly technical rules would be burdensome and costly.[28] One often refers to the capital adequacy and solvency requirements imposed on banks and insurance companies, which are much more demanding and do not relate to the concept of legal capital.[29]

It is not our intention to provide an extensive overview of the merits of the capital regime and the criticisms brought against it. Nevertheless, one should bear in mind that the legal capital rules embrace several elements which should be distinguished when assessing the merits of this regime.

14. ***Legal capital as a collective negative pledge.*** First, the capital rules prescribe a minimum legal capital, but the consensus opinion seems to be that this is of lesser relevance.[30] Indeed, the longer the company exists, the more irrelevant these initially contributed minimum funds become from a creditor protection perspective. Moreover, even at the time of incorporation, any link between the minimum capital and the financial needs of an individual company is missing.[31] It is therefore somewhat surprising that in 2004 the Belgian legislator took the initiative to increase the portion of the minimum capital of a private limited liability company with a single shareholder required to be paid up immediately upon constitution.[32] After all, it seems that such marginal anti-abuse legislation has only limited effects, if any.

Schön argues that, once the imposition of a minimum capital is disregarded, the capital amount set by the shareholders in the articles of association rather constitutes a voluntary guarantee offered by the company to its present and future creditors.[33] Of course, such a guarantee does not imply that the funds

[27] See W. SCHÖN, *l.c.*, 440. However, it should be noted that the maintenance of a substantial amount which is not available for distribution, and the maintenance of issuance premiums in particular, is most probably also inspired by the resultant tax status, which would – at least under Belgian law – be lost if issuance premiums were mixed up with distributable reserves.

[28] P. SANTELLA and R. TURRINI, "Capital Maintenance in the EU: Is the Second Company Law Directive Really That Restrictive?", *EBOR* 2008, 432. Referring in particular to the formalities imposed in the case of a contribution in kind: F. KÜBLER, "The Rules of Capital Under Pressure of the Securities Markets", *l.c.*, 101.

[29] E. WYMEERSCH, "Het statutaire kapitaal van de vennootschappen", in *Liber amicorum Lucien Simont*, Brussels, Bruylant, 2002, 915.

[30] M. LUTTER, "Legal capital of public companies in Europe. Executive summary of considerations by the expert group on 'Legal Capital in Europe'", in M. LUTTER (ed.), *Legal Capital in Europe, ECFR* 2006, special volume 1, Berlin, De Gruyter, 2006, 7.

[31] W. SCHÖN, *l.c.*, 437-438; P. SANTELLA and R. TURRINI, *l.c.*, 432.

[32] See Articles 213 and 223 of the Belgian Companies Code as amended.

[33] W. SCHÖN, *l.c.*, 438 et seq. See also the summary given by E. FERRAN, "The Place for Creditor

will be available at any time, but rather constitutes a collective negative covenant by which the shareholders renounce any appropriation of the corresponding amount by way of shareholder distribution. Naturally, important or powerful creditors can always agree with the company on individual terms to have their claims additionally secured, but the standards set by the company itself may reduce the need to do so. This should have a positive impact on overall transaction costs. From this perspective, the prohibition on paying up capital by rendering services, the value of which is difficult to determine, and the rules on expert valuation of contributions in kind are required to maintain confidence in the company's statement that it will not distribute the share capital amount to the shareholders. In such a way, one avoids each creditor individually having to assess the exact extent of the net asset position to which the company's negative pledge pertains. Furthermore, all creditors may benefit from the preventive effect provided by the capital regime, whereas involuntary creditors or creditors lacking bargaining power would be worse off if any individual creditor felt obliged to agree on financial covenants or ensure that its claim was sufficiently secured, thus reducing the company assets available to other – less powerful – creditors.[34]

Finally, the legal capital rules state which shareholder distributions are prohibited by the negative covenant and how to determine whether or not a proposed distribution conflicts with this restriction. The outcome of this – i.e. the identification of genuine profits – is of course largely dependent on the accounting methods that are used (a creditor-friendly conservative approach or a shareholder-oriented accounting method based on fair market value). Proponents of legal capital argue that these technical rules are clear and, if complied with, provide a higher degree of legal certainty than case by case assessments left to the directors but under the post factum control of the courts.[35]

15. ***Main criticism: rigidity and inadequacy of the capital rules aimed at creditor protection.*** Qualifying the legal capital as a negative guarantee which, to the extent that the capital exceeds the legal minimum, is provided by the company (and its shareholders) does not explain, however, why the regime is mandatory and not just a mechanism which is available to the company (as an opt-in or at least with the possibility of opting out).[36] Furthermore, this approach does not yet ensure that the costs related to the capital rules are proportionate to the aspired goal and the benefits actually achieved. This is

Protection on the Agenda for Modernisation of Company Law in the European Union", *l.c.*, 193 et seq.

[34] P. MANKOWSKI, "Does contract suffice to protect the creditors of a company and their assets?", in M. LUTTER (ed.), *Legal Capital in Europe*, *o.c.*, 400-401.

[35] M. LUTTER, "Legal capital of public companies in Europe. Executive summary of considerations by the expert group on 'Legal Capital in Europe'", *l.c.*, 4.

[36] See e.g. J. ARMOUR, "Share Capital and Creditor Protection. Efficient Rules for a Modern Company Law", *Modern Law Review* 2000, 375.

all the more the case since the capital rules are compulsory for public limited liability companies and many Member States, including Belgium, have also imposed these rules on private limited liability companies.

Opponents of the legal capital not only reject a minimum capital requirement but also consider the distribution restrictions to be inappropriate. The mandatory set of rules is seen as an impediment to efficient capital allocation, generating mismatch costs.[37] These costs could be avoided if creditor protection is left to contractual covenants focusing on what really matters to creditors at the time they establish the relationship with the company which underlies their claim. Assessing the creditworthiness of a company based on its legal capital or even its net-asset position only is basically defective. The entire asset and liability structure, the profitability of the business, its (free) cash flows, future prospects and financial ratios are considered much more important than a balance sheet test reflecting the historical net-asset position of the company.[38] Furthermore, the relationship between the amount of the share capital and its main purpose of creditor protection is merely coincidental: the legal capital is fixed by the statutory provisions or by the articles of association without any need to respect a proportionality requirement in view of the company's businesses.[39] The Belgian statutory provision requiring an adequate capital amount at incorporation is a well-known exception,[40] but in no way does it represent a permanent capital adequacy guarantee.[41]

5. Alternative regimes: a brief overview

5.1. Traditional mechanisms enhancing creditor protection

16. ***Mandatory disclosure.*** For a creditor, whether a financial institution or a commercial creditor, it is essential to be able to assess the creditworthiness of the debtor. Since limited liability companies present a particular agency problem because the interests of the shareholders and the company's creditors are not necessarily identical – the shareholder is not interested in an overcapitalised company while the creditors bear all the risk in case of excessive shareholder distributions – all jurisdictions require limited liability companies to maintain

[37] E. FERRAN, "The Place for Creditor Protection on the Agenda for Modernisation of Company Law in the European Union", *l.c.*, 199.

[38] J. ARMOUR, "Legal Capital: An Outdated Concept?", in H. EIDENMÜLLER and W. SCHÖN (eds.), *The Law and Economics of Creditor Protection. A Transatlantic Perspective*, *o.c.*, 14; E. WYMEERSCH, "Het statutaire kapitaal van de vennootschappen", *l.c.*, 916.

[39] See J. RICKFORD, "Legal Approaches to Restricting Distributions to Shareholders: Balance Sheet Tests and Solvency Tests", in H. EIDENMÜLLER and W. SCHÖN (eds.), *The Law and Economics of Creditor Protection. A Transatlantic Perspective*, *o.c.*, 141.

[40] Articles 440 and 456 of the Belgian Companies Code (for the *naamloze vennootschap/société anonyme*).

[41] For some critical observations, see H.J. DE KLUIVER, "Towards a Simpler and More Flexible Law of Private Companies. A New Approach and the Dutch Experience", *ECFR* 2006, 54-55.

proper accounting records and often require certified auditing and subsequent disclosure of the financial statements.[42] Transparency concerning the financial situation of the debtor creates creditor confidence and protection, generating an informed consent: the creditor can assess the risk factors and take the necessary precautions if need be (ask for a risk premium, security, etc.) and the debtor has access to external funding at a price reflecting its financial position and prospects.

Must disclosure be mandatory or can it be left to market forces? With respect to the securities markets, it has been argued that efficient allocation of resources is best served by mandatory disclosure.[43] Insiders might be reluctant to spread bad news, creating an agency problem between informed and non-informed market participants. This may lead to a "lemon" type failure[44] since the market is not in a position to assess the quality and completeness of the information disclosed. Finally, standardisation of the information with respect to format, content and quality will improve comprehensibility and comparability and therefore increase the value of the information to the market.

However, Merkt argues that current disclosure regulation does not provide the information that really matters to creditors such as: Is the debtor willing to meet its obligations? Does its operational cash flow suffice to do so? And what are its financial reserves? Therefore, a reform of the disclosure requirements should not only take into account the comprehensibility and timeliness of the information disclosed. Information on the expected solvency of the company would be even more useful.[45] This forward-looking element will also be included in the alternatives proposed to complement or replace the legal capital regime with respect to distribution restrictions (see 20-23 below).

These considerations should be taken into account when assessing the merits of the current proposal of the European Commission to exempt what it calls "micro-entities" from the scope of application of the Fourth Company Law Directive.[46] Here also, arguments exist to contest the one-size-fits-all approach established by the Fourth Directive, but one should carefully consider whether

---

[42] See H. MERKT, "Creditor Protection Through Mandatory Disclosure", in H. EIDENMÜLLER and W. SCHÖN (eds.), *The Law and Economics of Creditor Protection. A Transatlantic Perspective*, *o.c.*, 95.

[43] E.g. G. HERTIG, R. KRAAKMAN and E. ROCK, "Issuers and Investor Protection", in R. KRAAKMAN, P. DAVIES et al., *The Anatomy of Corporate Law. A Comparative and Functional Approach*, Oxford, University Press, 2nd ed., 2009, 277 et seq., 204; R. KRAAKMAN, "Disclosure and Corporate Governance: An Overview Essay", in G. FERRARINI, K. J.HOPT, J. WINTER and E. WYMEERSCH (eds.), *Reforming Company and Takeover Law in Europe*, Oxford University Press, 2004, 99-101; H. MERKT, "Creditor Protection Through Mandatory Disclosure", *l.c.*, 99; H. MERKT, "European Company Law Reform: Struggling for a More Liberal Approach", *ECFR* 2004, 11.

[44] See G. AKERLOF, "The Market for 'Lemons': Quality Uncertainty and the Market Mechanism", *Quarterly Journal of Economics* 1970, 488, analysing the pernicious impact of asymmetric information on market functioning.

[45] H. MERKT, "Creditor Protection Through Mandatory Disclosure", *l.c.*, 110 and 120.

[46] Proposal for a Directive of the European Parliament and of the Council amending Council Directive 78/660/EEC on the annual accounts of certain types of companies as regards micro-entities, COM (2009) 83 final 2, 18 March 2009.

the abolition of a European-wide requirement and its potential replacement with national requirements that may well complicate cross-border trade is the right option.[47] Besides, the debate remains open as to the extent to which disclosure of financial information should only supplement or may even replace substantive regulation.[48] Proponents of the latter option take the view that, if the relevant information is fully disclosed, companies will be directed automatically to compliance with standards that reflect the optimal level of self-restriction. However, as the recent financial crisis has shown, auto-regulation might be the appropriate technique to deal with corporate governance issues concerning internal policy and decision-making but it is less suited to compelling companies to comply with financial covenants and solvency requirements.

17. ***Mandatory insurance.*** An alternative to protect creditors – and in the first place involuntary (or so-called "non-adjusting") creditors – is mandatory liability insurance, whereby the monitoring cost of the level of risky activities (and moral hazard problems) is shifted to the insurer.[49] However, one can hardly imagine how such a system would work and how the insurer would be able to set its premium at an acceptable level. Once again, the one-size-fits-all approach does not suit.[50] Mandatory insurance seems feasible only with respect to well-defined risks relating to the particular risks the company and its stakeholders are exposed to given the nature of the company's activities.

5.2. Creditor protection: alternatives to the Second Directive distribution regime

18. ***Introduction.*** Criticism of the Second Directive mainly relates to the distribution rules that would needlessly restrict the company's flexibility by referring to a historical and static benchmark considered inappropriate for this purpose (see 15 above). Besides, the possibility of drawing up annual accounts in accordance with IFRS has already undermined the philosophy of the Second Directive, so that creditors might be better off with an alternative regime protecting against excessive distribution.

---

[47] With respect to this discussion, we refer to the contribution of K. Van Hulle and F. Hellemans.

[48] H. MERKT, "European Company Law Reform: Struggling for a More Liberal Approach", *l.c.*, 13-16.

[49] E.g. J. ARMOUR, "Share Capital and Creditor Protection: Efficient Rules for a Modern Company Law", *l.c.*, 372; F. EASTERBROOK and D. FISCHEL, *The Economic Structure of Corporate Law*, Harvard University Press, 1991, 61; see also R. KRAAKMAN, "Concluding Remarks on Creditor Protection", in H. EIDENMÜLLER and W. SCHÖN (eds.), *The Law and Economics of Creditor Protection. A Transatlantic Perspective*, *o.c.*, 474. With respect to tort claims: B. PETTET, "Limited Liability – A Principle for the 21st Century?", *Current Legal Problems* 1995, 157-158. Compare: H. HANSMANN and R. KRAAKMAN, "Towards Unlimited Shareholder Liability for Corporate Torts", *Yale Law Journal* 1990-91, 1879.

[50] P. MANKOWSKI, "Does contract suffice to protect the creditors of a company and their assets?", *l.c.*, 398-399.

In order to meet the objections raised against the Second Directive regime, several groups composed of academics have prepared an alternative to the balance sheet test established by the Second Directive. Below, we will briefly describe the current European regime and summarise the most important alternatives, which were also included in the feasibility report commissioned by the European Commission (see 6 above).

5.2.1. Second Directive: balance sheet test

19. ***Distribution rules established by the Second Directive.*** The distribution regime established by the Second Directive is based on a balance sheet test, limiting distributions to shareholders to "*the profits at the end of the last financial year plus any profits brought forward and sums drawn from reserves available for this purpose, less any losses brought forward and sums placed to reserve in accordance with the law or statutes.*" Put differently, a distribution to shareholders, other than in the framework of a capital reduction, is not permitted to the extent that "*on the closing date of the last financial year the net assets as set out in the company's annual accounts are, or following such a distribution would become, lower than the amount of the subscribed capital plus those reserves which may not be distributed under the law or the statutes.*" Both presentations of the distribution restriction are set out in the Second Directive, resulting in the same distributable amount,[51] which is exclusively derived from the company's balance sheet.

The Second Directive does not formally require that losses occurring after the closing of the last financial year (or following the approval of the last annual accounts) should be taken into account when determining the distributable amount. However, the better view is that such losses indeed affect the aggregate amount that is available for distribution.[52] Directors may therefore incur liability when proposing a shareholder distribution, in spite of the negative impact of intermediate losses on the current status of the distributable amount, provided that the directors were (or reasonably should have been) aware of such losses.

5.2.2. The High Level Group

20. ***Combined net asset and liquidity test as an optional alternative.*** The High Level Group of Company Law Experts proposed the introduction of an alternative solvency test, applicable to all forms of distributions (including dividends, share buybacks and capital reductions), which it considered to be at least as effective as the Second Directive regime.[53] To overcome the opposition against the abolition of the creditor protection regime provided for in the Second Directive, the High Level Group proposed that its alternative system

---

[51] Article 15(1)(a) and 15(1)(c) of the Second Directive. For the limited and rather theoretical differences that may result from these two presentations, see R. TAS, *Winstuitkering, kapitaalvermindering en -verlies in NV en BVBA*, Kalmthout, Biblo, 2003, 147, no. 201.

[52] R. TAS, *o.c.*, 208, no. 284 reporting a similar tendency in other European countries.

[53] Report of the High Level Group of Company Law Experts on a Modern Regulatory Framework for Company Law in Europe, 4 November 2002, 87-88.

should be optional, allowing Member States to replace the existing regime with the alternative technique but without any requirement to do so. The opt-in/ opt-out technique has already been successfully used to find a way out of the deadlock the Takeover Bid Directive was facing following its rejection by the European Parliament (see 3 above). It implies, however, that two systems may coexist, acknowledging the reality that the harmonisation efforts are confronted with insurmountable divergences of views which needs to be accounted for at the European level, at the risk of greater harm resulting from rigidity and non-decision making.

The proposed test comprises two elements: first, a balance sheet test which requires that the company's assets will still fully cover or exceed its liabilities following the contemplated distribution. Secondly, a liquidity test must prove that the company has sufficient liquid assets to make payments of its liabilities as they fall due in the following period, e.g. the forthcoming twelve months. The tests may be further reinforced by requiring a solvency margin (with respect to the net-asset and/or liquidity position of the company). Particular attention should be paid to the relevance of the valuation method applied (going concern or liquidation, not necessarily referring to national GAAP or IFRS[54]).

It is proposed that the directors of the company issue, on their responsibility, a solvency certificate based on these tests, explicitly confirming that the proposed distribution meets the test. No distribution would be allowed without such a certificate.

5.2.3. The Rickford proposal

21. *Solvency tests based on reasonable business expectations.* A similar but somewhat more radical approach is taken by the Interdisciplinary Group on Capital Maintenance, chaired by Prof. J. Rickford. The Rickford Group proposes a two-stage solvency test to determine the maximum amount available for distribution that would apply to all forms of distributions to shareholders (including dividends, share repurchases and capital reductions).

First, the solvency test requires issuing of a directors' certificate giving the assurance of the company's viability, confirming that, immediately after the payment, there would be no grounds on which a court could find that the company was unable to pay its debts. Contingent and prospective liabilities should be taken into account, as well as future and prospective assets. The directors' statement should determine whether the company can reasonably be expected to *meet its liabilities for the reasonably foreseeable future, taking account of its expected prospects in the ordinary course of business.*[55] Secondly, the certificate

[54] KPMG, *Feasibility study on an alternative to the capital maintenance regime established by the Second Company Law Directive 77/91/EEC of 13 December 1976 and an examination of the impact on profit distribution of the new EU-accounting regime*, January 2008, 272.

[55] J. RICKFORD (ed.), "Reforming Capital. Report of the Interdisciplinary Group on Capital Maintenance", *EBLR* 2004, 979.

should also indicate that, having regard to the intentions and resources likely to be available, the company will be able in the ordinary course of business to meet all its debts as they fall due as a going concern throughout the year immediately following the distribution. Auditor certification of both solvency tests is not required but, since the audit report, if any, will have to consider the legality of the distribution and the going-concern assurances given by the directors, it is advisable to consult the auditors.

A net asset test based on the balance sheet is not imposed. Such a test is considered to be too rigidly linked to the accounts to create added value in comparison to the more relevant solvency tests. However, if the simple balance sheet net-asset test (assets compared to liabilities including provisions) results in a deficit, the directors should explain why they consider the company still to be solvent in any case.

5.2.4. The Lutter proposal

22. *Additional solvency test adjusting IFRS balance sheet, if applicable.* Given its outspoken position in favour of the Second Directive, one should not be surprised that the Expert Group on Legal Capital in Europe, chaired by Prof. M. Lutter, came to the conclusion that the current regime does not require any changes provided that the company produces a balance sheet in accordance with commercial accounting principles (ordinary GAAP). This balance sheet, reviewed and certified, can then be used to determine the distributable amount.

However, if the balance sheet is drawn up according to IFRS, this may allow distribution of mere book profits (unrealised profits), which is not in line with the prudent distribution approach favoured by the Second Directive. In this case, an additional solvency test should be required, based on (i) all available information summarised in a financial budget and (ii) a longer term capital budget document. The test should demonstrate that after the intended distribution it is highly likely that the company will have sufficient funds to continue operating as a going concern for the next (one to two) years and should not indicate any risks potentially jeopardising the company's existence. Such a solvency test would avoid a full adjustment of the IFRS balance sheet which would, in practice, inevitably lead to requiring a new balance sheet and therefore annulling the possibility of drawing up the statutory balance sheet in accordance with IFRS.[56]

5.2.5. The Dutch proposal

23. *Combination of a simple balance sheet test and a liquidity test.* The Dutch Group, headed by Prof. J. Schutte-Veenstra, presented an alternative to

[56] M. LUTTER, "Legal capital of public companies in Europe. Executive summary of considerations by the expert group on 'Legal Capital in Europe'", *l.c.*, 11; B. PELLENS and T. SELLHORN, "Improving Creditor Protection through IFRS Reporting and Solvency Tests", in M. LUTTER (ed.), *Legal Capital in Europe*, *o.c.*, 389.

the Second Directive permitting a distribution (regardless of the form it takes) if it passes both a (simplified) balance sheet test and a liquidity test.[57]

The balance sheet test requires the company's equity to remain positive following the distribution to the shareholders. Unlike the balance sheet test provided for in the Second Directive, the balance sheet test required by the Dutch Group does not class subscribed capital or certain reserves as non distributable. The surplus, exceeding the company's debts and provisions, is eligible for distribution. The balance sheet test is performed by reference to the annual accounts, which can be drawn up in accordance with national GAAP, but also in accordance with IFRS.

The balance sheet test is supplemented by a liquidity test covering a fixed period following the distribution. The relevant criterion is whether the company, assuming that its operations continue, has sufficient cash available after the distribution to be able to meet the debts that fall due in the coming period (e.g. twelve months) as a result of its ordinary business operations.

The management board is required to provide and publish a solvency statement declaring that the distribution complies with both tests.

5.3. Initiatives at the European level

5.3.1. Second Directive to remain unchanged

24. *No initiative to reform distribution rules.* Following the publication of the report on the feasibility study, the European Commission announced that, since the capital maintenance regime did not seem to cause significant problems, no further amendments to the Second Directive were to be expected in the near future (see 7 above). It remains to be seen whether this approach will be maintained by the new Commission which will take office after the mid-2009 elections.

However, the decision not to propose amendments to the Second Directive – and *a fortiori* not to propose to simply repeal this Directive – does not mean that the Commission was convinced by the arguments advanced by the proponents of the legal capital regime. The proposal for a European Private Company is indeed a good test to scrutinise the Commission's inner convictions.

5.3.2. Proposal for a Regulation on the Statute for a European Private Company

25. *Draft Regulation: creditor protection moves away from the central concept of share capital.* The proposal for a Statute for a European Private Company (*Societas Privata Europaea* or *SPE*), submitted to the European Parliament on 26 June 2008, is meant to provide small and medium-sized enterprises with a flexible corporate form at European level, adapted to their

[57] H. BOSCHMA, M. LENNARTS and J. SCHUTTE-VEENSTRA, *Alternative systems for capital protection*, 18 August 2005, 69-72.

needs. The proposal does not make the creation of an SPE subject to a cross-border requirement (e.g. shareholders from different Member States or evidence of cross-border activity). Therefore, potentially all EU companies which do not intend to offer their shares to the public may be interested in taking the corporate form of an SPE.[58]

With respect to the capital requirements, the Commission took the view 'that "*in order to facilitate start-ups, the Regulation sets the minimum capital requirement at EUR 1 (..) [departing] from the traditional approach that considers the requirement of a high minimum of legal capital as a means of creditor protection.*"[59] Moreover, the Commission argues that director-shareholders of SMEs often offer personal guarantees to banks and that commercial counterparties use other methods to secure their claims (e.g. passing ownership of goods on payment only). Capital formation rules are thereby abandoned as far as the SPE is concerned.

With respect to distributions, the draft Regulation prescribes a balance sheet test: after the distribution, the company's assets should fully cover its liabilities (as defined in the Fourth Directive or in the IAS Regulation). Furthermore, the articles of association may restrict the distribution of certain reserves, but there is no general obligation to constitute such reserves. No solvency test is imposed either, since such a requirement has no common ground in the Member States' legislation. However, the articles of association may provide for an additional solvency test and may also require management to issue and disclose a solvency certificate prior to any distribution, certifying that the SPE will be able to pay its debts as they become due in the normal course of business within one year of the distribution.[60]

26. *Draft Regulation to be amended?* Given the current debate on the role and importance of legal capital as a tool of creditor protection, it is not surprising that the European Parliament proposed to mitigate the Commission's draft,[61] in particular with respect to the (absence of substantive) capital formation and maintenance rules.[62]

The European Parliament proposed to amend the minimum capital provision: a share capital of EUR 1 remains possible, provided that the articles of association require that the executive management body signs a solvency

---

[58] Commission staff working document accompanying the Proposal for a Council Regulation on the Statute for a European Private Company (SPE) - Impact assessment, 25 June 2008, SEC (2008) 2098, 18; see also *ex multos* R. DRURY, "The European Private Company", *EBOR* 2008, 125; A. DORRESTEIJN and O. UZIAHU-SANTCROOS, "The *Societas Privata Europaea* under the Magnifying Glass", *European Company Law* 2008, 277.

[59] Proposal for a Council Regulation on the Statute for a European Private Company, COM (2008) 396 final, 26 June 2008, 7.

[60] Article 21 of the draft Regulation.

[61] European Parliament legislative resolution of 10 March 2009 on the proposal for a Council regulation on the Statute for a European private company, 10 March 2009, P6_TA-Prov(2009)0094.

[62] The European Parliament also required the SPE to have at least a cross-border business *intention* and inserted new provisions on employee participation.

certificate before a distribution is made, certifying that the SPE will be able to pay its debts as they become due in the normal course of business within one year of the date of the distribution. Where the articles of association contain no provision to that effect, the capital of the SPE must be at least EUR 8,000. The Parliament also proposed to provide for shareholders' liability in the event that the value of a contribution in kind falls short (but without requiring prior expert valuation as is the case in the Second Directive). Last but not least, any shareholder who has received distributions made contrary to the applicable rules must return those distributions. The Parliament no longer requires the shareholder to be aware of the irregularity.

At this stage of the legislative process, it is too early to predict whether a consensus opinion will be reached and which capital requirements, if any, will eventually be imposed. However, it is noteworthy that both the European Commission and the European Parliament seem in principle to have accepted the idea of departing from most of the capital formation and maintenance rules by offering a corporate form with a merely symbolic share capital, combined with a balance sheet and solvency test with respect to distributions.[63]

6. Reasons for such a vigorous legal capital debate?

27. *Why the reform debate is about more than "detached arguments".* An outsider could be surprised by this vigorous debate on the usefulness of the concept of legal capital and, consequently, on the possible repealing of the Second Directive which only recently celebrated its thirtieth anniversary. Is it a conflict of the generations between those who successfully advocated the adoption of the Second Directive and want to preserve its inheritance by emphasising continental traditions on the one side and, on the other side, a new generation that no longer naturally tends towards a creditor-friendly company law policy considered to be too conservative to offer guidance for a European future that prioritises innovation?

When presenting their arguments, both sides acknowledge the value of the traditional law and economics approach focusing on what are called the "transaction costs" generated or avoided by the relevant model of creditor protection. However, there is a general awareness that other elements, too, are (to be) taken into consideration and the overtones sometimes become emotionally charged.

[63] Compare to the positions reported in 1995: H.J. DE KLUIVER, "Europe and the Private Company, An Introduction", in H.J. DE KLUIVER and W. VAN GERVEN (eds.), *The European Private Company?*, Antwerp, Maklu, 1995, 26 et seq.; M. LUTTER, "A Mini-Directive on Capital", in H.J. DE KLUIVER and W. VAN GERVEN (eds.), *The European Private Company?*, *o.c.*, 202 et seq.

28. ***Path dependence.*** The historical or cultural influence on the former preference for capital rules has been seen as an example of "path dependence". This refers to the fact that pre-existing rules and structures tend to persist if a major change would have undesirable consequences or would face opposition from powerful interest groups.[64] Furthermore, the changes that the abolition of legal capital would entail may by itself have an important deterrent effect. In this respect, Kübler recognises that "*even if it is true that a system like the American is less burdensome than a legal capital regime as the one imposed by the Second Directive, it may well be that the benefits achieved by the move to a more market-oriented model would be inferior to the costs of making the necessary changes.*"[65] Compare it to the creation of a governance model for a newly established state: in the twenty-first century, no one would opt for installing a monarchy, but this does not imply that all European countries would be better off removing their monarchs and adopting a presidential regime which might distort delicate inner state balances…

29. ***Economic and legal context.*** The economic environment also plays an important role. US jurisdictions are usually seen as more debtor-friendly, while continental Europe is more creditor-oriented.[66] This would stem from the role of the equity market as a financing source in the United States, whereas European enterprises tend more towards debt financing, which explains the legislative focus on creditor protection.[67] Kübler predicts that these differences may slowly fade away as globalising financial markets gain in importance.[68] The accounting policies reflect a similar shift in preferences. While traditional European GAAP favour a conservative approach, avoiding to a large extent a situation where unrealised profits are accounted for (or at least taken into consideration when deciding on shareholder distributions), the IAS accounting methods are entirely driven by the goal of complete and immediate transparency to the investor. Is it only a question of time before the Continent evolves in the direction of the American approach? We believe that the risk preference of continental Europe and the United States may be different, explaining – at least partially – the lesser importance of the European securities markets. In this respect, the recent financial crisis and the criticism brought against the self-amplifying effects of IAS may lead to further amendments to the accounting rules, resulting in a more balanced focus on the interests of creditors *and* equity holders.

---

[64] For an excessive interpretation, focusing on impediments to a so-called obvious reform: L. ENRIQUES and J. MACEY, *l.c.*, 1202-1204.

[65] F. KÜBLER, "The Rules of Capital Under Pressure of the Securities Markets", *l.c.*, 106.

[66] G. HERTIG and H. KANDA, "Creditor Protection", *l.c.*, 98.

[67] Identifying complementarity of legal rules as a cause of path dependence: K. HEINE and W. KERBER, "European Corporate Laws, Regulatory Competition and Path Dependence", *European Journal of Law and Economics* 2002, 63.

[68] See F. KÜBLER, "The Rules of Capital Under Pressure of the Securities Markets", *l.c.*, 108 et seq.; see also G. HERTIG and H. KANDA, "Creditor Protection", *l.c.*, 87; E. WYMEERSCH, "Het statutaire kapitaal van de vennootschappen", *l.c.*, 934-935.

Entirely in line with the previous contextual remark, the ownership structure of companies should also be taken into account. In this respect, the "open standards" for distributions to shareholders proposed by the Rickford Group are probably easier to implement in a context where shareholdings are rather dispersed, without a dominant shareholder (block) constantly monitoring and even actively intervening in all shareholder-related matters such as a dividend distribution. The sanction of directors' liability may be expected to have a more significant preventive effect in the absence of considerable shareholder pressure to decide on a distribution. Obviously, a stricter balance sheet approach is less convenient since it does not fully take into account the specific situation and the future prospects of a particular company. But the more objective (and therefore less flexible) rule brings comfort to a director whenever he is confronted with a shareholder who wants to stretch distributions to the limits of what is legally permissible.[69]

Finally, the impact of the law tradition cannot be ignored. Civil law countries tend to prefer applying legal rules rather than open-ended standards; the latter are felt to fit less comfortably with the civil law tradition, which does not officially recognise the binding value of precedents.[70]

7. Should creditor protection be ensured by corporate law?

30. *Functions of company law?* It is often argued that creditor protection should be offered by *company* law, since it is the corporate form, offering limited liability, that creates the duality between the beneficiaries of this organisational structure and its creditors. The shareholders can hope for a dividend if profits are generated, while the creditors should bear the risk if the business project fails. Furthermore, it has been argued that the power to (ab)use the limited liability to the detriment of the corporate creditors rests with the shareholders and/or directors (risk of moral hazard), so that any corrective mechanisms should be directly aligned to the use of those powers.[71]

However, this traditional approach has recently been strongly criticised by authors taking the view that legislation must primarily focus on business efficiency and competiveness: "*It can no longer simply be assumed that EC company law should protect creditors. Instead creditor-related concerns can only justifiably retain a place on the company law policy agenda where this is shown to*

[69] On the risk presented by managerial behaviour regarding an ad hoc test, compare: J. RICKFORD, "Legal Approaches to Restricting Distributions to Shareholders: Balance Sheet Tests and Solvency Tests", *l.c.*, 177 and W. SCHÖN, "Balance Sheet Tests or Solvency Tests – or Both?", in H. EIDENMÜLLER and W. SCHÖN (eds.), *The Law and Economics of Creditor Protection. A Transatlantic Perspective*, *o.c.*, 195.

[70] G. HERTIG and H. KANDA, "Creditor Protection", *l.c.*, 87; E. FERRAN, "The Place for Creditor Protection on the Agenda for Modernisation of Company Law in the European Union", *l.c.*, 199.

[71] See *inter alia* G. HERTIG and H. KANDA, "Creditor Protection", *l.c.*, 71.

be needed on efficiency and competitiveness grounds, and where subsidiarity and proportionality considerations are satisfied."[72]

31. *The influence of the corporate model.* It cannot be excluded that the different approach is at least partially based on the way a company is perceived. The Anglo-American tradition tends to treat a "corporation" as a nexus of contracts,[73] while continental scholars are, to some extent, more inclined to take into account the institutional aspect of the company, fostering mandatory rules to address the risks that are generated by the corporate institution as such.[74]

But even those who believe that creditor protection – and, in particular, the protection of involuntary creditors – is an issue that is too general and not sufficiently corporate-related to be dealt with by company law acknowledge that it is not only a matter of compensation for damages incurred as a result of their rights being impaired. It is also a matter of efficient cost accounting and protection of society as a whole.[75] We would like to add that it is also a matter of policy to what extent society as a whole is prepared to accept the burden of (financial) losses to foster risk-entailing activities that are indispensible to generate future wealth.

32. *How is creditor protection addressed outside the legal capital context?* Irrespective of whether the rules are found in company law, insolvency law or tort law, the following three types of sanctions are always present, though the intensity may differ considerably from one Member State to another: (i) shareholder liability, i.e. piercing the corporate veil, (ii) directors' liability for breach of the duty to respect creditors' interests in a pre-insolvency phase (including, as the case may be, a wrongful trading rule) and (iii) liability of counterparties due to fraudulent transfers.[76]

8. Alternative protective techniques

33. *Piercing the corporate veil.* The first sanction relates to the shareholders' behaviour upon incorporation of the company[77] or its subsequent management.[78] Rightly, the courts do not set aside the limited liability easily. That

[72] E. FERRAN, "The Place for Creditor Protection on the Agenda for Modernisation of Company Law in the European Union", *l.c.*, 181.

[73] F. EASTERBROOK and D. FISCHEL, *The Economic Structure of Corporate Law*, *o.c.*, 34-35, 41 et seq. Strongly criticised by M. EISENBERG, "The Structure of Corporation Law", *Columbia Law Review* 1989, 1461.

[74] See F. KÜBLER, "The Rules of Capital Under Pressure of the Securities Markets", *l.c.*, 104.

[75] R. KRAAKMAN, "Concluding Remarks on Creditor Protection", *l.c.*, 474.

[76] G. HERTIG and H. KANDA, "Creditor Protection", *l.c.*, 88 et seq.

[77] See 15 above (especially footnote 40) on shareholders' liability for undercapitalisation if the company goes bankrupt within the first three years after incorporation.

[78] See K. VANDEKERCKHOVE, *Piercing The Corporate Veil: A Transnational Approach*, Alphen a/d Rijn, Kluwer Law International, 2007, 765p.; H. MERKT and G. SPINDLER, "Direct Liability of

should remain a sanction for an obvious and generally deliberate abuse of the corporate form and the limited liability it confers. Therefore, such straight forward *non-recognition* of the limited liability is only appropriate when the controlling shareholder itself did not respect the legal entity, e.g. by mixing up assets outside any legal framework or by using the company as a mere shield without accepting the consequences of the asset partitioning that a separate legal entity entails.

More closely related to the traditional liability rules is the concept of "shadow directors". The High Level Group already advocated the introduction of a European framework rule on wrongful trading, alongside a concept of *shadow directors*.[79] Obviously, the majority shareholder who has taken over strategic management powers and actively oriented the corporate decision-making enters into the picture here if insolvency eventually follows. Although respondents to the consultation launched by the High Level Group believed that these issues should not be part of a reform of company law, the High Level Group rightfully argued that directors' liability should be considered together with the rules of company law that it tends to safeguard, including liability for *de facto* directors. This appeal has remained unsuccessful to date.

In Belgium, the legislator recently extended the use of the concept of a shadow director – which was already used in the context of a special liability provision exposing any (actual, former or *de facto*) director to personal liability for all unpaid debts if his "manifestly serious fault" contributed to the bankruptcy of the company[80] – to a new presumption of liability for unpaid withholding taxes, VAT and social security contributions. Moreover, limited liability of a shareholder selling an important participation in a so-called "cash company" has been set aside vis-à-vis the tax authorities. These (semi-) automatic remedies cannot be supported, even if the public authorities are fighting a just cause against fraudulent behaviour. Such legislative intervention constitutes a disproportionate – and therefore unacceptable – attack on the basics of limited liability, causing great harm to entrepreneurial confidence.

Finally, the High Level Group also proposed that subordination of insiders' claims should be considered as an alternative to creditor protection.[81] This technique, according to which the claims of certain insiders are only paid once all other creditors have been reimbursed, thereby converting such claims into quasi-equity, is well-known in some European countries, such as Germany,

---

Controlling Parties (Piercing the Corporate Veil) and Related Legal Constellations", in M. LUTTER (ed.), *Legal Capital in Europe*, *o.c.*, 166-231.

79 Report of the High Level Group of Company Law Experts on a Modern Regulatory Framework for Company Law in Europe, 4 November 2002, 86.

80 Originally a French liability ground, also known as "*action en comblement de passif*": Article 530 of the Belgian Companies Code.

81 Report of the High Level Group of Company Law Experts on a Modern Regulatory Framework for Company Law in Europe, 4 November 2002, 86.

Austria, Spain and Italy, but is nonexistent in others, like France and Belgium.[82] A European initiative in this field seems highly unlikely.

34. ***(Reinforcement of) directors' liability in the proximity of insolvency.*** The High Level Group's (unsuccessful) call for a pan-European wrongful trading rule was mentioned above.[83] What is crucial is the point in time at which such an extended liability rule comes into play. The shift from fiduciary duties towards the shareholders to a duty towards all creditors loses much of its efficacy if it only takes effect once the company is in a (virtual) state of insolvency. Filing for bankruptcy might well then be the only option. The creditors' interests should already be taken into account at a much earlier stage,[84] as soon as there is a realistic chance that the company may not be able to meet all its obligations. This does not imply that management should abandon a going concern approach too early and merely focus on creditors' reimbursement. Conversely, a going concern solution generally remains the preferred solution for all stakeholders, including creditors. The intensity of such a duty towards the creditors will of course depend on the financial position of the company, the chances of full recovery, and... applicable law.

The introduction of a directors' certificate confirming compliance with the envisaged solvency test shifts creditor protection to the reliability of the certificate and therefore, eventually, to directors' liability – and their solvency.

Finally, the High Level Group advocated a European regime for disqualification of directors, serving as an important deterrent alongside civil (and potentially criminal) liability.[85] The Rickford Group supported this recommendation.

35. ***Liability of counterparties due to fraudulent transfers.*** Creditors who have received payment or other benefits (e.g. collateral) to the detriment of other creditors and, for whatever reason, do not qualify for third party protection

---

82 U. HUBER and M. HABERSACK, "Special Rules for Shareholder Loans: Which Consequences Would Arise for Shareholder Loans if the System of Legal Capital Should be Abolished?", in M. LUTTER (ed.), *Legal Capital in Europe*, *o.c.*, 311 et seq.; D. SKEEL and G. KRAUSE-VILMAR, "Recharacterisation and Nonhindrance of Creditors", in H. EIDENMÜLLER and W. SCHÖN (eds.), *The Law and Economics of Creditor Protection. A Transatlantic Perspective*, *o.c.*, 261 et seq.; A. CAHN, "Equitable Subordination of Shareholder Loans?", in H. EIDENMÜLLER and W. SCHÖN (eds.), *The Law and Economics of Creditor Protection. A Transatlantic Perspective*, *o.c.*, 289 et seq.

83 Also supported by the Rickford Group: J. RICKFORD (ed.), "Reforming Capital. Report of the Interdisciplinary Group on Capital Maintenance", *EBLR* 2004, 971.

84 Concerning the crucial sense of timing, see P. DAVIES, "Directors' Creditor-Regarding Duties in Respect of Trading Decisions Taken in the Vicinity of Insolvency", in H. EIDENMÜLLER and W. SCHÖN (eds.), *The Law and Economics of Creditor Protection. A Transatlantic Perspective*, *o.c.*, 315; H. FLEISCHER, "The Responsibility of the Management and Its Enforcement", in G. FERRARINI, K.J. HOPT, J. WINTER and E. WYMEERSCH (eds.), *Reforming Company and Takeover Law in Europe*, *o.c.*, 402.

85 See also H. HIRTE, T. LANZIUS and S. MOCK, "Directors' disqualification and creditor protection", in M. LUTTER (ed.), *Legal Capital in Europe*, *o.c.*, 254 et seq.

(e.g. because they were or should have been aware of the insolvency and, consequently, of the violation of the creditors' right to equal treatment) can be forced to return the consideration under the continental *actio pauliana* doctrine.[86] This basic civil law provision was long neglected but has recently been enjoying a real revival. If restitution of the benefit itself has become impossible (because it has been mingled with the goods of the creditor or has been retransferred to a third party), a liability claim may be brought against the creditor, based on its participation in the unlawful act of the insolvent debtor. Bankruptcy law generally also entrusts the bankruptcy receiver with special powers to reconstitute the assets of the company if their prior transfer was detrimental to the creditors.

In Anglo-Saxon jurisdictions, a similar result is achieved through the fraudulent conveyance theory.[87]

9. Creditor protection: does Europe still want a level playing field?

36. *Creditor protection and company law: diversity rules.* We can only conclude that creditor protection through the concept of legal capital is no longer a compelling objective of European company law and that alternative protective mechanisms are very diverse and remain scattered and underdeveloped. The resistance to fundamentally amending or repealing the Second Directive was considered too great, but the reality will soon become apparent that the Second Directive – once an exponent of a creditor-friendly legislative approach – has lost most of its appeal.

Following the corporate mobility fostered by the Court of Justice's landmark decisions, many Member States are restricting the Second Directive regime to public limited liability companies, for which the capital regime still remains mandatory. So-called "flexible" private limited liability companies are emerging all over the European Union and Member States are hastily adapting their legislative framework to meet this demand from the business community, with a view to preventing a flood of English "Limiteds". The draft Statute for a European Private Company shows that the initial opposition to such a light vehicle, if any, has vanished completely over the last couple of years.

Proponents of the Second Directive may therefore be facing a difficult future. The economic environment, courts and legal scholars will have to get acquainted with the operational reality of the alternative and more flexible regime, including the (limited) distribution restrictions. When, within a couple of years, a new SLIM round is set up, it might be much harder to defend and

[86] See C. PAULUS, "Claw-back Rules and Creditors' Protection", in M. LUTTER (ed.), *Legal Capital in Europe*, *o.c.*, 325 et seq.

[87] G. BAIRD, "Legal Approaches to Restricting Distributions to Shareholders: The Role of Fraudulent Transfer Law", in H. EIDENMÜLLER and W. SCHÖN (eds.), *The Law and Economics of Creditor Protection. A Transatlantic Perspective*, *o.c.*, 199 et seq.; G. WAGNER, "Distributions to Shareholders and Fraudulent Transfer Law", in H. EIDENMÜLLER and W. SCHÖN (eds.), *The Law and Economics of Creditor Protection. A Transatlantic Perspective*, *o.c.*, 217 et seq.

obtain the status quo of the Second Directive. Justifying the different regime on the basis of the type of companies concerned (listed, open, private company) does not seem very convincing.

37. ***From an inclusive, preventive regulation to the "outsourcing" of protective mechanisms.*** It should be pointed out that the light vehicles, whether at the European or at the national level, have little in common. They are primarily corporate forms the status of which is left to the discretion of their founders. This does not raise any fundamental questions, but confirms our finding that the corporate entity is currently more and more perceived as an arrangement between corporate partners. Consequently, externalities need to be dealt with outside corporate law. The reluctance to address creditor protection concerns, irrespective of the corporate form, as part of European company law is not problematic *in se*, but this position deserves to be communicated openly. The creditor protection debate could only benefit from such transparency. Besides, it would only corroborate a position that is already largely supported by legal scholars who argue that insolvency-related creditor protection is rather a matter of insolvency law.[88]

Subsequently, the main question that remains unanswered to date is whether it is desired to address third party protection at the European level. This is not a legal issue nor should it be presented as a matter of subsidiarity favouring national action. In the end, it is primarily a policy decision.[89]

Would it not be contradictory that, on the one hand, a major part of our daily life is governed by rules of European origin – from the state deposit guarantee for our savings to the labelling requirements for a can of soup to the maximum price for a cross-border SMS and the cooling-off period for distance sales – while, on the other hand, despite all this consumer legislation, Europe would abdicate its role as legislator when it really matters in business law, i.e. in the vicinity of insolvency?

Whatever the political option may be, it should be stated openly. The current situation where the Second Directive regime coexists with balance sheet and/or solvency tests at national level (and in the future, potentially also at European level as far as the SPE is concerned), only creates confusion that could easily be avoided. Such an approach can only generate a false impression of harmonisation, producing community legislation that lists the various national or individual options (cf. the Takeover Bid Directive). In reality, replacing harmonisation by a menu of options constitutes an organised form of legal fragmentation.

---

88 E.g. H. HANSMANN and R. KRAAKMAN, "What is Corporate Law?", in R. KRAAKMAN, P. DAVIES et al., *The Anatomy of Corporate Law. A Comparative and Functional Approach*, *o.c.*, 17; J. RICKFORD, "Legal Approaches to Restricting Distributions to Shareholders: Balance Sheet Tests and Solvency Tests", *l.c.*, 139; W. SCHÖN, "The future of legal capital", *l.c.*, 431 and 447.

89 Strongly in favour of banning regulatory divergence regarding creditor protection: E. FERRAN, "The Place for Creditor Protection on the Agenda for Modernisation of Company Law in the European Union", *l.c.*, 214.

38. ***Is there a need for European insolvency legislation?*** Depending on whether one fosters a European or a national creditor protection regime, the relevant insolvency legislation may need to be amended to provide the aspired level of protection.

It should be noted that there is currently no substantive European insolvency legislation. The European Insolvency Regulation only harmonises the conflict-of-law issues relating to insolvencies and provides for jurisdictional cooperation. The content of insolvency law remains a national competence. However, given corporate mobility and the freedom of services, it could be worthwhile considering some kind of harmonisation of insolvency rules protecting third parties,[90] such as a common wrongful trading and fraudulent transfer regulation. Given the direct link to national tort and liability rules, this may well be a challenging initiative. However, the potential national opposition should not deter the European Commission from trying to reach a consensus on a minimum harmonisation, creating a new level playing field that is even more promising than what the Second Directive sought to achieve in the last century.

If a European initiative would not seem feasible, at least initially, the Member States will have to reflect on extending protective rules in their national insolvency legislation. Since the European Insolvency Regulation gives priority to the court and applicable law of the country where the debtor has its "centre of main interest" (COMI), this would to a large extent make the country of the COMI prevail over the corporate law governing the company.[91] If no such exercise is undertaken, the risk of a regulatory gap is imminent. Indeed, if a company from a country which bases its creditor protection mainly on insolvency law moves its COMI to a country that has dealt with creditor protection in its company law, neither of the two protective provisions will apply upon insolvency of the company.[92]

However, it has been argued that simply relabelling corporate creditor protection rules as insolvency protection rules might not withstand the scrutiny of the Court of Justice, which can be expected to take a functional approach rather than a merely formal one.[93] The "insolvencification" of creditor protection rules should therefore be conducted in such a way that the protective rules present sufficient features that link them to insolvency proceedings rather than

[90] For an example of an Italian company that transferred its registered office abroad just before its creditors filed a petition for insolvency: F. MUCCIARELLI, "The Transfer of the Registered Office and Forum-Shopping in International Insolvency Cases: an Important Decision from Italy", *ECFR* 2005, 512 et seq.

[91] For a detailed analysis, see L. ENRIQUES and M. GELTER, "Regulatory Competition in European Company Law and Creditor Protection", in H. EIDENMÜLLER and W. SCHÖN (eds.), *The Law and Economics of Creditor Protection. A Transatlantic Perspective*, *o.c.*, 441 et seq.; W. SCHÖN, "The future of legal capital", *l.c.*, 447.

[92] C. KERSTING, "Discussion Report", in H. EIDENMÜLLER and W. SCHÖN (eds.), *The Law and Economics of Creditor Protection. A Transatlantic Perspective*, *o.c.*, 236.

[93] J. ARMOUR, "Legal Capital: An Outdated Concept?", *l.c.*, 22-23; C. KERSTING, "Discussion Report", *l.c.*, 236.

to corporate issues.[94] This would require a profound rethinking of the applicable rules, exceeding by far a mere transposition into another legal framework. Even, if the European Union cannot swiftly agree on a minimum harmonisation of creditor protection rules applicable to all limited liability companies, we still believe that this exercise is absolutely necessary. Let us hope that we do not need another major crisis to create the required sense of urgency…

10. Concluding remarks: the way forward…

39. ***Need for a well-considered reform at the European level.*** Where the legal capital regime once was the omnipresent standard of creditor protection in limited liability companies in continental Europe, the "erosion of capital law" has gradually come from the inside. The rulings of the Court of Justice on corporate mobility and the general demand for deregulation have occasioned reflection on the added value of the capital regime set out in the Second Directive.

Apparently, the Member States could not find a better response to the expected rise of the UK-governed "Limiteds" than to modify (or announce the modification of) their national legislation to create a corporate form without any substantive minimum capital requirement, abolishing capital formation and maintenance rules. Creditor protection is not totally ignored but it is generally realised through non-harmonised solvency and/or liquidity tests. Under this regime, the board of directors is required to issue a distribution certificate and the directors are personally liable in case of unauthorised distributions.

In this respect, it is revealing that the draft regulation on the European Private Company presented by the European Commission only provided for a simple balance sheet test. Whether additional solvency tests are required was a matter to be resolved by the shareholders. The European Parliament insisted on the solvency test being compulsory if the share capital is below EUR 8,000. However, both approaches typically reflect the reluctance of the European legislator to impose a harmonised model for creditor protection throughout the European Union.

The current situation *de facto* results in a two-track policy. Smaller companies can opt for a light vehicle regime, adopting a flexible corporate form offered by national legislation or incorporating abroad and taking advantage of the (secondary) freedom of establishment guaranteed by European case law. On the other hand, public limited liability companies, and listed companies in particular, still have to comply with the highly technical and burdensome capital formation and maintenance rules on dividend distributions, share repurchases, cross-participations, financial assistance, etc. However, it is

---

[94] L. ENRIQUES and M. GELTER, "Regulatory Competition in European Company Law and Creditor Protection", *l.c.*, 454.

generally accepted that these rules are not always consistent or fully adequate. Indeed, the protective regime is entirely based on historically realised profits and disregards any forward looking statement. If future prospects are taken into account by national law, this is based on corporate interest standards, rather than on the technical rules for capital maintenance. Furthermore, legal capital is no longer the relevant standard of creditor protection for those companies that operate in regulated sectors such as banking and insurance, although they still have to observe the capital rules linked to their corporate form.

This dual situation is anything but optimal. Besides, it is likely that the capital regime imposed by the Second Directive will remain the subject of debate during the next decade, as the business community becomes increasingly acquainted with the alternative regimes concerning distributions organised at the national level. We therefore believe that a status quo is not the preferred option and that the European Union should aspire to a superior creditor protection regime which applies all over Europe, irrespective of the corporate form of the limited liability company.

40. ***Need for a Company Law Directive harmonising creditor protection.*** Creditor protection has been an important goal not only of the Second Directive, but also of the Third, Sixth and Tenth Directives on mergers, demergers and cross-border mergers. It has also been taken into account in the Statute for a European Company (SE).

In our view, European company law should not leave creditor protection entirely to the national legislator, as is the case at present for private limited liability companies. We would therefore warmly welcome any European initiative to harmonise the rules on distributions to shareholders, responding to the challenges that arise from the recent case law on corporate mobility. Such an initiative should address all forms of distributions to shareholders, including dividends, share repurchases, reimbursement of shareholder contributions, financial assistance and certain forms of directors' remuneration, and should apply irrespective of the corporate form of the limited liability company. Any distribution should be preceded by a directors' certificate issued on the basis of a solvency and liquidity test establishing that, for the foreseeable future, the proposed distribution does not prejudice creditors' rights to be paid in a timely manner. It may be advisable to require the tests to be performed on the basis of an (up-to-date) financial plan based on assumptions endorsed by the board of directors, with the board accepting liability for the reasonableness of the assumptions. Auditor certification could also be envisaged.

Distributions without such a certificate or in breach of the certificate should not be allowed. In this respect, directors' liability would be the first remedy. However, we believe that the distribution regime should also take account of the position of the directors who are asked to issue a distribution certificate. Reference is made to the position of non-executive directors, who *de facto* largely depend on the information provided by the company's management, and to the potential pressure that a reference shareholder could exert to have financial projections drawn up that enable the envisaged distribution. While these concerns may be partially addressed by adequate D&O insurance, we believe that European legislation harmonising the concepts of shadow directorship and fictitious dividends would greatly benefit a true European level playing field. Shareholders who were aware or reasonably should have been aware that a distribution jeopardised the rights of creditors should be compelled to reimburse the distribution, if need be. Likewise, shadow directors should be held liable alongside the formal directors if unauthorised distributions have occurred.

41. ***Minimal harmonisation of insolvency law.*** We support the idea of the High Level Group that rules on wrongful trading are needed at the European level. Moreover, we would suggest a minimal harmonisation of insolvency law, in particular with respect to the duties of directors vis-à-vis the corporate creditors in the vicinity of insolvency. Such harmonisation would counter the need for a national reform of insolvency law in order to avoid regulatory gaps which may result from the legislative approach taken by a Member State.[95] We believe that the harmonisation of substantive law is preferable to the cumulative application of creditor protection rules provided for by the insolvency law of the Member State of incorporation of the company and of the Member State where the insolvency proceeding is opened.

42. ***Practical considerations.*** The suggestions above express our preferences for new European initiatives harmonising creditor protection with respect to all European limited liability companies. However, we realise this may not be practically feasible in the short term. Therefore, priority should be given to (i) a minimal harmonisation of insolvency law, introducing uniform concepts of wrongful trading and fraudulent conveyance and (ii) harmonisation of the distribution requirements for private companies, based on a solvency and liquidity test rather than on the classical balance sheet test established by the Second Directive. Harmonisation of sanctions, providing for rules on shadow directorship and reimbursement of fictitious dividends, would also be beneficial. At a later stage, once this regime has been evaluated and, if necessary, refined, it could also be made applicable to public limited liability companies and replace the Second Directive.

---

[95] As stated above, this might be the case in a Member State that has provided for creditor protection rules in national company law rather than in its insolvency legislation, thereby incurring the risk of a lack of sufficient remedies in the event of an insolvency proceeding being opened on its territory with respect to a foreign company (see 38 above).

Bibliography

G. AKERLOF, "The Market for "Lemons": Quality Uncertainty and the Market Mechanism", *Quarterly Journal of Economics* 1970, 488-500;

J. ARMOUR, "Share Capital and Creditor Protection: Efficient Rules for a Modern Company Law", *Modern Law Review* 2000, 355-378;

J. ARMOUR, "Legal Capital: An Outdated Concept?", in H. EIDENMÜLLER and W. SCHÖN (eds.), *The Law and Economics of Creditor Protection. A Transatlantic Perspective*, The Hague, Asser, 2008, 3-25;

J. ARMOUR, H. HANSMANN and R. KRAAKMAN, "What is Corporate Law?", in R. KRAAKMAN, P. DAVIES et al., *The Anatomy of Corporate Law. A Comparative and Functional Approach*, Oxford, University Press, 2nd ed. 2009, 1-34;

G. BAIRD, "Legal Approaches to Restricting Distributions to Shareholders: The Role of Fraudulent Transfer Law", in H. EIDENMÜLLER and W. SCHÖN (eds.), *The Law and Economics of Creditor Protection. A Transatlantic Perspective*, The Hague, Asser, 2008, 199-215;

H. BOSCHMA, M. LENNARTS and J. SCHUTTE-VEENSTRA, *Alternative systems for capital protection*, 18 August 2005, 84p.;

A. CAHN, "Equitable Subordination of Shareholder Loans?", in H. EIDENMÜLLER and W. SCHÖN (eds.), *The Law and Economics of Creditor Protection. A Transatlantic Perspective*, The Hague, Asser, 2008, 289-302;

P. DAVIES, "Directors' Creditor-Regarding Duties in Respect of Trading Decisions Taken in the Vicinity of Insolvency", in H. EIDENMÜLLER and W. SCHÖN (eds.), *The Law and Economics of Creditor Protection. A Transatlantic Perspective*, The Hague, Asser, 2008, 303-339;

H.J. DE KLUIVER, "Europe and the Private Company, An Introduction", in H.J. DE KLUIVER and W. VAN GERVEN (eds.), *The European Private Company?*, Antwerp, Maklu, 1995, 21-41;

H.J. DE KLUIVER, "Inspiring a New European Company Law? Observations on the ECJ's Decision in *Inspire Art* from a Dutch Perspective and the Imminent Competition for Corporate Charters between EC Member States", *ECFR* 2004, 121-134;

H.J. DE KLUIVER, "Towards a Simpler and More Flexible Law of Private Companies. A New Approach and the Dutch Experience", *ECFR* 2006, 45-68;

A. DORRESTEIJN and O. UZIAHU-SANTCROOS, "The *Societas Privata Europaea* under the Magnifying Glass", *European Company Law* 2008, 277-283;

R. DRURY, "The European Private Company", *EBOR* 2008, 125-136;

F. EASTERBROOK and D. FISCHEL, *The Economic Structure of Corporate Law*, Harvard University Press, 1991, 370p.;

H. EIDENMÜLLER and W. SCHÖN (eds.), *The Law and Economics of Creditor Protection. A Transatlantic Perspective*, The Hague, Asser, 2008, 489p.

H. EIDENMÜLLER, B. GRUNEWALD and U. NOACK, "Minimum Capital in the System of Legal Capital", in M. LUTTER (ed.), *Legal Capital in Europe*, *ECFR* 2006, special volume 1, Berlin, De Gruyter, 2006, 17-41;

M. EISENBERG, "The Structure of Corporation Law", *Columbia Law Review* 1989, 1461-1525;

L. ENRIQUES and J. MACEY, "Creditors versus Capital Formation: the Case against the European Legal Capital Rules", *Cornell Law Review* 2000-01, 1165-1204;

L. ENRIQUES and M. GELTER, "Regulatory Competition in European Company Law and Creditor Protection", in H. EIDENMÜLLER and W. SCHÖN (eds.), *The Law and Economics of Creditor Protection. A Transatlantic Perspective*, The Hague, Asser, 2008, 421-457 E. FERRAN, "Legal Capital Rules and Modern Securities Markets - the Case for Reform, as Illustrated by the U.K. Equity Markets", in K.J. HOPT and E. WYMEERSCH (eds.), *Capital Markets and Company Law*, Oxford University Press, 2003, 115-143;

E. FERRAN, "The Place for Creditor Protection on the Agenda for Modernisation of Company Law in the European Union", *ECFR* 2006, 178-221;

H. FLEISCHER, "The Responsibility of the Management and its Enforcement", in G. FERRARINI, K.J. HOPT, J. WINTER and E. WYMEERSCH (eds.), *Reforming Company and Takeover Law in Europe*, Oxford University Press, 2004, 373-416;

H. FLEISCHER, "Legal Capital: A Navigation System for Corporate Law Scholarship", in H. EIDENMÜLLER and W. SCHÖN (eds.), *The Law and Economics of Creditor Protection. A Transatlantic Perspective*, The Hague, Asser, 2008, 27-36;

J. FREEDMAN, "Limited Liability: Large Company Theory and Small Firms", *Modern Law Review* 2000, 317-354;

S. GRUNDMANN, "Regulatory Competition in European Company Law – Some Different Genius?", in G. FERRARINI, K.J. HOPT and E. WYMEERSCH (eds.), *Capital Markets in the Age of the Euro. Cross-Border Transactions, Listed Companies and Regulation*, The Hague, Kluwer Law International, 2002, 561-595;

H. HANSMANN and R. KRAAKMAN, "Towards Unlimited Shareholder Liability for Corporate Torts", *Yale Law Journal* 1990-91, 1879-1934;

K. HEINE and W. KERBER, "European Corporate Laws, Regulatory Competition and Path Dependence", *European Journal of Law and Economics* 2002, 47-71;

G. HERTIG, R. KRAAKMAN and E. ROCK, "Issuers and Investor Protection", in R. KRAAKMAN, P. DAVIES et al., *The Anatomy of Corporate Law. A Comparative and Functional Approach*, Oxford, University Press, 2nd ed., 2009, 275-304;

H. HIRTE, T. LANZIUS and S. MOCK, "Directors' disqualification and creditor protection", in M. LUTTER (ed.), *Legal Capital in Europe*, *ECFR* 2006, special volume 1, Berlin, De Gruyter, 2006, 254-279;

U. HUBER and M. HABERSACK, "Special Rules for Shareholder Loans: Which Consequences Would Arise for Shareholder Loans if the System of Legal Capital Should be Abolished?", in M. LUTTER (ed.), *Legal Capital in Europe*, *ECFR* 2006, special volume 1, Berlin, De Gruyter, 2006, 308-324;

M. KAHAN, "Legal Capital Rules and the Structure of Corporate Law: Some Observations on the Differences Between European and U.S. Approaches", in K.J. HOPT and E. WYMEERSCH (eds.), *Capital Markets and Company Law*, Oxford University Press, 2003, 145-149;

R. KRAAKMAN, "Disclosure and Corporate Governance: An Overview Essay", in G. FERRARINI, K.J. HOPT, J. WINTER and E. WYMEERSCH (eds.), *Reforming Company and Takeover Law in Europe*, Oxford University Press, 2004, 95-113;

R. KRAAKMAN, "Concluding Remarks on Creditor Protection", in H. EIDENMÜLLER and W. SCHÖN (eds.), *The Law and Economics of Creditor Protection. A Transatlantic Perspective*, The Hague, Asser, 2008, 469-475;

C. KERSTING, "Discussion Report", in H. EIDENMÜLLER and W. SCHÖN (eds.), *The Law and Economics of Creditor Protection. A Transatlantic Perspective*, The Hague, Asser, 2008, 233-238;

F. KÜBLER, "The Rules of Capital Under Pressure of the Securities Markets", in K.J. HOPT and E. WYMEERSCH (eds.), *Capital Markets and Company Law*, Oxford University Press, 2003, 95-114;

M. LUTTER, *Kapital, Sicherung der Kapitalaufbringung und Kapitalerhaltung in den Aktien- and GmbH-Rechten der EWG: eine Untersuchung zur Ausfüllung von Artikel 54 Abs. 3 lit. g des Vertrages über die Errichtung einer Europäischen Wirtschaftsgemeinschaft*, Karlsruhe, Verlag C.F. Müller, 1964, 580p.;

M. LUTTER, "A Mini-Directive on Capital", in H.J. DE KLUIVER and W. VAN GERVEN (eds.), *The European Private Company?*, Antwerp, Maklu, 1995, 201-206;

M. LUTTER (ed.), *Legal Capital in Europe*, *ECFR* 2006, special volume 1, Berlin, De Gruyter, 2006, 701p.

M. LUTTER, "Legal capital of public companies in Europe. Executive summary of considerations by the expert group on 'Legal Capital in Europe'", in M. LUTTER (ed.), *Legal Capital in Europe*, *ECFR* 2006, special volume 1, Berlin, De Gruyter, 2006, 1-14;

P. MANKOWSKI, "Does contract suffice to protect the creditors of a company and their assets?", in M. LUTTER (ed.), *Legal Capital in Europe*, *ECFR* 2006, special volume 1, Berlin, De Gruyter, 2006, 394-410;

H. MERKT, "Der Kapitalschutz in Europa – ein rocher de bronze?", *Z.G.R.* 2004, 305-323;

H. MERKT, "European Company Law Reform: Struggling for a More Liberal Approach", *ECFR* 2004, 3-35;

H. MERKT and G. SPINDLER, "Direct Liability of Controlling Parties (Piercing the Corporate Veil) and Related Legal Constellations", in M. LUTTER (ed.), *Legal Capital in Europe*, *ECFR* 2006, special volume 1, Berlin, De Gruyter, 2006, 166-231;

H. MERKT, "Creditor Protection Through Mandatory Disclosure", in H. EIDENMÜLLER and W. SCHÖN (eds.), *The Law and Economics of Creditor Protection. A Transatlantic Perspective*, The Hague, Asser, 2008, 93-120;

M. MIOLA, "Legal Capital and Limited Liability Companies: the European Perspective", *ECFR* 2005, 413-486;

F. MUCCIARELLI, "The Transfer of the Registered Office and Forum-Shopping in International Insolvency Cases: an Important Decision from Italy", *ECFR* 2005, 512-533;

P. MÜLBERT and M. BIRKE, "Legal Capital – Is There a Case against the European Legal Capital Rules?", *EBOR* 2002, 695-732;

C. PAULUS, "Claw-back Rules and Creditors' Protection", in M. LUTTER (ed.), *Legal Capital in Europe*, *ECFR* 2006, special volume 1, Berlin, De Gruyter, 2006, 325-340;

B. PELLENS and T. SELLHORN, "Improving Creditor Protection through IFRS Reporting and Solvency Tests", in M. LUTTER (ed.), *Legal Capital in Europe*, *ECFR* 2006, special volume 1, Berlin, De Gruyter, 2006, 365-393;

B. PETTET, "Limited Liability – A Principle for the 21st Century?", *Current Legal Problems* 1995, 125-159;

J. RICKFORD (ed.), "Reforming Capital. Report of the Interdisciplinary Group on Capital Maintenance", *EBLR* 2004, 919-1027;

J. RICKFORD, "Legal Approaches to Restricting Distributions to Shareholders: Balance Sheet Tests and Solvency Tests", in H. EIDENMÜLLER and W. SCHÖN (eds.), *The Law and Economics of Creditor Protection. A Transatlantic Perspective*, The Hague, Asser, 2008, 135-179;

P. SANTELLA and R. TURRINI, "Capital Maintenance in the EU: Is the Second Company Law Directive Really That Restrictive?", *EBOR* 2008, 427-461;

W. SCHÖN, "The future of legal capital", *EBOR* 2004, 429-448;

W. SCHÖN, "Balance Sheet Tests or Solvency Tests – or Both?", in H. EIDENMÜLLER and W. SCHÖN (eds.), *The Law and Economics of Creditor Protection. A Transatlantic Perspective*, The Hague, Asser, 2008, 181-198;

D. SKEEL and G. KRAUSE-VILMAR, "Recharacterisation and Nonhindrance of Creditors", in H. EIDENMÜLLER and W. SCHÖN (eds.), *The Law and Economics of Creditor Protection. A Transatlantic Perspective*, The Hague, Asser, 2008, 261-287;

R. TAS, *Winstuitkering, kapitaalvermindering en -verlies in NV en BVBA*, Kalmthout, Biblo, 2003, 684p.;

C. TIMMERMANS, *Company Law as Ius Commune*, Antwerp, Intersentia, 2002, 23p.;

K. VANDEKERCKHOVE, *Piercing The Corporate Veil: A Transnational Approach*, Alphen a/d Rijn, Kluwer Law International, 2007, 765p.;

G. WAGNER, "Distributions to Shareholders and Fraudulent Transfer Law", in H. EIDENMÜLLER and W. SCHÖN (eds.), *The Law and Economics of Creditor Protection. A Transatlantic Perspective*, The Hague, Asser, 2008, 217-231;

E. WYMEERSCH, "Reforming the Second Company Law Directive", available at http://papers.ssrn.com/sol3/papers.cfm?abstract_id=957981;

E. WYMEERSCH, "Het statutaire kapitaal van de vennootschappen", in *Liber amicorum Lucien Simont*, Brussels, Bruylant, 2002, 913-935.

Transcripts of Capital and Creditor Protection Session

Paper: *Jean-Marie Nelissen Grade and Matthias Wauters*
Respondent: *Jonathan Rickford*
(British Institute of International and Comparative Law)
Chair: *Didier Martin (Bredin Prat, Paris)*
Rapporteur: *Anneleen Steeno (K.U.Leuven)*

A. Abstract

Current situation. The current situation of creditor protection is not optimal. The Second Directive for public companies imposing restrictive rules as to capital formation and capital maintenance does not provide adequate creditor protection. The capital requirements are not linked to the future business of the company and the distribution limitation is entirely based on a balance sheet test, which is backward-looking. For private companies the tendency exists, both at national and European level (draft Regulation on the Statute for a European Private Company) to create a company form without legal capital regime. However, the proposals on capital in the European Private Company proposal are found inadequate.

In the field of corporate law there is a problem with the UK Limited operating in the context of a commercial system outside the territory of its incorporation. It is often said that the UK Limited, having no minimum capital requirement, has no creditor protection and does not recognise capital maintenance. Professor Rickford argued that there is no evidence showing that the so-called invasion of Limiteds would lead to a real risk for creditor protection. Continental Europe wrongfully believes that distribution rules for Limiteds would be less protective.

The proposal of the paper. The paper proposed a harmonised European rule for private companies along the lines of the Rickford proposal: solvency certification certifying solvency over a foreseeable period and liquidity over a one-year period. However, in some jurisdictions the Second Directive-type regime is regarded as acceptable, familiar and still superior, so there should be room for flexibility. On the European Private Company, it is not clear whether the European Private Company imposes a solvency requirement or a balance sheet requirement and whether it indeed imposes a requirement for a capital cushion or not. The conclusion reached was that, whatever the regime is for the European Private Company, if there was to be a harmonised regime for private companies, it should be the same as the regime for the European Private Company. So that when it is debated what the capital maintenance regime should be for the

European Private Company, we need to bear in mind that we are at least setting a possible precedent for harmonisation in Europe at a later date.

The solvency test also requires adequate measurement rules with regard to the forward-looking financial information on the basis of which the directors have to issue the solvency certificate. As long as there are no generally accepted standards for such forward-looking test, the solvency test remains open-ended and provides a lesser degree of certainty to the directors as to which amount can be distributed.

Furthermore, the question arose whether only the certificate must be published or whether also the underlying assumptions should be made public to allow creditors to assess the correctness of the test and the reasonability of the assumptions.

It was suggested to impose the establishment of a financial plan, as is the case at incorporation of the company. The financial plan would not be made public, but would only be used in case of a liability claim.

Insolvency. The relevance of insolvency law was also discussed, and it was agreed that a measure of insolvency harmonisation was desirable. The main proposals in the paper were that there should be harmonisation on the liability of shadow directors and harmonisation on the liability of directors for wrongful trading (trading in neglect of the interests of creditors in the close vicinity of insolvency). It was agreed that those were desirable outcomes and that principles of justice militate in favour of harmonised principles within Europe in those two fields.

B. Response to paper by Jonathan Rickford

I have considerable difficulty in responding to this paper. The reason is that I very largely agree with it and I am struggling to find the basis for a response which is interesting and provocative. I am not going to dwell on the rival merits of Second Directive-tied balance sheet tests and forward-looking cash flow-based solvency tests because that is an argument that is being debated at length and it can continue to be debated later today, but I think it is rather worn out. It is in my opinion obvious that if you want security-interested creditors, you look to see whether the money will be available in the future, and the only question is whether you can find a good way of doing that. So there is no need to further elaborate on this.

I will talk about the paper and I am going to dwell on certain aspects of the paper where I think some questions and perhaps pressure can be brought to bear on whether the proposals lead to the right conclusion. I also want to cast perhaps a different light and a different perspective on some aspects of the paper.

Before I embark on that, I would like to make two personal reflections, if I may indulge myself. It is 37 years ago that I first came to Brussels, which was in 1972 before the UK joined the European Community, and the proposal on the table was the Second Directive, which should be applied to UK private companies. It was going to apply to public companies throughout Europe, except the UK where it was going to apply to UK private companies. It was explained to me that the justification for the Second Directive was a competitive one, that all companies of an equivalent standing should be subject to the same handicap or advantage, depending which way you look at it, as the German company was exposed to in terms of having a minimum capital. Otherwise it would be unfair that UK companies could trade in Germany and expose creditors to a different range of risks from those which would be exposed to the creditors of German companies in their reciprocal situation. It did occur to me to ask whether there was any evidence that, on the basis of the existing quite substantial international trade between the UK and Germany already, there was any difference in the effect on the protection of creditors for German companies in the UK as opposed to UK companies in Germany. It was explained to me that that was not the basis on which European harmonisation was done. Of course we fought hard on the UK side to ensure that we got what we regarded as parity of treatment for the more than a million private companies in the UK, not to be subjected to the same burdens that were exposed to the 1,000 or 2,000 public companies in Germany. We sought to establish, I think successfully, that the UK private company was the equivalent to the continental private company in all material respects. But one must speculate on what would have happened if the Second Directive had been applied fairly to all private companies throughout Europe and what the debate would be on these issues today if that had been the case.

The second point I want to make is about the race to the bottom. I see no national or commercial advantage to the United Kingdom in the UK Limited's popularity in continental Europe, with one possible exception which I will come to in a moment. I had the privilege of leading our company law reform programme, to revise the whole of our companies legislation over a three-year period between 1998 and 2001 and we looked at this issue. It never occurred to us remotely to consider the competitive advantages of a fleet of light vehicles invading the Continent (if I may mix my metaphors, I am not sure if light vehicles float, but you know what I mean). We were concerned, and we will always be concerned in the United Kingdom, with the adequacy of our company law, including its creditor protections, in the interest of our national economy. We will produce a set of rules which we think are optimal in terms of the competiveness of the economy, not the competiveness of company law, and I think that that leads to a thought which is of general application when considering the threat from the invading light vehicles: it is important to be specific and to state what it is which is defective in the national law system of these invading light vehicles.

Another thought which occurs to me is whether, now that we have French light vehicles and Dutch light vehicles, the threat is going to be any more from the UK light vehicle – and if it is from the UK light vehicles as opposed to the French and the Dutch, why? What is really going on, apart from the obvious, disreputable exploitation by certain company formation agents of the UK light vehicle as a kind of attractive device for attracting their customers into believing they are going to be able to get away with fraud and other disreputable conduct, which will pass.

I get to my presentation. As I said, I agree with the paper. I think we start from a situation where the European Commission has created a sort of stalemate in capital debate. There is the housemaid's baby excuse in relation to the Second Directive. You are familiar with the housemaid's baby excuse. The housemaid says to her mistress "Well, there is a baby but it is only a very little one". The Commission has concluded that the Second Directive causes little trouble. Having commissioned a report on whether it is efficient, it concludes that it causes little trouble, because by adopting a minimalist interpretation of the Second Directive – no requirement in particular for maintaining a capital cushion in relation to share premiums – the capital cushion turns into an almost entirely voluntary component of company financing. All that is left is the minimum capital, which the Commission describes as trivial, as indeed I think it is in the context of the Second Directive. The Winter Report took the same view and said that since it was trivial it was not worth worrying about. I think the trivial surplus is always worth repealing, but that is perhaps a marginal issue.

So we have a kind of stalemate on reforming the Second Directive but, as the authors of this paper rightly emphasise, there are other developments in the field. The housemaid's baby turns out already to be making rather a noise and rather a mess, and arguably the housemaid's baby is going to grow. The erosion is on a number of fronts: the UK Limiteds, the SPE (the European Private Company), and the difficult problems of resolving how to deal with international insolvencies in the context of the European Insolvency Regulation, and they then make a proposal.

Before I embark on looking at the erosions and the proposal, I had been minded to refer to the relevance, if any, of the Second Directive and the financial crisis. I think we have already had two remarks that it makes no difference. I think that is indeed the case but it is something perhaps we can discuss. To my mind, there is no discernable difference between the performance of banks which were subject to the Second Directive and those that were not, and I do not think we can imagine that those that were not would have performed any better if they had been. A second general observation is that we need to bear in mind the Treaty principles in relation to harmonisation of company law. The objective is not to produce uniformity; the objective is to produce equivalence of protection to the extent necessary and in a context of subsidiarity. There should only be Community action where it is better than state action. I will look at that at the end. A third general observation is the Anglo-American fallacy, which is something of a *bête noire* for me. I defy any of you to find any substantial issue of company law or corporate governance on which the English agree with the Americans. There is a very strong strand of doctrine or written empirical analysis which derives from the Unites States where you find particularly law and economics professors from the United States assuming that English law is the same as American. You need, whenever you see that, to question it. It is, in my experience, entirely false. It is very understandable that then Continental writers, commenting on that American writing, should assume that it is correct. What is unforgivable, and it happens, is for UK law and economics writers to reach the same assumption without troubling themselves with the British law. Now that does actually matter and - it is not just a *bête noire* of mine - it does lead to the next point.

I want to look very briefly at the position of the UK Limited and at capital maintenance law in the United Kingdom. We invented it. The notion of legal capital undistributable as a quid pro quo for limited liability was invented in the 1840s and 1850s in the United Kingdom. When we came to look at the Second Directive, it presented remarkably few problems for us. The big change was: a minimum capital for public companies, which we regarded as trivial; the capital constitution rules, particularly valuations, which we regarded as expensive and probably of not great value; and a more formalised distribution rule, which only reflected the rule we already had that the capital cushion should not be distributed including share premium account (so that all consideration for shares should not be distributed). It was only some years later that we discovered that it was not the intention of the Second Directive to make the share premium account non-distributable, which of course destroys the case for the capital cushion because it makes the capital cushion voluntary except to the extent of the minimum capital. When we discovered that, we did wonder whether we were really dealing with something that amounted to a coherent system at all in the Second Directive.

Now, the UK private company is subject to capital maintenance except that there is no minimum, and thus that the balance sheet test applies to a bare net asset test. The capital reduction rules for UK private companies are considerably stricter than required by the Second Directive. The 2006 reforms abolished financial assistance for UK private companies. We invented financial assistance in the first place, and a thoroughly bad invention it was. We also introduced a form of reduction of capital for private companies based on a solvency certificate, which is something quite closely corresponding to what for short I will refer to as a Rickford-style solvency certificate. That means that you can make distributions out of a UK private company by capital reduction via a solvency certificate.

The proposals that were made by my group for private companies were, of course, to adopt the solvency certificate and abandon the balance sheet test, even a bad balance sheet test, for private companies and those have already been described. It is worth emphasising that the distinction between a bad balance sheet test and a solvency test in terms of fundamental principle is actually quite hard to define. Both tests are seeking to secure there is enough resource in future to ensure that the company can cover its costs and expenditures. The values in a balance sheet, if they really corresponded to the values of the assets and liabilities to the company, would reach the same conclusion as a solvency test would. The reason why there is something wrong with the balance sheet test is because balance sheets are inherently defective as predictors of cash flows for the future. And that is the logic of the Rickford proposal. However, when we consider the competitive effects of the invasion of the UK light vehicles, we need to bear in mind that it is by no means a foregone conclusion, even in the United Kingdom, that the Rickford proposal will be accepted for private companies.

At the moment we have a capital maintenance regime for private companies of the kind that I described, which is traditional capital maintenance but with no minimum capital. So it looks remarkably like, to my eyes, what we are going to have in France and the Netherlands. The Rickford proposal is highly controversial and the major objection to it is that it is too strict. By depriving directors of the comfort blanket of the arithmetic test – add up your assets, add up your liabilities, if there is a surplus, it follows you can distribute it and you are safe – we are leaving them with a real responsibility to assure the public that their business is going to be capable, on the basis of the present evidence, on a reasonable commercial assessment, of meeting its liabilities. And the business community in the United Kingdom does not like that. They prefer the comfort blanket of the net asset test, the rigid and to my mind hopelessly imperfect linkage of the company's capacity to distribute with its balance sheet.

Incidentally, while we are on the subject of balance sheets, if we have the Commission proposal in place for exempting micro-companies from the obligation of preparing public annual accounts, where is the balance sheet going to come from? I am fundamentally opposed to that idea. One might also ask whether the justification for the Centros decision at all could still remain in place in relation to micro-companies because the Centros decision was fundamentally based on a notion that for creditor protection, subject to special considerations which were allowed by way of exception, creditor protection was secured in the main by publicity.

What is our policy objective? It is worth dwelling on this. Are we trying to protect creditors? Or are we trying to stifle Centros and to block the invasion of UK Limiteds? It is arguably contrary to the Treaty, but we need to look at the merits of blocking the UK Limiteds. There clearly is a problem, and it is a problem not just for UK Limiteds but for all company law vehicles where you have a company law vehicle from one jurisdiction operating entirely in the context of another jurisdiction's business environment. There might be a case for saying that it should be blocked. But of course it is only an issue of degree. Nobody is seriously arguing that where the head office of a company is in the jurisdiction of its law of incorporation, it should not be allowed to operate mainly or very heavily in other jurisdictions. The problem will arise whether we have a Centros-type choice or not. However, a blocking proposal does look as if it is contrary to the Treaty. And having a harmonised law that amounts to a blocking proposal will be just as much contrary to the Treaty. You cannot do by secondary legislation and the Treaty law what you are not permitted to do by national legislation in terms of stifling the operation of the fundamental freedoms. You cannot use the bootstraps of secondary European legislation to inhibit the operation of the fundamental freedoms.

I want to look at the SPE. Of course this is only a proposal, and to that extent dwelling on the uncertainties and unsatisfactory character of the drafting of the SPE might be regarded as a waste of time. But I think now is the time to debate both what the effect is of the Commission's proposal and, on the back of that debate, to debate what the SPE ought to have. The paper that we are discussing says that there are no capital maintenance rules provided by the SPE and that the Commission's inner convictions, revealed by the justification that it gives for the content of the SPE, in terms for example of no capital minimum and no capital formation rules for the SPE, seem to be clear from the proposal. On whether the SPE is subject to the capital cushion, the non-distributable share capital regime, it seems to me that the SPE proposals are ambiguous. I have included at the back of my slides a copy of the key texts: paragraph 11 of the Preamble and Article 21.1.

The Commission says that it is providing uniform rules based on a balance sheet test. The text says that the assets should fully cover the liabilities. The Commission goes on to say that the balance sheet will be a Fourth Directive or International Accounting Standards Regulation balance sheet. The first reflection on that is that that is not going to produce a uniform test. The second reflection is that what the Commission actually says is that the assets and liabilities should be defined by that balance sheet. It does at least leave open the possibility whether the assets fully covering the liabilities should be considered and determined by reference to their capacity to produce cash flows, rather than the mere arithmetical addition of their valuations. However, it seems clear from the Preamble that no capital cushion is required (paragraph 11 of the Preamble) Distributions that leave the European private company with liabilities that exceed its assets should be prohibited. "Liabilities that exceed its assets." It does not say anything about share capital so it looks as if there is no share capital cushion. It is not clear that the rules in the proposal for the European Private Company on reductions of capital enabling creditors to object to reductions on the grounds of their claims that are at stake, is consistent with the absence of a share capital cushion, but it may be. Similarly, if the European Parliament proposes to have a minimum capital adopted, is that consistent with the absence of a share capital cushion?

The conclusion I think we draw is that the distribution rules are obscure. I think the paper is a bit unfair in saying that there is nothing there at all. It is possible that we have a solvency requirement. It is possible that we have a bare net assets requirement. It is possible that we have a net assets plus capital cushion requirement. It is just hopelessly obscure.

On solvency certificates, of course, we have an explicit provision allowing solvency certificates for one year to be adopted in the European Private Company's articles. What that means is debatable. And it needs to be considered in the context of the fact that all these European Private Company rules are directly applicable Community law, which means that they take effect in national law in their own terms. And it is neither permissible nor desirable that Member States should elaborate the rules. It looks to me as if that means that no additional solvency requirement over and above the optional solvency requirement to be provided in the articles can be imposed. And the articles cannot impose a solvency requirement for more than a year. Whether that is the intention is debatable. I think that is the effect, and it seems to me to be thoroughly undesirable. Issues about the extent to which that provision pre-empts national law, in terms of sanctions, also arise. Article 22 provides one sanction. It is not clear whether Member States can provide more. On the face of it I would have thought not.

If the UK government does accept the Rickford proposal for the UK private company, the issue will arise whether the proposals on capital for the SPE will be competitive with the UK private company regime. But of course that depends on what the SPE regime on capital ultimately turns out to be. As it is at the moment, I think we do not know.

My next topic before my final slide, where I consider the proposal, is insolvency. It is clear that insolvency is highly relevant – particularly, incidentally, in the case of the small private companies. For the UK, and I do not know whether this is true for you, the distribution rule for small private companies is not very important. The owners are also the directors and they return what they get from the company by way of remuneration. And one asks oneself whether it makes the slightest difference whether you have one distribution rule or another or none at all, until you reach the point of insolvency.

Now, as we all know, the European Insolvency Regulation provides both a jurisdiction and a choice-of-law rule for insolvency which is territorial. It is territorial in terms of the main insolvency being conducted in the country of the centre of main interest, which is not unlike the real seat, with subordinate liquidations being possible, if it is worth it, in other jurisdictions of establishment. That enables one to consider a regime for insolvency which is colour-blind, so to speak, in terms of the nature of the incorporation of the insolvent company. It has been suggested by some that that is a way of blocking Centros. You can get over the problems of escape from national capital maintenance regulation by having stricter insolvency rules. The same principle applies to any such proposal as it applies to any other mechanism for blocking Centros. The European Insolvency Regulation confers a power of discretion on states to adapt their insolvency law to deal with insolvencies of foreign companies which have their centre of main interest within their jurisdiction. It does not confer the power on states to adopt an insolvency law that frustrates the operation of the fundamental freedoms. So insolvency law will fail to be justified in so far as it restricts freedom of movement in exactly the same way as any other restriction on freedom of movement.

It is suggested – or at least I think the paper suggests, but I believe it is not the authors' view - that capital maintenance and creditor protection are not really part of company law and are best dealt with by insolvency law. It seems to me that they need to work in parallel and the two need to be considered together. Each state needs to consider whether its insolvency law adequately supplements the capital maintenance law that applies to the companies within its jurisdiction. It makes excellent sense to allow company law to deal with distributions and the regulation of the relationship between directors and shareholders and creditors which that requires, on the one hand, and for insolvency law to deal with the relationship between the companies and creditors, primarily the creditors in the jurisdiction of the insolvency, on the other hand.

Now I am coming to a conclusion. I want to look at the paper's proposal. The paper argues for harmonisation of company law and insolvency law. The paper argues that so far as company law is concerned, the Second Directive is inadequate and a superior creditor protection regime is required. I agree with that. Then it argues that that superior creditor protection regime should be applied throughout the Community. Now, I have never advocated that. Perhaps the degree of excitement and hostility that the Rickford proposals provoked in some parts of continental Europe, particularly Germany, came as a surprise, but not as a complete surprise. And it seemed to me all along that for those states who wished to continue to apply a Second Directive type regime, they should be allowed to do so. It might be defective, but there were, as the paper argued, both path dependency and contextual reasons why one form of capital maintenance regime might be desirable in one state and another in another. I understand to a sufficient extent the uncertainties that are created by the operation of an alien corporate structure within the commercial context of another country. And the desire for an assurance that, at least at a minimum, there are assurances, there are protections for creditors on a going concern basis that are adequate for the purpose. But the question at the moment is only whether either the existing regime as it operates for the UK Limited in the UK or the very similar regimes, I would argue, that are going to operate in France and the Netherlands and perhaps other states as they adopt the abolition of the minimum capital and adopt the €1 private company, whether that or possibly a UK regime based on solvency certification, on Rickford lines, whether either one of those two is a sufficient assurance in terms of creditor protection for alien companies operating in jurisdictions which adopt a stricter view such as, for example, Belgium. That is the question. And it seems to me that it is only when one has resolved that question in the light of the principle that harmonisation is only required in order to produce, to the extent necessary, equivalent protection, that one can reach the conclusion that mandatory harmonisation Europe-wide is a good idea. Personally, I could live with it, but I am concerned about the interests of jurisdictions elsewhere in Europe.

What is clear, I think, is that if we are going to have an SPE – which I personally oppose, but that is another debate – if we are going to have an SPE and if we are going to have a harmonised rule, then the rule in the SPE regulation and the harmonised rule will have to be the same. We will have to have a harmonised rule that also harmonises the SPE. And for that reason, as we debate the capital maintenance regime for the SPE, we need to be conscious that if we have a harmonised rule, we are pre-empting what that rule will be. As for harmonised rules for insolvency and bankruptcy: the arguments in favour of shadow director regimes, which will also apply, incidentally, in corporate law and the arguments in favour of a wrongful trading standard on a harmonised basis seem to be stronger. The reason I believe that is twofold. First of all, both in the case of shadow directors and in the case of wrongful trading, it seems to me that the proposition appeals to a universal principle of justice that we can all recognise. People who act as directors to induce directors to breach their duties should be liable to a certain extent. And as a general principle, as directors approach the region of insolvency, it is clear that the focus of their concern should change away from the interests of shareholders and towards the interests of creditors. So I have much less difficulty with the proposal for a harmonised rule in those two areas.

I conclude by saying that I think it is a splendid paper and I almost entirely agree with it.

C. Discussion

Didier MARTIN

There is a link between minimum capital, insolvency rules and publicity of financial information. If you take the example of the new light vehicles in Europe, specifically in France, then it is possible to have a minimum capital of €1, no insolvency test (so there is no commitment of the board concerning the availability of funds for the next year), but on the other hand there is the cost of financial reporting. Do you see any link between these three?

Henri OLIVIER , University of Liège

I think the question you raise is one of two fundamental issues, namely the relationship between the global financial reporting system and the solvency test. The second issue has been made by Professor Nelissen Grade and is the problem of the liability. I think both issues are essential to the debate. I slightly disagree with Professor Rickford that we are discussing about competition here. We definitely need to consider consumer protection because we are trying to secure business relationships, to improve confidence in commercial transactions and to establish a unique single market in Europe. If that is the objective, we need to consider the best solution for securing creditor protection. I agree that the current situation is comfortable but unsatisfactory. I entirely agree with that conclusion. But now the point is: can the solvency test offer a solution? First we need to define the solvency test. We have exactly the same kind of difficulties in defining the method of the solvency test as we have for all financial reporting processes. As has been said already, if the measurement rules were exactly the same, we could arrive at the same conclusion with the balance sheet test as with the solvency test and the income statement approach. We have the same kind of measurement difficulties for financial reporting and also for any information which is forward-looking (information which is trying to define what will be the future of the company). And indeed, the crisis in the banking sector is a very easy argument, but I think it is a bit more complex. It is an easy argument to say that in the banking sector we had no support from the capital. I think it is a bit more complex than that. Basically, I am afraid that the issue of liability is absolutely central and in a Belgian context, there is some merit in looking at the financial plan at the outset of the company and how this system, which is far from being perfect, is applied, also for very small companies. What are the consequences of such financial plan, which is close to a solvency test, for the liability of those who are creating the company? I think that inevitably we will have a problem in the context of a solvency test about the disclosure, the publicity and the responsibility that the directors will take. Do we publish exclusively the certificate? Where is this certificate published? How is it made available to creditors? Is it accompanied by some supporting documents? Is the solvency test and the basis for establishing the solvency test also disclosed? Do you give the creditors the different elements to be able to judge whether this solvency test was made with the necessary care? These are questions that are still open, especially in a context outside the UK.

Jonathan RICKFORD

On the question of liability, I completely agree. This is absolutely fundamental. If we are going to adopt a solvency approach, then we have to strike a balance between a liability regime which secures proper compliance without so terrifying directors that they are scared to make distributions at all. Companies, directors are often tempted to hold cash and keep it under their own control and to resist the making of distributions. I make two observations on liability. First of all, on the solvency certificate that we have already got in our regime for capital reduction, there is criminal liability for issuing it in the absence of reasonable evidence on which it is based. After the event, when the company goes bust, the directors can be taxed with demonstrating the basis on which they reached the conclusion. I think that is quite a good way of dealing with it. As well as, of course, having civil liability on directors and civil liability on the shareholders who knowingly receive unlawful dividends, which is in the private company proposal and seems to me to be right. Going further and requiring business plans and additional disclosure seems to me to raise very serious confidentiality problems. Although Professor Olivier agrees with me, I want to repeat that the solvency test and the balance sheet test are both actually about the future; even the balance sheet test is about the future. The values in that balance sheet will only be true if it is the case that the cash flow to be realised by the resources in question will amount in current value to the value that is stated in the balance sheet. It is actually the same thing, and the problem that we have got with the balance sheet test at the moment is that the directors are let off the hook. All they have to do is to produce a number that the auditor will accept and that complies with accounting standards.

Didier MARTIN

I wish to dwell on a different matter. Have we really measured that the competition is driven by the light vehicles? The choice of the place of incorporation or the real seat can depend on tax reasons or participation rights of employees. Do we have any evidence that the share capital or the minimum capital plays a real role in the competition? The capital regime is obviously very important, but at the same time I hardly believe that it can be the critical criterion of choice of the location of the company. Do you have any figures?

Jonathan RICKFORD

There are certainly figures about the numbers of UK Limiteds in different jurisdictions. I do not have them off the top of my head, but there are now tens of thousands in Germany and there are significant populations in Denmark, the Netherlands and a few in Italy (these figures are published). What there is not, is any convincing evidence on what the motivation is for doing this. Some of it is pure salesmanship: people are being persuaded to buy UK Limiteds because they are represented as being a light vehicle, which is actually not the case. So some of it is that. We know from Centros that Mr and Mrs Bryde happily admitted that they were trying to avoid Danish capital maintenance law and they did not want to pay the capital. I am still astonished that Mr and Mrs Bryde thought it was worth going to England to incorporate a company, with all the trouble that that created, just in order to avoid Danish capital maintenance and minimum capital law. I think they must have been misled as to what they were getting, because I think the costs/benefits look different. The Dutch cases are different, I think. It looks as if in the case of the Dutch cases, the entrepreneurs in question were – if that is the right way of describing them – were influenced very much by the cheapness, the lack of cost and the lack of administrative burden in forming a UK limited company. Many jurisdictions have made their company registration system hugely more efficient. For example, it can be done online in many jurisdictions. And it is much quicker than it was, even five or six years ago. So that competitiveness has already had its effect, and that is a good reason for thinking that Centros was a good decision.

Karel VAN HULLE, K.U.Leuven and European Commission
I would like to make a few observations in this very interesting debate. I think that the paper shows clearly that the Second Directive is an unfinished symphony. It started a long time ago, and the Commission has not carried the logic of its thinking any further. Now if we were to do that at European level, and harmonisation is a very complex procedure today, even more than it ever was, we would all agree, probably, in Europe that companies with limited liability need to have a system in place whereby creditors are protected. I think it is pretty obvious that we would agree on that. But beyond that, we see the debate, and it is very much culturally implicated (the Germans will have great difficulties to delete their traditional maintenance regime). Could we not in Europe have a system whereby we have an option? We agree on the principle and then we leave it to the Member State to decide how it fills in that principle. You can have your solvency test, you could have your old capital maintenance system, you just have to make sure that it works. Now if we were to introduce such a proposal, the first thing we will face is an administrative burden. The Commission will have to come forward with a paper in which it shows what the advantages are of the solvency test compared to the capital maintenance regime. And I am absolutely certain that the cost of the solvency test, of introducing that and applying it, will be phenomenal and therefore the Commission will have great difficulty to come forward with that proposal without having a lot of opposition against it. I think that the suggestion to do something about insolvency is a very good one. It is an area where the financial crisis has shown now that we have a problem in Europe. And I think that maybe because of the financial crisis, Europe will be forced to do something within this area. If you take, for instance, major groups: why can we not have an efficient system of group supervision in the financial sector? Because we do not have rules to deal with the crisis situation. But again, if you want to deal with insolvency rules, it will be extremely complex, because the views are very different and we enter into areas of the law which are extremely disharmonised. And lastly, I do not think, Jonathan (Rickford), that I can agree with you when you say that the regime in the SPE should be the same as that in the Second Directive. I would believe that we could have a competition of systems whereby you have the SPE

regime that would be even better than what you have in the directive so as to allow the private company to have some attractive features, which might make it more likely that it is going to be used.

Philippe PELLE, European Commission

I would like to provide some information on where we stand on the European Private Company, the SPE. As Jonathan Rickford was saying, in the proposal on distribution we introduced, a bit as a way to test the water, the question whether a solvency test could fly. In our proposal, we left this as an option to the founders of the company. Through negotiation and counselling, which is far from being concluded, things have evolved and this option, which initially was intended to be left to the founders / shareholders, is moving to an option for Member States. But it will be on top of a balance sheet test, not as an alternative to the balance sheet test, and as Henri Olivier was saying, we do not even suggest what the solvency test should be. We say that directors could issue, if Member States so require, a solvency certificate. Why do we not go into the details of what a solvency test should be? Because some of the Member States are currently experimenting with such solvency tests, for instance Finland, and they were telling us that since this is still in the phase of experiment, they would not want us at a European level to come forward with a test that may not suit all the Member States. Also, as Karel Van Hulle was underlining, the complexity of it, at a time where one of the main priorities of the Commission is to come forward with simplification and reducing the administrative burden, makes us hesitant to define such solvency test. So as to the SPE proposal, I would see it as testing the water. We are waiting a bit.

Jonathan RICKFORD

There are a couple of things that Karel Van Hulle said I need to respond to. First of all, I am not advocating applying the Second Directive to the SPE. That would be, to my mind, an absolutely disastrous outcome. All I was arguing was that if we are going to have a harmonised rule for private companies, it has got to be the same as the harmonised rule for the SPE, whatever that is. I am personally not convinced that we need a harmonised rule for private companies. Like Karel Van Hulle, I think that giving options is appropriate. Particularly in the light of what Philippe Pelle says about the experiment of the Finns. But on the subject of experiment and cost, Karel Van Hulle suggested that introducing a solvency test would be hugely costly. We do have an experiment involving a medium-sized European-style economy in the shape of New Zealand, which introduced, instead of traditional capital maintenance (English capital maintenance), a solvency certification regime, with a net assets test, but not a binding net assets test (different from my proposals on net assets but not hugely different). That was introduced in 1994, if I remember rightly. The feedback in terms of the effects is a bit disappointing in the sense that they have had no problems with it. Nobody suggests that it is hugely expensive. It is generally agreed to be superior to what was there before, and it works. And although it is not necessary that something that works for New Zealand will work for us, it is a reasonable prospect that it would at least for the UK and it is generally regarded as convincing evidence for the UK. Of course it does not follow for other contexts and other jurisdictions. But one recognises that experimentation is probably desirable.

Marieke WYCKAERT, K.U.Leuven
I have three questions with regard to remarks that have been made. First of all, I heard Professor Rickford say that the balance sheet test and the solvency test would be the same thing if you would be able to conduct it on the basis of good balance sheet elements. So my question to all of you is, do we not also have to look at accounting rules as to their contents, not only to disclosure and publicity but also how do we make accounting? Second question, and that is more to Professor Nelissen Grade and Matthias Wauters: If you add a corporate interest test to the technical rules of dividend distribution, do we also add some element in the debate? The third question is, do we not, with the solvency test on the basis of a directors' certificate, shift the risk of solvency or insolvency to directors?

Didier MARTIN
On the last question, my answer is definitely yes. There is a shift in the liability. I would like to add some comments on the first question. I definitely agree that we have an issue about financial reporting. The issue is fundamental. What is the objective of financial reporting? Is it something backward-looking to provide some elements on the accountability of the directors to shareholders? Or do we have a forward-looking instrument or something which can be used for a forward-looking purpose? Of course, when we are preparing the financial statements and discussing about measurement rules, we will have a different approach. If we want definitely to have something which is useful for a forward-looking perspective, then we will go much more towards fair value measurements, toward different elements, and we will certainly not use extensively historical value as we are doing now. Historical value will be much more appropriate for a different purpose. If we are using a solvency test which is forward-looking, then I am afraid that the financial statements and the measurement in the financial statements are not appropriate.

Jean-Marie NELISSEN GRADE
I would like to comment on the two other questions that Marieke Wyckaert raised. We are fully aware that the solvency test would increase the risk of liability for the directors and we are a bit concerned about that. Adding an additional test such as a corporate interest test is not going to change a lot. The

decision clearly would have to meet the corporate interest. One of the things we had been thinking about, but that we have not developed yet because we have not thought it through, is whether it would not help to link this solvency test to a financial plan. The directors would have to develop a financial plan and would only be held liable if the assumptions appear later to not have been reasonably developed. In putting this idea on the table, we have certainly been inspired by the financial plan that you know with respect to the incorporation of the company (which also addresses the issue of disclosure that Jonathan Rickford mentioned). This financial plan is not meant to put an additional burden on the company but, on the contrary, to offer a certain protection against risks of liabilities. You could imagine a similar system in which the directors would issue a certificate of solvency that would have to be disclosed. The financial plan on which the solvency test would be based would be developed by the board, made available to the notary public (or another place in another jurisdiction), but not be published. It would be used only as a defence in case of a liability action against the directors.

Marieke WYCKAERT
I want to clarify that what I was trying to say with my question was that even if a balance sheet test is met, directors can be liable if the distribution is not in the corporate interest.

Jean-Marie NELISSEN GRADE
I agree. If you distribute whatever you can under article 617 of the Belgian Companies Code, there is still the risk of liability on the basis of violation of the corporate interest.

Jonathan RICKFORD
Just incidentally on the corporate interest in the UK: there is a clear recognition that there is an overriding duty of the directors to act prudently whatever test they apply. But the really interesting question is accounting standards, it seems to me. Our study in the UK was driven by impending International Accounting Standards mainly on directors' share options schemes, and on pensions. There were also problems on tax and financial instruments. But the key thing was that the expensing of share options threatened to result in a reduction of distributable profits. The other key introduction was the new full reserving for pension fund deficits which could lead to enormous hits on the balance sheet and thus on distributable profits. I will not trouble you with tax and financial instruments, mainly because I cannot remember. It is extremely debatable whether we would have even embarked on considering these issues in the UK had it not been for the threats paradoxically from the introduction of forward-looking financial statements to distributability. We thought that the introduction of forward-looking financial statements would risk reducing

unduly the scope for distribution. As we looked at it more closely, we discovered that it could work both ways. It could both reduce and unduly increase the scope for distribution. That is what drove us in the direction of a solvency test. It is paradoxical because you would expect that if International Financial Reporting Standards reflect a forward-looking view, they would be a better basis for determining distributions than historic cost ones. It emerged that, first of all, the share option issue was not an issue in the UK law because the fact that you put it in a profit and loss account did not mean that it was a realised loss, and it clearly was not a realised loss. The pension scheme problem, I think, illustrates the problem of identifying solvency with the balance sheet description. The problem is volatility. The effect of current International Financial Reporting Standards, although they are better than the equivalent English UK standards, is to produce the most phenomenal swings in the valuation of pension fund deficits. And they can produce in a matter of a few weeks a situation where at one point a company has a massive amount of distributable profits and at another point it is hugely in deficit. And the answer is that there is something wrong with the standard. But we hesitated in my group to conclude that there was something wrong with the standards, because we knew we would never persuade the International Financial Reporting Council to adapt its standards in order to suit a balance sheet based distribution test. I think the politics of it are still the same, and the result is that there is no comfort, unfortunately, in a route that would lead to more sensible accounting standards. Nor, I think, necessarily should the International Financial Reporting Council change its standards in order to respond to this point. Because they are trying to do a different thing, which is to produce a solid figure that is valid for the moment to which judgement can be applied.

Corporate Governance in a European Perspective

Hilde Laga[1] *and Floris Parrein*[2]
Jan Ronse Institute – K.U.Leuven

Abstract

Corporate governance has become an important issue at European level. Indeed, on the basis of the Winter Report, the Commission launched several initiatives aimed at enhancing corporate governance disclosure, the exercise of shareholders' rights and the independence of the board of directors. The question arises to what extent the European legislator should take action. This question is very intriguing. We argue for a rather limited role, since European corporate governance inevitably has to take the differing ownership structures into account. European corporate governance can formulate general principles, but filling in the details will remain a shared task.

Table of contents

1. Introduction

1. ***Separation of ownership and control.*** Corporate governance refers to the organization of the relationship between owners and managers of a corporation. It stands for the way in which corporations are directed and controlled[3] and deals

[1] Professor K.U.Leuven, Attorney Courtrai Bar (Laga).
[2] Ph. D. Candidate K.U.Leuven.
[3] This definition of corporate governance can be found in the Cadbury Report. The OECD Principles of Corporate Governance, which were revised in 2004, suggest a more general approach. According to these Principles, corporate governance "involves a set of relationships between a company's management, its board, its shareholders and other stakeholders. It also provides the structure through which

with the way in which suppliers of finance to corporations assure themselves of getting a return on their investment[4]. Framing this issue is necessary in a situation where the suppliers of finance do not run the company themselves but hire a management team that is responsible for the daily activities of the company. This separation of ownership and control lies at the heart of the need for corporate governance[5] [6], which is about optimizing the structure of decision-making within companies[7]. The separation of ownership and control is an old problem which was already pointed out by Adam Smith. He wrote that "the directors of companies however, being the managers rather of other people's money than of their own, it cannot well be expected, that they should watch over it with the same vigilance with which the partners in a private copartnery watch over their own"[8].

This does not mean that corporate governance only protects the private interests of investors. Indeed, the way in which a company is directed has an impact on its general economic setting. An indirect relationship between sound corporate governance and the financial stability of the market can be proven: the stability of firms and markets are essential elements for maintaining financial stability. Corporate governance tools contribute to the intermediate objectives at the firm level[9]. Therefore, the importance of sound corporate governance should not be underestimated.

---

the objectives of the company are set, and the means of attaining those objectives and monitoring performance are determined. Corporate governance essentially focuses on the problems that result from the separation of ownership and control, and addresses in particular the principal-agent relationship between shareholders and directors" (Preamble of the OECD Principles of Corporate Governance 2004).

4 H. OOGHE and T. DE LANGHE, "The Anglo-American versus the Continental European corporate governance model: empirical evidence of board composition in Belgium", *European Business Review* 2002, 437.

5 H. OOGHE and T. DE LANGHE, "The Anglo-American versus the Continental European corporate governance model: empirical evidence of board composition in Belgium", *European Business Review* 2002, 437; M. LITTGER, "Funktion und Verwendungschancen der neuen Kodizes am Beispiel von Corporate Governance", *Rechtstheorie* 2008, 496; P. NOBEL, "Stakeholders and the legal theory of the corporation", M. TISON et al. (eds.), *Perspectives in Company Law and Financial Regulation – Essays in Honour of Eddy Wymeersch*, Cambridge University Press 2009, 167; C. TEICHMANN, "Corporate Governance in Europa", *ZGR* 2001, 646.

6 For an overview of the different American crises caused by this separation, see: M.J. ROE, "The Inevitable Instability of American Corporate Governance", (September 2004). Harvard Law and Economics Discussion Paper No. 493. Available at SSRN: http://ssrn.com/abstract=615561 or DOI: 10.2139/ssrn.615561, 4-7.

7 S. GRUNDMANN, *European Company Law*, Antwerp/Oxford, Intersentia, 2007, no. 473, p. 268.

8 Adam SMITH, *The Wealth of Nations*, 1776, Book 5, Chapter 1, Part 3, Art. 1.

9 E. WYMEERSCH, "Corporate Governance and Financial Stability", Working Paper 2008-11, Financial Law Institute, University of Ghent, 13. A lot of research has been done on the correlation between firm value and good corporate governance. BEBCHUK, COHEN and FERRELL point out that there is a negative correlation: the "entrenching provisions" – i.e. provisions which protect incumbent management from removal – are bringing about lower firm valuation. These authors suggest that the correlation that poison pills and golden parachutes have with lower firm value at least partly reflects the greater tendency of managers of firms with lower firm value to adopt takeover readiness provisions: L. BEBCHUK, A. COHEN and A. FERRELL, "What Matters in Corporate Governance?" (1 September 2004). Harvard Law School John M. Olin Center Discussion Paper No. 491; 22 *Review of Financial Studies* 783-827 (2009).

2. Growing Interest in Corporate Governance at European Level

2. *Winter Report.* In the light of major corporate scandals[10], corporate governance has become a major issue globally. Regulators in most developed countries have started to propose different alternatives in order to restore market confidence[11]. Their approaches differ significantly: some provide for self-regulation in the form of codes of conduct with a "comply or explain" rule, others provide for a remedy at law[12]. Individual Member States of the European Union have also opted for different solutions. The vastness of corporate governance codes which are relevant for the European market is symbolic of the different legal cultures within the EU.

Besides these national initiatives, the EU has also taken a position on corporate governance. Its approach stems from the drive to create a single market[13] [14]. Between 1968 and 1989, the European Community adopted several Directives and one Regulation in the area of company law. This beginning of European company legislation can be described as a movement towards an "EU Companies Act"[15]. The proposal for a Fifth Company Law Directive[16] and the initial proposal for a Statute for a European Company (hereinafter: "SE")[17] included detailed rules in the field of internal corporate governance.

However, the initial idea of harmonizing differences in national law to achieve legal certainty was abandoned, since the enlargement of the European Community made such an approach more and more difficult to sustain. The different views on the role of labor within the corporation made such harmonization

---

[10] Several financial scandals in the US (Enron, WorldCom, Tyco, etc.) and Europe (Parmalat, Vivendi) shocked the international markets.

[11] M. LAMO DE ESPINOSA ABARCA, "The need for substantive regulation on investor protection and corporate governance in Europe: does Europe need a Sarbanes-Oxley?", *J.I.B.L.R.* 2004, 19(11) 419.

[12] M. LAMO DE ESPINOSA ABARCA, "The need for substantive regulation on investor protection and corporate governance in Europe: does Europe need a Sarbanes-Oxley?", *J.I.B.L.R.* 2004, 19(11) 419.

[13] K. LANNOO, "A European perspective on corporate governance", *Journal of Common Market Studies* 1999, 280.

[14] From a more general point of view, the purpose of harmonizing company law in Europe is to ensure that companies can establish themselves all over the Union, thereby creating a "common market" for their products and services: E. WYMEERSCH, "Company law in Europe and European company law", Financial Law Institute, University of Ghent, 2001, no. 15, p. 17.

[15] M. PANNIER and J. RICKFORD, "Corporate Governance Disclosures in Europe", (2005) *EBLR* 975. These authors refer in this context to the First proposal for a Fifth Directive concerning the structure of public limited companies and the powers and obligations of their organs, OJ 1972 C131/49.

[16] First proposal for a Fifth Directive concerning the structure of public limited companies and the powers and obligations of their organs, OJ 1972, C131/49. See also Amended proposal of 20 November 1991 for a Fifth Directive based on Article 54 of the EEC Treaty concerning the structure of public limited companies and the powers and obligations of their organs, COM (91) 372 final.

[17] Council Regulation (EC) No 2157/2001 of 8 October 2001 on the Statute for a European company (SE) (2001) OJ L 294/1.

impossible: the proposed Fifth Company Law Directive was never enacted because it promoted labor's role in corporate governance. The same issue held up the adoption of the SE for many years because of the concern that such a business organization would weaken labor protections[18].

Therefore, the European Community refrained for some years from pursuing plans for harmonization and regulation[19]. Some authors spoke of "the crisis of European company law". In a second phase, the Commission tended to follow a different harmonization concept in accordance with the White Book on completing the Internal Market (1985). This new approach focused on the mutual recognition[20] of national provisions[21]. In 2001, the European Community took up the thread and introduced the European Company Regulation and Directive[22]. However, the blockage in the same year of the Takeover Directive in the European Parliament caused major political problems, which the Commission tried to solve by establishing a High Level Group of Company Law Experts (hereinafter: "High Level Group") to make recommendations on a modern regulatory framework in the EU for company law[23].

This Group saw its mandate extended in 2002 to cover additional corporate governance issues in the light of issues raised by the collapse of Enron[24]. The Winter Report assumes that disclosure obligations are the most powerful tool for protecting market transparency and focuses on enhancing corporate governance disclosure requirements for listed companies. The Report differentiates between listed, open and close corporations. For each of them, a different regulatory approach is provided. Another key element is the convergence of various national

---

[18] A.R. PINTO, "The European Union's Shareholder Voting Rights Directive from an American Perspective: Some Comparisons and Observations" (15 September 2008). *Fordham International Law Journal*, Vol. 32, 2008; Brooklyn Law School, Legal Studies Paper No. 117. Available at SSRN: http://ssrn.com/abstract=1268454, 11.

[19] T. BAUMS, "European Company Law Beyond the 2003 Action Plan", ECGI - Law Working Paper No. 81/2007; *European Business Organization Law Review*, Vol. 8, 2007. Available at SSRN: http://ssrn.com/abstract=973456, 1.

[20] The concept of "mutual recognition" has been developed by the European Court of Justice: see ECJ Case 120/78 Cassis de Dijon (1979) ECR 649.

[21] Completing the Internal Market – White Paper from the Commission to the European Council of 14 June 1985, COM (85) 310 final. For this approach, see the later proposals for an SE Statute: A. WEHLAU, "The Societas Europaea: A critique of the Commission's 1991 amended proposal", 29 (1992) *CMLR* 473, 478.

[22] The adoption of the European Company can be seen as a major step forward. Moreover, the entire area of accounting law has a completely new foundation. The corpus of capital market law measures has been completely reformed. The case law of the European Court of Justice facilitates cross-border mobility. These successes are at the basis of what GRUNDMANN calls the "boom of European company law": S. GRUNDMANN, "The Structure of European Company Law: From Crisis to Boom", *EBOR* 5 (2004) 632.

[23] On the history of the High Level Group Reports, see K.J. HOPT, "Zur Arbeit der High Level Group of Company Law Experts" in P. NOBEL (ed.), *Internationales Gesellschaftsrecht einschliesslich internationales Kapitalmarktrecht*, Bern, 2004, p. 73.

[24] In a reaction to Enron, the European Council's meeting in June 2002 in Seville extended the mandate of the High Level Group to include issues related to best practices in corporate governance and auditing, in particular concerning the role of non-executive directors and supervisory boards, management remuneration, management responsibility for financial information, and auditing practices: Presidency Conclusions, Seville European Council, 21 and 22 June 2002, SN 200/02, p. 15.

corporate governance codes of Member States. The High Level Group makes some recommendations: (i) the inclusion of a corporate governance statement in the annual accounts of the corporation; (ii) additional disclosure obligations concerning corporate governance; (iii) the strengthening of the independent directors on the board; (iv) additional rules on voting information and access for shareholders. Responsibilities of institutional investors are revisited, mainly as regards their obligation to disclose investment policies and the exercise of voting rights.

3. *Action Plan.* The Winter Report laid the foundation of the Commission's Action Plan of 2003[25], the objectives of which are twofold. The first goal is to strengthen shareholders' rights and the protection of employees, creditors and other parties that listed companies deal with. Moreover, the Commission wants to foster the efficiency and competitiveness of business, with special attention to specific cross-border issues[26].

In the field of corporate governance, the Commission states that European corporate governance rules should fully respect the subsidiarity and proportionality principles of the Treaty and the diversity of many different approaches to the same questions in the Member States[27]. Moreover, European corporate governance rules should be flexible in application, but firm in the principles. The Commission emphasizes that the EU must define its own European corporate governance approach, tailored to its own cultural and business traditions. Indeed, the EU wants to develop its own response to the American Sarbanes-Oxley Act[28], which was adopted on 30 July 2002 in the wake of a series of scandals and created a series of problems due to its "outreach" effects on European companies and auditors[29]. The European "no size fits all" approach to

[25] The question arises as to why this kind of initiative has been taken so late. VAN HULLE and MAUL point to "tiredness" of the European legislator, after being very active in the field of capital markets and financial services regulation in the eighties: K. VAN HULLE and S. MAUL, "Aktionsplan zur Modernisierung des Gesellschaftsrechts und Stärkung der Corporate Governance", *ZGR* 2004, 485.

[26] European Commission, Communication from the Commission to the Council and the European Parliament "Modernising Company Law and Enhancing Corporate Governance in the European Union – A Plan to Move Forward", Brussels, 21.05.2003, COM (2003) 284, pp. 8-9.

[27] Indeed, for years different national concepts of employee representation on company boards blocked initiatives like the draft Fifth Directive, the SE Statute and the proposed directives on cross-border merger of companies and transfer of their registered seat: K.J. HOPT, "Europäisches Gesellschaftsrecht – Krise und neue Anläufe", (1998) *ZIP* 96, 99; M. PANNIER and J. RICKFORD, "Corporate governance disclosure in Europe", (2005) *EBLR* 977.

[28] The Sarbanes-Oxley Act contains far-reaching rules on accounting oversight, auditor independence, corporate responsibility, enhanced financial disclosure, analyst conflict of interest and corporate and criminal fraud accountability. Many rules – e.g. the mandatory division between audit and non-audit services – are very controversial. On the influence of the Sarbanes-Oxley Act on the European corporate governance practices and rules, see H.-J. HELLWIG, "The US Concept of Corporate Governance under the Sarbanes-Oxley Act of 2002 and Its Effects in Europe", *ECFR* 3/2007, 417-433 and C. STOLTENBERG, "A Comparative Analysis of Post-Sarbanes-Oxley Corporate Governance Developments in the US and European Union: The Impact of Tensions Created by Extraterritorial Application of Section 404, 53 *Am. J. Comp. L.* 457 2005, 457-492.

[29] European Commission, Communication from the Commission to the Council and the European Parliament "Modernising Company Law and Enhancing Corporate Governance in the European

good corporate governance which attaches great importance to flexibility and the use of non-binding legal instruments can be seen as an example of the so-called "Better Regulation Approach"[30].

The Action Plan provides the blueprint for recent and future changes in European company law. All the mentioned key elements of the Winter Report were included as priorities in the Commission's Plan, which was open for public consultation for several months. More than 110 contributions were received. In general, they were supportive of the scope and content of the actions announced[31]. Other EU institutions welcomed the Action Plan as well[32]. Accordingly, the European Commission and the Member States have taken initiatives to implement the Action Plan. In this article, we will focus on these initiatives[33].

3. General Outline: European Corporate Governance and Ownership Structures

4. *Corporate governance and ownership structures.* Before we examine these initiatives in detail, we want to point out the major difficulty in developing European corporate governance rules.

Such rules – whether binding or not – are about ensuring that a company is directed in its own interests and not in the interests of others[34]. Therefore,

Union – A Plan to Move Forward", Brussels, 21.05.2003, COM (2003) 284, p. 5.

[30] Better Regulation aims at the improvement of the quality and effectiveness of the acquis communautaire in such a way as to remove unnecessary burdens. D. WEBER-REY underlines that the European corporate governance policy is an excellent example of this approach. Indeed, by its principles-based approach, the European Commission wants to impose only as much of a burden as is necessary to reach the intended goals: D. WEBER-REY, "Effects of the Better Regulation Approach on European Company Law and Corporate Governance", *ECFR* 3/2007, 384.

[31] Synthesis of the responses to the Communication of the Commission to the Council and the European Parliament – Modernising Company Law and Enhancing Corporate Governance in the European Union – A Plan to Move Forward – COM (2003) 284 final of 21 May 2003. A Working Document of DG Internal Market, 15 November 2003.

[32] See Opinion of the European Economic and Social Committee on the Communication from the Commission to the Council and the European Parliament "Modernising Company Law and Enhancing Corporate Governance in the European Union – A Plan to Move Forward" (COM (2003) 284 final), OJ 2004 C 80/12. In its Resolution of 21 April 2004, the European Parliament welcomed the Action Plan as well and expressed strong support for most of the initiatives announced.

[33] See also: H. LAGA, "Europese initiatieven inzake corporate governance", *T.R.V.* 2006, 659-672.

[34] The question in whose interests a company should be governed is not easy to answer. In the US, contemporary corporate law is supposed to have as a central objective the protection of shareholder interests in the management-controlled firm. However, more than half the states have adopted "stakeholder" statutes that allow boards to take into consideration a variety of non-stockholder interests. In most continental European countries, it is not the exclusive, or even the primary, purpose of the board to protect the interests of the shareholders, but rather to promote the "interests of the firm", which is a far broader concept: T. BAUMS and K. SCOTT, "Taking Shareholder Protection Seriously? Corporate Governance in the United States and Germany". American Journal of Comparative Law, Vol. 53, Winter 2005; *ECGI* - Law Working Paper No. 17/2003; Stanford Law and Economics Olin Working Paper. Available at SSRN: http://ssrn.com/abstract=473185 or DOI: 10.2139/ssrn.473185, 2.

corporate governance provides for an effective system which monitors the management of a corporation. Different corporate governance actors contribute to this monitoring: the market, the (minority) shareholder, an independent board of directors and – possibly – the legislator.

The degree to which these actors can contribute to the monitoring of the management depends on the ownership structure of the company. Indeed, the differing degree to which a market relies on equity markets for its corporate finance has a major influence on the legal and other rules concerning the control and management of corporations[35]. Two main models of corporate governance can be distinguished. Liberal market economies subscribe to the Anglo-American model, while coordinated market economies in most cases feature the Continental model of corporate governance[36].

On the one hand, where corporate ownership is dispersed – which is the case in the United States[37] and the United Kingdom – the small, dispersed shareholders may lack capacity to monitor the managers of the corporation. Therefore, the importance of the role of the supervisory body – board of directors or supervisory board – consisting of monitoring the management is stressed. In this case, corporate governance rules will focus on supervisory body structures and practices to ensure that this body is a distinct entity which is capable of acting separately from the management.

On the other hand, when corporations are controlled by large shareholders – e.g. in Germany and Italy[38] – concern shifts to ensuring the fair treatment of

---

[35] LA PORTA et al. argue that the level of protection of minority shareholders and creditors is associated with lower concentrations of share ownership and is positively related to growth opportunities. In this view, good corporate governance is among the factors responsible for good performance. Common law systems based on transparency and arm's length relationships offer better protection than civil law systems. According to these studies, the latter should move towards the more efficient common law system: R. LA PORTA et al., "Investor protection and corporate governance", *Journal of Financial Economics* 58 (2000), 3-29. See also J. McCAHERY and E.P.M. VERMEULEN, "Role of corporate governance reform and enforcement in the Netherlands", M. TISON et al. (eds.), *Perspectives in Company Law and Financial Regulation – Essays in Honour of Eddy Wymeersch*, Cambridge University Press 2009, 323-3234.

[36] U. BERNITZ, "Special Issue on Corporate Governance in Europe in the Light of the Takeover Directive", (2004) EBLR 1363.

[37] However, A.R. PINTO refines this traditional point of view. He stresses that there are significant publicly traded corporations in the US in which there is a control group and the public are minority shareholders. They range from traditional family owned businesses (New York Times) to high-tech companies (Microsoft/Google). Therefore, he suggests describing the United States publicly traded corporations as a mixture of both dispersed and concentrated owners (A.R. PINTO, "The European Union's Shareholder Voting Rights Directive from an American Perspective: Some Comparisons and Observations" (15 September 2008). *Fordham International Law Journal*, Vol. 32, 2008; Brooklyn Law School, Legal Studies Paper No. 117. Available at SSRN: http://ssrn.com/abstract=1268454, 4).

[38] However, the number of widely held listed companies across France, Germany and Italy is growing. About one-third of this increase is due to a decline in family controlled companies in these countries. The rest is explained by the unwinding of majority blocks of widely held parent companies as well as privatizations of state owned companies: J.R. FRANKS, C. MAYER, P.F. VOLPIN and H.F. WAGNER, "Evolution of Family Capitalism: A Comparative Study of France, Germany, Italy and the UK" (18 March 2008). AFA 2009 San Francisco Meetings Paper. Available at SSRN: http://ssrn.com/abstract=1102475, 4-5.

minority shareholders. Since situations of dispersed ownership and concentrated ownership can both be found in the European markets, common European corporate governance rules are not easy to shape[39].

In what follows, we will focus on the way the European Union takes a position towards the various corporate governance actors. In its Action Plan, the Commission proposes (i) the enhancing of corporate governance disclosure, (ii) the strengthening of shareholders' rights and (iii) the modernizing of the board of directors. Which role the (European) legislator should play is another important issue[40]. We conclude by presenting a critical position on the current European corporate governance policy.

4. Monitoring by The Market

5. *Mandatory disclosure as a corporate governance instrument.* The market cannot efficiently control the way in which companies are governed without the relevant information. Mandatory public disclosure is an integral part of corporate governance, since it assists in the accurate pricing of corporate securities by economizing the information costs of investors[41]. Disclosure makes an "informed choice" by investors possible. Indeed, "publicity is justly commended as a remedy for social and industrial diseases. Sunlight is said to be the best of disinfectants; electric light the most efficient policeman"[42]. Therefore,

---

[39] ROE provides an intriguing analysis of the origin of this difference which exists through Europe. He underlines the influence of left-right political orientation on corporate governance institutions. Indeed, nations lodged towards the left would tend to disrupt managerial-shareholder alliances, and promote activities that favor employees with existing jobs. Firms would be encouraged to expand without regard to profitability, delay down-sizing when their production is misaligned with the product market, and go slow in taking profitable but disruptive risks. These pressures, and the denigration of some pro-shareholder tools, lead firms to have more concentrated ownership than otherwise, so that managers could be more directly controlled: M. ROE, "The Institutions of Corporate Governance" (August 2004). Harvard Law and Economics Discussion Paper No. 488. Available at SSRN: http://ssrn.com/abstract=612362 or DOI: 10.2139/ssrn.612362, 18.

[40] This question is very relevant, since company law and corporate governance are increasingly governed by sources other than legislation, such as self-regulation: E. WYMEERSCH, "Company law in Europe and European company law", Financial Law Institute, University of Gent, 2001, no. 21, p. 22.

[41] R. KRAAKMAN, "Disclosure and Corporate Governance: An Overview Essay", G. FERRARINI et al. (eds.), *Reforming Company and Takeover Law in Europe*, Oxford, Oxford University Press, 2004, 95 and 97. M.B. FOX examined the impact of required disclosure on corporate governance. This author emphasizes that this influence is indirect, through its positive effects on the functioning of four of the economy's key mechanisms for controlling corporate management: the market for corporate control, share-price-based managerial compensation, the cost of capital, and monitoring by external sources of finance. Through its effects on these mechanisms, disclosure improves the selection of proposed new investment projects in the economy and the operation of its existing productive capacity: M.B. FOX, "Required Disclosure and Corporate Governance", K.J. HOPT et al. (eds.), Comparative Corporate Governance – The State of the Art and Emerging Research, Oxford, Clarendon Press 1998, 709.

[42] L.D. BRANDEIS, Other People's Money – and How Bankers Use It (Jacket Library, New York 1914) 62. According to HOPT, this dictum of BRANDEIS had an early precedent in 1837 from the Prussian reformer HANSEMANN, who said that "among the means by which the management of a large company limited by shares can be kept law-abiding and efficient, is to be counted that it must be exposed to a certain degree to the public. This is the most effective control": K.J. HOPT, "Modern

disclosure is highly regulated under the securities laws of EU Member States. Disclosure requirements differ among Member States, and the variation in information can pose some impediment to a single European equity market[43]. Nevertheless, disclosure is becoming more similar, by way of efforts to promote better regulation of securities markets, broad use of International Accounting Standards and consolidation and coordination among listing bodies[44].

The movement towards disclosure rules for corporate governance regulation is not new at the European level. PANNIER and RICKFORD provide the historical context of the disclosure requirement. According to them, it can be traced back to case law of the European Court of Justice[45] [46]. Disclosure requirements can also be found in existing secondary legislation. The Merger Directive of 1978 and the Directive on Divisions of 1982 set out a system of disclosure rules which is based upon the idea of an informed choice by the shareholder and consists of three elements: information, authentication of the information and informed action. These Directives contain such rules: information through the draft terms of the merger established by the management of the company, often accompanied by a written report; correctness of the information by way of its control by an independent expert; the decision of the shareholders within the general meeting where a qualified majority is required.

6. *Winter Report and Action Plan on disclosure.* Disclosure can be an effective tool for the development of a European corporate governance policy, since lack of transparency was one of the leading factors in the recent corporate scandals both in the US and Europe[47]. It interferes least with freedom and com-

---

Company and Capital Market Problems: Improving European Corporate Governance After Enron" (January 2007). ECGI Law Working Paper No. 05/2002; ECGI Finance Working Paper. Available at SSRN: http://ssrn.com/abstract=356102 or DOI: 10.2139/ssrn.356102, 462.

[43] WEIL, GOTSHAL & MANGES LLP, "Comparative Study of Corporate Governance Codes Relevant to the European Union And Its Member States", on behalf of the European Commission, Internal Market Directorate General – Final Report, January 2002, 39.

[44] WEIL, GOTSHAL & MANGES LLP, "Comparative Study of Corporate Governance Codes Relevant to the European Union And Its Member States", on behalf of the European Commission, Internal Market Directorate General – Final Report, January 2002, 39.

[45] M. PANNIER and J. RICKFORD, "Corporate Governance Disclosures in Europe", (2005) *EBLR* 979; see also H. MERKT, "Disclosing Disclosure: Europe's Winding Road to Competitive Standards of Publication of Company-Related Information", G. FERRARINI et al. (eds.), *Reforming Company and Takeover Law in Europe*, Oxford, Oxford University Press, 2004, 127 et seq.

[46] In its famous *Cassis de Dijon* case, the Court held that a law laying down a minimum alcohol level was contrary to the free movement of goods because this measure was disproportionate. Other measures – labeling, for instance – were less restrictive and nevertheless sufficient for an informed consumer to be protected. Therefore, it is satisfactory to provide the market with information for making a rational and sound decision (ECJ Case C-120/*78 Cassis de Dijon* (1979) ECR 649). Similar reasoning lies at the basis of the *Centros* decision in which the Court stressed that creditors and contracting parties are informed for the purpose of dealing with a foreign company and that the disclosure of such information as required by the First, Fourth and Eleventh Directives already provides protection which is less restrictive than but a suitable equivalent of more restrictive capital requirements (ECJ Case C-212-97 *Centros Ltd v Erhvervs- og Selskabsstyrelsen* (1999) ECR I-1459).

[47] A. KOULORIDAS and J. VON LACKUM, "Recent Developments of Corporate Governance in the

petition of enterprises in the market. This is relevant since there is uncertainty and difference of opinion as to the question of what the European corporate governance rules should look like. Moreover, disclosure requirements can avoid the petrifying effect of European substantive law[48].

Indeed, the High Level Group emphasized that disclosure is an important tool for the development of a common European corporate governance policy. It even stated that "disclosure requirements can sometimes provide a *more efficient* regulatory tool than substantive regulation through more or less detailed rules. The regulatory effect of disclosure may in theory be more indirect and remote than with substantive rules. However, in practice enforcement of disclosure requirements as such is normally easier"[49]. The European Commission emphasizes the importance of disclosure as well.

However, the Action Plan avoids endorsing the Winter Report's proposition of the general superiority of disclosure over merit regulation[50].

Two disclosure instruments which were provided for in the Action Plan need to be examined: the Corporate Governance Statement and the Recommendation on directors' remuneration.

7. ***Corporate Governance Statement.*** In accordance with the Action Plan, which confirmed the importance of a Corporate Governance Statement[51], the European Parliament and the Council adopted Directive 2006/46/EC[52]. This Directive amends article 46*bis* of the Fourth Directive. Henceforth, companies whose securities are admitted to trading on a regulated market have to include a corporate governance statement in their annual report[53]. This statement

European Union and their Impact on the German Legal System", *German Law Journal* 2004, 1293.

48 K.J. HOPT, "Modern Company and Capital Market Problems: Improving European Corporate Governance After Enron" (January 2007). ECGI Law Working Paper No. 05/2002; ECGI Finance Working Paper. Available at SSRN: http://ssrn.com/abstract=356102 or DOI: 10.2139/ssrn.356102, 463.

49 Report of the High Level Group of Company Law Experts on a Modern Regulatory Framework for Company Law in Europe, Brussels, 4 November 2002, 34.

50 H. MERKT, "Disclosing Disclosure: Europe's Winding Road to Competitive Standards of Publication of Company-Related Information", G. FERRARINI et al. (eds.), *Reforming Company and Takeover Law in Europe*, Oxford, Oxford University Press, 2004, 133.

51 Many national corporate governance codes already demand reporting by the board on its governance by way of a "governance statement". In most codes, shareholders are informed about this statement, but do not have to approve it, although the general meeting can dismiss the board if it considers the statement unsatisfactory. Involvement of the auditor in verifying this statement is controversial. In some jurisdictions, the intervention of an auditor is part of the verification process, while in other Member States, the auditor should limit his role to verifying the figures that are mentioned in the governance report: E. WYMEERSCH, "Corporate Governance Codes and Their Implementation" (September 2006). University of Ghent Financial Law Institute Working Paper No. 2006-10. Available at SSRN: http://ssrn.com/abstract=931100, 5.

52 Directive 2006/46/EC of 14 June 2006 amending Council Directives 78/660/EEC on the annual accounts of certain types of companies, 83/349/EEC on consolidated accounts, 86/635/EEC on the annual accounts and consolidated accounts of banks and other financial institutions and 91/674/EEC on the annual accounts and consolidated accounts of insurance undertakings.

53 A separate statement in the consolidated annual report is not required, but risk management and internal control on a group-wide basis have to be considered; see Article 2 of Directive 2006/46/EC which amends Directive 83/349/EEC.

is a specific section of the annual report and must contain a reference to the corporate governance code to which the company is subject and/or the corporate governance code which the company may have voluntarily decided to apply. When a company departs from this corporate governance code, an explanation by the company as to which parts of the corporate governance code it departs from and the reasons for doing so have to be included as well. Where a company has decided not to apply any provisions of a corporate governance code, it has to explain the reasons[54]. This comes down to the codification of the "comply or explain" principle[55].

The question as to which corporate governance code the company has to apply is not easy to answer. The Directive leaves it to each Member State to decide whether to set up a compulsory national code. If there is no such mandatory provision, the company must refer in the statement to the code it is to apply[56].

This new obligation, applicable to all companies which are subject to the Accounting Directives, has been met with criticism in some Member States. HOPT refers to the German Lawyers Association which objected to the statement. It was said to be superfluous because much of the information to be included is already available from other sources. The *Arbeitsgruppe Europäisches Gesellschaftsrecht* draws attention to possible overlapping obligations stemming from the Takeover Directive or the Transparency Directive[57]. Moreover, critics assert that this new statement stretches disclosure too far, in particular regarding the concept of related parties. Finally, the statement in the annual report needs to be audited, and that could be difficult in some cases[58].

---

[54] The Corporate Governance Statement contains other information as well: (i) a description of the main features of the company's internal control and risk management systems in relation to the financial reporting process; (ii) the information required by Article 10(1)(c), (d), (f), (h) and (i) of Directive 2004/25/EC of the European Parliament and of the Council of 21 April 2004 on takeover bids, where the company is subject to that Directive; (iii) unless the information is already fully provided for in national laws or regulations, the operation of the shareholder meeting and its key powers, and a description of shareholders' rights and how they can be exercised; (iv) the composition and operation of the administrative, management and supervisory bodies and their committees. Directive 2004/25/EC – the "Takeover Directive" – requires the disclosure of some information: significant direct or indirect shareholdings, including those held through pyramid structures; holders of securities with special control rights and the description of these rights; restrictions on voting rights, such as limitations on the number of votes that can be cast; rules on appointment and replacement of board members and on amending the articles of association; the powers of board members, especially the rules on issuing or buying back shares.

[55] M. KORT, "Standardization of Company Law in Germany, other EU Member States and Turkey by Corporate Governance Rules", *ECFR* 4/2008, 403. The comply-or-explain principle has already been codified in some Member States, such as the Netherlands. In Germany as well, the members of the two boards must declare annually whether the recommendations of the Corporate Governance Code have been and are being followed, or which recommendations have not been followed or are not being followed, according to section 161 of the Stock Corporation Act 1965.

[56] M. PANNIER and J. RICKFORD, "Corporate Governance Disclosures in Europe", (2005) *EBLR* 992.

[57] K. VAN HULLE and S. MAUL, "Aktionsplan zur Modernisierung des Gesellschaftsrechts und Stärkung der Corporate Governance", *ZGR* 2004, 490.

[58] WYMEERSCH notes that the Directive contains little information about the way the codes have to be enforced. Whether the data on governance have to be audited, and the extent of this audit or of any other type of external monitoring are left to the Member States: E. WYMEERSCH, "Implementation

In this context, attention has to be drawn to the amending Directive of 14 June 2006 which reaffirms the collective responsibility of board members for financial statements and key non-financial information[59]. Member States must ensure that board members are collectively responsible at least towards the company. This guarantees a minimum standard for appropriate sanctions and civil liability for non-respect of the requirements of the Accounting Directive for drawing up the annual accounts and the annual report[60]. By creating this rule, the European legislator consciously takes a different direction from that of the US Sarbanes-Oxley Act, which focuses responsibility on a company's CEO and CFO[61]. Member States are not prevented from extending the responsibility directly to shareholders and other stakeholders. On the other hand, a system of responsibility limited to individual board members would be prohibited[62].

8. *Belgian corporate governance statement.* Recently, the Belgian Federal Government has launched several initiatives on corporate governance. According to the Draft Corporate Governance Law 2009, a corporate governance statement is to be included in the annual report of listed companies. The joint and several liability of directors guarantees the observance of this new obligation. Under Belgian law, directors can be released from liability for any breach in which they had no part if no fault can be imputed to them and they denounced the breach at the first general meeting after they became aware of it[63]. The Belgian legislator delegates the power to designate an applicable corporate governance code to the Government. The comply-or-explain principle remains in force. Nevertheless, that executive remuneration disclosure rules will be codified (see below).

9. *Directors' remuneration.* Another European corporate governance instrument based on disclosure is the Recommendation on directors' remuneration (hereinafter: "Remuneration Recommendation")[64]. Executive remuneration has

of the Corporate Governance Codes", K.J. HOPT et al. (eds.), *Corporate Governance in Context – Corporations, States, and Markets in Europe, Japan, and the US*, Oxford, Oxford University Press 2005, 418.

59 See Articles 50b, 50c and 60a of the Accounting Directive and Articles 36(a) and 48 of the Consolidated Account Directive.

60 M. PANNIER and J. RICKFORD, "Corporate Governance Disclosures in Europe" (2005), *EBLR* 984.

61 T. BAUMS, "European Company Law Beyond the 2003 Action Plan", ECGI - Law Working Paper No. 81/2007; European Business Organization Law Review, Vol. 8, 2007. Available at SSRN: http://ssrn.com/abstract=973456, 6.

62 Recital 2 Directive 2006/46/EC of 14 June 2006 amending Council Directives 78/660/EEC on the annual accounts of certain types of companies, 83/349/EEC on consolidated accounts, 86/635/EEC on the annual accounts and consolidated accounts of banks and other financial institutions and 91/674/EEC on the annual accounts and consolidated accounts of insurance undertakings; M. PANNIER and J. RICKFORD, "Corporate Governance Disclosures in Europe" (2005), *EBLR* 984.

63 Article 528 Belgian Companies Code.

64 Commission Recommendation 2004/913/EC of 14 December 2004 fostering an appropriate regime for the remuneration of directors of listed companies, OJ 2004 L 385, p. 55. Agreement on this Rec-

become a major issue in corporate governance. It is a difficult topic because of the conflict between allowing executive directors to be remunerated adequately, whilst at the same time curbing possible excesses in remuneration levels[65]. Corporate governance scandals have prompted major reforms and changes to commercial policy in relation to executive pay in European Member States[66]. FERRARINI, MOLONEY and VESPRO examined the different approaches of the various Member States. They emphasize that both public and private rules on executive pay appear to be more highly developed in the UK and Ireland than on the Continent. This difference stems from the differing ownership structures. Indeed, the remuneration problem is more acute in diffuse ownership systems[67]. However, a tendency towards convergence can be noted: the merits of the Anglo-Saxon full disclosure of executive remuneration and the use of remuneration committees are increasingly being recognized, and their use is on the rise in continental Europe[68].

The European Commission builds on this tendency towards convergence in its Remuneration Recommendation. Indeed, on the one hand, it is inspired by Anglo-American best practices, but on the other hand it tries to take the realities of continental corporate governance into account. The Remuneration Recommendation has no binding force according to Article 249(4) of the EC Treaty. Member States are invited to apply the principles of the Remuneration Recommendation at least to listed companies registered in their territory and to listed companies which are not registered in an EU Member State (third countries) but have their primary listing on a regulated market established in their territory[69] [70].

---

ommendation was reached in October 2004 (IP/04/1183 of 6 October 2004). For a discussion of a draft version, see S. MAUL and G. LANFERMANN, "Europäische Corporate Governance – Stand der Entwicklungen", *BB* (59) 2004, 1866-1867.

65 C. DE GROOT, "Executive Directors' Remuneration", *European Company Law* 2006, 62.

66 J.G. HILL, "Regulating Executive Remuneration: International Developments in the Post-Scandal Era", *European Company Law* 2006, 67.

67 G. FERRARINI, N. MOLONEY and C. VESPRO, "Executive Remuneration in the EU: Comparative Law and Practice" (June 2003). ECGI - Law Working Paper No. 09/2003. Available at SSRN: http://ssrn.com/abstract=419120 or DOI: 10.2139/ssrn.419120, 42.

68 However, this does not mean that corporate practices regarding executive remuneration will soon be uniform: many companies still refuse to implement the principle of full disclosure. Moreover, the remuneration committee is not easily transplanted into systems which are characterized by concentrated ownership or two-tier governance structures: G. FERRARINI, N. MOLONEY and C. VESPRO, "Executive Remuneration in the EU: Comparative Law and Practice" (June 2003). ECGI - Law Working Paper No. 09/2003. Available at SSRN: http://ssrn.com/abstract=419120 or DOI: 10.2139/ssrn.419120, 42.

69 Secs. 1.1. and 1.2. Remuneration Recommendation.

70 The effects for third countries have been criticized by PANNIER and RICKFORD. According to them, it raises doubts whether the EU standards can efficiently be applied to third countries. They spot a lacuna in the case where a company incorporates in Member State A but is only listed in Member State B. The Recommendation seems to suggest that Member State A is in charge of regulating the corporate governance standards of this company. However, it is not always clear whether the law of incorporation or the law of listing prevails, for instance if the listing rules are applicable regardless of the place of incorporation: M. PANNIER and J. RICKFORD, "Corporate Governance Disclosures in Europe" (2005), *EBLR* 993.

The Remuneration Recommendation provides for three key measures. All listed companies should disclose in a statement their policy on directors' remuneration for the following year and, if appropriate, the subsequent years (remuneration statement)[71]. Particular emphasis should be laid on any significant changes in the listed company's remuneration policy as compared to the previous financial year[72]. The remuneration statement should include information on the relative importance of the variable and non-variable components of directors' remuneration, on performance criteria and on the parameters for annual bonus schemes or non-cash benefits. It should also explain the company's contract policy. The company should not have to disclose commercially-sensitive information.

Moreover, the Recommendation suggests that the remuneration of each director should be disclosed individually and also in detail[73]. The statement should include the total amount of salary paid and/or emoluments of each director, the shares or rights to share options granted to them, their contribution to supplementary pension schemes, and any loans, advances or guarantees to each director[74].

Finally, the Recommendation suggests that shareholders have a role in the decision-making process[75]. Remuneration policy should be an item on the agenda of the shareholders' general meeting and there should be a vote which may be either mandatory or advisory. Member States can provide that this vote will only be organized upon the request of at least 25 percent of the votes held by shareholders or represented in the annual meeting[76]. If so, companies should inform shareholders about the possibility to table such a resolution. The Recommendation provides that variable remuneration, such as shares, share option schemes and other rights to acquire shares, should be subject to the prior approval of the annual general meeting[77]. Any substantial change in the terms and conditions of the schemes should also be approved[78]. The approval would only relate to the system providing for individual remuneration but not the individual remuneration itself[79]. It should set a time limitation for such types

71 Secs 3.1 and 3.2 Remuneration Recommendation.

72 Sec 3.2 Remuneration Recommendation.

73 Sec 5 Remuneration Recommendation. FERRARINI, MOLONEY and VESPRO argue that the Remuneration Recommendation will not be followed by some Member States on this point. In some Member States, a tradition of opaqueness is followed as to executive remuneration and only aggregate data are published. The publication of detailed and individualized information in all countries will be obtained only if required by EU legislation: G. FERRARINI, N. MOLONEY and C. VESPRO, "Executive Remuneration in the EU: Comparative Law and Practice" (June 2003). ECGI - Law Working Paper No. 09/2003. Available at SSRN: http://ssrn.com/abstract=419120 or DOI: 10.2139/ssrn.419120, 64.

74 Sec 5.3 Remuneration Recommendation.

75 Sec 4 Remuneration Recommendation.

76 Sec 4.2 Remuneration Recommendation.

77 Secs 6.1 and 6.2 Remuneration Recommendation.

78 Sec 6.4 Remuneration Recommendation.

79 Sec 6.1 Remuneration Recommendation.

of remuneration[80]. General employee share options are exempted from these provisions[81]. An information notice concerning the resolution should be made available to shareholders. This should contain the full text of the share-based remuneration schemes or a description of their principal terms, and the names of the participants[82].

10. *Belgian remuneration statement.* The Belgian legislator will introduce the legal obligation to disclose a remuneration statement. Indeed, the Draft Corporate Governance Law 2009 imposes on listed companies the duty to provide a remuneration statement, which will be part of the corporate governance statement. Interestingly enough, Belgian law will require much more information than is provided for in the Remuneration Recommendation. These elements are inspired by – currently non-binding – provisions of the Belgian Code on Corporate Governance[83], which demonstrates the importance of the question of whether the legislator should intervene in the corporate governance debate (see below, no. 26). The remuneration statement will be made subject to the approval of the shareholders' meeting. This approval determines the framework in which the board of directors must exercise its power in the area of the remuneration policy. If the general meeting rejects the statement, the board of directors will be obliged to change this policy.

5. The Shareholders in the Corporate Governance Debate

11. *Rational apathy and the Wall Street rule.* The legal role of the shareholders is similar in most EU Member States[84]. They have the authority to amend the articles of association or other organic documents, approve new share issues, approve the selection of the external auditors, approve the annual accounts, approve the distribution of dividends, approve transactions such as mergers, acquisitions and takeovers, and elect the supervisory body. Regardless

[80] Sec 6.3 Remuneration Recommendation.
[81] Sec 6.6 Remuneration Recommendation.
[82] Sec 7.1 Remuneration Recommendation.
[83] Exposition of Motives, Preliminary Draft Law on the Corporate Governance Statement and the Remuneration Committee, p. 6. The legislator justifies the enactment of these provisions by pointing out that "these obligations have in large degree been accepted by the business world, since they were already part of the Belgian Code on Corporate Governance". This argument is not convincing.
[84] It is clear that fundamental decisions and significant transactions (mergers, alterations of the company charter) are for the shareholder, while many other decisions are delegated to the board. HOPT underlines that the line between what is to be decided by the board and what should remain for the shareholders is difficult to draw and is drawn rather differently in national company laws: K.J. HOPT, "Modern Company and Capital Market Problems: Improving European Corporate Governance After Enron" (January 2007). ECGI Law Working Paper No. 05/2002; ECGI Finance Working Paper. Available at SSRN: http://ssrn.com/abstract=356102 or DOI: 10.2139/ssrn.356102, 452.

of the size of their holdings, they have the right to participate and vote in the general meeting.

Despite this important role, successful corporate governance rules on the strengthening of shareholders' rights are said to be difficult to imagine since the average shareholder is known for his "rational apathy"[85]. This problem has been analyzed by BERLE and MEANS, who stated that "as his personal vote will count for little or nothing at the meeting unless he has a very large block of stock, the stockholder is practically reduced to the alternative of no voting at all or else of handing over his vote to individuals over whom he has not control and in whose selection he did not participate[86]. CLARK identified this problem as "the shareholders' rational apathy"[87]. Later, EASTERBROOK and FISCHEL analyzed the shareholders' apathy as a collective choice problem: "when many are entitled to vote, none expects his votes to decide the contest"[88].

ZETZSCHE considers concentrated ownership as an obvious solution to this passivity claim: the more shares shareholders have, the more likely they are to exercise their rights. However, large shareholders tend to pursue their own agenda. They may, for instance, limit the expansion of the company despite the fact that there are profitable opportunities – if these could entail a loss of influence for the large shareholder through additional capital being supplied by outsiders[89].

Institutional investors traditionally tend to follow the "Wall Street rule", which is to move out of their investment rather than to monitor within the company[90]. However, this traditional view has to be refined in the light of the emergence of a new breed of institutional investors in the late nineties: the "hedge funds" and "private equity funds"[91].

---

85 K.J. HOPT, "Modern Company and Capital Market Problems: Improving European Corporate Governance After Enron" (January 2007). ECGI Law Working Paper No. 05/2002; ECGI Finance Working Paper. Available at SSRN: http://ssrn.com/abstract=356102 or DOI: 10.2139/ssrn.356102, 451; M. SIEMS, "Shareholder Protection Across Countries - Is the EU on the Right Track?", DICE-Report - Journal for Institutional Comparisons, Vol. 4/3, pp. 39-43, 2006. Available at SSRN: http://ssrn.com/abstract=940567, 41. Rational apathy is an old problem. Indeed, SIEMS refers to Adam Smith, who wrote that "the greater part of those proprietors seldom pretend to understand anything of the business of the company; and when the spirit of faction happens not to prevail among them, give themselves no trouble about it, but receive contentedly such half-yearly or yearly dividend as the directors think proper to make to them": A. SMITH, *An Inquiry into the Nature and Causes of the Wealth of Nations*, 1776, 71)

86 A.A. BERLE and G.C. MEANS, *The Modern Corporation and Private Property*, New Brunswick & London, Transaction Publ., 2003, 80.

87 R.C. CLARK, "Vote Buying and Corporate Law", (1979) 29 *Case Western Res. Law Review*. 776, 779.

88 F.H. EASTERBROOK and D. FISCHEL, *The Economic Structure of Corporate Law*, Harvard University Press, Ca., MA & London, England, 1991, 66-67.

89 D. ZETZSCHE, "Shareholder Passivity, Cross-Border Voting and the Shareholder Rights Directive", 15.

90 K.J. HOPT, "Modern Company Law and Capital Market Problems: Improving European Corporate Governance after Enron", Law Working Paper no. 5/2002, ECGI, 451.

91 For an analysis of this new trend, see: E. WYMEERSCH, "Shareholders in Action", Working Papers, Financial Law Institute, February 2007, 1-11 and M. KAHAN and E. ROCK, "Hedge Funds in Corporate Governance and Corporate Control", U of Penn, Inst for Law & Econ Research Paper No. 06-16; NYU, Law and Economics Research Paper No. 06-37; ECGI - Law Working Paper No.

These funds ride on the under-pricing in the market that is due to corporate governance deficiencies or detect under-pricing due to lack of focus in the business. They hold a large block of shares and, bearing in mind the passivity of the small investor, this means that they are the new masters of the general meeting. Analogous to this increasing "shareholder activism"[92] is the strengthening of the shareholders' position in law. Their position has been improved, both as a consequence of financial (especially disclosure) regulation, and on the basis of company law rules: more transparency, better governance, stronger auditing[93].

12. ***Directive 2007/36/EC.*** Following the High Level Group[94], the European Commission emphasized the importance of the shareholders in the EU corporate governance debate in its Action Plan. Indeed, shareholders are the ultimate risk-bearers in a company. The Commission indicated that new tailored initiatives should be taken with a view to enhancing shareholders' rights in listed companies and that problems relating to cross-border voting should be solved as a matter of urgency[95]. It is possible to take such initiatives, since

---

76/2006; University of Pennsylvania Law Review, Vol. 155, No. 5, 2007. Available at SSRN: http://ssrn.com/abstract=919881. The "short-termism" of the hedge funds can cause serious problems. Therefore, the question arises whether legal intervention is necessary. The authors mentioned take a different view on this issue. KAHAN and ROCK argue that a sufficient case for legal intervention cannot be made, given the uncertainties about whether short-termism is a real problem. Nevertheless, WYMEERSCH points out that there is one point where a different approach is appropriate, and that is when the activist shareholder imposes a radical change in the business plan. When a hedge fund manifests itself as a dominating shareholder, this may be a fundamental change for the other minority shareholders. This might lead to granting them the right to opt out. WYMEERSCH calls this a kind of "pre-emptive sell-out right": E. WYMEERSCH, "Shareholders in Action" (February 2007). University of Ghent Financial Law Institute Working Paper No. 2007-03. Available at SSRN: http://ssrn.com/abstract=965661, 11.

92 See W.W. BRATTON, "Hedge Funds and Governance Targets" (2007) 95 *Georgetown Law Journal* 1375 (2007) and S.T.W. BRIGGS, "Corporate Governance and the New Hedge Fund Activism: An Empirical Analysis", 32 *Iowa J. Corp. L.* 681 (2007). ZETZSCHE underlines that since these funds rely on high leverage, debt is the basis of their voting power. To the extent that debt is becoming more scarce (due to refinancing issues on the side of the lending banks) and more expensive (due to high interest rates for risky investments), this author expects the new watchdogs' activism to disappear: ZETZSCHE, "Shareholder Passivity, Cross-Border Voting and the Shareholder Rights Directive", 17.

93 E. WYMEERSCH, "Shareholders in Action", Working Papers, Financial Law Institute, February 2007, 8.

94 In its second report, the High Level Group considered whether European company law should also give the shareholders a role in fixing the principles and limits of board remuneration. Shareholder decision-making on the principles and limits of board remuneration seems beneficial for the European internal market because of the need to maintain public confidence in remuneration and decision-making on remuneration: K.J. HOPT, "Modern Company and Capital Market Problems: Improving European Corporate Governance after Enron", Law working paper no. 5/2002, ECGI, 453.

95 However, SIEMS doubts whether a European initiative is really necessary. He points out that the German, French and British law on the "active shareholder" has improved without European directives. Therefore, the Directive does not significantly change the situation in these countries, because many of its suggestions already correspond to their law: M. SIEMS, "Shareholder Protection Across Countries - Is the EU on the Right Track?", DICE-Report - Journal for Institutional Comparisons, Vol. 4/3, pp. 39-43, 2006 . Available at SSRN: http://ssrn.com/abstract=940567, 41.

modern technology allows much faster and better shareholder information, communication, and decision-making[96].

According to the Commission, strengthening shareholders' rights should be based on (i) the provision of comprehensive information on what the various existing rights are and how they can be exercised and (ii) the development of the facilities necessary to make sure that these existing rights can be effectively exercised[97]. These facilities should be offered to shareholders across the EU by means of a Directive, since effective exercising of these rights requires a number of legal difficulties to be resolved[98].

In the area of the protection of shareholders' rights, the Action Plan finds its realization in Directive 2007/36 of the European Parliament and of the Council of 11 July 2007 on the exercise of certain rights of shareholders in listed companies (hereinafter: "Directive on Shareholders' Rights")[99]. With this Directive, the European legislator aimed to facilitate the exercise of the voting rights by holders of shares.

Obstacles which deter shareholders from voting, such as making the exercise of voting rights subject to the blocking of shares during a certain period before the general meeting, should be removed[100]. The existing obstacles which hinder the access of non-resident shareholders to the information relevant to the general meeting and the exercise of voting rights without physically attending the general meeting should be removed as well[101]. Existing Community legislation in this field is not sufficient to achieve this objective[102]. Therefore, the European legislator provides some minimum standards which aim to remove the obstacles to cross-border voting. Member States are free to go beyond these standards.

---

[96] K. J. HOPT, "Modern Company and Capital Market Problems: Improving European Corporate Governance After Enron" (January 2007). ECGI Law Working Paper No. 05/2002; ECGI Finance Working Paper. Available at SSRN: http://ssrn.com/abstract=356102 or DOI: 10.2139/ssrn.356102, 451.

[97] European Commission, Communication from the Commission to the Council and the European Parliament "Modernising Company Law and Enhancing Corporate Governance in the European Union – A Plan to Move Forward", Brussels, 21.05.2003, COM (2003) 284, p. 14. The Commission points out that this approach is fully consistent with the OECD Principles on Corporate Governance.

[98] European Commission, Communication from the Commission to the Council and the European Parliament "Modernising Company Law and Enhancing Corporate Governance in the European Union – A Plan to Move Forward", Brussels, 21.05.2003, COM (2003) 284, p. 14.

[99] Directive 2007/36/EC of the European Parliament and of the Council of 11 July 2007 on the exercise of certain rights of shareholders in listed companies, *Pb. L.* 184/17.

[100] Recital 3 Directive on Shareholders' Rights.

[101] Recital 5 Directive on Shareholders' Rights.

[102] Recital 4 Directive on Shareholders' Rights. Indeed, Directive 2001/34/EC of the European Parliament and of the Council of 28 May 2001 on the admission of securities to official stock exchange listing and on information to be published on those securities focuses on the information issuers have to disclose to the market and accordingly does not deal with the shareholder voting process itself. Moreover, Directive 2004/109/EC of the European Parliament and of the Council of 15 December 2004 on the harmonization of transparency requirements in relation to information about issuers whose securities are admitted to trading on a regulated market imposes on issuers an obligation to make available certain information and documents relevant to general meetings, but such information and documents are to be made available in the issuer's home Member State. Therefore, certain minimum standards should be introduced with a view to protecting investors and promoting the smooth and effective exercise of shareholder rights attaching to voting shares.

13. ***Equal treatment.*** In its Article 4, the Directive on Shareholders' Rights contains a universal principle on the equal treatment of shareholders. Shareholders who are in the same position with regard to participation and the exercise of voting rights in the general meeting have to be treated in the same way[103].

14. ***Information prior to the meeting and agenda.*** Shareholders should be able to cast informed votes at, or in advance of, the general meeting, no matter where they reside. They should have sufficient time to consider the documents intended to be submitted to the general meeting and determine how they will vote[104]. Therefore, Article 5 of the Directive on Shareholders' Rights provides a detailed regulation on the information prior to the general meeting. The European legislator grants shareholders the right to put items on the agenda of the general meeting, provided that each such item is accompanied by a justification or a draft resolution to be adopted in the general meeting[105] [106]. Moreover, shareholders have the right to table draft resolutions for items included or to be included on the agenda of a general meeting.

15. ***Requirements for participation and voting.*** Article 7 of the Directive on Shareholders' Rights affects the requirements for participation and voting in the general meeting. Member States must ensure that the rights of a shareholder to participate in a general meeting and to vote in respect of any of his shares are not subject to any requirement that his shares be deposited with, or transferred to, or registered in the name of another natural or legal person before the general meeting[107].

The European legislator mandates Member States to introduce a record date requirement[108]. The rights of a shareholder to participate in a general meeting and to vote in respect of his shares have to be determined with respect to the shares held by that shareholder on a specified date prior to the general meeting[109]. In general, a single record date must be applied to all compa-

---

[103] This provision refers to the requirement of equal treatment found in the Transparency Directive which states that ongoing information of holders of securities admitted to trading on a regulated market should continue to be based on the principle of equal treatment. Such equal treatment only relates to shareholders in the same position and does not therefore prejudice the issue of how many voting rights may be attached to a particular share.

[104] Recital 6 Directive on Shareholders' Rights.

[105] Article 6 Directive on Shareholders' Rights. Member States may provide that this right may be exercised only in relation to the annual general meeting. In that case, shareholders should have the right to call, or to require the company to call, a general meeting that is not an annual general meeting, with an agenda including at least all the items required by those shareholders.

[106] Member States can require a minimum stake in the share capital of the issuer. This minimum stake may not exceed 5% of the share capital or a nominal value of EUR 10 million, whichever is the lower.

[107] Article 7.1(a) Directive on Shareholders' Rights.

[108] Article 7.2, 7.3, 7.4 Directive on Shareholders' Rights.

[109] Member States need not apply this obligation to companies that are able to indentify the names and addresses of their shareholders from a current register of shareholders on the day of the general meeting.

nies[110]. During the period between the record date and the general meeting, the rights of a shareholder to sell or otherwise transfer his shares may not be subject to any restriction to which they are not subject at other times[111]. This means the end of different share blocking schemes which the laws of some Member States required (at either the corporate or the intermediary level) and which constituted an alternative to a record date system for shareholder identification. They prevented institutional shareholders from exercising their voting rights, because these investors want or are required to retain their ability to respond to market reactions by trading their shares[112].

The relationship between the company and its shareholders as to shareholder identification is subject to the principle of proportionality. According to Article 7(4) Directive on Shareholders' Rights, proof of qualification as a shareholder may be made subject only to such requirements as are necessary in order to ensure the identification of shareholders and only to the extent that they are proportionate to achieving that objective.

These European rules on identification and authorization of shareholders do not take into consideration the fact that the securities may be held through a chain of intermediaries. Indeed, the European legislator failed to mandate an efficient regime governing the identification and authorization of shareholders who hold their shares within a chain of intermediaries[113] [114]. Therefore, one may doubt whether the Directive on Shareholders' Rights will be able to enhance shareholders' democracy in practice.

The European legislator stresses the importance of participation in the general meeting by electronic means. Under the regime of the new Directive,

---

[110] According to the Directive on Shareholders' Rights, this date must be at least 8 days after the convocation, and it must not be more than 30 days before the day of the general meeting.

[111] Article 7.1 Directive on Shareholders' Rights.

[112] D. ZETZSCHE, "Shareholder Passivity, Cross-Border Voting and the Shareholder Rights Directive", 36 and D. ZETZSCHE "Virtual Shareholder Meetings and the European Shareholder Rights Directive - Challenges and Opportunities" (26 June 2007). CBC-RPS No. 0029. Available at SSRN: http://ssrn.com/abstract=996434, 51-52.

[113] D. ZETZSCHE "Virtual Shareholder Meetings and the European Shareholder Rights Directive - Challenges and Opportunities" (26 June 2007). CBC-RPS No. 0029. Available at SSRN: http://ssrn.com/abstract=996434, 9; J. WINTER, "*Ius Audacibus*. The Future of EU Company Law", M. TISON et al. (eds.), *Perspectives in Company Law and Financial Regulation – Essays in Honour of Eddy Wymeersch*, Cambridge University Press 2009, 58.

[114] The European legislator is aware of the problem. However, it is underlined that "further consideration should be given to this issue by the Commission in the context of a Recommendation, with a view to ensuring that investors have access to effective voting services and that voting rights are exercised in accordance with the instructions given by these investors (Recital 11 Directive on Shareholders' Rights). The questions of who is the shareholder, the approach which should be required for authentication, and who should bear the costs of the authentication procedure were discussed. No agreement could be found on all these issues: D. ZETZSCHE "Virtual Shareholder Meetings and the European Shareholder Rights Directive - Challenges and Opportunities" (26 June 2007). CBC-RPS No. 0029. Available at SSRN: http://ssrn.com/abstract=996434, 52. WINTER stresses that such a Recommendation in itself, by definition, will not be able to solve the problem, as Member States can choose to ignore it and not impose any obligation on securities intermediaries: J. WINTER, "*Ius Audacibus*. The Future of EU Company Law", M. TISON et al. (eds.), *Perspectives in Company Law and Financial Regulation – Essays in Honour of Eddy Wymeersch*, Cambridge University Press 2009, 58.

companies will be granted the right to offer their shareholders any form of participation in the general meeting by electronic means[115].

16. ***Right to ask questions.*** According to Article 9, every shareholder has the right to ask questions related to items on the agenda of the general meeting[116]. The company is obliged to answer the questions formulated by shareholders. Member States may take, or allow companies to take, measures to ensure the identification of shareholders, the good order of general meetings and their preparation and the protection of confidentiality and business interests of companies[117]. They may allow companies to provide one overall answer to questions having the same content and can provide that an answer is deemed to be given if the relevant information is available on the company's Internet site in a question and answer format.

17. ***Voting by proxy.*** Article 12 of the Directive on Shareholders' Rights gives shareholders the possibility of voting by correspondence in advance of the general meeting.

More innovative and important is the introduction of European rules on voting by proxy[118]. Following the example of the United States, the European legislator has introduced the right for every shareholder to appoint any other natural or legal person as a proxy holder to attend and vote at a general meeting in his name[119]. Proxy voting individually and through securities accounts are both allowed[120]. Proxy holders may be appointed by electronic means[121].They

[115] Some forms are explicitly mentioned in the Directive on Shareholders' Rights: real-time transmission of the general meeting, real-time two-way communication enabling shareholders to address the general meeting from a remote location, a mechanism for casting votes, whether before or during the general meeting, without the need to appoint a proxy holder who is physically present at the meeting.

[116] PINTO observes that no similar specific requirement can be found in US law. If a company refuses to allow shareholders to ask questions, it is unclear whether that would violate the law in the US. Nevertheless, such behavior is unlikely since it would violate accepted norms of corporate behavior: A.R. PINTO, "The European Union's Shareholder Voting Rights Directive from an American Perspective: Some Comparisons and Observations" (15 September 2008). Fordham International Law Journal, Vol. 32, 2008; Brooklyn Law School, Legal Studies Paper No. 117. Available at SSRN: http://ssrn.com/abstract=1268454, 24.

[117] This provision has to be read in the light of legislation enacted in various Member States. The German Stock Corporation Act allows German companies to provide in their articles or by-laws authorization for the chairman of the meeting to restrict a shareholder's right to speak and ask questions.

[118] Article 10 et seq. Directive on Shareholders' Rights.

[119] In the United States, the use of proxy voting is very frequent and this is the reason why the Securities and Exchange Act of 1934 gave the SEC broad powers to regulate proxies. The federal proxy rules are very detailed with their focus on disclosure, with publicly traded corporations required to comply when proxies are solicited. In addition to companies soliciting proxies, there can be proxy fights where a shareholder group seeks votes for the shareholder meeting on issues opposed by the company's management. In this way, proxy fights create a market mechanism to monitor managers either by replacing them or by influencing their behavior: A.R. PINTO, "The European Union's Shareholder Voting Rights Directive from an American Perspective: Some Comparisons and Observations" (15 September 2008). Fordham International Law Journal, Vol. 32, 2008; Brooklyn Law School, Legal Studies Paper No. 117. Available at SSRN: http://ssrn.com/abstract=1268454, 22-23.

[120] Article 13 Directive on Shareholders' Rights.

[121] Article 11 Directive on Shareholders' Rights.

enjoy the same rights to speak and ask questions in the general meeting as those to which the represented shareholder would be entitled. The proxy holder is obliged to cast votes in accordance with the instructions issued by the appointing shareholder[122].

Member States are allowed to formulate some limitations. They can limit the appointment of a proxy holder to a single meeting, or to such meetings as may be held during a specified period. Moreover, they may limit the number of persons whom a shareholder may appoint as proxy holders in relation to any one general meeting. Finally, Member States can restrict or allow companies to restrict the exercise of shareholder rights through proxy holders to address potential conflicts of interest between the proxy holder and the shareholder[123], in whose interest the proxy holder is bound to act[124].

The fact that the Directive on Shareholders' Rights deals with proxy voting is very important, since proxy rules have so far been regulated quite differently in different Member States[125]. Despite the existing differences, GRUNDMANN analyses three trends at the national and European level. He points out that the emerging rules are all about (i) having a disinterested, professional representative, (ii) providing a clear insight into the proposals to the shareholder and (iii) reducing the representative's options via a mandatory vote[126]. The European legislator is developing a level playing field in the area of organized shareholder representation by taking some important positions: (i) the prohibition of any outright exclusion of one or the other type of organized shareholder representation; (ii) a reduction of the grounds on which regulations or restrictions for such organized representation may be based; (iii) a priority rule for specific instructions given by shareholders[127].

---

[122] Article 10, 4 Directive on Shareholders' Rights.

[123] According to Article 10, 3 Directive on Shareholders' Rights, a conflict of interest may arise where the proxy holder: (i) is a controlling shareholder of the company, or is another entity controlled by such shareholder; (ii) is a member of the administrative, management or supervisory board of the company, or of a controlling shareholder or controlled entity referred to in point (i); (iii) is an employee or an auditor of the company, or of a controlling shareholder or controlled entity referred to in (i); (iv) has a family relationship with a natural person referred to in points (i) to (iii).

[124] The Directive on Shareholders' Rights prescribes which measures Member States can take. They may (i) prescribe that the proxy holder disclose certain specified facts which may be relevant for the shareholders in assessing any risk that the proxy holder might pursue any interest other than the interest of the shareholder; (ii) restrict or exclude the exercise of shareholder rights through proxy holders without specific voting instructions for each resolution in respect of which the proxy holder is to vote on behalf of the shareholder; (iii) restrict or exclude the transfer of the proxy to another person. This cannot prevent a proxy holder who is a legal person from exercising the powers conferred upon it through any member of its administrative or management body or any of its employees.

[125] S. GRUNDMANN, "The renaissance of organized shareholder representation in Europe", M. TISON et al. (eds.), *Perspectives in Company Law and Financial Regulation – Essays in Honour of Eddy Wymeersch*, Cambridge University Press, 2009, 190-192.

[126] S. GRUNDMANN, "The renaissance of organized shareholder representation in Europe", M. TISON et al. (eds.), *Perspectives in Company Law and Financial Regulation – Essays in Honour of Eddy Wymeersch*, Cambridge University Press, 2009, 193.

[127] S. GRUNDMANN, "The renaissance of organized shareholder representation in Europe", M. TISON et al. (eds.), *Perspectives in Company Law and Financial Regulation – Essays in Honour of Eddy Wymeersch*, Cambridge University Press, 2009, 198-199.

6. Monitoring by an Independent Board of Directors

18. *Importance of the board in the corporate governance debate.* In the corporate governance literature, the importance of a knowledgeable, well-informed and powerful board of directors has always been stressed[128].

When a company has a dispersed ownership structure, the management needs to be supervised because the various shareholders are not in a position to monitor the management themselves[129]. When the ownership is concentrated, the major shareholder will have an influence on the board, which could constitute a hazard to the interests of the minority shareholder. Therefore, the management function should be subject to an effective and sufficiently independent supervisory function in both cases[130].

19. *Non-executive directors.* Anglo-Saxon corporate governance found an answer to this problem by bringing in non-executive directors who have no material relationship with the corporation and its management to serve on the (unitary) board of directors. This created a functional distinction between management (executive directors) on the one hand and control (non-executive directors) on the other hand[131].

The non-executive director found his way to Continental Europe, where he took up the role of counterweight to the dictatorship of the majority shareholder.

Most European corporate governance codes attach great importance to the position of the non-executive director[132], although there are important differences in this area as well. Moreover, criteria of substantive independence have been discussed and developed, which means that there are three groups of

---

[128] See for instance: G. CARRIERE, ANDREW COWEN et al., "European Corporate Governance: A changing landscape?", *MIT Sloan School of Management 50th Anniversary Research Project* – October 2002 Celebrations, 22. The predecessor of the British Combined Code (the Hampel Report) already stated that corporate governance "puts the directors of a company at the centre of any discussion": Committee on Corporate Governance ("Hampel Committee"), Final Report, January 1998, para. 1.15.

[129] R. KRAAKMAN, P. DAVIES et al., *The Anatomy of Corporate Law, A Comparative and Functional Approach*, Oxford, Oxford University Press, 2004, 11, 34 et seq.

[130] Recital 7 Commission Recommendation 2005/162/EC of 15 February 2005 on the role of non-executive or supervisory directors of listed companies and on the committees of the (supervisory) board, *Pb.* L. 25.02.2005, 52/51.

[131] This is clearly expressed in the Cadbury Report: "Every public company should be headed by an effective board which can both lead and control the business (...) This means a board made up of a combination of executive directors, with their intimate knowledge of the business, and of outside, non-executive directors, who can bring a broader view to the company's activities, under a chairman who accepts the duties and responsibilities which the post entails". See also: K.J. HOPT and P. LEYENS, "Board Models in Europe - Recent Developments of Internal Corporate Governance Structures in Germany, the United Kingdom, France, and Italy. ECGI - Law Working Paper No. 18/2004; Available at SSRN: http://ssrn.com/abstract=487944 or DOI: 10.2139/ssrn.487944, 11.

[132] For an overview, see WEIL, GOTSHAL & MANGES LLP, "Comparative Study of Corporate Governance Codes Relevant to the European Union And Its Member States", on behalf of the European Commission, Internal Market Directorate General – Final Report, January 2002, 53 et seq.

directors to be distinguished: executive; non-executive; and non-executive and independent directors[133].

In the UK and the Netherlands, the requirements for independence are rather strict, focusing on ensuring the independence of non-executive/supervisory directors from the company itself and its management[134]. Employees and representatives of shareholders are not seen as independent. Therefore, in Germany, neither the code nor legislation contains substantial independence requirements for supervisory board members[135].

The initial enthusiasm for outside directors has been dampened since no clear correlation has yet been found between having independent directors and the welfare of the firm. Moreover, it is clear that non-executive directors may be less familiar with the company's affairs and less competent than executive directors[136]. Nevertheless, their significance for the monitoring of the management by the board has been emphasized by the European Commission. It promulgated its Recommendation of 15 February 2005 on the role of non-executive or supervisory directors of listed companies and on the committees of the (supervisory) board (hereinafter: "Non-Executive Directors Recommendation")[137], which is partly comparable to the provisions of the Sarbanes-Oxley Act and the SEC Rule[138].

The Non-Executive Directors Recommendation has the same non-binding nature as the Remuneration Recommendation. The two Recommendations can also be compared in terms of scope: national provisions should at least

[133] S. GRUNDMANN, *European Company Law*, Antwerp/Oxford, Intersentia, 2007, no. 412, p. 226.

[134] For the UK, see Sec. A.3.1. Combined Code (2006): A person who has been an employee of the company within the previous five years or has had a material business relationship with it in the previous three years is not categorized as independent. See P. DAVIES, Gower and Davies' Principles of Modern Company Law, London, Sweet & Maxwell 2008, 407.

[135] K.J. HOPT, J. GARRIDO GARCIA, J. RICKFORD, G. ROSSI, J.S. CHRISTENSEN, J. SIMON and J. WINTER, "European Corporate Governance in company law and codes", *Report prepared for the European Corporate Governance Conference of October 18*, The Hague, The Netherlands, 61. HOPT points out that the tendency toward independent non-executive directors is less marked in countries with a two-tier board system, because this system as such provides for mutual exclusivity of membership of the two boards. However, this is only true insofar as there is a mandatory separation between the two boards. In practice, this does not preclude the movement of a former chairman of the management board onto the supervisory board after retirement. Therefore, the German Corporate Governance Code recommends that no more than two former members of the management board should be members of the supervisory board: K.J. HOPT, "Modern Company and Capital Market Problems: Improving European Corporate Governance After Enron" (January 2007). ECGI Law Working Paper No. 05/2002; ECGI Finance Working Paper. Available at SSRN: http://ssrn.com/abstract=356102 or DOI: 10.2139/ssrn.356102, 459.

[136] K.J. HOPT, "Modern Company and Capital Market Problems: Improving European Corporate Governance After Enron" (January 2007). ECGI Law Working Paper No. 05/2002; ECGI Finance Working Paper. Available at SSRN: http://ssrn.com/abstract=356102 or DOI: 10.2139/ssrn.356102, 459.

[137] Commission Recommendation 2005/162/EC of 15 February 2005 on the role of non-executive or supervisory directors of listed companies and on the committees of the (supervisory) board, *Pb.* L. 25.02.2005, 52/51. For the influence of this Recommendation on Dutch law, see: M. VAN HARTEN, "Europese corporate governance beginselen met betrekking tot commissarissen", *V&O* April 2005, no. 4, 70-73.

[138] H.-J. HELLWIG, "Effects of US Corporate Governance in Europe", *ECFR* 3/2007, 426.

cover listed companies incorporated in the territory and also companies with a primary listing regardless of their place of incorporation[139]. However, the Non-Executive Directors Recommendation follows a comply-or-explain approach, while the Remuneration Recommendation aims at establishing a mandatory disclosure regime. Thus, like its other initiatives, the approach of the Commission to board structure is based on transparency rather than regulating substantive details[140]. When Member States implement the Non-Executive Directors Recommendation, they can follow the same comply-or-explain approach: in view of the complexity of many of the issues at stake, the adoption of binding rules at national level is not necessary.

According to the Non-Executive Directors Recommendation, the management function should be subject to an effective and sufficiently independent supervisory function[141]. Therefore, the (supervisory) board should comprise a sufficient number of committed non-executive or supervisory directors, who play no role in the management of the company or its group and who are independent in that they are free of any material conflict of interest[142].

The Commission attaches great importance to the profile of the independent non-executive or supervisory directors. Therefore, it defines the conditions for a director to be independent: this is the case "when he is free from any business, family or other relationship – within the company, its controlling shareholder or the management of either – that creates a conflict of interest such as to jeopardize exercise of his judgment"[143]. Although independence in the legal sense of absence of financial ties to the company does not guarantee that a director's decision-making will be independent, it does mitigate somewhat against bias[144]. Apart from that, the determination of independence is an issue for the (supervisory) board itself to decide. The Non-Executive Directors Recommendation requests the company to disclose the relevant information. This broad definition has to be seen in the light of the different role an independent director plays in the different European corporate governance systems[145].

---

[139] Preamble 6 Non-Executive Directors Recommendation.

[140] M. PANNIER and J. RICKFORD, "Corporate Governance Disclosures in Europe" (2005), *EBLR* 987.

[141] Recital 7 Non-Executive Directors Recommendation.

[142] Recital 8 Non-Executive Directors Recommendation.

[143] Sec 13.1 Non-Executive Directors Recommendation.

[144] T. BAUMS and K. SCOTT, "Taking Shareholder Protection Seriously? Corporate Governance in the United States and Germany". American Journal of Comparative Law, Vol. 53, Winter 2005; ECGI - Law Working Paper No. 17/2003; Stanford Law and Economics Olin Working Paper. Available at SSRN: http://ssrn.com/abstract=473185 or DOI: 10.2139/ssrn.473185, 14.

[145] The broadness of this definition has to be seen in the light of major differences between European Member States in this regard. In particular, according to HOPT, formulating the criteria for the independence of a director creates difficulties for countries with co-determination. Indeed, if the independence requirement were applied solely to the shareholders' representatives in the board, this would weaken their voice. If it is also applied to the labor side, this would be even worse for the shareholders because the consequence would be to weaken the voice of the employees, who know the company best and have a keen interest in its prosperity. Instead, even more labor union representatives would move in, with interests that do not necessarily coincide with those of the particular company:

20. ***Chairman of the board.*** Effective monitoring of the management by an independent board of directors requires a strong position for its chairman. However, in unitary board structures, it was not unusual for the chairman of the board to also serve simultaneously as an executive of the company, often the CEO. This can give rise to problems: if the leader of the body which is charged with supervision is also the leader of the body under supervision, that person faces a conflict of interest. Therefore, separating these roles is another common recommendation in European corporate governance codes[146]. The same position has been taken by the European Commission in its Non-Executive Directors Recommendation[147].

21. ***One-tier vs. two-tier board systems.*** In some European Member States, the separation of the managerial and supervisory roles within the board of directors takes a formal shape. Indeed, corporate boards can be structured according to two basic systems[148]. In the "one-tier system" – e.g. in the United Kingdom – one unitary board, consisting of executive and non-executive directors, is at the head of the company and combines the functions of management and

K.J. HOPT, "Modern Company and Capital Market Problems: Improving European Corporate Governance After Enron" (January 2007). ECGI Law Working Paper No. 05/2002; ECGI Finance Working Paper. Available at SSRN: http://ssrn.com/abstract=356102 or DOI: 10.2139/ssrn.356102, 461.

[146] For instance, the Combined Code advocates separation: "There are two key tasks at the top of every public company – the running of the board and the executive responsibility for the running of the company's business. There should be a clear division of responsibilities at the head of the company which will ensure a balance of power and authority, such that no one individual has unfettered powers of decision (Principle A.2). A decision to combine the posts of chairman and chief executive officer in one person should be publicly justified (Principle A.2.1).

[147] For dual systems, these roles are already separated. Therefore, the Non-Executive Directors Recommendation suggests that the chairman of the management board should not immediately become the chairman of the supervisory board. Moreover, such a director would not be regarded as independent. PANNIER and RICKFORD emphasize that the appointment of the departing CEO is still common practice in German companies. Supporters refer to the advantages of this solution: continuity and transfer of know-how. On the other hand, a CEO could have problems changing the strategy introduced by his predecessor who now chairs the supervisory board. The solution of the Recommendation is disclosure (Sec 3.2 Non-Executive Directors Recommendation): M. PANNIER and J. RICKFORD, "Corporate Governance Disclosures in Europe" (2005), *EBLR* 998.

[148] HANSEN distinguishes a third, Nordic system. This model, which applies in Denmark, Sweden, Finland, Norway and Iceland, appears to be a two-tier model: there are two company organs below the general meeting (the board of directors and the management board). However, several features indicate that the Nordic executive system relates to the one-tier model. The Nordic system is strictly hierarchical. The board of directors is the senior organ and can instruct the management board. The upper level appoints and dismisses members of the lower level. The general meeting appoints the directors, who hire and fire the managers. This strict hierarchy is different from the German two-tier model, where the power of shareholders is limited and the management board is entrenched. Another difference is that under the Nordic system managers can serve as directors, which is unlawful under the German model. HANSEN underlines that the Nordic system is related to the one-tier model, although it has characteristics which set it apart from that model. Most notable is the allocation of powers between two different organs with distinct powers and responsibilities: J. L. HANSEN, "The Nordic corporate governance model – a European model?", in M. TISON et al. (eds.), *Perspectives in company law and financial regulation – Essays in Honour of Eddy Wymeersch*, Cambridge University Press, 2009, 151-153.

supervision[149]. In other European countries, the management function is performed by the management board (which consists of executive directors) while the supervisory function is performed by another body, the supervisory board (which consists of supervisory directors)[150]. The best-known example of this system in Europe is in Germany, where this board model (including co-determination) is rooted in statutory regulation[151]. The main intention of this duality is to promote the supervision of the management[152]. The German two-board system is based on the presumption that the owners in a public company are not only incapable of running the business themselves but also of supervising it[153]. Therefore the independence of the members of the supervisory board is essential for the proper functioning of the dual board system[154].

Subsequently, the dual board structure serves other purposes as well. Indeed, some jurisdictions saw the possibility of placing influence in one organ or the other. This influence is given to key shareholders or to stakeholders such as employees[155]. Indeed, the organization of the German supervisory board is heavily influenced by the co-determination rules. According to these rules,

---

[149] A.F.M. DORRESTEIJN and C. DE GROOT, "Corporate Governance Codes: Origins and Perspectives", *European Company Law* 2004, 49; S. GRUNDMANN, European Company Law, Antwerp/Oxford, Intersentia, 2007, no. 412, p. 225; K.J. HOPT and P. LEYENS, "Board Models in Europe - Recent Developments of Internal Corporate Governance Structures in Germany, the United Kingdom, France, and Italy". ECGI - Law Working Paper No. 18/2004; Available at SSRN: http://ssrn.com/abstract=487944 or DOI: 10.2139/ssrn.487944, 11. Theoretically, a supervisory board could be created in the memorandum or the articles of a UK company: S. GRUNDMANN, *European Company Law*, Antwerp/Oxford, Intersentia, 2007, no. 412, p. 225.

[150] A.F.M. DORRESTEIJN and C. DE GROOT, "Corporate Governance Codes: Origins and Perspectives", *European Company Law* 2004, 49-50.

[151] §§ 95 et seq. in conjunction with § 23 para 5 (1) Aktiengesetz (for a public limited liability company). The two-tier board is also prescribed mandatorily for a private limited liability company when it is subject to codetermination (§ 1 para. 1 no. 1 and § 7 of the Codetermination Law). The German two-tier board model is discussed in detail by HOPT and LEYENS: K.J. HOPT and P. LEYENS, "Board Models in Europe - Recent Developments of Internal Corporate Governance Structures in Germany, the United Kingdom, France, and Italy. ECGI - Law Working Paper No. 18/2004; Available at SSRN: http://ssrn.com/abstract=487944 or DOI: 10.2139/ssrn.487944, 4.

[152] The effective oversight of management in the German system is hindered by the obligatory size of supervisory boards. For larger corporations, a 20-member supervisory board is required. BAUMS and SCOTT underline that if one includes the members of the management board, the company is saddled with a directorate of about 30 members or more, which points to an inefficiency of the German system in comparison to the smaller boards common in international practice: T. BAUMS and K. SCOTT, "Taking Shareholder Protection Seriously? Corporate Governance in the United States and Germany". *American Journal of Comparative Law*, Vol. 53, Winter 2005; ECGI - Law Working Paper No. 17/2003; Stanford Law and Economics Olin Working Paper. Available at SSRN: http://ssrn.com/abstract=473185 or DOI: 10.2139/ssrn.473185, 12.

[153] S. GRUNDMANN, *European Company Law*, Antwerp/Oxford, Intersentia, 2007, no. 413, p. 227.

[154] According to German legislation, membership of the supervisory board of the *Aktiengesellschaft* is incompatible with simultaneous membership of the management board (§ 105 AktG). In practice, this independence is difficult to achieve due to the practice of mandating representatives of banks for the supervisory board. Moreover, former managers sitting on the supervisory board can also hamper this independence.

[155] S. GRUNDMANN, *European Company Law*, Antwerp/Oxford, Intersentia, 2007, no. 411, p. 225.

employees must be represented on the boards of companies employing more than 500 employees[156].

The question which board system is the most efficient is difficult to answer. Some argue that the British one-tier model might guarantee more intensive supervision, since supervision is more closely integrated into the flow of decision-making[157]. On the other hand, one can argue that in countries with a high incidence of dominant or controlling shareholders – such as Germany – there should be quite intensive informal supervision. In any case, the existence of the two different board systems within the European Union could be "a major corporate governance difference among Member States"[158].

However, both models are said to be converging[159]. Indeed, the British board of directors is moving towards becoming a de facto supervisory board through the introduction of non-executive directors[160]. Moreover, the practice of delegating day-to-day management and major operational questions to a "management board" is becoming common in the UK. Thus, the formal similarities in current board practices are significant. However, this convergence thesis is nuanced by DAVIES who points out that differences still exist as between Britain and Germany in relation to what boards do in addition to monitoring. While the UK board sets the corporate strategy, the function of leading the German company is allocated to the management board. Therefore, he argues that at the level of function, divergence is still the case[161].

[156] These requirements depend upon the number of employees in the company. Where the company has more than 500 workers, one-third of the members of the supervisory board are employee representatives. Where it employs more than 2,000 workers, half the members are employee representatives. See: P. DAVIES, "Board Structure in the UK and Germany: Convergence or Continuing Divergence?", available at SSRN: http://ssrn.com/abstract=262959 or DOI: 10.2139/ssrn.262959, 1.

[157] M. SCHIESSL, "Leitungs- und Kontrollstrukturen im internationalen Wettbewerb", *ZHR* 2003, 235; S. GRUNDMANN, *European Company Law*, Antwerp/Oxford, Intersentia, 2007, no. 415, p. 228.

[158] WEIL, GOTSHAL & MANGES LLP, "Comparative Study of Corporate Governance Codes Relevant to the European Union And Its Member States", on behalf of the European Commission, Internal Market Directorate General – Final Report, January 2002, 43.

[159] See e.g. R. BREUER, spokesman for the Deutsche Bank Group Board, who stresses that "in the past, it was more or less esoteric when comparing the American one tier system to the European two tier system". According to BREUER, "this discussion is obsolete, even in academia, because both board models have converged globally": R. BREUER, "Corporate Governance in Europe", Forum Financier/Revue Bancaire et Financière 2001/5, 259. See also M. KORT, "Standardization of Company Law in Germany, other EU Member States and Turkey by Corporate Governance Rules", ECFR 4/2008, 383 and C. TEICHMANN, "Corporate Governance in Europa", *ZGR* 2001, 668.

[160] K.J. HOPT and P. LEYENS, "Board Models in Europe - Recent Developments of Internal Corporate Governance Structures in Germany, the United Kingdom, France, and Italy". ECGI - Law Working Paper No. 18/2004; Available at SSRN: http://ssrn.com/abstract=487944 or DOI: 10.2139/ssrn.487944, 19.

[161] P. DAVIES, "Board Structure in the UK and Germany: Convergence or Continuing Divergence?", Available at SSRN: http://ssrn.com/abstract=262959 or DOI: 10.2139/ssrn.262959, 23.

This tendency towards – formal – convergence is accompanied by a tendency towards flexibility. In several Member States – e.g. in France[162] [163] – the legislator left the choice of a one-tier or two-tier board model open to the companies[164]. In other Member States, some authors plead for the introduction of this option[165].

This same tendency towards flexibility can now be observed at the European level[166]. Indeed, the Winter Report recommended that at least listed companies in the EU should have the option of choosing between a one-tier board structure (with executive and non-executive directors) and a two-tier board structure[167]. In its Action Plan, the Commission welcomed the idea of offering additional

---

[162] A choice between the one-tier model (*conseil d'administration*) and the two-tier model (*directoire* (management board) and *conseil de surveillance* (supervisory board)) was introduced in 1966. The *Loi Nouvelle Régulations Economiques* (NRE) of 2001 offers a third option: a traditional one-tier structure that nevertheless breaks with the formerly mandatory concentration of powers in the hands of the PDG, who took the position of both chairman of the board and CEO (Nouvelles Régulations Economiques, no. 2001-420, 15.05.2001, Journal Officiel 16.05.2001, 7776; see M. KORT, "Standardization of Company Law in Germany, other EU Member States and Turkey by Corporate Governance Rules", *ECFR* 4/2008, 405 and M. STORCK, "Corporate Governance à la Francaise – Current Trends", *ECFR* 1/2004, 36 et seq.

[163] The vast majority of companies stuck to their one-tier model. Nevertheless, a significant number of listed and multinational companies chose the division between management and control (4% of all public companies but 20% of the companies making up the CAC-40 index): M. COZIAN, A. VIANDIER and F. DEBOISSY, Droit des sociétés, Paris, Litec, 2005, no. 611; K.J. HOPT, "Modern Company Law and Capital Market Problems: Improving European Corporate Governance after Enron", Law Working Paper no. 5/2002, ECGI, 454; P. LE CANNU, "Pour une evolution du droit des sociétés anonymes avec directoire et conseil de surveillance", *Bulletin Joly* 2000, 483; C. TEICHMANN, "Corporate Governance in Europa", *ZGR* 2001, 664.

[164] This legal option may be acceptable from an economic point of view. Empirical research indicates that both systems can be effective means of control. According to JUNGMANN, it is therefore not possible to assign superiority to either of them (C. JUNGMANN, "The Effectiveness of Corporate Governance in One-Tier and Two-Tier Board Systems", *ECFR* 4/2006, 426). The debate is heavily influenced by national preferences: the overwhelming majority of German commentators are convinced of the superiority of the two-tier system, just as the British and others are convinced of the effectiveness of their own system: K.J. HOPT, "The German Two-Tier Board: Experience, Theories, Reforms", K.J. HOPT et al. (eds.), *Comparative Corporate Governance – The State of the Art and Emerging Research*, Oxford, Clarendon Press 1998, 254-255.

[165] See e.g. for Germany: T. BAUMS and K. SCOTT, "Taking Shareholder Protection Seriously? Corporate Governance in the United States and Germany". *American Journal of Comparative Law*, Vol. 53, Winter 2005; ECGI - Law Working Paper No. 17/2003; Stanford Law and Economics Olin Working Paper. Available at SSRN: http://ssrn.com/abstract=473185 or DOI: 10.2139/ssrn.473185, 19.

[166] See e.g. K.J. HOPT, "Modern Company and Capital Market Problems: Improving European Corporate Governance After Enron" (January 2007). ECGI Law Working Paper No. 05/2002; ECGI Finance Working Paper. Available at SSRN: http://ssrn.com/abstract=356102 or DOI: 10.2139/ssrn.356102, 454 and M. KORT, "Standardization of Company Law in Germany, other EU Member States and Turkey by Corporate Governance Rules", *ECFR* 4/2008, 403.

[167] This position differs from previous European proposals. Indeed, the first Proposal for a Fifth Directive (Company Structure Directive) sought to impose a two-tier board on all Member States. In a later phase, this structure only served as a starting point: Member States could leave it open to companies to choose the one-tier structure. HOPT underlines that it is certainly not for the European corporate governance law to make either one of the two systems mandatory, since practitioners on both sides of the Channel believe that their own system is clearly the better one: K.J. HOPT, "Modern Company and Capital Market Problems: Improving European Corporate Governance After Enron" (January 2007). ECGI Law Working Paper No. 05/2002, ECGI Finance Working Paper. Available at SSRN: http://ssrn.com/abstract=356102 or DOI: 10.2139/ssrn.356102, 454.

organizational freedom to listed companies, but recognized that the implications of such a proposal should be carefully studied. The recommendation made by the High Level Group will be followed up in the medium term[168] but for the time being, the possibility of opting for a one-tier or two-tier board system is not part of "hard" European law, except in the case of the SE[169].

22. ***European perspectives on board committees.*** In the context of the organization of the board of directors, special attention should be given to the nomination, remuneration and audit committees.

Nominating the members of the board and fixing their remuneration is a competence of the shareholders. When a company has a dispersed ownership structure, management can use its control to influence the agenda of the general meeting. Therefore, corporate governance provides for committees consisting of non-executive directors to deal with these issues. On the other hand, in a concentrated ownership structure, the executives have to be protected from the influence of the majority shareholder by the non-executive directors[170].

The European Commission has stressed the role of committees in the Non-Executive Directors Recommendation, which suggests that companies should create within the board a nomination committee, a remuneration committee and an audit committee[171]. The Recommendation is not intended to establish separate independent bodies; the decision-making power stays with the (supervisory) board. For smaller companies, exceptions are provided, which allows some flexibility. The main characteristic of these committees is that they are dominated by independent non-executive directors: the nomination committee should be composed of at least a majority of independent non-executive directors, whereas the remuneration[172] and audit committees should be composed exclusively of non-executive directors of which a majority should be independent[173].

---

168 European Commission, Communication from the Commission to the Council and the European Parliament – "Modernising Company Law and Enhancing Corporate Governance in the European Union – A Plan to Move Forward", Brussels 21.05.2003, COM (2003) 284, 15-16.

169 This proposal has met with some enthusiasm in Germany – although such a choice appeared unthinkable until very recently, due to German labor co-determination, which was felt to be incompatible with a one-tier board system: K.J. HOPT, "European Company Law and Corporate Governance: Where Does the Action Plan of the European Commission lead?", working paper no. 52/2005, ECGI, 2005, 19.

170 K. GEENS, "Over corporate governance, aandeelhoudersstructuren en vennootschapsrecht", *Knelpunten van dertig jaar vennootschapsrecht*, Kalmthout, Biblo, 1999, 762.

171 Sec 6.1 Non-Executive Directors Recommendation.

172 There are some reasons why the presence of independent directors on the remuneration committee might not have the desired effect. They may lack expertise on pay or have insufficient time to become expert. Moreover, they may be reluctant to disturb the status quo, being friends of the CEO, or incentivized to set pay in a manner beneficial to them where they are serving executive directors: G. FERRARINI, N. MOLONEY and C. VESPRO, "Executive Remuneration in the EU: Comparative Law and Practice" (June 2003). ECGI - Law Working Paper No. 09/2003. Available at SSRN: http://ssrn.com/abstract=419120 or DOI: 10.2139/ssrn.419120, 12.

173 Secs 2.1.1, 3.1.2, 4.1 Non-Executive Directors Recommendation.

23. *Audit committee.* The Action Plan does not expressly refer to the replacement of the Eighth Company Law Directive (hereinafter: "Audit Directive"[174]).

Nevertheless, the Audit Directive has a major influence on the European corporate governance landscape since it requires "public-interest entities", which includes listed EU companies, financial institutions and insurance undertakings, to establish an audit committee[175]. This audit committee consists of non-executive or supervisory directors, and at least one member has to be competent in accounting and/or auditing[176]. The committee should *inter alia* monitor the financial reporting process and the effectiveness of the company's internal control, internal audit (where applicable) and risk management systems, monitor the statutory audit of the annual and consolidated accounts and review and monitor the independence of the statutory auditor or audit firm[177]. It plays an important role in the appointment of a statutory auditor or audit firm. Indeed, the proposal of the administrative or supervisory body for this appointment must be based on a recommendation made by the audit committee. This rule has met with criticism. PANNIER and RICKFORD argue that the Audit Directive creates a mandatory organ with decision-making power which is separate from the board in a unitary system. Therefore, it sets up substantive defaults rather than a flexible system which allows modifications and which is accompanied by disclosure of these modifications[178].

The Belgian legislator has introduced the obligation to install an audit committee in its Act of 17 December 2008[179]. This new obligation applies to listed companies[180], credit institutions, insurance companies, investment com-

[174] Directive 2006/43/EC of the European Parliament and of the Council of 17 May 2006 on statutory audits of annual accounts and consolidated accounts, amending Council Directives 78/660/EEC and 83/349/EEC and repealing Council Directive 84/253/EEC, OJ 2006, L 157/87.

[175] HOPT underlines that some Member States take a different view of the mandatory audit committee. In the United Kingdom and in other countries with a one-tier board, audit committees are common. On the other hand, they are less common in Germany than in other Member States, which is partly due to the two-tier system and partly because the tasks of the audit committee are carried out by other committees such as the presidential committee or the finance committee. Despite these differences, this author suggests that in the light of Enron and the general crisis of confidence, there is a case for a European rule requiring listed companies to have audit committees: K. J. HOPT, "Modern Company and Capital Market Problems: Improving European Corporate Governance After Enron" (January 2007). ECGI Law Working Paper No. 05/2002; ECGI Finance Working Paper. Available at SSRN: http://ssrn.com/abstract=356102 or DOI: 10.2139/ssrn.356102, 456.

[176] Article 41.1 Audit Directive.

[177] Article 41.2 Audit Directive.

[178] M. PANNIER and J. RICKFORD, "Corporate Governance Disclosures in Europe" (2005), EBLR 998.

[179] Act of 17 December 2008 concerning the installation of an audit committee in listed companies and financial undertakings, Belgian Official Gazette of 29 December 2008. See C. VAN DER ELST and I. DE POORTER, "Upgrading corporate governance: auditcomités in het Wetboek van Vennootschappen", *T.R.V.* 2009, 397-415.

[180] Small and medium-sized listed companies are not obliged to set up an audit committee. If they do not set up an audit committee, its tasks are carried out by the entire board of directors, provided that at least one member of the board of directors is independent. Where the chairman of the board is an executive member of the board, he cannot preside over the board when it acts in its capacity as audit committee. Listed companies retain the choice whether or not to establish an audit committee if, on a consolidated basis, at least two of the following three criteria are met: i) fewer than 250 employees on average during the financial year; ii) balance sheet total not exceeding EUR 43,000,000; iii) net

panies and management companies of institutions for collective investment[181]. All members are non-executive directors[182] and one member has to be an independent director in the sense of the new article 526*ter* Belgian Companies Code. The criteria for the independence of this director, which are based on the Non-Executive Directors Recommendation, are stricter than the already existing criteria of article 524 Belgian Companies Code[183].

24. ***Belgian remuneration committee.*** Under European law, the creation of an audit committee is compulsory while the remuneration and nomination committees are mere possibilities. However, the Belgian legislator will go further. Indeed, the Draft Corporate Governance Law 2009 *obliges* listed companies to set up a remuneration committee. This committee should consist exclusively of non-executives, the majority of whom should qualify as independent directors. At least one member of the committee should have three years' experience in remuneration policy. Meeting at least twice a year, the remuneration committee is to present proposals for the overall remuneration policy regarding directors and members of the management committee, as well as for their individual remuneration, including variable remuneration, long-term incentives, stock options, and termination arrangements. Moreover, it will draw up the obligatory remuneration statement (see no. 10).

7. Monitoring by the Legislator

25. ***Non-binding corporate governance codes.*** The question of whether the legislator should intervene in the corporate governance debate by enacting binding corporate governance legislation is rather controversial, since corporate governance traditionally attaches great importance to the market for monitoring the way in which a company is governed.

The belief that the market is able to control the management of publicly held companies is expressed in the various corporate governance codes developed in most European Member States. These codes, which are applicable to listed

annual turnover not exceeding EUR 50,000,000.

[181] In small and medium-sized credit institutions and insurance undertakings, the functions assigned to the audit committee can be performed by the board of directors as a whole. These financial institutions are defined in the same way as small and medium-sized listed companies (see above). The same criteria apply, although for these financial institutions they are not applied on a consolidated basis. Small and medium-sized investment undertakings and management companies of undertakings for collective investment are not required to have an audit committee and do not have to assign the audit functions to the board of directors. Two specific entities are exempt from the obligation to set up an audit committee: (i) collective investment undertakings with variable numbers of participation rights and (ii) entities whose sole business is to act as issuers of asset-backed securities.

[182] The members of the day-to-day management and the management committee are excluded.

[183] Under article 524 Belgian Companies Code, which is applicable to listed companies, decisions and transactions between the listed company and any associated enterprise have to be examined by a committee of three independent directors.

companies[184], developed as private initiatives[185]. Listing rules can be another source of corporate governance rules. Even government's involvement cannot be totally excluded from the creation of corporate governance codes[186]. Forty or so corporate governance codes relevant to the European Union have been adopted with the aim of better protecting the interests of shareholders and/or stakeholders[187].

These codes are non-binding[188] and start out from the same comply-or-explain approach. Even when a "comply or explain" disclosure mandate exists, a company is generally free to choose not to follow the code's prescriptions, so long as it discloses and explains such non-compliance[189]. Companies are not bound to follow the provisions of the code. This principle allows the diversity of individual situations to be taken into account. It is up to the market to control the way in which companies are complying with its rules[190].

---

184 The ambit of corporate governance codes is a subject of discussion. The application of these codes to large non-listed companies is controversial. Nevertheless, some codes are addressed to unlisted, especially family owned companies (e.g. the Belgian Buysse Code). Another difficult subject is that of governance of state-owned enterprises. WYMEERSCH reports that states are unwilling to abandon their influence on this group of enterprises, sometimes until market competition brings the enterprise down. Good governance should be a guarantee for ensuring the survival of this kind of enterprise: E. WYMEERSCH, "Implementation of the Corporate Governance Codes", K.J. HOPT et al. (eds.), *Corporate Governance in Context – Corporations, States, and Markets in Europe, Japan, and the US*, Oxford, Oxford University Press 2005, 408.

185 For thorough research on the origins of corporate governance codes, see E. WYMEERSCH, "Corporate Governance Codes and Their Implementation" (September 2006). University of Ghent Financial Law Institute Working Paper No. 2006-10. Available at SSRN: http://ssrn.com/abstract=931100, 2.

186 Indeed, some codes are linked with the public authorities (the initiative to draw up the code was taken with the participation of ministries; the drafting committee was appointed by the ministry, ...): E. WYMEERSCH, "Corporate Governance Codes and Their Implementation" (September 2006). University of Ghent Financial Law Institute Working Paper No. 2006-10. Available at SSRN: http://ssrn.com/abstract=931100, 2.

187 This interest in corporate governance improvement started in the United Kingdom after a series of financial scandals and related failures of listed companies. The Cadbury Report (1992) was the starting point for a series of European codes. The "code activity" in Europe accelerated after the publication of the OECD Business Sector Advisory Group on Corporate Governance Report (the "Millstein Report") and the issuance of the OECD Principles of Corporate Governance in 1999. For a short overview of different European corporate governance codes, see A. DORRESTEIJN and C. DE GROOT, "Corporate Governance Codes: Origins and Perspectives", *European Company Law* 2004, 46-48.

188 However, these non-binding recommendations can have an influence on the entire body of legally binding rules through various mechanisms. Therefore, "soft law" can be a misnomer for these "recommendations". Indeed, a non-binding corporate governance code can become a listing requirement. Moreover, incorporation in "hard law" can be possible by means of a reference in company law itself. When a judge interprets legally binding open rules (e.g. "good faith"), he may take the content of a corporate governance code into account. Finally, institutional investors tend to disclose which governance principles are important for them (or even a precondition) when they invest: S. GRUNDMANN, *European Company Law*, Oxford/Antwerp, Intersentia, 2007, no. 480-481, p. 271-272.

189 This comply-or-explain principle has been given legal force by the European legislator (Directive 2006/46/EC). This does not mean that the contents of the various corporate governance codes will lose their voluntary nature.

190 Research indicates that most provisions of codes are complied with, with the exception of some sensitive provisions – e.g. on disclosure of directors' remuneration. Therefore, most authors suggest that the codes are being implemented under the pressure of the markets: good governance practices are considered to have a positive influence on the price evolution. However, the phenomenon of market

26. *Action by the legislator.* These non-binding rules may be as effective as legal rules[191], sometimes even more effective since voluntary compliance is better than forced obedience[192].

However, HOPT stresses that voluntary rules have their drawbacks: they can present problems of compliance, liability, relationship to legal rules, free-riding and anti-trust issues[193]. Nevertheless, it remains to be seen whether legislative action would be able to solve these problems. There are serious doubts in this regard since, inevitably, legislation not only takes economic efficiency into account but can be ideologically inspired. Moreover, one can argue that the general character of obligations imposed by the legislator in the field of corporate governance cannot take the complexity of modern corporations into account[194]. Therefore, we suggest that every legislator should generally exercise restraint in the area of corporate governance.

This does not mean that action by the legislator in this area should be totally excluded. Indeed, legislation can have its intrinsic advantages. It is appropriate to ensure that the essential legal infrastructure is available and operates efficiently (e.g. facilitating shareholder voting) and to set generally accepted minimum standards. Finally, disclosure requires legislation and not a flexible approach.

influence is broader than the direct impact on price formation, since it also relates to opinion building through the media, as well as the rating agencies and the financial analysts: E. WYMEERSCH, "Implementation of the Corporate Governance Codes", K. J. HOPT et al. (eds.), *Corporate Governance in Context – Corporations, States, and Markets in Europe, Japan, and the US*, Oxford, Oxford University Press 2005, 406-407. This author nevertheless acknowledges that "nothing is mathematical. Some of the most successful companies simply refuse to follow the governance precepts, without negative effect on their financial results of their market valuation" (E. WYMEERSCH, "Implementation of the Corporate Governance Codes", K. J. HOPT et al. (eds.), *Corporate Governance in Context – Corporations, States, and Markets in Europe, Japan, and the US*, Oxford, Oxford University Press 2005, 406).

191 However, this effectiveness has been questioned by Dutch research on the role of self-regulation in Corporate Governance in the Netherlands. A. DE JONG points out that the private sector initiative on corporate governance (the Peters Committee Report) had no substantive effect on corporate governance characteristics of companies. Moreover, according to this research, it was impossible to prove a relationship between the corporate governance initiatives and firm value. Therefore, it suggests that little can be expected from initiatives that rely on monitoring without enforcement: A. DE JONG, D. DEJONG, G. MERTENS and C. WASLEY, "The Role of Self-Regulation in Corporate Governance: Evidence and Implications from The Netherlands" (December 2001). Simon School of Business Working Paper No. FR 00-20; ERIM Report Series Reference No. ERS-2001-87-F&A. Available at SSRN: http://ssrn.com/abstract=246952.

192 K. J. HOPT, "Comparative Company Law", M. REIMANN and R. ZIMMERMAN (eds.), *The Oxford Handbook of Comparative Law*, Oxford, 2006, 1183. However, the effectiveness of these non-binding rules has been questioned by others. NOWAK, ROTT and MAHR do not find a correlation between compliance with these rules and the share price: E. NOWAK, R. ROTT and T. MAHR, "Wer den Kodex nicht einhält, den bestraft der Kapitalmarkt? Eine empirische Analyse der Selbstregulierung und Kapitalmarktrelevanz des Deutschen Corporate Governance Kodex", *ZGR* 2/2005, 252-279.

193 K. J. HOPT, "Comparative Company Law", M. REIMANN and R. ZIMMERMAN (eds.), *The Oxford Handbook of Comparative Law*, Oxford, 2006, 1183.

194 M. LITTGER, "Funktion und Verwendungschancen der neuen Kodizes am Beispiel von Corporate Governance", *Rechtstheorie* 2008, 497.

Where it is decided that disclosure makes sense, companies should not have the option of explaining why they do not disclose certain information[195] [196].

27. ***Towards a European corporate governance code?*** At the European level, the effectiveness of corporate governance codes can be questioned, since the various European codes differ: they were introduced in the various European Member States with their diverse cultures, financing traditions, ownership structures and legal origins.

At first sight, this could create uncertainty and costs for both issuers and investors. However, recent research indicates a growing convergence in this area between the EU Member States. Indeed, in 2003, WOJCIK analyzed the dynamics of European corporate governance between 2000 and 2003 using a dataset of corporate governance ratings of the 3,000 largest European companies from 17 countries. He emphasizes that continental companies are narrowing the gap in relation to the UK and Ireland, and there is evidence of convergence within individual countries and industries[197] [198].

This evolution towards convergence is relevant to the discussion on the desirability of a *European* corporate governance code. Because of these fundamental similarities, neither the minor differences between codes nor the number of potentially competing codes appear to burden an integrated European equity market. Therefore, the High Level Group concluded in its Winter Report that an EU corporate governance code is not needed. The diversity in underlying company law structures and systems in Member States is still so great that attempting to produce a common EU code would either be futile because it would not be able to set out best practices at a level which is of real practical importance, or the result would be a very complex document

---

[195] K. J. HOPT, J. GARRIDO GARCIA, J. RICKFORD, G. ROSSI, J.S. CHRISTENSEN, J. SIMON and J. WINTER, "European Corporate Governance in company law and codes", *Report prepared for the European Corporate Governance Conference of October 18*, The Hague, The Netherlands, 63.

[196] KRAAKMAN points out why binding legislation is necessary in the field of disclosure. The first explanation concerns the agency problem between shareholders and corporate insiders; the worse the news, the less likely managers are to disclose it voluntarily. Controlling shareholders are equally loath to disclose bad news, since this will reduce the value of their shares. Moreover, in the absence of mandatory disclosure, the capital markets would expect corporate insiders to withhold bad news, and would discount the share prices of companies accordingly. Finally, there is a divergence between the private benefits of disclosure to the company and the social benefits. Although disclosure enhances the welfare of diversified investors, it may be a burden for the company. Therefore, voluntary disclosure cannot work: R. KRAAKMAN, "Disclosure and Corporate Governance: An Overview Essay", G. FERRARINI et al. (eds.), *Reforming Company and Takeover Law in Europe*, Oxford, Oxford University Press 2004, 100.

[197] D. WOJCIK, "Convergence in Corporate Governance: Empirical Evidence from Europe 2000-2003" (June 2004). Available at SSRN: http://ssrn.com/abstract=559424.

[198] This evolution has its influence on the company legislation of Member States. Indeed, according to STORCK, the recent evolution of the practice of corporate governance in France reveals a manifest convergence with the guiding principles preached by Anglo-Saxon law, although in France it is by way of legislation that the principles of corporate governance have been imposed: M. STORCK, "Corporate Governance à la Francaise – Current Trends", *ECFR* 1/2004, 36 et seq.

containing all sorts of different applications and exemptions to accommodate local practices and rules[199].

The Commission shares this view and stresses that the existence of many codes in the EU is not generally perceived as a difficulty by issuers. It considers that the adoption of a European code would not achieve full information for investors about the key corporate governance rules applicable to companies across Europe, as these rules would still be based on – and part of – national company laws that are in certain respects widely divergent. Trying to harmonize all the elements of a European code would take years and would not be achievable in a reasonable timeframe[200]. Moreover, some argue that efforts to achieve broad agreement among Member States on detailed best practices that fit well with varying legal frameworks is more likely to express a negotiated "lowest common denominator" of "acceptable" practice rather than true "best" practice[201]. Finally, one may wonder whether a European corporate governance code would lead to more convergence in reality, since the greatest distinctions in corporate governance practices among Member States emanate from differences in national company law[202].

Some authors criticize this option taken by the EU. ZAFIROVA demonstrates that the Commission's explanations are not in fact all that convincing. Even if it is true that a European corporate governance code would not provide investors with full information because of the underlying divergence of national company and securities laws, there is no reason why operating with a single code and a variety of company and securities laws would not be easier than also having to deal with a number of corporate governance codes[203].

Moreover, ZAFIROVA brings another contradiction into the limelight. On the one hand, the Commission's position reiterates the finding that corporate governance codes around Europe are largely convergent while, on the other hand, it claims that they are so different that agreement on a common document will not be possible. Therefore, she foresees the creation of a European corporate governance code[204].

---

[199] K. J. HOPT, J. GARCIA et al., "European Corporate Governance in company law and codes", *Report prepared for the European Corporate Governance Conference of October 18,* The Hague, The Netherlands, 2.

[200] European Commission, Communication from the Commission to the Council and the European Parliament "Modernising Company Law and Enhancing Corporate Governance in the European Union – A Plan to Move Forward", Brussels, 21.05.2003, COM (2003) 284, p. 11.

[201] WEIL, GOTSHAL & MANGES LLP, "Comparative Study of Corporate Governance Codes Relevant to the European Union And Its Member States", on behalf of the European Commission, Internal Market Directorate General – Final Report, January 2002, 7.

[202] The greatest difference in corporate governance practice among EU Member States relates to the role which employees play in company law: WEIL, GOTSHAL & MANGES LLP, "Comparative Study of Corporate Governance Codes Relevant to the European Union And Its Member States", on behalf of the European Commission, Internal Market Directorate General – Final Report, January 2002, 3 and 34.

[203] Z. ZAFIROVA, "A Uniform Corporate Governance Code?", working paper, University of Groningen, 2007, 2.

[204] Z. ZAFIROVA, "A Uniform Corporate Governance Code?", working paper, University of Groningen, 2007, 2.

8. What Should Be on the European Agenda?

28. *Demand for convergence.* It is widely accepted that a national focus on corporate governance is too narrow, because of the growing demand for convergence of corporate governance practices in the market.

Indeed, in its Working Party Report "Corporate Governance in Europe" of June 1995, the CEPS enumerates developments which are increasingly having the effect of reducing the specificities of corporate governance systems, opening national markets to international competition and augmenting the importance of stock markets[205]. The growing role of institutional investors[206], the worldwide integration of capital markets and the increased activism of shareholders all lead to a growing demand for the integration of corporate governance rules and practices. Moreover, several continental European countries launched large-scale rounds of privatization of state assets in the nineties. This evolution will increase the importance of stock markets and augment their capitalization as well[207].

As has been emphasized above, the market finds an answer to this challenge in the convergence of the national corporate governance codes. The question remains as to what position the EU should take in this debate. What kind of role can and should Europe play[208]? This question is difficult to answer. Indeed, as has been underlined by HOPT, identifying the key elements of corporate governance is difficult enough, but the challenge reaches further. The fact that a rule may be good or even necessary for good corporate governance is not yet an answer to the question of whether such a rule is appropriate on the European level[209].

---

[205] "Corporate Governance in Europe", Report of a CEPS (Centre for European Policy Studies) Working Party, June 2005, p. 30.

[206] The trend for institutional investors to increase their share of listed companies in several European countries will continue, due to developments in retirement financing and health care. The European "pay-as-you-go financed" pension schemes are becoming more and more untenable due to the growing pensioner-to-worker ratios and the restraints on public spending. This will lead to an increase in the demand for equity by institutional investors, acting as the depositors of pension funds. They will have an influence on the financing methods and internal corporate governance structures of companies. Since American pension funds are increasingly investing outside the US, they are bringing their corporate governance standards with them ("Corporate Governance in Europe", Report of a CEPS (Centre for European Policy Studies) Working Party, June 2005, p. 31). GRUNDMANN also emphasizes that "there is increasingly a standard-setter via demand-side power, i.e. institutional investors" (S. GRUNDMANN, *European Company Law*, Antwerp/Oxford, Intersentia, 2007, no. 481, p. 272).

[207] "Corporate Governance in Europe", Report of a CEPS (Centre for European Policy Studies) Working Party, June 2005, p. 39.

[208] In the field of shareholder protection, SIEMS underlines that legal harmonization is not the only method of legal convergence. Indeed, as the social, political and economic conditions that form the background to shareholder law come closer internationally, the law itself will also grow more similar ("convergence through congruence"). Moreover, this author expects individual interest groups to press for a greater approximation of laws ("convergence through pressure"): M. SIEMS, "Shareholder Protection Across Countries - Is the EU on the Right Track?", DICE-Report - Journal for Institutional Comparisons, Vol. 4/3, pp. 39-43, 2006 . Available at SSRN: http://ssrn.com/abstract=940567, 39

[209] K. J. HOPT, "Modern Company and Capital Market Problems: Improving European Corporate

29. ***Flexibility and restraint.*** The question of which role Europe *should* play leads to another question: how can the current policy be assessed? This *current position* (i) tends towards greater flexibility and (ii) can be described as "restraint".

On the one hand, European corporate governance attaches great importance to flexibility. European companies are able to choose their governance model by moving their place of incorporation[210]. Moreover, national corporate law tends to allow freedom of choice between different corporate governance models[211]. The same option was taken at European level by the creation of the SE. Indeed, the governance of the SE can be designed based on a menu of different choices. BECHT emphasizes that this competition may have its benefits. However, he points out that there are costs as well: the danger is that companies switch in favor of a model that reinforces the power of its block-holders or their managerial entrenchment[212].

On the other hand, the EU action on corporate governance can be described as "restraint".

Partly, this restraint goes back to the subsidiarity principle, according to which the Community is to take action "only if and in so far as the objectives of the proposed action cannot be sufficiently achieved by the Member States and can therefore, by reason of the scale or effects of the proposed action, be better achieved by the Community". Moreover, any action of the Community should not go beyond what is necessary to achieve the objectives of the Treaty. Although there are indications that the European Court of Justice will not lightly overturn Community action on the ground that it does not comply

Governance After Enron" (January 2007). ECGI Law Working Paper No. 05/2002; ECGI Finance Working Paper. Available at SSRN: http://ssrn.com/abstract=356102 or DOI: 10.2139/ssrn.356102, 449.

[210] Indeed, in the European context, special attention should be given to the case law of the European Court of Justice on corporate mobility. Historically, convergence through regulatory competition was not available in Europe because the application of the "real seat" doctrine dictated that the corporate law – and corporate governance rules – of the country in which the corporation's principal place of business was located governed its internal affairs regardless of the country of incorporation (R.J. GILSON, "Globalizing Corporate Governance: Convergence of Form or Function", 49 *Am. J. Comp. L.* 350 2001). This changed fundamentally after the *Centros* decision of the European Court of Justice, in which the Court introduced regulatory competition into the European Union. The possible voluntary selection of different formal – corporate governance – rules will lead to more convergence of the corporate governance rules and practices of the various Member States.

[211] WINTER calls this the "privatization of company law". The regulation of corporate governance is to a large extent left to companies and their shareholders. Member States adopt corporate governance codes, which are drafted by committees consisting of representatives of companies, shareholders and other private entities. They are not binding upon companies, although companies must explain any non-compliance with them. Therefore, the enforcement is primarily in the hands of the shareholders: J. WINTER, "*Ius Audacibus*. The Future of EU company law", M. TISON et al. (eds.), *Perspectives in Company Law and Financial Regulation – Essays in Honour of Eddy Wymeersch*, Cambridge University Press 2009, 47.

[212] M. BECHT, "Current issues in European Corporate Governance", Background Note prepared for the Euro 50 Group Meeting on Corporate Governance, European Investment Bank, Luxembourg, 10 July 2003, 8.

with the subsidiarity principle[213], it must be acknowledged that the principle has a role to play in the debate concerning whether the EU should take action in the field of corporate governance[214]. De facto, this restraint can even be explained by another, more historical reason. Indeed, the more the EU wanted to harmonize internal corporate governance in the past, the less successful it was[215]. Finally, economic reasoning could give this restraint a scientific basis: it is not yet established that the risk-reducing factor of corporate governance outweighs the costs of compliance with more stringent rules, including the cost of inflexibility[216]. This is another reason for not fixing corporate governance developments through mandatory harmonization at EU level[217].

30. *Freedom of choice.* This restraint makes the emphasis of the Commission on national corporate governance initiatives clear. However, this does not mean that the EU does not take a position at all. Indeed, the Commission emphasizes the importance of a framework of rules which will bring about convergence, whereby the principle is that the EU should facilitate freedom of choice between these alternative systems for companies across Europe[218], rather than trying to agree upon one specific EU system or leaving the option to Member States. Indeed, sound competition between corporate governance arrangements could

---

[213] P. CRAIG and G. DE BURCA, *EU Law. Text, cases and materials*, Oxford, Oxford University Press, 2003, 137.

[214] WINTER underlines the importance of the strong emphasis on subsidiarity in the European company law debate. He stresses that this trend can be seen from abandoning the Fifth and Ninth Directives. It is also clear from the efforts to simplify current directives, in particular the Second Directive on capital maintenance. Finally, this trend can be seen from the development of not imposing certain elements of legislation on Member States but either giving them options to apply or not apply certain EU rules or leaving core elements of regulation out of an EU legislative instrument. WINTER refers to the Thirteenth Directive on Takeover Bids and the opt-outs that Member States have been given from the rules on defense against takeovers, provided they give opt-in rights to companies and to the SE Statute, leaving anything contentious to Member States to regulate themselves in their legislation implementing the SE Statute: J. WINTER, "*Ius Audacibus.* The Future of EU company law", M. TISON et al. (eds.), *Perspectives in Company Law and Financial Regulation – Essays in Honour of Eddy Wymeersch*, Cambridge University Press 2009, 46-47. See also J. L. HANSEN, "The Nordic corporate governance model – a European model?", in M. TISON et al. (eds.), *Perspectives in company law and financial regulation – Essays in Honour of Eddy Wymeersch*, Cambridge University Press, 2009, 149.

[215] K. LANNOO and A. KHACHATURYAN, "Reform of Corporate Governance in the EU", *EBOR* 5 (2004) 44.

[216] There is no empirical evidence to suggest that a superior corporate governance system exists. Nor it is likely that one could be identified by academics or lawmakers when the market participants themselves have been unable to do so through generations of competitive market behavior: J. L. HANSEN, "The Nordic corporate governance model – a European model?", in M. TISON et al. (eds.), *Perspectives in company law and financial regulation – Essays in Honour of Eddy Wymeersch*, Cambridge University Press, 2009, 150.

[217] K. J. HOPT, J. GARRIDO GARCIA, J. RICKFORD, G. ROSSI, J.S. CHRISTENSEN, J. SIMON and J. WINTER, "European Corporate Governance in company law and codes", *Report prepared for the European Corporate Governance Conference of October 18*, The Hague, The Netherlands, 63.

[218] BAUMS underlines that Commissioner McCreevy strongly supported the use of "enabling legislation", which leaves as many options as possible between various legal forms open to the undertakings: T. BAUMS, "European Company Law Beyond the 2003 Action Plan", ECGI - Law Working Paper No. 81/2007; European Business Organization Law Review, Vol. 8, 2007. Available at SSRN: http://ssrn.com/abstract=973456, 16.

bring the best possible results for investors[219]. This option fits in with the wider liberalization agenda of the Internal Market Directorate, and with the case law of the European Court of Justice. The European Corporate Governance Forum, set up by the Commission to enhance the convergence of national codes of corporate governance, gives shape to this policy[220].

31. ***European corporate governance heavily influenced by Anglo-American standards?*** This could give the impression that the European Community takes a neutral stand. However, some authors point out that this is not the case. They suggest that the European corporate governance policy attaches too much importance to Anglo-American corporate governance tools[221] [222].

(i) The first critique concerns the emphasis on shareholders' rights in current European policy. Symptomatic in this context is the way in which the EU stresses the protection of the shareholder in its Directive on Shareholders' Rights. If shareholder voting is enhanced, it could encourage more proxy fights that try to change management or policy. Increasing shareholder democracy and activism, which often means a louder voice for shareholders, is not uncontroversial but has become an international phenomenon. Enhanced shareholder protection may lead to more pressure for companies to focus on shareholders' interests and thus have an effect on other stakeholders[223].

---

[219] S. MAVROMATTI and C. PAPATHANASSIOU, "A Modified Open Method of Coordination in Corporate Governance", 2006 *EBLR* (1637) 1645.

[220] Commission Decision 2004/706/EC of 15 October 2004 establishing the European Corporate Governance Forum, OJ 2004 L 321, 53.

[221] The influence of Anglo-American corporate governance standards on the corporate governance practices on the Continent has been examined by BAUER, BRAUN and CLARK. They argue that the Anglo-American governance system serves as a market-reference point for the government of large continental European firms: R. BAUER, R. BRAUN and G. CLARK, "The Emerging Market for European Corporate Governance: The Relationship between Governance and Capital Expenditures, 1997-2005" (9 November 2007). Available at SSRN: http://ssrn.com/abstract=1030771, 22. See also S. MAUL and E. EGGENHOFER, "Aktionsplan der Europäischen Kommission zur Reform des Europäischen Gesellschaftsrechts", *Betriebs-Berater* 2002, (1289) 1295, who underline that "zahlreiche Vorschläge in wichtigen Bereichen an die anglo-amerikanische Gedankenwelt anknüpfen" and S. MAUL and G. LANFERMANN, "Europäische Corporate Governance – Stand der Entwicklungen", *Betriebs-Berater* 2004, 1868. BURBIDGE points out that this convergence is not a matter of one-way communication. Indeed, he argues that the UK is inching towards the continental model under the influence of a series of EC directives imposing consultation rights: P. BURBIDGE, "Creating High Performance Boardrooms and Workplaces – European Corporate Governance in the Twenty-First Century", *E.L. Rev.* 2003, 28(5) 644.

[222] SCHMIDT emphasizes the gradual nature of this influence. Therefore, he suggests that a possible breakdown of the traditional (German corporate governance) system would not imply that a market-based governance system is already in place and functioning. It might create a lack of any form of functioning governance: R. SCHMIDT, "Corporate Governance in Germany: An Economic Perspective" (August 2003). CFS Working Paper No. 2003/36. Available at SSRN: http://ssrn.com/abstract=477761 or DOI: 10.2139/ssrn.477761, 35.

[223] A.R. PINTO, "The European Union's Shareholder Voting Rights Directive from an American Perspective: Some Comparisons and Observations (15 September 2008). Fordham International Law Journal, Vol. 32, 2008; Brooklyn Law School, Legal Studies Paper No. 117. Available at SSRN: http://ssrn.com/abstract=1268454, 34.

In any case, enhancing shareholders' rights by mandatory law fits into a governance system that is more market-oriented because it strengthens self-help by shareholders and investors[224]. This relates to a particular concept of best practice, which is represented by the principal-agent model of corporate governance. The OECD Principles and, to a large degree, US and British practice have had a huge influence on the European policy on corporate governance[225]. Enhancing shareholders' rights is of great value when the ownership of a company is dispersed, but does not address the problem of minority shareholders on the Continent, who have no real influence even if they vote[226].

(ii) Moreover, the implicit preference for the Anglo-Saxon corporate governance system can also be found in the EU's emphasis on disclosure as an important corporate governance tool. This emphasis may however ignore the ownership structure of companies on the Continent. In the UK, the factual conditions are better suited to a corporate governance system which is mainly based on disclosure rules and a comply-or-explain mechanism[227].

Controlling shareholders have no need for mandatory disclosure, since they are familiar with their companies in any case. The added value of disclosure is therefore likely to be minimal. The real contribution of disclosure in controlled companies is to alert minority shareholders to the company's ownership structure before they invest, and to restrain controlling shareholders from extracting illicit private benefits afterwards[228]. The High Level Group is aware of this peculiarity and recommends disclosure of major shareholdings, shareholder agreements and potential shareholder coalitions as well as documentation of the economic relationships between companies and their major shareholders.

For minority shareholders, disclosure can only be a source of added value if they can act upon the information obtained. According to the Winter Report, a European Framework Rule granting "special investigatory rights to minority shareholders" should be adopted[229]. Possible

---

224 K.J. HOPT, "European Company Law and Corporate Governance: Where Does the Action Plan of the European Commission lead?", Working Paper no. 52/2005, ECGI, 2005, 12.

225 S. DEAKIN, "Reflexive Governance and European Company Law", CLPE Research Paper Series, 2007, 25.

226 S. SHEIKH, "A modern regulatory framework for European company law", The Company Lawyer Vol. 24 No. 12 2003, 366.

227 M. PANNIER and J. RICKFORD, "Corporate Governance Disclosures in Europe" (2005), *EBLR* 999; J. RICKFORD, "Fundamentals, Developments and Trends in British Company Law – Some Wider Reflections for Europe. Second Part: Current British Priorities and Wider Reflections" (2005), *ECFR* 1, 38.

228 R. KRAAKMAN, "Disclosure and Corporate Governance", G. FERRARINI et al. (eds.), *Reforming Company and Takeover Law in Europe*, Oxford, Oxford University Press, 2004, 104.

229 This has also been defended by the Forum Europaeum Corporate Group Law. This Group is in favor of a framework rule that leaves it to the Member States to fit the special investigation into their particular procedural laws: Forum Europaeum Corporate Group Law, "Corporate Group Law for Europe", 2002 EBOR, 165.

sanctions should be determined by the Member States. The likelihood of this European investigatory right being born under a lucky star seems rather remote, since the Winter Report suggests that disqualification of directors might be a useful sanction. However, KRAAKMAN points out that disqualification seems to be more suitable for disciplining directors and managers of widely-held companies than for policing the conduct of directors handpicked by controlling shareholders[230].

(iii) The European tendency towards the Anglo-Saxon corporate governance system finds another expression in the emphasis placed on the role of non-executive directors in monitoring the management. Again, some argue that this feature of the British and American systems was presented as if it had universal validity. DEAKIN argues that the distinctive roles of worker directors and community representatives in two-tier boards were shoehorned in this supposedly universal model[231].

32. *Final comments – European corporate governance: quo vadis?* For all these reasons, LANNOO and KHACHATURYAN argue that the Commission fails to promote the strength of the diversity of Europe's corporate governance systems[232]. This critique is not fully correct[233]. Anglo-American corporate governance tools can be effective in the context of the concentrated ownership structure as well, provided that they are adapted to this different setting. In the light of globalization, any corporate governance system has to meet a sufficient standard of objectivity, which means that it must be able to adapt to differing ownership structures[234]. A fortiori, this is the case for a European corporate governance system.

The intrinsic limit of such a European corporate governance system comes into the limelight: because of the difference in problems European companies are confronted with, European corporate governance should limit itself to formulating general principles – the independence of the board of directors, protecting the "shareholders' voice", the protection of the minority sharehold-

[230] R. KRAAKMAN, "Disclosure and Corporate Governance", G. FERRARINI et al. (eds.), *Reforming Company and Takeover Law in Europe*, Oxford, Oxford University Press, 2004, 105.

[231] S. DEAKIN, "Reflexive Governance and European Company Law", CLPE Research Paper no. 20/2007, 14.

[232] K. LANNOO and A. KHACHATURYAN, "Reform of Corporate Governance in the EU", *EBOR* 5 (2004), 53.

[233] Reference should be made to L. CERIONI and A. KEAY, who deny this so-called "victory for the shareholder model". They suggest a new definition of corporate governance, and emphasize that a corporate objective should consist of the survival and development of the business activity under sound economic and financial conditions. It is possible that this result may be better enforced by some (such as the shareholders) rather than by others (other stakeholders). However, this does not mean that the latter are deemed to be less important: L. CERIONI and A. KEAY, "Corporate Governance and the Corporate Objective in the European Community: Proposing a Re-Definition in the Light of EC Law", (2008) *EBLR* 405-445.

[234] K. GEENS, "Over corporate governance, aandeelhoudersstructuren en vennootschapsrecht", *Knelpunten van dertig jaar vennootschapsrecht*, Kalmthout, Biblo, 1999, no. 14, p. 751.

er[235]. WINTER stresses that the substance of corporate governance is linked directly to the core of company law. Since this core is designed differently across Member States, agreement at European level on a single model is very unlikely[236]. Nevertheless, this does not mean that Europe cannot play an important role in the ongoing corporate governance debate. According to WINTER, the EU can coordinate the efforts of Member States to protect and improve the integrity of their national corporate governance models[237].

In a broad sense, "corporate governance" is dealt with in an enormous body of different rules – corporate governance codes, national company law, securities law, social law[238] . Therefore, and in the light of some national particularities[239], filling in the details based on the general principles we have discussed will always remain a task for the European Union… and the Member States.

---

[235] See K.J. HOPT, "Gemeinsame Grundsätze der Corporate Governance in Europa?", *ZGR* 6/2000, 814.

[236] J. WINTER, "*Ius Audacibus.* The Future of EU company law", M. TISON et al. (eds.), *Perspectives in Company Law and Financial Regulation – Essays in Honour of Eddy Wymeersch*, Cambridge University Press 2009, 49.

[237] J. WINTER, "*Ius Audacibus.* The Future of EU company law", M. TISON et al. (eds.), *Perspectives in Company Law and Financial Regulation – Essays in Honour of Eddy Wymeersch*, Cambridge University Press 2009, 49.

[238] Therefore, transplanting some governance mechanisms from one legal system to another may not be effective since they may be incompatible with the underlying legal structure: C. JORDAN, "The Conundrum of Corporate Governance", 30 *Brook. J. Int'l L.* 993 2004-2005, 1010.

[239] A complete harmonization of corporate governance is not desirable in the light of some national particularities, e.g. German co-determination rules, which demonstrate the strong "path dependence" of company law and corporate governance: M. KORT, "Standardization of Company Law in Germany, other EU Member States and Turkey by Corporate Governance Rules", *ECFR* 4/2008, 406. See also TEICHMANN, who states that "jedes [Corporate Governance-]System reagiert möglicherweise spezifisch auf die vorherrschenden wirtschaftlichen und kulturellen Anforderungen, denen es an seinem Anwendungsort gerecht werden muß": C. TEICHMANN, "Corporate Governance in Europa", *ZGR* 2001, 675.

Bibliography

R. BAUER, R. BRAUN and G. CLARK, "The Emerging Market for European Corporate Governance: The Relationship between Governance and Capital Expenditures, 1997-2005" (9 November 2007). Available at SSRN: http://ssrn.com/abstract=1030771, 40 p.

T. BAUMS, "European Company Law Beyond the 2003 Action Plan", ECGI - Law Working Paper No. 81/2007; European Business Organization Law Review, Vol. 8, 2007. Available at SSRN: http://ssrn.com/abstract=973456, 25 p.

T. BAUMS and K. SCOTT, "Taking Shareholder Protection Seriously? Corporate Governance in the United States and Germany". American Journal of Comparative Law, Vol. 53, Winter 2005; ECGI - Law Working Paper No. 17/2003; Stanford Law and Economics Olin Working Paper. Available at SSRN: http://ssrn.com/abstract=473185 or DOI: 10.2139/ssrn.473185, 20 p.

R. BREUER, "Corporate Governance in Europe", Forum Financier/Revue Bancaire et Financière 2001/5, 259

L. CERIONI and A. KEAY, "Corporate Governance and the Corporate Objective in the European Community: Proposing a Re-Definition in Light of EC Law", (2008) EBLR 405

P. DAVIES, "Board Structure in the UK and Germany: Convergence or Continuing Divergence?", available at SSRN: http://ssrn.com/abstract=262959 or DOI: 10.2139/ssrn.262959, 24 p.

Y. DE CORDT and C. BRÜLS, "La protection des actionnaires en droit communautaire", JTDE 2007, 129

A. DORRESTEIJN and C. DE GROOT, "Corporate Governance Codes: Origins and Perspectives", European Company Law 2004, 43

G. FERRARINI and N. MOLONEY, "Executive Remuneration and Corporate Governance in the EU: Convergence, Divergence, and Reform Perspectives", G. FERRARINI et al. (eds.), Reforming Company and Takeover Law in Europe, Oxford, Oxford University Press, 2004, 267

G. FERRARINI, N. MOLONEY and C. VESPRO, "Executive Remuneration in the EU: Comparative Law and Practice" (June 2003). ECGI - Law Working Paper No. 09/2003. Available at SSRN: http://ssrn.com/abstract=419120 or DOI: 10.2139/ssrn.419120, 67 p.

K. GEENS, "Over corporate governance, aandeelhoudersstructuren en vennootschapsrecht", JAN RONSE INSTITUUT (ed.), Knelpunten van dertig jaar vennootschapsrecht, Kalmthout, Biblo 1999, 735

S. GRUNDMANN, "The Structure of European Company Law: From Crisis to Boom", EBOR (5) 2004, 601

S. GRUNDMANN, European Company Law, Intersentia, Antwerp/Oxford, 2007, 807 p.

J. L. HANSEN, "The Nordic corporate governance model – a European model?", M. TISON et al. (eds.), Perspectives in Company Law and Financial Regulation – Essays in Honour of Eddy Wymeersch, Cambridge University Press, 2009, 145

J. HILL, "Regulating Executive Remuneration: International Developments in the Post-Scandal Era", European Company Law 2006, 64

K. J. HOPT, "Modern Company and Capital Market Problems: Improving European Corporate Governance After Enron" (January 2007). ECGI Law Working Paper No. 05/2002; ECGI Finance Working Paper. Available at SSRN: http://ssrn.com/abstract=356102 or DOI: 10.2139/ssrn.356102, 446, also in: Journal of Corporate Law Studies 3 (2003) 221

K. J. HOPT, "Labor Representation on Corporate Boards: Impacts and Problems for Corporate Governance and Economic Integration in Europe", 14 International Review of Law and Economics, 1994, 203

K. J. HOPT, "The German Two-Tier Board (Aufsichtsrat), A German View on Corporate Governance", K. J. HOPT and E. WYMEERSCH (eds.), Comparative Corporate Governance – Essays and Materials, Berlin/New York, De Gruyter, 1997, 3

K. J. HOPT, "Gemeinsame Grundsätze der Corporate Governance in Europa?", ZGR 6/2000, 779 and "Common Principles of Corporate Governance in Europe?", J.A. MCCAHERY et al. (eds.), Corporate Governance Regimes, Convergence and Diversity, Oxford, Oxford University Press 2002, 175

K. J. HOPT and P. LEYENS, "Board Models in Europe - Recent Developments of Internal Corporate Governance Structures in Germany, the United Kingdom, France, and Italy." ECGI - Law Working Paper No. 18/2004; Available at SSRN: http://ssrn.com/abstract=487944 or DOI: 10.2139/ssrn.487944, 24 p., also in: ECFR 2004, 135

K. J. HOPT, "European Company Law and Corporate Governance: Where Does the Action Plan of the European Commission Lead?", K. J. HOPT, E. WYMEERSCH et al. (eds.), Corporate Governance in Context, Oxford, Oxford University Press, 2005, 119

K. J. HOPT, "Comparative Company Law", M. REIMANN and R. ZIMMERMANN (eds.), The Oxford Handbook of Comparative Law, Oxford, Oxford University Press 2006, 1161

C. JORDAN, "The Conundrum of Corporate Governance", 30 Brook. J. Int'l. L. 983 2004-2005, 983

C. JUNGMANN, "The Effectiveness of Corporate Governance in One-Tier and Two-Tier Board Systems", ECFR 4/2006, 426

M. KAHAN and E. ROCK, "Hedge Funds in Corporate Governance and Corporate Control", U of Penn, Inst for Law & Econ Research Paper No. 06-16; NYU, Law and Economics Research Paper No. 06-37; ECGI - Law Working Paper No. 76/2006; University of Pennsylvania Law Review, Vol. 155, No. 5, 2007. Available at SSRN: http://ssrn.com/abstract=919881, 54 p.

M. KORT, "Standardization of Company Law in Germany, other EU Member States and Turkey by Corporate Governance Rules", ECFR 4/2008, 379

H. LAGA, "Bestuur: monistisch of duaal", JAN RONSE INSTITUUT (ed.) Knelpunten van dertig jaar vennootschapsrecht, Kalmthout, Biblo 1999, 469

M. LAMO DE ESPINOSA ABARCA, "The Need for Substantive Regulation on Investor Protection and Corporate Governance in Europe: Does Europe Need a Sarbanes-Oxley?", JIBLR 2004, 19(11), 419

K. LANNOO and A. KHACHATURYAN, "Reform of Corporate Governance in the EU", EBOR 5 (2004) 37

M. LITTGER, "Funktion und Verwendungschancen der neuen Kodizes am Beispiel von Corporate Governance", *Rechtstheorie* 2008, 495

M. LUTTER et al., "Stellungnahme der Group of German Experts on Corporate Law zum Konsultationspapier der High Level Group of Experts on Corporate Law", Zeitschrift für Wirtschaftsrecht (ZIP) 2002, 1310

S. MAUL and E. EGGENHOFER, "Aktionsplan der Europäischen Kommission zur Reform des Europäischen Gesellschaftsrechts", Betriebs-Berater 2003, 1289

S. MAUL and G. LANFERMANN, "Europäische Corporate Governance – Stand der Entwicklungen", Betriebs-Berater 2004, 1861.

S. MAVROMATTI and C. PAPATHANASSIOU, "A Modified Open Method of Coordination in Corporate Governance", 2006 EBLR 1637

M. PANNIER and J. RICKFORD, "Corporate Governance Disclosures in Europe", (2005) EBLR 975

A. PINTO, "The European Union's Shareholder Voting Rights Directive from an American Perspective: Some Comparisons and Observations" (15 September 2008). Fordham International Law Journal, Vol. 32, 2008; Brooklyn Law School, Legal Studies Paper No. 117. Available at SSRN: http://ssrn.com/abstract=1268454, 35 p.

S. SHEIKH, "A modern regulatory framework for European company law", The Company Lawyer 2003, 362

M. SIEMS, "Shareholder Protection Across Countries - Is the EU on the Right Track?", DICE-Report - Journal for Institutional Comparisons, Vol. 4/3, pp. 39-43, 2006. Available at SSRN: http://ssrn.com/abstract=940567, 39

C. TEICHMANN, "Corporate Governance in Europa", *ZGR* 2001, 645

D. THIENPONT, "Corporate Governance in the EU: the Commission's Approach", European Company Law 2004, 57

K. VAN HULLE and S. MAUL, "Aktionsplan zur Modernisierung des Gesellschaftsrechts und Stärkung der Corporate Governance", ZGR 2004, 484

D. WEBER-REY, "Effects of the Better Regulation Approach on European Company Law and Corporate Governance", ECFR 3/2007, 370

J. WINTER, "*Ius audacibus*. The future of EU Company Law", M. TISON et al. (eds.), Perspectives in Company Law and Financial Regulation – Essays in Honour of Eddy Wymeersch, Cambridge University Press, 2009, 43

D. WOJCIK, "Convergence in Corporate Governance: Empirical Evidence from Europe 2000-2003" (June 2004). Available at SSRN: http://ssrn.com/abstract=559424, 22 p.

E. WYMEERSCH, "Shareholders in Action" (February 2007). University of Ghent Financial Law Institute Working Paper No. 2007-03. Available at SSRN: http://ssrn.com/abstract=965661, 11p.

E. WYMEERSCH, "Corporate Governance Codes and Their Implementation" (September 2006). University of Ghent Financial Law Institute Working Paper No. 2006-10. Available at SSRN: http://ssrn.com/abstract=931100, 11 p.

E. WYMEERSCH, "Enforcement of Corporate Governance Codes" (June 2005). ECGI - Law Working Paper No. 46/2005. Available at SSRN: http://ssrn.com/abstract=759364, 26 p.

E. WYMEERSCH, "Implementation of the Corporate Governance Codes", K.J. HOPT et al. (eds.), Corporate Governance in Context – Corporations, States, and Markets in Europe, Japan, and the US, Oxford, Oxford University Press 2005, 403

D. ZETZSCHE "Virtual Shareholder Meetings and the European Shareholder Rights Directive - Challenges and Opportunities" (26 June 2007). CBC-RPS No. 0029. Available at SSRN: http://ssrn.com/abstract=996434, 75 p.

Transcripts of Corporate Governance Session

Paper: *Hilde Laga and Floris Parrein*
Respondent: *Eddy Wymeersch (University of Ghent)*
Chair: *Paul Davies (University of Oxford)*
Rapporteur: *Sofie Cools (K.U.Leuven)*

A. Abstract

Independent Directors – The problem with independent directors is twofold. First, they are often ill-informed and not knowledgeable about the business of the company. Second, even if they are informed, it requires a great deal of courage to stand up against the executives and challenge their proposals, especially if the executives are very powerful. Yet failure of a company is not always and exclusively the fault of the independent directors, or even the entire board. One cannot evaluate the role of independent directors without considering the responsibility of other corporate constituencies, such as the shareholders' meeting. Consideration should be given to introducing internal inquirers or ad hoc committees to investigate issues, rather than paying too much attention to the role of independent directors.

Limits of Corporate Law – There are limits to the possibilities of corporate law: the performance of a company depends to a large extent on the individual behaviour of the directors and managers. However, this should not be an argument for abstaining from any legal intervention designed to promote good decision-making.

Soft Law – The value of soft law is that it allows a judge to apply general principles in concrete situations. In other words, it can make the (hard) law better enforceable, without unduly burdening efficient governance. For that reason, many issues should not be taken up in hard law. They could be addressed in best practice guidelines. In that respect, it was also argued that the European legislator should set out some high level principles for national corporate governance codes.

Director Liability – It was proposed to distinguish between executive and non-executive directors. There are arguments for the position that a non-executive director, who must remain an outsider and thus does not spend as much time becoming informed, should be evaluated according to less stringent standards.

Empty Voting – Empty voting should be avoided, but this is not easy to regulate. This is partly due to the difficulty in determining what is covered by the term "empty voting". Obviously, the general meaning is voting of shares by people who have no economic interest in the shares. However, there are several rules, such as record date mechanisms, which were introduced for good reasons, but which can be abused as a means to engage in empty voting.

B. Response to paper by Eddy Wymeersch

My first reaction is that we should also look at these issues from the perspective of the financial crisis. The financial crisis reveals significant shortcomings in the governance of those institutions that have suffered the most. Claiming the existence of corporate governance shortcomings afterwards is always rather easy, because the company has gone down, the board has been removed, the CEO has almost been killed, etc.

I propose to deal first with financial stability, i.e. the link between corporate governance and financial stability. Although this has not yet been sufficiently explored, it must be emphasised that the international institutions, such as the IMF, FSF and others, are showing increasing interest in corporate governance issues. They are right. The second item I will deal with is the exercise of cross-border voting rights, and the third one is empty voting.

The first point is financial stability. In my view, it is obvious that in all the big failures which we have seen and that created systemic risks, governance shortcomings of all kinds have been of paramount importance. I can recommend a few books written by journalists. There is one book on Northern Rock and two books, written by Jeroen Smit, on Ahold and ABN Amro respectively. They are not highly technical accounts, but they are very informative as to the governance process.

What we see in all of these descriptions – and I am sure there are many others – is that boards have been utterly ineffective. Nonexistent monitoring, no guidance: it is really very disappointing. In the case of Northern Rock, the board was constituted of members originating from two predecessor entities, one being a corporate entity and the other one a building society owned by the local gentry. There was a clash between two totally different cultures: on the one hand the corporate world of the small savers and on the other hand the traditional and rich gentry. They were unable to talk to each other, but moreover, they did not meet (or they met in terms of socialising but not effectively). That board was clearly ineffective.

An ineffective board with, in addition, an overly powerful CEO or chairman is even more dangerous. That was the case in Northern Rock too. In the last two years before it collapsed, Northern Rock grew by a factor of five, stronger than any competitor. Anybody seeing that must have realised that something was wrong. What was wrong is very simple. It is the typical banking failure, namely making long out of short. Short funds, essentially interbank funds, which are transformed into long-term credits. As has been very well documented in economic literature, especially in the United States, overly powerful CEOs who monopolise power are not accountable to their board. They do whatever they like and they spend their money especially for their private purposes, such as perks.

The third point is in fact a summary of the two previous ones: insufficient checks and balances. The dialogue between the board and the CEO or the management did not function. Even at a lower level, Northern Rock obviously had a good CFO, but the man was on sick leave for months before the collapse. He saw in advance that things were going awry, but nevertheless he was unable to communicate that to the CEO, because he did not want to listen, or to the board, because the board was not interested. As a consequence, he quit. Well, he took sick leave, which is almost the same. We know of other examples of the same kind of sick leave, of course.

Independent directors are not a real help. The problem with independent directors is not only that they are not competent. They could be competent, but another problem is their subservience to the CEO. Indeed, it is de facto the CEO who selects the independent directors. Very often, "you become an independent director on my board and I will then become an independent director on your board". That certainly is a situation of conflict of interests which we should not accept. The question is what to do. Well, we need better procedures for the selection of independent directors.

Let me touch on another subject which has also been mentioned and which is of course very much in the centre of our preoccupation incentives. In the financial crisis, people got the wrong incentives. Mortgage brokers received fees for mortgages that did not exist, or that were taken on debtors that were absolutely insolvent. They were only interested in the fee and once they cashed the fee, they sold the mortgage and that was it for them. This is not a good system. The same problem existed at the top and in the intermediate management. If people are remunerated based on the company's growth, there are certainly problems ahead. Management engages in excessive risk taking and pursues short term business. This is not only a problem at management level. Indeed, it is part of the whole organisation. In banks, for instance, traders are remunerated by way of a fee or a bonus on the basis of the profits they have made. Think of Mr Kerviel. Although we still do not know the full story, I would not be astonished to find out that his bonus was also linked to the volume and to the profits he made. Consequently, he took increasingly bigger risks to earn even more or to hide his previous losses. That is what we have observed in hundreds of cases: traders in trading rooms are dangerously encouraged to take risks. Therefore, they should be strictly governed by specific rules and one should make sure that they stay within these rules.

Remuneration committees, which we believed would take care of the incentives and of the remuneration, have not worked at all. Why not? Because they were working on the basis of advice of so-called remuneration agents or specialist remuneration advisers, and of course, these advisers have a strong interest in pushing up the level of remuneration. Indeed, they will necessarily go from one firm to another. Therefore, their reputation is based on a company's generosity in its remuneration policy. Secondly, in continental Europe we have started disclosing remuneration. The consequence has been very clear: remuneration has increased tremendously. Was this the purpose? Is that the benefit of disclosure obligations? Why do we need disclosure of remuneration, provided it is reasonable? An investor does not need this information. The only thing he wants to know is his own return, not the return for the management. I know this statement is not politically correct, but the essence is to separate remuneration from risk taking.

Shareholders have been suffering and continue to suffer very much. The question is: have they been well informed? The answer is clearly, yes, they have been informed *ex post*, not *ex ante*. When the firm collapsed then of course they got all the facts, but before they did not.

The last point in my list on the shareholders' rights is the matter of rights issues. Capital has been raised by placing shares or other securities privately and the shareholders had no right to participate. Of course they were very angry afterwards. Some people argue they should be very pleased today because they have avoided the losses, but that is an *ex post judgment*. The question is whether we need a good procedure to protect investors' rights even in difficult situations and cases of high stress.

The second point of discussion, the participation of shareholders in decision-making, is not directly linked to the crisis. In our European systems, participation is poor and unreliable. Very often, shareholders do not take part in general meetings, either directly or indirectly. Except in the recent shareholders' meeting of Fortis, normally the general meetings are mainly composed of the stable or controlling shareholders. What is the reason for that? Partly, this is caused by the disinterest of the shareholders. A lack of information can explain this as well. Shareholders have not been contacted, they do not know the meeting is taking place, they do not know its agenda. How can we make sure that shareholders are informed in a cross-border context? We know today that, certainly with dematerialisated shares, all shares are held in bank accounts. Do the banks inform the shareholders? The answer is no. So we do not know when general meetings are taking place; much less are we solicited to vote at the general meeting. Therefore, we should change this system to ensure there is direct contact between the issuer, the company and the shareholder. That can be done relatively easily, although eliminating the intervention of the bank is of course needed. This would probably lead to a cut in the bank's revenues. That is probably the reason why this is not well organised.

Short selling is another issue. It came on the agenda in late September 2008. The SEC and the FSA started to enact regulations on short selling. The aim was financial stability: bank shares plunged heavily, which led to loss of confidence, and the supervisors tried to limit this lack of confidence. I think they were not very successful but at least the message was given. It raises the fundamental question: should one allow investors for good or bad reasons to start campaigning for short selling and then destroy, especially for banks, the firm itself? This question is especially important for banks, since short selling pushes down the share price, which necessarily has an impact on the position of the creditors, in the form of CDSs or otherwise. Do shareholders have a duty with regard to the future of the firm?

The last point is empty voting. For a couple of years now, in more and more companies general meetings are taking place with shareholders who vote, but who do not have any financial stake. They are entitled to vote – legally there is no question there – but if you ask them if they also have money, if they "have their skin in the game", then the answer is no. There are all kinds of techniques, three or four in total. For instance, this can be done using the registration date, which was introduced for good reasons in 2002. However, we see that some shareholders are registered on the registration date, but the day after they have left and at the date of the general meeting they have no stake whatsoever. Nevertheless, they can vote in any direction, whether in – or against – the interest of the firm or in their own interest. The same situation arises with securities lending. That is voting with the shares of somebody else, or by means of put options, contracts for differences, indexes with put options, whatever you can imagine. From a philosophical point of view, we should wonder whether our companies, our economic entities, can be run by parties who have no economic interest but are merely formal, legal owners, and whose interests are therefore not aligned with those of the company. And if they take decisions, are these decisions in the interest of the company or merely in their personal interest, which in some cases has clearly been the opposite of the interest of the company? This is a question that, in my view, has a high priority, also in practice. One of the proposals to be made to the European Commission concerns that what is usually called "empty voting".

C. Discussion

Paul DAVIES

It seems to me that there were two broad areas that the papers and the respondent raised: one in relation to the effectiveness of boards and the other in relation to the effectiveness (or abuses) of shareholder voting. Let's take the board first. The papers gave us an account of all the changes that have been made, at Community level and to some extent at national level, to try to make boards more effective. These measures include in particular the requirements or recommendations for more independent non-executive directors and for giving those independent non-executive directors a bigger role in the running of the company. All of that happened, and yet Professor Wymeersch in his account of Northern Rock criticises that company for having an overly powerful CEO. Similarly, if you go back to the Cadbury Committee in the UK, which in the early 1990s made certain recommendations to increase the number of independent non-executives and to give them bigger tasks, the criticisms which the Cadbury Committee made were exactly the ones that Professor Wymeersch has made in his criticism today. Yet the recommendations made by the Cadbury Committee for dealing with that problem, in particular the introduction of the independent directors, have been implemented, with apparently no significant impact on the functioning of boards. Thus, the first question is whether we have put too much faith in board reform, in reforming the structure and composition of boards, as a way of dealing with the problem of overly powerful CEOs. And if that is true, where do we go from here? Does a set of options for the board structure exist, or should we say that within company law this type of reform has proved to be a failure, possibly opening the argument in favour of much stronger external regulation of companies' operations? Has this been a complete waste of time and should we be thinking in a totally different way?

Peter MONTAGNON, Association of British Insurers
This is a very important question, but I think it actually should not be treated in isolation. The failure is not only in the board, but also with shareholders. I am holding them to account. I think it was always the envisaged standard Cadbury approach that the shareholders would have a role to play. In some cases, the shareholders have not managed to hold the board to account. We do need some kind of examination as to why this is the case. In the USA, the reasons are obvious: the shareholders have no real rights to hold the boards to account, so they cannot dismiss them. In the UK, where we do have very dispersed ownership, maybe the long-term shareholders do not have the critical mass any more. However, if you just look at the board failure in isolation, you will not necessarily get the right answer. I think the answer we ought to strive for is one in which the accountability chain is made to work. I agree that if we cannot get there, we will have regulation with a totally wrong approach. Probably, looking at what happens with shareholders is important to try to make them work better. That may mean examining the governance of shareholder entities as well as the governance of the companies they control. I just think that has to be part of the debate. Otherwise we will not get very far.

Walter VAN GERVEN, K.U.Leuven
I am not a true believer at all in external members of the board of directors. I have been an external director, and I fully subscribe to what I have heard. These directors are not competent. They may have *some* use, but they are dependent on management: when they have a question to ask, they must depend on management to formulate the question the correct way. Sometimes it is worthwhile because they are asking for the most evident things and a

lot of people within a company have forgotten reality. I have one personal experience where an external board director was very useful and that was in the pharmaceutical sector, namely Janssen Pharmaceutica. But that was because the board of directors was composed of no more than five people, with the legendary Paul Janssen, who was a great scientist, and a few other people who were extremely transparent.

Having said that, I am a believer in ad hoc committees, appointed either by a court or otherwise, and who then have all the powers to investigate, to see all documents, to interview all the people from the top down to the drivers who will tell you much more than the directors often do. That works. I have two examples where I served on a committee like that, both of which worked well. The first was the committee on the Santer Commission. The Santer Commission resigned after receiving the report of the committee, which had worked no longer than five weeks. Secondly, under the Paul Volcker chairmanship at the World Bank two years ago, we investigated the institutional integrity department, anti-corruption division. The same methods were used and the same results were achieved. Now we have the Fortis committee. I do not know whether there will be any results there, but I am sure that ad hoc committees are better than any external members on the board of directors.

Jaap WINTER, University of Amsterdam

Just two or three small comments on your question. I do not think that another crisis supports the position that boards in general fail to operate as they should. We have had two consecutive crises: the first crisis could be called the "governance crisis". Now, we are confronted with the financial crisis. We responded to the governance crisis by requiring very explicitly that boards behave better – more independence, more time investment, etc. The fact that the financial crisis has now occurred and that the boards of those financial institutions at least have not been able to prevent this crisis for their institutions does not mean that the improvements that we have seen are completely valueless. It is basically our human tendency to always respond to a crisis by saying that the system has failed.

The problem with the system is not the system, but the human beings that have to work in it. This is the case for boards as well. We considered the governance practices to have failed and we made sure that independent directors would act as a countervailing power, checking the overly powerful CEO. In some cases it definitely has worked. In other cases, it hasn't. These failures are not caused by a lack of authority. Their behaviour was simply not up to standard. How can one deal with this situation? I think that is the crucial question. My intuition is that we can only very partially at best respond to this issue by introducing more rules and regulations in company law. The main problem is much more related to individual personal behaviour of people on a board and group behaviour on that board. Individual and group psychology are key issues. The way people act and behave on boards is driven by their own individual understanding and expectations of what they are supposed to do and what they see that others are doing, what they see that the group is doing. Psychology and group dynamics studies can offer a clear insight into the functioning of the board. The "poverty" of the board is located in that area, not in the applicable rules. If we think hard, we can imagine two, three or even five different sets of rules, or changes to the current rules and practices that probably would be very sensible. But even then, boards would continue to fail under certain circumstances in certain cases. That is something we cannot prevent by creating company law or other types of rules. I believe people who are really interested in good board performance, as well as the boards themselves, should be the first to be interested in their own performance. They should not look too much at the legal rules, the responsibilities, duties and regulations concerning the board and its committees. These rules do not make much of a difference. The personal behaviour is going to make a difference, and that requires a different set of experts, not corporate governance specialists.

Bruno LAFORCE, GIMV NV

I tend to agree that not all boards have worked in a bad way. I also tend to agree with Professor Winter that the way they behave is important. We already touched on their lack of information. Independent directors often have a more neutral role on the board. Therefore, the question arises whether there is not now a place for a kind of "counter-director". This morning, Professor Swennen launched the idea in the session on "one share, one vote" that dispersed shareholders could have a kind of representative on the board who looks after the interests of the smaller shareholders. Even if that would be the case, the question remains how the directors will be well informed. I tend to have a lot of sympathy for the proposal of Professor Van Gerven, who favours the creation of committees that can interview the whole organisation. Nevertheless, I believe it is important to keep in mind that all these people one is going to interview still depend on the CEO. They work for and are paid by the CEO. The question is – and this may be a far-fetched idea – whether the solution could be found in a kind of "shadow management" in which people are working who are not accountable to the CEO but accountable to the directors. I do not believe this is a good solution, since a lot of tension will be created within the company. But what is the solution, then? How does one ensure that board members are well informed? Board members often want a one-size solution for a problem. If a board meeting takes too much time, the quality of the discussion also deteriorates. A further question is how the shareholders, who are even more remote than the members of the board, can be informed. If the board members cannot be informed in a proper manner, how can the shareholders be well informed?

Philippe PELLE, European Commission
The last intervention leads to the problem of measuring the performance of some German companies, in which rules on co-determination apply. The boards of these companies include employee representatives. Perhaps they should be more independent... Well, they are not that independent, because they are also employees. Have those companies outperformed others?

Klaus J. HOPT, Max Planck Institute
At least in the management case, the workers were not really that efficient when it came to being able to react. Theoretically, of course, many of them have good and early knowledge of what is happening in the company. Exploiting that aspect could be interesting. However, I am not convinced that the German co-determination model is the answer. There should be a different solution.

As far as the board is concerned, I agree with Jaap Winter, at least based on the German experience. If one compares what boards did ten years ago and what they do nowadays, there is a huge difference. They not only sit much longer, but they also undertake committee work. Moreover, liability rules are becoming more important and public attention is growing. These are improvements, probably partly thanks to the corporate governance codes. Of course, these codes are not a full solution, but they pushed companies in the right direction.

As far as the ad hoc committees of Walter Van Gerven are concerned, the question arises who will appoint these committees. Appointment by supervisory agencies is an option. I have, for a long time, been an advocate of special inquiry rights within the company. If an expert is appointed by a court or by a minority shareholder, he will or could be able to check things out. If this is really what is wanted, one should keep a kind of group dimension in mind, as difficult as that may be. If that is done properly, it could be a good solution. Some countries, e.g. the Netherlands, are good examples of how this works.

Finally, with regard to powerful CEOs: one needs courage. It is very difficult to swim against the stream. It is very difficult to stand up as an independent director and say that you do not fully understand something. Therefore, we need courage.

José GARRIDO GARCIA, University of Castilla-La Mancha
I do not agree with the position that the whole corporate governance movement has been a failure. In Spain, for instance, one is better off than twenty years ago. Boards today function far better than twenty years ago. That is important to underline. Nevertheless, some things remain to be done. One of these things concerns the complexity of many companies. In these companies, sitting on the board is not a part-time job. Being a member of the board of six different companies at the same time is not possible. The main problem here concerns the non-executive directors. They may not be that independent, since they receive their income from the company – although they have to devote more

time to the company. That is important. The question of powerful CEOs – a phenomenon which I believe is prevalent in many countries – raises another fundamental question, on which we need further legal research, namely the question how we can reconcile the unitary board with the liability regime. A CEO with absolute power should have absolute liability for what happens in his company. The liability of a part-time board member, by contrast, should be measured in a different way. Judges still respond with the old rule of the fiction that the board of directors rules the company which means that all members of the board respond in the same way. I think this problem should be given more thought.

Didier MARTIN, Bredin Prat, Paris

I do not agree that independent directors and non-independent directors should be treated in a different way. Nevertheless, I fully agree with what has been said concerning behaviour. It is essentially a question of behaviour sometimes. In this area, there is no magic answer to the question how the board can control the company efficiently. Consider French corporate law. The answer to this question remains unclear, since there are only a few leading cases that go into detail. However, soft law and corporate governance codes may help. Let us take the example of the audit committee. For this committee, it could be useful to have a chart that can be followed in order to know exactly how to control. I am not saying this guarantees right and efficient control. Nevertheless, avoiding it could be a mistake. Similarly, even if competence and behaviour within the board of directors are essential, the board can at the same time benefit from having the help of recommendations on how to work efficiently.

Paul DAVIES

Well, we reached agreement on the fact that boards do not work in the best possible way. I agree with the position that the initial idea behind independent directors was not only their independence in their relationship to the management. They may be dependent on shareholders as well. Corporate governance documents pay much more attention to the independence of the independent director in his relationship to the management than to the controlling shareholder. Very little is said about their relationship to the shareholder. Indeed, doesn't that rather suggest that the whole notion of independent directors may operate differently in different shareholding structures? If you've got highly atomised shareholdings, there seems little chance of even the most effective independent directors being able to build effective relationships with the shareholders: there are simply too many of them. When you have semi-concentrated shareholdings, as has traditionally been the case in the UK, building such relationships could be possible. I do not think this issue is any less relevant on the other side of the Channel. In companies with concentrated shareholdings, the question for independent directors is presumably the kind of relationship they develop with the non-controlling shareholders. You do not need to worry about the controlling shareholder. The non-controlling shareholder poses the most problems. So again the same question arises: is the structure of the non-controlling shareholders in a block holding regime one which facilitates interaction between the independent directors and the non-controlling shareholders? Thus, one thing we have to think about is the role of shareholders in making independent director regimes operate effectively.

We also discussed mechanisms that do not depend upon the shareholders, such as the independent inquiry. Jaap Winter not only advocates independent directors, he is also in favour of independently minded directors. That still raises the question of what structural mechanisms will ensure that we get such people. In other words, what sort of appointment process is likely to lead to this result?

What about hard law versus soft law, which was one of the big topics in the paper? I think this is an academic debate. Isn't it a pretty meaningless question?

Hilde LAGA
It is not a meaningless question. However, what I wanted to stress is that this issue is not a question of hard law. The choice between hard law or soft law is not obvious, since there is a migration from soft law towards hard law undertaken by the legislator, and recently by the judges. We were confronted with this migration in the Fortis case. Indeed, the corporate governance charter of Fortis was a key element in the judgment. Companies may be very confident with soft law, because they can comply and if they don't, they can explain why. However, I do not believe that not complying will always be accepted by the courts. The contradiction between hard law and soft law could be false.

Paul DAVIES
Do you think it is a good and appropriate development that judges should start looking at soft law when interpreting liability?

Hilde LAGA
I think it is a good evolution because judges want to know what the board has to do. It can also be meaningful when the Company Code remains silent on a certain topic. Judges will take these corporate governance codes into account when judging whether a director took the wrong or the right decisions.

Paul DAVIES
I think that might be a partial answer to Professor Garrido's question (should the same liability standard apply to non-executive as to executive directors?). In a very broad, abstract way the same formulation of the law is applied. However, the exact content of this broad formulation surely varies from director to director according to the function of the director. How is the judge supposed to know what the function of the director is? Well, maybe the corporate governance

codes are of some help there. Justice Austin of the Sydney Court of Chancery recently had to work out what the functions of the chairman of the board were. Now, under the British tradition of common law or statutory law, indeed absolutely nothing is said in the statutes about what the directors are supposed to do, and certainly nothing about what the chairman of the board is supposed to do. So the judge looked at various corporate governance codes around the world in order to deduce the answer to this question. It seems he came up with a sensible answer.

This raises the broader question: where do we see liability rules fitting in a sort of corporate governance structure? The debates are all about structure and composition, but very little about liability. Do you have views about the role of liability rules in improving corporate governance performance of companies? Is it much used in Belgium? Do you have lots of suits against incompetent directors, and when you are advising members of the board do you say, you must be wary about this or that because you may end up being liable?

Walter VAN GERVEN

I would like to come back to the point which I made and Hilde Laga was making as well. Codes of ethics, even more than soft law, are useful for a judge to know where he has to look for something. Indeed, we have, like in the common law tradition, very general notions like fault, etc. It helps a lot when self-regulating devices are filling up these gaps. It is useful that we do not have to find them in books, where you do not find them, but in real life. For that reason, I think it is useful to have codes of ethics. I would even prefer them to soft law, because they allow a judge to be more flexible in using them.

Eddy WYMEERSCH

Indeed, I would like to continue on the same track. I was not trying to tell you that the existing corporate governance codes have no value. They have a value, absolutely, but we should ensure that they work better. For instance, our remuneration committees, the nomination committees, etc. should work. The value of these codes – and that is what the legislator does not understand – is precisely to get a framework in which these fine psychological, social, human elements can develop. Conversely, if you would put that in the law itself, the good functioning of the boards may often be hindered. Therefore, I am very much in favour of having most of these rules outside the legal system. The same holds true for remuneration, a topic on which the legislator is now taking a lot of initiatives. The consequence will be an explosion of new techniques and an increase in remuneration, although that is not the purpose. If one wants to make these codes more efficient, it needs to be ensured that the codes are lived up to, which is not the case today. The monitoring is very light-footed, except perhaps in the Netherlands. So work has to be done there.

José GARRIDO GARCIA

This is a very interesting question, because actually it is difficult to make a clear distinction between hard law and soft law. In Spain this distinction is very difficult to make. Indeed, next to the existence of corporate governance recommendations, every listed company is expected to have a board regulation and a general meeting regulation. The company decides which recommendations it will follow in these regulations. The chosen regulations become hard law. For instance, a board agreement approving a related party transaction which is not approved by the audit committee can be effectively challenged, because it goes against internal regulations of the company.

Hendrik DE SCHEEMAEKER, Deloitte Belgium

I would like to respond to the earlier remark on the consequences of soft law. It is said that directors can be sanctioned for not complying with rules of soft law since soft law is nothing more or less than good practice, and good practice is just what directors are expected to do. Nevertheless, I would like to disconnect it from liability. I am not convinced that liability is the real motive for good directorship. Directors do not keep liability in mind when doing their job day-to-day. They may worry at night sometimes. However, this is not the real motive, especially in countries like Belgium, where a tradition of liability cases against directors does not really exist.

I think there are more modern motives that are equally or more important and which would emphasise the importance of soft law and render it much more important even in the absence of liability. Over the last ten years, different aspects of company behaviour which determine good functioning and the success of a company have been observed. They are all a kind of soft law. Corporate social responsibility rules make a company attractive to the outside world, as well as HR policies on correct behaviour with employees. It can ruin the reputation of a company if the company systematically exploits people. The Nike case is a fine example. Environmental policy should also be mentioned: these days, companies are competing to go beyond the rules, just to make a good impression on their stakeholders and the public at large. Companies that highlight in their annual report their good practices in corporate governance will be much more attractive. A modern company which has a generous information policy is far more interesting for investors and other people the company is working with. I believe all these elements have become more important in practice, especially over the last ten years. This evolution - and not just the threat of liability - lies at the heart of the strength of the soft rules. The effectiveness and the success of the whole company, with all these different elements, are far more important.

Peter MONTAGNON

I just want to reflect on the meaning of "soft law" and something I noticed in the paper with which I fundamentally disagree, namely where it describes codes as self-regulation – that is not the point as far as I am concerned. The point about having a code in the comply-or-explain process is that actually a company has to explain to the people who own it and to whom the company is accountable. Actually, this is a completely different approach compared to "soft law" which is about a code of good behaviour that a company respects because it is in its own interest. I think we are looking in the wrong place if we try to attach liability consequences to failures to live up to codes. If companies do not live up to codes, the shareholders ought to hold the directors to account and the shareholders ought to act in a way that concentrates the minds of the board. Unfortunately, this has not worked as well as it should have because, for one reason or another, shareholders have not been willing to remove directors who infringe best practice or to vote against them at general meetings in a way which exposes them. This is the dimension we really need to look at. The ability to explain and to have somebody who actually owns the business considering that explanation and accepting or rejecting it does introduce very good flexibility. However, this system cannot work when the board members know that at the end of the day the shareholders will actually not take them on. The key is to make the shareholders really work at this.

Paul DAVIES

On that particular point there is an article by Roberta Romano from Yale on corporate governance codes, in which she makes the point that if we were really interested in just self-regulation, we might require companies to adopt corporate governance codes but we would not develop a model against which they were to be judged. She points out that corporate governance codes go one step further than self-regulation. These codes are saying to companies: in effect, this is what you ought to be doing, you do not have to do it, but you do need to explain why you are not doing it. You need to explain it to your shareholders and see if you can convince them, so there is a little bit more "steel fist" in the velvet glove of the corporate governance code as it appears at first sight.

There is one additional topic that Eddy Wymeersch raised, namely the issue of empty voting: are there any thoughts on the regulation of empty voting?

Peter MONTAGNON

Indeed, I think it must be clear that empty voting is an abuse which is unacceptable in a social sense. By "empty voting" we mean voting with shares which do not really represent an economic interest in order to further an economic interest in the sort of counter-party situation, for example. It is extremely difficult to imagine an appropriate procedure. Indeed, the use of derivatives can lead to a separation of control and economic ownership. Taking away the legal right to vote of people who have this right on the basis that they do not have "economic ownership" is very difficult. All that can – and should – be done is to ensure more transparency. It should be obvious when somebody is perpetrating this sort of abuse. I still have enough faith in the markets' human nature to believe that if people were seen to be doing this, the markets themselves would punish those people in one way or another. Therefore, I believe transparency is the answer, plus general public understanding that empty voting is not acceptable.

Eddy WYMEERSCH
I agree with Peter Montagnon. The only thing to do is early disclosure and to avoid having cases where all of a sudden somebody has a controlling stake that nobody knew about (e.g. the Continental and Volkswagen cases in Germany). In the old days, we had criminal provisions on voting with somebody else's shares, but these rules have been abolished. Disclosure probably is the only thing we can do – I do not see very much else we could do. That being said, if the rules are violated, the sanctions should be very strict. However, finding out and proving it remains extremely difficult. Nevertheless, once you have been able to prove it in a convincing way, a very strict response is essential.

Paul DAVIES
The example of somebody buying the controlling stake without disclosing this transaction, isn't that in some way the opposite end of the spectrum from empty voting?

Eddy WYMEERSCH
That is true. However, the question remains: when is something a case of empty voting? Empty voting is difficult to define. If one keeps in mind some general meetings where decisions were taken with a huge number of shareholders present and with a huge majority, I am a little bit distrustful.

José GARRIDO GARCIA
I believe a resolution which is passed in the general meeting with the majority at least partially based on empty voting to be challengeable since it is, from a strictly legal point of view, an abuse of right. Voting rights serve to protect the shareholders' interest. Therefore, if a person has the votes and has no interest and is yet determining the result of the vote, I think that would be an abuse of right.

Jaap WINTER
The following question demonstrates the difficulty of the ongoing debate. It is a question on a more conceptual level, rather than concerning the technique of empty voting. What is the fundamental difference between empty voting with derivative structures on the one hand and a record date of thirty days in

advance of the meeting on the other hand? A former shareholder may not be a shareholder at the time of the meeting any more, but it remains possible for him to vote since he was a shareholder thirty days before. This person has no economic or other interest any more but he still votes. I am not saying this means that no instrument allowing for some form of empty voting should be abolished or that you should not do anything about it, but it is not so easy to cover.

Paul DAVIES
Presumably, it is less easy for a shareholder to manipulate the record date system, which is set by the company, than to acquire votes by buying derivatives.

Jaap WINTER
You can very easily manipulate the record date system. This is actually possible for companies which are listed on different exchanges. Manipulating the record date system can be done with own shares. This happens in European companies that are listed in the United States. American companies typically work with a record date 45 to 60 days in advance of the meeting. Under Delaware law it is between that 45 to 60-day period. When a European company has a listing in the United States and it wants to allow its American investors to vote those shares, they vote on the basis of a record date between those brackets, 45 to 60 days in advance of the meeting. A smart US pension fund or mutual investor then exchanges its US shares for underlying European shares before the record date in Europe and votes again. It does not happen very frequently, but it happens. Companies are vulnerable to this. If hedge funds find this out, they will use this too. It has just to do with the record date. There is no manipulation with derivatives at all. They really hold shares at different moments and can vote twice. It may be an abuse, but what can be done?

Eddy WYMEERSCH
But in plenty of cases, if someone wants to have the 1% to start a minority procedure, he does not buy shares, he just borrows it and that is it. It costs 1% of the original price.

Didier MARTIN
I fully agree concerning the record date because there has been a lot of discussion concerning the borrowing of votes. In an American case, some hedge funds voted against a specific resolution by virtue of the record date, although they had sold their shares just before the general meeting. It was just in favour of a competitor in which they had a larger stake. So, for empty voting, it is true that it is easy to borrow shares but also to use a record date.

Peter MONTAGNON
Bringing the record dates as close as possible to the meeting is the answer. This is possible thanks to modern technology.

Didier MARTIN
Empty voting raises an important question which is obviously more difficult to answer: can we leave the vote to shareholders who are no longer shareholders when the general meeting of shareholders takes place? The legitimacy of such a vote is questionable.

Hilde LAGA
Indeed, this is a very delicate problem. Moreover, one can wonder whether multiple voting rights are not a kind of empty voting as well.

Eddy WYMEERSCH
The last question you raise is not just a fundamental one, but a philosophical one. What can we do if, in our corporate decision-making procedures, decisions are taken by people who have no interest involved? I think that is an anomaly. Of course, you can say it does not matter, since, provided decisions are taken, they should not be taken by the shareholders. Nevertheless, it creates an issue of aligning interests, which disciplines conduct towards a common goal.

Philippe PELLE
The situation becomes almost absurd. When we worked on the Shareholders' Rights Directive, we attached great importance to a record date system at the European level. Indeed, institutional investors wanted to be able to sell their stakes at any time. They were not exercising their voting rights because they wanted to have the freedom to sell their stake. That is why we introduced a period during which they can still express themselves, while having the flexibility to sell. Some people may take abusive advantage of this. At the end of the day, it is a "Catch-22" situation. I have not discovered any real solutions in the ongoing debate. I remember Peter Montagnon, and perhaps other investor institutions as well, advocating against legislation regarding stock lending, because there are already codes of proper governance within institutional investors to limit stock lending if the only purpose is to influence without having an economic interest in the company.

Stef OOSTVOGELS, Oostvogels Phister Feyten
I agree that in principle empty voting can be abusive. Nevertheless, to the extent that the people concerned have played according to the rules, one cannot simply bar their votes. Otherwise one should be consistent and say that a company which is run by a majority representing 10% of the shares also does not take decisions that are supported by a majority of the shareholders. Maybe

a solution could be that a company that is afraid of empty voting should be a little bit more proactive and try to set up some kind of proxy voting system to ensure that at least somebody other than just the empty voters is voting.

Floris PARREIN
It was remarkable that in a lot of answers and responses given by the audience, the importance of (group) psychology was underlined. Perhaps this demonstrates that the crisis cannot be completely reduced to a failure of the system itself. Equally important are the human beings working in the system. This leads to the conclusion that corporate governance touches upon the limits of the law. The question arises whether the legal system is able to solve problems of that kind in the area of human behaviour. Perhaps this is the most important problem of the whole issue.

Hilde LAGA
I might have given the impression that I did not believe in independent directors and in the effectiveness of boards, but of course that was provocative. I truly believe in the effectiveness of boards and in the fact that they can have added value. It is all a question of incentives. Sometimes I have the impression that everybody in a company has an incentive to do his job. The management, because they have huge stock option plans; the other employees, because they will be paid better. The only ones who are poorly paid, have no stock options, come six times a year and have another career outside the company –are the outside directors. The question is then: how can we encourage them to do their job properly? Can we encourage them by legal provisions? The answer is probably yes. Saying that is it a question of behaviour is far too easy an answer. If everyone behaves well, we do not need legislation and procedures. We have to think about incentives. Why not pay them with stock options? I know it is very provocative. Why not pay them in shares instead of in stock options? Is this such a bad idea? Is this so much against the orthodox principles of corporate governance?

Eddy WYMEERSCH
I think I have four conclusions – or messages to the European Commission. The first one is: no hard law. I think we do not need hard law in terms of corporate governance. I think there is very wide agreement on that. Secondly, we have to strengthen the existing rules in soft law and make the system work better. Thirdly, we have to make the rules better enforceable, which can be achieved with soft law mechanisms. There is no incompatibility between enforcement and soft law, for instance through disclosure and internal reporting. And the last message for the EU, although it has not been discussed today, is the importance of some high level principles for national corporate governance codes, which are not so difficult to find. The national corporate governance codes can then be

valued against these principles. For instance, "Boards should be appointed by the general meeting", which is not always the case today.

Paul DAVIES

Like all good discussions, I don't think one can say we came to very firm conclusions. We devoted our time to three main issues. One was the composition of boards, in particular the role of non-executive directors; the second was the role of soft law; and the third was empty voting – a shareholder issue rather than a board issue.

Let me begin with empty voting. My impression was that in the group we were struggling quite hard to work out how to define empty voting. Obviously the general meaning is voting of shares by people who have no economic interest in the shares. There was general agreement that empty voting was a "bad" thing, but no clear proposals emerged as to how it should be regulated. There was a clear awareness amongst participants that regulation certainly has to deal with other rules or institutions for which there is a prima facie good reason, such as setting a record date for voting at general meetings.

The other two matters, board structure and hard and soft law, corporate governance code, etc. have been going on now for a couple of decades. Overall, we were a bit more sceptical about how well these institutions were working than we would have been at a conference, say, eighteen months or two years ago. The recent events have put those institutions – independent directors and soft law – under some sort of stress. However, there was no strong argument in my view for moving in any significant way from soft law to hard law – more a tendency to feel we should be strengthening soft law. What we did concentrate on was the underlying conditions under which independent non-executive directors and soft law might operate more effectively. I was much impressed by the point that there is an underlying assumption with independent non-executive directors and soft law, namely that the shareholders (either the dispersed shareholders in a British context or the non-controlling shareholders in a Continental context) should have a good relationship with the independent directors if the institution is going to work well. That relationship with the shareholders, I think, is under-researched and under-theorised. In addition, this may be changing as shareholder structures change. We thought one could not assume that the way these institutions were operated in the past would continue to be the way in which they would operate in the future if shareholding structures changed as well.

One Share One Vote: Fairness, Efficiency and EU Harmonisation Revisited

Koen Geens[1] *and Carl Clottens*[2]
Jan Ronse Institute – K.U.Leuven

Abstract

One of the most controversial aspects of the Company Law Action Plan of 2003 was the European Commission's ambition to establish real shareholder democracy and to impose the principle of proportionality between capital and control – One Share One Vote (1S1V) – for listed companies in the EU. This paper considers the arguments that have been raised in the animated debate between advocates and critics and analyses whether such a rule – either a general and permanent 1S1V or a breakthrough rule (BTR) limited to takeover situations – could be justified from the viewpoint of efficiency and/or fairness. Starting from the premise that the law can have an impact on ownership structure, this paper argues that the EU legislator, by imposing a mandatory bid rule, has expressed a preference for dispersed ownership of listed companies. In the long run, the continental EU will therefore gradually converge towards the UK model. The mandatory bid rule reduces the odds that a BTR or a general 1S1V rule would result in more concentrated ownership. A consistently formulated BTR has an added value in speeding up this process, because it exposes existing block-holders to the market for corporate control. Whereas contestability of control would solve most of the problems which 1S1V remedies, the merits of 1S1V are not limited to takeovers and therefore a general 1S1V rule should at least be reconsidered. A Fifth or Ninth Directive, while perhaps not feasible politically, would be useful to resolve closely related issues (e.g. board rules, pyramids) and could constitute a less intrusive means of achieving more uniform capital and voting structures while allowing for some flexibility. Finally, if the EU legislator remains unwilling or unable to advance further on the path towards 1S1V, the case law of the European Court of Justice on the free movement of capital and the freedom of establishment could prove to be a useful substitute for secondary EU legislation.

---

[1] Professor and Director of the Jan Ronse Institute for Company Law, K.U.Leuven, attorney Brussels Bar (Eubelius).

[2] Ph.D. candidate K.U.Leuven; attorney Brussels Bar (Eubelius).

Table of contents

1. Introduction

1. *The Company Law Action Plan 2003.* The European Commission, in its Company Law Action Plan of 2003, considered that there was a strong case for promoting the principle of proportionality between capital and control – One Share One Vote ("1S1V") – as a means of achieving, in the medium to long term, real shareholder democracy in the EU[3]. This proposal was part of a broader set of corporate governance measures intended to strengthen shareholders' rights.

2. *The true meaning of "shareholder democracy" is efficiency.* Shareholder democracy is in itself a rather vague notion which may sound appealing but only creates confusion[4]. Indeed, it is capital that reigns in a stock corporation, not people; a company is therefore more akin to a plutocracy[5]. If the EU is to

---

[3] Communication from the Commission to the Council and the European Parliament – Modernising Company Law and Enhancing Corporate Governance in the European Union – A Plan to Move Forward, COM (2003) 284 final, Brussels, 21 May 2003, no. 3.1.2.

[4] H. MANNE, "The 'Corporate Democracy' Oxymoron", Wall Street Journal, 2 January 2007.

[5] Historically, 1S1V has not always been the rule. See e.g. C. DUNLAVY, "Corporate Governance in Late 19th-Century Europe and the U.S.: The Case of Shareholder Voting Rights", in K.J. Hopt,

take any legislative action, it should most probably do so on efficiency grounds and not merely on the basis of fairness considerations. But this is not to say that proportionality between capital and control is only about fairness[6]. The proportionality principle is based on the intuitive notion that shareholders are best placed to make certain discretionary decisions regarding the running of a company since they are residual claimants and thus bear the ultimate economic risk[7]. A logical consequence is thus proportionality of voting rights to equity stake. Although for the purpose of decision-making on a day-by-day basis it may be efficient to delegate powers to the board of directors (subject to shareholder oversight), it makes sense to let shareholders at least decide on key matters such as the outcome of a takeover bid (also because directors themselves may be conflicted).

3. ***The story so far: unsuccessful attempts at harmonisation.*** Already in the early 1990s, the European Commission had identified the absence of proportionality as an obstacle to takeovers and tried to promote 1S1V in the Draft Fifth Directive, which was never adopted[8]. Article 33, paragraph 1 of the last draft proposal[9] – which was eventually withdrawn[10] – stated that "the shareholders' right to vote shall be proportionate to the fraction of the subscribed capital which the shares represent"; paragraph 2 allowed for a limited exception for non-voting shares; paragraph 3 provided for suspension of voting rights attached to shares which have not been paid-up after calls have been made by the company[11].

H. Kanda, M. Roe, E. Wymeersch and S. Prigge (eds.), *Comparative Corporate Governance: The State of the Art and Emerging Research*, Oxford, Clarendon Press, 1998, 5-39 (the common law standard of "one vote per person" was gradually abandoned for companies in the late 19th century).

6 It is clear that 1S1V expresses a notion of equality (albeit relative to equity contribution) and, in a certain way, acts as a complement to the majority rule, which in turn derogates from the unanimity requirement under general contract law: K. GEENS and M. WYCKAERT, "Les espaces de liberté contractuelle dans le droit des sociétés à responsabilité limitée: entre rapprochement et palliation", in Commission Royale Droit et Vie des Affaires (ed.), *Les espaces de liberté en droit des affaires*, Brussels, Bruylant, 2007, 139-189.

7 F. EASTERBROOK and D. FISCHEL, *The Economic Structure of Corporate Law*, Cambridge, Harvard University Press, 1991, 63 et seq.

8 Bangemann Report, 14 May 1990. This report identified the lack of proportionality between the amount of capital investment and voting rights as one of the major obstacles for takeover bids and led to a second amendment to the proposal for a Fifth Directive which introduced a limit for shares without voting rights (i.e. they may not be issued for an amount exceeding 50% of subscribed capital) and a prohibition on voting caps, thus strengthening proportionality. The latter in particular met with criticism: see B. BASTUCK and C. KOENIG, "The Concept of 'One Share – One Vote' in EC Company Law", *Butterworths Journal of International Banking and Financial Law* 1991, 170-174; P. LE CANNU, "Limitations du droit de vote et contrôle des sociétés anonymes (réflexions sur la proposition modifiée de cinquième directive en droit des sociétés)", *Bull. Joly* 1991, 263.

9 Proposal for a Fifth Council Directive based on Article 54 of the EEC Treaty concerning the structure of public limited companies and the powers and obligations of their organs, COM (91) 372 final, 20 November 1991, OJ 1991, C 321, p. 9.

10 OJ 2004, C 5, p. 20.

11 Although it eventually failed to be adopted, the draft Fifth Company Law Directive directly inspired the Belgian legislator in 1991 to introduce non-voting preference shares and to make mandatory voting caps optional: J. WOUTERS, "European Company Law: Quo Vadis?", *CMLR* 2000, 261-262.

In 2002, after the compromise proposal for a Takeover Directive had been voted down by the European Parliament, the Winter Group, asked for technical advice on how to create a level playing field for takeovers within the EU, came up with the novel concept of breakthrough, which involves a limited application of 1S1V in the context of a takeover bid (more specifically in the vote on the authorisation of defensive measures and at the first general meeting after completion of the bid)[12]. Although the Takeover Directive was finally adopted in 2004, it has failed as far as the breakthrough rule (and thus proportionality) is concerned. In order to reach a political compromise, the original proposal was watered down in the final text of the Directive and, in addition, it was made merely optional for Member States or companies.

Undoubtedly influenced by past experience of strong opposition by Member States, 1S1V did not figure in the Final Report of the Winter Group on Company Law[13], which formed the basis for the Action Plan of 2003. Nevertheless, the Action Plan proposed to give further effect to the principle first put forward by the Winter Group in its prior Report on Takeover Bids and to extend its application even beyond takeover situations. Before considering the introduction of a general 1S1V rule, the European Commission proposed to call for a study on the possible consequences of such an approach aimed at achieving full shareholder democracy, at least for listed companies.

A fact-finding study was carried out in 2007[14], after such an approach had been endorsed in the 2006 consultation on Future Priorities for the Action Plan[15]. This study was then followed by an opinion from the European Corporate Governance Forum[16] and an impact assessment by the European Commission[17]. After having taken into account the rather inconclusive results of the study and the impact assessment, the EU Commissioner for the Internal Market, Charlie McCreevy, decided to step back from his push for 1S1V[18]. For the time being, no further action is to be expected. But the debate on 1S1V is bound to continue. Indeed, the subject will have to be tackled again in 2011 at the latest, when the Takeover Directive is scheduled for revision[19]. Moreover,

---

[12] Report of the High Level Group of Company Law Experts on Issues Related to Takeover Bids, Brussels, 10 January 2002.

[13] Final Report of the High Level Group of Company Law Experts on a Modern Regulatory Framework for Company Law in Europe, Brussels, 4 November 2002.

[14] ISS Europe, ECGI, Shearman & Sterling LLP, Report on the Proportionality Principle in the European Union, 18 May 2007; Shearman & Sterling LLP, Proportionality between Ownership and Control in EU Listed Companies: Comparative Legal Study, 18 May 2007.

[15] DG Internal Market and Services, Summary report on the consultation and hearing on future priorities for the Action Plan on the Modernisation of Company Law and Corporate Governance, p. 8.

[16] Paper of the European Corporate Governance Forum Working Group on Proportionality, June 2007; European Corporate Governance Forum Statement on Proportionality, August 2007.

[17] Impact Assessment on the Proportionality between Capital and Control in Listed Companies, SEC (2007) 1705, Brussels, 12 December 2007.

[18] Speech by Commissioner McCreevy at the EP Legal Affairs Committee, Brussels, 3 October 2007 (SPEECH/07/592); A. Bounds, "EU scraps plan for 'one share one vote' reform", Financial Times, 4 October 2007.

[19] Article 20 of the Takeover Directive.

the Commission staff report on the implementation of the Takeover Directive has indicated that this review may start even sooner[20]. This could possibly be as soon as the end of 2009, after the new Commission has taken office.

4. ***Purpose of the present paper.*** The time has come, therefore, to reassess the 1S1V debate. This paper will discuss the merits of a breakthrough rule ("BTR") in takeover situations and the shortcomings of Article 11 of the Takeover Directive in its present state. However, the scope of this paper will not be limited to takeovers. Since the Action Plan itself adopted a broader approach, we will also reflect on possible grounds for a general and permanent 1S1V rule which would apply outside takeover situations as well.

5. ***Overview.*** The remainder of this paper is structured as follows: section 2 provides a basic overview of ownership and control structures and corporate governance models; section 3 describes how the mandatory bid rule affects these ownership and control structures; section 4 presents a summary of the theoretical and empirical evidence on 1S1V; section 5 describes the effects of 1S1V on ownership and control structures (in connection with the mandatory bid rule); sections 6 and 7 discuss the BTR, its current limits and its added value in connection with the mandatory bid rule; section 8 then moves on to discuss the merits of a general 1S1V rule and explores some alternative rationales for 1S1V; section 9 considers negative harmonisation by the case law of the European Court of Justice as an alternative – and perhaps more realistic – way of achieving 1S1V; section 10 concludes.

2. Models of Corporate Ownership and Control

6. ***The corporate ownership and control continuum.*** As with company law and corporate governance in general, 1S1V cannot be discussed properly without having regard to the ownership and control structures of companies, since the latter determine which agency problems may occur, which the law in turn has to remedy. The different ownership and control structures that may occur can be situated on a continuum with, at one end, a company with a single proprietor and, at the opposite extreme, a widely held company with many small shareholders none of whom holds a large block of shares. For listed companies, of course, the position at the extreme left of the continuum corresponds to the situation where a person or entity holds a large block of shares conferring an absolute or *de facto* majority of the votes, but where there are also minority shareholders. These two extremes correspond to two different models of corporate governance.

[20] Report on the implementation of the Directive on Takeover Bids, SEC (2007) 268, 21 February 2007, p. 10-11.

7. *Agency problems in dispersed and concentrated ownership structures.* In a widely held company with dispersed shareholders none of whom has the incentive to closely monitor the board of directors, management will tend *de facto* to control the company. Since management tends to be too autonomous in the absence of monitoring, this creates possible scope for abuse of shareholders by the managers (i.e. the "agency problem" between management and the shareholders as a class)[21]. Already in 1932, this situation was characterised by Berle & Means in terms of a "separation of ownership and control"[22] and today it is still typical of most US and UK corporations.

In the continental EU and in the rest of the world, share ownership has been historically – and still is – conspicuously more concentrated[23]. This creates a totally different situation. A majority block-holder will both have the incentives (as a result of his investment) and the power (as a result of his voting rights) to monitor management closely and, if he does so, this will benefit all shareholders. However, at the same time this large block-holder, whilst he is in control, may be tempted to act for his own private benefit rather than for the benefit of all shareholders. Here the "agency problem" runs between controlling and minority shareholders[24]. Management, in contrast, will tend to have too little autonomy in running the company because the controlling block-holder will *de facto* dominate the board of directors through his power to appoint and remove directors.

8. *Principal devices limiting agency costs.* How this problem of exploitation of (minority) shareholders is resolved depends precisely on the ownership structure. When ownership is widely dispersed, the market for corporate control is supposed to discipline management[25]. A bidder can emerge who buys a block of shares and votes and then ousts the incumbent management. Alternatively, a proxy fight can be mounted, in which case only voting rights are assembled. Other devices for disciplining management include performance-based compensation and all sorts of corporate governance measures designed to reduce the autonomy of management (independent directors, board committees, increased transparency, etc.).

When ownership is concentrated, the market for corporate control will be inoperative; but at least minority shareholders have the reassurance that the

---

[21] M. JENSEN and W. MECKLING, "Theory of the Firm: Managerial Behavior, Agency Costs and Ownership Structure", *Journal of Financial Economics* 1976, 305-360.

[22] A. BERLE and G. MEANS, *The Modern Corporation and Private Property*, New York, MacMillan, 1933, 2-3.

[23] See e.g. M. FACCIO and L. LANG, "The separation of Ownership and Control: An Analysis of Ultimate Ownership in Western European Companies", Working Paper (2000).

[24] See e.g. R. KRAAKMAN et al., *The Anatomy of Corporate Law. A Comparative and Functional Approach*, Oxford, Oxford University Press, 2004, 22.

[25] H. MANNE, "Mergers and the Market for Corporate Control", *Journal of Political Economy* 1965, 110-120.

controlling shareholder has himself invested a large amount of money, so that he will have incentives not to extract too many private benefits deriving from his control. Indeed, to the extent that these private benefits reduce the company profits, this would be to his own detriment.

9. ***Control-enhancing mechanisms.*** The spectrum outlined above is still incomplete. A controlling shareholder who is financially constrained will tend to employ certain devices which allow him to leverage his voting power above the level of his financial investment, in order to retain control with less equity invested. This allows the company to access the capital market in order to finance its growth, without the controlling shareholder having to relinquish control. Instead, he can retain control with a lower ownership stake and thus at lower cost of under-diversification. For other shareholders as well, liquidity may increase when more shares can be floated. These control-enhancing mechanisms (or CEMs as they are commonly referred to) result in a separation of voting rights from cash-flow rights. This situation corresponds to the centre of the aforementioned continuum where, despite ownership of shares being dispersed, a controlling shareholder is still present. A wide variety of CEMs exist, ranging from legal structures provided for by law or by the articles of association (e.g. dual class shares) to factual or contractual structures (e.g. pyramids, cross-shareholdings, shareholder agreements). In essence, the debate on 1S1V is about eliminating these CEMs in order to establish strict proportionality between voting rights and cash-flow rights.

At first sight, this "middle" situation could be seen as combining the best of both worlds (growth, liquidity and shareholder monitoring), but upon closer inspection the opposite is true. Under 1S1V (i.e. when voting rights are strictly tied to cash-flow rights), the two models of management discipline are mutually exclusive: the alignment of the controlling shareholder's interests with those of the minority shareholders through the former's high equity exposure eliminates the market for corporate control. The trouble with CEMs, however, is that they may give rise to a controlling minority situation, in which both models are excluded[26]. A controlling shareholder holding a majority of voting rights with less than a majority of cash-flow rights is shielded from hostile takeovers and, at the same time, his reduced equity stake makes it more profitable for him to extract private benefits at the expense of other shareholders since he can externalise more of the associated costs. This explains the potential danger of deviations from 1S1V (cf. *infra*, section 4.1.1).

[26] L. BEBCHUK, R. KRAAKMAN and G. TRIANTIS, "Stock Pyramids, Cross-Ownership, and Dual Class Equity – The Mechanisms and Agency Costs of Separating Control from Cash-Flow Rights", in R. Morck (ed.), *Concentrated Corporate Ownership*, Chicago, University of Chicago Press, 2000, 295-315.

10. *What determines ownership structure?* It is not certain what determines ownership structure. Some scholars argue that law matters[27], others have advanced alternative political, socio-economic or even cultural explanations[28]. Within the first theory there is further disagreement as to *how* law matters, i.e. which particular legal rules influence the (choice of) ownership structure (e.g. rules on investor protection[29] or distribution of powers[30]).

Nor is it obvious which ownership structure and corresponding corporate governance model is best. So far, no conclusive evidence has been found that one model is superior to the other and thus the debate remains unsettled. Perhaps there is no clear-cut answer to the question of whether the market or a large shareholder is better suited to monitoring management, i.e. it may depend on the circumstances (e.g. country, industry or company-specific factors). What is clear, though, is that both models have their drawbacks[31].

11. *The mandatory bid rule.* Nonetheless, EU policy – and in particular the Takeover Directive – is undeniably influenced by the UK model. In the UK, the mandatory bid rule favours dispersed ownership by discouraging the emergence of a controlling shareholder, which in turn induces management disciplining and minority protection through (the threat of) hostile takeovers. Although doubts can be cast on the actual disciplinary effect of the market for corporate control[32], at least the Takeover Directive appears to be convinced of its potential benefits[33] since it contains a mandatory bid rule (Article 5) and attempts to stimulate hostile takeovers through the board passivity/neutrality rule and the BTR (Articles 9 and 11, which are optional pursuant to Article 12). Although other factors undoubtedly contribute(d) to the dispersed ownership structure

[27] See in particular the series of papers by R. LA PORTA et al., "Law and Finance", *Journal of Political Economy* 1998, 1113 (legal origin, in part through a difference in the degree of investor protection, influences ownership structure). Although controversial, this approach has significantly influenced later research. See also J. COFFEE, Jr., "The Rise of Dispersed Ownership: The Role of Law in the Separation of Ownership and Control", *Yale Law Journal* 2001, 1 et seq.

[28] M. ROE, *Political Determinants of Corporate Governance*, New York, Oxford University Press, 2003; A. LICHT et al., "Culture, Law and Corporate Governance", *International Review of Law and Economics* 2005, 229 et seq.

[29] R. LA PORTA et al., "Investor Protection and Corporate Governance", *Journal of Financial Economics* 2000, 3-27; R. GILSON, "Controlling Shareholders and Corporate Governance: Complicating the Comparative Taxonomy", *Harvard Law Review* 2006, 1641-1679.

[30] L. BEBCHUK, "A Rent-Protection Theory of Corporate Ownership and Control", NBER Working Paper No. 7203, (1999); S. COOLS, "The Real Difference in Corporate Law between the United States and Continental Europe: Distribution of Powers", *Delaware Journal of Corporate Law* 2005, 697-766; A. PACCES, *Featuring Control Power: Corporate Law and Economics Revisited*, Ph.D. thesis, Erasmus Universiteit Rotterdam, 2008.

[31] This explains the popularity on both sides of the Atlantic of corporate governance measures, which can mitigate both situations. Quite interestingly, the remedies advanced in this respect are often very similar (e.g. independent directors, board committees, etc.).

[32] See e.g. C. BLANAID, "Articles 9 and 11 of the Takeover Directive (2004/25) and the Market for Corporate Control", *Journal of Business Law* 2006, 356-362.

[33] See also the Winter Report on Takeover Bids, no. 1.

in the UK[34], our analysis is based on the premise that at least the mandatory bid seems to matter[35].

We will start with a summary of the existing mandatory bid rule before analysing the merits of 1S1V and/or the BTR, which at present can hardly be considered rules of European law[36].

3. The Mandatory Bid Rule

12. *The mandatory bid.* Article 5 of the Takeover Directive obliges a shareholder who, alone or in concert with others, has acquired more than a given percentage (generally 30 or 33.3%) of the shares with voting rights of a listed company (conferring control over the company) to make a bid for all the remaining shares with voting rights at the highest price paid for the same shares in the last 6 to 12 months[37]. As a result, the minority shareholders get the opportunity to exit at a fair price. To guarantee that the shareholders will get a fair price for their shares, the threshold triggering a mandatory bid is set sufficiently low that a counterbid remains possible. This way, the fair price presumption provided for by law can still be rebutted by the market when a counterbid is actually launched.

13. *The goal of the mandatory bid rule: minority protection.* The mandatory bid rule ensures minority protection as well as (more or less) efficient allocation of control. The full bid requirement causes the bidder to internalise all the external effects that result from the extraction of private benefits. This not only improves the competitive position of a value-enhancing bidder but even places all bidders on an equal footing[38]. On the other hand, as the controlling shareholder will not sell unless he is paid a control premium, the mandatory bid rule forces a bidder to pay that premium on all shares. The resulting redistribution of wealth

---

[34] Regulatory disfavour of controlling shareholders is also exemplified by the UK Listing Rules ("Yellow Book") governing substantial shareholders (defined in Appendix 1 of the Listing Rules as shareholders accounting for more than 10% of the voting rights): e.g. § 11 of the Listing Rules (independent shareholder approval of all significant related-party transactions). See also § A.3.1 of the Combined Code on Corporate Governance (majority of board members must be independent from significant shareholders).

[35] Admittedly, ownership was already dispersed in the UK before the mandatory bid rule was introduced. Still, we believe that the deterrence effect of the mandatory bid should not be underestimated. This view seems to be confirmed by the fact that nowadays ownership in the UK is even more dispersed than in the US, where a mandatory bid rule generally does not exist (with a few exceptions). See e.g. LA PORTA et al., "Corporate Ownership Around the World", *Journal of Finance* 1999, 471-517.

[36] G. FERRARINI, "One Share – One Vote: A European Rule?", *ECFR* 2006, 165-166 (arguing that, at present, 1S1V is more an aspirational principle of EU law than an effective one).

[37] Article 5 of the Takeover Directive.

[38] P. MÜLBERT, "Make It or Break It: The Break-Through Rule as a Break-Through for the European Takeover Directive?", in G. Ferrarini, K.J. Hopt, J. Winter and E. Wymeersch (eds.), *Reforming Takeover and Company Law in Europe*, Oxford, Oxford University Press, 2004, p. 732.

from bidder to minority shareholders makes a control transfer more expensive, thereby preventing all value-reducing transactions but also deterring some value-enhancing bidders[39]. As a result, allocation of control may not be entirely optimal (in the sense that a controlling block may not always be owned by the most efficient user), but at least the minority shareholders are well protected by the rule. As a final observation it should be pointed out, though, that the beneficial effect of the mandatory bid rule holds true only if the mandatory bid extends to all classes of shares, including non-voting shares[40], and if there is no room for price discrimination between different classes[41].

14. *A less obvious (and unintended?) effect of the mandatory bid rule: ownership dispersion.* The mandatory bid rule indirectly brings about dispersed ownership. The application of the rule itself will of course lead to more ownership concentration (*ex post* effect), but at the same time the existence of the rule makes it unattractive to obtain a controlling stake (*ex ante* effect). In the long run[42], the mandatory bid rule will therefore lead to a situation where only companies with dispersed ownership are listed in the EU and where controlled companies are privately held (like in the UK).

We will come back to the mandatory bid rule later. It is important to keep these effects of the mandatory bid in mind when we discuss (the added value of) 1S1V and/or the BTR. Now, we will turn to 1S1V and examine how it fits into this framework.

---

[39] E. BERGLÖF and M. BURKART, "European Takeover Regulation", *Economic Policy* 2003, p. 196.

[40] This is already the case in the UK. However, according to some interpretations of the Takeover Directive, the mandatory bid is to be addressed only to the holders of the class of shares used to acquire control. See P. MÜLBERT, "Make It or Break It: The Break-Through Rule as a Break-Through for the European Takeover Directive?", in G. Ferrarini, K.J. Hopt, J. Winter and E. Wymeersch (eds.), *Reforming Takeover and Company Law in Europe*, Oxford, Oxford University Press, 2004, 733. In Belgium, the mandatory bid does not extend to non-voting shares. At the same time, non-voting shares are disregarded when calculating the 30% threshold, therefore causing it to be crossed sooner by holders of voting shares.

[41] According to Article 5.4 of the Takeover Directive, the fair price is to be calculated based on the highest price paid for the "same securities". See J. RICKFORD, "Invisible Hand or Dead Hand? – Reflections on the EU One Share One Vote", in G. Mather (ed.), *One Share One Vote? – Tomorrow's Companies: One Universal Model or Tailored Equity Structures*, London, European Policy Forum, 2006, 82.

[42] In the short run, the opposite may be true: a Belgian study found that the transition period for the new mandatory bid rule actually led to an increase of ownership concentration on Euronext Brussels because existing block-holders raised their stake above the 30% threshold in anticipation of the new rule: "Referentieaandeelhouder dominanter in Brussel", De Tijd, 29 October 2008.

4. The Effects of 1S1V on Control Allocation and Operational Governance

4.1. Theoretical Approach

15. ***Overview.*** From a theoretical perspective, there is a double efficiency rationale for 1S1V: CEMs are bad because they lead to inefficient allocation of control and to inefficient operational decisions, both of which are partially caused by entrenchment[43].

4.1.1. The impact of deviations from 1S1V on operational decisions (outside a takeover situation)

16. ***The problem of "rent" extraction.*** CEMs provide controlling shareholders with more incentives to extract private benefits of control (PBs)[44]. There are many types of PBs and many ways to extract them, ranging from the inefficient use of assets (empire building) to more or less sophisticated forms of theft (tunnelling). Although not all PBs are necessarily bad, the assumption is that at least some firm value is destroyed by the extraction of PBs. When a shareholder uses a CEM to control the company, he owns a disproportionately small equity stake and consequently he does not bear a proportional cost in the event of extraction of PBs. In addition, since company profits are distributed in accordance with equity stake and not voting power, the controlling shareholder will have even stronger incentives to extract PBs rather than to distribute profits. Under a 1S1V rule, by contrast, the controlling shareholder would be required to own a large equity stake and as a result he would bear a larger part of the costs from the extraction of PBs. He would be less interested in extracting PBs and more interested in dividends and other profit distributions. The theory predicts that the larger the gap between voting rights and cash-flow rights, the greater the chance that inefficient decisions will be made as to project choice (i.e. incentives are distorted in favour of projects with lower value but higher PBs), company size (i.e. incentives are distorted against distribution of free cash flows) and sale of control (i.e. incentives are distorted in favour of control transactions which lead to lower firm value but higher PBs)[45]. The potential agency costs of CEMs rise at a sharply increasing rate as the gap grows. These

---

[43] For an overview of theoretical literature, see: M. BURKART and S. LEE, "The One Share One Vote Debate: A Theoretical Perspective", ECGI Finance Working Paper No. 176 (2007).

[44] PBs can be defined as "any benefits that a controlling shareholder derives from his control of a company that are not shared proportionally with other shareholders". See J. COATES, "Ownership, Takeovers and EU Law: How Contestable Should EU Corporations Be?", in G. Ferrarini, K.J. Hopt, J. Winter and E. Wymeersch (eds.), *Reforming Takeover and Company Law in Europe*, Oxford, Oxford University Press, 2004, 690.

[45] L. BEBCHUK, R. KRAAKMAN and G. TRIANTIS, "Stock Pyramids, Cross-Ownership, and Dual Class Equity – The Mechanisms and Agency Costs of Separating Control from Cash-Flow Rights", in R. Morck (ed.), *Concentrated Corporate Ownership*, Chicago, University of Chicago Press, 2000, 295-315.

agency costs are thus not simply a matter of low investor protection: it cannot fully explain the problem, although can perhaps mitigate it. This seems to be confirmed by empirical research[46].

17. ***The problem of "entrenchment".*** This agency problem may be aggravated by the fact that control is not contestable. Indeed, 1S1V also has an indirect impact on operational decisions to the extent that it makes control contestable. In that case, the mere threat of a hostile takeover ensures that the incumbent block-holder will strive to maximise shareholder value.

4.1.2. The impact of deviations from 1S1V on control transfers (both on the outcome of public takeover bids and on private sales of control)

18. ***Public takeover bids for firms with dispersed ownership.*** The impact of dual class shares on the outcome of public takeover bids for firms with dispersed shareholders was first analysed by US scholars in the 1980s. This strand of research shows that CEMs can in some cases be beneficial, to the extent that they can help a value-enhancing bidder to overcome the "free rider" condition by providing scope for extraction of PBs[47]. However, on the other hand, PBs can also allow value-decreasing takeovers to succeed as a result of the "pressure to tender" problem (which is the reverse of the free rider problem). Moreover, there are several other ways to overcome the collective action problem among dispersed shareholders (e.g. building a toehold before making the bid, organising a shareholder vote on the bid[48]). Most notably, the free rider condition ceases to exist in the event of a bidding contest. In that scenario, CEMs can lead to inefficient outcomes where a value-decreasing bidder with higher PBs than the incumbent can triumph and, conversely, where a value-enhancing bidder with lower PBs than its rival can fail to obtain control[49]. Then again, a full bid requirement neutralises this effect because it forces a successful bidder to internalise more of the consequences of his operational decisions once in control[50].

---

[46] R. MASULIS, C. WANG and F. XIE, "Agency Problems at Dual-Class Companies", ECGI Finance Working Paper No. 209, (2008); M. HOLMEN and P. HÖGFELDT, "Pyramidal Discounts: Tunnelling or Agency Costs?", ECGI Finance Working Paper No. 73 (2005).

[47] S. GROSSMAN and O. HART, "Takeover Bids, the Free-Rider Problem and the Theory of the Corporation", *Bell Journal of Economics* 1980, 42-64. The "free rider" or collective action problem in takeovers is due to a lack of coordination among dispersed shareholders. Due to this situation, shareholders may demand a higher price for their shares than they are actually prepared to sell at, in the hope of improving their own individual position, and socially inefficient allocation of control is likely to ensue.

[48] L. BEBCHUK, "Toward Undistorted Choice and Equal Treatment in Corporate Takeovers", *Harvard Law Review* 1985, 1695-1808.

[49] S. GROSSMAN and O. HART, "One-Share/One-Vote and the Market for Corporate Control", *Journal of Financial Economics* 1988, 175 et seq.; M. HARRIS and A. RAVIV, "Corporate Governance: Voting Rights and Majority Rules", *Journal of Financial Economics* 1988, 203 et seq.

[50] Unlike in the US, partial bids are not allowed in Belgium. For the impact of the mandatory bid: cf. *infra*, section 7.

19. *Private sales of control.* More relevant for the continental EU, however, are private sales of control. Since a controlling shareholder can easily thwart a takeover bid by not tendering his control block, a negotiated sale by an incumbent controlling shareholder is in fact the only option. Private transfers of control tend to be suboptimal because the incumbent shareholder does not take into account the position of minority shareholders when tendering, thus *de facto* reducing them to non-voting shareholders[51]. Although 1S1V does not achieve an optimal outcome for private transfers of control (in the sense that the bidder with the highest sum of share value and PBs always obtains control), the result under 1S1V is still clearly better than under CEMs[52]. Due to CEMs, incentives are even more distorted in favour of control transactions which lead to lower firm value but higher PBs (cf. *supra*, section 4.1.1).

In conclusion, although 1S1V may not always be optimal under dispersed ownership, at least it does not do any harm; and although 1S1V is only a second-best solution for private control transfers, socially (as opposed to privately) it is in any case better than the use of CEMs.

4.2. Empirical Evidence

20. *Inconclusive evidence on the impact of CEMs.* The empirical evidence about the impact of CEMs on firm value and/or performance is less conclusive. This is partially due to a number of methodological problems which are fairly difficult to remedy[53]. However, some of the regression analyses that have been carried out thus far indicate that deviations from 1S1V are associated with a negative impact on firm value (as measured by Tobin's Q or market-to-book value)[54]. This seems to confirm the above hypothesis that disproportional structures are inefficient. However, not all results of these early studies are mutually consistent and they must be interpreted with caution (due to difficulties in defining and measuring disproportionality, possibility of omitted variables, issues of reverse causality, etc.).

Even if all these methodological problems were resolved, there would still remain doubts about the effects of CEMs on welfare and about the hypothesis of inefficient controlling shareholders. Indeed, Tobin's Q is only a measure of the value of outside equity and does not take into account the value of control. PBs have to be added up in order to calculate total firm value and to measure

---

51 M. KAHAN, "Sales of Corporate Control", *Journal of Law, Economics, and Organization* 1993, 368-379; L. BEBCHUK, "Efficient and Inefficient Sales of Corporate Control", *Quarterly Journal of Economics* 1994, 957-994.

52 Cf. *infra*, section 7, for a comparison with impact of mandatory bid.

53 For an overview, see: R. ADAMS and D. FERREIRA, "One Share, One Vote: The Empirical Evidence", ECGI Finance Working Paper No. 177/2007, (2007).

54 For the EU, see e.g. M. BENNEDSEN and K. MEISNER NIELSEN, "The Principle of Proportional Ownership, Investor Protection and Firm Value in Western Europe", ECGI Finance Working Paper No. 134, (2006). However, this study found no impact of disproportional ownership structures on operating performance.

the impact of CEMs. The value of PBs is much more difficult to measure. Usually the control premium for block trades or the price difference between share classes with disproportionate voting rights is presumed to provide some measure, but here too caution is warranted since price differences between separate share classes may also reflect other inequalities (different cash-flow rights, liquidity). Moreover, the pyramidal discount is notoriously enigmatic[55]. As a result, it is not inconceivable that the value of PBs for the controlling shareholder would (more than) offset the loss of firm value (as measured by Tobin's Q) to outside investors. In this situation, CEMs would increase total welfare[56]. Still, this situation would not seem desirable from the viewpoint of investors[57]. The mere fact that CEMs lead to a lower Tobin's Q could thus warrant legislative intervention.

21. ***Evidence on the negative impact of entrenchment.*** To be sure, there is some US evidence that entrenchment leads to lower firm value[58]. The fact that control is not contestable leads to a discount in the stock price, reflecting the fact that investors cannot benefit from a hostile takeover. The market anticipates that the company will not be run efficiently or by the most efficient party as it is shielded from the discipline of hostile takeovers. In the US, entrenchment is achieved mainly by a combination of staggered boards and poison pills. In the EU, by contrast, entrenchment follows mainly from concentration of voting rights and is facilitated by CEMs.

It is fair to conclude that the empirical evidence concerning the effects of CEMs is indecisive and provides results in support of either view.

---

[55] B. COLMANT et al., *La décote boursière des holdings belges : décrypter l'énigme financière*, Cahiers Financiers, Brussels, De Boeck & Larcier, 2003. As of February 2009, Belgian holding companies listed on Euronext traded at an average discount of 40% compared to their portfolio: "Holdings noteren 40% onder intrinsieke waarde", De Tijd, 26 February 2009. This discount is subject to fluctuations: in August 2007, the average was 15% and in July 2008 it was 25%: "Holdings kwart goedkoper dan portefeuille", De Tijd, 24 July 2008.

[56] Indeed, this situation corresponds with what welfare economists term Kaldor/Hicks efficiency, a more sophisticated version of Pareto efficiency. See implicitly: I. LEE, "Fairness, Finance and Dual Class Share Structures", in G. Mather (ed.), *One Share One Vote? – Tomorrow's Companies: One Universal Model or Tailored Equity Structures*, London, European Policy Forum, 2006, 9-10; J. RICKFORD, "Invisible Hand or Dead Hand? – Reflections on the EU One Share One Vote", in G. Mather (ed.), *One Share One Vote? – Tomorrow's Companies: One Universal Model or Tailored Equity Structures*, London, European Policy Forum, 2006, 80.

[57] Nor would it necessarily be desirable from the perspective of issuers: cf. *infra*, section 8.2. (potentially negative impact of CEMs on welfare through an increased cost of capital).

[58] L. BEBCHUK, A. COHEN and A. FERRELL, "What Matters in Corporate Governance?" (2005) (negative impact of entrenchment for the US, which mainly results from staggered boards in combination with poison pills).

5. The Effects of 1S1V on Ownership Structure

22. *The "ex ante" effects on (choice of) ownership structure.* Even if, on the basis of the above evidence, 1S1V could be considered an efficient rule, its introduction will not necessarily lead to efficient operational decisions and control transfers. This is due to the fact that 1S1V, in turn, also influences the choice of the ownership and control structure. To the extent that controlling shareholders respond dynamically to the introduction of 1S1V in order to avoid contestable control, the final outcome may be even worse than the *status quo*. Below we will review the effects of 1S1V on (choice of) ownership structure.

23. *One Share One Vote, by itself, is not biased towards creating dispersed ownership...* A 1S1V regime (i.e. a total ban on CEMs) only affects controlling minority structures, while it cannot reach either of the extremes on the aforementioned corporate ownership continuum (i.e. a controlling shareholder holding more than 50% of both voting rights and cash-flow rights vs. dispersed ownership); a ban on CEMs can prevent those extreme situations from evolving towards the centre. By itself (*ceteris paribus*), 1S1V does not favour dispersed ownership over concentrated ownership as long as the ownership concentration does not result from the use of CEMs. Even if the introduction of a 1S1V regime could just as well lead to more dispersion as it could produce more concentrated ownership, the latter outcome appears more plausible nonetheless (at least in the absence of a mandatory bid rule – cf. *infra*). Our view on this point is, admittedly, influenced by the Belgian experience. Belgium already adopted a mandatory 1S1V rule as early as 1934, albeit limited to the prohibition of multiple voting rights shares[59]. This ban on multiple voting rights, in combination with the division of savings and investment banks[60], has led to a massive flight towards pyramid structures[61]. Nowadays, because of the prevalence of holding companies, corporate ownership in Belgium is more concentrated and the free float is more limited than in most other EU countries[62].

---

[59] Royal Decree No. 26 of 31 October 1934 (now art. 541 of the Belgian Companies Code); J. BAUGNIET, *La réglementation du droit de vote dans les sociétés anonymes*, Brussels, Bruylant, 1935; H. WILLEMS, "Multiple voting right in the general meeting of shareholders in Belgium during the interbellum period", London School of Economics, BHU Occasional Paper Series, (2005), 69-95.

[60] Royal Decree No. 2 of 22 August 1934. This legislation was inspired by the Glass Steagall Act of 1933, which introduced a similar prohibition of mixed banks in the US.

[61] M. BECHT et al., "Shareholding Cascades: The Separation of Ownership and Control in Belgium", in F. Barca and M. Becht (eds.), *The Control of Corporate Europe*, Oxford University Press, 2001, 71-105.

[62] A study recently found that the largest shareholder holds on average 36% of the capital and voting rights in companies listed on Euronext Brussels and the free float on Euronext Brussels has dropped just below 50%: "Referentieaandeelhouder dominanter in Brussel", De Tijd, 29 October 2008. The transition period for the new mandatory bid rule in particular has led to an increase of ownership concentration (because large shareholders raised their stake above the 30% threshold in anticipation of the new rule).

24. ... *but the mandatory bid rule favours dispersed ownership.* However, this *ex ante* effect of 1S1V should not be assessed separately from the mandatory bid rule, which tends to favour dispersed ownership[63]. Indeed, in the long run, when controlling shareholders will have disappeared altogether, a 1S1V rule will become largely – although perhaps not completely[64] – redundant.

At present, most CEMs are already covered by the mandatory bid rule. This is most obviously the case for dual class shares. The mandatory bid threshold is expressed in terms of (actual) voting rights; cash-flow rights are irrelevant for calculating the threshold. A mandatory bid is triggered as soon as a shareholder holds more than the specified percentage of voting rights, irrespective of the amount of cash-flow rights. Accordingly, a controlling position derived from the use of multiple voting rights shares does not escape the mandatory bid. Non-voting shares are not considered in calculating the threshold, which will trigger a mandatory bid even sooner. At least in Belgium, the mandatory bid obligation is extended to indirect acquisitions, i.e. to persons who acquire control over a "mono-holding" which in turn holds a threshold percentage of voting shares in a listed company[65]. This extension was introduced in order to prevent circumvention by abusive pyramids[66]. Thus, the use of holding companies to acquire or strengthen control can in some cases trigger a mandatory bid. Furthermore, the broad definition of acting in concert covers most shareholder agreements, and the issuance of depository certificates can also trigger a mandatory bid (unless the holders of certificates have an unlimited right to convert their certificates for the underlying voting shares). As a result, 1S1V has little added value in preventing an evasion of the mandatory bid rule.

25. *Shortcomings of the mandatory bid rule.* However, it may still take a long time before ownership will be dispersed, especially since EU Member States, when implementing the Takeover Directive, have generously allowed for grandfathering[67] and for a range of derogations from the mandatory bid

[63] Cf. *supra*, section 3.

[64] Cf. *infra*, section 8.

[65] A "mono-holding" is defined as a company that owns more than 30% of a listed company, provided that these shareholdings represent 50% or more of that holding company's net assets or more than 50% of its net results (art. 1, 6° of the Royal Decree of 27 April 2007).

[66] E. WYMEERSCH, "The New Belgian Law on Takeover Bids", UGent Financial Law Institute Working Paper No. 2008-04, (2008), p. 6.

[67] Such exemption of existing controlling positions by way of a transitional measure is not explicitly regulated by the Takeover Directive but is referred to in its Recital 10, which states that "the obligation to make a bid to all holders of securities should not apply to those controlling holdings already in existence on the date on which national legislation transposing this Directive enters into force". In Belgium a permanent exemption of existing controlling positions as of 1 September 2007 was granted, irrespective of subsequent incremental acquisitions (except those acquisitions tilting a single concert party above the control threshold) (art. 74 of the Belgian Law of 1 April 2007). This radical form of grandfathering appears open to challenge: see J. MEYERS, "Agenda Items for the Revision of the European Takeover Bid Directive", *Van alle markten. Liber Amicorum Eddy Wymeersch*, Antwerp, Intersentia, 2008, 702.

rule[68]. It would, as a minimum, be useful to delineate the scope for possible exemptions from the mandatory bid rule[69]. But even if the exemptions would be limited, the mandatory bid rule could still tend to freeze existing control structures rather than encourage dispersion. Indeed, while the mandatory bid rule prevents or at least restricts the emergence of new controlling shareholders, existing control structures remain largely unaffected (unless control changes hands on a voluntary basis). Hence, 1S1V could perhaps play a valuable role in speeding up the process of creating dispersed ownership by exposing "leveraged" block-holders to the market for corporate control[70].

In the next sections we will review the added value, if any, of the BTR in view of the mandatory bid rule. Thereafter, the potential merits of 1S1V outside the takeover context will be examined.

6. The Breakthrough Rule

26. *The concept of Breakthrough.* In order to break the existing deadlock in the adoption of the Takeover Directive, the Winter Group proposed a breakthrough rule (BTR), which has a more limited scope than a general 1S1V. Whereas a general 1S1V abolishes CEMs overall, a BTR only renders them inoperative during or immediately after a takeover bid.

The focus of the Winter Group was on achieving contestable control and a level playing field for (hostile) takeovers[71]. The ultimate goal was to facilitate the market for corporate control. Takeovers are not only an instrument of corporate restructuring, but also a means of disciplining management[72]. As mentioned above, a market for corporate control requires dispersed ownership: a controlling shareholder can easily thwart a hostile takeover attempt by not tendering his controlling block. This prevents hostile takeovers from effectively

---

[68] Article 5.4 of the Takeover Directive. Report on the implementation of the Directive on Takeover Bids, SEC (2007) 268, 21 February 2007.

[69] As suggested by J. MEYERS, "Agenda Items for the Revision of the European Takeover Bid Directive", *Van alle markten. Liber Amicorum Eddy Wymeersch*, Antwerp, Intersentia, 2008, 701-702; P. MÜLBERT, "Make It or Break It: The Break-Through Rule as a Break-Through for the European Takeover Directive?", in G. Ferrarini, K.J. Hopt, J. Winter and E. Wymeersch (eds.), *Reforming Takeover and Company Law in Europe*, Oxford, Oxford University Press, 2004, 732, note 48.

[70] Cf. the goal of the Lisbon strategy to create the world's most competitive economy by 2010, through reform of the capital market and the market for corporate control.

[71] M. BECHT, "Reciprocity in Takeovers", in G. Ferrarini, K.J. Hopt, J. Winter and E. Wymeersch (eds.), *Reforming Takeover and Company Law in Europe*, Oxford, Oxford University Press, 2004, 647-675; J.C. COATES, "Ownership, Takeovers and EU Law: How Contestable Should EU Corporations Be?", in G. Ferrarini, K.J. Hopt, J. Winter and E. Wymeersch (eds.), *Reforming Takeover and Company Law in Europe*, Oxford, Oxford University Press, 2004, 677-709; P. MÜLBERT, "Make It or Break It: The Break-Through Rule as a Break-Through for the European Takeover Directive?", in G. Ferrarini, K.J. Hopt, J. Winter and E. Wymeersch (eds.), *Reforming Takeover and Company Law in Europe*, Oxford, Oxford University Press, 2004, 711-736.

[72] Cf. *supra*, section 2.

performing a disciplinary function, although it does not constitute an obstacle to corporate restructuring through friendly bids or private sales. The BTR transforms a target company with a controlling minority shareholder into a company with dispersed ownership for the purpose of facilitating takeover bids. To be sure, for hostile takeover bids to be feasible, dispersed ownership alone is not sufficient. Indeed, general company law, the articles of association of a target company or shareholder agreements can contain provisions which may obstruct a bid (e.g. transfer or voting restrictions). The BTR also needed to address these obstacles[73]. Furthermore, the BTR had to complement the board passivity rule, which only deals with post-bid defences[74]. The board passivity rule by itself is clearly not sufficient to achieve a level playing field. It is a useful tool to make control contestable when share ownership is already dispersed, but the requirement for shareholder approval of takeover defences after a bid has been launched or as soon as a bid is imminent does not impose any real constraint on a controlling shareholder.

Thus, the BTR, as conceived by the Winter Group, dispenses with the following types of impediments to takeovers: (i) legal structures and mechanisms that prevent shareholders from reacting to a takeover bid either by tendering their shares (transfer restrictions) or by voting on the authorisation of defensive measures (voting restrictions and pre-completion breakthrough); and (ii) legal structures and mechanisms that prevent a bidder from exercising control once he has successfully completed his bid and acquired a significant block that would normally confer control (transfer and voting restrictions and post-completion breakthrough).

By making control contestable, the BTR also protects the minority shareholders. The fact that control is not contestable often leads to a discount in the stock price, reflecting that investors cannot benefit from a hostile takeover. In fact, the only plausible bidder for the minority shares would be the incumbent controlling shareholder in a voluntary bid and in this case the offered bid price may well be too low in the absence of a feasible counterbid. The market anticipates that the company will not be managed efficiently or by the most efficient party as it is shielded from the discipline of hostile takeovers. The BTR ensures that minority shareholders get their share of the control premium. To some extent, this is comparable to the protection offered by the mandatory bid rule[75]. But, differently, a bid does not actually need to take place in order for the BTR to protect the minority. In an efficient capital market, the mere fact that control is contestable (i.e. the mere possibility of a future bid) will be reflected in the stock price, thus giving minority shareholders an exit at a fair price at all times. This is a powerful rationale for a BTR. Unlike a general 1S1V rule, though, a BTR does not protect minority shareholders against the

[73] Article 11.2 and 11.3 of the Takeover Directive.
[74] Article 9 of the Takeover Directive.
[75] Cf. *supra*, section 3, and *infra*, section 7.

detrimental effects of CEMs on operational governance (except to the extent that the mere threat of hostile takeovers may provide discipline).

While the BTR does not necessarily make takeovers cheaper[76], it does ensure an efficient allocation of control under certain circumstances by requiring the bidder to purchase a larger fraction of the cash-flow rights[77]. This increases the likelihood that a more efficient bidder will gain control. This also leads the successful bidder to internalise more of the consequences of his operational decisions once in control. The mandatory (full) bid has a comparable effect[78]. At least when partial bids are allowed, CEMs can facilitate takeovers by making them cheaper (since a bidder has to buy a smaller fraction of shares to obtain control), but at the same time CEMs increase the likelihood of an inefficient outcome.

27. *Shortcomings of the Breakthrough rule.* The BTR laid down in Article 11 of the Takeover Directive has been criticised as not being a suitable means of achieving the objectives stated above, in particular contestable control. However, in our view this is mainly due to the fact that the Winter Group proposal, while itself not yet perfect, was amended to such an extent in the course of the legislative process that the text finally adopted barely resembles the original proposal.

First, a large number of exceptions were admitted (CEMs which are carved out include non-voting (preference) shares, voting securities other than shares, double voting rights shares[79], priority shares, golden shares, etc.)[80]. These numerous exceptions leave plenty of scope for evasion and, as a result, the BTR in its present form is unlikely to achieve a level playing field[81]. The present BTR creates an unbalanced situation which is especially to the detriment of Scandinavian countries as multiple voting rights shares seem to be one of the few CEMs actually covered, if not the only one[82].

---

[76] For numerical examples, see P. MÜLBERT, "Make It or Break It: The Break-Through Rule as a Break-Through for the European Takeover Directive?", in G. Ferrarini, K.J. Hopt, J. Winter and E. Wymeersch (eds.), *Reforming Takeover and Company Law in Europe*, Oxford, Oxford University Press, 2004, 719-720. This author stresses the fact that the BTR will not make control transfers cheaper. However, lowering the control premium in order to facilitate takeovers should not be a goal of takeover regulation if this would lead to an inefficient allocation of control. The BTR cannot be criticised for making control changes more expensive as long as it ensures an efficient allocation of control (or at least goes some way towards this goal – as the author acknowledges).

[77] G. FERRARINI, "One Share – One Vote: A European Rule?", *ECFR* 2006, 153 et seq.

[78] Cf. *supra*, section 3, and *infra*, section 7.

[79] Report on the implementation of the Directive on Takeover Bids, SEC (2007) 268, 21 February 2007, p. 8, note 21; J. RICKFORD, "The Emerging European Takeover Law from a British Perspective", *EBLR* 2004, 1391.

[80] J. RICKFORD, "The Emerging European Takeover Law from a British Perspective", *EBLR* 2004, 1391-1393.

[81] J. COATES, "Ownership, Takeovers and EU Law: How Contestable Should EU Corporations Be?", in G. Ferrarini, K.J. Hopt, J. Winter and E. Wymeersch (eds.), *Reforming Takeover and Company Law in Europe*, Oxford, Oxford University Press, 2004, 682 et seq.

[82] For a Scandinavian perspective, see U. BERNITZ, "The Attack on the Nordic Voting Rights Model: The Legal Limits under EU Law", *EBLR* 2004, 1423-1437; R. SKOG, "The Takeover Directive, the

Furthermore, in order to reach a political compromise, the BTR had to be made optional for Member States (or companies)[83]. This optional nature of the rule has incited most Member States to preserve the *status quo*[84]. Only the Baltic States have imposed the BTR. This tendency to opt out of the BTR is not surprising in the light of its unbalanced and incomplete nature, and this is reinforced by the uncertainty on the issues of reciprocity[85] and compensation[86].

Nonetheless, the initial proposal did not have a solution for factual structures – as opposed to legal structures – deviating from 1S1V (most notably pyramids and cross-shareholdings)[87]. More radical and/or complementary measures would be required in this respect (e.g. delisting of holding companies whose sole or main assets are their shareholding in another listed company, rules on conflicts of interest in groups of listed companies with cross-holdings[88], tax measures). Such measures would extend beyond takeover situations and even beyond the realm of company law[89]. Similar concerns are raised by purely contractual deviations from 1S1V (e.g. derivatives that allow for a decoupling of voting rights from cash-flow rights)[90].

The BTR threshold raises another question. At present, the BTR is triggered when a bidder obtains 75% of the cash-flow rights. This still allows for some disproportionate control. Indeed, the BTR is ineffective against a controlling shareholder who holds at least 25% of the share capital of the company. This also provides scope for evasion, not by having recourse to other CEMs but simply by increasing or maintaining the ownership stake above the 25% level (provided that the controlling shareholder is not facing wealth constraints). It could be argued that a bidder who has obtained 50% of the cash-flow rights should be able to appoint (the majority of) the board of directors. Then again,

'Breakthrough' Rule and the Swedish System of Dual Class Common Stock", *EBLR* 2004, 1439-1451; J.L. HANSEN, "The Nordic Corporate Governance Model – A European Model?", in M. Tison, H. De Wulf, C. Van der Elst and R. Steennot (eds.), *Perspectives in Company Law and Financial Regulation. Essays in Honour of Eddy Wymeersch*, Cambridge, Cambridge University Press, 2009, 156-158.

83 Article 12.1 and 12.2 of the Takeover Directive. Opt-in by companies requires a decision of the general meeting with a supermajority for amendment of the articles. As a result, existing control blocks are ordinarily in a position to vote down such a voluntary opt-in to the BTR. An opt-out default rule would have been better.

84 Report on the implementation of the Directive on Takeover Bids, SEC (2007) 268, 21 February 2007, p. 7-8.

85 Article 12.3 of the Takeover Directive.

86 Article 11.5 of the Takeover Directive. Although the Winter Group considered that compensation was not necessary, concerns about Article 1 of the First Protocol to the ECHR have led to the insertion of this vague provision.

87 Report of the High Level Group of Company Law Experts on Issues Related to Takeover Bids, para. 3. As pyramids and cross-holdings are arguably worse than dual class shares, the problem would even be exacerbated by the BTR: L. BEBCHUK and O. HART, "A Threat to Dual Class Shares", Financial Times, 31 May 2002.

88 Cf. art. 524 of the Belgian Companies Code.

89 Cf. *infra*, section 8 on general application of 1S1V.

90 A. KHACHATURYAN, "Trapped in Delusions: Democracy, Fairness and the One-Share-One-Vote Rule in the European Union", *EBOR* 2007, 353-355.

the 75% threshold makes sense for amendment of the company articles[91]. Two separate thresholds could be used. Or perhaps the threshold should be aligned with the thresholds for the mandatory bid[92] or the sell out right[93]?

But even if all CEMs were to be included and the threshold were to be lowered to 50% by an improved BTR, such a rule would not affect a controlling shareholder holding more than 50% of both votes and cash-flow rights. The introduction of the BTR might lead to even higher ownership concentration, above the 50% level. While this may arguably be better than having CEMs[94], it could also have a negative impact on the stock price, since control would remain incontestable and liquidity would be hampered even more[95].

28. *Summary: need for a more consistent approach.* From the foregoing analysis it follows that the problem with the BTR is its *ex ante* effect. This is very similar to the *ex ante* effect of a general 1S1V regime, which would not only render CEMs ineffective during or immediately after a takeover bid, but abolish them altogether[96]. At first glance, the BTR does not prevent the use of CEMs outside takeovers (unlike a general 1S1V regime), but tries to reconcile the advantages of both concentrated and dispersed ownership structures (i.e. shareholder monitoring in ordinary course of business and the market for corporate control) without imposing a choice of either structure. However, because CEMs are overridden in a takeover situation, they become less attractive overall[97]. As with a general 1S1V rule, it is therefore not certain whether an improved BTR would actually produce dispersed ownership and contestable control or, on the contrary, lead to a higher degree of ownership concentration *ex ante* (as opposed to *ex post*, i.e. as a result of a successful takeover bid).

At any rate, if the BTR is intended to make control contestable, it needs to be formulated in a more radical way, because CEMs which are not covered

---

[91] The Winter Report on Takeover Bids took the view that the threshold for the BTR should not be set at a level higher than required for special shareholder resolutions such as amendments of the articles (para. 4.2).

[92] M. PRADA, "A Modern Regulatory Framework for Company and Takeover Law in Europe", in G. Ferrarini, K.J. Hopt, J. Winter and E. Wymeersch (eds.), *Reforming Company and Takeover Law in Europe*, Oxford, Oxford University Press, 2004, 94 (proposing a threshold of 2/3, in line with the mandatory bid threshold at 1/3).

[93] P. MÜLBERT, "Make It or Break It: The Break-Through Rule as a Break-Through for the European Takeover Directive?", in G. Ferrarini, K.J. Hopt, J. Winter and E. Wymeersch (eds.), *Reforming Takeover and Company Law in Europe*, Oxford, Oxford University Press, 2004,725-726 (in order to alleviate the "pressure to tender" problem, the sell out right should be triggered once the bidder obtains voting control). Also, in Belgium, the threshold triggering the mandatory reopening of a bid (set at 90% of voting rights) should be lowered.

[94] Cf. *supra*, section 2.

[95] Introducing a "one vote per person" rule or a combination of a mandatory voting cap and a BTR (as suggested by M. BECHT, "Reciprocity in Takeovers", in G. Ferrarini, K.J. Hopt, J. Winter and E. Wymeersch (eds.), *Reforming Takeover and Company Law in Europe*, Oxford, Oxford University Press, 2004, 654), would move us even further away from 1S1V. In addition, such an approach would disadvantage, and thus deter, all large investments.

[96] Cf. *supra*, section 5.

[97] G. FERRARINI, "One Share – One Vote: A European Rule?", *ECFR* 2006, 176.

by the BTR provide an easy escape, and it needs to be complemented by a mandatory bid rule in order to deter recourse to concentrated ownership of both voting rights and cash-flow rights.

7. Added Value of the Breakthrough Rule in the light of the Mandatory Bid Rule

29. *Different levels of minority protection.* Another argument that is often raised against the BTR is that it is unnecessary in view of the mandatory bid rule[98]. As mentioned above, both minority protection and efficient allocation of control are already assured by the mandatory bid rule[99]. Since a shareholder who reaches the relevant threshold has to address an offer for all outstanding shares and has to spread the control premium, if any, among all shareholders, the mandatory bid rule goes at least as far as the BTR – and, to be sure, it goes even further when a voluntary bid is not subject to a full bid requirement. Some scholars have therefore argued that the BTR would, to a certain extent, undo the minority protection provided by the mandatory bid rule[100]. A party that wants to acquire control could in certain circumstances opt for a voluntary bid with application of the BTR instead of a negotiated block trade followed by a mandatory bid. This would be the case in a company where the incumbent shareholder holds 30% or more of the voting rights but less than 25% of the cash-flow rights. As a result, the more stringent rules of the mandatory bid with respect to minimum bid price, cash alternative and conditions of the bid could be avoided by opting for a voluntary bid and application of the BTR. As a result, minority shareholders could be harmed. On the other hand, this might encourage some efficient bids to take place which would otherwise not be undertaken under the overly protective mandatory bid rule[101]. However, it is not certain whether the application of the BTR would actually make a transfer of control cheaper than a negotiated block trade followed by a mandatory bid. This would depend, among other things, on the equitable compensation that the bidder may have to pay under Article 11.5 of the Takeover Directive to shareholders whose rights have been broken through[102]. It will also depend

---

[98] P. MÜLBERT, "Make It or Break It: The Break-Through Rule as a Break-Through for the European Takeover Directive?", in G. Ferrarini, K.J. Hopt, J. Winter and E. Wymeersch (eds.), *Reforming Takeover and Company Law in Europe*, Oxford, Oxford University Press, 2004, 732-733.

[99] Cf. *supra*, section 3.

[100] E. BERGLÖF and M. BURKART, "European Takeover Regulation", *Economic Policy* 2003, 200; J. McCAHERY, L. RENNEBOOG, P. RITTER and S. HALLER, "The Economics of the Proposed European Takeover Directive", in G. Ferrarini, K.J. Hopt, J. Winter and E. Wymeersch (eds.), *Reforming Takeover and Company Law in Europe*, Oxford, Oxford University Press, 2004, 625.

[101] Cf. *supra*, section 3.

[102] J. MEYERS, "Agenda Items for the Revision of the European Takeover Bid Directive", *Van alle markten. Liber Amicorum Eddy Wymeersch*, Antwerp, Intersentia, 2008, 707.

on the possibility of partial bids and price discrimination between classes of shares[103].

30. ***Should the Breakthrough rule equally apply in a mandatory bid situation?*** Another question is whether the BTR should also apply to the mandatory bid. Due to the low threshold triggering a mandatory bid (30% in most Member States), it is possible that such a bid will not actually confer control on the bidder, because a third party already holds a majority of the voting rights or a higher stake than the party that is crossing the threshold. This used to be – and remains – one of the most common exemptions from the mandatory bid rule[104]. However, it remains to be clarified whether it is in fact allowed under the Takeover Directive[105]. If it would indeed be considered desirable to guarantee that a party who has to make a mandatory bid can in all circumstances effectively obtain control, the BTR could to some extent help to ensure that this will be the case (instead of granting an outright exemption). Indeed, some CEMs may prevent a party from obtaining control as a result of a mandatory bid (e.g. priority shares granting special veto or nomination rights, voting caps, supermajority rules). But the BTR alone cannot ensure that a mandatory bid will always confer control. For example: when a bidder does not manage to obtain 75% of the cash-flow rights triggering the application of the BTR, takeover defences contained in the articles of association and locked in by a block of at least 25% of the cash-flow rights remain out of reach. The mandatory bid is unconditional, hence a bidder cannot withdraw his bid when the threshold triggering the BTR is not reached or when takeover defences are not voluntarily removed.

8. Added Value of 1S1V in the light of the Mandatory Bid and Breakthrough Rules

31. ***The view of the Winter Report.*** The Winter Group did not advocate the mandatory general application of a 1S1V rule outside the takeover context. On the one hand, the Group did not believe that universal adoption was necessary

[103] P. MÜLBERT, "Make It or Break It: The Break-Through Rule as a Break-Through for the European Takeover Directive?", in G. Ferrarini, K.J. Hopt, J. Winter and E. Wymeersch (eds.), *Reforming Takeover and Company Law in Europe*, Oxford, Oxford University Press, 2004, 734.

[104] As mentioned above (cf. *supra*, section 3), the threshold was deliberately set at around 30% to allow for counterbids. The equitable price can thus still be corrected by the market. However, when there is already a large(r) shareholder present, the market for corporate control will be blocked.

[105] J. MEYERS, "Agenda Items for the Revision of the European Takeover Bid Directive", *Van alle markten. Liber Amicorum Eddy Wymeersch*, Antwerp, Intersentia, 2008, 701-702 (implicitly considering that it is a justified exemption). Contra: M.P. NIEUWE WEME, *Het verplicht bod op effecten* [The mandatory bid for securities], Van der Heijden Instituut no. 80, Deventer, Kluwer, 2004, 183-184 and 214 (considering that it is a deliberate choice to cross the threshold – and otherwise the exemption for temporary crossing still applies – and refuting several arguments for such an exemption).

to solve the takeover problem. On the other hand, the Group recognised that complete restructuring in line with 1S1V would be a huge, expensive and controversial exercise since departures from 1S1V might well be justified in some cases (depending on country, industry or company-specific conditions) and separation of voting rights and cash-flow rights could also be achieved by other means (pyramids, derivatives)[106].

However, in our view, an effective BTR would inevitably have some consequences outside takeover situations.

First, the post-completion BTR, as proposed by the Winter Group, implies that a bidder who has acquired at least 75% of the cash-flow rights can call a general meeting of shareholders in order to appoint directors to the board and to amend the articles. In this vote, 1S1V would apply. Whereas the pre-completion BTR relating to the shareholder vote on the authorisation of defensive measures would only temporarily affect the normal distribution of voting rights, the post-completion BTR would inevitably lead to a permanent alteration since the bidder would thus be entitled to install 1S1V on a permanent basis by abolishing multiple voting rights shares and voting caps and by transforming non-voting (preference) shares into voting shares (presumably without preference). Thereafter, the bidder will be able to exercise control rights on a 1S1V basis, in accordance with his acquired stake of risk-bearing capital[107].

Furthermore, an effective BTR would somehow have to address the problem of pyramids as well[108]. If pyramids and similar factual structures are also regulated, one ends up in a situation where 1S1V finds permanent application.

32. *The Company Law Action Plan 2003.* Apart from these considerations relating to the BTR, the question arises what further benefits, if any, could result from a general application of 1S1V in addition to the BTR. Since both the Action Plan itself (although it proposed a broad 1S1V) and the fact-finding study of 2007 remain silent on this question, we have to provide our own answers against the background of the EU policy objectives.

[106] Winter Report on Takeover Bids, no. 3; J. RICKFORD, "Invisible Hand or Dead Hand? – Reflections on the EU One Share One Vote", in G. Mather (ed.), *One Share One Vote? – Tomorrow's Companies: One Universal Model or Tailored Equity Structures*, London, European Policy Forum, 2006, 70-71.

[107] P. MÜLBERT, "Make It or Break It: The Break-Through Rule as a Break-Through for the European Takeover Directive?", in G. Ferrarini, K.J. Hopt, J. Winter and E. Wymeersch (eds.), *Reforming Takeover and Company Law in Europe*, Oxford, Oxford University Press, 2004, 728. However, this will not necessarily be the scenario. After having abolished existing CEMs, the bidder could, for example, also insert new CEMs into the articles, this time to his own benefit. These would remain locked in until the bidder's stake dropped below 25% of risk-bearing capital.

[108] The Winter Report on Takeover Bids acknowledged the problem of abusive pyramids but considered that it would be impossible to extend the BTR to such structures: alternative measures would be needed (para. 4.3.3).

8.1. Minority Protection (Outside the Takeover Situation)

33. *Introduction.* One reason for a general 1S1V regime – in addition to a BTR – could be that minority protection is also needed outside the specific takeover context, since disproportionate ownership and control structures also affect operational decisions by providing scope for undue minority abuse[109].

Nonetheless, the agency problems caused by the use of CEMs may already be tempered when control is made contestable by an effective BTR[110]. Indeed, the BTR arguably has an indirect impact on operational decisions to the extent that it makes control contestable. In that case, the mere threat of a hostile takeover ensures that the incumbent block-holder will strive to maximise shareholder value.

34. *Need for minority protection.* An often raised counter-argument states that there is no need for minority protection against CEMs since apparently there is a market for non-voting or low-voting shares[111]. Investors will buy such shares voluntarily if the price is right, and in fact they will apply a discount. There is nothing unfair about disproportionate structures as long as investors are well informed and as long as they are free (not) to invest in those companies. This explains the calls for more disclosure[112]. However, disclosure alone cannot substitute for a BTR or a 1S1V rule because it cannot make control contestable and, in fact, it is quite useless when control is entrenched[113]. A few further points need to be raised as to the limits of disclosure.

This argument applies only to those situations where investors actually have a free choice whether or not to invest (e.g. IPOs), but the problem remains in the case of midstream changes to the capital and voting structure. Later issuances of (or conversions into) new share classes with disproportionately higher voting rights can dilute the voting power of the existing minority shareholders against their will. In the US, where 1S1V was heavily debated in the 1980s and early 1990s, later issuances of share classes with higher voting rights and dual class recapitalisations (conversions of ordinary shares into non-

---

[109] J. RICKFORD, "Invisible Hand or Dead Hand? – Reflections on the EU One Share One Vote", in G. Mather (ed.), *One Share One Vote? – Tomorrow's Companies: One Universal Model or Tailored Equity Structures*, London, European Policy Forum, 2006, 73.

[110] Cf. *supra*, section 4.1.1.

[111] I. LEE, "Fairness, Finance and Dual Class Share Structures", in G. Mather (ed.), *One Share One Vote? – Tomorrow's Companies: One Universal Model or Tailored Equity Structures*, London, European Policy Forum, 2006, 9-10.

[112] European Corporate Governance Forum Statement on Proportionality, August 2007. See also E. WYMEERSCH, "'One share, one vote' ou proportionnalité du droit de vote des actions", *Liber Amicorum Guy Keutgen*, Brussels, Bruylant, 2008, 223-225.

[113] For this reason the enforcement of corporate governance codes through a "comply or explain" approach raises questions in the continental EU: J. WINTER, "Ius Audacibus – The Future of EU Company Law", in M. Tison, H. De Wulf, C. Van der Elst and R. Steennot (eds.), *Perspectives in Company Law and Financial Regulation. Essays in Honour of Eddy Wymeersch*, Cambridge, Cambridge University Press, 2009, 50.

voting preference shares) were considered as the main problem and only they were addressed, whereas subsequent issuances of share classes with lesser voting rights are in principle permitted[114]. For the US, therefore, the question is not whether dual class shares are allowed, but under which procedural conditions[115]. In the EU, on the other hand, dual class recapitalisations are less of a problem, since regulation of share capital and in particular the pre-emption right of existing shareholders prevents controlling shareholders from diluting the minority[116]. In addition, dual class recapitalisations are financially less attractive for controlling shareholders than for managers as a way of reinforcing control through a dilution of minority shareholders, since they would ultimately have to replace a block of common stock with comparatively weakened voting rights in a discounted sale, thus bearing the effect of outside investors' discount[117]. As far as midstream changes are concerned, pyramids are worse than dual class shares. New layers can be added either at the bottom or at the top of the control chain. Minority shareholders of the newly added entity will not be affected since they will only buy stock at a discount, but minority shareholders at any intermediate level will see the value of their investment diminish by the added potential for PBs extraction, without being able to do anything about it. The Winter Report suggested a ban on multiple listings to get rid of abusive pyramids[118]. The question would then be how to distinguish abusive pyramids from groups which also serve legitimate business purposes. In Belgium, the use of holding structures to acquire or strengthen control can in some cases trigger a mandatory bid[119]. This underscores our point that a general 1S1V regime may not be feasible without a mandatory bid rule in place. In the US, pyramids have

[114] For an overview of the US history of 1S1V, see G. FERRARINI, "One Share – One Vote: A European Rule?", *ECFR* 2006, 162-164. It should be noted that 1S1V is primarily a matter of state law in the US. See S. BAINBRIDGE, "The Scope of the SEC's Authority over Shareholder Voting Rights", UCLA School of Law Research Paper No. 07-16, (2007), (http://papers.ssrn.com/abstract=985707). In 1990 it was decided by the US Court of Appeals that federal securities law is limited to matters of disclosure: *Business Roundtable vs. SEC*, 905 F.2d 406 (DC Cir. 1990). Although SEC Rule 19c-4 was thereby invalidated, the major stock exchanges voluntarily adopted to a similar listing standard, albeit with some greater flexibility (see Rule 313 NYSE Listed Company Manual; Rule 4351 NASDAQ Marketplace Rules; Section 122 et seq. AMEX Company Guide).

[115] Not all authors are satisfied with the present state of the law. For a more lenient approach (only targeting coercive recapitalisations): S. BAINBRIDGE, *Corporation Law and Economics*, New York, Foundation Press, 2002, 457-461 (disinterested shareholder approval); P. FLOCOS, "Toward a Liability Rule Approach to the One Share, One Vote Controversy: An Epitaph for the SEC's Rule 19c-4?", *University of Pennsylvania Law Review* 1990, 1761-1816 (appraisal remedy). For a more stringent approach: P.L. SIMMONS, "Dual Class Recapitalizations and Shareholder Voting Rights", *Columbia Law Review* 1987, 106-124.

[116] B. ARRUÑADA and C. PAZ-ARES, "The Conversion of Ordinary Shares into Non-Voting Shares", in D. HEREMANS and H. COUSY (eds.), *Essays in Law and Economics, III Financial Markets and Insurance*, Antwerp, Maklu, 1996, 129-161.

[117] A. PACCES, *Featuring Control Power: Corporate Law and Economics Revisited*, Ph.D. thesis, Erasmus Universiteit Rotterdam, 2008, 471.

[118] Similar rules are already in place in the UK (Listing Rules 6.1.19R and 6.1.20G) and Italy: see Shearman & Sterling LLP, Comparative Legal Study (2007), synthesis, p. 13; exhibit B, p. 37-42; C.I, p. 331 (Italy) and C.II, p. 268-270 (UK).

[119] Cf. *supra*, section 5.

historically been less common, even in the absence of a mandatory bid rule. At least partially, this is due to the taxation of intra-group dividends which was introduced in the 1930s by Franklin D. Roosevelt as part of the New Deal[120].

This line of reasoning furthermore presumes that, in cases where they have a free choice, investors act rationally upon the available information. Leaving aside the criticism of the rationality presumption articulated by the "behavioural" economics and finance schools, this raises the question as to whether the current transparency around CEMs is sufficient to enable investors to make an informed investment decision. Article 10 of the Takeover Directive requires listed companies to disclose annual information on a comprehensive list of pre-bid defences and, at least for disclosure purposes, establishes 1S1V as the EU standard[121]. The Transparency Directive requires market participants to disclose major holdings in terms of voting rights. However, the amount of cash-flow rights in relation to voting rights (i.e. the gap between both as a measure of the degree of disproportionality) is not required to be disclosed[122]. Nor is any justification (i.e. non-neutral disclosure) required from listed companies themselves for the presence of CEMs. Furthermore, a number of technical difficulties arise in relation to derivatives, which in fact constitute alternative ways of separating voting rights from the underlying cash-flow rights and thus, ultimately, of undermining 1S1V[123]. For instance, cash-settled equity swaps (contracts for difference) currently escape disclosure under the transparency rules, even though possible delivery of the underlying shares or influence on the exercise of the voting rights attached thereto may derive from informal understandings[124]. Pyramids remain less transparent than dual class shares. Perhaps the higher visibility of shares with multiple voting rights explains why they generate a relatively larger discount in some empirical studies[125], even though they are usually associated with higher liquidity and lower administration costs than pyramids.

---

[120] J. BONRIGHT and G. MEANS, *The holding company: its public significance and its regulation*, New York, McGraw-Hill, 1932; R. MORCK, "Why some double taxation might make sense: the special case of inter-corporate dividend", University of Alberta Center for Financial Research Working Paper No. 03-01 (2003). Other factors that contributed to the elimination of pyramids probably include strict antitrust rules (Sherman Act of 1890 and Clayton Act of 1914) and the prohibition against savings banks owning more than 5% of shares in industrial companies (Glass Steagall Act of 1933).

[121] G. FERRARINI, "One Share – One Vote: A European Rule?", *ECFR* 2006, 165-166; H. HIRTE, "The Takeover Directive – a Mini-Directive on the Structure of the Corporation: Is it a Trojan Horse?", *ECFR* 2004, 10 and 18.

[122] Some Member States (e.g. France, the Netherlands and Sweden) provided for additional disclosure of holdings of capital in order to measure the impact of multiple voting rights shares.

[123] H. HU and B. BLACK, "Hedge Funds, Insiders, and Decoupling of Economic and Voting Ownership in Public Companies", ECGI Law Working Paper No. 56, (2006).

[124] At present, these contracts do not fall under Article 13 of the Transparency Directive as implemented by Article 11 of Directive 2007/14/EC: see e.g. J. MEYERS, "Agenda Items for the Revision of the European Takeover Bid Directive", *Van alle markten. Liber Amicorum Eddy Wymeersch*, Antwerp, Intersentia, 2008, 704-705.

[125] M. BENNEDSEN and K. MEISNER NIELSEN, "The Principle of Proportional Ownership, Investor Protection and Firm Value in Western Europe", ECGI Finance Working Paper No. 134, (2006), 23-25.

Last but not least, even if investors correctly anticipate the potential extraction of PBs by controlling minority shareholders by applying a discount to shares in such companies, this still leaves us with the macro-economic question of whether CEMs might have a negative impact on firm value and/or performance and even on the economy as a whole.

8.2. Cost of Capital

35. ***The constraints of the market for capital and the wider macro-economic impact of CEMs.*** Even when minority shareholders are not directly harmed, CEMs could impair total welfare by increasing the cost of capital. The potential for extraction of PBs through the use of CEMs could have a negative impact on the willingness of rational, informed outside investors to buy shares in companies where such CEMs are present. The discount thus applied by these investors could increase the cost of capital market financing[126]. Hence 1S1V could assist in reducing the discount and thus the cost of capital. In addition, in companies where CEMs are absent 1S1V could function as a "commitment device" by ensuring that investors will not be diluted and expropriated in the future through the subsequent introduction of CEMs (i.e. after the IPO stage, by the incumbent block-holder or his successor). This extra discount applied at the IPO stage, reflecting the uncertainty regarding future deviations from 1S1V, would thus be eliminated.

However, the macro-economic effects of 1S1V are also ambiguous. According to some views, capital market development could be hampered if the prohibition against using CEMs prevented entrepreneurs who are unwilling to relinquish control from taking their company public, but instead encouraged them to reincorporate elsewhere or to search for other sources of financing (debt, private equity)[127]. Which of these two effects dominates will have to be established empirically.

36. ***Need for "structural" measures to reduce the cost of capital.*** Some authors contend that 1S1V would in any case be a disproportionate measure: if PBs are the real problem, then it would be a better alternative to focus directly on improving the level of investor protection against extraction of PBs[128]. This

[126] In the recent ISS survey, 80% of institutional investors stated that they would expect a discount on the share prices of companies with CEMs, ranging from 10% to 30% (ISS Europe, ECGI, Shearman & Sterling, *Report on the Proportionality Principle in the European Union*, 18 May 2007, p. 96). However, empirical studies do not demonstrate that such a discount is actually applied in practice.

[127] At least as far as Belgium is concerned, we are not aware of any legal or listing rule that would prevent an entrepreneur from floating less than 50% of the shares on the stock exchange. A ban on CEMs would only restrict the number of shares that can be floated without giving up control. According to the famous "pecking order" theory, equity finance will be the last resort in any case.

[128] G. PSARAKIS, "One Share – One Vote and the Case for a Harmonised Capital Structure", *EBLR* 2008, 721; E. WYMEERSCH, "'One share, one vote' ou proportionnalité du droit de vote des actions", *Liber Amicorum Guy Keutgen*, Brussels, Bruylant, 2008, 225-226.

would also reduce the discount for CEMs. Instead of relying on structural measures which aim to eliminate or at least discourage the use of CEMs, this approach would focus more on standards, disclosure and (public and private) enforcement. Ultimately, this comes down to improving the quality of the legal system by introducing typical corporate governance measures (e.g. independent directors or procedures for dealing with conflicts of interest), by stimulating shareholder activism and litigation, etc.[129] Studies suggest that pyramids emerge when external financing is more expensive than internal financing and when the controlling shareholder is expected to extract substantial PBs, both of which conditions hold in an environment of low investor protection[130].

This argument implicitly assumes that increased investor protection will automatically disperse ownership (due to a changed trade-off between the cost and benefits of CEMs) and thus make a 1S1V rule redundant. However, corporate governance reforms can work rather slowly and, as a result, structural measures may still be needed[131]. Moreover, while it is probably true that investor protection limits the possibilities for tunnelling and thus the utility of CEMs for a controlling shareholder, other forms of PBs probably cannot be removed simply by increased investor protection[132]. Therefore, it seems that investor protection only tells part of the story. It can perhaps explain the willingness of outside investors to provide equity financing at low charge, but not a controlling shareholder's decision to relinquish control: a controlling shareholder is unlikely to part with control simply because he knows that he will be protected adequately once reduced to holding a minority stake himself. He is likely to be motivated (more) by concerns of protection of his PBs[133], and besides, the degree of ownership dispersion seems to be influenced (also) by the legal distribution of powers between shareholders and management[134].

[129] This line of reasoning is influenced by the work of R. LA PORTA et al. See also R. GILSON, "Controlling Shareholders and Corporate Governance: Complicating the Comparative Taxonomy", *Harvard Law Review* 2006, 1641-1679.

[130] H. ALMEIDA and D. WOLFENZON, "A Theory of Pyramidal Ownership and Family Business Groups", *Journal of Finance* 2006, 2637-2681 (pyramids allow the entire cash flow of a company to be used in order to control another company without the need to access the capital markets and the costs of PB extraction to be externalised onto the minority shareholders of the parent company).

[131] As recognised by R. GILSON, "Controlling Shareholders and Corporate Governance", in G. Mather (ed.), *One Share One Vote? – Tomorrow's Companies: One Universal Model or Tailored Equity Structures*, London, European Policy Forum, 2006, 40-42.

[132] E.g. more subtle forms of PB extraction resulting from suboptimal decision-making (cf. *supra*, section 4.1.1) or even "good" PBs that are efficient (J. COATES, "Ownership, Takeovers and EU Law: How Contestable Should EU Corporations Be?", in G. Ferrarini, K.J. Hopt, J. Winter and E. Wymeersch (eds.), *Reforming Takeover and Company Law in Europe*, Oxford, Oxford University Press, 2004, 692-693; A. PACCES, *Featuring Control Power: Corporate Law and Economics Revisited*, Ph.D. thesis, Erasmus Universiteit Rotterdam, 2008, 318 et seq.).

[133] L. BEBCHUK, "A Rent-Protection Theory of Corporate Ownership and Control", NBER Working Paper No. 7203, (1999).

[134] L. BEBCHUK, "The Case for Increasing Shareholder Power", *Harvard Law Review* 2005, 833 et seq.; S. COOLS, "The Real Difference in Corporate Law between the United States and Continental Europe: Distribution of Powers", *Delaware Journal of Corporate Law* 2005, 697-766; A. PACCES, *Featuring Control Power: Corporate Law and Economics Revisited*, Ph.D. thesis, Erasmus Universiteit Rotterdam, 2008, 403 et seq.

If minority protection and cost of capital are not convincing grounds for a full 1S1V rule, could there perhaps be other justifications for introducing such a general regime? A few alternative rationales for 1S1V will be explored in some detail below.

8.3. Shareholder Participation

37. As argued above, the case for 1S1V is primarily about creating shareholder value, not some vague ideal of shareholder democracy. Nevertheless, democracy can be understood in a procedural sense. In that case, 1S1V could be one of the preconditions for a higher degree of active participation by shareholders in corporate governance – not by giving shareholders more information or facilities for exercising their rights (matters already dealt with in the Shareholders' Rights and Transparency Directives), but precisely by giving them more voting rights[135]. The underlying assumption is that shareholders will be encouraged to (attend and) participate more actively at the general meeting if they are given equal voting rights.

This rationale was implicit in the Fifth Company Law Directive[136], but it is questionable. At best, it could convince institutional investors to choose "voice" over "exit", but it is implausible that retail investors would become more active under 1S1V, since they are "rationally apathetic" (i.e. they do not have enough at stake to make close monitoring worth the time and money and giving them more voting rights would thus be irrelevant). But even as far as institutional investors are concerned, one may wonder whether they would in fact be able and/or willing to perform such a monitoring role, since they also face conflicts of interest with the companies they invest in[137] and collective action problems (albeit on a higher level, as a result of competition amongst themselves)[138].

38. ***Voting by institutional investors.*** If institutional investors are the most prominent advocates of 1S1V, should they not be obliged to systematically exercise their voting rights? Such a requirement was not considered desirable in the Action Plan, in view of its potentially counterproductive effects. Indeed, due to a lack of time or resources, institutional investors might simply vote

[135] G. BACHMANN, "Strengthening Shareholders' Rights: A Comment on the EU Action Plan", *ERA Forum* 2005, 359.

[136] See the 13th Recital, as introduced by the Second Amendment to the proposal for a Fifth Council Directive based on Article 54 of the EEC Treaty concerning the structure of public limited companies and the powers and obligations of their organs, OJ 11 January 1991, C 7, p. 4. See also A. POUTIANEN, "Shareholders and Corporate Governance: The Principle of One Share One Vote" *EBLR* 2001, 67-75.

[137] Winter Report on Company Law, Chapter 3, para. 3.3.

[138] G. BACHMANN, "Strengthening Shareholders' Rights: A Comment on the EU Action Plan", *ERA Forum* 2005, 362.

in favour of any proposed resolution in order to satisfy the requirement[139]. Instead, the Action Plan suggested they should be obliged to disclose their investment policy and their policy with respect to the exercise of voting rights in companies in which they invest, and to disclose to their beneficial holders on request how these rights have been used in a particular case. This would improve the internal governance of institutional investors themselves and increase participation by institutional investors in the affairs of the companies in which they invest.

39. *Voting by hedge funds.* Hedge funds have emerged recently to give a new meaning to shareholder activism. But they predominantly use their potential voting rights as a threat, in order to influence management and without actually having to exercise them. Sometimes they are accused of engaging in "empty voting" (i.e. through various stock market transactions, such as stock borrowing or derivative transactions, they try to obtain voting power without the corresponding economic risk)[140]. This ultimately undermines the premises of 1S1V and insofar as these transactions are undertaken for the sole purpose of obtaining voting rights separate from the underlying cash-flow rights, they should be prohibited.

40. *Loyalty shares as a solution - or rather as a problem?* The above argument about increased shareholder participation can also be reversed: certain deviations from 1S1V could be explained as a way of strengthening shareholder participation. The renewed interest in "loyalty shares" fits into this framework. The typical French double voting rights shares[141], which grant an extra voting right to "loyal" shareholders whose shares have been registered for at least two years, are ardently defended by proponents as increasing the democratic degree of shareholder decision-making[142], especially when the double voting right is made subject to conditions relating to the presence or participation of shareholders at the general meeting (as in a recent Belgian proposal[143]).

---

[139] Action Plan 3.1.1. ("Information about the role played by institutional investors").

[140] H. HU and B. BLACK, "Hedge Funds, Insiders, and Decoupling of Economic and Voting Ownership in Public Companies", ECGI Law Working Paper No. 56, (2006), (http://ssrn.com/abstract=874098).

[141] Art. L. 225-123 Code de commerce.

[142] E.g. Paris Chamber of Commerce and Industry, "Une action = une voix" – Faut-il imposer une égalité entre participation au capital et détention du pouvoir? (Report Norguet), 24 May 2007, available at http://www.etudes.ccip.fr/archrap/rap07/une-action=une-voix-nor0705.htm.

[143] Belgian Governance Institute, Een Belgisch model van aandelen met meervoudig stemrecht verenigbaar met deugdelijk bestuur [A Belgian model for multiple voting rights shares compatible with corporate governance], Brussels, October 2006, www.guberna.be (study and proposal commissioned by the Belgian Parliament Committee on Economic Affairs); H. DE WULF, "Meervoudig stemrecht in vennootschappen: flexibiliteit gewenst", *Van alle markten. Liber Amicorum Eddy Wymeersch*, Antwerp, Intersentia, 2008, 369-395.

An alternative way to reward faithful shareholders is a loyalty dividend. This is also allowed in France[144] and it was recently considered in Germany[145] and the Netherlands[146]. The loyalty dividend raises fundamental issues of equal treatment under Article 42 of the Second Company Law Directive[147] as well as many technical questions. For now, we will limit ourselves to two general observations. First, the law of most EU Member States tends to be more flexible as to unequal treatment in relation to dividend rights than voting rights. Secondly, a financial incentive seems to be a more effective measure for inducing shareholder loyalty than an extra voting right.

The unique feature of loyalty shares is that they do not constitute a separate class[148]: the extra voting/dividend rights are vested in the person rather than being attached to the share itself. As a rule, any shareholder who satisfies certain requirements can obtain the extra rights. Accordingly, the extra rights are usually lost when the shares are transferred. Although, in principle, the extra voting right cannot be valorised in a private sale of control since it is lost upon transfer of the underlying shares, it nevertheless provides an incumbent block-holder with protection against hostile takeovers as long as he holds on to his shares. In other words, the question remains whether loyalty shares do not amount to a disguised measure for the benefit of incumbents, for whom it will be less of a sacrifice to register their shares and to attend the general meeting than for retail investors, whose only protection often results from the fact that they can freely sell their shares[149]. Voting caps raise the same objection: although, in theory, they can be used in order to enhance the position of minority shareholders – and were originally introduced by the legislator for this purpose – by imposing an upper limit on the number of votes any shareholder can cast at a general meeting, they are in fact utilised to achieve the opposite effect (i.e. entrenchment

[144] Art. L. 232-14 Code de commerce.

[145] Bundesministerium der Justiz, Bericht über die Entwicklung der Stimmrechtsausübung in börsennotierten Aktiengesellschaften in Deutschland seit Inkrafttreten des Namensaktiengesetzes, p. 24 (http://www.bdi-online.de/de/fachabteilungen/7469.htm); M. STORCK and U. SCHNEIDER, "Doppeltes Stimmrecht für langfristig investierte Aktionäre im französischen Recht", *AG* 2008, 700-706.

[146] In the recent DSM case, the loyalty dividend was upheld under Dutch law: The Netherlands Supreme Court, 14 December 2007, JOR 2008, 11 (overruling Enterprise Chamber of the Amsterdam Court of Appeal, 28 March 2007, JOR 2007, 118). For comment, see: M.L. LENNARTS and M.S. KOPPERT-VAN BEEK, "Loyalty Dividend and the EC Principles of Equal Treatment of Shareholders", *ECL* 2008, 173-180.

[147] Although this point was not under scrutiny in the DSM case, it was addressed by Advocate General Timmerman in his advice; he believed that the loyalty dividend can be justified in the light of the envisaged aim of promoting long-term shareholding. Some commentators disagree, however, arguing that there is no legitimate aim, or that the measure is disproportionate.

[148] However, there remains some controversy on this point in France: see M. STORCK and T. DE RAVEL D'ESCLAPON, "Faut-il supprimer les actions à droit de vote double en droit français?", *Bull. Joly Sociétés* 2009, 92.

[149] If retail investors were to register their shares on a large scale, this could hamper liquidity.

of an existing block-holder). For this reason[150], double voting rights and voting caps are perceived negatively by institutional investors[151].

To summarise, whereas increased shareholder participation is a rather dubious motive for introducing 1S1V, it is equally dubious as a justification for the French system of double voting rights.

8.4. Restructuring (Other than in a Takeover Situation)

41. *Corporate mobility.* 1S1V could stimulate cross-border mobility of companies (freedom of establishment). To the extent that it could make control contestable, a 1S1V rule would facilitate hostile takeovers, which are a common means of establishing a subsidiary company (secondary establishment)[152]. The Takeover Directive (including the BTR) is indeed based on Article 44(1) in conjunction with 44(2)(g) of the EC Treaty[153]. However, the BTR is incomplete in the transactions it covers[154]. Other forms of corporate restructuring, such as cross-border mergers and transfers of seat, are subject to a qualified majority decision of the general meeting of shareholders without any reallocation of voting rights. Hence, these transactions may continue to be blocked by a minority holding less than 25% of voting rights. In addition, these transactions are almost inconceivable without endorsement by the board of directors, which is likely to be the captive of the leveraged shareholder. Thus, increased mobility could be an extra argument for 1S1V.

8.5. Uniformity: Level Playing Field and Legal Certainty

42. *Level playing field.* Another merit of 1S1V is that it attempts to achieve a certain degree of uniformity of capital and voting structures within the EU – although, admittedly, at the same time this may come at a cost of rigidity. A greater degree of uniformity would reduce the scope for regulatory arbitrage and competition. This is the classical rationale for company law harmonisation. A level playing field may be needed more than ever, now that companies can easily

[150] Time-phased voting rights also complicate the calculation of relative voting power, which can lead to unpleasant surprises (e.g. a shareholder can suddenly cross the mandatory bid threshold after the relevant time period has lapsed or even simply because another shareholder had sold his double voting rights shares).

[151] M. STORCK and T. DE RAVEL D'ESCLAPON, "Faut-il supprimer les actions à droit de vote double en droit français?", *Bull. Joly Sociétés* 2009, 90-96.

[152] See G.-J. VOSSESTEIN, *Modernisation of European Company Law and Corporate Governance: Some Considerations on its Legal Limits*, Ph.D. thesis, Universiteit Leiden, 2008, 102.

[153] G. KEMPERINK and J. STUYCK, "The Thirteenth Company Law Directive and Competing Bids", *CMLR* 2008, 99-101.

[154] J. RICKFORD, "Invisible Hand or Dead Hand? – Reflections on the EU One Share One Vote", in G. Mather (ed.), *One Share One Vote? – Tomorrow's Companies: One Universal Model or Tailored Equity Structures*, London, European Policy Forum, 2006, 73. Cf. the broad scope of art. 556 of the Belgian Companies Code (requiring specific shareholder approval for all decisions granting rights to third parties in respect of company assets or creating debts or obligations for the company that are subject to a takeover bid or a change of control).

change the applicable law through cross-border merger and/or the formation of an SE[155]. CEMs may constitute a primary consideration in the decision where to (re-)incorporate and, in turn, this may prompt Member State legislators to maintain or even expand the number of available CEMs. 1S1V would then be justified in order to avoid a European "Delaware effect". However, it is not certain whether such a race to the bottom is actually taking place[156].

43. *Legal certainty.* Alternatively, a uniform 1S1V regime could also be justified as promoting freedom of establishment and free movement of capital, simply by providing a greater degree of legal certainty. Legal certainty would be favourable not only for corporate restructuring but also for cross-border investments. Foreign investors in particular are often said to be deterred by CEMs since they are not familiar with them. Although the benefit of 1S1V would thus be mainly psychological in nature, uniform and transparent capital and voting structures would also reduce transaction costs.

First, increased uniformity and transparency could facilitate corporate restructuring. A lack of uniformity may cause legal uncertainty, especially in cases of migration where the applicable law changes[157]. An example will illustrate this: What happens if a Swedish SE, after having issued multiple voting rights shares, wants to move its seat to Belgium, where multiple voting rights shares are prohibited? What about Swedish public company with multiple voting rights shares that is planning to merge with a Belgian company? In these cases, 1S1V would allow companies to migrate more easily by providing a similar legal framework and thus legal certainty. 1S1V would thus justify harmonisation under Article 44 of the EC Treaty because it facilitates the free movement of companies as such, i.e. without focusing on the coordination of safeguards such as the protection of (minority) shareholders, creditors or other constituencies.

Secondly, 1S1V could also stimulate cross-border investments[158]. The free movement of capital (Article 56 of the EC Treaty) covers portfolio investments (for purely financial motives) as well as direct investments (with a view to participating in the management or control of a company)[159]. In this case, Article 95 of the EC Treaty could be used as an additional legal basis for positive harmonisation with a view to the completion of the internal market[160].

---

[155] See with specific regard to 1S1V: L. ENRIQUES, "Silence is Golden: The European Company Law Statute as a Catalyst for Company Law Arbitrage", *Journal of Corporate Law Studies* 2004, 77-95.

[156] For some observers, the trend seems to be rather in the opposite direction: G. FERRARINI, "One Share – One Vote: A European Rule?", *ECFR* 2006, 171-172 (citing the examples of Italy and Germany). However, in other Member States (e.g. Belgium) there is clearly a protectionist tendency, which has been amplified by the financial and economic crisis.

[157] G. PSARAKIS, "One Share – One Vote and the Case for a Harmonised Capital Structure", *EBLR* 2008, 731-732.

[158] G. PSARAKIS, "One Share – One Vote and the Case for a Harmonised Capital Structure", *EBLR* 2008, 726-727.

[159] Cf. the nomenclature set out in Annex I to Council Directive 88/361/EEC of 24 June 1998, which still informs the definition of free movement of capital.

[160] In this respect it can be noted that the Directive on Shareholders' Rights was based on both Article 44

44. ***Minimum harmonisation as a more realistic alternative?*** It is doubtful whether this rationale would be any more acceptable politically. From a legal viewpoint, the question is whether harmonisation on this basis could be justified in the light of the principles of subsidiarity and proportionality[161]. These principles seem to have gained significance[162]. More uniformity could also be achieved through minimum harmonisation of some CEMs (e.g. procedures for implementation, limits and safeguards). Such an approach would be less intrusive than a general 1S1V regime as some deviations would still be allowed. It would achieve more uniformity while at the same time allowing for some flexibility. But, as the failure of the draft Fifth Directive has shown, even then success is not guaranteed[163].

9. Negative Harmonisation of 1S1V and the Role of the European Court of Justice

45. ***Does One Share One Vote follow directly from the EC Treaty?*** If the pursuit of 1S1V through legislative measures would not be a realistic prospect in the light of the resistance of Member States[164], perhaps the emerging case law of the ECJ on golden shares could prove to be a powerful tool for reshaping EU company law and bringing down barriers to cross-border restructuring and investment that derive from national company law. This would amount to negative harmonisation, i.e. the removal of obstacles to free movement of capital[165]. Indeed, to the extent that 1S1V should already follow directly

and Article 95 of the EC Treaty.

[161] G. PSARAKIS, "One Share – One Vote and the Case for a Harmonised Capital Structure", *EBLR* 2008; V. DE BEAUFORT, "One Share – One Vote, Le Nouveau Saint Graal?" ESSEC Business School, Working Paper No. DR 06019, (2006).

[162] J. WINTER, "Ius Audacibus – The Future of EU Company Law", in M. Tison, H. De Wulf, C. Van der Elst and R. Steennot (eds.), *Perspectives in Company Law and Financial Regulation. Essays in Honour of Eddy Wymeersch*, Cambridge, Cambridge University Press, 2009, 46 et seq.; D. WEBER-REY, "Effects of the Better Regulation Approach on European Company Law and Corporate Governance", *ECFR* 2007, 404-407 (arguing that the EU, in pursuing 1S1V, would be in blunt violation of Better Regulation principles).

[163] Cf. *supra*, section 1.

[164] Cf. past experience with the Fifth Directive (general 1S1V) and the Takeover Directive (limited BTR).

[165] Arguably, golden shares also fall within the scope of freedom of establishment (Article 43 of the EC Treaty), but unlike in other areas of company law (e.g. cross-border transfer of seat, cross-border merger) the ECJ seems to give preference to free movement of capital. A contrary view was however expressed in the Opinion of AG Ruiz-Jarabo Colomer in Case C-112/05, *Commission v. Germany* [2007] ECR I-8995, paras. 57-60. Since no specific line of argument in support of a restriction on freedom of establishment was brought forward by the EC, the ECJ declined to rule on the basis of Article 43 of the EC Treaty. See G.-J. VOSSESTEIN, "Volkswagen: the State of the Art of Golden Shares, General Company Law and the Free Movement of Capital", *ECFR* 2008, 128-129; E. WERLAUFF, "Safeguards against Takeovers after Volkswagen – On the Lawfulness of such Safeguards under Company Law after the European Court's Decision in Volkswagen", *EBLR* 2009, 105-107.

from the EC Treaty, there would be no immediate need for secondary EU legislation[166].

46. *The "goldes share" cases.* The European Commission believes that golden shares have a negative impact on the completion of the internal market[167]. Since the late 1990s it has therefore instituted several infringement proceedings against Member States who were unwilling to give up their golden shares[168].

In its jurisprudence[169], the ECJ has adopted a broad approach in defining what measures constitute a "golden share": in short, the scope of the prohibition under Article 56 of the EC Treaty extends to legal structures applying to individual companies which contribute to preserving an influence of a public authority over such companies that is not based on, and proportional to, its investment and that is liable to impede or to deter investors from other Member States from investing in such companies. Golden share powers typically include the right to veto strategic management decisions, the right to appoint board members and the right to block takeovers or acquisitions by undesirable parties, even if the State's shareholding is reduced to a minimum or no longer exists[170]. These powers can be granted by or under public law provisions deviating from general company law or they can be attached to actual shares issued in accordance with private law (i.e. national company law itself may allow for deviations from 1S1V that can be exploited by the Member State *qua* shareholder)[171].

[166] See G. KEMPERINK and J. STUYCK, "The Thirteenth Company Law Directive and Competing Bids", *CMLR* 2008, 99-101 (comparable analysis of the implications of primary EC law with regard to competing bids, which were also left out of the Takeover Directive).

[167] Commission staff working document, Special rights in privatised companies in the enlarged Union – a decade full of developments, Brussels, 22 July 2005.

[168] As mentioned above, golden shares were excluded from the scope of the BTR (Article 11.7 of the Takeover Directive), although this was not intended by the Winter Group (Report on Takeover Bids, para. 4.2).

[169] Case C-367/98, *Commission v. Portugal* [2002] ECR I-04731; Case C-483/99, *Commission v. France* [2002] ECR I-04781; Case C-503/99, *Commission v. Belgium* [2002] ECR I-04809; Case C-463/00, *Commission v. Spain* [2003] ECR I-4581; Case C-98/01, *Commission v. United Kingdom* [2003] ECR I-4641; Case C-174/04, *Commission v. Italy* [2005] ECR I-4933 and Cases C-282/04 and C-283/04, *Commission v. the Netherlands* [2006] ECR I-9141; Case C-112/05, *Commission v. Germany* [2007] ECR I-8995; Cases C-463/04 and 464/04, *Federconsumatori v Commune di Milano* [2007], ECR I-10419.

[170] The fact that golden shares confer a disproportionate influence compared to the level of investment was stressed by the ECJ in *Commission v. Netherlands* (para. 22) and *Commission v. Germany* (para. 61-64). The nature of this disproportionality test remains obscure: J. RICKFORD, "Free Movement of Capital and Protectionism after Volkswagen and Viking Line", in M. Tison, H. De Wulf, C. Van der Elst and R. Steennot (eds.), *Perspectives in Company Law and Financial Regulation. Essays in Honour of Eddy Wymeersch*, Cambridge, Cambridge University Press, 2009, 73-75 and 78-79.

[171] See in particular Case C-98/01, *Commission v. United Kingdom* [2003] ECR I-4641 and Case C-283/04, *Commission v. Netherlands* [2006] ECR I-9141. Accordingly, it does not matter whether the Member State is acting as a legislator or simply as a shareholder: even when only acting within the realm of general company law, a Member State cannot grant itself special rights (J. VAN BEKKUM, J. KLOOSTERMAN and J. WINTER, "Golden Shares and European Company Law: the Implications of Volkswagen", *ECL* 2008, 9). Member States thus seem to have less freedom than private individuals when acting as shareholders. In both cases the ECJ still qualified the golden shares as "state measures". This would have been unnecessary if the free movement of capital also applied horizontally

47. *Horizontal effect?* So far, the case law has dealt with Member States rather than companies and citizens. An important question that needs to be answered is whether the free movement of capital also applies horizontally, in relationships between private parties exercising autonomous private law powers. If the prohibition of Article 56 of the EC Treaty would extend to all legal structures provided for in national company law which are liable to deter investors, this would help to create a level playing field[172].

Several scholars have taken this view[173], especially since, in its initial judgments, the ECJ nowhere stated that the scope of the prohibition was limited to legal structures that served to preserve special rights of Member States over privatised companies. Almost inevitably, in subsequent cases, the question was raised as to whether legislation which enables some shareholders to obtain certain special rights in order to shield them from the market for corporate control may itself constitute a restriction on the free movement of capital[174].

For other freedoms, the ECJ has already addressed the question of their horizontal effect. On the one hand, the Court has ruled that the prohibition against restrictions on the free movement of workers and services also applies to private bodies exercising rule-making functions with semi-public implications[175], and that the prohibition against discrimination even applies to any private individual[176]. On the other hand, as regards free movement of goods[177], the ECJ has judged that, even when Member States are not involved, they may still be responsible for guaranteeing the full scope and effect of the

(J. RICKFORD, "Free Movement of Capital and Protectionism after Volkswagen and Viking Line", in M. Tison, H. De Wulf, C. Van der Elst and R. Steennot (eds.), *Perspectives in Company Law and Financial Regulation. Essays in Honour of Eddy Wymeersch*, Cambridge, Cambridge University Press, 2009, 83 and 86).

172 Thus reducing the scope for regulatory competition and arbitrage that was set in motion by the ECJ case law on freedom of establishment: Case C-212/97, *Centros Ltd v. Erhvervs- og Selskabsstyrelsen*, [1999] ECR I-1459; Case C-208/00, *Überseering BV v. Nordic Construction Company Baumanagement GmbH*, [2002] ECR I-9919 Case C-167/01, *Kamer van Koophandel en Fabrieken voor Amsterdam v. Inspire Art Ltd*, [2003] ECR I-10155.

173 J. ADOLFF, "Turn of the Tide? The 'Golden Share' Judgments of the European Court of Justice and the Liberalization of the European Capital Markets", *German Law Journal* 2002, No. 8, para. 31-36; M. ANDENAS, T. GUTT and M. PANNIER, "Free Movement of Capital and National Company Law", *EBLR* 2005, 757-787; S. GRUNDMANN and F. MÖSLEIN, "Golden Shares – State Control in Privatised Companies: Comparative Law, European Law and Policy Aspects", *Euredia* 2001-2002, 623 et seq.

174 E.g. Opinion of AG Poiares Maduro in Cases C-282/04 and C-283/04, *Commission v. Netherlands* [2006] ECR I-9141, para. 24.

175 Case C-36/74, *Walrave* [1974] ECR 1405; Case C-415/93, *Bosman* [1995] ECR I-4921. This case law has also been applied to the freedom of establishment: see e.g. Case C-309/99, *Wouters* [2002] ECR I-1577, and recently Case C-438/05, *Viking Line* [2007] ECR I-10779.

176 Case C-281/98, *Angonese* [2000] ECR I-4139. The ECJ was more hesitant as to a pure horizontal effect in a recent case on the violation of the freedom of establishment by trade unions: Case C-438/05, *Viking Line* [2007] ECR I-10779, paras. 56-66 (compare the Opinion of AG Poiares Maduro, para. 31-48).

177 Case C-265/95, *Commission v. France* [1977] ECR I-6959; Case C-112/00, *Schmidberger v. Germany* [2003] ECR I-5659. The same reasoning was applied to freedom of services: see e.g. Cases C-94/04 and C-202/04, *Cipolla v Portolese* [2006] ECR I-11421.

freedoms under the EC Treaty. In other words, they may be responsible for not taking the necessary measures in order to prevent the Treaty's freedoms from being violated in relations between private parties[178].

At first sight, there is no reason why the extension into the private sphere could or should not apply to the free movement of capital as well[179]. The case law on the free movement of capital has traditionally trailed behind, but it has picked up quite a bit over the past decade[180].

The ECJ basically has two options if it decides to expand the free movement of capital into the private sphere: it can either endow Article 56 of the EC Treaty with a direct horizontal effect[181], or – less sweeping and thus perhaps more plausible – it can proclaim an indirect horizontal effect (i.e. an obligation on Member States based on Article 10 in conjunction with Article 56 of the EC Treaty).

48. ***Hesitation by the European Court of Justice.*** However, in the Volkswagen case[182], the ECJ seems to have implicitly rejected the hypothesis that all legal structures which are liable to deter investors would fall within the scope of Article 56 of the EC Treaty[183]. The ECJ did not have to address the issue because the Volkswagen Law was clearly a state measure. Nevertheless, it was neutral legislation, laying down a special regime deviating from general company law (voting cap and supermajority provisions) without explicitly granting Lower Saxony any special rights. But instead of ruling that the Volkswagen Law itself was liable to deter investors, the ECJ explicitly relied on

---

[178] For a discussion, see P. OLIVER and W.-H. ROTH, "The Internal Market and the Four Freedoms", *CMLR* 2004, 422-423; G. FERRARINI, "One Share – One Vote: A European Rule?", *ECFR* 2006, 169-171.

[179] J. WINTER, "Ius Audacibus – The Future of EU Company Law", in M. Tison, H. De Wulf, C. Van der Elst and R. Steennot (eds.), *Perspectives in Company Law and Financial Regulation. Essays in Honour of Eddy Wymeersch*, Cambridge, Cambridge University Press, 2009, 55; J. RICKFORD, "Free Movement of Capital and Protectionism after Volkswagen and Viking Line", in M. Tison, H. De Wulf, C. Van der Elst and R. Steennot (eds.), *Perspectives in Company Law and Financial Regulation. Essays in Honour of Eddy Wymeersch*, Cambridge, Cambridge University Press, 2009, 85-86.

[180] L. FLYNN, "Coming of Age: The Free Movement of Capital Case Law 1993-2002", *CMLR* 2002, 773-805.

[181] A "pure" direct effect in relations between private individuals may be a bridge too far in the present state of EC law. Indeed, private individuals cannot rely on the justifications relating to public policy and public security (G. KEMPERINK and J. STUYCK, "The Thirteenth Company Law Directive and Competing Bids", *CMLR* 2008, 118). But things could be different for private institutions with quasi-regulatory powers (e.g. stock exchanges).

[182] Case C-112/05, *Commission v. Germany* [2007] ECR I-8995.

[183] J. VAN BEKKUM, J. KLOOSTERMAN and J. WINTER, "Golden Shares and European Company Law: the Implications of Volkswagen", *ECL* 2008, 11-12; G.-J. VOSSESTEIN, "Volkswagen: the State of the Art of Golden Shares, General Company Law and the Free Movement of Capital", *ECFR* 2008, 129-131; E. WERLAUFF, "Safeguards against Takeover after Volkswagen – On the Lawfulness of such Safeguards under Company Law after the European Court's Decision in Volkswagen", *EBLR* 2009, 111; P. ZUMBANSEN and D. SAAM, "The ECJ, Volkswagen and European Corporate Law: Reshaping the European Varieties of Capitalism", *German Law Journal* 2007, 1027 et seq.

the specific shareholding percentage of Lower Saxony[184]. As to the voting cap, the ECJ also noted that there is "a difference between a power made available to shareholders, who are free to decide whether or not they wish to use it, and a specific obligation imposed on shareholders by way of legislation, without giving them the possibility to derogate from it"[185], suggesting that CEMs which are introduced in the articles of association and which can be removed by a shareholder vote are in principle not covered by the free movement of capital[186].

Also in the recent AEM case[187], which is the first golden share judgment on the basis of a preliminary question, the ECJ declined to rule on the applicability of Article 56 of the EC Treaty to provisions of general company law[188].

For now, the question of whether all legal structures which are liable to deter investors infringe upon Article 56 of the EC Treaty remains unanswered. We can only hope that on the next occasion the ECJ will explicitly address it. If the ECJ were to decide that 1S1V follows directly from Article 56 of the EC Treaty, this would reduce the immediate need for legislative measures, while at the same time motivating Member States to address the issue of 1S1V themselves through positive (minimum) harmonisation.

49. *Limits of negative harmonisation.* Whatever the chances of the ECJ coming to the rescue, at best its rulings could ban all legal structures which are liable to deter investors, but factual structures such as pyramids would remain out of reach. Nor would its jurisprudence be likely to extend to non-listed companies, since for those companies it would be more difficult to demonstrate an impact on free movement of capital[189].

---

[184] J. RICKFORD, "Free Movement of Capital and Protectionism after Volkswagen and Viking Line", in M. Tison, H. De Wulf, C. Van der Elst and R. Steennot (eds.), *Perspectives in Company Law and Financial Regulation. Essays in Honour of Eddy Wymeersch*, Cambridge, Cambridge University Press, 2009, 80; J. VAN BEKKUM, J. KLOOSTERMAN and J. WINTER, "Golden Shares and European Company Law: the Implications of Volkswagen", *ECL* 2008, 11-12; G.-J. VOSSESTEIN, "Volkswagen: the State of the Art of Golden Shares, General Company Law and the Free Movement of Capital", *ECFR* 2008, 123.

[185] *Commission v. Germany*, para. 40.

[186] E. WERLAUFF, "Safeguards against Takeovers after Volkswagen – On the Lawfulness of such Safeguards under Company Law after the European Court's Decision in Volkswagen", *EBLR* 2009, 107-108.

[187] Cases C-463/04 and 464/04, *Federconsumatori v Commune di Milano* [2007], ECR I-10419.

[188] In the AEM case, a special nomination right was inserted in the articles of association by a decision of the general meeting and with the public authority acting as an ordinary shareholder. However, the ECJ stressed that it was not ruling on the applicability of Article 56 of the EC Treaty to provisions of general company law because, pursuant to art. 2449 of the Italian Civil Code, only the State or a public authority were entitled to such a special nomination right (provided that it had been adopted in the articles).

[189] S. GRUNDMANN and F. MÖSLEIN, "Golden Shares – State Control in Privatised Companies: Comparative Law, European Law and Policy Aspects", *Euredia* 2001-2002, 657-658.

10. Conclusion

50. ***Need for harmonisation.*** The EU legislator, by imposing a mandatory bid rule for all Member States, has expressed a preference for dispersed ownership of listed companies. In the long run, the continental EU will gradually converge towards the UK model. The mandatory bid rule reduces the probability that a BTR or a general 1S1V would lead to greater ownership concentration *ex ante* (unlike what happened, for example, in Belgium in the 1930s). A consistent BTR has an added value in speeding up this process, slowed down in part by grandfathering and exemptions from the mandatory bid rule, because it exposes existing block-holders to the market for corporate control. While contestability of control would solve most of the problems, the merits of 1S1V are not limited to takeovers and therefore a general 1S1V rule should at least be reconsidered. A Fifth or Ninth Directive would be useful to resolve closely related issues (e.g. board rules and structure, pyramids) and would constitute a less intrusive means of achieving a higher degree of uniformity while allowing for some flexibility. Finally, if the political support for further legislative action continues to be lacking, the ECJ case law on the free movement of capital could be a promising substitute for secondary EU legislation.

Bibliography

R. ADAMS and D. FERREIRA, "One Share, One Vote: The Empirical Evidence", ECGI Finance Working Paper no. 177/2007, 2007 (http://ssrn.com/abstract=987488).

J. ADOLFF, "Turn of the Tide?: The 'Golden Share' Judgments of the European Court of Justice and the Liberalization of the European Capital Markets", *German Law Journal* 2002/8 (http://germanlawjournal.com/article.php?id=170).

H. ALMEIDA and D. WOLFENZON, "A Theory of Pyramidal Ownership and Family Business Groups", *Journal of Finance* 2006, 2637-2681.

M. ANDENAS, T. GUTT and M. PANNIER, "Free Movement of Capital and National Company Law", *EBLR* 2005, 757-787.

B. ARRUÑADA and C. PAZ-ARES, "The Conversion of Ordinary Shares into Non-Voting Shares", in D. HEREMANS and H. COUSY (eds.), *Essays in Law and Economics, III Financial Markets and Insurance*, Antwerp, Maklu, 1996, 129-161.

G. BACHMANN, "Strengthening Shareholders' Rights: A Comment on the EU Action Plan", *ERA Forum* 2005, 352-362.

S. BAINBRIDGE, "The Scope of the SEC's Authority over Shareholder Voting Rights", UCLA School of Law Research Paper No. 07-16 (2007) (http://papers.ssrn.com/abstract=985707).

B. BASTUCK, and C. KOENIG, "The Concept of 'One Share – One Vote' in EC Company Law", *Butterworths Journal of International Banking and Financial Law* 1991, 170-174.

J. BAUGNIET, *La réglementation du droit de vote dans les sociétés anonymes*, Brussels, Bruylant, 1935, 114 p.

V. BEAUFORT DE, "One Share – One Vote, Le Nouveau Saint Graal?" ESSEC Business School, Working Paper no. DR 06019, 2006 (http://ideas.repec.org/p/ebg/essewp/dr-06019.html).

L. BEBCHUK, "The Case for Increasing Shareholder Power", *Harvard Law Review* 2005, 833-914.

L. BEBCHUK, R. KRAAKMAN, and G. TRIANTIS, "Stock Pyramids, Cross-Ownership, and Dual Class Equity – The Mechanisms and Agency Costs of Separating Control from Cash-Flow Rights", in R. Morck (ed.), *Concentrated Corporate Ownership*, Chicago, University of Chicago Press, 2000, 295-315.

L. BEBCHUK, A. COHEN, and A. FERRELL, "What Matters in Corporate Governance?", Harvard Discussion Paper No. 49109, 2004, revised 03/2005 (http://papers.ssrn.com/abstract_id=593423).

L. BEBCHUK, "A Rent-Protection Theory of Corporate Ownership and Control", NBER Working Paper No. 7203, 1999 (http://www.nber.org/papers/w7203).

L. BEBCHUK, "Efficient and Inefficient Sales of Corporate Control", *Quarterly Journal of Economics* 1994, 957-994.

L. BEBCHUK, "Toward Undistorted Choice and equal Treatment in Corporate Takeovers", *Harvard Law Review* 1985, 1695-1808.

M. BECHT, "Reciprocity in Takeovers", in G. FERRARINI, K.J. HOPT, J. WINTER and E. WYMEERSCH (eds.), *Reforming Takeover and Company Law in Europe*, Oxford, Oxford University Press, 2004, 647-675.

M. BECHT, A. CHAPELLE, and L. RENNEBOOG, "Shareholding Cascades: The Separation of Ownership and Control in Belgium", in F. BARCA and M. BECHT (eds.), *The Control of Corporate Europe*, Oxford University Press, 2001, 71-105.

M. BENNEDSEN, and K. MEISNER NIELSEN, "The Impact of a Break-Through Rule on European Firms", CEBR Discussion Paper, 2002 (http://papers.ssrn.com/abstract_id=328020).

M. BENNEDSEN and K. MEISNER NIELSEN, "The Principle of Proportional Ownership, Investor Protection and Firm Value in Western Europe", ECGI Finance Working Paper No. 134, 2006.

E. BERGLÖF and M. BURKART, "European Takeover Regulation", *Economic Policy* 2003, 173-213.

A. BERLE and G. MEANS, *The Modern Corporation and Private Property,* New York, MacMillan, 1933.

C. BLANAID, "Articles 9 and 11 of the Takeover Directive (2004/25) and the Market for Corporate Control", *Journal of Business Law* 2006, 355-374.

J. BONRIGHT and G. MEANS, *The holding company: its public significance and its regulation*, New York, McGraw-Hill, 1932.

M. BURKART and S. LEE, "The One Share One Vote Debate: A Theoretical Perspective", ECGI Finance Working Paper No. 176/2007, May 2007 (http://ssrn.com/abstract=987486).

J. COATES, "Ownership, Takeovers and EU Law: How Contestable Should EU Corporations Be?", in G. FERRARINI, K.J. HOPT, J. WINTER and E. WYMEERSCH (eds.), *Reforming Takeover and Company Law in Europe*, Oxford, Oxford University Press, 2004, 677-709.

J. COFFEE Jr., "The Rise of Dispersed Ownership: The Role of Law in the Separation of Ownership and Control", *Yale Law Journal* (2001), 1.

B. COLMANT, A. DETOURNAI and L. SERVATY, *La décote boursière des holdings belges : décrypter l'énigme financière*, Cahiers Financiers, Brussels, De Boeck & Larcier, 2003, 150 p.

S. COOLS, "The Real Difference in Corporate Law between the United States and Continental Europe: Distribution of Powers", *Delaware Journal of Corporate Law* 2005, 697-766.

H. DE WULF, "Meervoudig stemrecht in vennootschappen: flexibiliteit gewenst" [Multiple voting rights in companies: flexibility wanted], *Van alle markten. Liber Amicorum Eddy Wymeersch*, Antwerp, Intersentia, 2008, 369-395.

C. DUNLAVY, "Corporate Governance in Late 19th-Century Europe and the U.S.: The Case of Shareholder Voting Rights", in K.J. HOPT, H. KANDA, M. ROE, E. WYMEERSCH and S. PRIGGE (eds.), *Comparative Corporate Governance: The State of the Art and Emerging Research*, Oxford, Clarendon Press, 1998, 5-39.

F. EASTERBROOK and D. FISCHEL, *The Economic Structure of Corporate Law*, Cambridge, Harvard University Press, 1991.

L. ENRIQUES, "Silence is Golden: The European Company Law Statute as a Catalyst for Company Law Arbitrage", *Journal of Corporate Law Studies* 2004, 77-95.

M. FACCIO and L. LANG, "The Separation of Ownership and Control: An Analysis of Ultimate Ownership in Western European Companies", Working Paper 2000 (http://papers.ssrn.com/abstract_id=222429).

G. FERRARINI, "One Share – One Vote: A European rule?", *European Company and Financial Law Review* 2006, 147-177.

L. FLYNN, "Coming of Age: The Free Movement of Capital Case Law 1993-2002", *Common Market Law Review* 2002, 773-805.

K. GEENS and M. WYCKAERT, "Les espaces de liberté contractuelle dans le droit des sociétés à responsabilité limitée: entre rapprochement et palliation", in Commission Royale Droit et Vie des Affaires (ed.), *Les espaces de liberté en droit des affaires*, Brussels, Bruylant, 2007, 139-189 (http://www.cdva.be/).

R. GILSON, "Controlling Shareholders and Corporate Governance: Complicating the Comparative Taxonomy", *Harvard Law Review* (2006), 1641-1679; and (abbreviated version): "Controlling Shareholders and Corporate Governance", in G. MATHER (ed.), *One Share One Vote? – Tomorrow's Companies: One Universal Model or Tailored Equity Structures*, London, European Policy Forum, 2006, 27-43.

S. GROSSMAN and O. HART, "One-Share/One-Vote and the Market for Corporate Control", *Journal of Financial Economics* 1988, 175.

S. GROSSMAN and O. HART, "Takeover Bids, the Free-Rider Problem and the Theory of the Corporation", *Bell Journal of Economics* 1980, 42-64.

S. GRUNDMANN and F. MÖSLEIN, "Golden Shares – State Control in Privatised Companies: Comparative Law, European Law and Policy Aspects", *Euredia* 2001-2002, 623.

J.L. HANSEN, "The Nordic Corporate Governance Model – A European Model?", in M. TISON, H. DE WULF, C. VAN DER ELST and R. STEENNOT (eds.), *Perspectives in Company Law and Financial Regulation. Essays in Honour of Eddy Wymeersch*, Cambridge, Cambridge University Press, 2009, 145-161.

M. HARRIS and A. RAVIV, "Corporate Governance: Voting Rights and Majority Rules", *Journal of Financial Economics* 1988, 203.

H. HIRTE, "The Takeover Directive – a Mini-Directive on the Structure of the Corporation: Is it a Trojan Horse?", *European Company and Financial Law Review* 2004, 1-19.

M. HOLMEN and P. HÖGFELDT, "Pyramidal Discounts: Tunnelling or Agency Costs?", ECGI Finance Working Paper 73/2005.

H. HU and B. BLACK, "Hedge Funds, Insiders, and Decoupling of Economic and Voting Ownership in Public Companies", ECGI Law Working Paper No. 56, 2006 (http://ssrn.com/abstract=874098).

M. JENSEN and W. MECKLING, "Theory of the Firm: Managerial Behavior, Agency Costs, and Ownership Structure", *Journal of Financial Economics* 1976, 305-360.

M. KAHAN, "Sales of Corporate Control", *Journal of Law, Economics, and Organization* 1993, 368-379.

G. KEMPERINK and J. STUYCK, "The Thirteenth Company Law Directive and Competing Bids", *Common Market Law Review* 2008, 93-130.

A. KHACHATURYAN, "Trapped in Delusions: Democracy, Fairness and the One-Share-One-Vote Rule in the European Union", *European Business Organisation Law Review* 2007, 333-367.

R. KRAAKMAN, P. DAVIES, H. HANSMANN, G. HERTIG, K.J. HOPT, H. KANDA and E. ROCK, *The Anatomy of Corporate Law – A Comparative and Functional Approach*, Oxford, Oxford University Press, 2004, 231 p.

R. LA PORTA, F. LOPEZ DE SILANES, A. SHLEIFER, and R. VISHNY, "Investor Protection and Corporate Governance", *Journal of Financial Economics* 2000, 3-27.

R. LA PORTA, F. LOPEZ DE SILANES, and A. SHLEIFER, "Corporate Ownership Around the World", *Journal of Finance* (1999), 471-517.

R. LA PORTA, F. LOPEZ DE SILANES, A. SHLEIFER and R. VISHNY, "Law and Finance", NBER Working Paper No. 5661, 1996; and *Journal of Political Economy* 1998, 1113-1155.

P. LE CANNU, "Limitations du droit de vote et contrôle des sociétés anonymes (réflexions sur la proposition modifiée de cinquième directive en droit des sociétés)", *Bulletin Joly* 1991, 263.

I. LEE, "Fairness, Finance and Dual Class Share Structures", in G. MATHER (ed.), *One Share One Vote? – Tomorrow's Companies: One Universal Model or Tailored Equity Structures*, London, European Policy Forum, 2006, 9-10.

M.L. LENNARTS, and KOPPERT-VAN BEEK, M.S., "Loyalty Dividend and the EC Principles of Equal Treatment of Shareholders", *European Company Law* 2008, 173-180.

A. LICHT, C. GOLDSCHMIDT and S. SCHWARTZ, "Culture, Law and Corporate Governance", *International Review of Law and Economics* 2005, 229.

H. MANNE, "Mergers and the Market for Corporate Control", *Journal of Political Economy* 1965, 110-20.

R. MASULIS, C. WANG and F. XIE, "Agency Problems at Dual-Class Companies", ECGI Finance Working Paper no. 209/2008, 2008.

G. MATHER, (ed.), *One Share One Vote – Tomorrow's Companies: One Universal Model or Tailored Equity Structures*, London, European Policy Forum, 2006, 84 p.

J. McCAHERY, L. RENNEBOOG, P. RITTER, and S. HALLER, "The Economics of the Proposed European Takeover Directive", in G. FERRARINI, K.J. HOPT, J. WINTER and E. WYMEERSCH (eds.), *Reforming Takeover and Company Law in Europe*, Oxford, Oxford University Press, 2004, 575-645.

J. MEYERS, "Agenda Items for the Revision of the European Takeover Bid Directive", in X. (ed.), *Van alle markten. Liber Amicorum Eddy Wymeersch*, Antwerp, Intersentia, 2008, 693-709.

R. MORCK, "Why some double taxation might make sense: the special case of inter-corporate dividend", University of Alberta Center for Financial Research Working Paper No. 03-01 (2003) (http://papers.ssrn.com/abstract_id=369220).

P. MÜLBERT, "Is There a Case for One Share One Vote?", in G. MATHER (ed.), *One Share One Vote? – Tomorrow's Companies: One Universal Model or Tailored Equity Structures*, London, European Policy Forum, 2006, 1-6.

P. MÜLBERT, "Make It or Break It: The Break-Through Rule as a Break-Through for the European Takeover Directive?", in G. FERRARINI, K.J. HOPT, J. WINTER and E. WYMEERSCH (eds.), *Reforming Takeover and Company Law in Europe*, Oxford, Oxford University Press, 2004, 711-736.

M.P. NIEUWE WEME, *Het verplicht bod op effecten* [The mandatory bid for securities], Van der Heijden Instituut no. 80, Kluwer, Deventer, 2004.

P. OLIVER and W.-H. ROTH, "The Internal Market and the Four Freedoms", *Common Market Law Review* 2004, 407-441.

A. PACCES, *Featuring Control Power: Corporate Law and Economics Revisited*, Ph.D. thesis, Erasmus Universiteit Rotterdam, RILE, 2008, 821 p.

A. POUTIANEN, "Shareholders and Corporate Governance: The Principle of One Share One Vote" *European Business Law Review* 2001, 67-75.

G. PSARAKIS, "One Share – One Vote and the Case for a Harmonised Capital Structure", *European Business Law Review* 2008, 709-733.

S. RAMMELOO, "Past, Present (and Future?) of the German Volkswagengesetz under the EC Treaty", *European Company Law* 2007, 118-121.

J. RICKFORD, "Free Movement of Capital and Protectionism after Volkswagen and Viking Line", in M. TISON, H. DE WULF, C. VAN DER ELST and R. STEENNOT (eds.), *Perspectives in Company Law and Financial Regulation. Essays in Honour of Eddy Wymeersch*, Cambridge, Cambridge University Press, 2009, 61-90.

J. RICKFORD, "Invisible Hand or Dead Hand? – Reflections on the EU One Share One Vote", in G. MATHER (ed.), *One Share One Vote? – Tomorrow's Companies: One Universal Model or Tailored Equity Structures*, London, European Policy Forum, 2006.

J. RICKFORD, "The Emerging European Takeover Law from a British Perspective", *European Business Law Review* 2004, 1379-1421.

M. ROE, *Political Determinants of Corporate Governance*, New York, Oxford University Press, 2003. R. SKOG, "The Takeover Directive, the 'Breakthrough' Rule and the Swedish System of Dual Class Common Stock", *European Business Law Review* 2004, 1439-1451.

M. STORCK, and U. SCHNEIDER, "Doppeltes Stimmrecht für langfristig investierte Aktionäre im französischen Recht", *Aktiengesellschaft* 2008, 700-706.

M. STORCK and T. DE RAVEL D'ESCLAPON, "Faut-il supprimer les actions à droit de vote double en droit français?", *Bulletin Joly Sociétés* 2009, 90-96.

J. VAN BEKKUM, J. KLOOSTERMAN and J. WINTER, "Golden Shares and European Company Law: the Implications of Volkswagen", *European Company Law* 2008, 6-12.

G.-J. VOSSESTEIN, "Volkswagen: the State of the Art of Golden Shares, General Company Law and the Free Movement of Capital", *European Company and Financial Law Review* 2008, 115-133.

G.-J. VOSSESTEIN, *Modernisation of European Company Law and Corporate Governance: Some Considerations on its Legal Limits*, Ph.D. thesis, Universiteit Leiden, 2008, 237 p.

E. WERLAUFF, "Safeguards against Takeover after Volkswagen – On the Lawfulness of such Safeguards under Company Law after the European Court's Decision in Volkswagen", *European Business Law Review* 2009, 101-117.

H. WILLEMS, "Multiple voting right in the general meeting of shareholders in Belgium during the interbellum period", in C. BRAUTASET (ed.), Business History Unit Occasional Paper Series, London School of Economics, 2005, 1, 69-95 (www.scob.be).

J. WINTER, "Ius Audacibus – The Future of EU Company Law", in M. TISON, H. DE WULF, C. VAN DER ELST and R. STEENNOT (eds.), *Perspectives in Company Law and Financial Regulation. Essays in Honour of Eddy Wymeersch*, Cambridge, Cambridge University Press, 2009, 43-60.

J. WOUTERS, "European Company Law: Quo Vadis?", *Common Market Law Review* 2000, 257-307.

E. WYMEERSCH, "The Takeover Bid Directive, Light and Darkness", UGent Financial Law Institute Working Paper No. 2008-01, January 2008.

E. WYMEERSCH, "The New Belgian Law on Takeover Bids", UGent Financial Law Institute Working Paper No. 2008-04, February 2008 (http://papers.ssrn.com/sol3/papers.cfm?abstract_id=1109048).

E. WYMEERSCH, "'One share, one vote' ou proportionnalité du droit de vote des actions", *Liber Amicorum Guy Keutgen*, Brussels, Bruylant, 2008, 209-226.

P. ZUMBANSEN and D. SAAM, "The ECJ, Volkswagen and European Corporate Law: Reshaping the European Varieties of Capitalism", CLPE Research Paper 30/2007 (http://ssrn.com/abstractid=1030652) and *German Law Journal* 2007, 1027.

Transcripts of One Share, One Vote Session

Paper: *Koen Geens and Carl Clottens*
Respondent: *José M. Garrido Garcia (University of Castilla-La Mancha)*
Chair: *Peter Montagnon (Association of British Insurers)*
Rapporteur: *Deborah Janssens (K.U.Leuven)*

A. Abstract

Dispersed versus concentrated ownership in the EU? The group first focused on the speakers' proposition that, by introducing the mandatory bid rule (MBR) in the Thirteenth Company Law Directive, the EU "chose clearly for a dispersed shareholder structure". The respondent and the intervening speakers seemed to agree that no such conscious decision was taken at EU level. Rather, minority protection was the EU rationale for the introduction of the MBR. The group also seemed to agree that the speakers' proposition needed to be nuanced in that the MBR had the effect of freezing concentrated ownership existing at the time of its introduction (potential acquirers of the stake being deterred by the threat of the MB), but probably did increase the obstacle to acquiring controlling stakes after its introduction, thus favouring dispersed ownership. Regardless of whether or not there was a conscious or unconscious EU decision to favour dispersed ownership, the question is whether or not the EU is heading in this direction. Generally, the group's sense was that this was the case, for a variety of reasons including the fact that the EU needed to increase the size of its companies to remain competitive (assuming that bigger companies need more capital from a variety of investors). For the time being, however, the EU legislators have to cater for both systems (dispersed and concentrated ownership) and draft "one-size fits all" legislation, which is challenging.

One share, one vote (1S1V). A narrow majority seemed to support the introduction of a 1S1V system, but it is widely acknowledged that there is no political support, certainly not in the light of the financial crisis which drives politicians to favour concentrated (national) ownership. Opponents of the 1S1V system pointed to the importance of rewarding long-term investors, certainly in times of crisis and short selling, but the group seemed to agree that the distinction between long-term and short-term investors was difficult to draw, exacerbated by the fact that a historic investor would not necessarily (commit to) stay on in the long term, and that both types of investors were important in the market. In this connection, the group also stressed the importance of tackling the issue of pyramids, but there was insufficient time to explore this topic in further depth. Workshop members seemed to agree that what cannot be achieved by positive (or negative) harmonisation will likely be remedied by the market itself (as experienced in Germany and the UK). In times of crisis or restructuring, minority shareholders may impose 1S1V conditions for investing more capital. There may be a growing consensus towards neutral, or even non-neutral, disclosure of control-enhancing mechanisms (CEMs) and deviations from the 1S1V principle. 1S1V is, intuitively and implicitly, a way to promote further internal market integration.

B. Response to paper by José M. Garrido Garcia

This is a very controversial topic indeed and I am afraid that my position is also going to be very controversial and very provocative. The basic aim of my contribution is twofold. I will first discuss the unfortunate 1S1V proposal by the European Commission and then I will add some thoughts on what the proportionality principle, in my opinion, really means. I will conclude with what lies ahead in the future.

Let me begin with the history of the initiative. The Winter Group purposely left proportionality out of the Company Law Action Plan. The experience with the Takeover Directive (particularly the optional breakthrough rule) had shown that, politically, Europe was unwilling to advance further on the principle of proportionality. Even the Takeover Directive's breakthrough rule is not a full implementation of the proportionality principle, because if one is able to retain 25% of the capital of the company one is able to block the breakthrough. The breakthrough rule is therefore a type of "diminished proportionality". For these reasons, the prevalent idea of the high-level group was that the one share/one vote principle was not ripe. But Commissioner Bolkenstein had a different idea and thought that it was important to give a signal and include this principle in his study and, later, to everyone's surprise, Commissioner McCreevy announced that "the shareholder is king" and that he would investigate the possibility of introducing the proportionality principle. I believe most of us knew in advance what was going to happen sooner or later.

In respect of the study on proportionality that was then made, I would like to mention first that I have a lot of respect for everybody who participated in the study: the people involved are very prestigious academics and professionals. But nevertheless, I was very disappointed with the study.

I have a number of observations on the study in general. First, the study is not really a study on proportionality. It is a study on "control enhancement mechanisms" (CEMs), a very popular notion. To me, the term "control enhancement mechanisms" is used as the corporate law equivalent of "collateral damage". The word is often used, but what is really meant is management entrenchment, abuse of minorities, tunnelling, etc. I was not convinced either about the methodology of the study, which drew up confusing "smoke curtains" and was obsessed with the "Egyptian syndrome". This calls for some further explanation. First, "smoke curtains": the study included so many different CEMs that it was totally confusing. For instance, some of the statistics in the study state the number of control enhancement mechanisms available in each jurisdiction. This information does not really add any value. What does it mean that there are eleven control enhancement mechanisms in one country and three in another? One would have to assess each such mechanism individually: each mechanism is totally different, and the effects are different. Second, the "Egyptian syndrome": The Egyptian syndrome ironically refers to the fact that if you are obsessed with pyramids you will find them everywhere. For the authors of the study, a pyramid is any indirect holding of more than 20% in a public [listed?] company. This is a low and absurd threshold and, logically, the study found pyramids everywhere. In Spain, the study reported four pyramids while actually none of them is a real pyramid. In my opinion a pyramid exists when one controls a holding company which controls the underlying public company or companies. In the absence of control, I would not consider it a pyramid. The study also included a review of the relevant economic literature. This part of the study was also troubling because, while the efficiency debate seemed to indicate that it was more efficient to have 1S1V, the authors would then conclude that 1S1V vote should not be pursued. The study also included an investor survey, which was perhaps the most unfortunate part of the study, and this for the following reasons. First, the investor survey was taken among institutional investors and had a very clear bias mainly in favour of the opinion of Anglo-Saxon institutional investors, which does not help the debate in Europe. Secondly, and most importantly, we did not have the opinion of shareholder associations (for instance, in Scandinavia, shareholders' associations are very much against dual-class companies), which would have been very useful.

The result of the study proved very unfavourable for the debate because, first, it created the impression that one share/one vote is a very strong limitation of freedom of contract, putting rules before contract. Secondly, the study conveyed the impression that it was the intent of the European Union bureaucrats and international investors to disrupt the national economies, local culture and finance and so on. Thirdly, the study concluded that the European Union would be producing rules unsupported by empirical evidence. And finally, according to the study, the proliferation of control enhancement mechanisms in Europe would imply that the initiative would be futile because there are so many techniques for locking control that there is no use in imposing 1S1V.

In the aftermath of the study, we tried to find a way out of the problem at the European Corporate Governance Forum, at the level of the Forum Special Group, by proposing that disclosure of all deviations from proportionality would be enhanced, and, importantly, that such disclosure should not be neutral – i.e. the disclosure would be framed in a sort of comply-or-explain recommendation from the Commission. This would give a signal to the market that proportionality is positive and best practice. The mere fact that you have to provide explanations means that deviations are not the best practice but that the best practice is proportionality. Personally, I defended this idea. But the final position of the Forum was that they did not want to express any value judgement about proportionality or disproportionality. The end conclusion was that there ought to be disclosure but neutral disclosure, i.e. that no position, not even an implied position, should be taken as to what constitutes the better practice.

Finally, Commissioner McCreevy, as everybody had expected, changed his mind dramatically and announced that no action should be taken on 1S1V.

To me, the most worrying element in the entire initiative was the impact assessment made by the European Commission, which expressly stated that no rule should be introduced because there was no empirical evidence. If we are going to apply this sort of impact assessment from now on, I would venture that we will not have any European company law rule or corporate governance recommendation any more. The impact assessment may say that there is no empirical evidence about proportionality but what is the empirical evidence about minimum capital, or about, in fact, any company law rule? Is this a test that we will have to satisfy in the future? If we do have to satisfy that test, we are in fact favouring the status quo. It is notable that this impact assessment has not been applied to other kinds of rules recently enacted, for instance the Shareholders' Rights Directive: there are many rules in the Shareholders' Rights Directive that seem arbitrary at the least, but for which no impact assessment was made. In addition, the impact assessment also suggests that the cost of disclosure on disproportionality would be very high, which I do not understand: there is disclosure of corporate governance all over the European Union, there would be no incremental cost to insert this into disclosure. So, I was personally very disappointed: I believe that, from a corporate governance point of view, the most important thing is the control of a company by its shareholders and if we are abandoning this principle, I believe trouble lies ahead.

Now, some words about proportionality. I think the basis of proportionality is very clear: one's power should be proportionate to one's risk in the company. This is fundamental in capitalism in general. There is no contradiction in this case between efficiency and fairness. Proportionality, in my view, is a principle and one has to distinguish between rules and principles. A principle is general in nature, underpinning various rules and admitting different implementations. A rule is clear-cut, admitting no exceptions.

This proportionality principle, in fact, is implicit in many European rules. Of course, first of all there is the breakthrough rule, but that is optional. Secondly, the compulsory bid rule is only really effective with proportionality because, for instance, in a dual-class company, the price paid for the controlling stake is not reflected in the price paid for the other shares. In other words, the policy of the directive, which is to allow minority shareholders to share in the control premium, fails for this type of company. In a 1S1V company, minority shareholders receive their share of the control premium because the price is the same for all shares. Instead, in a dual-class company, the price will be different, so there will be a compulsory bid at a different price, resulting in minority shareholders not sharing the control premium. The same is true for companies where there is a voting cap. In such companies, the compulsory bid rule produces strange results: for instance, the buyer of a 30% stake in a Spanish company is forced to make a compulsory bid, but will not have control because the buyer will be limited to 10% of the votes. In other words, there are a lot of dysfunctionalities of the compulsory bid rule in a non-proportionality setting. A third example of a rule where the proportionality principle is implicit is the Shareholders' Rights Directive. The Shareholders' Rights Directive assumes that it is very important that shareholders in Europe are able to exercise their respective rights. One could question its use, considering that in many cases these votes are meaningless. A fourth example is our corporate governance policy. As opposed to the United States, our corporate governance policy relies on shareholders to assess the comply-or-explain statements. We do not rely on the control of agencies. This policy assumes that there is real control by shareholders.

I agree with most of the arguments that have been set out today in favour of proportionality. There are the arguments of the general fairness and efficiency of the principle, the simplicity of the capital structure and the fact that controlling shareholders need to invest heavily in the company, so that incentives are generally aligned with minority shareholders. Another important argument is that proportionality allows for an indefinite expansion of the shareholder base, which is much more difficult in the absence of proportionality (e.g. dual-class companies require intricate and difficult arrangements for growth if one wishes to maintain the voting power of the families). In addition, I believe that crises are much easier to solve under a proportionality regime. When there is a crisis in a company and recapitalisation is needed, it is very difficult to convince investors to invest in a company where they have no votes or very reduced voting power. In such instances, one of the first demands of the investors is changing to a 1S1V regime. Finally, proportionality allows the market for corporate control to work because votes by shareholders are or become meaningful.

One may query what the opposing paradigm is to proportionality. I do not believe that it is freedom of contract, because freedom of contract explains very little in company law. Actually, if freedom of contract were the main principle behind company law, company law would not exist.

"One man/one vote" is the opposing paradigm for companies in which the personal qualities of members prevail, such as partnerships. This is logical because in partnerships there is unlimited liability for partners. If a partner has unlimited liability, it is logical that he desires one man/one vote. This is confirmed by the corporate form of the *société en commandite par actions*, where the investors, shareholders, cannot remove the person in charge of the company who has unlimited liability.

One should also centre the proportionality debate correctly. There are true and false exceptions to the proportionality principle. One can achieve a functional equivalent result to disproportionality through different means. False exceptions are, for instance, preference shares, lacking voting right but entitling the holder to a special dividend. The voting right will be recovered if the dividend is not paid out. This is not a true exception to the proportionality principle because the holder of the preference share has less risk, and in return for less risk, he has less voice. He will be more exposed when he does not receive the dividend and will then recover his voting power. Other false exceptions are pyramids and derivatives. Shareholder agreements, even change-of-control clauses were also included in the study as exceptions to the proportionality rule. For me, these are equally false exceptions: there is no relation between the change-of-control clause and proportionality. Of course, some of these techniques or false exceptions heavily influence the control in a company but they are not directly related to proportionality. True exceptions to the proportionality principle are dual-class structures, voting and ownership caps, double voting rights, and non-voting shares.

The discussion on proportionality is often focused on dual-class structures and in my view that has some disadvantages. Firstly, because it is perceived as an attack on several economies in different countries and, secondly, it is my impression that some countries and companies are relying on, and hiding behind, others to make a strong defence on non-proportionality mechanisms. In Spain, for instance, the real exception to proportionality is the voting cap. Spain is quite happy to let the Scandinavians do the fighting and defend their dual-class structure companies, because if they succeed, Spain benefits and if they do not, they will attract all the attention and nothing will happen to Spain.

We discussed the question of pyramids and the difficulty of defining them before, in the context of the "Egyptian syndrome". I do not think that proportionality is marking a move to pyramids, since many factors contribute to the existence of pyramids. Aside from Belgium and Italy, there are countries in which proportionality is prevalent but there are no pyramids. This has been explained in the U.S., for instance, by the existence of tax rules on intercorporate dividends. In Germany the law on groups may have some influence, given the fact that there are fewer pyramids there than in other parts of Europe. Finally, it often goes unnoticed that pyramids are easier to build in a dual-structure system. For instance, the study revealed that the country with the largest number of pyramids is Sweden. I would like to conclude that the fact that there would be some alternative ways to arrive at the result that we consider undesirable is not a justification for inaction, because otherwise there would be almost no rules under private law.

The problem of deviations from proportionality exists, and it affects the integration of European capital markets because it is preventing international mergers in many cases. It is also preventing the creation of a European market for corporate control in many respects and affecting the protection of shareholders in the European Union. The solutions to the problem in many cases are not realistic. I think that, as I said before, the best approach would be a non-binding Commission recommendation to "comply or explain", with a strong position in favour of proportionality. So, to conclude, I am in basic agreement with the paper by Professor Geens and Mr Clottens, but are we representative of the academic, legal and financial community? I would say no: finding a round table with four people in favour of proportionality is difficult in the European Union these days.

I would like to add some points of debate: I do not believe that there is a conscious and articulated policy towards dispersed ownership in European companies. I followed the making of the Takeover Directive, also as member of the council and nobody said a word about having to create dispersed ownership. Actually, when the compulsory bid was discussed, the protection of minorities was the objective.

Finally, I would say that our problem today is that after the failed initiative we are in a sort of "scorched earth" situation and there is a sort of nihilism in corporate governance, because if you are not able to express a view in favour of shareholders having voting rights proportionate to the risk in companies, it is very difficult to argue for instance that the company should have independent directors, that there should be remuneration committees and so on. We are therefore back to square one. We face the challenge of rebuilding or building a European corporate governance system while avoiding the cornerstone of the system. I believe this was a big mistake – the time is not ripe for this problem now, but certainly will emerge again in the future.

C. Discussion

Peter MONTAGNON

I think that there is one thing that actually one can say with certainty on this subject: it is just about the most controversial issue that has been discussed in company law in Europe in a very long time and it is not entirely surprising that that should be the case, because it raises issues that are fundamental to the way that European capitalism works and, I believe, even fundamental to the way that some societies in Europe are constructed. At the extreme, this debate implies a choice, conscious or otherwise, between two systems: on the one hand, a system that favours block holders by giving them additional rights of control, which may then lead to better monitoring of management and possibly less short-termism, though it obviously also – and Professor Hopt alluded to this earlier – introduces the risk of extraction of private benefits and board entrenchment. On the other hand, there is a more dispersed ownership system which protects minority shareholders from expropriation and facilitates, I would argue, cross-border flows and therefore more of a creation of a unified European capital market, but which may actually be less effective in enabling the management to be monitored by shareholders. Supporters of the dispersed ownership system, of course, argue that the latter risk is offset by the proper operation of a market for corporate control, which acts as a continuing constraint on management, whereas the block holder system can actually lead to more management entrenchment. I do not think that we are going to reach final agreement on 1S1V this morning – it would be nice if we could – but what I hope we will be able to do in this discussion is to understand better the nature and the implications of the choices we are facing, and this, I think, is the important contribution of the paper that we are just about to discuss. What, for example, really is the impact of the mandatory bid rule introduced in the Takeover Directive, especially if accompanied by an effective – and I think the word "effective" needs to be underscored here – breakthrough rule? Is it the same, essentially, as introducing a 1S1V regime during takeovers? How far are we heading in that direction and what are the relative impacts of these various measures, and how do they interact, not just on companies, but also on the share ownership structure? Is Europe moving any way in the direction of dispersed ownership, and what should we do about that? Does the mandatory bid rule push us more inevitably in that direction? It is quite clear from what we have heard that our speakers are in favour of 1S1V, but I would really like to know whether the other participants of this workshop are in favour of one share/one vote. [*Follows a poll on the proportionality principle, in which about half of of the audience is sympathetic towards the general concept (irrespective of the question of legislation) whereas a small number of participants opposes it*].

I would just like somebody who has actually disagreed with what has been said to stand up and give us some alternative points of view to get the discussion going.

Gerard HERTIG, ETH Zürich

If you look at the current financial crisis, I am most convinced that the problem is having dispersed shareholders at the moment. In most companies one would prefer to have a controlling shareholder with a firm hand on the company: that is the way to raise capital, not the other way around. We should definitely be against a reform at this moment. More generally, the reason why it is so hard to argue in favour of 1S1V is that we do not have any empirical data and the empirical data we have are contradictory. From a political perspective, if you go out there, and you propose something which the opposition can counter with data, you will get murdered by the interest groups. This is the reason why the debate is not moving. So you have two ways: either you are against 1S1V and you are happy with the result now; or you are in favour of it, which implies that you will have to "shut up for the next ten years, gather your data, and come back when you have it".

Peter MONTAGNON

I would actually just like to put one thought that I consider quite important forward: there are market solutions that actually evolve over time and I think it is useful to consider the British experience in the 1990s. Before, in the UK, we had a lot of CEMs. At some point, a number of companies which had them wanted to raise capital, which the institutional investors in Britain refused, unless these companies would abandon this control. A discussion followed with these companies around the compensation that would be offered to remove the control enhancing mechanisms. In the end, the control enhancing mechanisms were removed and, in compensation, those who helped remove them got extra shares and the minority was further diluted. The minority felt that they would actually recuperate that loss through a corporate governance premium, which is, I believe, what happened. In sum, there was an amicable negotiation – never a legal pressure – which evolved to a situation where it is permitted by law to have CEMs, but basically very few companies actually use them, and it is not expected that a UK company will. But I think the point that is being made on raising capital is quite an important one. It may or may not be true that in the present crisis it is harder to raise capital if you do not have a controlling shareholder who protects you. I would postulate that within the present crisis, as people defend their national interests, they would be less interested in running the risk of outsiders coming in and therefore, at least politically, controlled ownership may become more important.

Another point to be considered is the one about dispersed ownership as being the model in Europe, or having a controlling shareholder as the model in Europe and whether we have made a choice in Europe to go towards dispersed ownership, and, if so, whether we have done so deliberately or as it were by accident through the mandatory bid rule, and what that might mean.

Paul DAVIES, University of Oxford

I would like to address the particular point about the relationship between the mandatory bid rule and the shareholder structure because I find it a very difficult question. I would like to formulate three propositions and see whether it is possible to go beyond these propositions.

The first proposition is that if you have actually got an existing dispersed shareholding structure, then it may well be that the mandatory bid rule makes it more difficult to move towards a concentrated structure for obvious reasons. But that is rather different from saying, as I think it said in the paper, that a mandatory bid rule induces a dispersed shareholding structure: my proposition is more a negative one than a positive one.

The second proposition is that in presence of a mandatory breakthrough rule, or even a mandatory 1S1V rule, a mandatory bid rule makes it slightly more difficult for an existing controlling shareholder to respond to that new rule by buying more shares in the company. In most cases, though, I believe that such controlling shareholder could move to having a blocking position in the company in terms of changes of the articles of association without triggering a mandatory bid rule.

The third proposition is that if there is already a concentrated shareholder structure, a mandatory bid rule makes control shifts actually less likely to happen because a potential acquirer who, say, has a dispersed shareholding structure and wishes to acquire a target with a concentrated shareholder structure has two options under a mandatory bid rule: (i) either he has to pay the minority shareholders the control premium, i.e. he has to pay them for something that they do not have, being control, or (ii) he fails to pay the controlling shareholder the full value of the control premium, which makes it presumably less likely that the existing controlling shareholder will sell out.

In sum, in the context of an existing controlling structure, I wonder whether a mandatory bid rule does not actually tend to freeze the structure rather than encourage dispersion. One final point: it seems to me that the impact of the mandatory bid rule might depend on whether it applies to shareholders which have already got existing blocks when the rule comes in, or whether they were grandfathered out of it, and perhaps even more important, I have a question as to what you do about shareholders with controlling blocks which acquire more shares after they have introduced the rule? I think this is something the Takeover Directive is unclear about.

Koen GEENS
Of course, everybody speaks from the national tradition he or she is familiar with. In Belgium, we have known the mandatory bid rule for a long time, but in a somewhat different context and it is because the context changed that maybe we came to make this provocative statement. In Belgium, mandatory bids were a matter of equality and of minority protection, because the mandatory bid was only triggered when a controlling shareholder was selling its shares to a new controlling shareholder, with a premium, i.e. when the price paid was higher than market price. So there was a lot of case law in Belgium, hard cases and bad cases indeed, centred around the question whether a control premium had been paid and "control" had actually been acquired. Indeed, it was not a matter of an objective percentage, it was not a matter of a market for corporate control that we wanted to maintain, it was just a matter of transfer of control by somebody who already had 50% and sold to somebody else who bought that 50%. So when the UK rule came in, we were amazed because on the one hand the control requirement was replaced by an objective percentage, as it is required by the Directive (in most countries now 30% to 33.3%), and, on

the other hand, there was no longer a premium requirement. I had thought that what the rule wanted to achieve was to guarantee in those companies a market for corporate control, i.e. when you have to launch a bid from 30% onwards, it automatically implies that a counter bid at that moment should still be possible because 30% is only 30% and does not necessarily imply control. The result is rivalling bidders who create a market price. So our view is that the mandatory bid rule as it is expressed now in the "Thirteenth" Directive is trying to maintain a market for corporate control in listed companies and that therefore one should be consistent by introducing 1S1V.

As to the second proposition, I completely agree. 25%, for instance, in Belgium is sufficient to block amendments to the articles of association.

Your third proposition touches on the grandfathering question, which Belgium knows a lot about. We could devote hours to this subject, because the Belgian legislation implementing the "Thirteenth Directive" was written in such a way that a lot of exemptions were made, not only in order to go beyond the 30% in certain ways without triggering the need to launch a mandatory bid (in case of certain capital increases, for instance), but also to grandfather existing situations. We did not address this issue in our paper because the issue is so Belgium-specific. But indeed, we think that, in Belgium, we will still live 30 to 40 years at least with companies in which control is frozen, even more frozen than before because the big fear of the controlling shareholders, of course, is to go below 30%. Since these shareholders do not want to go below 30%, it might even make growth by capital increases more difficult than before.

Klaus J. HOPT, Max Planck Institute

I will reiterate what we believed in the High Level Group, being that the topic is not really ripe, at least as far as politics is concerned. Now, of course that does not really prevent academia from thinking ahead, so I am grateful for both reporters and respondents to do that. I want to underline what Peter Montagnon said, namely that there are market solutions, maybe not immediately but certainly in the longer run. For instance, if I look to what happened in Germany, and compare it to what we had ten years ago, this classical capitalism has not disappeared, of course, but has been clearly weakened. Before, you could say basically that the Germany corporate landscape consisted of groups and banks. The evolution of the banks is noteworthy. Take Deutsche Bank: Deutsche Bank purposely reduced its seats on the supervisory boards of industrial companies. As a policy, they retreated from major participations and this set an example. Other banks followed voluntarily (others not so voluntarily). Private banks in Germany are a relatively small percentage compared to other countries and there is a realignment now between savings banks and state banks, so this also reduces bank capitalism. Thirdly, the financial market crisis made both the private banks (which were stabilizing the system) and the state banks lose credibility so this pillar is also breaking down. Now, as for the groups, of course they are still there, but the latest figures suggest that the public companies in the real sense (i.e. not controlled) are really on the way forward. I did not yet look at these figures closely and I do not know how representative they are but if it is true, this is a considerable change. I agree with Professor Gerard Hertig that the financial crisis requires strong boards and controlling shareholders, but what I do not think is that that this will take ten years.

José M. GARRIDO GARCIA

I think that the mandatory bid rule is definitely very important, but I do not think it guarantees dispersed ownership. What happened is the phenomenon that Paul Davies was describing before: a potential buyer of a larger stake in a company is, when negotiating the price, already taking into account that he will have to launch a mandatory bid so he is possibly not offering the price that he would have offered in the absence of the mandatory bid rule. From a cynical point of view, one could say that in the European countries where the European Takeover Directive imposed the mandatory bid rule, controlling shareholders have been expropriated: before, they were able to sell their shares at a control premium; now they have to share the control premium with the minority shareholders.

On dispersed ownership in general, I believe that what we should be concerned about in Europe is the size of our companies. If Europe needs to compete with companies in other parts of the world, it needs larger companies. We therefore need to favour integration. In my opinion, dispersed ownership is in many cases just a function of the sheer size of the companies. It is almost impossible to create a very large company which is controlled. From the point of view of the law, one cannot have legislation designed for dispersed ownership only or for concentrated ownership only. Legislation has to deal with everything because that is the current situation. Take Spain, for instance. In Spain we have lots of concentrated ownership companies and few dispersed ownership companies (which are the largest and the most important ones), so we cannot craft a legal system to deal with specific problems of dispersed ownership or the other way. We have to deal with everything, because we have everything.

Peter MONTAGNON

I do think that this seems to be rather an important point, actually, that we are facing a situation in Europe where we do have this mixture of systems, of dispersed ownership and concentrated ownership. The questions are (a) how do you get a framework fitting the whole when you have got this mix, and (b) to decide whether we are evolving in a particular direction. If we consider that we are evolving in a particular direction, the question is how far do we want to facilitate the evolution. In addition, if one is evolving any way, one would actually need to think ahead and have a framework which actually fits the situation where we will end up.

Hans DE WULF University of Ghent
First I would like to briefly mention that I agree with Paul Davies. I think one of the most interesting points in the paper by Koen Geens and Carl Clottens is their thesis that the mandatory bid rule induces dispersed ownership. I doubt that this will happen in the near future in systems which already have concentrated ownership.

According to Professor Garrido, a mandatory bid rule does not work in a system that allows dual-class companies and I see his point, but as he rightfully stressed, the main problem is that there will be no equal share in the control premium of the two or several classes of shareholders. My question is why should they share in the same way in the control premium? If there is a pre-existing dual-class system, this is not evident to me.

José M. GARRIDO GARCIA
I will give an easy example. For instance, imagine that you have a family here in Belgium, and you have the same family in Sweden, and both families decide to take their company public. Both families want to retain control. The Belgian family retains 51% of the capital, and the Swedish family creates a dual-class structure, whereby they have 10% of the capital and more than 50% of the votes. Twenty years thereafter, the Swedish family sells the 10% at a control premium to an investor and the investor buys the 10% at a premium and makes a bid to the remaining shareholders at a differing price (fixed according to quotation averages). At the same moment, the Belgian family decides to sell its 51% and the remaining shareholders get the possibility of selling at the same price. This does not make any sense. In the Takeover Directive you have very clear statements in the recitals that the compulsory bid is needed to ensure fair treatment of minority shareholders. If the objective is to try to ensure fair treatment of minority shareholders, I would respond that one can only guarantee fair treatment of minority shareholders under proportionality because under dual-class structures, the compulsory bid procedure offers no protection at all for minorities. That is the only point I am making.

In the case of preference shares, I do not see a reason to extend a compulsory bid to those shares because those shares are totally different from many points of view.

Piet BEVERNAGE, Ackermans & Van Haaren NV
Although it is intellectually attractive, I think I am only a cold lover of the concept of 1S1V. It starts from the principle that powers should be allocated in proportion to the risks that the shareholder bears. Now, we all know that there are shareholders with a long-term view and shareholders with a very short-term view. I will just refer to the Fortis case where we have shareholders who have voted in favour of the capital increase of the bank because they believed in the project and in the long-term business plan of management and so they put the

money on the table. They are now the losers in this case, and the winners are the short sellers, the funds who knew this was a very big bank in a very small country. There were two capital increases and they speculated on a decrease of the stock price and they ended up being the winners in this case. They have earned a lot of money in this terrible crisis. It may be interesting to discuss this conflict between long-term and short-term shareholders. Do they bear the same type of risk and should they therefore be allocated the same voting rights?

Peter MONTAGNON

I think it is very difficult to know in advance who is a long-term and who is a short-term shareholder. ("But maybe, if I like you, you can be a long-term shareholder.

Carl CLOTTENS

Your question reminds me of the French system of loyalty shares where a distinction is drawn between "loyal" shareholders and short-term shareholders. I personally think that is a dangerous distinction. Why would a long-term investor know better what the right decision is for a company? I also believe that double voting shares are not a practical solution in terms of transparency towards the market, in knowing how many votes a person has and whether or not this entails control (as this situation can alter suddenly when someone else sells his block of shares). I am personally not convinced that loyalty shares are the solution.

José M. GARRIDO GARCIA

I always have this discussion with my French colleagues. In a way, it looks like an attractive proposition; in reality what you get is a very subtle way of entrenching shareholders. In my opinion, a real long-term shareholder is the one who is going to stay in the future, not the one who has been there in the past. The fact that you have been there for so many years should not give you an entitlement to have more power in the future. So, I think, if your proposed system were to be logical – and this will sound very strange – one would have to gain votes not because one has been a shareholder for many years, but because the shareholder has a commitment to stay. I think nobody would like to give such commitment: no investor would like to sign a commitment to stay in a company for five years and receive double voting rights in return. I think that would not be popular.

Koen GEENS
Of course, I am very open to what Piet Bevernage is saying, because we have in Belgium a long tradition of controlled ownership in general. Let me pursue the example you gave: we have another Belgian listed bank which is more than 50% controlled, being KBC, and it survived the crisis somewhat better than Fortis – but of course it is always a question whether that is empirically and statistically relevant. We do know, on the other hand, that Fortis was able to grow much faster in the last ten years because of its dispersed ownership. It could, amongst other things, buy ABN Amro, which KBC could never have done because it was controlled and the shareholders would not have been able to follow. In conclusion, both models have their merits, and in different times, probably different merits. We live with a very complex reality in Europe, with different shareholder structures. The question is whether, with a level playing field in view, we should not try to find some coherent rules which we try to apply everywhere in the market because when you intervene with a mandatory bid rule, as we have now done, whatever it may have as a goal and as a purpose, and it intervenes in totally different situations, you get totally different effects. Therefore, I would hope that one day we would have a level playing field and 1S1V is certainly an element there.

Peter MONTAGNON
One must not consider the debate on 1S1V in isolation, and certainly in the Forum, we became very clear about this over the time we looked at it. I think it is very difficult to distinguish between who really is a long-term shareholder and a short-term shareholder, and I think it is terribly difficult to ever draw that distinction. But I think you can actually give people some comfort, for example, by having transparency arrangements that very clearly show empty voting and abuse through use of derivatives. I think that if you put those measures in place, as stand-alone measures or in tandem with moving towards one share/one vote, I think the market would become more comfortable with it. So there are things that you can do.

Henri SWENNEN, University of Antwerp
As I understand it, the ultimate question is whether the shareholders in the general assembly of shareholders exercise control on the board of directors. One of the problems with dispersed ownership in a company that is a possible target of a hostile takeover is that the only defence is making the share price sufficiently high, which is done by distributing huge profits annually to the shareholders to keep them happy. This has led to a lack of necessary investments in a lot of companies and leads to some kind of creeping winding up of the company by distributing profits time and again and not making investments. If these investors, after having taken the money, leave when there is no money left to be distributed, you may have a problem. As far as solutions to address this

problem are concerned, may I remind of something possibly horrible: in France under Mitterrand, in Belgium in the 1930s and 1980s, in the Netherlands in 1920 and in Great Britain in 1920, socialist governments proposed to have a *de iure* representation of absent shareholders at the general meeting by some kind of government official or a trustee. These proposals were buried, but one of the distinguished professors of the K.U.Leuven knew of these proposals and applied this concept in the first international Eurobasket debt issue where there was no control by the creditors. Because there was no general meeting of creditors holding debt papers (or "*obligations*" as it is called in our Belgian Companies Code), they created a trustee in the debt issuance contract. Why not encourage companies, within the framework of a corporate governance, to provide for a trustee in their articles of association who would represent long-term interest limited to a certain amount of votes, limited to interventions where it would appear that dispersed ownership will have a negative effect on the investments of the company and the economy as a whole?

Peter MONTAGNON

I suspect this is quite a controversial proposition. May I make one quick point about distribution policies and long-termism? I believe that to have a dividend distribution which is based on a company's ability to generate cash and whereby the company is committed to generate cash over the long term is a very good discipline for management. That is why we have always been quite worried about introducing solvency tests for dividends, because it allows for the sort of manipulation you are suggesting. I believe that if management knows that the company has to generate the cash to pay dividends over the long term, it helps them focus on the business. This is another way of looking at it.

José M. GARRIDO GARCIA

I think that the 1S1V debate just shows that Europe has become a place where there are very different legal systems. When the European Community was much smaller, you could dare to draft the Fifth Directive and to have an explicit provision imposing 1S1V. This is impossible to achieve today. Of course the academic debate must go on, for sure, but the problem is that from the point of view of politics, we are now in a dead end. There is no way we are going to advance. My principal concern now is how we are going to advance on corporate governance in the European Union, in particular because the 1S1V debate has done a lot of damage in two ways. The first damage done is that we now lack a real base for a corporate governance system. How should we explain our corporate governance system, and its enforcement, to Americans when we meet them? The Americans will tell us: in the U.S. we have this strict system of corporate governance (which we in Europe dislike profoundly), controlled by agencies. The Europeans will respond: we have corporate governance which is roughly based on a comply-or-explain regime, i.e. there is disclosure of corporate governance practices and "comply or explain" is applied. The Americans will query who judges this comply-or-explain rule, to which the Europeans will respond: the shareholders. However, if one digs in deeper, one realises that in many European companies shareholders do not have a real possibility of influencing management or the board, or influencing the controlling shareholders of the company. In sum, there is an enforcement problem. The other damage done is that the "empirical evidence" requirement currently applied for corporate governance initiatives makes it very unlikely that we will be able to advance. Funnily enough, now there are talks about introducing fair remuneration measures. Remuneration is not the most important part of corporate governance, but it is politically attractive. I am convinced that for remuneration, the policymakers are not going to apply the same test that they applied to proportionality: I am sure that we will not have empirical evidence of which remuneration regime is best. In conclusion, the problem is that when you have a difficult political situation, you will always be able to hide behind the lack of empirical evidence to defend inertia and preserve the *status quo*. This is really worrying because that will prevent progress in the area of corporate governance.

Koen GEENS

I would like to underline three things. First of all, 1S1V does not prevent controlled ownership; there is only a higher price to control. If I may reiterate this point: if you would do an IPO, a full IPO (not retaining 35% or 50%), and list the company on the stock exchange, this company will have to remain dispersed, because otherwise it will be taken private by a (mandatory) bid. But in all other situations, and there I agree completely with what Professor Davies said, 1S1V does not necessarily prevent controlled ownership.

Secondly, we did not have the debate on pyramids, which is a very complex debate, and I can tell you that in Belgium, as opposed to Spain, there are real pyramids. These pyramids had very good results in a certain way, but you have to admit that when you allow pyramids in the way we have them, it is difficult not to allow, in certain instances, multiple voting rights, because as far as I am concerned, the economic effect is rather identical. I understood José Garrido Garcia's argument that there are true and false exceptions to the 1S1V rule and I see the difference between pyramids and the 1S1V rule. I also realise that it is very difficult to develop rules that would forbid pyramids, such as obliging them to de-list the parent and the ultimate parent. In Belgium, we only have a rule extending the mandatory bid rule to acquisitions of mono-holdings so as to avoid the evasion of the mandatory bid rule, but for the rest we have no rules to constrain pyramids. Nevertheless, I consider the economic effect of pyramids and dual-class companies to be identical.

Last but not least, of course it is true that in the European Community only politically attractive things will pass. In this respect I understand and share the disappointment of José Garrido Garcia and appreciate his honesty. The Fifth Directive did not pass, because of the *Mitbestimmung* and other topics, but also because politicians understood what it was about. When it is really technical, such as the 30% mandatory bid rule, I do not think that most politicians really understand, which allows a rule to be adopted. For 1S1V, though, all politicians will understand, so it will be impossible, I fear, to have more than a recommendation within this and a number of years.

Belgian and European Accounting Law 30 years after the Fourth EC Directive

A route planner in a landscape scattered with (a growing number of) crossroads

Karel Van Hulle[1] *and Frank Hellemans*[2]
Jan Ronse Institute – K.U.Leuven

Abstract

Although financial reporting is, strictly speaking, not included in the Action Plan of the European Commission of 21 May 2003 on "Modernising company law and enhancing corporate governance within the European Union", the objectives of the Action Plan can only be achieved by means of a "fully integrated approach". Financial reporting is to be considered an important element of this fully integrated approach.

While having been a preoccupation of the Commission for over thirty years, European legislation on accounting has undergone drastic changes since the Communication of the Commission of 13 June 2000 on financial reporting.

In the present article, the authors focus on the evolution of European legislation on financial reporting since the aforementioned Communication and on the implementation of these European rules into Belgian legislation.

Considering that the European Commission radically changed its policy on financial reporting in its Communication of 13 June 2000, the authors investigate the reasons behind this policy change. They come to the conclusion that the main objectives of the Fourth Directive of 25 July 1978 on the annual accounts of certain companies and of the Seventh Directive of 13 June 1983 on consolidated accounts, namely equivalence and comparability of financial information published by limited liability companies, have only been met to a limited extent after the implementation of the two aforementioned directives.

An analysis by the authors of the European legislation on financial reporting since the Communication of the Commission of 13 June 2000 (the IAS/IFRS Regulation and the "modernisation wave" of the Fourth and Seventh Directives), and of the implementation thereof in Belgian law, shows that for the consolidated accounts of listed companies, the aforementioned legislation has largely provided a uniform

---

1 Professor K.U.Leuven, Head of Unit European Commission. The views expressed in this paper are entirely those of the author.
2 Professor K.U.Brussels and K.U.Leuven.

reporting framework. However, for non-listed companies, the objectives of equivalence and comparability of financial information have not been furthered by the aforementioned legislation – quite the opposite, in fact. The European rules issued since the Communication of the Commission of 13 June 2000 have led to even more divergence in financial reporting for non-listed companies than was the case under the old Fourth and Seventh Directives.

The authors also briefly analyse two issues the Commission has recently been dealing with (creation of a simplified business environment for companies in the area of accounting law; modification of IAS 39 and IFRS 7 with respect to mark-to-market accounting of financial instruments), thus evidencing the Commission's efforts to create a new reporting framework for SMEs and to improve the existing IAS/IFRS reporting framework for listed companies.

Table of contents

Introduction

1. ***The European Action Plan on modernising company law and the European Strategy regarding financial reporting: two sub-initiatives, one common objective.*** Looking at the European Commission's Action Plan of 21 May 2003 on "Modernising company law and enhancing corporate governance within the European Union"[3], it is already apparent from the introduction that the Commission has adopted a rather narrow interpretation of the concept of "company law" in this context. This immediately explains why accounting law

[3] Communication from the Commission to the Council and the European Parliament - Modernising Company Law and Enhancing Corporate Governance in the European Union – A Plan to Move Forward, COM (2003) 284.

or, to use the Commission's terminology, "financial reporting", is not included in the Action Plan.

However, the foregoing does not mean that from the Commission's perspective company law and financial reporting are not interlinked. Neither does it imply that the Commission's policy leaves (modernisation of) financial reporting unconsidered.

As a matter of fact, according to the Commission, the dual objective of the Action Plan, namely (i) increasing efficiency and competitiveness of companies and (ii) strengthening shareholders' rights and reinforcing third-party protection, can only be achieved by means of a "*fully integrated approach*". And it is precisely within the framework of this integrated approach that (among other things) financial reporting is addressed. In terms of policy, however, financial reporting is the subject of another, earlier Communication from the Commission – the Communication of 13 June 2000, explaining its "*Strategy*" regarding "*further measures*" in the field of financial reporting[4].

2. *Overview of the structure of this article.* In this paper, we will mainly discuss the developments in European and Belgian accounting law since the Commission's Communication of 13 June 2000.

However, in order to properly understand these developments, it is appropriate to look back at the situation before 13 June 2000. Indeed, recent developments in European and Belgian accounting law and the particular questions they generate can only be properly understood if they are situated against the background of the "Fourth" and "Seventh" Directives (the "Accounting Directives") concerning annual and consolidated accounts respectively. Indeed, the developments since the turn of the century and the proposals which are currently being developed imply a reconsideration of policy decisions that were made earlier. For this reason, we will first discuss the question of whether and, if so, why the Fourth and Seventh Directives have not or have only insufficiently achieved their objectives (section 1).

Then we will examine the European developments, both in the field of IAS/IFRS (section 2) and the corresponding amendments to the Fourth and Seventh Directives (section 3).

Next, we will discuss in detail how the Belgian legislator has transposed the European legislation into national law (section 4).

[4] Communication from the Commission to the Council and the European Parliament - EU Financial Reporting Strategy: the way forward, *COM* (2000) 359.

On the basis of the (current) situation of the European and Belgian legislation, we will then present an overview of the many different ways in which annual and consolidated accounts can be prepared within the European Union today (section 5). This overview will show that, at least with respect to non-listed companies, the situation that currently exists is very different from the harmonisation that was planned 30 years ago with the Fourth and Seventh Directives.

In the sixth and final section, we will examine the two "hot issues" that are currently being discussed at the European level: the special treatment of "micro entities" and the amendments to IAS 39.

We will conclude with some general considerations regarding the development of accounting law in the last three decades and the likely developments in the future.

1. Harmonisation under the Fourth and Seventh Directives: (why) a bridge too far?

1.1 The main objectives of the Fourth[5] and Seventh[6] Directives

3. ***General. Why harmonise accounting standards?*** Harmonisation of accounting standards is not specifically provided for in the EC Treaty. It is part of the company law harmonisation programme initially provided for in Article 54(3)(g) of the EC Treaty (now Article 44(1)).

In general, the harmonisation of company law should promote freedom of establishment for companies and firms by providing an equivalent level of protection for members (shareholders and employees) and other persons (mainly creditors) in all Member States.

The harmonisation of accounting standards also serves a number of specific objectives[7]. It should facilitate trade within the EU as well as cross-border transactions. It should also help to bring about a European capital market.

As stated in the Preamble to the Fourth Directive[8], it is necessary to establish in the Community minimum equivalent legal requirements as regards the

---

[5] Fourth Council Directive 78/660/EEC of 25 July 1978 based on Article 54(3)(g) of the Treaty on the annual accounts of certain types of companies, *O.J.* L 222 of 14 August 1978, 11-31.

[6] Seventh Council Directive 83/349/EEC of 13 June 1983 based on Article 54(3)(g) of the Treaty on consolidated accounts, *O.J.* L 193 of 18 July 1983, 1-17.

[7] See A. HALLER, "Financial accounting developments in the European Union: past events and future prospects", *European Accounting Review* 2002, 153-190; K. VAN HULLE, "Das Europäische Bilanzrecht. Entwicklungen und Herausforderungen", *Wirtschaftsprüferkammer-Mitteilungen* 1994, 9-17; K. VAN HULLE , "Harmonisatie van de regels inzake financiële verslaggeving: Eenheid in verscheidenheid", *Maandblad voor Accountancy en Bedrijfseconomie* 1992, 400-406; K. VAN HULLE, "Harmonisatie van de regels inzake financiële verslaggeving in de EG: Een getrouw beeld in een kleurenpalet", *De Accountant* 1989, 540-545.

[8] Recitals 2 and 3 of the Fourth Directive.

extent of the financial information that should be made available to the public by companies that are in competition with one another. This is particularly true for limited liability companies, because the activities of such companies frequently extend beyond the frontiers of their national territories and because such companies offer no safeguards to third parties beyond the amounts of their net assets. The different methods for the valuation of assets and liabilities must be coordinated to the extent necessary to ensure that annual accounts disclose comparable and equivalent information.

4. *The main objectives of the Fourth Directive.* Equivalence and comparability of the financial information published by limited liability companies were the main objectives of the Fourth Directive[9].

Equivalence was preferred over uniformity because the latter would not have been possible and was not even considered desirable. Because of different socio-economic and legal traditions, it was impossible in 1978 to go beyond the definition of those accounting rules that could be considered equivalent. The Directive therefore includes a large number of options both for companies and for Member States. The coexistence of so many different rules was considered acceptable because the various approaches were regarded as equivalent.

Comparability played a more limited role. It was established through note disclosures, a new approach in harmonisation. For instance, where a building had been revalued on the balance sheet, its historical cost had to be shown in the notes. Another important element in comparability was the introduction of standard formats for the balance sheet and for the profit and loss account. However, because the Fourth Directive only established minimum harmonisation and because of the recognition of a large number of options, financial statements prepared on the basis of the Directive were only comparable to a limited extent.

Today, it is considered necessary to build accounting standards on a conceptual framework which lays down the objectives and main characteristics of financial information[10]. Although the Fourth Directive does not contain such a conceptual framework, there was a great deal of agreement on some major aspects of financial reporting:

---

9 K. VAN HULLE and L. VAN DER TAS, "European Union – Individual Accounts", in D. ORDELHEIDE and KPMG (eds.), *Transatlantic Accounting,* Second Edition, Volume I, Basingstoke, Palgrave, 2001, 773-877.

10 See for instance, IASB, "Framework for the Preparation and Presentation of Financial Statements", London, 1989 and D. DAMANT, "The IASB Framework – creator of wealth", in H.-G. BRUNS, R.B. HERZ, H.-J. NEUBÜRGER and D. TWEEDIE (eds.), *Globale Finanzberichterstattung / Global Financial Reporting,* Stuttgart, Schäffer-Poeschel, 2008, 17-27. See also M. BONHAM and others, "The Quest for a conceptual framework for financial reporting", in ERNST & YOUNG (eds.), *International GAAP 2007,* London, LexisNexis, 2006, 77-167.

- The accounting rules should interfere as little as possible with tax rules, i.e. where tax rules required a certain treatment, such treatment should also be possible in the financial statements (for instance, provisions and amortisation)[11];
- Capital maintenance should be furthered: the basis of valuation should be historical cost, and prudence should be a principle and not merely an attitude[12];
- Some recognition should be given to economic reality through the adoption of the "true and fair view" override, i.e. the provisions of the Directive should be departed from if their application would not lead to a true and fair view of the company's assets, liabilities, financial position and profit or loss[13];
- The profit and loss account was considered an important element of the financial statements because financial statements had to be seen in the context of reporting to the shareholders (stewardship approach)[14];
- It was not considered necessary to formulate more detailed, specific rules for listed companies;
- The simplifications introduced for small and medium-sized companies were not aimed at deregulation, but more at establishing a level playing field in terms of the information delivered to the market (considering small and/or medium-sized players' needs for confidentiality) and at resolving a potential problem in the field of auditing (the fear that there would not be enough qualified auditors)[15].

Probably one of the biggest achievements of the Fourth Directive was the introduction of a requirement for all limited liability companies to make their financial statements available to the public. This was a major problem in Germany, which had to be taken to the Court of Justice in order to enforce this requirement[16]. Another major achievement of the Fourth Directive was the introduction in all Member States of a comparable set of rules governing financial reporting for all limited liability companies.

---

[11] K. VAN HULLE, "Convergences in accounting rules and income tax legislation", in F. ABRAHAM, J. STUYCK and F. VANISTENDAEL (eds.), *Tax Policy and the Impending Economic and Monetary Union,* Leuven Law Series 12, Leuven, Leuven University Press, 1999, 117-126.

[12] K. VAN HULLE, "Prudence: a principle or an attitude?", *European Accounting Review* 1996, 375-382.

[13] J. ARDEN, "True and fair view: a European perspective", *European Accounting Review* 1997, 675-679; K. VAN HULLE, "The true and fair view override in the European Accounting Directives", *European Accounting Review* 1997, 711-720; P. WALTON, "The true and fair view and the drafting of the Fourth Directive", *European Accounting Review* 1997, 721-730.

[14] H. BECKMAN, "Jaarrekening en verantwoording", *Ondernemingsrecht* 2007, 226-230.

[15] K. VAN HULLE and L. VAN DER TAS, "European Union – Individual Accounts", in D. ORDELHEIDE and KPMG (eds.), *Transatlantic Accounting,* Second Edition, Volume I, Basingstoke, Palgrave, 2001, 818.

[16] Court of Justice 29 September 1998 (Commission of the European Communities v Federal Republic of Germany), No C-191/95, *European Court Reports* 1998, I, 05449.

5. *The main objectives of the Seventh Directive*[17]. The Seventh Directive follows the same approach as the Fourth Directive. The main objectives are equivalence and comparability. There are no specific rules for listed companies. Tax coloration is also allowed subject to disclosure in the notes[18]. There are fewer options in the Directive because consolidation was a new practice for most Member States. There was therefore less need to accept different accounting treatments. It is interesting that the Seventh Directive gives clear preference to the economic group concept (i.e. consolidation is required whenever a parent controls a subsidiary) rather than to the legal power of control concept – i.e. consolidation is required whenever a parent has the legal power to control a subsidiary – which, at the time of adoption of the Directive, was the leading approach internationally[19].

1.2 The transposition of the Fourth and Seventh Directives: more diversity than unity

6. *The setting up of the Contact Committee and the need for further harmonisation.* Although the transposition of the Fourth and Seventh Directives led to important changes to the legal requirements for financial reporting in all Member States, it is clear that the harmonisation resulting from these Directives was far from perfect.

In order to promote further harmonisation, the Directives set up a Contact Committee composed of representatives from the Member States and chaired by a Commission representative. The functions of the Contact Committee were to facilitate the harmonised application of the Directives through regular meetings (dealing in particular with practical problems arising in connection with their application) and to advise the Commission, if necessary, on additions or amendments to the Directives.

The Contact Committee met at regular intervals (two to three times a year) and arrived at a number of conclusions concerning the interpretation of provisions in the Directives, which were included in an Interpretative Communication published by the Commission[20]. However, it is fair to say that the Committee did not make much progress with further harmonisation, particularly because of resistance from two Member States.

---

[17] K. VAN HULLE and L. VAN DER TAS, "European Union – Group accounts", in D. ORDELHEIDE and KPMG (eds.), *Transatlantic Accounting*, Second Edition, Volume I, Basingstoke, Palgrave, 2001, 881-951.

[18] Article 29(5) of the Seventh Directive.

[19] M. PETITE, "The conditions for consolidation under the Seventh Company Law Directive", *CMLR* 1984, 81-121; C.W.A. TIMMERMANS, "Les comptes consolidés dans la CEE", *Revue de droit international et de droit comparé* 1977, 341-354; K. VAN HULLE, "Het groepsbegrip in de zevende richtlijn", in *Liber Amicorum Jan Ronse*, Brussels, Story-Scientia, 1986, 335-356.

[20] Interpretative communication concerning certain Articles of the fourth and seventh Council Directives on accounting (98/C16/04), *O.J.* C 16 of 20 January 1998, 0005 - 0012.

7. ***Different views about the way forward.*** Germany had experienced serious difficulties in transposing the Accounting Directives, because small and medium-sized companies (mainly of the GmbH type) opposed the requirement to disclose their financial statements. Germany's official position was that the objectives of the EC Treaty concerning harmonisation of accounting requirements had been fulfilled with the adoption and transposition of the Accounting Directives. After all, the Treaty only required minimum harmonisation. There was no need for further work[21].

The United Kingdom considered the Accounting Directives as an unhelpful limitation of the creativity of its Accounting Standards Board which preferred to cooperate with the other leading standard setters in the world, i.e. Canada, the United States and Australia/New Zealand within the "Group of 4" and with organisations such as the International Accounting Standards Committee (IASC)[22]. Ideally, the EU should adopt international standards and stop further independent work at the EU level.

Other Member States, such as Belgium, France, Spain and Italy would have preferred to continue the harmonisation process.

8. ***The 1990 Conference of the Commission on the future of the harmonisation of accounting standards.*** Because the process was not really moving forward, the Commission organised a Conference in 1990 on the future of the harmonisation of accounting standards in the EU[23]. Experts from the various ministries of the Member States, academics, representatives of European organisations of the main users and preparers of accounts, of the accounting profession and of national accounting standard-setting bodies were invited to express their views on what, if anything, needed to be done at the EU level to further harmonise accounting standards.

A number of important conclusions came out of this Conference, which was the first of its kind ever organised in the EU:

- There is no need to reduce the options in the Accounting Directives: the options reflect real differences between the Member States. Their existence does not prevent comparability;
- Harmonisation should be continued so as to avoid further diversity, particularly on topics not yet covered by the Directives;
- Stakeholders should be more closely associated with further initiatives taken by the Commission in the field of accounting.

---

21 H. BIENER, "Procedural reforms", in Commission of the European Communities (ed.), *The future of Harmonization of Accounting Standards within the European Communities,* Luxembourg, Office for Official Publications of the European Communities, 1990, 109-110.

22 See M. BONHAM and others, "The influence of the G4 + 1 Group of standard setters on international accounting", in H.-G. BRUNS, R.B. HERZ, H.-J. NEUBÜRGER and D.TWEEDIE (eds.), *Globale Finanzberichterstattung / Global Financial Reporting,* Stuttgart, Schäffer-Poeschel, 2008, 11.

23 The proceedings of this Conference were published on the website of the Commission at the address listed in footnote 24.

9. ***The setting up of the Accounting Advisory Forum.*** Following the Conference, the Commission decided to set up a new advisory body, the Accounting Advisory Forum. The Forum was chaired by the Commission and comprised twenty-two members. These members represented both the accounting standard-setting bodies of Member States and the European organisations for the main users and preparers of accounts (industry, trade-unions, banks, insurance companies, stock exchanges and financial analysts), as well as the accounting profession and academia.

The Forum discussed a number of accounting issues that had been identified as major lacunae in the Fourth Directive: foreign currency translation, government grants and leasing. The Forum produced a working paper on each of those topics. These papers were published by the Commission[24]. The documents stated clearly that the Forum was not a standard-setting body. Rather, its main function was to advise the Commission on accounting matters and possible ways to facilitate further harmonisation. The purpose of the publications was to stimulate discussions among standard-setters, preparers, users and auditors of accounts in Member States. The last publications of the Forum dealt with prudence and matching and with environmental issues in financial reporting. The conclusions of the Forum on the latter topic were included in a Recommendation published by the Commission in 2001[25].

In fact, the Forum can be seen as the predecessor of EFRAG (see no. 18 below). An important reason why the EU's contribution to the international accounting standard-setting debate has been rather minimal was the absence of a body that could speak on behalf of the EU on the international scene. Such a body was difficult to establish, as the views on accounting issues among Member States and stakeholders were very different. Indeed, the Accounting Directives did not provide a framework that was sufficiently harmonised to allow them to serve as a basis for negotiations on accounting issues at the international level.

[24] These documents as well as all other official EU documents referred to in this article can be consulted on the Commission's website at the following address: http://ec.europa.eu/internal_market/accounting/index_en.htm.

[25] Recommendation of the Commission No 2001/453/EC of 30 May 2001 on the recognition, measurement and disclosure of environmental issues in the annual accounts and annual reports of companies, *O.J.* L 156 of 13 June 2001, 0033 - 0042.

2. The IAS/IFRS Regulation[26]: a response to increasing demand for uniformity in financial reporting

2.1 The growing pressure from capital markets

10. ***New demands in a changing (financial) world.*** It is most probable that the accounting scene in the EU would not have changed dramatically if there had not been pressure from capital markets. Indeed, most companies in the EU continued to report on the basis of the Accounting Directives[27]. Only a minority of companies produced, in addition to their statutory accounts, financial statements based upon either International Accounting Standards (IAS) or United States Generally Accepted Accounting Principles (US GAAP).

The collapse of the Soviet Union, the changes in Central and Eastern Europe and the prospect of the creation of an economic and monetary union in the EU in the early 90s provided a major impetus for change: large companies in the EU needed sizeable amounts of capital. The banking system could no longer provide these amounts at a reasonable cost. The only alternative was the capital market. But capital markets were demanding financial information that was more investor oriented[28]. Financial statements prepared on the basis of the Accounting Directives did not provide the information which capital markets wanted. Companies were therefore required to produce two sets of financial statements, i.e. one set as required under national law transposing the Accounting Directives and another set based upon either IAS or US GAAP[29].

It became increasingly clear that a special solution needed to be developed for listed companies. The Commission therefore proposed, in a Communication published in 1995[30], to put its weight behind the international harmonisation

---

[26] Regulation (EC) No 1606/2002 of the European Parliament and of the Council of 19 July 2002 on the application of international accounting standards, *O.J.* L 243 of 9 September 2002, 1–4.

[27] VERMOESEN and SCHUMESCH mention that at the time of writing their article, only a limited number of companies had used the option – granted to "global players" – to publish their consolidated accounts on the basis of an international standard for financial reporting and that, when these companies did so, it was mostly because they wanted to get access to international capital markets: P. VERMOESEN and P. SCHUMESCH, "L'utilisation des normes comptables internationales par les entreprises belges: bilan et perspectives", *Liber Amicorum Henri Olivier*, Bruges, Die Keure, 2000, 653-654.

[28] R. KROCKAERT, "Les normes IAS/IFRS, leurs perspectives et les conséquences peut-être imprévisibles de leur application, dans la convergence avec la modernisation du droit comptable belge", *Liber Amicorum Guy Horsmans*, Brussels, Bruylant, 2004, 597: K. VAN HULLE, "De Europese jaarrekeningrichtlijnen en de internationale verslaggevingsstandaarden van het IASC", in X (ed.), *Ondernemingsfinancieringsrecht*, Deventer, Kluwer, 1999, 24-26.

[29] Note that the difference between accounts drafted according to the Directives and accounts drafted according to US GAAP was sometimes great. See K. VAN OOSTVELDT, "De Belgische boekhoudwetgeving in een internationale veranderende omgeving", *Liber Amicorum Henri Olivier*, Bruges, Die Keure, 2000, 595; C. POURBAIX, "Levée de capitaux internationaux. Clarté et comparabilité des états financiers (normes EU / IAS / US GAAP)", *Liber Amicorum Henri Olivier*, Bruges, Die Keure, 2000, 417-419.

[30] Communication from the Commission - Accounting Harmonisation: a new strategy vis-à-vis international harmonisation, *COM* 95 (508); K. VAN HULLE, "De strategie van de Europese Commissie

process, which was already well under way in the International Accounting Standards Committee (IASC). Global players in Europe should be allowed to prepare a single set of financial statements, preferably drawn up in accordance with IAS and possibly with a distinction between annual and consolidated accounts.

11. *The Commission's (pragmatic) position in view of the specific demands of the capital markets.* In the Commission's opinion, the production of two sets of financial statements was not only costly, but also confusing. The publication of different figures for different purposes would undermine the investor's confidence in the published financial information. Therefore, it was of the utmost importance that European companies could satisfy differing requirements by producing only one set of financial statements. These financial statements would preferably have to be prepared on the basis of IAS, as there was a clear prospect that financial statements based upon these standards would ultimately be accepted by IOSCO (International Organisation of Securities Commissions) for listing on capital markets throughout the world[31].

The Commission was well aware that, for many companies in Europe, the preparation of financial statements in accordance with IAS would mean that they would have to distinguish between annual accounts and consolidated accounts. Indeed, this pragmatic solution would be required for companies based in Member States where there was a close linkage between accounting and taxation. In those Member States, the annual accounts that companies are required to prepare for approval by the shareholders are attached to the tax return and form the basis for corporate taxation. Thus, any change in the accounting rules was likely to have immediate (and mostly negative) consequences in terms of the amount of taxes to be paid.

On the other hand, in most instances, consolidated accounts have the advantage of not being the basis on which the distributable or taxable profit is determined. In those Member States that had introduced the option provided for in Article 29(2) of the Seventh Directive, it was already possible for parent companies to adopt different accounting policies in their parent entity and consolidated accounts. The use of different valuation rules was possible as long as the rules were in conformity with those of the Fourth Directive.

---

voor de harmonisering van financiële verslaggeving", *Acc.Bedr.* 1998, 6-14; K. VAN HULLE, "Die Reform des europäischen Bilanzrechts: Stand, Ziele und Perspektiven", *ZGR* 2000, 537-549.

31 On the Commission's choice for IAS, see N. SOFIANOS and M. PELIDIS, "Corporate governance and international accounting standards: summary of presentation", in UAE, *Corporate Governance. Transparency and investors protection in listed companies*, Brussels, Bruylant, 2005, 65; K. VAN HULLE, "De strategie van de Europese Commissie voor de harmonisering van financiële verslaggeving", *Acc. Bedr. (M)* 1998, 6-7; K. VAN HULLE, "Het beleid van de Europese Unie inzake boekhoudrecht", *Bull. C.B.N.* 1997, ed. 40-41, 251-252.

12. *The (conditional) approval by the Council of Ministers of the Commission's proposal.* The Council of Ministers endorsed the Commission's proposed new accounting strategy subject to two conditions[32]:

(1) The influence of the EU in the work of the IASC had to be increased. As a result, the Commission was granted an observer seat on the Board of the IASC, on the Standards Advisory Council (SAC) and on the Standards Interpretations Committee (SIC);

(2) The preparation of consolidated accounts using IAS was only possible to the extent that there were no conflicts between IAS and the Accounting Directives. After careful analysis, the Commission came to the conclusion that there were no major conflicts between IAS and the Accounting Directives and that, accordingly, a European company could prepare its consolidated accounts in conformity with IAS without being in conflict with the Accounting Directives[33].

The fact that there were no major conflicts between IAS and the Accounting Directives did not mean that there were no conflicts with national law. The Accounting Directives contained a significant number of options. It was perfectly possible for Member States to have chosen an option that was not allowed under IAS. In the same way, it was presumed that in those cases where the Accounting Directives gave companies a choice, companies would apply the option that conformed with IAS. The absence of major conflicts also resulted from the fact that IAS contained a number of options. Companies could then select those options that were in conformity with the Accounting Directives[34].

Following the Commission's recommendation in the 1995 Communication, seven Member States (Austria, Belgium, Finland, France, Germany, Italy and Luxembourg) adopted legislation or measures that allowed listed companies to depart from the national rules on consolidation and to prepare their consolidated financial statements in accordance with IAS (and US GAAP).

13. *The Commission's 1999 Financial Services Action Plan.* Because of the growing importance of capital markets for corporate financing in the EU, and to allow EU companies and citizens to benefit fully from the advantages of the

---

[32] K. VAN HULLE, "From Accounting Directives to IAS", in CH. LEUZ, D. PFAFF and A. HOPWOOD (eds.), *The Economics and Politics of Accounting*, Oxford, Oxford University Press, 2004, 349.

[33] European Commission, *An examination of the conformity between the IAS and the European Accounting Directives*, Luxembourg, *Office for Official Publications of the European Communities,* 1996, 22 p.; for an overview of the results of this examination, see X. "Europese en internationale ontwikkelingen inzake boekhoudnormering", *Bull. C.B.N.* 2000, ed. 46, 15-17; K. VAN HULLE, "De Europese jaarrekeningrichtlijnen en de internationale verslaggevingsstandaarden van het IASC", in X?? (ed.), *Ondernemingsfinancieringsrecht*, Deventer, Kluwer, 1999, 26-31; K. VAN HULLE, "De strategie van de Europese Commissie voor de harmonisering van financiële verslaggeving", *Acc. Bedr. (M) 1998,* 9-10; see also: X., "Dossier: Harmonisation comptable internationale", *C&FP* 1996, ed. 9, 1-35.

[34] At regular intervals, the Commission published position papers on the conformity between newly adopted IAS and Interpretations by the SIC and the Accounting Directives. These positions were published on the Commission's website referred to in footnote 24.

introduction of a common currency, the Commission presented its Financial Services Action Plan in 1999[35].

In the area of financial reporting, the Financial Services Action Plan proposed that all listed EU companies report under the same accounting framework. Applying a common framework for financial reporting should not only improve the comparability between financial statements of companies operating on the same (European) capital market; it should also allow EU companies to use the same set of financial statements for listing purposes throughout the world.

The efficiency of capital markets in the EU was seriously hampered by the lack of comparability between financial statements published by listed companies. Indeed, it was not uncommon for companies listed on the same exchange to apply different accounting frameworks (national standards of any EEA Member State, IAS or US GAAP). In addition, because of the options in the Directives and the minimum level of harmonisation, national standards were still very different. It had become clear that, as a result of the lack of harmonisation of accounting standards within the EU, listed companies in the EU had to bear a higher cost to obtain capital. The EU's position was further weakened by a lack of proper enforcement of the standards applied by companies.

Lack of comparability and inadequate enforcement were the main reasons why the Commission proposed a radical change in a new Communication published on 13 June 2000[36] which contained the following proposals:

- All listed EU companies would have to prepare their consolidated accounts in accordance with IAS;
- The requirement to apply IAS would take effect at the latest from 2005 onwards;
- Member States would be allowed to extend the application of IAS to unlisted companies and to individual accounts;
- IAS would be introduced into the legal environment of the EU on the basis of a decision by an endorsement mechanism to be set up at EU level;
- A proper enforcement infrastructure would have to be developed to ensure the application of accounting standards in the same way in all Member States;
- The Accounting Directives would be modernised.

2.2 The principles governing the IAS/IFRS Regulation

14. ***General. Objective of the IAS/IFRS Regulation.*** With the Regulation of 19 July 2002, the European legislator has created a legal framework allowing

[35] Communication from the Commission - Implementing the framework for financial markets: action plan, *COM* (1999) 232.

[36] Communication from the Commission to the Council and the European Parliament - EU Financial Reporting Strategy: the way forward", *COM* (2000) 359.

for the IAS/IFRS standards to be integrated into EU law. In practice, this allows a uniform system of valuation and reporting standards to be introduced in an identical way throughout the European Union[37].

It goes without saying that this constitutes an important change with respect to the harmonisation approach envisaged by the Accounting Directives, which has failed to deliver the ultimate objective, namely ensuring comparability and equivalence of annual accounts throughout the European Union[38]. The fact that additional support was sought from a set of standards developed by a private organisation – the IASC Foundation – makes the change in approach all the more remarkable. Apart from the pressure from capital markets (see subsection 2.1 above), the growing importance of the IAS/IFRS standards internationally undoubtedly also had an impact on the EU's decision.

15. ***Three cornerstones of the IAS/IFRS Regulation.*** Three cornerstones of the Regulation should be highlighted in particular:

(i) the creation of an institutional and procedural framework for the introduction of IAS/IFRS standards (see nos. 16-22 below);

(ii) the introduction of a requirement for listed companies to use IAS/IFRS standards when preparing their consolidated accounts (see no. 23 below); and

(iii) the introduction of an option for Member States, on the one hand, to permit or require application of IAS/IFRS standards in cases other than those stipulated by the Regulation and, on the other hand, to postpone the required application of IAS/IFRS standards during a transitional period in certain cases (see no. 24 below).

16. ***First cornerstone: creation of a framework for the introduction of IAS/IFRS standards.*** It should be emphasised that the Regulation only creates an institutional and procedural framework for the introduction of IAS/IFRS standards into EU law. In other words: IAS/IFRS standards are not as such introduced by the Regulation. This introduction only occurs after an endorsement process, with a technical and a (restricted) political phase[39], in application of the Council Decision of 28 June 1999 "*laying down the procedures for the exercise of the implementing powers conferred on the Commission*"[40] (specifically in application of Articles 5, 7 and 8 of that Decision).

---

[37] See also Article 1 of the IAS/IFRS Regulation.

[38] See especially Recital 3 of the IAS/IFRS Regulation.

[39] Articles 6 and 7 of the IAS/IFRS Regulation.

[40] Council Decision No 1999/468/EC of 28 June 1999 laying down the procedures for the exercise of implementing powers conferred on the Commission, *O.J.* L 184 of 17 July 1999, 23-26. See in this context K. GEENS, "De nieuwe harmonisatiedynamiek van het vennootschapsrecht: een 'eerste klas' begrafenis van het Europees vennootschapsrecht na vijftig jaar?", *T.R.V.* 2006, 83 and K. VAN HULLE, "De toekomst van de Europese harmonisatie inzake het vennootschapsrecht", *T.R.V.* 2006, 158-159 and 162.

Indeed, although most people agreed that the choice in favour of IAS/IFRS was right, there was considerable opposition to handing over the accounting standard-setting for listed companies to a private body that was largely self-regulated. It was therefore clear from the outset that the standards adopted internationally would have to be officially endorsed before they could be integrated into the EU legal environment[41].

At the same time, it was unthinkable that an international standard adopted by the IASB would subsequently need to be renegotiated at EU level. The policy should be that, once an international standard had been adopted by the IASB, in principle it should be acceptable to the EU. Therefore, it was extremely important to build into the process a number of guarantees that would contribute to the success of that policy[42].

17. *The first guarantee* relates to (i) the position of the EU within the IASC Foundation's structure and (ii) the governance of the Foundation in general and the IASB in particular.

(i) On the first issue, it was agreed that the European Commission would keep an observer seat on the Standards Advisory Council and on the International Financial Reporting Interpretations Committee (IFRIC) and that close contacts would be maintained on a permanent basis between the Commission and the IASB. As most Board positions had become full-time after the reform of the structure of the IASC, there was no more room for observers on the Board. Although the Commission does not formally represent the EU in this area, Member States and the European Parliament both insisted that the Commission should be an active participant on behalf of the EU. The representation of the EU within the IASC Foundation has remained an issue because it is felt that the EU's influence in the process of adoption of international standards does not reflect the fact that the EU was the first major jurisdiction to make IFRS mandatory for its listed companies and that EU representation in the structure of the IASC Foundation remains insufficient.

The Trustees of the IASC Foundation have responded to these concerns by publishing, in July 2008, a discussion document entitled "*Review of the Constitution: Public Accountability and the Composition of the IASB – Proposals for Change*". Among the envisaged measures (to enter into effect as of 1 January 2009) are the establishment of a formal link between the IASC Foundation and a Monitoring Group, representing the European Commission, the IMF,

---

[41] K. VAN HULLE, "From Accounting Directives to IAS", in CH. LEUZ, D. PFAFF and A. HOPWOOD (eds.), *The Economics and Politics of Accounting,* Oxford, Oxford University Press, 2004, 366.

[42] K. VAN HULLE, "IFRS as accounting standards for Europe", in H.-G. BRUNS, R.H. HERZ, H. J. NEUBÜRGER and D. TWEEDIE (eds.), *Globale Finanzberichterstattung / Global Financial Reporting,* Stuttgart, Schäffer-Poeschel, 2008, 79-83.

IOSCO, the FSA of Japan, the SEC and the World Bank, as well as an increase of the membership of the IASB to 16 members and the addition of new guidelines regarding the geographical diversity of the members of the IASB. Further changes to the IASC Foundation's Constitution are envisaged to take effect from 1 January 2010[43].

(ii) On the second issue, the situation remains difficult and has become even more politically sensitive in the context of the present financial crisis. There was a general feeling that the IASB was not sufficiently responsive to the concerns expressed by governments and prudential regulators, particularly in relation with the application of the fair value rules to financial instruments. An international accounting standard-setter should also take into account public interest issues and should not disregard financial stability aspects that might arise from the application of its standards. The issue has now also moved up from the EU level to the level of the G20. At the request of the Council, the Commission Services present at regular intervals a report on IASB/IASCF governance developments[44]. The European Parliament is also actively following governance issues and has reported on this on its own initiative.

18. ***The second guarantee*** relates to the upstream technical input from interested parties in the EU in the international accounting standard-setting process.

Through the creation of the European Financial Reporting Advisory Group (EFRAG)[45], representing the main parties interested in financial reporting (industry, accounting profession, standard-setters, stock exchanges, banking and insurance sector and financial analysts), it is hoped that one of the main weaknesses of the EU's harmonisation approach, i.e. the absence of a common view on financial reporting issues, could at least be partly remedied. The best way to prevent possible rejection of a standard by the EU is to ensure that there has been proper input from the very beginning and that all arguments have been properly discussed. Although EFRAG as such has not yet been officially recognised and is not mentioned in the IAS/IFRS Regulation, the Commission nevertheless has undertaken to endorse an IAS/IFRS standard only after consultation with EFRAG[46].

---

[43] See the press release of the IASB of 21 July 2008 available on their website: www.iasb.org.

[44] These reports can be found on the Commission website, referred to in footnote 24.

[45] For the structure and operation of EFRAG, see their website: www.efrag.org.

[46] See K. VAN HULLE and N. LYBAERT, *Boekhoud- en jaarrekeningenrecht*, Bruges, Die Keure, 2005, 100-102.

Moreover, the role of EFRAG is likely to increase in the future[47]. A new structure agreed after extensive consultations is currently being put in place and the Commission has announced the provision of EU funding for up to 50% of the EFRAG budget from 2010 onwards[48]. With the increasing importance of IFRS worldwide, it is clear that the EU needs to devote more resources to the development of a common view on financial reporting issues[49].

19. ***The third guarantee*** is specifically provided for in the Regulation. International standards can only become mandatory after endorsement by the European Commission on the basis of the "comitology" procedure provided for in a Council Decision of 28 June 1999. On the basis of that Decision, it is the Commission that makes the final decision on endorsement.

The Commission is assisted in this task by the Accounting Regulatory Committee (ARC), which is presided over by the Commission and which comprises representatives from the Member States. The ARC in turn will only decide after having received the advice of EFRAG.

It was also agreed that the European Parliament would have to be closely associated with the endorsement process. Since the amendment in 2006 of the 1999 Council Decision, the European Parliament now has a right of scrutiny[50]. Before a Commission endorsement decision becomes final, the Parliament may express its own opinion on the standard. It is currently being considered whether a "fast track" procedure could be used in cases where a swift endorsement is needed.

The various Commission Regulations with the relevant standards are published in the Official Journal of the European Communities in all (22) official languages of the EU as well as on the Commission's website.

20. Within the framework of the endorsement process, the Commission must verify whether the standards concerned are in accordance with the principle of a true and fair view (in the meaning of the Fourth and Seventh Directives, i.e. they must be in conformity with European accounting thinking), as well as

---

47 EFRAG launched a public consultation on "Strengthening the European contribution to the international standard-setting process" with a comment deadline of 22 September 1988 with concrete proposals to enhance the role of EFRAG through additional resources. See also S. ENEVOLDSEN and TH. OVERSBERG, "Importance of a European voice in international standard setting", in H.-G. BRUNS, R.H. HERZ, H.-J. NEUBÜRGER and D. TWEEDIE (eds.), *Globale Finanzberichterstattung / Global Financial Reporting,* Stuttgart, Schäffer-Poeschel, 2008, 89-106.

48 For more information on the enhancement of EFRAG (new structure and funding), see http://www.efrag.org/projects/detail.asp?id=134.

49 This is also the view expressed by the European Parliament. See especially paragraphs 26 and 53 of the own-initiative report of MEP Alexander RADWAN available at http://tinyurl.com/6ddah5.

50 Decision 2006/512/EC of the Council of 17 July 2006, *O.J.* L 200 of 22 July 2006, 11. See the consequent amendment of the IAS Regulation: Regulation (EC) No 297/2008 of the European Parliament and of the Council of 11 March 2008 amending Regulation (EC) No 1606/2002 on the application of international accounting standards, as regards the implementing powers conferred on the Commission, *O.J.* L 97 of 9 April 2008, 62-63.

whether they serve the European public interest. Only when a positive answer is given to these questions and when the standards concerned also meet a number of basic criteria which financial information must comply with (for example in terms of understandability, relevance, reliability and comparability[51]) may the Commission adopt a standard and issue a new Regulation, thereby introducing the standard into EU law[52].

In practice, the Commission can adopt an IAS/IFRS standard, as well as the associated interpretations developed by the Standards Interpretations Committee with respect to the IAS standards and by the International Financial Reporting Interpretations Committee with respect to the IFRS standards. Furthermore, the Commission can also adopt any modification of standards or interpretations[53]. Because a standard must be adopted before companies are required to apply it, companies applying international standards in their financial statements are advised to specifically refer to the preparation of these financial statements "in accordance with IFRSs as adopted by the EU". This reference should make clear that the standards applied are those adopted by the Commission following the endorsement process.

Because of the complexity of the endorsement procedure, it is possible that the IASB may publish a standard before the balance sheet date of a company and that the endorsement procedure has not yet been finalised. The adopted international standard will normally include an effective date for its application with an encouragement for early application of the standard. As EU listed companies are only required to apply endorsed IAS/IFRS standards, the question was raised as to whether they could already apply a standard for which the endorsement procedure had not yet been finalised. After discussion with Member States, the Commission has advised that Regulations published in the Official Journal endorsing IAS/IFRS standards and entering into force after the balance sheet date but before the date the financial statements are signed can be used by companies where early application is permitted in the Regulation and the related international standard. Companies are not, however, obliged to apply such standards[54].

---

[51] These criteria are contained in and based upon the "IASB Framework" which was adopted by the International Accounting Standards Board in April 2001. As this Framework is not an IAS/IFRS standard, it was not included as such in European Community law. Nevertheless, it is used as a base document to resolve issues in the field of financial reporting. See in this context the Memorandum from the European Commission, "Comments concerning certain Articles of the Regulation (EC) No 1606/2002 of the European Parliament and of the Council of 19 July 2002 on the application of international accounting standards and the Fourth Council Directive 78/660/EEC of 25 July 1978 and the Seventh Council Directive 83/349/EEC of 13 June 1983 on accounting", November 2003, pp. 5-6, the Annex of which contains the complete IASB Framework (pp. 14-37) (available at http://ec.europa.eu/internal_market/accounting/docs/ias/200311-comments/ias-200311-comments_en.pdf).

[52] See Article 3(2) of the IAS/IFRS Regulation.

[53] See Article 2 of the IAS/IFRS Regulation.

[54] See the extract from the minutes of the meeting of the Accounting Regulatory Committee of 30 November 2005 published on the Commission's website at the address referred to in footnote 24.

21. Between 29 September 2003 and 15 October 2008, the Commission had issued no less than 19 Regulations[55]. As a consequence, the (endorsed) IAS/

---

[55] Specifically, these Regulations are:

(i) Commission Regulation (EC) No 1725/2003 of 29 September 2003 adopting certain international accounting standards in accordance with Regulation (EC) No 1606/2002 of the European Parliament and of the Council, *O.J.* L 261 of 29 September 2003, 1–420;

(ii) Commission Regulation (EC) No 707/2004 of 6 April 2004 amending Regulation (EC) No 1725/2003 adopting certain international accounting standards in accordance with Regulation (EC) No 1606/2002 of the European Parliament and of the Council, *O.J.* L 111 of 6 April 2004, 3-17;

(iii) Commission Regulation (EC) No 2086/2004 of 19 November 2004 amending Regulation (EC) No 1725/2003 on the adoption of certain international accounting standards in accordance with Regulation (EC) No 1606/2002 of the European Parliament and of the Council as regards the insertion of IAS 39, *O.J.* L 363 of 19 November 2004, 1-65;

(iv) Commission Regulation (EC) No 2236/2004 of 29 December 2004 amending Regulation (EC) No 1725/2003 adopting certain international accounting standards in accordance with Regulation (EC) No 1606/2002 of the European Parliament and of the Council as regards International Financial Reporting Standards (IFRSs) Nos 1, 3 to 5, International Accounting Standards (IASs) Nos 1, 10, 12, 14, 16 to 19, 22, 27, 28, 31 to 41 and the interpretations by the Standard Interpretation Committee (SIC) Nos 9, 22, 28 and 32, *O.J.* L 392 of 29 December 2004, 1-145;

(v) Commission Regulation (EC) No 2237/2004 of 29 December 2004 amending Regulation (EC) No 1725/2003 adopting certain international accounting standards in accordance with Regulation (EC) No 1606/2002 of the European Parliament and of the Council, as regards IAS No 32 and IFRIC 1, *O.J.* L 393 of 29 December 2004, 1-41;

(vi) Commission Regulation (EC) No 2238/2004 of 29 December 2004 amending Regulation (EC) No 1725/2003 adopting certain international accounting standards in accordance with Regulation (EC) No 1606/2002 of the European Parliament and of the Council, as regards IASs IFRS 1, IASs Nos 1 to 10, 12 to 17, 19 to 24, 27 to 38, 40 and 41 and SIC Nos 1 to 7, 11 to 14, 18 to 27 and 30 to 33, *O.J.* L 394 of 29 December 2004, 1-175;

(vii) Commission Regulation (EC) No 211/2005 of 4 February 2005 amending Regulation (EC) No 1725/2003 adopting certain international accounting standards in accordance with Regulation (EC) No 1606/2002 of the European Parliament and of the Council as regards International Financial Reporting Standards (IFRS) 1 and 2 and International Accounting Standards (IASs) No 12, 16, 19, 32, 33, 38 and 39, *O.J.* L 2005, ep. 41,1-24;

(viii) Commission Regulation (EC) No 1073/2005 of 7 July 2005 amending Regulation (EC) No 1725/2003 adopting certain international accounting standards in accordance with Regulation (EC) No 1606/2002 of the European Parliament and of the Council, as regards IFRIC 2, *O.J.* L 175 of 8 July 2005, 3-11;

(ix) Commission Regulation (EC) No 1751/2005 of 25 October 2005 amending Regulation (EC) No 1725/2003 adopting certain international accounting standards in accordance with Regulation (EC) No 1606/2002 of the European Parliament and of the Council, as regards IFRS 1, IAS 39 and SIC 12, *O.J.* L 283 of 25 October 2005, 3-8;

(x) Commission Regulation (EC) No 1864/2005 of 15 November 2005 amending Regulation (EC) No 1725/2003 adopting certain international accounting standards in accordance with Regulation (EC) No 1606/2002 of the European Parliament and of the Council, as regards International Financial Reporting Standard No 1 and International Accounting Standards Nos. 32 and 39, *O.J.* L 299 of 15 November 2005, 45-57;

(xi) Commission Regulation (EC) No 1910/2005 of 8 November 2005 amending Regulation (EC) No 1725/2003 adopting certain international accounting standards in accordance with Regulation (EC) No 1606/2002 of the European Parliament and of the Council, as regards International Financial Reporting Standard 1 and 6, IASs 1, 16, 19, 24, 38, and 39, International Financial Reporting Interpretations Committee's Interpretations 4 and 5, *O.J.* L 305 of 8 November 2005, 4-29;

(xii) Commission Regulation (EC) No 2106/2005 of 21 December 2005 amending Regulation (EC) No 1725/2003 adopting certain international accounting standards in accordance with Regulation (EC) No 1606/2002 of the European Parliament and of the Council, as regards

IFRS standards are today available in all (22!) official languages of the European Union[56].

Until recently, this plurality of Regulations seriously hampered access to the standards in practice. In fact, anyone consulting the various Regulations, as well as being confronted with a strikingly large number of provisions, soon discovered that later Regulations often amended previous Regulations, as there was no consolidated version of the IAS/IFRS standards that were endorsed by the European Commission[57].

To resolve this coordination problem and facilitate access to the standards, the European Commission decided on 3 November 2008 to issue a consolidated text of all IAS/IFRS standards it had endorsed between 29 September 2003 and

---

International Accounting Standard (IAS) 39, *O.J.* L 337 of 21 December 2005, 16-19;

(xiii) Commission Regulation (EC) No 108/2006 of 11 January 2006 amending Regulation (EC) No 1725/2003 adopting certain international accounting standards in accordance with Regulation (EC) No 1606/2002 of the European Parliament and of the Council as regards International Financial Reporting Standards (IFRS) 1, 4, 6 and 7, International Accounting Standards (IAS) 1, 14, 17, 32, 33, and 39, International Financial Reporting Interpretations Committee's (IFRIC) Interpretation 6, *O.J.* L 24 of 27 January 2006, 1-36;

(xiv) Commission Regulation (EC) No 708/2006 of 8 May 2006 amending Regulation (EC) No 1725/2003 adopting certain international accounting standards in accordance with Regulation (EC) No 1606/2002 of the European Parliament and of the Council as regards International Accounting Standard (IAS) 21 and International Financial Reporting Interpretations Committee's (IFRIC) Interpretation 7, *O.J.* L 122 of 8 May 2006, 19-23;

(xv) Commission Regulation (EC) No 1329/2006 of 8 September 2006 amending Regulation (EC) No 1725/2003 adopting certain international accounting standards in accordance with Regulation (EC) No 1606/2002 of the European Parliament and of the Council as regards the International Financial Reporting Interpretations Committee's (IFRIC's) Interpretations 8 and 9, *O.J.* L 247 of 9 September 2006, 3-8;

(xvi) Commission Regulation (EC) No 610/2007 of 1 June 2007 amending Regulation (EC) No 1725/2003 adopting certain international accounting standards in accordance with Regulation (EC) No 1606/2002 of the European Parliament and of the Council as regards International Financial Reporting Interpretations Committee's (IFRIC) Interpretation 10, *O.J.* L 141 of 2 June 2007, 46-48;

(xvii) Commission Regulation (EC) No 611/2007 of 1 June 2007 amending Regulation (EC) No 1725/2003 adopting certain international accounting standards in accordance with Regulation (EC) No 1606/2002 of the European Parliament and of the Council as regards International Financial Reporting Interpretations Committee's (IFRIC) Interpretation 11, *O.J.* L 141 of 2 June 2007, 49-52;

(xviii) Commission Regulation (EC) No 1358/2007 of 21 November 2007 amending Regulation (EC) No 1725/2003 adopting certain international accounting standards in accordance with Regulation (EC) No 1606/2002 of the European Parliament and of the Council as regards International Financial Reporting Standard (IFRS) 8, *O.J.* L 304 of 22 November 2007, 9-20;

(xix) Commission Regulation (EC) No 1004/2008 of 15 October 2008 amending Regulation (EC) No 1725/2003 adopting certain international accounting standards in accordance with Regulation (EC) No 1606/2002 of the European Parliament and of the Council as regards International Accounting Standard (IAS) 39 and International Financial Reporting Standard (IFRS) 7, *O.J.* L 275 of 15 October 2008, 37-41.

[56] See also Article 3(4) of the IAS/IFRS Regulation expressly stipulating this requirement, following a long period of discussion on this matter.

[57] See F. HELLEMANS, "De IAS/IFRS-normen en de nieuwe Audit-Richtlijn", *T.R.V.* 2006, 640, no. 13.

15 October 2008[58]. This consolidated text replaces the 19 Regulations listed in footnote 55[59].

---

[58] Commission Regulation (EC) No 1126/2008 of 3 November 2008 adopting certain international accounting standards in accordance with Regulation (EC) No 1606/2002 of the European Parliament and of the Council, *O.J.* L 320 of 3 November 2008, 1-481.

[59] Meanwhile, in the period between 3 November 2008 and 20 October 2009, fifteen new regulations have been issued by the Commission:

(i) Commission Regulation (EC) No 1260/2008 of 10 December 2008 amending Regulation (EC) No 1126/2008 adopting certain international accounting standards in accordance with Regulation (EC) No 1606/2002 of the European Parliament and of the Council as regards International Accounting Standard (IAS) 23, *O.J.* L 338 of 17 December 2008, 10–16;

(ii) Commission Regulation (EC) No 1262/2008 of 16 December 2008 amending Regulation (EC) No 1126/2008 adopting certain international accounting standards in accordance with Regulation (EC) No 1606/2002 of the European Parliament and of the Council as regards International Financial Reporting Interpretations Committee's (IFRIC) Interpretation 13, *O.J.* L 338 of 17 December 2008, 21–24;

(iii) Commission Regulation (EC) No 1263/2008 of 16 December 2008 amending Regulation (EC) No 1126/2008 adopting certain international accounting standards in accordance with Regulation (EC) No 1606/2002 of the European Parliament and of the Council as regards International Financial Reporting Interpretation Committee's (IFRIC) Interpretation 14, *O.J.* L 338 of 17 December 2008, 25–30;

(iv) Commission Regulation (EC) No 1261/2008 of 16 December 2008 amending Regulation (EC) No 1126/2008 adopting certain international accounting standards in accordance with Regulation (EC) No 1606/2002 of the European Parliament and of the Council as regards International Financial Reporting Standard (IFRS) 2, *O.J.* L 338 of 17 December 2008, 17–20;

(v) Commission Regulation (EC) No 1274/2008 of 17 December 2008 amending Regulation (EC) No 1126/2008 adopting certain international accounting standards in accordance with Regulation (EC) No 1606/2002 of the European Parliament and of the Council as regards International Accounting Standard (IAS) 1, *O.J.* L 339 of 18 December 2008, 3–44;

(vi) Commission Regulation (EC) No 53/2009 of 21 January 2009 amending Regulation (EC) No 1126/2008 adopting certain international accounting standards in accordance with Regulation (EC) No 1606/2002 of the European Parliament and of the Council as regards International Accounting Standard (IAS) 32 and IAS 1, *O.J.* L 17 of 22 January 2009, 23–36;

(vii) Commission Regulation (EC) No 69/2009 of 23 January 2009 amending Regulation (EC) No 1126/2008 adopting certain international accounting standards in accordance with Regulation (EC) No 1606/2002 of the European Parliament and of the Council as regards amendments to International Financial Reporting Standard (IFRS) 1 and International Accounting Standard (IAS) 27, *O.J.* L 21 of 24 January 2009, 10–15;

(viii) Commission Regulation (EC) No 70/2009 of 23 January 2009 amending Regulation (EC) No 1126/2008 adopting certain international accounting standards in accordance with Regulation (EC) No 1606/2002 of the European Parliament and of the Council as regards Improvements to International Financial Reporting Standards (IFRSs), *O.J.* L 21 of 24 January 2009, 16–37;

(ix) Commission Regulation (EC) No 254/2009 of 25 March 2009 amending Regulation (EC) No 1126/2008 adopting certain international accounting standards in accordance with Regulation (EC) No 1606/2002 of the European Parliament and of the Council as regards International Financial Reporting Interpretations Committee's (IFRIC) Interpretation 12, *O.J.* L 80 of 26 March 2009, 5-13;

(x) Commission Regulation (EC) No 494/2009 of 3 June 2009 amending Regulation (EC) No 1126/2008 adopting certain international accounting standards in accordance with Regulation (EC) No 1606/2002 of the European Parliament and of the Council as regards International Accounting Standard (IAS) 27, *O.J.* L 149 of 12 June 2009, 6-21;

(xi) Commission Regulation (EC) No 495/2009 of 3 June 2009 amending Regulation (EC) No 1126/2008 adopting certain international accounting standards in accordance with Regulation (EC) No 1606/2002 of the European Parliament and of the Council as regards International Financial Reporting Standard (IFRS) 3, *O.J.* L 149 of 12 June 2009, 22-59;

(xii) Commission Regulation (EC) No 460/2009 amending Regulation (EC) No 1126/2008 adopting certain international accounting standards in accordance with Regulation (EC) No

22. Most standards and interpretations were endorsed without difficulties. The endorsement of IAS 39 (Financial instruments: recognition and measurement) proved very difficult, however[60]. Because of major opposition, particularly from the banking industry, no agreement could be reached on full endorsement of the standard. After extensive consultations with all parties concerned, the Commission decided to introduce a carve-out in the standard, which basically meant that certain provisions in the standard were scoped out and were not adopted "for mandatory use". The Commission provided extensive justification for its decision and pointed out that preference would always be given to full endorsement of international standards, but that IAS 39 represented an exceptional situation caused by particular prudential and technical complexities which had not been resolved.

It was alleged that the inability of EFRAG to arrive at a decision was due to a lack of independence of the experts represented in the Technical Expert Group of EFRAG. The Commission therefore decided to set up a group of non-governmental experts in accounting (the Standards Advisory Review Group) which advises the Commission, before it takes a decision on endorsement, on whether EFRAG's opinion on the endorsement of a particular standard or interpretation is well-balanced and objective. The group must deliver its advice to the Commission within three weeks from the date of receiving EFRAG's opinion[61].

1606/2002 of the European Parliament and of the Council as regards International Financial Reporting Interpretations Committee's (IFRIC) Interpretation 16, *O.J.* L 139 of 5 June 2009, 6-14;

(xiii) Commission Regulation (EC) No 636/2009 of 22 July 2009 amending Regulation (EC) No 1126/2008 adopting certain international accounting standards in accordance with Regulation (EC) No 1606/2002 of the European Parliament and of the Council as regards International Financial Reporting Interpretations Committee's (IFRIC) Interpretation 15, *O.J.* L 191 of 23 July 2009, 5-9;

(xiv) Commission Regulation (EC) No 824/2009 of 9 September 2009 amending Regulation (EC) No 1126/2008 adopting certain international accounting standards in accordance with Regulation (EC) No 1606/2002 of the European Parliament and of the Council as regards International Accounting Standard (IAS) 39 and International Financial Reporting Standard (IFRS) 7, *O.J.* L 239 of 10 September 2009, 48-50;

(xv) Commission Regulation (EC) No 839/2009 of 15 September 2009 amending Regulation (EC) No 1126/2008 adopting certain international accounting standards in accordance with Regulation (EC) No 1606/2002 of the European Parliament and of the Council as regards International Accounting Standard (IAS) 39, *O.J.* L 244 of 16 September 2009, 6-9.

As of 20 October 2009, no consolidated version integrating the modifications made by the above Regulations to Regulation 1126/2008 has been published on the web site of the European Commission.

[60] K. VAN HULLE, "Internationaliseren: een moelijke opdracht", *Liber Amicorum Erik De Lembre. Accountancy tussen onderzoek en praktijk*, Mechelen, Kluwer, 2007, 188-189.

[61] Commission Decision No 2006/505/EC of 14 July 2006 setting up a Standards Advice Review Group to advise the Commission on the objectivity and neutrality of the European Financial Reporting Advisory Group's opinions, *O.J.* L 199 of 21 July 2006, 36-38. The members of the SARG were appointed by Commission Decision No 2007/73/EC of 20 December 2006 on appointment of members of the Standards Advice Review Group created by the Commission Decision 2006/505/EC of 14 July 2006 setting up a Standards Advice Review Group to advise the Commission on the objectivity and neutrality of the European Financial Reporting Advisory Group's (EFRAG's) opin-

The endorsement procedure has also been complicated by the requirement, introduced at the request of the European Parliament, to present an assessment of the likely impact of the new standard or interpretation for stakeholders. The use of impact assessments has become the normal practice in the EU as a result of the Better Regulation Agenda. It has now been extended to endorsement decisions. In practice, many impact assessments are carried out by EFRAG[62].

23. ***Second cornerstone: the introduction of a requirement for EU listed companies to use IAS/IFRS standards when preparing consolidated accounts.*** The IAS/IFRS Regulation does more than just create a framework for the endorsement of IAS/IFRS standards.

Indeed, as a basic rule, the Regulation states that *listed companies,* being subject to the laws of a Member State[63], *with respect to their financial years commencing on or after 1 January 2005, are obliged to draw up their consolidated accounts in accordance with the IAS/IFRS standards* (as endorsed by the European Union)[64].

The requirement to use endorsed IAS/IFRS standards in the EU was extended (i) to third country issuers making a public offer of securities in the EU by the Prospectus Regulation[65] and (ii) to third country issuers with securities traded on an EU regulated market by the Transparency Directive[66]. Under these legal instruments, the issuers must prepare their financial information in accordance either with IFRS or with a third country's national accounting standards framework (third country GAAP) that is "equivalent" to endorsed

---

ions, *O.J.* L 32 of 6 February 2007, 181-182. See also S. ENEVOLDSEN and TH. OVERSBERG, "Importance of a European voice in international standard setting", in H.-G. BRUNS, R.H. HERZ, H.-J. NEUBÜRGER and D. TWEEDIE (eds.), Globale Finanzberichterstattung / Global Financial Reporting, Stuttgart, Schäffer-Poeschel, 2008, 96.

[62] K. VAN HULLE, "IFRS as accounting standards for Europe", in H.-G. BRUNS, R.H. HERZ, H.J. NEUBÜRGER and D TWEEDIE (eds.), *Globale Finanzberichterstattung / Global Financial Reporting,* Stuttgart, Schäffer-Poeschel, 2008, 82.

[63] Therefore, an American company with securities listed in Europe does not fall within the scope of the Regulation. This principle is intended to serve as an example to non-EU countries (especially the US), to encourage them to adopt a similar principle.

[64] See Article 4 of the IAS/IFRS Regulation, which also further specifies the concept of a "listed company". See also the Memorandum from the European Commission, "Comments concerning certain Articles of the Regulation (EC) No 1606/2002 of the European Parliament and of the Council of 19 July 2002 on the application of international accounting standards and the Fourth Council Directive 78/660/EEC of 25 July 1978 and the Seventh Council Directive 83/349/EEC of 13 June 1983 on accounting", November 2003, pp. 6-7, where the concept of "companies" is discussed in further detail (available at http://ec.europa.eu/internal_market/accounting/docs/ias/200311-comments/ias-200311-comments_en.pdf).

[65] Commission Regulation (EC) No 809/2004 of 29 April 2004 implementing Directive 2003/71/EC of the European Parliament and of the Council of 4 November 2003 as regards information contained in prospectuses as well as the format, incorporation by reference and publication of such prospectuses and dissemination of advertisements, *O.J.* L 215 of 16 June 2004, 3-103.

[66] Directive 2004/109/EC of the European Parliament and of the Council of 15 December 2004 on the harmonisation of transparency requirements in relation to information about issuers whose securities are admitted to trading on a regulated market and amending Directive 2001/34/EC, *O.J.* L 390 of 31 December 2004, 38-57.

IAS/IFRS. Those requirements were initially subject to a transitional exemption until 1 January 2007.

Subsequently, in the light of the (convergence) efforts of the national accounting standard-setters of Canada, Japan, the USA and other jurisdictions, and considering the positive efforts for convergence towards IFRS already under way[67], it was agreed to postpone this date for a further two years. Therefore, on 4 December 2006, the Commission adopted two legal measures under which third country issuers can continue using certain third country GAAP, for the purposes of the Prospectus Regulation, in all prospectuses filed before 1 January 2009 and, for the purposes of the Transparency Directive, for all financial years starting before January 2009[68].

On 21 December 2007, the Commission adopted a Regulation which sets out the definition of equivalence and establishes an equivalence mechanism in relation to third country GAAP[69]. In its advice delivered in March, May and October 2008, the Committee of European Securities Regulators ("CESR") recommended finding US GAAP and Japanese GAAP equivalent to IFRS for use within the Community. Furthermore, CESR recommended the acceptance of financial statements using the GAAP of China, Canada, South Korea and India within the Community on a temporary basis, no longer than until 31 December 2011. The Commission therefore adopted, on 12 December 2008, two new legal measures[70] which determine that the GAAP of the USA and the GAAP of Japan are found to be equivalent to IFRS and that the GAAP of China, Canada, South Korea and India can be accepted until 31 December 2011. The Commission will continue to monitor, with the technical assistance of CESR, the development of the GAAP of these third countries. The ultimate

---

67 See Commission of the European Communities, "First Report to the European Securities Committee and to the European Parliament on convergence between IFRS and third country national GAAP", *COM* (2007) 405 final of 6 July 2007, 11 p. See also H. OLIVIER, "Le concept d'équivalence des normes, une réponse à la mondialisation des marchés de capitaux?", in *Van alle markten. Liber Amicorum Eddy Wymeersch*, Antwerp, Intersentia, 2008, 731-748.

68 Commission Regulation (EC) No 1787/2006 of 4 December 2006 amending Commission Regulation (EC) 809/2004 implementing Directive 2003/71/EC of the European Parliament and of the Council as regards information contained in prospectuses as well as the format, incorporation by reference and publication of such prospectuses and dissemination of advertisements, *O.J.* L 337 of 5 December 2006, 17-20 and Commission Decision (EC) No 2006/891 of 4 December 2006 on the use by third country issuers of securities of information prepared under internationally accepted accounting standards, *O.J.* L 343 of 8 December 2006, 96-98.

69 Commission Regulation (EC) No 1569/2007 of 21 December 2007 establishing a mechanism for the determination of equivalence of accounting standards applied by third country issuers of securities pursuant to Directives 2003/71/EC and 2004/109/EC of the European Parliament and of the Council, *O.J.* L 340 of 22 December 2007, 66-68.

70 Commission Regulation (EC) No 1289/2008 of 12 December 2008 amending Commission Regulation (EC) No 809/2004 implementing Directive 2003/71/EC of the European Parliament and of the Council as regards elements related to prospectuses and advertisements, *O.J.* L 340 of 19 December 2008, 17-19; Commission Decision (2008/961/EC) of 12 December 2008 on the use by third countries' issuers of securities of certain third country's national accounting standards and International Financial Reporting Standards to prepare their consolidated financial statements, *O.J.* L 340 of 19 December 2008, 112-114.

goal should be the adoption of IFRS by those countries. Intense discussions are taking place between the Commission and these countries to encourage them to take effective measures to secure timely and complete transition to IFRS by 31 December 2011. The EU may indeed decide that the national standards of third countries which have been determined to be equivalent (as has been the case for the US and Japan) may no longer be used for the purpose of preparing information under the Prospectus Regulation or the Transparency Directive when these countries have adopted IFRS as their sole accounting standard.

When third country companies present financial information on the basis of IFRS, the notes to the audited financial statements must contain an explicit and unreserved statement that the information complies with IFRS in accordance with IAS 1 *Presentation of financial statements.* This means that full compliance with IFRS must be ensured.

24. *Third cornerstone: the introduction of an option for Member States to extend and in some cases postpone the use of IAS/IFRS standards.* The IAS/IFRS Regulation allows Member States *to extend the field of application of the IAS/IFRS standards* (as adopted by the European Union) *or*, at least during a limited transition period, *to restrict the use of those standards.*

Specifically, a Member State can opt to permit or even require listed companies falling within its jurisdiction to also prepare their annual accounts in accordance with IAS/IFRS[71].

In addition, or possibly in combination with this first option, a Member State can also opt to permit or require other, non-listed companies, to prepare their consolidated accounts and/or their statutory annual accounts in accordance with the international standards[72].

Both options were, strictly speaking, not necessary as Member States are free to impose further accounting requirements as long as these requirements are in conformity with EU law. As IAS/IFRS were considered to be in conformity with the Accounting Directives, companies could apply these standards in their annual or consolidated accounts if so allowed by Member States. There was no need for a specific authorisation in EU law. The explicit introduction of an option to extend the use of IAS/IFRS was an indication of the wish of the EU legislator to expand the use of IAS/IFRS within the EU.

Experience has shown that, up to now, a (limited) number of Member States permit listed or unlisted companies to apply IAS/IFRS in their annual accounts (for instance, Denmark, Estonia, Finland, Ireland, the Netherlands, the United Kingdom). Only two Member States (Cyprus and Malta) require the use of IAS/IFRS also in the annual accounts of listed and unlisted companies.

However, for banks and insurance undertakings, a number of Member States require the use of IAS/IFRS both in the annual and in the consolidated

[71] See Article 5, a) of the IAS/IFRS Regulation.
[72] See Article 5, b) of the IAS/IFRS Regulation.

accounts. Prudential supervisors want the institutions in these regulated sectors to produce comparable data.

Finally, the Regulation offered the possibility of granting listed companies a temporary exemption from the obligation to prepare their consolidated accounts in accordance with IAS/IFRS standards, in two specific cases. This possibility of exemption only existed up to the financial year commencing on or after 1 January 2007[73].

25. *Impact of the IAS/IFRS Regulation. Relation to the Fourth and Seventh Directives. Absence of a specific sanctions system.* To summarise, it can be said that the Regulation has brought about an evolutionary development on a massive scale, both in terms of content –because for the first time a framework was created to implement a uniform set of rules on financial reporting, binding on listed companies when drawing up consolidated accounts – and in terms of procedure – more specifically because it involves the adoption of standards originating outside the political structure of the EU, although the endorsement of the standards is preceded by a (limited) political and technical decision-making process.

Although the Regulation thus seriously affects the harmonisation concept underlying the Fourth and Seventh Directives, these Directives remain fully effective. Considering the Regulation's limited scope of application, both in terms of the types of companies and the financial statements concerned, these Directives continue to have an important function for a large number of companies and for most financial statements. Moreover, these Directives also continue to play a role with respect to the companies and the financial statements that fall within the scope of the Regulation. For instance, the question of whether a company is required to prepare consolidated accounts is still to be answered on the basis of the (national) provisions enacted in transposition of the Seventh Directive. In addition, certain references in the notes to the consolidated accounts, the content of the annual report on the consolidated accounts, the audit of the consolidated accounts and their disclosure are still governed by the national provisions that were introduced in transposition of the Seventh Directive[74].

Somewhat remarkable in this respect is the fact that not a single provision of the Regulation refers to (a system of) sanctions for non-compliance with the IAS/IFRS standards. Although Recital 16 of the Regulation very rightfully

[73] See Article 9 of the IAS/IFRS Regulation, as well as Recital 17 of the IAS/IFRS Regulation.

[74] See in this context the Memorandum from the European Commission, "Comments concerning certain Articles of the Regulation (EC) No 1606/2002 of the European Parliament and of the Council of 19 July 2002 on the application of international accounting standards and the Fourth Council Directive 78/660/EEC of 25 July 1978 and the Seventh Council Directive 83/349/EEC of 13 June 1983 on accounting", November 2003, 10-13, the Annex of which contains the complete IASB Conceptual Framework (14-37) (available on the Commission's website at the address referred to in footnote 24).

stipulates that "*an appropriate and rigorous enforcement system (is) of essential importance*", the same Recital restricts itself to repeating that, pursuant to Article 10 of the Treaty, Member States are required to take "*appropriate measures*" with a view to ensuring compliance with the IAS/IFRS standards. Despite the uniform nature of the standards, each Member State can therefore set up its own enforcement mechanism.

Although a common approach in this respect is not being considered at this stage, the consistent application of IAS/IFRS has been a concern for the Commission from the very beginning. The International Financial Reporting Interpretations Committee ("IFRIC") has been reluctant to play an active role in providing guidance on how to apply the standards. There was fear that a too active approach might lead to rule-based financial reporting as has been the case in the US. However, CESR has taken a number of initiatives and the Commission has set up a temporary Roundtable for the consistent application of IFRS in the EU. The Roundtable is chaired by the Commission. It comprises in addition a total of seventeen representatives from the IASB, CESR, EFRAG, FEE, Business Europe, the audit firms, national accounting standard-setters and preparers. In addition to the three representatives of the national standard-setters of France, Germany and the UK, any other national standard setter can participate by giving advance notice to the Commission[75].

By virtue of EU law, it is up to the Court of Justice to settle in last instance the interpretation and application issues that may arise from the IAS/IFRS standards (adopted by the European Commission)[76].

3. The (first) "modernisation wave" of the Fourth and Seventh Directives

26. *Modernisation of the Fourth and Seventh Directives.* As mentioned above (no. 25), the Fourth and Seventh Directives will continue to be fully effective, in addition to the IAS/IFRS Regulation. Considering this situation, the European legislator has "modernised" the Fourth and Seventh Directives, both prior to the adoption of the IAS/IFRS Regulation (and thus prior to the implementation of IAS/IFRS standards) and also subsequently.

This "modernisation wave" was essentially aimed on the one hand at bringing European accounting law closer to the IAS/IFRS standards, and on the other hand at further increasing harmonisation by requiring that the financial statements or any related documents (annual report/audit report) should con-

---

[75] K. VAN HULLE, "IFRS as accounting standards for Europe", in H.-G. BRUNS, R.H. HERZ, H.J. NEUBÜRGER and D. TWEEDIE (eds.), *Globale Berichterstattung / Global Financial Reporting*, Stuttgart, Schäffer-Poeschel, 2008, 84-85.

[76] See in this context the study by the Central Council of Economy ("*Centrale Raad voor het Bedrijfsleven*"), "IAS/IFRS: toelichting voor de leden van de ondernemingsraden", 13 September 2006, 15-16 (available on the website of the Institute of Auditors: www.ibr-ire.be).

tain certain specific references. The three phases of the "modernisation wave" are briefly discussed below (subsections 3.1, 3.2 and 3.3).

3.1 The "Fair Value Directive" of 27 September 2001

27. ***Objective and priorities of the Fair Value Directive.*** Even prior to the adoption of the IAS/IFRS Regulation and, as it were, in preparation for the implementation of the IAS/IFRS standards, the European legislator introduced quite a significant amendment to the Fourth and Seventh Directives.
This was done with the adoption on 27 September 2001 of the "Fair Value Directive"[77]. This Directive was necessary to ensure that companies applying international standards would still comply with the Accounting Directives. The Commission had indicated that it would not hesitate to propose amendments to these Directives so as to maintain the conformity between IAS and the Accounting Directives[78]. The main stumbling block was IAS 39 which had recently been adopted and required certain financial instruments to be measured at fair value. This was a siginicant departure from the historical cost principle which was the main principle for valuation of assets and liabilities under the Fourth Directive[79].

In essence, two innovations were introduced by the Fair Value Directive:

- On the one hand, it authorises Member States to permit – and possibly, if so desired by a Member State, to require – companies to *value certain financial instruments at their fair value* instead of at their historical cost. Member States may restrict this permission or requirement to the consolidated accounts. With respect to the annual accounts, these new provisions were incorporated in a new Section 7a of the Fourth Directive ("Valuation at fair value")[80], whereas with respect to the consolidated accounts they are contained in Article 29(1) of the Seventh Directive[81] (which contains a reference to Section 7a of the Fourth Directive).
- On the other hand, it introduces *new information requirements with respect to certain financial instruments both in the notes to the accounts and in the annual report.* With respect to the notes to the annual accounts

[77] Directive 2001/65/EC of the European Parliament and of the Council of 27 September 2001 amending Directives 78/660/EEC, 83/349/EEC and 86/635/EEC as regards the valuation rules for the annual and consolidated accounts of certain types of companies as well as of banks and other financial institutions, *O.J.* L 283 of 27 October 2001, 28-32.

[78] See in this context the Communications from the Commission entitled "Accounting harmonisation: a new strategy vis-à-vis international harmonisation" (COM (1995) 508) and "EU Financial Reporting Strategy: the way forward" (COM (2000) 359).

[79] On the impact of fair value accounting on the need for modification of the Fourth and Seventh Directive, see H. OLIVIER, "L'adaptation des normes comptables aux besoins des marchés de capitaux", Diegem, Ced. Samson, 2000, 141-145.

[80] See more precisely Articles 42a to 42d of the Fourth Directive, as amended by Article 1.1 of the Fair Value Directive.

[81] As amended by Article 2(1) of the Fair Value Directive.

and the annual report, these new requirements are included in Article 43(1) (new point 14) and in Article 46(1) (new point f) of the Fourth Directive[82], and with respect to the notes to the consolidated accounts and the consolidated annual report they are incorporated into Article 34 (new points 14 and 15) and Article 36(2) (new point e) of the Seventh Directive[83].

3.2 The "Modernisation Directive" of 18 March 2003

28. ***Objective of the Modernisation Directive.*** In order to avoid the creation within the European Union of a regulatory regime for annual accounts operating "at two different paces" (which could potentially constitute an element of distortion of competition), the Commission, in parallel with (the preparations for) the adoption of the IAS/IFRS Regulation, also proposed a new Directive, intended to bring the existing Accounting Directives into closer conformity with IAS/IFRS.

This initiative resulted in the Directive of 18 June 2003, which is often designated as the "Modernisation Directive"[84]. This Directive essentially[85] amends the Fourth and Seventh Directives by offering Member States supplementary options, allowing them, if so desired, to have their national accounting laws (developed in application of the Accounting Directives) brought closer in line with the approach that is typical of IAS/IFRS. Whereas the Fourth and Seventh Directives were characterised from the start by a vast freedom of choice offered to Member States and companies (see no. 4 above), as a consequence of the Modernisation Directive this freedom of choice was even further expanded.

29. ***Scope of the Modernisation Directive.*** Pursuant to the Fourth and Seventh Directives, as amended by the Modernisation Directive, Member States may opt:

- to permit or require that the annual or consolidated accounts are presented in a manner that is more in line with international practice, as laid down in the IAS/IFRS standards[86], as well as

---

[82] As amended by Article 1(2) of the Fair Value Directive.

[83] As amended by Article 2(2) of the Fair Value Directive.

[84] Directive 2003/51/EC of the European Parliament and of the Council of 18 June 2003 amending Directives 78/660/EEC, 83/349/EEC, 86/635/EEC and 91/674/EEC on the annual and consolidated accounts of certain types of companies, banks and other financial institutions and insurance undertakings, *O.J.* L 178 of 17 July 2003, 16-22.

[85] As the title of the Modernisation Directive indicates, it also amends the Directives that contain the specific accounting provisions for financial institutions and insurance undertakings. However, discussion of these amendments falls outside the scope of this article.

[86] See Articles 2, 4, 8, 10a and 22 of the Fourth Directive, as amended by Article 1(1) to 1(3), 1(6) and 1(9) of the Modernisation Directive, as well as Articles 16 and 17 of the Seventh Directive, as amended by Article 2(7) and 2(8) of the Modernisation Directive.

- to permit or require revaluation and valuation at fair value for assets other than financial instruments[87].

The amendments in this category are worded to the effect that "*the Member States may permit or require that …*". In other words, Member States are entirely free to decide whether they want to make these new provisions available to companies within their jurisdiction.

In addition, the Directive also contains new provisions relating to the annual report and the auditor's report, both with respect to the annual accounts and the consolidated accounts[88].

A final series of amendments aims at preventing listed companies from further using the accounting exemptions for small and medium-sized companies[89].

Unlike the first category, these last two categories of amendments require Member States to adjust their legislation.

3.3 The "Second Modernisation Directive" of 14 June 2006

30. ***General. Objectives of the Second Modernisation Directive.*** Those who had thought that the European legislator would fit in a period of rest after the (first) Modernisation Directive soon discovered that this was not to be the case. Indeed, on 14 June 2006, a new Directive was adopted, once more (essentially) amending the Fourth and Seventh Directives in various respects[90]. This Directive, which we will refer to as the "Second Modernisation Directive", is not only aimed at further closing the gap with IAS/IFRS. It is also intended to introduce new, specific arrangements in the field of *corporate governance* and director liability within the framework of the "*modernisation of company law*"[91]. These last amendments were introduced as a reaction to a number of major corporate failures, particularly Enron and Parmalat.

31. ***Amendments in terms of accounting law.*** In terms of accounting law, four amendments were introduced.

---

[87] See Articles 33, 42e and 42f of the Fourth Directive, as amended by Article 1(10), 1(12) and 1(13) of the Modernisation Directive. Pursuant to Article 29(1) of the Seventh Directive, this freedom of choice in terms of valuation rules also applies to the consolidated accounts.

[88] See Articles 46, 48, 51 and 51a of the Fourth Directive, as amended by Article 1(14) and 1(16) to 1(18) of the Modernisation Directive, as well as Articles 36 and 37 of the Seventh Directive, as amended by Article 2(10) and 2(11) of the Modernisation Directive.

[89] See Article 53a of the Fourth Directive, as inserted by Article 1(20) of the Modernisation Directive.

[90] Directive 2006/46/EC of the European Parliament and of the Council of 14 June 2006 amending Council Directives 78/660/EEC on the annual accounts of certain types of companies, 83/349/EEC on consolidated accounts, 86/635/EEC on the annual accounts and consolidated accounts of banks and other financial institutions and 91/674/EEC on the annual accounts and consolidated accounts of insurance undertakings, *O.J.* L 224 of 16 August 2006, 1-7.

[91] See in particular the three first Recitals of the Second Modernisation Directive.

First of all, the thresholds for the definitions of "small company" and "medium-sized company" are once again adjusted[92]. Pursuant to the new arrangements, Member States can increase the minimum balance-sheet total for small companies up to EUR 4,400,000 and the net sales figure up to EUR 8,800,000. With respect to medium-sized companies, they can apply a threshold of EUR 17,500,000 for the balance-sheet total and EUR 35,000,000 for the net sales figure[93].

A second novelty is directly related to IAS/IFRS. This involves a further expansion of the possibility introduced by the Fair Value Directive with respect to the valuation of certain financial instruments at their fair value (see no. 27 above). From now on, Member States can simply determine that all financial instruments (including financial assets and financial liabilities) may be valued in accordance with the IAS/IFRS standards (adopted by the European Commission)[94].

In addition, and once again in line with IAS/IFRS, the minimum content of the notes to the annual accounts and the notes to the consolidated accounts is expanded. In order to increase transparency, new disclosure requirements are introduced for off-balance-sheet arrangements and transactions with related parties[95].

Finally, the minimum content of the annual report is also expanded for reasons going beyond accounting law *sensu strictu*: listed companies are required to include a *corporate governance* statement in their annual report on the annual accounts[96]. In their consolidated annual report, they have to describe "*the main features of the Group's internal controls and risk management systems in relation to the process for preparing consolidated accounts*"[97].

32. *Amendments in terms of company law.* In addition to the amendments in terms of accounting law and, in line therewith, in terms of corporate governance, the Second Modernisation Directive also requires Member States to ensure that the members of the "*administrative, management and supervisory bodies*" are collectively responsible for the proper preparation and publication of the annual and consolidated accounts and the annual and consolidated annual report and that they are at least liable towards the company for failure to do so[98].

---

92 For the record: the previous adjustment was made in Council Directive 2003/38/EC of 13 May 2003, *O.J.* L 120 of 15 May 2003, 22-23.

93 New Articles 11 and 27 of the Fourth Directive.

94 New Article 42a(5a) of the Fourth Directive.

95 New Article 43(1),7a) and 7b) of the Fourth Directive and new Article 34,7a) and 7b) of the Seventh Directive.

96 New Article 46a of the Fourth Directive.

97 New Article 36(2), f) of the Seventh Directive.

98 New Articles 50b and 50c of the Fourth Directive and new Articles 36a and 36b of the Seventh Directive.

4. Transposition of the IAS/IFRS Regulation and of the (first) "modernisation wave" for the Fourth and Seventh Directives into Belgian accounting law

4.1 Transposition of the IAS/IFRS Regulation

33. ***Initiatives of the Belgian legislator pursuant to the IAS/IFRS Regulation. General.*** As the requirement for listed companies to prepare their consolidated accounts in accordance with IAS/IFRS for each financial year commencing on or after 1 January 2005 is stipulated by the Regulation and is therefore directly applicable, strictly speaking no intervention by the Belgian legislator was required.

Nevertheless, the Belgian legislator did take some initiatives, partly to facilitate transition to the required application of IAS/IFRS, and partly to create additional options and obligations for the transposition of IAS/IFRS with respect to companies that are not referred to in the Regulation. A total of four Royal Decrees were issued in this respect, three of which are essentially still important today[99].

Below we will first discuss the rules with respect to the application of IAS/IFRS, as incorporated by means of the Royal Decree of 18 January 2005[100] into the Royal Decree of 30 January 2001 implementing the Company Code (section 4.1.1).

We will then discuss the specific rules for credit institutions and investment companies (section 4.1.2) and for closed-end real estate investment companies (section 4.1.3).

4.1.1 Article 114 of the Royal Decree of 30 January 2001 implementing the Company Code: indication of the optional or required application of IAS/IFRS with respect to the consolidated accounts

34. ***General.*** Article 114 of the Royal Decree of 30 January 2001 contains the general rules with respect to the application of IAS/IFRS by Belgian companies.

This provision is part of Volume II ("Annual accounts, consolidated accounts and formalities with respect to disclosure") of the Royal Decree of 30 January 2001, which essentially further implements Volume IV, Title VI of the Company Code ("The annual accounts and consolidated accounts"). More

---

[99] The first Royal Decree is dated 4 December 2003 (Royal Decree implementing article 10, § 1, 2° of the Act of 2 August 2002 on supervision of the financial sector and financial services (*B.S.*, 9 January 2004) and is today, although it has not yet been repealed, mainly of historical significance. As a matter of fact, the major objectives of this Royal Decree have been incorporated into the general principles of Belgian accounting law dealing with consolidated accounts, as introduced by the Royal Decree of 18 January 2005 (see nos. 34-37 below).
Regarding this Royal Decree of 4 December 2003, see: F. HELLEMANS, "De IAS/IFRS-normen en de nieuwe Audit-Richtlijn", *T.R.V.* 2006, 642-643, no. 18.

[100] Royal Decree of 18 January 2005 concerning the application of international accounting standards (*B.S.* 9 February 2005, second edition).

specifically, Volume II, Title II ("Consolidated accounts") considers first the provision of the "Undertakings to be consolidated" (Chapter I) and then the "General principles" (Chapter II). It is in this last chapter that article 114 was incorporated.

The provision is essentially based on three principles, which we will discuss below.

35. *First principle: free choice for IAS/IFRS is allowed. Relation to the Fair Value Directive.* Pursuant to article 114 of the Royal Decree implementing the Company Code, the administrative body of each company, regardless of whether it is a listed or non-listed company, may decide to depart from the principle that the consolidated accounts must be prepared in accordance with the provisions of Volume II, Title II[101], and instead opt for preparation of the consolidated accounts "*in accordance with the entirety of international accounting standards as issued by the International Accounting Standards Board*" and "*adopted by the European Commission at the balance sheet date*" pursuant to the IAS/IFRS Regulation[102].

Thus the legislator grants the administrative bodies of all companies a great deal of freedom to decide in accordance with which accounting standards they wish to prepare their consolidated accounts – the Belgian standards in transposition of the Seventh Directive, or the IAS/IFRS standards.

This freedom is not unlimited, however: as a matter of fact, if the administrative body decides to shift to the IAS/IFRS system, then the shift is "*irrevocable*"[103]. In practice, this means that if, for example, a company intends to apply for an official listing and considers reporting under IAS/IFRS more appropriate in anticipation of this, its administrative body, without any additional approval (from, for example, the shareholders' meeting or the statutory auditor or any other supervisory authority) may modify the reporting from "Belgian GAAP" to IAS/IFRS, at least with respect to its consolidated accounts. If, however, it later turns out that a listing will not be feasible or becomes inappropriate, the company cannot switch back to Belgian GAAP.

If an administrative body makes use of this option, an indication must be included in the notes to the consolidated accounts that the company "*possesses the necessary administrative and organisational means*" to apply the IAS/IFRS standards (as adopted by the European Commission) as well as a description of these means and that the company applies all IAS/IFRS standards as adopted by the European Commission at the balance sheet date[104]. Although not explicitly stipulated, it may reasonably be assumed that these additional references only need to be incorporated into the notes to the first set of consolidated accounts that are prepared in accordance with IAS/IFRS. Furthermore, the positioning

[101] Article 114, § 1, first subparagraph R.D. implementing the Belgian Companies Code.
[102] Article 114, § 2, first subparagraph R.D. implementing the Belgian Companies Code.
[103] Article 114, § 2, second subparagraph R.D. implementing the Belgian Companies Code.
[104] Article 114, § 2, third subparagraph R.D. implementing the Belgian Companies Code.

of the new provisions indicates that these additional references in the notes are only required if the decision to prepare consolidated accounts in accordance with the IAS/IFRS standards was made on a voluntary basis.

By means of this general provision which expresses an "all-or-nothing" attitude, the Belgian legislator has first of all made use of the freedom offered by the IAS/IFRS Regulation to extend the scope of application of IAS/IFRS standards to companies other than listed companies (cf. no. 24 above). However, at the same time the Belgian legislator also transposed the first part of the Fair Value Directive (cf. no. 27 above). Thus, although technically speaking the Belgian legislator has correctly transposed the Fair Value Directive, it must nevertheless be emphasised that the final objective of the Directive, namely to bring national accounting law (following from the Fourth and Seventh Directives) a step closer to IAS/IFRS, has not been achieved. Indeed, a Belgian company will have to choose whether to prepare its consolidated accounts under Belgian GAAP (in which case financial instruments are valued in accordance with the provisions of Belgian GAAP), or on the basis of IAS/IFRS standards (in which case these standards will (also) apply to financial instruments).

36. *Second principle: certain companies are required to apply IAS/IFRS.* In addition to the voluntary "entry option" as discussed above (see no. 35), the Royal Decree of 18 January 2005 also contains the requirement for Belgian companies whose financial instruments are admitted to trading on a regulated market at the balance sheet date[105] to prepare their consolidated accounts in accordance with IAS/IFRS standards (adopted by the European Commission), as from the financial year commencing on or after 1 January 2005.

At the same time, certain listed companies were exempted from this requirement until the financial year commencing on or after 1 January 2007[106].

By means of this double arrangement, the legislator thus truly and fairly transposes the IAS/IFRS Regulation into Belgian accounting law[107].

37. *Third principle: required additional references in the notes if a company opts for IAS/IFRS.* Regardless of whether the preparation of consolidated accounts in accordance with IAS/IFRS is done on a voluntary basis or pursuant to an express statutory obligation, the notes to the annual accounts, according to Belgian law[108], must always contain, in addition to the information required by IAS/IFRS, the following four elements of information:
(i) the name, registered office and (with respect to Belgian companies) the

[105] This concept is defined in the same way as in the IAS/IFRS Regulation, i.e. by referring to Article 1(13) of Council Directive 93/22/EEC of 10 May 1993 on investment services in the securities field.
[106] This relates to companies for which Article 9 of the IAS/IFRS Regulation allowed Member States to introduce a transitional regime (see no. 24 above, *in fine*). As the transitional period has already expired, we will not discuss this any further.
[107] See article 114, § 3 R.D. implementing the Belgian Companies Code.
[108] See article 114, § 4 R.D. implementing the Belgian Companies Code.

enterprise number of all companies included or excluded from the consolidation and of all associated companies;
(ii) the average number of staff members employed by the companies included in the consolidation, with a breakdown by category;
(iii) the overall remuneration paid to all directors or managing directors of the consolidating company for the positions occupied by them at that company, its subsidiaries and its associated companies; the amounts of retirement pension paid to former directors or managing directors, as the case may be, must also be included in this overall remuneration;
(iv) the overall amount of the advances and loans granted to directors or managing directors of the consolidating company by that company, a subsidiary, or an associated company.

These references are not "new": as a matter of fact, the same references, as well as a number of other references, are also included in the notes to the consolidated accounts prepared in accordance with Belgian accounting law[109]. The references concerned were specifically incorporated in article 114, §4 of the Royal Decree implementing the Company Code because they refer to provisions of the Seventh Directive that continue to be applicable to companies preparing their consolidated accounts in accordance with IAS/IFRS (cf. no. 25 above).

4.1.2 The Royal Decree of 23 September 1992: required application of IAS/IFRS with respect to the consolidated accounts of credit institutions and investment companies

38. The Royal Decree of 23 September 1992 contains specific rules with respect to the consolidated accounts of credit institutions (and, in line with that, of investment companies).

When amending this Royal Decree by means of the Royal Decree of 5 December 2004[110], the legislator (once more) made use of the freedom offered by the IAS/IFRS Regulation by requiring all credit institutions and investment companies, even if they are not listed, to apply IAS/IFRS standards for the preparation of their consolidated accounts, as from the financial year commencing on or after 1 January 2006[111].

As listed credit institutions and investment companies, by virtue of the IAS/IFRS Regulation (subject to exceptional cases), were already obliged to prepare their consolidated accounts in accordance with IAS/IFRS as from the financial year commencing on or after 1 January 2005, in practice this Decree is especially important for non-listed credit institutions and investment companies.

[109] See article 165, II to V, XIV.B and XVII R.D. implementing the Belgian Companies Code.
[110] Royal Decree of 5 December 2004 amending Royal Decree of 23 September 1992 on the consolidated accounts of credit institutions, *B.S.* 28 December 2004.
[111] See article 5 of the Royal Decree of 23 September 1992 on the consolidated accounts of credit institutions, applicable as from 1 January 2006 (pursuant to articles 7 and 14 of the R.D. of 5 December 2004). See also the Report to the King preceding the R.D. of 5 December 2004 (*B.S.* 28 December 2004, 85.877).

4.1.3 The Royal Decree of 21 June 2006: required application of IAS/IFRS with respect to the annual accounts of closed-end real estate investment companies

39. *Application of IAS/IFRS standards to the consolidated accounts by virtue of the general provisions of the accounting law. Extension of the use of IAS/IFRS standards to the annual accounts by the Belgian legislator.* Article 75 of the Act of 20 July 2004 on certain forms of collective management of investment portfolios requires that the rights to participation in closed-end real estate investment companies are traded on a regulated market. By virtue of the general provisions of the accounting law (see no. 36 above), closed-end real estate investment companies must therefore prepare their consolidated accounts in accordance with IAS/IFRS standards.

The Belgian legislator was in no case whatsoever obliged to introduce additional requirements with respect to closed-end real estate investment companies, but the legislator decided to do so anyway, for two reasons.

First of all, the legislator had established that, of the limited number of closed-end real estate investment companies operating in Belgium, some prepared consolidated accounts and others did not. As a result, it was very difficult or even impossible to compare the annual accounts of these closed-end real estate investment companies – which were prepared on the basis of different standards (IAS/IFRS or Belgian GAAP respectively).

The same problem of comparability obviously also applies to (other) listed companies, whether or not they prepare consolidated accounts. Unlike those companies, however, closed-end real estate investment companies are not taxed on the basis of their normal profits (derived from rental income and/or capital gains on transfers of real property), but only on their non-deductible expenses, other than impairments and capital losses on equity shares. That is why the annual accounts of closed-end real estate investment companies do not serve as a basis for completion of the tax computation, but rather have an informational function. It is precisely "*the absence of obstacles in terms of fiscal law*" that made the legislator decide to extend the use of IAS/IFRS standards to the annual accounts of closed-end real estate investment companies.

This is exactly what article 2 of the Royal Decree of 21 June 2006[112] has done. Pursuant to this provision, closed-end real estate investment companies must "*prepare their annual accounts on the basis of the international standards that are adopted by the European Commission at the balance sheet date*" in application of the IAS/IFRS Regulation.

40. *Specific technique to make the IAS/IFRS standards applicable to the annual accounts of closed-end real estate investment companies.* Although the Belgian legislator could perfectly well have achieved this extension of the

---

[112] Royal Decree of 21 June 2006 on the bookkeeping, the annual accounts and the consolidated accounts of public closed-end real estate investment companies and amending Royal Decree of 10 April 1995 concerning real estate investment companies, *B.S.* 29 June 2006.

IAS/IFRS standards to the annual accounts of closed-end real estate investment companies as part of the implementation of the IAS/IFRS Regulation (see no. 24 above), the legislator deliberately chose not to do this. As a matter of fact, a direct application of the IAS/IFRS standards pursuant to Article 5 of the IAS/IFRS Regulation would have meant losing any opportunity to make subtle distinctions or modifications.

Instead, the Belgian legislator chose, with respect to the annual accounts of closed-end real estate investment companies, to refer to the use of IAS/IFRS standards in national law. This approach, which is perfectly possible in the light of the Modernisation Directive of 18 March 2003[113], allows the legislator to require all closed-end real estate investment companies to use a standard balance sheet and income statement format for the preparation of their annual accounts[114]. This would not have been possible under IAS/IFRS (which do not introduce standard formats for the financial statements).

These standard formats are especially necessary because closed-end real estate investment companies on the one hand are subject to a limited overall debt burden and on the other hand have to comply with minimum requirements in terms of profit distribution. Both obligations were incorporated in the Royal Decree of 21 June 2006 through the introduction of standard formats – a typical feature of Belgian GAAP. As such formats would cease to apply when making the IAS/IFRS standards applicable, it was considered desirable to find a means of preserving them, and this was actually achieved. This approach is especially interesting because it might also be used in the future, if the Belgian legislator should (ever) decide to require that companies other than closed-end real estate investment companies should prepare their annual accounts in accordance with IAS/IFRS. In that case, for example, the company law provisions with respect to capital maintenance (which currently refer to the concepts defined in the Fourth Directive) would also have to be adjusted.

Finally, it should be noted that the Belgian legislator also introduced some standard formats for the consolidated accounts of closed-end real estate investment companies. Unlike for the annual accounts, however, the standard for mats for the consolidated accounts are only optional[115]. Given the direct effect of the IAS/IFRS Regulation with respect to listed companies, the national leg

[113] See the Memorandum of the European Commission, "Comments concerning certain Articles of the Regulation (EC) No 1606/2002 of the European Parliament and of the Council of 19 July 2002 on the application of international accounting standards and the Fourth Council Directive 78/660/EEC of 25 July 1978 and the Seventh Council Directive 83/349/EEC of 13 June 1983 on accounting", November 2003, 10-12, to which the Report to the King (which precedes the Royal Decree of 21 June 2006) explicitly refers.

[114] See article 3 of the Royal Decree of 21 June 2006 on the bookkeeping, the annual accounts and the consolidated accounts of public closed-end real estate investment companies and amending Royal Decree of 10 April 1995 concerning real estate investment companies.

[115] Article 4 of the Royal Decree of 21 June 2006 on the bookkeeping, the annual accounts and the consolidated accounts of public closed-end real estate investment companies and amending Royal Decree of 10 April 1995 concerning real estate investment companies, *B.S.* 29 June 2006.

islator is not allowed to impose mandatory formats (which do not exist under IAS/IFRS).

4.2 Transposition of the (first) "modernisation wave" for the Fourth and Seventh Directives

41. ***General. The (minimalistic) transposition of the Fair Value and Modernisation Directives into Belgian law.*** A closer examination of the way the Belgian legislator has transposed the Fair Value and Modernisation Directives immediately reveals that the legislator opted for a decidedly minimalistic transposition of these Directives.

For example, the legislator only adopted the second part of the Fair Value Directive, i.e. the extended disclosure requirements with respect to certain financial instruments by means of the annual report (see no. 44 below) and the notes (see nos. 47-48 below) to the (annual or consolidated) accounts.

With respect to the transposition of the Modernisation Directive, the legislator also adopted a very minimalistic approach. The Explanatory Memorandum accompanying the draft which became the Act of 13 January 2006, transposing this Directive[116], makes no secret of this fact. It expressly states that the draft Act only refers to the transposition "*of the provisions of the directive that are required to be integrated*", i.e. (i) the requirement for all listed companies to prepare full accounts (see no. 43 below) and (ii) the additional disclosures required in the annual report (see no. 45 below) and in the statutory auditor's report (see no. 46 below). According to the Government, the question of whether, at a later stage, Belgium would adopt all or some of the Directive's options will be *"the subject of debate and deliberations on the modernisation of Belgian law in terms of annual and consolidated accounts within the scope of the proposals made by the Accounting Standards Commission to the Government"*[117]. So far, however, no such proposals have been formulated.

42. ***No transposition of the Second Modernisation Directive as yet.*** The Second Modernisation Directive, at the time of writing, has not yet been transposed into Belgian law. An answer to a recent parliamentary question[118] indicates that this transposition will be finalised shortly, the intention being to make the new provisions applicable to the financial years commencing on (or after) 1 September 2008.

[116] Note that in application of the Royal Decree of 19 November 2005 amending the Royal Decree of 30 January 2001 implementing the Belgian Companies Code (*B.S.* 2 December 2005), article 108 of the Royal Decree of 30 January 2001 implementing the Belgian Companies Code was amended in order to transpose Article 2(6) of the Modernisation Directive.

[117] Explanatory Memorandum, *Gedr.St.*, Kamer, 2004-2005, no. 2017/1, 4-5.

[118] Oral question from Mr Jenne De Potter to Minister Vincent Van Quickenborne regarding the "transposition of Directive 2006/46/EC".

4.2.1 Removal of the possibility for listed companies to use the accounting and audit exemptions for small companies

43. Within the scope of the transposition of the Modernisation Directive, the legislator first amended a number of provisions so that listed companies can no longer use the accounting and audit exemptions for small companies. As a consequence of these amendments, listed companies, even if they are "small" in the sense of article 15 of the Company Code, must always prepare full accounts and an annual report and must publish them[119], and they will always have to appoint a statutory auditor as well[120].

4.2.2 Additional disclosure required in the annual reports on the annual and consolidated accounts (articles 96 and 119 of the Company Code)

44. Regarding the annual report and the consolidated annual report, the legislator first of all reproduced the text of the corresponding sections of the Fair Value Directive word for word, which partly explains why the new articles 96, 8° and 119, 5° of the Company Code[121]are difficult to understand.

Thus, pursuant to the new regulation, "*with respect to the company's use of financial instruments and where material for the assessment of its assets, liabilities, financial position and profit or loss*", the annual reports on the annual and consolidated accounts respectively must contain the following data:

- "*The company's financial risk management objectives and policies, including its policy for hedging each major type of forecasted transaction for which hedge accounting is used, and*
- *The company's exposure to price risk, credit risk, liquidity risk and cash flow risk*".

Although not expressly stated in either the Fair Value Directive or the Belgian provisions transposing the Directive, it can be assumed that the concept of "*financial instruments*" must be interpreted in the light of IAS 32 and IAS 39 on the disclosure of information and the recognition and measurement of financial instruments respectively[122]. As a matter of fact, it is essentially to these standards that the Directive was intended to refer.

In practice, one should therefore use the (broad) definition of "financial instrument" contained in paragraph 11 of IAS 32 and further expanded in the "IAS 32 Implementation Guideline", which was published as Annex A

[119] Articles 93, last subparagraph, 94, first subparagraph, 1°, 99 and 100, 6° of the Belgian Companies Code transposing Article 1(20) of the Modernisation Directive.

[120] Article 141, 2° of the Belgian Companies Code, also transposing Article 1(20) of the Modernisation Directive.

[121] More specifically, the text of the last-mentioned provisions corresponds word for word with the amended Articles 46(2) and 36(2) of the Fourth and Seventh Directives.

[122] See also the Comments of the Accounting Standards Commission of 25 April 2005, concerning the transposition into Belgian law of Directive 2001/65/EC of the European Parliament and of the Council of 27 September 2001 amending Directives 78/660/EEC, 83/349/EEC and 86/635/EEC as regards the valuation rules for the annual accounts and consolidated accounts of certain types of companies as well as of banks and other financial institutions (available at http://www.cnc-cbn.be).

to IAS 32 and illustrates the definition by means of examples. In addition, paragraph 52 of IAS 32 also constitutes a convenient source of inspiration for the application of the new provisions: this paragraph specifies the risks that need further explanation in the annual report.

45. Furthermore, within the scope of the transposition of the Modernisation Directive, a more specific disclosure requirement was included in the annual report. In particular, the old provision requiring the annual report to contain a "*comment on the accounts (...) presenting a fair review of the development of the business and of its position*" was replaced with a new, more detailed provision according to which the annual report is to contain the following information:

"*at least a fair review of the development and performance of the company's business and of its position, together with a description of the principal risks and uncertainties that it faces. The review shall be a balanced and comprehensive analysis of the development and performance of the company's business and of its position, consistent with the size and complexity of the business.*

To the extent necessary for an understanding of the company's development, performance or position, the analysis shall include both financial and, where appropriate, non-financial key performance indicators relevant to the particular business, including information relating to environmental and employee matters. In providing its analysis, the annual report shall, where appropriate, include references to and additional explanations of amounts reported in the annual accounts."[123]

The same requirement is also introduced *mutatis mutandis* for the annual report on the consolidated accounts[124]. Furthermore, it is specified that when the annual report on the consolidated accounts is combined with the annual report on the annual accounts[125], it may be appropriate when preparing this unified report "*to give greater emphasis to those matters which are significant to the undertakings included in the consolidation taken as a whole*"[126].

Following these new provisions, the usual, general comment on the annual accounts, which in practice was nothing more than the reproduction of the major items from the balance sheet and the profit and loss account, can no longer constitute the rule. Instead, the annual reports must be prepared in a much more company-specific and more risk-oriented way. This is to allow the reader of the annual report to obtain a more accurate view of the development, performance and position of the company or the group to which it belongs.

---

[123] New article 96, 1° of the Belgian Companies Code implementing Article 1(14) of the Modernisation Directive.

[124] New article 119, second subparagraph (1) of the Belgian Companies Code implementing Article 2(10), a) of the Modernisation Directive.

[125] This was already possible under the old provisions of company law and remains possible under the new provisions of company law provided that the required data are furnished separately with respect to the consolidating company and the entities included in the consolidation.

[126] New article 119, third subparagraph of the Belgian Companies Code, implementing Article 2(10), b) of the Modernisation Directive.

4.2.3 Additional disclosure required in the statutory auditor's reports on the annual and consolidated accounts (articles 144 and 148 of the Company Code)

46. In line with the modifications with respect to the annual report, the content of the statutory auditor's report was also amended. Although for that reason both article 144 of the Company Code (with respect to the statutory auditor's report on annual accounts) and article 148 of the Company Code (with respect to the statutory auditor's report on consolidated accounts) were entirely rewritten[127], the impact of the changes is less dramatic than it appears at first sight. The most important difference with respect to the "old" statutory auditor's report is that from now on the statutory auditor's report must clearly indicate:

(i) the financial reporting framework in accordance with which the (annual or consolidated) accounts subject to the statutory audit are prepared;

(ii) the scope of the statutory audit and in accordance with which auditing standards the statutory audit was conducted;

(iii) whether the statutory audit results in an unqualified opinion, a qualified opinion, an adverse opinion, or, if the statutory auditor is unable to express an audit opinion, in a disclaimer of opinion;

(iv) the matters to which the statutory auditor draws attention by way of emphasis without qualifying the audit opinion[128].

In addition, it is also expressly stipulated that the statutory auditor must sign and date his report.

As the rest of the required references in the statutory auditor's report remain (almost) the same, it seems to us that in practice the "new" statutory auditor's reports will differ only slightly from those that existed before.

4.2.4 Additional disclosure required in the notes to the annual and consolidated accounts (articles 91, 97 and 116 of the Royal Decree of 30 January 2001 implementing the Company Code)

47. The notes on the (full) annual and consolidated accounts must mention "*where valuation at fair value of financial instruments has not been applied (...) for each class of <u>derivative financial instruments</u>, the <u>fair value</u> of the instruments, if such a value can be determined by any of the methods prescribed in article 97 C (of the Royal Decree implementing the Company Code)*", together with "*information about the extent and the nature of the instruments*" (articles 91, A, XX and 165,

[127] Implementing Articles 1(18) and Article 2(11) of the Modernisation Directive.

[128] Please note that, from now on, the information mentioned under points (iii) and (iv) also needs to be included if, in application of article 105 of the Belgian Companies Code, abridged annual accounts have been published: see article 105, *in fine* of the Belgian Companies Code as amended following transposition of Article 1(16) of the Modernisation Directive.

XVIII of the Royal Decree implementing the Company Code[129]; emphasis ours).

Although under current Belgian accounting law only companies preparing consolidated accounts in accordance with IAS/IFRS standards are entitled to measure their financial instruments at fair value[130], this new disclosure requirement is applicable to all Belgian companies that must prepare full[131] annual accounts or that prepare consolidated accounts in accordance with Belgian GAAP.

48. Article 97 C of the Royal Decree implementing the Company Code further defines the two basic concepts determining the scope of the new disclosure requirement.

First, it indicates what "*(correct*[132]*) fair value*"[133] means. This corresponds to the market value if "*a reliable market can readily be identified*" for the financial instrument concerned. If this is not the case, but there is a reliable market for the components of the financial instrument concerned or for a similar financial instrument, then the market value can be calculated on the basis of the market value of its components or that of the similar instrument. If no such alternative reference values are available, then the value of the financial instrument concerned is to be calculated "*by means of generally accepted valuation models and techniques*". These valuation models and techniques "*shall ensure a reasonable approximation of the market value*".

In addition, article 97 C of the Royal Decree implementing the Company Code defines the concept of "*derivative financial instruments*". More specifically, these comprise "*commodity-based contracts that give either contracting party the right to settle in cash or (in*[134]*) some other financial instrument (...), except when a) they were entered into and continue to meet the company's expected purchase, sale*

---

[129] These articles correspond almost word for word with Articles 43(14), a) and 34(15), a) of the Fourth and Seventh Directives, as amended by the Fair Value Directive.

[130] As mentioned above (no. 40), the closed-end real estate investment companies constitute the only exception.

[131] Please note that an exemption from this requirement for the notes to the abridged annual accounts is made possible by Article 44(1) of the Fourth Directive, as amended by Article 1(3) of the Fair Value Directive.

[132] We have added these brackets. As a matter of fact, in our opinion the word "correct" was added as a consequence of an inaccurate and inconsistent translation of the French term "*juste valeur*". Whereas everywhere else in the R.D. of 8 March 2005 this is consistently translated as "*fair value*", when it comes to article 97 C of the R.D. implementing the Belgian Companies Code this is suddenly (and unnecessarily) translated as "*correct fair value*". The Fair Value Directive also only uses the term "*fair value*".

[133] This section of Article 97 C of the R.D. implementing the Belgian Companies Code corresponds almost word for word with Article 42b(1) of the Fourth Directive which, pursuant to Article 29(1) of the Seventh Directive, also applies to the consolidated accounts.

[134] Please note that this word ("in") is not used in the Dutch text of article 97 C of the R.D. implementing the Belgian Companies Code. However, when comparing this text with the French version, it is clear that this also refers to the settling in cash or by means of any other financial instrument ("*dénouer en numéraire ou au moyen d'un autre instrument financier*" (emphasis ours)).

or usage requirements, b) they were designated for such purpose at their inception, and they are expected to be settled by delivery of the commodity". It is clear from the text of this provision that commodity-based contracts are only excluded (and therefore exempted from a specific disclosure requirement) if they meet the above three conditions cumulatively.

Although, unlike the provision concerning the annual report, the new provisions with respect to the notes contain some additional details regarding the meaning of the terms used, it is recommended to interpret the new provisions in the light of IAS 32 and IAS 39.

49. It should be clear from the two previous points that *none* of the newly introduced provisions *implies a requirement or permission for measurement of financial instruments at fair value*. This is despite the fact that (at least) permitting this valuation method was one of the objectives of the Fair Value Directive (see no. 27 above).

Does this mean that the Belgian legislator has not transposed the Directive in this respect? No, it does not. The answer to the question which companies are required or permitted to measure their financial instruments at fair value in Belgium is to be found in the answer to another question: which companies are required or permitted to prepare their consolidated accounts in accordance with IAS/IFRS standards ?

It is true that the Belgian legislator has failed to specifically transpose the first part of the Fair Value Directive (see no. 27 above). As a matter of fact, such specific transposition would have meant that companies preparing their annual or consolidated accounts in accordance with Belgian GAAP (and therefore not in accordance with IAS/IFRS standards) would have been allowed (or, as the case may be, even required) to measure their financial instruments at fair value. Rather than creating such permission (or requirement), the Belgian legislator has decided to determine in a general way the conditions under which Belgian companies may apply all IAS/IFRS standards (as adopted by the European Commission) (see no. 34ff. above, especially no. 35).

5. Overview of the (numerous) crossroads in the accounting landscape in 2008-2009

50. ***Available options regarding consolidated accounts***

EU

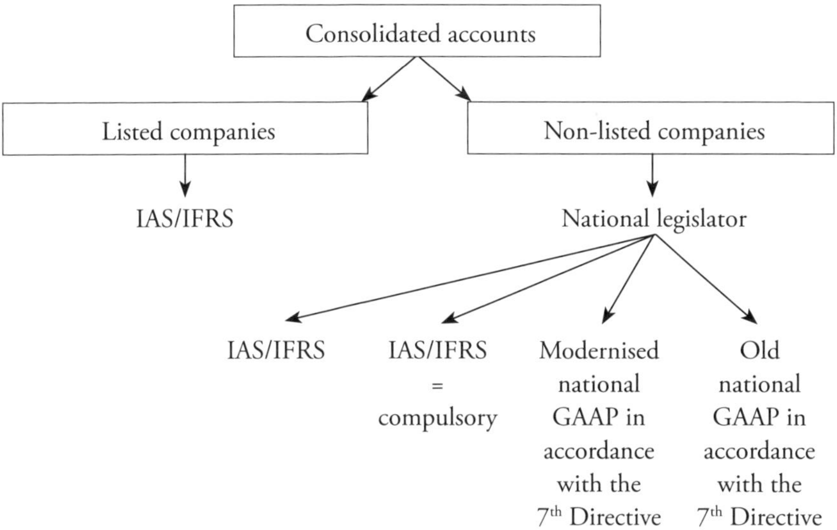

Belgium

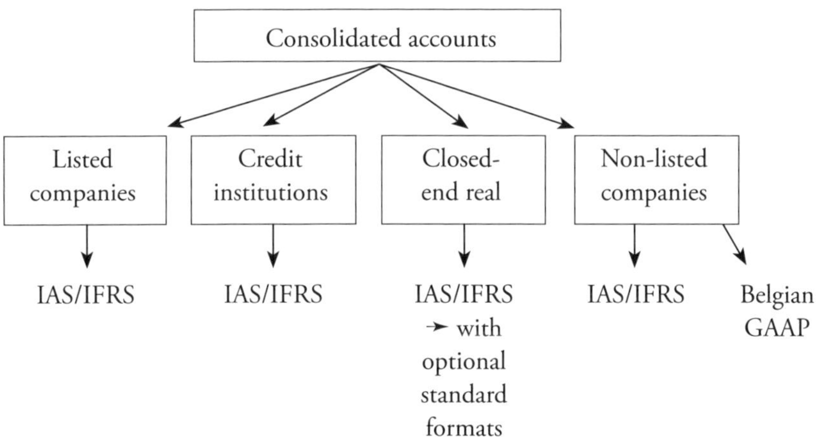

51. ***Available options regarding annual accounts***

EU

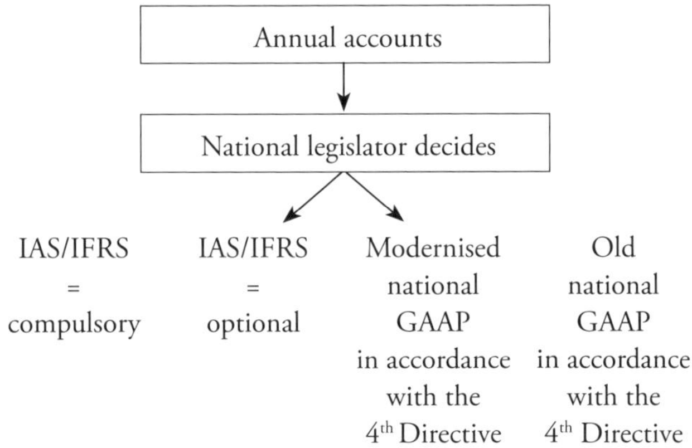

Belgium

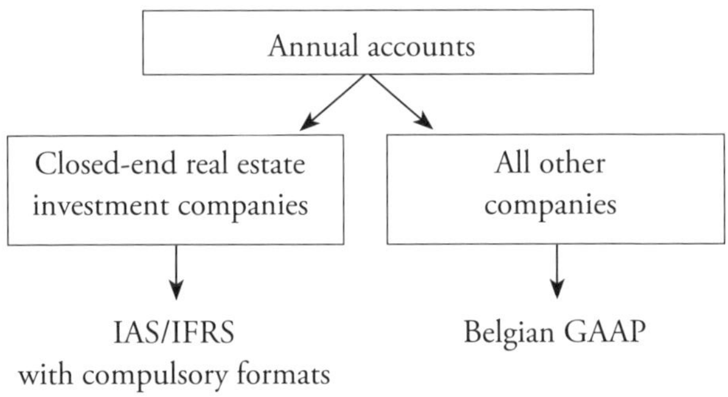

52. ***The financial reporting policy within the EU: does an "integrated approach" still exist?*** The above diagrams show that, both with respect to the consolidated accounts of non-listed companies and with respect to the annual accounts of all companies, there are a large number of options available for the national legislators. In this respect, it should be emphasised that these options come in addition to the options already contained in the "old" Fourth and Seventh Directives (see no. 4 above).

This immediately exposes the weakness of the current EU policy in the field of financial reporting for non-listed companies. Essentially, this policy consists in granting the national legislators, with respect to non-listed companies, very extensive powers to specify the applicable reporting standards. This will have an impact in terms of achieving comparability and equivalence of financial information. It seems that this objective for non-listed companies is now more remote than ever before.

53. *Basic options for the Belgian legislator: driven by fiscal concerns.* A comparison of the numerous options that exist within the EU regarding the preparation of (consolidated) accounts and the approach used by the Belgian legislator in this respect indicates that tax considerations played an important role.

The legislator used its best endeavours to retain the annual accounts without any changes, as far as this was possible[135]. It was only with respect to the notes to the annual accounts that a number of modifications were introduced (see nos. 47-48 above). In addition, new requirements were also imposed with respect to the annual report and the statutory auditor's report on the annual accounts (see nos. 44-45 above). No modifications were introduced with respect to the balance sheet or the profit and loss account. As a consequence, for the time being the approximation of Belgian GAAP and IAS/IFRS, as desired by the European legislator, appears to consist only of additional disclosure requirements that must be met and which, in essence, are all aimed at determining the fair value of certain assets and the real risk of the company's activities. As indicated (see no. 39 above), the reason for this conservative approach of the Belgian legislator lies in the link between accounting law and fiscal law[136].

Partly because there is no such link in the field of consolidated accounts, when transposing the European provisions on consolidated accounts, the legislator opted for an approach that was frankly liberal, sometimes even revolutionary. For example, not only Belgian listed companies but also all Belgian credit institutions and investment companies (whether they are listed or not) are required to apply the IAS/IFRS standards (adopted by the Commission). Furthermore, all Belgian companies that are required to prepare consolidated accounts are entitled to apply the IAS/IFRS standards (adopted by the Commission).

6. Difficult issues to resolve

6.1 Amendments to the Accounting Directives

54. *The EU approach for listed versus non-listed companies: a radical difference.* Since the adoption of the IAS/IFRS Regulation, the issue of how to deal with those companies which remain fully covered by the Accounting

[135] The situation is different (e.g.) in France, where the rules applicable to the annual accounts converge towards the IAS/IFRS standards. See J-L. ROSSIGNOL and M. DE WOLF, "La comptabilité des PME face à la normalisation internationale en France et en Belgique", 2006, ed. 10, 324-325.

[136] For an analysis of the link between (Belgian) accounting law and fiscal law, and between accounting law and company law, see, H. LAMON and A. VAN BAVEL, "IAS/IFRS pour les comptes sociaux de toutes les sociétés belges?", 2006, ed. 80, 348-383. On the impact which the application of IAS/IFRS to the annual accounts would have from the viewpoint of Belgian company law, see, D. SZAFRAN, "Quelques incidences en droit des sociétés de l'application des normes comptables internationales IAS/IFRS", 2006, ed. 4, 379-403.

Directives (mainly non-listed companies) has preoccupied the Commission and Member States. Indeed, the approach followed by the EU for the 8,000 listed companies is radically different from that which remains in place for the 7,158,000 companies covered by the Accounting Directives.

For listed companies, the EU now has uniform financial reporting rules, whilst minimum harmonisation with a wide range of options remains the framework for unlisted companies. Whilst the modernisation of the Accounting Directives allowed Member States to bring these companies totally or partially within the scope of IFRS, most Member States have remained rather prudent in this area, considering in particular the great (and increasing) complexity of IFRS.

55. ***The draft IFRS for Small and Medium-Sized Entities.*** Some people had hoped that the IASB would have provided a solution which could also have been picked up by the EU. Indeed, in February 2007, the IASB published an Exposure Draft of a proposed IFRS for Small and Medium-Sized Entities, which was published as a new Financial Reporting Standard (*IFRS for SMEs)* on 9 July 2009. The standard is a simplified, self-contained set of accounting principles that are considered appropriate for smaller, non-listed companies. Whilst the IASB's 2007 Bound Volume of IAS/IFRS standards is over 2,600 pages in length, the IFRS for SMEs is 230 pages, plus a separate Basis for Conclusions (48 pages) and accompanying Illustrative Financial Statements and Disclosure Checklist (80 pages) with pages 20% smaller in size than the pages in the Bound Volume[137].

Although this new standard might provide a solution for medium-sized and large non-listed companies, most commentators in the EU have concluded that this could never be a suitable standard for the smaller companies[138].

For a number of years now, the debate has been dominated by concerns of deregulation and simplification. The Accounting Directives have been identified as particularly burdensome for small and medium-sized companies and the Commission has been very active in trying to respond to the concerns raised by stakeholders and also by the European Parliament.

[137] See P. PACTER, "IFRS for SMEs: meeting user needs and reducing preparer burdens", in H.-G. BRUNS, R.H. HERZ, H.-J. NEUBÜRGER and D. TWEEDIE (eds.), *Globale Finanzberichterstattung / Global Financial Reporting,* Stuttgart, Schäffer-Poeschel, 2008, 255-272.

[138] See for instance the December 2007 synthesis of the reactions received by the Commission to its Communication on a simplified business environment for companies in the areas of company law, accounting and auditing, published on the Commission's website, 15. See also, P. HOMMELHOFF, "Modernisiertes HGB-Bilanzrecht im Wettbewerb der Regelungssysteme", *ZGR* 2008, 272-274.

6.1.1 Communication from the Commission on a simplified business environment for companies in the areas of company law, accounting and auditing

56. *The growing (political) pressure to reduce the administrative burden.* Already in 2005, the Commission launched a programme for measuring administrative costs and reducing administrative burdens in order to improve the business environment for EU companies and to make the EU economies fit to meet the challenges of the more competitive global business environment in which they have to operate. The Commission outlined the way to achieve this by adopting, on 14 November 2006, an updated simplification programme[139] and the main elements for measuring administrative costs and reducing administrative burdens[140]. Both programmes emphasised the need to generate tangible economic benefits. They were complemented by the Action Programme adopted on 24 January 2007 which set the aim of a 25% reduction in the administrative burdens on businesses in the EU by the year 2012 and launched the first package of fast-track proposals.

57. The European Council of 8/9 March 2007 endorsed the Action Programme, emphasising that reducing administrative burdens is important in boosting Europe's economy, especially given the potential benefits this can bring for SMEs. It stressed that a strong joint effort of the EU and the Member States is necessary to reduce administrative burdens within the EU. European company law, accounting and auditing had been identified as priority areas within this initiative. Preliminary analyses carried out by a number of Member States had shown that administrative costs caused by EU rules in these areas were particularly high[141].

In its Communication of 10 July 2007[142], the Commission stresses that a successful reduction of the administrative burden for SMEs in the areas of accounting and auditing requires action at both EU and national levels. Indeed, it makes no sense to increase the exemptions at the EU level when these exemptions are not passed on to companies at the national level. In addition, financial reporting should also be seen in the context of reporting for other purposes such as tax, statistics, social security and employment. Eventually the introduction of electronic reporting formats such as XBRL might provide a suitable answer.

---

[139] Communication from the Commission to the Council, the European Parliament, the European Economic and Social Committee and the Committee of the Regions - A strategic review of Better Regulation in the European Union, *COM* (2006) 689 final.

[140] Commission working document of 14 November 2006 – "Measuring administrative costs and reducing administrative burdens in the European Union", *COM* (2006) 691.

[141] See also the Study on Administrative Costs of the EU Company Law Acquis carried out on behalf of the Internal Market and Services Directorate General by Ramboll Management (July 2007), available on the Commission's website at the address referred to in footnote 24.

[142] Communication from the Commission, "A simplified business environment for companies in the areas of company law, accounting and auditing, *COM* (2007) 394 final.

58. ***Possible measures to reduce the administrative burden.*** Having recognised that the IASB standard for SMEs is unlikely to provide sufficient elements to simplify the life of European SMEs, the Commission identifies a number of other measures that could lead to tangible simplification for SMEs:

- To exempt "micro entities", i.e. companies with fewer than ten employees, with a balance sheet total below EUR 500,000 and a turnover below EUR 1,000,000, from the scope of application of the Accounting Directives;
- To extend the transition period for SMEs crossing the thresholds from two to five years;
- To exempt small entities from the requirement to publish their accounts;
- To make it possible for certain medium-sized entities to use exemptions currently available only for small entities;
- To simplify the procedure for the adaptation of the thresholds;
- To allow certain companies which do not have a wide range of external users of financial statements, such as owner-managed companies and unlimited liability companies (GmbH&Co KG) to use the regime applicable for small companies;
- To exempt certain subsidiaries included in consolidated accounts from the requirement to prepare annual accounts (Article 57 of the Fourth Directive);
- To exempt a parent undertaking from the requirement to prepare consolidated accounts if none of its subsidiaries is material;
- To exempt SMEs from the requirement to disclose information on deferred taxes (Article 43(1)(14) of the Fourth Directive);
- To exempt medium-sized companies from the requirements to provide an explanation of formation expenses (Article 34(2) of the Fourth Directive) and to disclose the breakdown of net turnover into categories of activity and geographical markets (Article 43(1)(8) of the Fourth Directive).

From the reaction of stakeholders[143], it became apparent that there was a great deal of support for allowing Member States to exempt micro entities from the scope of application of the Fourth Directive. A preference was expressed for extending the transition period for SMEs crossing the thresholds from two to three years. A majority of respondents opposed exempting small companies from publishing their accounts, and there was no majority support for an extension of exemptions for companies without particular external users of financial statements. The other proposed simplifications received a great deal of support[144].

---

143 See the document referred to in footnote 138.

144 For a critical viewpoint on some of the aforementioned proposals for simplification, see Y. STEMPNIERWSKY, "La réduction des charges administratives des PME par une 'simplification' de leurs obligations comptables: un objectif louable mais une méthode inadéquate et des propositions dangereuses", 2007, 17-27.

6.1.2 Fast-track amendment of the Accounting Directives

59. *(Limited) simplifications proposed by the Commission. European Parliament calling for a more far-reaching proposal.* Following the reactions to its proposed simplifications in the Communication, the Commission decided to go ahead, in a fast-track procedure, with those simplifications that had received a great deal of support and did not require further examination.

In its proposal adopted on 17 April 2008[145], the Commission proposes three amendments to the Accounting Directives:

- To exempt medium-sized companies from the requirement to provide an explanation of formation expenses;
- To exempt medium-sized companies from the requirement to disclose a breakdown of net turnover into categories of activity and geographical markets;
- To exempt a parent undertaking from the requirement to prepare consolidated accounts if none of its subsidiaries is material.

In its impact assessment[146], the Commission concludes that the potential overall savings from the three measures would lie between EUR 11 and 21 million, provided of course that the exemptions would be passed on to companies by the Member States.

Both Rapporteurs in the European Parliament (on the Economic and Monetary Affairs Committee and on the Legal Affairs Committee), whilst supporting the Commission's proposal, call for a more far-reaching proposal. In its Resolution, the European Parliament invites the Commission to come forward with a uniform EU accounting framework before the end of 2009.

60. *Further initiatives regarding micro entities announced by Commissioner McCreevy.* On both issues, Commissioner McCreevy has recently announced further action. In a statement made on 29 September 2008[147], he announced that he will propose a further amendment of the Fourth Directive which would allow Member States to exempt micro entities from its scope of application.

---

[145] Proposal for a Directive of the European Parliament and of the Council amending Council Directives 78/660/EEC and 93/349/EEC as regards certain disclosure requirements for medium-sized companies and obligation to draw up consolidated accounts, *COM* (2008) 195 final.

[146] Commission Staff Working Document accompanying the Proposal for a Directive of the European Parliament and of the Council amending Council Directives 68/151/EEC and 89/666/EEC as regards publication and translation obligations of certain types of companies and the Proposal for a Directive of the European Parliament and of the Council amending Council Directives 78/660/EEC and 83/349/EEC as regards certain disclosure requirements for medium-sized companies and obligation to draw up consolidated accounts - Summary of the Impact Assessment, *SEC* (2008) 467.

[147] See the press release of 29 September 2008 "McCreevy announces major initiatives on accounting rules for small businesses", available on the Commission's website at the following address:http://ec.europa.eu/internal_market/company/simplification/index_en.htm.

This would represent a cost saving for each micro entity of about EUR 1,200 per year. Furthermore, the Commissioner has announced an overhaul of the Accounting Directives.

61. ***The need for a bottom-up approach.*** It is clear that the two issues are interlinked. Whilst the introduction of a micro exemption is likely to remove the bulk of the companies from the mandatory scope of the Accounting Directives in several Member States, there will still be a need for rules covering these companies, as many Member States will not use the option to exempt micro entities. If the present rules are considered too burdensome, the question then is how to proceed. The only sensible way forward seems to be to start from the bottom and define what the accounting needs are for small companies, and to increase the requirements moving up the ladder (for medium-sized and large companies). This approach is different from the present approach in the Fourth Directive which follows a top-down approach. The development of such a uniform framework will be complex, as it will require a number of important questions to be answered[148]:

- Should the EU continue to follow a company law approach in defining the accounting requirements (capital maintenance, profit distribution, creditor protection)?
- Should the EU favour a financial reporting model whereby accounting requirements and fiscal requirements are in principle separate?
- Should the EU favour a balance sheet approach (as preferred by the IASB) or continue to put more emphasis on the profit and loss account or on a cash flow statement?
- Should IFRS be used as a basis to develop the EU framework?
- Should the EU favour a valuation model based upon historical cost or move towards a full or partial fair value model?
- Should there still be options left to Member States or to companies?
- Should the uniform model be introduced by way of a Regulation or a Directive?
- Should the uniform model be optional or mandatory?
- How to ensure a smooth transition for companies moving from the EU framework to the IFRS framework (for instance, in the case of listing)?

[148] The Commission has created a working party of experts which has contributed to the development of a draft working paper that was published for consultation in February 2009. A meeting with stakeholders was held on 12 June 2009. Following the publication by the IASB of an International Financial Reporting Standard for SMEs on 9 July 2009, the Commission has decided to take more time to review the Accounting Directives to allow it to carry out consultations on this IFRS and, more generally, on specific needs of EU financial reporting. See the announcement published on the Commission's website.

62. ***Exempting micro entities from the Accounting Directives: a (real) cost-saving ?*** A study conducted on behalf of the Commission in January 2008[149] shows that exempting micro entities from the scope of the Accounting Directives would mean – if one were to adopt the criteria listed above – that 5,369,738 companies out of the 7,158,000 companies covered by the Fourth Directive would fall outside the scope of the Accounting Directives. The number of companies that would remain covered by the Fourth Directive would be reduced to between 1.68 million and 1.89 million. The study also concludes that this exercise would result in a total cost saving of EUR 5,976 million.

These figures are impressive. They should, however, be looked at in a proper perspective. Not all Member States are likely to make use of the option to exempt micro entities from the scope of the Directives. And even if an exemption is introduced, it is unlikely that the exempted undertakings will no longer be subject to national accounting requirements. These may over the course of time become even more burdensome than those following from the Directives.

From a Community point of view, the question is whether the internal market will be furthered by such an exercise. In this respect, particular attention will have to be paid to the disclosure of financial information. Especially in Germany, where there has always been opposition against the disclosure of financial statements by small and medium-sized enterprises, there is a risk that an exemption might make financial statements of German companies even less readily available to interested parties, particularly from other Member States. This would make cross-border trade more difficult. However, as the requirement to disclose financial information results from the First Company Law Directive, the optional exemption of micro entities from the scope of the Accounting Directives would not normally result in an exemption from disclosure.

63. ***The need for a public debate on the basic options.*** Before an exemption is introduced, there should be clear agreement between all parties concerned on the ultimate objectives of the exercise. Exemption at the EU level should not lead to the reintroduction at the national level of alternative rules that are even more burdensome than those of the Fourth Directive. Exemption should not lead to a situation where cross-border trade becomes more difficult. One should not forget that disclosure of financial information is regarded in many EU countries as the price to be paid for limited liability. If micro entities are no longer publishing financial data, the first victims of such a policy are likely to be their trading partners – which will mostly be other micro entities. Consideration should therefore be given to ensuring an appropriate level of disclosure of financial data by all companies with limited liability.

[149] Evaluation of Thresholds for Micro-Entities, Final Report produced on behalf of the Commission (DG Internal Market and Services) by the Centre for Strategy and Evaluation Services, January 2008, 91 p.

6.2 Financial crisis: modification of IAS 39 and IFRS 7

64. ***The risk of procyclicality.*** For years, EU supervisors and central banks have been voicing concerns about the need to include the objective of financial stability in IFRS. While recognising the benefits of the application of fair value to financial instruments for conveying the true economic situation of an undertaking to investors, they worried about the implications of increased volatility for financial stability (procyclicality). The current financial crisis has highlighted several shortcomings of applying in the financial sector an accounting framework based on a strict notion of fair value understood as the market exit price. In fact, as a result of the crisis, certain financial instruments were no longer traded or the related markets had become inactive or distressed, a situation which had not been foreseen in IAS 39.

The problem facing the EU was that, on the one hand, the IASB did not seem in a hurry to come up with an appropriate solution and that, on the other hand, action was taken in the US to remedy the situation, thereby creating an unlevel playing field between financial institutions in the US and financial institutions in the EU.

65. ***Action in the US.*** On 30 September 2008, the SEC issued accounting guidance which made it easier for US banks to move from fair value based on market price to fair value determined by models. US GAAP already provided the possibility of reclassifying financial instruments from fair value accounting to cost accounting regimes. This was either impossible or very difficult under IFRS. On 3 October 2008, the US administration approved the Troubled Asset Relief Programme (TARP). The relevant Act confirmed the SEC's authority to suspend mark-to-market accounting. This authority gave the SEC considerable flexibility to tailor the rules for a company, a sector or all entities.

66. ***Action by the IASB.*** The IASB, recognising the EU's concerns, issued press releases on 2 and 3 October 2008, stating that the SEC accounting guidance was consistent with IAS 39 and that the IASB would assess any remaining inconsistencies between IAS 39 and US GAAP on reclassifications of assets in order to eliminate differences. As the crisis worsened, and following the mini-G8 Summit in Paris on 4 October 2008 and the ECOFIN Council meeting on 7 October 2008, the Commission asked the IASB to change certain rules in IAS 39 in order to allow a reclassification out of the "fair valued asset" category so as to establish a level playing field between IFRS and US GAAP.

On 13 October 2008, the IASB adopted amendments to IAS 39 and IFRS 7 (Financial instruments: disclosures). These amendments allow the reclassification of certain financial instruments out of the "held-for-trading" category in rare circumstances. The current financial crisis is considered to be one of the rare circumstances which would justify the use of this possibility for companies. In accordance with the amendments, companies are allowed to reclassify these financial instruments as from 1 July 2008, thereby making it possible to positively influence their third quarter results.

67. ***Action by the EU.*** After consulting EFRAG and the ARC in a fast track procedure, on 15 October 2008 the Commission adopted a Regulation introducing the relevant amendments and allowing EU financial institutions to immediately apply the amended rules[150]. In order to obtain speedy endorsement, the Commission had to issue a declaration indicating the need to take further steps. The Commission organised a stakeholders meeting on 21 October 2008 to examine which further measures needed to be taken. Following that meeting, the Commission wrote to the IASB on 27 October 2008 requesting further action on the following issues:

- Guidance on the application of fair value in illiquid markets and particularly on the use of mark-to-model;
- The possibility of reclassifying financial assets currently classified under the Fair Value Option into other categories not measured at fair value;
- Clarification as to whether synthetic Collateralised Debt Obligations (CDOs) include embedded derivatives;
- A change in the approach to impairment losses for available-for-sale debt securities;
- The possibility of reversing impairment losses for equity instruments.

On 31 October 2008, the IASB published guidance on fair value when markets become inactive. This was welcomed by the Commission. However, on 14 November 2008, twenty national accounting standard-setters sent a communiqué to the IASB and to the IASC Foundation expressing support for the work of the IASB and insisting that due process should be followed in addressing accounting issues. Indeed, the Board had been criticised for having relaxed its due process rules in order to respond to the urgent requests from the Commission.

Following the G20 Summit Declaration, further work will have to be carried out by the IASB in order to address issues such as fair value guidance, off-balance sheet commitments, disclosures on financial instruments and risk exposure, IASB governance, best practices on hedge funds, convergence of standards and consistent application and enforcement.

It is interesting to observe that a large majority of Member States and stakeholders in the EU were clearly in favour of finding solutions for the

[150] Commission Regulation (EC) No 1004/2008 of 15 October 2008 amending Regulation (EC) No 1725/2003 adopting certain international accounting standards in accordance with Regulation (EC) No 1606/2002 of the European Parliament and of the Council as regards International Accounting Standard (IAS) 39 and International Financial Reporting Standard (IFRS) 7, *O.J.* L 275 of 16 October 2008, 37-41.

accounting problems resulting from the crisis within the international context of the IASB rather than coming forward with EU-specific solutions, for instance through the use of a new carve-out. On the other hand, it is striking that so much pressure needed to be exercised on the IASB before the Board moved into action in a situation which would clearly have called for leadership. The debate on improved governance of the IASB will therefore continue in the coming months.

Final considerations: European and Belgian accounting law: quo vadis?

68. ***IAS/IFRS as the uniform regime for (consolidated) financial reporting by listed companies.*** The Fourth and Seventh Directives stood the test of time until capital market pressure forced the EU to change its approach: from minimum harmonisation with options to a uniform regime of financial reporting. Because the EU did not have the means to develop its own standards in a short period of time and because there was a firm belief that the world needed a global set of accounting standards, the decision was made to join the efforts of the IASB to develop such a global set of accounting standards. With one stroke – the IAS/IFRS Regulation – international standards became part of EU law. Their ultimate adoption was however made subject to an endorsement procedure involving both a technical and a political part.

The introduction of the requirement for about 8,000 listed companies to prepare their consolidated accounts in conformity with IAS/IFRS was a success. Several studies that were conducted on this issue have come to that conclusion. Of course, the situation is still far from perfect because the magnitude of the change from national GAAP to IAS/IFRS was sometimes considerable. Improvements are certainly possible in the area of enforcement. Weaknesses in the system are likely to become apparent in times of economic crisis.

The procedure for the adoption of IAS/IFRS has become very complex. The process is still just about manageable. The attitude of the IASB has not made things easier. If the Board had been more responsive, it might have been possible to avoid some of the political interference that has occurred in connection with the endorsement of certain standards. Whilst an improvement of the governance of the IASB remains an important task for the future, it is equally important for the EU to ensure that the endorsement process does not become more burdensome. The upstream input of EFRAG into the work of the IASB is particularly important in this respect[151]. If the EU can speak with

[151] On 10 December 2008, EFRAG published its final report on the enhancement of EFRAG which contains a number of proposals aiming at making Europe a more important player in the financial reporting world. Of importance is the establishment of a three-tier funding model: European organisations, national funding mechanisms and the European Commission. The shared financial responsibility should ensure the commitment of all parties concerned to make EFRAG a success.

one voice at the international table, it will become much easier to convince stakeholders afterwards that the standard or interpretation is appropriate.

With its choice in favour of international standards, the EU has put the IASB on the map. Many countries have followed or are in the process of following the EU's lead in this area. If the EU had decided otherwise, the prospect of one set of accounting standards for the world would still have been very remote. The question remains whether it will be possible in the end to have only one set of identical standards for all major countries in the world. It is not clear whether comparability requires identical standards. What is important is that the starting point remains the same, i.e. the objectives of financial reporting and the conceptual framework on which the standards are based must be largely the same. Variations will be difficult to avoid because they are linked to the enforcement regime, which is likely to remain different in different parts of the world.

When transposing the European provisions on consolidated accounts, Belgium has taken a liberal approach. As a consequence, not only Belgian listed companies but also all Belgian credit institutions and all closed-end real estate investment companies (whether they are listed or not) are required to apply the IAS/IFRS standards (adopted by the Commission). Furthermore, all Belgian companies that are required to prepare consolidated accounts are entitled to apply the IAS/IFRS standards (adopted by the Commission).

69. *The difficult way forward for financial reporting by non-listed companies.* It is clear that the EU has difficulties in deciding on the way forward for the financial reporting requirements of non-listed companies. Although a clear message was given by the Commission to Member States that IAS/IFRS was the way forward, only a minority of Member States have decided to follow this route.

The minimalistic approach taken by the Belgian legislator – implementing only those European provisions concerning the annual accounts that must be transposed – is therefore certainly not exceptional within the EU. As in other Member States, a close linkage exists in Belgium between accounting and taxation. As the annual accounts form the basis for corporate taxation, any change in the accounting rules risks having immediate consequences in terms of the amount of taxes to be paid. Under these circumstances, any move towards applying IAS/IFRS standards in the annual accounts will only be seriously considered after an in-depth examination of other possible legal measures that are needed to guarantee the tax neutrality of such a reform. It seems that, at least for the time being, there is no real political or economic pressure to embark on such an exercise and to carry out such an examination.

Meanwhile, there is, at the EU level, serious pressure on the Commission to relax the reporting requirements for small and medium-sized companies. The Commission has carried out the preparatory work and has decided to follow the wishes of a clear majority of Member States and of the European Parliament. The proposal, which was officially introduced on 26 February 2009[152], has already proven to be controversial. It will however have the advantage of putting the issue clearly on the table so that all parties concerned can decide on the basis of facts and figures. The internal market perspective, however, cannot be overlooked: deregulation must not lead to a situation where cross-border trade becomes more difficult. There is room here for some creative thinking. Deregulation at EU level should not lead to re-regulation at national level. That would be the worst possible solution. Some guarantees will have to be built into the system to avoid such a situation.

70. ***The financial crisis and the need for a renewed debate on fundamental principles of financial reporting.*** The financial crisis has shown that the existing international standards dealing with financial instruments are still far from perfect. Particularly for financial institutions, it is important to avoid procyclical effects of the standards. Whilst over-prudence might have been a problem in the past, a lack of prudence is also a problem. The prohibition on creating a provision unless there is a present obligation at the balance sheet date may need to be looked at again. On the other hand, it would be wrong to put all the blame on fair value. It is not so much the fair value rule itself but the way in which it is being applied that has led to difficulties. More importance will have to be attached to capital maintenance and the stewardship approach., concepts which are firmly enshrined in the European approach towards financial reporting. In the same way as sustainability has become a key issue for the environment, sustainability should also receive more attention in financial reporting. The short-termist approach combined with a distribution of short term profits needs to be reversed in favour of a more sustainable model whereby companies can or have to reserve certain "profits" to prepare for bad times.

Finally, there is the question of the role of communication in financial reporting, which does not seem to receive sufficient attention. Financial reporting is the technique through which the financial situation of an entity is communicated to a broader audience. This must be done with care. If accounting standards become too sophisticated, the communication with the broader audience is bound to suffer and the financial information is likely to be misunderstood.

---

[152] Proposal for a Directive of the European Parliament and of the Council amending Directive 78/660/ EEC of the Council on the annual accounts of certain types of companies as regards micro-entities, (2009) 83 final.

Bibliography

J. ARDEN, "True and fair view: a European perspective", *European Accounting Review* 1997, 675-679.

H. BECKMAN, "Jaarrekening en verantwoording", *Ondernemingsrecht* 2007, 226-230.

H. BIENER, "Procedural reforms", in Commission of the European Communities (ed.), *The future of Harmonization of Accounting Standards within the European Communities,* Office for Official Publications of the European Communities, Luxembourg, 1990, 109-110.

M. BONHAM and others, "The Quest for a conceptual framework for financial reporting", in ERNST & YOUNG (eds.), *International GAAP 2007,* London, LexisNexis, 2006, 77-167.

M. BONHAM and others, "The influence of the G4 + 1 Group of standard setters on international accounting", in H.-G. BRUNS, R.B. HERZ, H.-J. NEUBÜRGER and D. TWEEDIE (eds.), *Globale Finanzberichterstattung / Global Financial Reporting,* Stuttgart, Schäffer-Poescheol, 2008, 11.

Central Council of Economy ("*Centrale Raad voor het Bedrijfsleven*"), "IAS/IFRS: toelichting voor de leden van de ondernemingsraden", 13 September 2006, 44 p. (available on the website of the Institute of Auditors: www.ibr-ire.be).

Comments of the Accounting Standards Commission of 25 April 2005, concerning the transposition into Belgian law of Directive 2001/65/EC of the European Parliament and the Council of 27 September 2001 amending Directives 78/660/EEC, 83/349/ EEC and 86/635/EEC as regards the valuation rules for the annual accounts and consolidated accounts of certain types of companies as well as of banks and other financial institutions (available at http://www.cnc-cbn.be).

D. DAMANT, "The IASB Framework – creator of wealth", in H.-G. BRUNS, R.B. HERZ, H.-J. NEUBÜRGER D. TWEEDIE (eds.), *Globale Finanzberichterstattung / Global Financial Reporting,* Stuttgart, Schäffer-Poeschel, 2008, 17-29.

S. ENEVOLDSEN and TH. OVERSBERG, "Importance of a European voice in international standard setting", in H.-G. BRUNS, R.H. HERZ, H.-J. NEUBÜRGER and D. TWEEDIE (eds.), *Globale Finanzberichterstattung/ Global Financial Reporting,* Stuttgart, Schäffer-Poeschel, 2008, 89-106.

K. GEENS, "De nieuwe harmonisatiedynamiek van het vennootschapsrecht: een 'eerste klas' begrafenis van het Europees vennootschapsrecht na vijftig jaar?", *T.R.V.* 2006, 75-89.

A. HALLER, "Financial accounting developments in the European Union: past events and future prospects", *European Accounting Review* 2002, 153-190.

F. HELLEMANS, "De IAS/IFRS-normen en de nieuwe Audit-Richtlijn", *T.R.V.* 2006, 631-658.

P. HOMMELHOFF, "Modernisiertes HGB-Bilanzrecht im Wettbewerb der Regelungssysteme", *ZGR* 2008, 250-274.

R. KROCKAERT, "Les normes IAS/IFRS, leurs perspectives et les conséquences peut-être imprévisibles de leur application, dans la convergence avec la modernisation du droit comptable belge", in X. (ed.), *Liber amicorum Guy Horsmans,* Brussel, Bruylant, 2004, 591-621.

H. LAMON and A. VAN BAVEL, "IAS/IFRS pour les comptes sociaux de toutes les sociétés belges?", *DAOR* 2006, ed. 80, 348-383.

J-L. ROSSIGNOL and M. DE WOLF, "La comptabilité des PME face à la normalisation internationale en France et en Belgique", *C&FP* 2006, ed. 10, 321-332.
H. OLIVIER, "L'adaptation des normes comptables aux besoins des marchés de capitaux", in X. (ed.), *25 jaar Boekhoudwet, Liber amicorum Michel vander Linden*, Diegem, Ced. Samson, 2000, 133-158.
H. OLIVIER, "Le concept d'équivalence des norms, une réponse à la mondialisation des marches de capitaux?", in *Van alle markten. Liber Amicorum Eddy Wymeersch*, Antwerpen, Intersentia, 2008, 731-748.
P. PACTER, "IFRS for SMEs: meeting user needs and reducing preparer burdens", in H.-G. BRUNS, R.H. HERZ, H.-J. NEUBÜRGER and D. TWEEDIE (eds.), *Globale Finanzberichterstattung / Global Financial Reporting*, Stuttgart, Schäffer-Poeschel, 2008, 255-272.
M. PETITE, "The conditions for consolidation under the Seventh Company Law Directive", *CMLR* 1984, 81-121.
C. POURBAIX, "Levée de capitaux internationaux. Clarté et comparabilité des états financiers (normes EU / IAS / US GAAP)", in X. (ed.), *Liber amicorum Henri Olivier*, Brugge, Die Keure, 2000, 417-441.
N. SOFIANOS and M. PELIDIS, "Corporate governance and international accounting standards: summary of presentation", in X., *Corporate Governance. Transparency and investors protection in listed companies*, Brussel, Bruylant, 2005, 61-74.
Y. STEMPNIERWSKY, "La réduction des charges administratives des PME par une "simplification" de leurs obligations comptables: un objectif louable mais une méthode inadéquate et des propositions dangereuses", *Rev. B. Compt.* 2007, 17-29.
D. SZAFRAN, "Quelques incidences en droit des sociétés de l'application des normes comptables internationales IAS/IFRS", *T.B.H.* 2006, ed. 4, 379-403.
C.W.A. TIMMERMANS, "Les comptes consolidés dans la CEE", *Revue de droit international et de droit comparé* 1977, 341-354.
K. VAN HULLE, "Het groepsbegrip in de zevende richtlijn", in *Liber Amicorum Jan Ronse*, Brussel, Story-Scientia, 1986, 345-356.
K. VAN HULLE., "Harmonisatie van de regels inzake financiële verslaggeving in de EG: Een getrouw beeld in een kleurenpalet", *De Accountant* 1989, 540-545.
K. VAN HULLE , "Harmonisatie van de regels inzake financiële verslaggeving: Eenheid in verscheidenheid", *Maandblad voor Accountancy en Bedrijfseconomie* 1992, 400-406.
K. VAN HULLE, "Das Europäische Bilanzrecht. Entwicklungen und Herausforderungen", *Wirtschaftsprüferkammer-Mitteilungen* 1994, 9-17.
K. VAN HULLE, "Prudence: a principle or an attitude?", *European Accounting Review* 1996, 375-382.
K. VAN HULLE, "The true and fair view override in the European Accounting Directives", *European Accounting Review* 1997, 711-720.
K. VAN HULLE, "Het beleid van de Europese Unie inzake boekhoudrecht", *Bull. C.B.N.* 1997, ed. 40-41, 249-258.
K. VAN HULLE, "De strategie van de Europese Commissie voor de harmonisering van financiële verslaggeving", *Acc. Bedr. (M) 1998,* 6-14.
K. VAN HULLE, "De Europese jaarrekeningrichtlijnen en de internationale verslaggevingsstandaarden van het IASC", in X (ed.), *Ondernemingsfinancieringsrecht*, Deventer, Kluwer, 1999, 11-36.

K. VAN HULLE, "Convergences in accounting rules and income tax legislation", in F. ABRAHAM, J. STUYCK and F. VANISTENDAEL (eds.), *Tax Policy and the Impending Economic and Monetary Union,* Leuven Law Series 12, Leuven, Leuven University Press, 1999, 117-126.

K. VAN HULLE., "Die Reform des europäischen Bilanzrechts: Stand, Ziele und Perspektiven", *ZGR* 2000, 537-549.

K. VAN HULLE and L. VAN DER TAS, "European Union – Individual Accounts", in D. ORDELHEIDE and KPMG (eds.), *Transatlantic Accounting,* Second Edition, Volume I, Basingstoke, Palgrave, 2001, 773-877.

K. VAN HULLE and L. VAN DER TAS, "European Union – Group accounts", in D. ORDELHEIDE and KPMG (eds.), *Transatlantic Accounting,* Second Edition, Volume I, Basingstoke, Palgrave, 2001, 881-951.

K. VAN HULLE, "From Accounting Directives to IAS", in CH. LEUZ, D. PFAFF and A. HOPWOOD (eds.), *The Economics and Politics of Accounting*, Oxford, Oxford University Press, 2004, 349-376.

K. VAN HULLE and N. LYBAERT, *Boekhoud- en jaarrekeningenrecht*, Brugge, Die Keure, 2005, 744 p.

K. VAN HULLE, "De toekomst van de Europese harmonisatie inzake het vennootschapsrecht", *T.R.V.* 2006, 150-167.

K. VAN HULLE, "Internationaliseren: een moeilijke opdracht", in X. (ed.), *Liber Amicorum Erik De Lembre. Accountancy tussen onderzoek en praktijk*, Mechelen, Kluwer, 2007, 183-197.

K. VAN HULLE, "IFRS as accounting standards for Europe", in H.-G. BRUNS, R.H. HERZ, H. J. NEUBÜRGER and D. TWEEDIE (eds.), *Globale Finanzberichterstattung / Global Financial Reporting,* Stuttgart, Schäffer-Poeschel, 2008, 71-89.

K. VAN OOSTVELDT, "De Belgische boekhoudwetgeving in een internationale veranderende omgeving", in X. (ed.), *Liber amicorum Henri Olivier*, Brugge, Die Keure, 2000, 593-601.

P. VERMOESEN and P. SCHUMESCH, "L'utilisation des normes comptables internationales par les entreprises belges: bilan et perspectives", in X. (ed.), *Liber amicorum Henri Olivier*, Brugge, Die Keure, 2000, 651-670.

P. WALTON, "The true and fair view and the drafting of the Fourth Directive", *European Accounting Review* 1997, 721-730.

X., "Dossier: Harmonisation comptable internationale", *C&FP* 1996, ed. 9, 1-35.

X. "Europese en internationale ontwikkelingen inzake boekhoudnormering", *Bull. C.B.N.* 2000, ed. 46, 11-18.

Transcripts of Financial Reporting Session

Paper: *Karel Van Hulle and Frank Hellemans*
Respondent: *Peter Van der Zanden (University of Tilburg) and Hans Beckman (University of Amsterdam and University of Groningen)*
Chair: *Henri Olivier (University of Liège)*
Rapporteur: *Sven Bogaerts (K.U.Leuven)*

A. Abstract

Purposes of financial reporting. Financial reporting is a technique through which the financial situation of an entity is communicated to a broader audience. At present we are living in a complex world and we cannot expect financial reporting to be very simple. However, if accounting standards become too sophisticated – which they currently are – the communication with the broader audience is bound to suffer and the financial information is likely to be misunderstood or even wrongfully communicated. And it is a general feeling that we have some problems ahead of us with the current development in accounting standards.

Scope of the different systems for financial reporting. There is a discussion ongoing about the possibility of fully exempting so-called "micro-entities" from the scope of the Fourth Directive (which has nothing to do with the usefulness of accounting as an internal management tool). The European Commission has identified a number of measures that could be considered to simplify the legislation and to reduce the administrative burdens imposed on "small" and "medium-sized" companies There was overall agreement during the session that the exemption of small entities from the EU legislation would certainly not be applied in all Member States and would possibly have a counter-effect. There was also general agreement that indeed, if the current system of disclosure (publication) of financial statements were to be abolished, this would result in a significant increase in administrative burdens and costs for "small and medium-sized companies". That is why the participants to the workshop agreed to recommend sticking to the current system.

Competent body and process. This issue was not discussed at large, except by the authors of the paper presented to the panel and in the response thereto. The issue finds its origin in the success of IFRS and the fact that IFRS are gradually becoming the global accounting standards. The challenge ahead of us is to make sure that the role of Europe will be safeguarded in future development of 'global' legislation.

Enforcement mechanism and consistent application of the International Financial Reporting Standards. The role of the securities organisations is quite important. The database that CESR (Committee of European Securities Regulators) has developed on IFRS interpretation issues was discussed with somewhat mixed feelings because there remains a fear that we are on the way to developing a new kind of "rules based" approach, such as the SEC has done with the "pre-clearance" system in the US. On the other hand, it was generally recognised that, in the end, the last word will remain with the court, since we are dealing with EU law. Given the fact that IFRS now forms part of the EU legislation, the possibility exists that in the end the European Court of Justice may have to interpret International Financial Reporting Standards. Such judicial review may again lead to diversity.

B. Response to paper by Hans Beckman and Peter Van der Zanden

Hans BECKMAN

With great interest and appreciation, I have read the paper prepared by my colleagues VAN HULLE and HELLEMANS. It is self-evident that, while reading this paper, various remarks and thoughts have come to the surface, several of which I have summarised.

1. The application of IAS/IFRS is, as far as the European Union is concerned, only possible through the IAS Regulation of 2002. For IAS/IFRS to become applicable in the Member States, an endorsement process has to be followed, whereby the "true and fair view" concept as laid down in the Fourth and Seventh Directives has to be verified, as well as several quality requirements.

In this respect, it is strange to note that the quality requirements enumerated in the IAS Regulation cannot be found in these Accounting Directives, but are derived from the International Financial Reporting Standards themselves, whereas the "true and fair view" concept does find its origin in the Accounting Directives.

This means – in my opinion – that the "true and fair view" test, when applying this concept in relation to IFRS, should be the test of the "true and fair view" concept as it is laid down in the Accounting Directives and not as this "true and fair view" concept has been formulated by the IASB (International Accountancy Standards Board) itself.

2. In practice, it appears that the IASB itself claims all power and authority, since over and over again it seems that the IASB fiddles with its own set of concepts, each time extending their scope and interpretation.

Here are some examples:

- "Consolidated annual accounts": the IAS Regulation refers to the concept of consolidated accounts as defined by the Seventh Directive, as a consequence of which, when preparing the consolidated accounts, even though prepared on the basis of IFRS, the consolidation circle has to be determined on the basis of the Seventh Directive and not on the basis of the concept of consolidated accounts as described in IFRS rules.

- "Valuation of participations" in the statutory annual accounts: such valuation has to take place in accordance with national GAAP. The IASB) follows this approach as far as it concerns a non-affiliated entity. However, when confronted with a participation in an affiliated entity, a joint venture or a subsidiary, the statutory annual accounts are then denominated as "*separate financial statements*", with the IASB imposing separate requirements for the valuation of such participations in those statements. In my opinion, by requiring this, the IASB exceeds the boundaries of its competences in view of the fact that such statements – given their nature – are not consolidated accounts. Under this position of the IASB, the valuation of such participations against "equity value" – an option under the Accounting Directives – would not be permissible for statutory annual accounts with participations.

- "Subsidiaries not to be consolidated": it is possible under IAS/IFRS that no consolidated accounts are needed where the relevant subsidiary serves a sales function. In that event, there will be no consolidated accounts and IFRS cannot be mandatorily applicable, unless the national legislation would impose otherwise. In the view of the IASB there would nevertheless be a need for consolidated accounts – and thus the applicability of IFRS – if a listed company is involved.

- Relation to the annual report: the IASB has no authority in relation to the annual report. According to the Accounting Directives, information must be provided on the risks associated with the relevant company. The annual report – and the information required to be reported therein – is also required for listed companies. However, suddenly all kinds of disclosure requirements in relation to risk are now also incorporated in IAS 1 – to a large extent the same requirements as laid down in the Seventh Directive for the consolidated annual report. As a consequence, listed companies must apparently disclose this information both in the annual report and in the consolidated accounts.

- "Intermediate holding companies": under IAS, an intermediate holding company which is listed cannot invoke an exemption not to consolidate. If it were not listed, such exemption would exist. However, under the IAS rules the ultimate parent company must consolidate in compliance with IFRS. In my opinion, these provisions are not relevant – what is decisive are the rules laid down in the Seventh Directive. Under the rules of the Seventh Directive, an intermediate holding company is not required to prepare consolidated accounts if it is included in the consolidated accounts of the ultimate parent company and these accounts comply with equivalent requirements, such as US GAAP (Generally Accepted Accounting Principles).

3. The next remark relates to the choice between the mandatory or optional use of IAS/IFRS for the statutory annual accounts. The Dutch legislator deemed it opportune to create a mixed form which cannot be found in the IAS Regulation. In the statutory annual accounts under Dutch law, one or various valuation methods derived from IFRS may be used if the relevant company also provides consolidated accounts drawn up under IFRS. The aim is to ensure that the statutory and consolidated equity remains the same. This is an option which most probably is recommendable for other Member States. But even then, the question remains whether in such a situation the legislator should not require that all IFRS valuation rules should be used rather than leaving the choice to only pick the then most convenient valuation rules.

4. As to the specific requirements for drafting the annual accounts, the size of the relevant company/companies is also important – this is determined in accordance with the thresholds laid down in the Accounting Directives. Although it would seem plausible that in the Fourth Directive the statutory annual accounts are envisaged, there are various Member States that determine "small", "medium-sized" and "large" by comparing the consolidated figures with these thresholds. In these Member States, the relevant companies will be considered more quickly as "large" or "medium-sized" than in those Member States that compare the statutory figures with these thresholds. It is to be recommended that clear guidelines are created to ensure that the information on "size" ("small", "medium-sized" or "large") would become more comparable and "informative". In addition, the use under IFRS of criteria to distinguish between "small", "medium-sized" or "large" seems undesirable. The *summa division* should rather be and remain whether a company is "listed" or not.

As to "small" companies, I note that the Dutch legislator allows "small" legal entities to use their "tax" accounts as their "annual accounts".

5. Finally, a closing remark on "fair value": "Fair value" is a valuation method which exists, under both IFRS and the Accounting Directives, besides "historical costs" valuation and "current value" valuation. Both under the Accounting Directives and under IFRS, the revaluation reserves and current value alternatives of the Accounting Directives cannot be used in case of fair value. Nevertheless, the Dutch legislator did consider the "fair value" valuation as a form of "current value" and linked to it a revaluation reserve which is broader than the "fair value" reserve. Consequently, under Dutch law, revaluation reserves will be much more readily accepted than in other Member States. The desirability of this can be questioned. This being said, it can even be questioned whether the notion of "fair value" is altogether desirable.

Peter VAN DER ZANDEN

First of all, I gladly concur with the appreciation that Hans BECKMAN expressed for the contribution of our Belgian colleagues VAN HULLE and HELLEMANS.

In addition to what Hans BECKMAN pointed out with respect to the power that the IASB usurps, I would like to draw your attention to the recently published "*Exposure Draft 10 - Consolidated Financial Statements*" in which the IASB has proposed to extend the concept of "control" – again, you see, the same "extending" attitude to which Hans BECKMAN already drew the attention – a concept which lies at the basis of the consolidation obligation. It is the clear intention of the IASB, as stated in that Exposure Draft, to choose a "principles based" approach. However when one studies the documentation, it quickly becomes clear that IASB cannot escape having to formulate all sorts of specific criteria which will again result in a "rules based" approach.

Then let me share some observations that came up when reading the paper.

1. With respect to several issues, the paper focuses on the distinction in the legislation with respect to, on the one hand, listed companies which are (at least) for their consolidated figures subject to the IAS Regulation and, on the other hand, companies that are still subject to the Fourth and Seventh Directives.

First of all, I would rather see a distinction between listed (public) companies and non-listed (private) companies, and in each category there would then exist "large", "medium-sized" and "small" companies. In my opinion, the question that we should ask ourselves is whether and, if so, what the difference in external accounting should be for those different categories and on which basis we account for them?

To my understanding, in the IAS as well as in the paper, for the category of listed companies, the distinction between "large", "medium-sized" and "small" is irrelevant. However, the paper presented to us nowhere underpins this starting point and neither does, in my opinion, the IASB. If, for the sake of argument, we assume that making this distinction would be justified and that listed companies were to be regarded as one category, would this special status of listed companies in such a case not imply – as I argued before – that the legislation for the financial reporting of these listed companies should be included in securities law, rather than in company law in order to get the same position as is the case – I think – in the United States?

2. We should then introduce an "opt-out" possibility for the Seventh Directive for these companies. The consolidated annual financial statements could then – as a figure of speech – be "privatised", whereas the single (statutory) annual accounts could keep the function that they have in the company laws of several European jurisdictions. As a result there would be a clear distinction for the consolidated accounts, which would be solely regulated by the securities laws. This would better allocate the responsibilities for legislation and would also result in easier harmonisation of enforcement. The single (statutory) annual accounts could keep their legal status and their function in capital maintenance. In other words, the application of IFRS to the single (statutory) annual accounts keeps on presenting problems which are sometimes solved for Member States. This is beautifully demonstrated by the way in which the Dutch legislation described certain legal reserves and the way in which this is formulated in the Fourth Directive.

3. If non-listed companies were regarded as a separate category, the legislation for such companies could be based on the principle of "stewardship" for all involved. Indeed, in that case one could make the distinction between "large", "medium-sized" and "small" companies. This distinction seems to be explained by the balance between costs and benefits. It might well be that a separate category of micro-companies would indeed be an efficient solution because the weighing of costs and benefits in such a case is again different. The approach chosen by the authors appeals to me.

Often the form of the legal entity is not chosen for the limitation of liability but is merely tax driven. For that reason, companies also have to draw up financial accounts for tax purposes. Perhaps a solution may be found in also using these documents for financial reporting purposes. I refer to Hans BECKMAN's observations with respect to the situation in the Netherlands where the accounting of small companies on a tax basis has recently been allowed.

In this context, I would also like to point to the developments concerning the common consolidated corporate tax base that currently seems to have been put in the fridge but that could also be involved in this discussion.

4. In my opinion, studies and papers that express opinions regarding the development of rules and legislation for financial reporting should also put more focus on the difference that exists as to the "essence" of a company between the views in continental Europe on the one hand and the Anglo-Saxon world on the other hand. The Anglo-Saxon world uses an instrumental approach in which the company is regarded as the property of the shareholders as well as an instrument in their hands for carrying out entrepreneurship. Accordingly, financial reporting focuses on that concept: it is addressed to shareholders and investors. Continental Europe uses a more institutional approach in which a company is regarded as an independent institution with its own corporate interest. This implies that the financial reporting also has a different focus. The role of the general interest is much bigger.

5. Due to the fact that legislation is embedded in company law and the enforcement thereof differs per country, the risk of different interpretation by local courts is real, especially in the area where we strive for a higher degree of comparability, in particular in the field of listed companies that all have to apply IFRS. In the Netherlands, we are currently confronted with this issue. The most important adviser to our Supreme Court, the Attorney General, who is participating in this conference, opined on 24 December 2008 in his advice for the Supreme Court – in a case instigated by the Dutch Financial Market Supervisory Authority against the Dutch company Spyker – that a uniform interpretation still leaves room for some discretion in the decisions by the local courts[1]. If enforcement for IFRS consolidated statements would be in the hands of the financial market supervisory authorities in Europe, it would be much easier to harmonise decisions.

6. Finally, a somewhat separate remark. The authors postulate that the Fourth Directive does not have a conceptual framework like IASB. I would like to draw their attention to a study by F.E.E. (European Federation of Accountants) which compares the implicit conceptual framework in continental Europe to the explicit framework in the Anglo-Saxon world.

In their final observations, the authors point to the increasing complexity of financial reporting. In that context I cannot refrain from referring to a contribution in the magazine of the Dutch auditing profession, *De Accountant*, by the CFO of Shell Nederland B.V. She argues that "*the complexity clouds the picture that the annual accounts are to paint while it is clarity we desire*". I agree with her that we should return to the basis of the annual accounts.

[1] The judgement of the Dutch Supreme Court (Hoge Raad der Nederlanden) in this case was rendered on 24 April 2009 (LJ/BG8790), and it confirmed the opinion of the Attorney General and of the Judge in First Instance (Ondernemingskamer).

C. Discussion

Karel VAN HULLE

First of all, I entirely agree with what Hans BECKMAN says that if we have to test whether the International Accounting Standards are in conformity with the "true and fair view" concept, this should indeed be the "true and fair view" concept as it is laid down in the Accounting Directives. The European Commission has worded this in this way in the IAS Regulation because a direct reference to the Accounting Directives would have created difficulties, as then the Commission would have had to examine each international standard and compare it with the text of the various articles in the Accounting Directives. So the Commission said that the reference to the "true and fair view" under the Accounting Directive means that it must be broadly in line with European accounting thinking.

I do accept that there are a number of issues where the relationship between the IAS Regulation – and therefore the International Accounting Standards or International Financial Reporting Standards – and the Seventh Directive could be problematic. And that is the reason why the European Commission issued a paper in 2003 in which it identified some of these issues, and I am sure that in the future we will even discover more such issues, so I accept your analysis that it is a very complex issue to make these two legal frameworks work together.

On Peter VAN DER ZANDEN's point on integrating the accounting requirements for listed companies into the securities directives, I'm not so sure that I would agree. The European Commission did think about whether to integrate these accounting requirements for listed companies into the securities directives rather than to keep them in the Accounting Directives. The European Commission has decided not to do that because it wanted to keep the scheme for the accounting as a whole in one place. You made the comparison with the United States, but the United States does not have an accounting framework for non-listed companies, so it does not really have that issue.

Enforcement and consistent application of IAS/IFRS

Karel VAN HULLE

I agree with Peter VAN DER ZANDEN that enforcement is an issue that the European Commission needs to look at. Fortunately, we have not had a case yet where there have been discussions and disputes on the basis of the use of International Accounting Standards. But if that were to happen, I think we would discover a whole world of interesting issues. But I am not so certain that it is very likely. There exists very little case law on the Accounting Directives over the last 30 years. The only cases there have been were related to tax issues, but no real financial reporting issues. I think it is certainly a problem that the European Commission needs to look into.

Peter VAN DER ZANDEN
On this issue, in the Netherlands we indeed have the problem that it is the Financial Market Authority that is in charge of looking after the financial reporting by listed companies. If the Financial Market Authority believes that the financial reporting is not in conformity with IFRS, it has to bring the case to court. And that is what the Financial Market Authority has done in the "Spyker"-case. Currently, this dispute has been brought before the Dutch Supreme Court where the Attorney General has defended the position that the possibility exists that one can agree that the accounts are not in conformity with IFRS but that it can be accepted that the annual accounts are not changed[2]. And I do not know how the Supreme Court will decide, but it is an odd thing: if in other countries the competent court would decide otherwise, you lose the "level playing field". Whereas if it were only the financial market authorities that were the competent authority, then they would have to deal with it within the (CESR) and I believe that then you would get the same decision in all Member States.

Henri OLIVIER
I'm afraid that M. Van der Zanden is a bit optimistic. I tend to agree that this enforcement issue and the interpretation of International Financial Reporting Standards are quite an issue. It is really a challenge for the securities organisations to keep a uniform and consistent interpretation of the standards, because in some cases there is this possibility of getting a "pre-clearance". This is certainly the solution applied in France, to some extent also in Belgium; certainly also in the United States – not in the UK. But "pre-clearance" means that you create a kind of administrative jurisprudence. Severe issues will arise if you have an enforcement body deciding on the interpretation of IFRS in one jurisdiction which is different compared to the "pre-clearance" opinion delivered in another jurisdiction. That is why within both IOSCO (International Organisation of Securities Commissions) and CESR there is a kind of database of cases where the most important decisions are put together. In this respect, it is interesting to note that the securities organisations are not publishing all their decisions. They are making a selection only. On what basis? What kind of transparency is achieved in this way? What is the impact thereof? That remains an open question, I'm afraid.

Karel VAN HULLE
I think we need to clarify a couple of points. First of all, the database set up by CESR aims at promoting a uniform interpretation and it is not meant to be a "rule" – which has been made quite clear. There is a lot of reluctance worldwide against "rules based regulation". People want the International

2 As pointed out above, on 24 April 2009, the Dutch Supreme Court took the same position as its Attorney General and ruled against the Financial Market Authority.

Financial Reporting Standards to be a "principle based" system. "Pre-clearance" is in principle not accepted in the European environment because in Europe we wanted to do away with what the SEC has been doing. The SEC has thousands of cases: they pass a standard every second of the day on something ... And so the European Commission did not want to do that and CESR is finding a kind of middle way. But in the end you must not forget that uniform interpretation is ensured in the European context through the European Court of Justice. For example, eventually the European Court of Justice may have to decide on the "Spyker"-case referred to by the Dutch Supreme Court[3].

Henri OLIVIER

You should know that the European Commission tried to find a solution to possible interpretation issues and channelled the various questions which it was aware of to "IFRIC", the "International Financial Reporting Interpretations Committee". They, however, were a bit disappointed because they had just about no questions at all. The point is that between the four major audit firms there existed a kind of procedure, very informal but very effective, in order to avoid major difficulties in the first-time application of IFRS and this informal process has continued ever since. So when an issue arises, it is dealt with within this informal consultation process to see whether the same kind of answer would be given by all audit firms to avoid major differences in interpretation. All that is and remains very informal but it seems to be very effective for the moment.

Karel VAN HULLE

I can only confirm that indeed the European Commission has organised a round table that dealt with questions of interpretation to stimulate the market to take up this duty. Everybody indeed feared that IAS would be something like US GAAP. In the US, before you publish your financial statements, the SEC gives you a kind of green light after it has sent you a letter with 50, 60 or 200 questions on your accounts which need to be properly answered. That is something that we wanted to avoid in Europe. We do not want to have a system which is entirely "rules based". We want to have a system where people are forced to think before they apply the standards. Whether in the end that will be possible remains to be seen and I think that once we have some cases in enforcement, we may see where the limits of that approach are, but clearly there is an intention to move away from "rules based" accounting standards.

Peter VAN DER ZANDEN

But you can wonder whether it is a good thing that interpretations are dealt with within a close informal (secret) group. I think that from a rule-of-law perspective, the decision-making process regarding the interpretation questions

---

[3] Hoge Raad der Nederlanden (Dutch Supreme Court), 24 April 2009, LG/BG8790 (see preceding footnotes)

should be public. As I have been working with one of the major firms, I know the system but I do not think it is a democratic system.

Henri OLIVIER
That is probably true, but the question was whether we have a number of "problems" with the interpretation and apparently we do not. And let me confirm that Karel VAN HULLE really has been instrumental in bringing IAS/IFRS into the legislation in Europe. He has made something which is now accepted worldwide: we already have the evidence that we have an equivalent system in a number of countries, we have other countries joining, etc. For example, I recently received in my office people from Japan saying that they can no longer do anything else but join. It will be IFRS that will apply throughout the world. The decision of the SEC to allow IFRS as an experimental solution for the financial statements for 2009 is unbelievable; to allow some of their companies in the US to use IFRS is an incredible achievement. Nevertheless, the issue of uniformity, the issue of consistent interpretation will become even much worse at a global level than it is at the EU level. Because at the EU level securities organisations are meeting within CESR, they know each other, they have frequent contacts, making it possible to solve a number of problems within a similar cultural environment. But as soon as you will, with the same kind of interpretation problem, have to deal with Chinese people, with Russian people, with Indian people, basically with a different cultural environment, I am afraid that we will most probably encounter some quite different issues about interpretation and enforcement.

Administrative burden of financial reporting - exemption for "micro-entities"

Karel VAN HULLE
I think that you are right that analyses which are based on costs-benefits are very difficult to carry out. There is a lot of expertise developed in the Netherlands on calculating the "costs", but the other side of the equation – the benefits – is a lot more difficult to calculate. What the deregulation aims at is basically to avoid a rigid financial reporting regime like what is imposed by the Fourth Directive with a balance sheet format, a profit and loss account format and specific rules. The people behind the deregulation calculate that the production of each of these items implies a number of costs. Whether they have thought their arguments completely through in terms of what is the most ideal situation where the costs will be reduced to the basics, I'm not so sure that they have carried out that analysis completely.

Frank HELLEMANS
Every change will lead in the end to an additional "formation" cost and I believe that very often that formation cost is forgotten. I think that many formation

costs still need to be incurred in order to inform not only auditors – present auditors but also future ones – but also, for instance, the members of the companies' administrative bodies about the complexity of the International Accounting Standards. A recent study by the Belgian Banking, Finance and Insurance Commission shows that 50% of the listed companies do not give information on the risks that the companies are faced with. This is clearly a lack of application of the rules and I think that formation is too often forgotten in this whole debate. If you just look at the new regulation which has consolidated 19 previous separate regulations endorsing the various International Accounting Standards, you will see that it counts over 850 pages of rules. Everyone who teaches from time to time will know how difficult it is to explain those rules: they are very detailed and the language is all but easy …

That is one part of the formation cost. The other part relates to the proposed deregulation itself. If one would follow the proposed route for simplification of the accounting regime, we will finally end up with three different sets of standards: one for the "micro-entities", one for the "small and medium-sized" entities and then one for the "large" entities with, within this last category, possibly still another set for the listed companies. This will become a very difficult situation and I believe it is time to think about that.

Henri OLIVIER

I would like to add a few words. I do not believe that anybody has said in the European Commission or in all ongoing debates that accounting is not a necessary management tool, even for the smallest companies. That is not the issue. European legislation does not deal with bookkeeping or with accounting systems – there are only rules about financial reporting to external parties, not internally to the management. Indeed, the issue is all about "publishing" financial statements. And that is where people believe that it is possible to get some savings, but I cannot agree more with Karel VAN HULLE when he says that as soon as, at European level, we have got rid of these (European) publication requirements for the financial statements, we will be asked by the local tax authorities to provide them with financial statements for taxation purposes, or by the national bank which will need information for statistical purposes, or by our bank which will need this information in order to assess whether or not we are creditworthy … At this very moment we have, at least in Belgium, the advantage that everybody is picking up the financial statements from one single source: a company has to push the button to transfer electronically its financial statements to the National Bank once a year, and then all parties can obtain that information from there. If you abolish this system, a company will have the costs of communicating this information multiple times. This is exactly the kind of thing that has not been taken into account by those who are in favour of the "micro-system" and wish to exempt all the small companies from disclosing their financial statements. And it was very surprising and very hard to understand that the competent High Level Group of experts at the European

Commission could not grasp why organisations representing "small" and "medium-sized" companies were against their proposals. The latter understood that, without this single publication of financial statements, it will represent an increase in their costs and not a simplification.

Karel VAN HULLE
An additional word on these administrative burdens. One of the reasons why the European Commission will in the end introduce a proposal on this issue is that it believes that the subject should be on the table. On the one hand you have the political authorities (European Parliament, Member States) putting pressure on the Commission to deregulate and then, on the other hand, when the Commission comes up with a proposal, everybody criticises the proposal put forward. So the only way to deal with a debate like that is to put a proposal clearly on the table so that all parties have a chance to express their concerns. I hope that this will purify some of these discussions, which I readily accept are not all as sincere and transparent as they could have been.

Henri OLIVIER
To stay on this issue of administrative burden, maybe it is interesting to know the evolution in the Netherlands in order to know a bit more about what Peter VAN DER ZANDEN briefly addressed in his presentation. Because one of the arguments of those who are complaining about the administrative burdens is the fact that in a number of countries a very small company has to produce different sets of accounts, on the one hand for commercial purposes and on the other hand for tax purposes. So if you get rid of one of the two, you would achieve real simplification. What was the response to that in the Netherlands?

Peter VAN DER ZANDEN
That was exactly what happened in the Netherlands: we had traditionally two sets of accounts, one for commercial purposes and one for tax purposes. And at a certain moment in time there was a study started for XBRL (eXtensible Business Reporting Language) to come up with a Dutch "taxonomy" to be used in XBRL. There the problem of the difference between tax accounting and commercial accounting came on the table. From that study it became clear that there were only a few differences for most companies, and especially for small companies. The Minister of Justice took this opportunity to simplify the legislation by allowing the smallest companies to use their tax accounting for the purpose of publishing accounts in so far as they are in conformity with the Fourth Directive. The exemption is not that they have to be in conformity with Dutch law but only in conformity with all the options in the Fourth Directive. Consequently, when a Dutch company chooses to use its tax accounts and looks into the Fourth Directive and chooses well, then it has only one set of accounts, which is clearly less burdensome.

Henri OLIVIER
That is indeed similar to the situation in Belgian law where an effort has been made to combine both the accounting and the tax system. We should recommend the solution for the UK and maybe it will be one of the options that we will consider in the group which is thinking about the solution to revisit the Fourth Directive at the moment.

Who should be the standard setter - due process - governance?

Karel VAN HULLE
A lot of things can be said about the governance of the IASB. The whole debate is about the so-called "independence" of an international accounting standards setter. Everybody agrees that the standard-setter should be independent, but does independence mean that you no longer have to take account of the public interest? For instance, if you have a major financial crisis and your standards are the subject of discussion, can you then just stay away and just look at what the world is doing with your standards instead of intervening and responding to the crisis? There are a lot of critical things that can be said about the IASB, such as its lack of responsiveness or the lack of democracy in the system, as exemplified by the fact that the Board of Trustees is self-selected. Currently an international monitoring group is being set up above the Board of Trustees. They would be involved in the selection of the members of the Board of Trustees and that might improve the situation. There is e.g. also the fact that the Board members that we have today have never actually applied the standards which they promulgate.

Henri OLIVIER
In my opinion the following issue will probably become the most challenging for the future. It has been mentioned already during this discussion that we have unreadable documents and that is correct. We are publishing 400 to 600-page prospectuses that nobody will ever read, which are incredibly complex and very expensive indeed. We are using a technology of the past for these documents. So are we meeting the objectives of the financial statements and can we expect some very different evolution for the future? Can we get out of this traditional format of financial reporting towards a new system with the use of new technology, such as XBRL or others? Is it a realistic perspective?

Karel VAN HULLE
Well, I can't give the final answer to that but I have a couple of thoughts. I have difficulties with the financial reporting standards setting regime that is based on a conceptual framework and that is trying to deduce all possible accounting issues from that framework as if this were to be a mathematical exercise. If you take part in a meeting of the IASB, for instance, it requires a great deal of preparation because it is like living in a different world. They speak a language

which most people do not understand and if you use one of the expressions in the wrong way, the mathematical equation does not lead to the same result any more because everything is defined and sub-defined and sub-sub-defined. That is what I meant by "communication". Because if that is your financial reporting, then everybody who reads these 600 pages will have to spend three years on a full-time training course to understand all these concepts, and how they fit together and so on. That cannot be right ...

Coming back to the point of governance, when the world was discussing the reform of the structure of the IASC, everybody said that the standard-setter should be more professional, that one therefore needed to follow the American model. The US have the Financial Accounting Standards Board, which has a great deal of knowledge on accounting. There is virtually no issue that has not yet been discovered or discussed by them. That was the model which people wanted the IASB to adopt, having a full-time standard-setting board. We in Europe wanted a model which was a combination of full-time people with part-time people: people who have practical day-to-day experience. I think that the model which is based on full-time professional standard-setters is probably not the best model. It will automatically lead to very complex standards and to a situation where the communication with the outside world – the people who do not spend 365 days a year dealing with these issues – becomes more difficult. It becomes "incommunicado". I think that is the problem that needs to be addressed. The world is complex but we should try to develop standards that are not overly complex. IAS 39 is a complex standard dealing with a complex subject. Financial instruments are also extremely complex. The question has therefore been raised, following the financial crisis, whether one should not oblige the people who put these instruments on the market, before they put them on a market, to explain what they are putting on the market. This in order to make sure that they indeed know what they are putting on the market and that the market knows it as well. That is a way to reduce the complexity. But on a number of issues, unfortunately, the world is complex and we cannot deal with it more simply. I nevertheless think if we had a more pragmatic way of accounting standards setting, maybe it would improve things.

Frank HELLEMANS

Indeed, everything is becoming more complex but we have to be honest here, too. It is related to our society – we are living in a complex society and people look at those documents, not at the moment that they are drafted (to inform them) but only afterwards, when there is a corporate failure. It is clear that only now people are looking at the accounts of Fortis. And they will review whether all the standards were complied with or not. And then it becomes like a doctoral thesis – *post factum* – and people will have to make a link with the legislative framework where all the rules are set. Under Belgian law, these rules are part of company law and if you do not respect one of these rules, it is seen as a violation of a corporate law rule, leading to liability of all the members of the administrative body. Today many directors who sign and approve the accounts certainly do not understand all the rules. So they trust their auditors, they trust their management, but finally they have to assume the liability.

Henri OLIVIER

I have the feeling that we have four main issues in financial reporting and the architecture of the standards:

- Firstly, what are the objectives and what is the meaning of the financial statements? What can we do to make them more understandable and readable?
- Secondly, what is the scope and do we need to have different systems according to the size of the companies?
- Thirdly, who has to set the scene, to set the rules and what is the due process therefore? Can we have in Europe enough influence on standards which are becoming more and more global?
- Finally, what are the enforcement mechanisms and the solutions to ensure consistent interpretation?

I think these four issues are absolutely vital for the future of the system.

Corporate Mobility

Marieke Wyckaert[1] *and Filip Jenné*[2]
Jan Ronse Institute – K.U.Leuven

Abstract

Starting from the right of primary and secondary establishment embedded in the EC Treaty, and the presence, throughout the Member States of the European Union, of two possible connecting factors that have equally been recognized in the EC Treaty, this paper aims at analysing and systematizing the current understanding of the concept of "corporate mobility" on the basis of European legislation and the case law of the European Court of Justice. Such analysis shows in the very first place that a lot of confusion still exists about the various applications of the right for a company to be mobile throughout the European Community. We have therefore rigorously set out all possible scenarios. This, in turn, leads to the conclusion that the case law of the European Court of Justice only covers very few of these scenarios, that it does so in a much more consistent manner than is generally perceived, and that it continues to scrupulously respect the connecting factors accepted in the EC Treaty, as they are embedded in the national law of the individual Member States. On the one hand, the Court rigorously accepts the expansionism of the incorporation doctrine states; on the other hand, the Court also respects the more conservative cautiousness of the real seat doctrine states. It is therefore not predictable how the Court will rule if other scenarios are submitted to it, since its position will largely be influenced by the national law involved. In fact, this clearly demonstrates the void in European legislation: apart from a few – recently introduced – regulations with regard to corporate mobility that cover one specific situation, i.e. a cross-border merger of an SE or of any other corporate form that is allowed by its own corporate law to merge cross-border, the Commission does not seem to have a clear view where it wants to end up with corporate mobility. Two options seem possible: either the European Union evolves towards the interstate competition model that already exists in the United States; or a choice is made for one single connecting factor and its consequences. In both cases, further harmonization in the field of company law as well as in neighbouring fields, e.g. tax and insolvency law, would considerably facilitate the process.

1 Professor, KULeuven; Attorney Brussels Bar (Eubelius).
2 Teaching assistant, KULeuven; Attorney Brussels Bar (Eubelius).

Table of contents

1. Introduction[3]

1. ***Where it all starts: the EC Treaty.*** Pursuant to Article 43 of the Treaty establishing the European Community, restrictions on the freedom of establishment of nationals of a Member State in the territory of another Member State are prohibited (the "*right of primary establishment*"). This prohibition also applies to restrictions on setting up agencies, branches or subsidiaries by nationals of a Member State established in the territory of any Member State (the "*right of secondary establishment*").

Article 43, 2nd section further provides that the freedom of establishment also includes the right to set up and manage companies or firms[4] under the same conditions laid down for its own nationals by the law of the country where such establishment is effected (*non-discrimination*), and subject to Articles 56-60 of the EC Treaty regarding the movement of capital. Such companies or firms should be treated in the same way as natural persons who are nationals of Member States if they are (i) formed in accordance with the law of a Member State and (ii) have their registered office, central administration or principal place of business within the European Community (Article 48, 1st section of the EC Treaty). By virtue of such equal treatment, companies should in principle also be allowed, with a view to taking up and pursuing activities as self-employed persons, to move to any other Member State, but in accordance

[3] This text is a slightly revised version of the draft text we presented at the Conference on 9 January 2009. It has been adapted only to take into account certain comments, remarks or criticisms expressed by the Chairman, the Respondent and the participants in the "Cross Border Mobility" workshop, as well as some comments on the Cartesio case that have been published in the meantime (up to 1 September 2009). While the authors are very grateful for all constructive remarks they received, they remain solely responsible for the contents of this final text.
Finally, the authors also draw the reader's attention to the doctoral thesis of G.-J. VOSSESTEIN, successfully defended in autumn 2008 at the University of Leiden, the Netherlands on *Modernisation of European Company Law and Corporate Governance – Some considerations on its legal limits*, which provides very interesting reading on some aspects treated in this text but in a broader context and from a wider angle.

[4] Companies or firms are defined in Article 54, 2nd section of the EC Treaty as "*companies or firms constituted under civil or commercial law, including cooperative societies, and other legal persons governed by public or private law, save for those which are non-profit-making*".

with the conditions laid down in the law of that Member State for its own nationals.

Article 46 of the EC Treaty however refines the general rule of Article 43, by allowing special treatment for foreign nationals on grounds of "*public policy, public security or public health*". Moreover, the Court of Justice has developed the "*rule of reason*", according to which national measures hindering or restricting fundamental freedoms guaranteed by the EC Treaty are allowed if certain conditions are met (see below, under 17).

In order to achieve the freedom of establishment, the European Council and the European Commission are requested to coordinate and make equivalent, to the necessary extent, the safeguards which are required by Member States of companies or firms for the protection of the interests of members and other parties. The question of what the exact intentions of the founding fathers of the EU with regard to the timing of the harmonization of EU law were – a condition for the freedom of establishment or only an accompanying measure – when they approved this (then Article 54.3(g), now) Article 44.2(g) of the EC Treaty has lost its relevance with the Reyners case[5], where the Court of Justice ruled that since the end of the transitional period, (then Article 52, now) Article 43 of the EC Treaty is a directly applicable provision despite the absence in a particular sphere of the directives prescribed by Articles (then 54(2), now) 44.2 and (then 57(1), now) 47.1 of the EC Treaty.

It is noteworthy that Article 293 of the current EC Treaty version encouraging Member States to enter into negotiations "*with a view to securing for the benefit of their nationals [...] the mutual recognition of companies or firms [...], the retention of legal personality in the event of transfer of their seat from one country to another, and the possibility of mergers between companies or firms governed by the laws of different countries*" will be abolished when the last consolidation following the Treaty of Lisbon enters into force[6].

The right of primary establishment (i.e. the right for companies to transfer their seat from one Member State to another Member State, or to incorporate in any Member State) thus needs to be distinguished from the right of secondary establishment (i.e. the right to set up agencies, branches or subsidiaries in

---

5 ECJ, 21 June 1974, C-2/74 (Reyners), §32. Article 50.2(g) provides that "[now also the European Parliament,] the Council and the Commission shall carry out the duties devolving upon them under the preceding provisions, in particular, [...] by coordinating to the necessary extent the safeguards which, for the protection of the interests of members and others, are required by Member States of companies or firms within the meaning of the second paragraph of Article 54 with a view to making such safeguards equivalent throughout the Union". At that time harmonization was certainly (also) perceived as a protective measure compensating the freedom of establishment. See C. TIMMERMANS, "Chapter Three, Methods and Tools for Integration" in R.M. BUXBAUM, G. HERTIG, A. HURSCH, K.J. HOPT (eds.), *European Business Law*, W. De Gruyter & Co, Berlin, 1991, 132 (3).

6 See the Consolidated version of the Treaty on the Functioning of the European Union, OJ C115/47 (9 May 2008), not yet in force. This seems to definitively limit the harmonization exercise to the promulgation of new EC legislation, but, as will be demonstrated, it does not take away the relevance of the Daily Mail case (ECJ, 27 September 1988, C-81/87 (Daily Mail and General Trust Plc) ("**Daily Mail**"), §23 where both future legislation and conventions are mentioned).

another Member State)[7].

It is important to stress that the EC Treaty explicitly refused to make a choice between the variety in national legislation existing in the European Community as regards the factor providing a connection to the national territory required for the incorporation of a company and the question of whether a company incorporated under the law of a given Member State may subsequently modify this connecting factor. In Article 48, by placing the registered office, the central administration and the principal place of business of a company all on the same footing as a connecting factor for enjoying the right of establishment, the EC Treaty encompasses all possibilities[8].

Moreover, it is important to keep in mind that companies, as "*creatures of national law*", "*exist only by virtue of the national legislation which determines their incorporation and functioning*"[9]. This has, probably more than one realizes, influenced the Court of Justice in its case law on the freedom of establishment.

2. *The issue: where do we stand with regard to corporate mobility?* Corporate mobility can generally speaking be defined as the freedom of a company to operate in different countries and to choose the company law model that best fits its entrepreneurial needs[10]. The concept of corporate mobility finds its origin in the United States, where corporations are in principle free to choose their state of incorporation, and where corporations are subject to the corporate law of the state in which they have chosen to be incorporated (see below, under 3)[11].

Traditionally[12], the following types of corporate mobility are identified:

---

[7] K. LENAERTS and P. VAN NUFFEL, *Europees Recht in Hoofdlijnen*, Maklu, Antwerp, 1999, 212. In that case there seems to be no doubt that the import state can impose its own national law as regards the specific functioning of these local establishments (for Belgium, see the references cited by D. VAN GERVEN, "Kroniek vennootschappenrecht 2007-2008", *Tijdschrift voor Rechtspersoon en Vennootschap* 2008, 471, no. 13); see however also further, under 19, the Inspire Art case.

[8] Daily Mail, §§20-21; ECJ, 16 December 2008, C-210/06 (Cartesio Oktató és Szolgáltató bt) ("Cartesio"), §106.

[9] Daily Mail, §19; Cartesio, §104.

[10] K. MARESCEAU doubts whether the choice of the most appropriate law is covered by the right of establishment under Article 43 of the EC Treaty ("Het vrij vestigingsrecht, de problematiek van de zetelverplaatsing en zijn impact op het internationaal privaatrecht: een stand van zaken na de zaak Cartesio", *Tijdschrift voor Belgisch Handelsrecht* 2009/6, 607, no. 50).

[11] L. BEBCHUCK and A. COHEN, "Firms' decisions where to incorporate", http://papers.ssrn.com/abstract_id=304386, 1 (also published in 46 *Journal of Law and Economics* 383-425 (2003)); J. MCCAHERY and E. VERMEULEN, "Does the European Company Prevent the 'Delaware Effect'?", http://papers.ssrn.com/sol3/papers.cfm?abstract_id=693421, 789; M. SIEMS, "Convergence, Competition, Centros and Conflicts of Law: European Company Law in the 21st Century", http://papers.ssrn.com/sol3/papers.cfm?abstract_id=853865, 2.

[12] E. WYMEERSCH, "Is a Directive on Corporate Mobility Needed?", *European Business Organization Law Review,* 2007, 163. We have slightly adapted this enumeration, in order include the concept of de facto moving businesses from one state to another.

(i) a company is formed in one jurisdiction and conducts business in another jurisdiction;
(ii) a company migrates from one state ("home state") to another state ("host state"), subjecting itself – voluntarily or otherwise – (to a greater or lesser extent) to the company law of the host state. Within this type, a distinction can be made between different forms of migration:
    a. the establishment of an agency or branch in the host state[13];
    b. the incorporation of a subsidiary in the host state;
    c. the transfer of the "real seat" to the host state, or the change of the applicable company law (for the different scenarios, see below, under 5);
(iii) the cross-border merger of two companies, whereby the surviving entity becomes subject to a different legal regime.

3. *Two different conflict of law theories.* Even though the EC Treaty explicitly recognizes the freedom of establishment for companies, the implementation of corporate mobility in the European Union has been the subject of controversy for decades. This controversy is to be placed against the background of the two different conflict of law theories[14] for determining the connecting factor for the "*lex societatis*" existing in the European Union and between which no choice has ever been made[15]. Moreover, each of these theories comes in different shades[16]:

- the **incorporation theory**[17] [18] (adopted *inter alia* in the United Kingdom, Ireland, Denmark and the Netherlands): a company is governed by the laws of its place of incorporation (i.e. where it acquired a legal personality) or registration (i.e. where its registered seat is located). Besides a registered office (mainly for receipt of legal proceedings), no

[13] See in this respect the Eleventh Council Directive 89/666/EEC of 21 December 1989 concerning disclosure requirements in respect of branches opened in a Member State by certain types of company governed by the law of another State.

[14] WYMEERSCH identifies a third theory in international private law. This third theory is a variation of the incorporation theory, and refers to the corrections made voluntarily by some countries "*to take into account the potential danger to their reputation*" (E. WYMEERSCH, "The transfer of the company's seat in European Company Law", *Common Market Law Review 2003,* 662).

[15] For an historical overview, see J. MCCAHERY and E. VERMEULEN, "Does the European Company Prevent the 'Delaware Effect'?", http://papers.ssrn.com/sol3/papers.cfm?abstract_id=693421, 791.

[16] For an overview, see K. MARESCEAU, "Het vrij vestigingsrecht, de problematiek van de zetelverplaatsing en zijn impact op het internationaal privaatrecht: een stand van zaken na de zaak Cartesio", *Tijdschrift voor Belgisch Handelsrecht* 2009/6, 582, no. 3. As he points out, in those jurisdictions where the incorporation theory is understood as a determination of applicable law on the basis of the place of incorporation only, a company can as a rule never change the law applicable to it, regardless of a move of its (registered or real) seat.

[17] We will refer to "registered seat" when speaking of a company whose governing law is determined by its place of incorporation or registration solely.

[18] Also called "theory of foundation" or "Gründungstheorie", see P. RYAN, "Will there ever be a 'Delaware of Europe'?" http://papers.ssrn.com/sol3/papers.cfm?abstract_id=763164, 188.

other connection with the country of incorporation is required: whatever activities the company may develop in other states, it will not lose its original status. Similarly, companies incorporated under foreign law are recognized if the law of the country of incorporation or registration confers validity upon them. Under the pure incorporation theory, it is theoretically extremely difficult for a company to ever lose its original governing law, wherever it establishes itself.

- the **real seat theory**[19] (adopted *inter alia* in Germany, France, Spain, Portugal, Greece, Luxembourg and Belgium): a company is formed under and governed by the laws of the country where it has its "real seat". If there is no substantial territorial connection between the real seat (i.e. the "head office" or the "principal place of business", the place where the company is administered and governed)[20] and the jurisdiction of incorporation, recognition by reference to the laws of the country of incorporation is denied[21].

The advantage of the incorporation theory is that it creates legal certainty and enhances cross-border transactions and the smooth development of international commercial relations[22]. It needs no further reasoning to see that the incorporation doctrine, much better than the real seat doctrine, allows a company to easily establish itself wherever it wishes to establish itself, without having to worry about its legal status. The downside of this theory is clearly that it encourages, or at least allows, the creation of "letterbox companies", and that it could result in a "race to the bottom" of company law (see also below, under 26).

This is at the same time what constitutes the appeal of the real seat doctrine: it is embedded in the social and economic reality and discourages the creation of letterbox companies and the possible associated abuse, by applying the laws of the jurisdiction which is most concerned by the activities of the company. The major disadvantages of the real seat theory, however, are that it complicates international transactions: a change of corporate law implies a change of real

19 We will refer to "real seat" when speaking about companies that are governed by the law of the Member State where their main activities or central administration are situated.

20 Also called "theory of domicile" or "Sitztheorie", see P. RYAN, "Will there ever be a 'Delaware of Europe'?", http://papers.ssrn.com/sol3/papers.cfm?abstract_id=763164, 188.

21 Again, this real seat concept comes in many variations: in its purest and now almost abandoned form, it implies that a company can only change applicable law by winding up in its original jurisdiction and reincorporation in its new jurisdiction; the current more alleviated version accepts that a company can, with continuity, change its real seat provided it adapts to the legislation of its new jurisdiction (K. MARESCEAU, "Het vrij vestigingsrecht, de problematiek van de zetelverplaatsing en zijn impact op het internationaal privaatrecht: een stand van zaken na de zaak Cartesio", *Tijdschrift voor Belgisch Handelsrecht* 2009/6, 584-586, no. 6-7.

22 M. SIEMS, "Convergence, Competition, Centros and Conflicts of Law: European Company Law in the 21st Century", http://papers.ssrn.com/sol3/papers.cfm?abstract_id=853865. 2.

seat, and vice versa. Moreover, it is not always clear – and in future it will become less and less clear – where the "real seat" of a company is located[23].

4. ***Can the two theories coexist?*** As a general rule, one can say that coexistence will be more acceptable for incorporation states than for real seat states, because they are ready to separate the regulation of company law and the regulation of a company's economic activities. Real seat Member States are not used to thinking in terms of incorporation as a choice of the corporate law by which companies want to be governed, regardless of where they pursue their activities. On the contrary, their reflex is to consider that a company should develop its main activities under the same law as its corporate law[24]. If a foreign company exports such activities to a real seat Member State, the latter will refuse to recognize the company (or will consider that its members are cooperating without the protection of a legal form conferring limited liability), unless it adapts to local law. Under the incorporation doctrine, there is no need for such a link: once the company is validly incorporated under the law of incorporation, it continues to be governed by that law, regardless of the localisation (from the outset or following a later move) of its activities. Incorporation states have however sometimes introduced corrective legislation imposing certain additional requirements on companies incorporated abroad but active in their country[25]. This reflex may be interpreted as the need felt, even by incorporation states, to be able to rely on minimum standards of quality for imported companies.

It should therefore not come as a surprise that most of the case law of the European Court of Justice up to now relates to companies incorporated in incorporation states seeking recognition after having developed activities in other Member States (see below, under 19). Companies incorporated in a real seat state are much less inclined to develop such a reflex.

It would be unfair to assert that the failure to take adequate action on corporate mobility within the European Union is solely caused by the failure to make a choice between the real seat doctrine and the incorporation doctrine, but it can hardly be denied that this has played an important role and continues to do so, even if it is true that other politically sensitive issues, such as the lower level of tax law harmonization, employee participation or, to a lesser degree, the

---

[23] One may expect this problem to increase, both with the further development of new technologies and with the globalization of business where firms will more and more be active in different countries.

[24] See the opinion of Advocate General Poiares Maduro in the Cartesio case, paragraph 23, with a reference to Edwards: "*the real seat doctrine 'inextricably entwines a company's nationality and residence*". For this link under Belgian law, see article 110, 1st section of the Code of International private law; Ph. DE PAGE and B. VAN DE WALLE DE GHELCKE, "Les personnes morales étrangères et le droit public international belge", *Revue Pratique des Sociétés* 1979, 6-7.

[25] J. MEEUSEN, "De werkelijke zetel-leer en de communautaire vestigingsvrijheid van vennootschappen - analyse van het arrest Überseering van het Hof van Justitie", *Tijdschrift voor Rechtspersoon en Vennootschap* 2003, 100, no. 13; as regards specifically the Netherlands, H.-J. DE KLUIVER, "Inspiring a New European Company Law? – Observations on the ECJ's decision in *Inspire Art* from a Dutch perspective and the Imminent Competition for Corporate Charters between EC Member States", *ECFR* 1/2004, 121 et seq.; see also the Centros and Inspire Art cases, below, under 19.

choice between a one-tier or a two-tier board system, have been slowing down the process[26].

5. ***When real seat and incorporation clash.*** Coexistence of the two theories most visibly becomes problematic when companies cross state borders[27]. Such crossing of state borders can occur in the following scenarios; in each of them the question arises whether (i) the company can change the corporate law applicable to it or whether (ii) the company must accept that the corporate law applicable to it changes, even if it is not seeking such a change. This distinction is not always clearly made.

(a) The company does not intend to change the company law applicable to it

1. **Move of real seat from incorporation state A to incorporation state B.** At first glance this should not be an issue, either for the states concerned or for third parties[28]. However, in reality several incorporation states do (or at least did) provide palliative or corrective measures aimed at governing economic activities taking place on their territory (see above, under 4, and below, under 19).
2. **Move of real seat from incorporation state A to real seat state B.** At first glance this leads to double nationality.
3. **Move of real seat from real seat state A to real seat state B.** At first glance, state A should allow the company to leave its territory and move to state B, provided that the company also accepts a change of corporate law; the question is: how and under what conditions is such a move allowed?
4. **Move of real seat from real seat state A to incorporation state B.** In a strict application of both theories, this would lead to the company being stateless, unless state B would, one way or another, allow the company to re-establish itself in state B.

For the sake of simplification of our reasoning, we are not taking into account the possibility of "*renvoi*", i.e. the possibility that a host state or a third state, following its own conflict of law referral rules, ends up applying the law of another Member State which in turn considers itself to be applicable[29].

---

[26] E. WYMEERSCH, "Is a Directive on Corporate Mobility Needed?", *European Business Organization Law Review,* 2007, 162. see also C. TIMMERMANS, *Company Law as Ius Commune,* Antwerp, Intersentia, 2002, 3.

[27] For an overview of specific situations where the application of the two theories is especially difficult, see the Report of the High Level Group of Company Law Experts on a Modern Regulatory Framework for Company Law in Europe, 4 November 2002 (the "**Winter Report**"), 102-103.

[28] See the Winter Report, 102.

[29] G. VAN HECKE and K. LENAERTS, *Internationaal privaatrecht,* Story-Scientia, Ghent, 1989, no. 312-319, pp. 160-165, and no. 753, p. 348. Belgian conflict of law rules accept the "*renvoi*": J.-P BLUMBERG, "Over het grensoverschrijdend associatieconcern, zetelverplaatsing en internationale

(b) The company intends to change the company law applicable to it

1. **Intention to change applicable company law from incorporation state A to incorporation state B.** Such intention may exist without the company wishing to change its real seat (wherever located) or with the company wishing to also move its real seat (wherever located). In this scenario, location and/or transfer of the real seat are neutral, since the incorporation theory does not attach importance to the real seat. The question arises under which circumstances the change of company law the company wishes to obtain would be allowed[30].
2. **Intention to change applicable company law from incorporation state A to real seat state B.** Such a change will in any event not be allowed by state B if the company does not also transfer its real seat. In this case there may also be a risk of double nationality, since for state A the transfer of the real seat is in fact irrelevant.
3. **Intention to change applicable company law from real seat state A to real seat state B.** Again, both for state A and state B, such a change will not be admissible without a change of the real seat. The question again arises under which circumstances the change of company law the company wishes to obtain would be allowed.
4. **Intention to change applicable company law from real seat state A to incorporation state B.** If the real seat stays in state A, state A will consider its own law to continue to be applicable. If the real seat is transferred to state B, state A should not object, but then the question again arises whether and if so, how it is technically possible to re-incorporate in an incorporation state if the company has originally been incorporated elsewhere.

6. *The Winter Report.* The Consultative Document of the High Level Group of Company Law Experts[31] preceding the Winter Report already points to a

fusie", *Tijdschrift voor Privaat Recht* 1992, 817 (with references); J. ERAUW, *Handboek Belgisch Internationaal Privaatrecht*, Kluwer, Mechelen, 2006, 566; K. LENAERTS, "Het personeel statuut van een Belgische vennootschap bij overbrenging van de werkelijke zetel naar het buitenland", annotation of RvSt. 19 June 1987, *Tijdschrift voor Rechtspersoon en Vennootschap* 1988, 112. See also the Winter Report, 106.

30 In the US a transfer of registered seat is mostly achieved through a merger of the company with a newly incorporated company registered in the host state (E. WYMEERSCH, "Is a Directive on Corporate Mobility Needed?", *European Business Organization Law Review,* 2007, 162). In an extreme application of the incorporation doctrine, this is indeed the only way to get rid of the applicable law of the original state of incorporation, since that state does not attach any consequences to the move of the real seat. See also, with respect to the need for a registered office within the incorporation state, mainly for legal proceedings, the Consultative Document of the High Level Group of Company Law Experts, http://ec.europa.eu/internal_market/company/docs/modern/consult_en.pdf, 32.

31 See pp. 31-34 of the Consultative Document. For the expert report of KPMG in 1993, see J. BELLINGWOUT, "Company Migration in Motion: the KPMG Report 1993", in J. WOUTERS and H. SCHNEIDER (eds.), *Current issues of cross-border establishment in the European Union*, Maklu-Nomos-Bruylant, Ius Commune Europaeum Series No 14, Antwerp, 1995, 75-88.

1997 draft Fourteenth Directive on transfer of seat as a means for a company to change its internal law/corporate status. It calls for a common EU approach taking into account shareholder and creditor protection when a company moves its "head office" or "central administration" cross-border, whether or not the Member States involved also require changing the law of incorporation. It points out the existence of the incorporation doctrine and (the various versions of) the real seat doctrine, and is of the opinion that the requirement of the incorporation states to keep a place for service of process and maintenance of public documents within the territory of formation is a proportionate measure, while the real seat states are not acting proportionately when requiring that the main activities of a company must be maintained in a given state in order for that state's company law to be applicable. It concludes by calling for further harmonization in this field, but is not convinced that a Fourteenth Directive should be based on a change of applicable law upon each "*transfer of registered office or de facto head office*" to another Member State, as the draft directive stated at that time, because in many cases that could be "*unnecessary and produce anomalies*".

The Winter Report itself sets out several guiding principles that would need to be applied in the case of a change of corporate seat or domicile. However, it does not always make a clear distinction between the different scenarios that may present themselves (see above, under 5):

(i) Member States are not allowed to adopt a version of the real seat doctrine which automatically denies recognition to a company with its real seat in a country other than that of its incorporation (see also below, under 19, the Überseering case).

(ii) The transfer of the real seat between two "incorporation" Member States is considered as the simplest scenario: the company continues to be governed by the home state, and none of the Member States involved has an interest in inhibiting the move (see however above, under 4, for the presence of corrective measures and below, under 19, for the Centros and Inspire Art cases). As the regulations on the European Interest Grouping and on the European Company "*make it unlawful for such entities to have their 'real seat' in a state other than their state of incorporation*", the Winter Report calls for this to be corrected[32].

(iii) In the case of a transfer of the real seat to another real seat state (i.e. where a company moves its real seat to a host state where the effect of its law of incorporation is inconsistent with local mandatory requirements), the host state is allowed to take measures overriding

[32] See also K. MARESCEAU, "Het vrij vestigingsrecht, de problematiek van de zetelverplaatsing en zijn impact op het internationaal privaatrecht: een stand van zaken na de zaak Cartesio", *Tijdschrift voor Belgisch Handelsrecht* 2009/6, 603, no. 39, pointing out that the Court of Justice does not seem to find this requirement contrary to its interpretation of the right of establishment (Cartesio, §117).

the law of incorporation of the guest company, provided that such measures[33] (see below, "the rule of reason", under 17):

a. are imposed only to support a requirement of *legitimate general interest*;
b. are not disproportionate *(proportionality principle)*;
c. require no more than is necessary and appropriate to secure the interest concerned *(principle of minimum intervention)*;
d. are non-discriminatory compared to the rules applicable to "national" companies formed in the host state *(non-discrimination principle)*;
e. are sufficiently transparent to inhibit to the minimum extent necessary the exercise in practice of the fundamental freedom of establishment *(transparency principle)*.

(iv) The transfer of the real seat out of a real seat state can be regarded as a means of escaping the law of the home country, provided that any sanctions applied by the home country must comply with the principles mentioned under (iii). The Winter Report even mentions that if the host state is a Member State which has adopted the incorporation theory and which has applied the law of origin, the home state should not be able to take special measures on the ground of the transfer of the real seat (see however below, under 19, §112 of the Cartesio case). In the event of a conflict law between the home state and the host state, the reciprocity principle applies.

(v) Third states should apply the law of the state of incorporation, with a "*renvoi*" to the law of the host state where appropriate (see above, under 5).

7. *The Action Plan.* In its Action Plan of 21 May 2003[34], the European Commission assessed the current position and prospects of European company law, and provided an outline of the approach that it intended to follow in the area of company law and corporate governance. The Commission set forth the following "guiding criteria" for future action in the field of company law:

(i) full respect for the subsidiarity and proportionality principles of the EC Treaty;
(ii) any action must be flexible in application, but firm in the principles;
(iii) any action should help shape international regulatory developments.

[33] According to the Winter Report, justification must thus be provided for requirements imposed with respect to the internal governance, the protection of creditors or the external representation of the company.

[34] Communication to the Council and the European Parliament entitled "Modernising Company Law and Enhancing Corporate Governance in the European Union – A Plan to Move Forward" (the "**Action Plan**"), 21 May 2003, COM (2003) 284 final.

In view of the fact that companies increasingly do business across national borders and the need for alignment of their structure to their activities, the Action Plan announced the following measures in respect of corporate mobility:

(i) the presentation of a new proposal for a Tenth Company Law Directive on cross-border mergers and a Fourteenth Company Law Directive on the transfer of the seat from one Member State to another[35].
(ii) simplification of restructuring transactions by amending the Third Directive and Sixth Directive (although this was not an immediate priority);
(iii) simplification of the Second Directive in the short term.

Today all these measures have been put in place except for one: there is still no Directive on the cross-border transfer of seat. The public consultation on the proposed Fourteenth Directive[36] reaffirmed the need for legislative action to regulate cross-border seat transfers, by way of freedom of establishment, of the registered office of a limited liability company already formed under the law of a Member State, whereby the case of a transfer of the real seat should be addressed both for Member States adhering to the incorporation doctrine and for Member States opting for the real seat doctrine. At the 2006 consultation and hearing on the Action Plan[37], a very large majority again confirmed the need for a Fourteenth Directive, but a minority expressed doubt as to its practical value, albeit merely in view of obstacles of another nature that should be dealt with, such as employee participation and taxation.

8. *December 2007: No need for further action. October 2008: Request for draft Fourteenth Company Law Directive.* Confronted with the very outspoken case law of the Court of Justice, the Commission changed its mind with respect to the need for a directive regarding the transfer of seat. In a Working Document dating from year-end 2007[38], the Commission analysed the various

[35] The Commission announced its intention to present a proposal for a Fourteenth Directive on the transfer of the seat from one Member State to another, "*in order to implement the freedom of establishment in the manner intended by the Treaty*", and justified its intention by arguing that "*in the absence of legislation governing the cross-border transfer of seat, such an operation is currently impossible or at least contingent on complicated legal arrangements*", and that the "*Member States laws do not provide the necessary means and [...] there are frequent conflicts between those laws because of the different connecting criteria applied in the Member States*".

[36] http://ec.europe.eu/internal_market/company/seat-transfer/2004-consult_en.htm.

[37] Directorate General for Internal Market and Services, Consultation and hearing on future priorities for the Action Plan on Modernising Company Law and Enhancing Corporate Governance in the European Union, 3 May 2006, http://ec.europa.eu/internal_market/company/docs/consultation/final_report_en.pdf.

[38] Commission Staff Working Document – Impact assessment on the Directive on the cross-border transfer of registered office, SEC(2007)1707, http://ec.europa.eu/internal_market/company/docs/shareholders/ia_transfer_122007_part1_en.pdf. This document also describes in detail the various steps that had been taken since the Action Plan's announcement that the Fourteenth Directive on cross-border transfer of seat would be an absolute priority.

options available, and came to the conclusion that in order to achieve the policy objectives either a directive or "no action" would be suitable, but that, under the proportionality test, "no action" was preferable: first, the effect of Directive 2005/56/EC on cross-border mergers should be ascertained, and furthermore the case law of the Court of Justice on transfer of seat should be awaited.

Recently Committees of the European Parliament have reinitiated the debate, by issuing two draft documents urging the Commission to reconsider the matter[39]. The Parliament's Committee on Legal Affairs is concerned that at present there is still insufficient legal certainty that a cross-border transfer of seat will not lead to a (taxable) winding up in the home state and a reincorporation in the host state, and it pleads for application of the law of the host state after the transfer. It also requests that specific attention be paid to the rights of shareholders, employees and creditors. However, it does not take any position or give any indication regarding how to resolve the conflicts of law resulting from the fact that some Member States opt for the incorporation doctrine and the others for the real seat doctrine. Apparently, in its view, a company is under all circumstances allowed to transfer its registered office cross-border, and thus change applicable law. "*Where appropriate*", the procedure must provide for "*detailed information on the transfer of the central administration or principal place of business*" (recommendation 2): this seems to imply that a Member State may still require companies governed by its law to have their real seat in its territory.

9. *Scope of our analysis.* In section 2 below we will analyse the typical means currently available to companies to organize their cross-border activities otherwise than through a secondary establishment. They include the European Company (subsection 2.1), cross-border mergers (subsection 2.2) and cross-border transfer of seat (subsection 2.3). We will also briefly turn our attention to other types of cross-border transactions which have so far received little or no attention at the European level but which nevertheless often occur in practice (subsection 2.4).

In the concluding section we will evaluate the current status of European company law with regard to corporate mobility, and put forward some suggestions and issues for further consideration.

[39] Draft Opinion of the Committee on Economic and Monetary Affairs for the Committee on Legal Affairs, 23 September 2008 (2008/2196(INI) (http://www.europarl.europa.eu/RegData/commissions/econ/projet_avis/2008/412191/ECON_PA(2008)412191_EN.doc) and Draft Report of the Committee on Legal Affairs of 17 October 2008, 2008/2196 (INI), (http://www.europarl.europa.eu/RegData/commissions/juri/projet_rapport/2008/414360/JURI_PR(2008)414360_EN.doc).

2. Moving companies and corporate activities across Europe: techniques

2.1. The European Company

10. ***Creation of the European Company.*** The European Company (also known as the "Societas Europaea" or "SE") was created by Council Regulation No 2157/2001 of 8 October 2001 on the Statute for a European company (the "**SE Council Regulation**"), supplemented by Council Directive 2001/86/EC of 8 October 2001 containing specific rules for the Statute for a European company with regard to the involvement of employees, and entered into force on 8 October 2004.

The creation of the European Company Statute[40] was a major step in the legislative evolution of European company law regarding corporate mobility[41] and came into effect over 30 years after negotiations for the creation of a European company were initiated, as it had required finding common ground between Member States with a tradition of worker involvement and those Member States where worker involvement is not imposed.

11. ***Cross-border mergers with a view to creating a European Company.*** The first reason why the European Company can be considered as a crucial step in the development of European company law with regard to corporate mobility is the fact that, for the first time, the European Company Statute explicitly provides rules for mergers between public companies from different Member States via the incorporation of an SE. The procedure for such mergers is laid down in Articles 20-31 of the SE Council Regulation and is similar to the procedure for "national" mergers set out in the Third Directive. In this respect, the SE Council Regulation explicitly mentions that the laws of the Member State governing each merging company must apply as in the case of a merger of public limited liability companies, with regard to the protection of the interests of (a) creditors of the merging companies; (b) holders of bonds of the merging companies; and (c) holders of securities, other than shares, which carry special rights in the merging companies. Moreover, Member States are specifically allowed to adopt provisions designed to ensure appropriate protection for minority shareholders who have opposed the transaction[42]. Moreover, such

---

[40] In this paper we will not elaborate on the European Cooperative Company, a corporate form which will most probably very rarely be used and the rules for which are quite similar to the rules regarding corporate mobility for the European Company.

[41] L.L. HANSEN, "Merger, Moving and Division Across National Borders – When Case Law Breaks through Barriers and Overtakes Directives", *European Business Law Review*, 2007, 181; J. MCC-AHERY and E. VERMEULEN, "Does the European Company Prevent the 'Delaware Effect'?", http://papers.ssrn.com/sol3/papers.cfm?abstract_id=693421, 797; C. TIMMERMANS, *Company Law as Ius Commune*, Antwerp, Intersentia, 2002, 9.

[42] On this topic, see K. GEENS and M. WYCKAERT, "Cross Border Merger and Minority Protection: an Open-Ended Harmonisation", *Utrecht Law Review*, volume 4, issue 1, March 2008; also published in

merger is tax-neutral under the (amended) Merger Tax Directive of 23 July 1990[43].

12. ***Transfer of seat by a European Company.*** A second reason for the importance of the European Company Statute for corporate mobility within the European Union is that under the SE Council Regulation, the registered office of a European Company may be transferred to another Member State without prior liquidation and without new establishment (and thus without liquidation or incorporation taxes)[44] [45].

The rules on the transfer of the seat of a European Company set out in Article 8 of the SE Council Regulation can be summarized as follows:

(i) the management organ must draw up a transfer proposal (including *inter alia* the timetable for the transfer and the protection of shareholders and/or creditors) and a special report (explaining and justifying the legal and economic aspects of the transfer and the implications for shareholders, creditors and employees), to be made available to shareholders and creditors;

(ii) Member States are allowed to provide for protection for minority shareholders who oppose a transfer;

(iii) The competent authority of the Member State in which the European Company has its registered office issues a certificate attesting the completion of all necessary acts and formalities before the transfer. The new registration may not be effected until this certificate has been submitted and evidence is produced that the formalities required for registration in the country of the new registered office have been completed.

(iv) The transfer of an SE's registered office and the consequent amendment of its articles of association take effect on the date on which the SE is registered in the register for its new registered office. As from publication of an SE's new registration, the new registered office may be relied on as against third parties. However, as long as the deletion of the SE's registration from the register for its previous registered office has not been publicized, third parties may continue to rely on the previous registered office unless the SE proves that such third parties were aware of the new registered office.

European Company Law volume 5, issue 6, December 2008, 288-296.

43 Council Directive 90/434/EEC of 23 July 1990 on the common system of taxation applicable to mergers, divisions, transfers of assets and exchanges of shares concerning companies of different Member States.

44 Such transfer is not allowed if proceedings for winding up, liquidation, insolvency or suspension of payments or other similar proceedings have been brought against the relevant European Company.

45 See also K. GEENS, "De zetelverplaatsing van de Europese vennootschap als vrij vestigingsvehikel", in *Liber Amicorum Lucien Simont*, Brussels, Bruylant, 2002, 1025-1039.

(v) The laws of a Member State may provide that the transfer of a registered office which would result in a change of the applicable law will not take effect if any of that Member State's competent authorities opposes it. Such opposition may be based only on grounds of public interest.

It is important to stress however that, under the European Company Statute, a European Company must have its registered office in the same Member State as its head office (Article 7). Failure to comply with this requirement may lead to the imposition of appropriate sanctions to oblige the European Company to regularize its position, by moving either its head office or its registered office (Article 64[46]). To put it differently, the SE Council Regulation only had to consider one of the scenarios set out under 5: the move of the real seat (starting from a – specifically for the European Company – real seat state) with the corresponding change of the applicable law.

13. ***Success of the European Company?*** Almost 300 European Companies were incorporated between 2004 and 2008, and 24 companies were reported to be in the process of registering as an SE[47]. While perhaps not disappointing, this is not an impressive number. On the whole, it is felt that the European Company is only suitable for large companies[48]. Moreover, the onerous procedure with regard to employee participation, as good a compromise as it may be, is not applied with enthusiasm by those Member States in which employee participation is limited to information or, at the most, consultation.

We did not find any information in relation to transfers of seat by any European Company. There are indications that in some cases the European Company was used merely because it offered the possibility of a cross-border merger in Member States where this was not possible – or at least not with tax neutrality – before the transposition of the Tenth Directive. If this is correct, the success of the European Company may be on the verge of decreasing rather than increasing.

2.2. Cross-border mergers

14. ***Lack of European legislation on cross-border mergers for more than 30 years.*** The founding fathers of the EC included a provision in the EC Treaty (previously Article 220 EEC, now Article 293 EC Treaty, on the verge of being abolished) that the Member States would, as far as necessary, enter

[46] The procedure it should comply with to do so is not entirely clear, since Article 8 was drafted to take account of the regular situation where the registered seat and the real seat are located in the same Member State.

[47] See the website of the European Trade Union Institute for Research, Education and Health and Safety (ETUI-REHS), http://ecdb.worker-participation.eu.

[48] The Commission is developing the private limited-liability alternative (see below, under 28).

into negotiations with a view to securing the possibility of mergers between companies governed by the laws of different countries.

The scope of the Third and Sixth Company Law Directives, adopted in 1978 and 1982 respectively, was explicitly limited to "national" mergers and demergers[49]. Indeed, for a long time, a European solution for cross-border mergers seemed impossible, in particular because some of the Member States were afraid that the procedure would be abused to place a company under a foreign legal system with (more) limited employee involvement[50]. A second, but less clearly voiced cause of the lack of enthusiasm was most certainly the fear that national tax authorities would lose taxable basis because of the disappearance from their territory of the companies being merged. As a result, European company law did not contain any legal basis for mergers between companies from different countries until 2005.

In spite of this gap, a legal basis providing for tax neutrality of cross-border mergers was already put in place with the Merger Tax Directive.

In the absence of harmonized company law rules, the organization of cross-border mergers was complex and led to legal uncertainty, despite the increasingly cross-border nature of companies' activities. More specifically, the exclusion of cross-border mergers from the Third Directive often resulted in unfavourable tax treatment of cross-border mergers, in particular by the Member State which was abandoned following the cross-border merger[51].

15. ***Impulse given by the SE Council Regulation.*** It was only in connection with the SE Council Regulation of 2001 that a first legal basis was created for cross-border mergers under European law, providing for the creation of a European Company by merger of two or more public limited liability companies from different Member States, setting out detailed regulation of the procedure for such mergers and laying down the associated rules for worker involvement (see above, under 11)[52].

However, under the European Company Statute, a cross-border merger was only possible if (i) the merging companies were public limited liability companies and (ii) a European Company was created. In view of this, the Commission announced in the Action Plan that it was desirable to adopt a Tenth Company Law Directive on cross-border mergers which was open to other types of companies and which did not require the creation of a European Company.

---

[49] Article 2 of the Third Directive; Article 1.1 of the Sixth Directive.

[50] For an historical overview of the discussions regarding a Cross-Border Directive, see P. BEHRENS, annotation of ECJ 13 December 2005, no. C-411/03, SEVIC Systems AG, *CML Review* 2006, 1670 and J. WOUTERS, "Grensoverschrijdende fusie en vrijheid van vestiging van vennootschappen in de Europese Unie", *Tijdschrift voor Belgisch Handelsrecht* 2006, 410.

[51] By treating a cross-border merger as (i) a liquidation of the disappearing company under national law (subject to liquidation taxes) followed by (ii) the incorporation of a new company under the "foreign law", national tax legislation deterred parties from entering into cross-border mergers.

[52] A. UGLIANO, "The New Cross-Border Merger Directive: Harmonisation of European Company Law and Free Movement", *European Business Law Review*, 2007, 588.

16. *Adoption of the Tenth Directive. Summary of rules.* Eventually, the Tenth Directive (Directive 2005/56/EC of the European Parliament and of the Council on cross-border mergers) was adopted on 26 October 2005. It entered into force on 15 December 2005 and had to be implemented by the Member States by 15 December 2007[53].

The rules applicable to cross-border mergers set out in the Tenth Directive are inspired by the principles laid down in the Third Directive regarding national mergers, and can be summarized as follows:

(i) the Tenth Directive (only) applies to mergers of limited liability companies formed in accordance with the law of a Member State and having their registered office, central administration or principal place of business within the European Community, and where at least of two of them are governed by the laws of different Member States.
(ii) Cross-border mergers are only possible between types of companies which may merge under national laws of the relevant Member States, and each company has to comply with the provisions of the national law to which it is subject.
(iii) Article 16 of the Tenth Directive provides for a procedure relating to employee participation within the company resulting from the cross-border merger. As a principle (and subject to certain exceptions), the national rules (if any) regarding employee participation of the law governing the company resulting from the merger will apply.

It is remarkable how little attention the Tenth Directive pays to the issue of the connecting factor in this context. A cross-border merger by definition means that shareholders opt for the applicability of the corporate law of the surviving entity, regardless of where its head office is located. Also, the former head office of the disappearing company takes on the status of a permanent establishment of the surviving entity (this at least demonstrates the relativity of a head office – see also above, under 3, on the difficulty of determining the location of the head office).

17. *The Sevic case.* Shortly before the promulgation of the Tenth Directive, the Court of Justice, in its Sevic decision[54], ruled that in principle EU Member States must allow cross-border mergers between a company established on their

[53] On 5 June 2008 and 16 October 2008, the European Commission sent reasoned opinions to various Member States (including Belgium) in connection with their failure to implement the Tenth Directive in a timely manner.

[54] ECJ 13 December 2005, C-411/03 (SEVIC Systems AG) ("**Sevic**"), *Jur.* 2005, I-10805; for a more elaborate discussion of this judgment, see A. UGLIANO, "The New Cross-Border Merger Directive: Harmonisation of European Company Law and Free Movement", *European Business Law Review*, 2007, 591.

territory and a company established in another Member State. In this case, Germany had refused to register a merger effected through the acquisition of a Luxembourg company by a German company because the merger did not involve two German companies.

The Court of Justice decided that "*the right of establishment precludes registration in the national commercial register of the merger by dissolution without liquidation of one company and transfer of the whole of its assets to another company from being refused in general in a Member State where one of the two companies is established in another Member State, whereas such registration is possible, in compliance with certain conditions, where the two companies participating in the merger are both established in the territory of the first Member State*"[55].

This means that cross-border mergers are indeed recognized as a method of exercising the right of establishment[56] and free movement of capital set out in the EC Treaty[57]. Restrictions on the freedom of establishment in the public interest are allowed if they pass the "*rule of reason*" test: they should pursue a legitimate objective compatible with the EC Treaty and should be justified by imperative reasons in the public interest. Furthermore, the application of any such restriction must be appropriate to ensure the attainment of the objective thus pursued and must not go beyond what is necessary to attain that[58].

As will be demonstrated below (under 21 and 22), in our view, the Sevic case remains important for companies and for cross-border transactions which do not fall within the scope of the Tenth Directive[59]. The fact that it confirms the possibility of cross-border merger as a means of exercising the right of establishment – with an even broader scope of application than the Tenth Directive promulgated a short while thereafter – has created some doubt among practitioners as regards the utility of the Tenth Directive: after all, by providing for minority and employee protection it makes life more complicated than would have been the case under a mere application of the right of establishment. The battle of national tax authorities protecting their taxable basis might have lasted a little longer, but it would have subsided all the same.

---

[55] Sevic, §31.

[56] According to the opinion of Advocate General Tizzano, cross-border mergers "*could be seen not only as a case of primary establishment, but also as a case of secondary establishment*" (para. 35).

[57] On the different geographical scope of the two provisions, see T. DELVAUX, "Fusion internationale et libertés de circulation", *Journal des Tribunaux* 2006, 147

[58] Sevic, no. 23.

[59] See also M. RAAIJMAKERS, "Sevic: grensoverschrijdende fusie binnen de EU", *Ars Aequi* (Ned.) 2006, 632 and K. MARESCEAU, "Het vrij vestigingsrecht, de problematiek van de zetelverplaatsing en zijn impact op het internationaal privaatrecht: een stand van zaken na de zaak Cartesio", *Tijdschrift voor Belgisch Handelsrecht* 2009/6, 594-595, no. 22-25. Of particular interest is the issue raised by this author whether the Sevic case only allows a company absorbing a foreign company to invoke the right of establishment (inbound merger) (comparable to the recognition issue) or whether the right of establishment can also be invoked by the disappearing company vis-à-vis the Member State of the surviving entity (outbound merger).

2.3. Cross-border transfer of seat / freedom of establishment

18. ***Definition of the problem.*** As indicated above, the difficulties in reconciling the two theories on the connecting factor for company law (real seat vs. incorporation) arise in particular in the context of a company wishing to transfer its seat from one Member State to another Member State or wishing to change its corporate law.

19. ***Milestone judgments of the Court of Justice.*** This issue of the transfer of the real seat has resulted in several milestone judgments by the Court of Justice: Daily Mail, Centros[60], Inspire Art[61], Überseering[62] and Cartesio[63] [64].

Below we analyse the case law of the Court in chronological order. Since these cases cannot be properly understood outside the specific factual context the Court had to assess in each of them, we briefly summarize the relevant facts. Also, the reader should keep in mind from the outset that Daily Mail and Cartesio on the one hand, and Centros, Inspire Art and Überseering on the other hand should be read together[65].

In the **Daily Mail** case, and also in Cartesio, only the law of the home state (in Daily Mail: the United Kingdom; in Cartesio: Hungary) is at stake. The United Kingdom is an incorporation state. Daily Mail and General Trust Plc, a company incorporated and having its registered seat in the United Kingdom, intended to establish its central management and control outside the United Kingdom without however losing its legal personality or ceasing to be a company incorporated in the United Kingdom[66].

---

[60] ECJ, 9 March 1999, C-212/97 (Centros Ltd vs. Erhvervs- og Selskabsstyrelsen) ("**Centros**").

[61] ECJ, 30 September 2003, C-167/01 (Kamer van Koophandel en Fabrieken voor Amsterdam vs. Inspire Art Ltd.) ("**Inspire Art**").

[62] ECJ, 5 November 2002, C-208/00 (Überseering BV vs. Nordic Construction Company Baumanagement GmbH (NCC)) ("**Überseering**").

[63] For an overview of these cases (except for Cartesio), ; U. KLINKE, "European Company Law and the ECJ: The Court's Judgments in the Years 2001 to 2004", *ECFR* 2005, 270; P. RYAN, "Will there ever be a 'Delaware of Europe'?", http://papers.ssrn.com/sol3/papers.cfm?abstract_id=763164, 187-198; E. WYMEERSCH, "Chapter 7. Cross-border transfer of the seat of a company – recent EU case law and the SE Regulation", in J. RICKFORD (ed.), *The European Company – developing a community law of corporations*, Intersentia, Antwerp, 2003, 83-94.

[64] In an earlier judgment, the Court of Justice had already ruled that the fact that a company has no activities in a Member State where its registered office is located (i.e. the United Kingdom, an incorporation state), does not allow the Member State where its real activities are exercised (i.e. the Netherlands, an incorporation state), to impose restrictions on the freedom of establishment (ECJ, 10 July 1986, 79/85, (D. H. M. Segers vs. Bestuur van de Bedrijfsvereniging voor Bank- en Verzekeringswezen, Groothandel en Vrije Beroepen) ("**Segers**"). We also think one should distinguish the tax cases, such as Cadbury Schweppes (ECJ, 12 September 2006, C-196/04), or Avoir fiscal (ECJ, 28 January 1986, 270/83, France) because they do not so much concern the right of transfer as the right to organize a European-wide group (secondary right of establishment).

[65] In this respect, P. RYAN makes a distinction between "outbound cases" (e.g. Daily Mail and Cartesio) and "inbound cases" (e.g. Centros, Überseering and Inspire Art) (P. RYAN, "Will there ever be a 'Delaware of Europe'?", http://papers.ssrn.com/sol3/papers.cfm?abstract_id=763164, 187).

[66] Daily Mail, §3.

Only companies which are resident for tax purposes in the United Kingdom are as a rule liable for United Kingdom corporation tax. A company is resident for tax purposes in the place in which its central management and control are located and cannot cease to be so resident without the consent of the tax authorities[67].

The intended move of its central management and control to the Netherlands was only inspired by tax motives: a certain tax that would have been applicable would no longer apply under the Dutch regime, and the tax authorities were only willing to let the company go provided that it realized at least part of the operations triggering such tax while still resident in the United Kingdom, which the company in turn refused to do[68].

The Court held as follows: "*the Treaty regards the differences in national legislation concerning the required connecting factor and the question whether – and if so how – the registered office or real head office*[69] *of a company incorporated under national law may be transferred from one Member State to another as problems which are not resolved by the rules concerning the right of establishment but must be dealt with by future legislation or conventions.*

Under these circumstances, [the right of establishment] cannot be interpreted as conferring on companies incorporated under the law of a Member State a right to transfer their national administration to another Member State [B] while retaining their status as companies incorporated under the legislation of the first Member State [A].

In the present state of community law [the right of establishment confers] no right on a company incorporated under the legislation of a Member State [A] and having its registered office there to transfer its central management and control to another Member State [B]"[70].

The Daily Mail case is however somewhat special in that, normally, an incorporation state would not be opposed to a company developing its real activities elsewhere without ceasing to be governed by the corporate law of the state. Here, however, the issue was not the further application of a rule of company law, but a taxation issue, which is quite a different matter[71].

In the **Centros** case, the Court is in fact dealing with the question whether a Member State must recognize a company validly formed under the company law of another Member State. The case concerned once more a company incorporated under the law of England and Wales (an incorporation state) but conducting its activities (quasi-solely) in its Danish branch[72]. Danish law (Denmark being an incorporation state) requires foreign branches to register

---

67 Daily Mail, §§ 4-5.

68 Daily Mail, §§7-8.

69 Emphasis ours; see also below, the Cartesio case.

70 Daily Mail, §§23-25 and ruling.

71 K. MARESCEAU, "Het vrij vestigingsrecht, de problematiek van de zetelverplaatsing en zijn impact op het internationaal privaatrecht: een stand van zaken na de zaak Cartesio", *Tijdschrift voor Belgisch Handelsrecht* 2009/6, 589, no. 13 for a similar comment.

72 Centros, §3.

in Denmark, but in this case such registration was refused because it was considered that Centros was in fact a Danish company circumventing Danish minimum capital rules[73].

The Court held as follows: "*It is contrary to [the right of establishment] for a Member State [B] to refuse to register a branch of a company formed in accordance with the law of another Member State [A] in which it has its registered office but in which it conducts no business where the branch is intended to enable the company in question to carry on its entire business in the state in which that branch is to be created, while avoiding the need to form a company there, thus evading application of the rules governing the formation of companies which, in that State [B], are more restrictive as regards the paying up of a minimum share capital. That interpretation does not, however, prevent the authorities of the Member State concerned [B] from adopting any appropriate measure for preventing or penalising fraud, either in relation to the company itself, if need be in cooperation with the Member State where it was formed [A], or in relation to its members, where it has been established that they are in fact attempting, by means of the formation of a company, to evade their obligations towards private or public creditors established in the territory of the Member State concerned [B]*"[74].

In **Überseering**, the Court was also confronted with an issue of recognition. Überseering was a company incorporated in the Netherlands (an incorporation state). Its shares were at a certain point in time acquired by German residents, and thereafter it was in fact mainly active in Germany and held its general meetings in Germany. However, it did not – and did not intend to – move its registered seat, and thus intended to continue to be governed by Dutch law[75]. Germany, a real seat state, refused legal standing to Überseering, claiming that it in fact had its real seat in Germany and thus had to reincorporate in Germany.

According to the Court, "*where a company formed in accordance with the law of a Member State ('A') in which it has its registered office is deemed, under the law of another Member State ('B'), to have moved its actual centre of administration to Member State B, [the right of establishment precludes] Member State B from denying the company legal capacity and, consequently, the capacity to bring legal proceedings before its national courts for the purpose of enforcing rights under a contract with a company established in Member State B. Where a company formed in accordance with the law of a Member State ('A') in which its has its registered office exercises its freedom of establishment in another Member State ('B'), [the right of establishment requires] Member State B to recognise the legal capacity, and consequently, the capacity to be a party to legal proceedings which the company enjoys under the law of its state of incorporation, Member State A*"[76].

[73] Centros, §8.
[74] Centros, §39 and ruling.
[75] Überseering, §50.
[76] Überseering, §§94-95 and ruling.

As is the case for Centros and Überseering, **Inspire Art** is also a recognition issue, in nature more comparable to Centros than to Überseering. Inspire Art was a company incorporated under the law of England and Wales but conducted its activities (solely) in its Dutch branch. The Netherlands is an incorporation state but nevertheless imposes certain additional requirements on foreign companies operating within its territory. Such requirements go beyond what is prescribed for foreign branches by the Eleventh Directive, and in fact oblige them (at least) to comply with some rules applicable to Dutch private limited liability companies with regard to capital formation and director liability[77].

The Court decided that "*it is contrary to [the right of establishment] for national legislation [...] to impose on the exercise of freedom of secondary establishment in that State by a company formed in accordance with the law of another Member State certain conditions provided for in domestic company law in respect of company formation relating to minimum capital and directors' liability. The reasons for which the company was formed in that other Member State, and the fact that it carries on its activities exclusively or almost exclusively in the Member State of establishment, do not deprive it of the right to invoke the freedom of establishment guaranteed by the EC Treaty, save where the existence of an abuse is established on a case-by-case basis*"[78].

In **Cartesio**, as in Daily Mail, only the law of the home state (in Cartesio: Hungary) was at stake. Hungarian law adheres to the real seat doctrine, whereby the concept of "seat" has to be understood as the place where a company has its central administration[79]. Cartesio intended to move its real seat to Italy but continue to be governed by Hungarian law[80]. Hungarian law, however, does not allow a company incorporated in Hungary to transfer its (real) seat abroad while continuing to be subject to Hungarian law[81], which is normal under a real seat doctrine[82].

---

77 Inspire Art and the Commission even argued that the rules on the joint and several liability of directors imposed by the Netherlands on Inspire Art were discriminatory, (i) as directors of Inspire Art would be jointly and severally liable if the company's minimum capital dropped below the limit set out in the Dutch WFBV, whereas, by contrast, the directors of a limited liability company governed by Dutch law would not be subject to that same strict liability, and (ii) the circle of potentially liable persons is extended to those who actually conduct the company's activities. The Court of Justice has not dealt with this argument.

78 Inspire Art, §143.

79 Cartesio, §48.

80 Cartesio, §§47 and 99-100.

81 Cartesio, §102.

82 It is worth noting that some authors contest whether the Advocate General and the Court have correctly interpreted Hungarian law as it stands today (see V. KROM and P. METZINGER, "Freedom of Establishment for Companies: the European Court of Justice confirms and refines its Daily Mail Decision in the Cartesio Case C-210/06", *ECFR* 2009/6, no. 1, 125 et seq.) We have deliberately followed the understanding of the Court because that understanding solely is at the basis of its decision (see also F. JENNÉ, "Grensoverschrijdende zetelverplaatsing: de determinerende invloed van het land van oorsprong", to be published in *Tijdschrift voor Rechtspersoon en Vennootschap* 2009/6).

The Court held as follows:

"*Thus a Member State has the power to define both the connecting factor required of a company if it is to be regarded as incorporated under the law of that Member State and, as such, capable of enjoying the right of establishment, and that required if the company is to be able subsequently to maintain that status. That power includes the possibility for that Member State not to permit a company governed by its law to retain that status if the company intends to reorganise itself in another Member State by moving its seat to the territory of the latter, thereby breaking the connecting factor required under the national law of the Member State of incorporation.*"[83]

"*As community law now stands, the right of establishment is to be interpreted as not precluding legislation of a Member State under which a company incorporated under the law of that Member State may not transfer its seat to another Member State whilst retaining its status as a company governed by the law of the Member State of incorporation.*"[84],

However, without being invited or even challenged to do so, the Court added that "*the power [to define the connecting factor], far from implying that national legislation on the incorporation and winding-up of companies enjoys any form of immunity from the rules of the EC Treaty on freedom of establishment, cannot, in particular, justify the Member State of incorporation, by requiring the winding-up or liquidation of the company, in preventing that company from converting itself into a company governed by the law of the other Member State, to the extent that it is permitted under that law to do so*"[85].

The Court thus seems to issue an important warning to Hungary and all other Member States which may have far-reaching consequences: if a company does intend to change its corporate law, and the national law of the host state allows the company to convert itself into a company governed by the law of the host state, the home state will not be in a position to preclude that. The Court does not indicate under which conditions the host state may allow conversion, but Articles 43 and 58 of the EC Treaty will in any event apply: the host state may not impose stricter conditions on such companies than it imposes on the companies that are already governed by its law. This leaves at least one crucial question unanswered: what about liquidation or other exit taxes?

---

[83] Cartesio, §110.

[84] Cartesio, §124 and ruling. It should be noted that in this ruling the Court deviated entirely from the opinion of Advocate General Poiares Maduro, who had suggested that the Court should rule that the freedom of establishment precludes national rules which make it impossible for a company constituted under national law to transfer its operational headquarters to another Member State. The Advocate General was also of the opinion that it was difficult, if not impossible, to reconcile Daily Mail with Centros, Inspire Art and Überseering. As this overview shows, that is not necessarily the case, provided one carefully takes the facts into account. However, one may have negative feelings on the maintenance of the "semantic" logic adhered to by the Court, and leading to a considerably different approach to inbound (Centros, Überseering, Inspire Art) and outbound (Daily Mail and Cartesio) situations (see K. MARESCEAU, "Het vrij vestigingsrecht, de problematiek van de zetelverplaatsing en zijn impact op het internationaal privaatrecht: een stand van zaken na de zaak Cartesio", *Tijdschrift voor Belgisch Handelsrecht* 2009/6, 598 et seq., no. 31 et seq).

[85] Cartesio, §112.

20. ***What can be learned from the milestone judgments of the Court of Justice?*** In Daily Mail and Cartesio, the issue at stake was whether a company could continue to be governed by the law of its home state, under conditions not acceptable to the home state. Daily Mail concerns an incorporation state, but the move of the real activities to the Netherlands had nothing to do with any desire to change the applicable corporate law: on the contrary, the United Kingdom company wanted to remain governed by United Kingdom law, while at the same time moving its centre of administration to the Netherlands in order to no longer qualify as a tax resident for United Kingdom law purposes. In Cartesio (where a real seat state was involved), the company wanted to continue to be governed by Hungarian law, even after having moved its real seat to Italy. In these two cases, no recognition issues arose – though they could have arisen if the Netherlands or Italy had questioned the moves.

In Centros and Inspire Art, the only question that was raised is whether a United Kingdom (incorporation state) company can exercise its (sole) activities in another Member State without having to comply with specific requirements imposed by the host state. In Überseering, a similar question was at stake: could a company incorporated in the Netherlands (incorporation state) exercise activities in Germany without German law imposing a reincorporation under German law? In all three of these cases, the Court held that the host state had to recognize the legal personality as it existed in the home state, given that the home state (being an incorporation state) allowed the company concerned to be governed by it without conducting its (main) activities in the home state.

When one considers the case law in the light of the different scenarios for corporate mobility listed above (under 5), one realizes that in fact only very few of them have so far been submitted to the Court.

(a) The company does not intend to change the company law applicable to it

1. **Move of real seat from incorporation state A to incorporation state B**: At first glance this should not be an issue, either for the states concerned or for third parties[86]. However, Centros and Inspire Art show that even incorporation states must refrain from imposing additional conditions, and that state B must recognize the company without imposing additional requirements, except in cases where a specific abuse is established (see above, under 19)[87]. Protection of creditors is not a valid argument for refusing recognition under the law of the host state, since creditors are on notice that the company is not governed by the law of the host state and they can obtain information through the national legislation implementing the Fourth and Eleventh Directives. Public creditors could be given specific

[86] See the Winter Report, 102.

[87] Such abuse could exist, for example, if the company was established in its home state in an attempt to evade its obligations towards private or public creditors established in the host state (Centros, §8).

guarantees[88]. Disclosure requirements for the "branch" in the host state stretching beyond the requirements laid down in the Eleventh Directive are likewise not admissible, nor are additional capitalization requirements and enforcing director liability for the protection of creditors, even if they do not go beyond what is required for companies established in the host state[89].

2. **Move of real seat from incorporation state A to real seat state B**: In Überseering the Court ruled that real seat state B must recognize (the capacity and thus also the capacity to bring legal proceedings of) the company, and cannot impose reincorporation except in cases where specific abuse is established (see above, under 19). Enhancement in general of legal certainty and creditor protection does not suffice; neither does protection of minority shareholders, nor even employee protection or tax interests[90]. To put it differently, if the ruling of the Court that the host state must recognize the legal capacity of a company validly incorporated in its home state is to be understood in its fullest extent, this takes away the risk of double nationality.

3. **Move of real seat from real seat state A to real seat state B:** State A is allowed to determine the connecting factor (and can thus state that the company is not allowed to be governed by its law if the real seat is no longer located in state A), but would nevertheless not be allowed to prohibit the company from converting itself into a company governed by the law of state B if the law of state B so allows: this is the lesson to be learned, partially from Daily Mail but most certainly from Cartesio.

4. **Move of real seat from real seat state A into incorporation state B:** So far, this situation has never been submitted to the Court of Justice. As set out above (under 5), in a strict application of both theories, this would lead to the company being stateless, unless state B would, one way or another, allow the company to re-establish itself in state B.

(b) The company intends to change the company law applicable to it

In none of the cases so far submitted to the Court of Justice did the company intend to change the corporate law applicable to it. Therefore, it is very difficult to predict under what circumstances the Court would allow a change of company law.

---

88 Centros, §§36-37.
89 Inspire Art, §106 et seq.
90 Überseering, §§92-93.

Only in the scenario of a company intending to change applicable company law to the law of a real seat state (see above, under 5, hypotheses (b)2 and (b)3) does the Cartesio case seem to offer some guidance: since a real seat state may require that the real seat continues to be located in state A for the company law of state A to be applicable, one can probably be inclined to believe that the Court would also accept that real seat host state B can rightfully impose the condition that the real seat should be moved to state B in order for state B's company law to be applicable[91]. Moreover, the Court indicates that, if a conversion is possible under state B's company law, state A may not refuse to allow the conversion of the company into a company governed by state B's company law. The question remains how the Court would judge in the event that B's company law did not allow such a conversion. Secondly, the question remains as to which protective measures should or may accompany such a conversion, taking into account the interests (shareholders, creditors, tax authorities, etc.) at stake[92].

2.4. Other cross-border reorganizations

21. ***(Partial) de-merger.*** The Sixth Directive provides for specific rules regarding national (partial) de-mergers. However, no such company law rules exist for cross-border de-mergers (i.e. de-mergers whereby one of the acquiring companies is governed by a Member State other than the home Member State of the de-merging company): these transactions are covered by the Merger Tax Directive, but not by the Tenth Directive.

Current European company law already indirectly enables companies to proceed to a cross-border de-merger, by (i) first de-merging a company under the applicable national laws (harmonized after the Sixth Directive) and (ii) then merging one of the companies resulting from the de-merger with a company newly incorporated in another Member State (in accordance with the rules based on the Tenth Directive)[93].

Although the outcome of such transactions is the same as in the event of a de-merger, the question arises whether one is allowed, on the basis of the freedom of establishment, to carry out a cross-border (partial) de-merger directly (without dividing the transaction into two separate "transactions").

---

[91] See also Cartesio, §112. For a detailed discussion of possible issues that could arise and on which no clear answer can be provided on the basis of the Court's case law to date: K. MARESCEAU, "Het vrij vestigingsrecht, de problematiek van de zetelverplaatsing en zijn impact op het internationaal privaatrecht: een stand van zaken na de zaak Cartesio", *Tijdschrift voor Belgisch Handelsrecht* 2009/6, 600-602, no. 35-37.

[92] For the European Company, these measures are referred to in Article 8, §2 to §16 of the SE Council Regulation.

[93] See also the Winter Report, 108. As a matter of fact, this procedure is similar to the procedure generally applied in the United States for a transfer of seat: incorporating a new company in the host state, and then merging the initial company with the new company (see above, footnote 26).

In the Sevic decision, the Court of Justice explicitly stated that "*cross-border merger operations, like other company transformation operations, [...] constitute particular methods of exercise of the freedom of establishment*". Arguably, (partial) de-merger also qualifies as a particular method of exercising freedom of establishment: on the one hand, in principle the transfer of part of the assets to a company in another Member State constitutes, for the de-merging company, a means of exercising the right of primary establishment; on the other hand, the acquiring company exercises its right of secondary establishment (especially if the assets and liabilities it acquires constitute a secondary place of business abroad)[94].

Limiting the scope of the (partial) de-merger legislation to national de-mergers and prohibiting cross-border (partial) de-mergers, would therefore, in our view, constitute a restriction on the freedom of establishment which is only allowed if it passes the "rule of reason" test (see above, under 17).

22. *Contribution or transfer of a branch of activities.* Under Belgian law, a branch of activities[95] can be transferred to one or more (new or existing) companies, while the transferring company continues to exist. The consideration can consist of cash (sale) and/or shares (contribution). The procedure for the transfer or contribution of a branch of activities is similar to the procedure for mergers and de-mergers. The main advantage of this transaction is that all assets and liabilities connected with the branch are automatically deemed to be transferred to the acquiring company and, except in respect of specific agreements[96], IP rights, real estate and permits, the transfer is enforceable vis-à-vis third parties as of publication in the Belgian Official Gazette without any further formalities.

The contribution of assets is covered by the Merger Tax Directive, but not by either the Third or the Sixth Directive. As a result, hardly any European harmonization is in place regarding the transfer of a branch of activities. This lack of harmonization complicates the frequently occurring cross-border transfers of branches of activities, especially with respect to the formalities necessary to make the transfer enforceable vis-à-vis third parties[97].

---

[94] For a more detailed analysis, see L.L. HANSEN, "Merger, Moving and Division Across National Borders – When Case Law Breaks through Barriers and Overtakes Directives", *European Business Law Review*, 2007, 191-196. See also above, footnote 59, on the doubt that may arise as regards the exact scope of the Sevic case, precisely in view of its link to the right of establishment.

[95] For the purposes of this transaction, a branch of activities ("branch") is defined as a technical and organizational entity which exercises an autonomous activity and can function by itself (disconnected from the other activities of the transferring company).

[96] i.e. the agreements which provide for enforceable change of control clauses that also apply in the event of a transfer of a branch.

[97] Under the conflict of law rules, the enforceability of a transfer is governed by the "*lex rei sitae*": for each asset to be transferred as part of the branch of activities, the transfer formalities have to be examined (M. WYCKAERT, "De toepasselijkheid van de artikelen 759 e.v. W.Venn. bij grensoverschrijdende herstructureringen: het water mag niet langer te diep zijn voor Belgische juristen", *Tijdschrift voor Rechtspersoon en Vennootschap* 2001, 214).

In our view, there is therefore a case for harmonizing at European level the rules regarding national and cross-border transfers of branches of activities, in a similar manner as for mergers.

For the sake of completeness, it should be mentioned that cross-border activity is also often organized through a simple sale of shares. Therefore, transfers of shares would only be relevant to the topic covered in this paper if the law of a Member State considered that the nationality of the shareholders had an impact on the applicable corporate law (see above, under 19, for the Überseering case).

3. Some concluding remarks – Where do we go from here?

23. *European Company, European Cooperative Company and Cross-Border Mergers.* Although it is too early to assess the effectiveness of the cross-border possibilities offered by the European Company, the European Cooperative Company and the Tenth Directive, it is probably fair to say that they will enhance corporate mobility in Europe, and have created, to a large extent, legal certainty. The real added value of these measures however will have to be demonstrated in practice: it may be that the European Company in particular has mainly had the honour of "preparing the ground".

24. *Where does the case law of the Court of Justice bring us?* We believe that the analysis above leads to the following conclusions:

a) the Court of Justice fully respects Article 48 of the EC Treaty by equally accepting the registered seat, central administration or principal place of business as connecting factors.

b) The Court of Justice also fully respects the principle that the company law of the state of incorporation determines whether a company validly exists; if this is the case, other states have to fully respect this.

c) The Court of Justice has accepted that companies have the freedom of choice between the creation of a subsidiary or a branch.

d) Nevertheless, and in line with the first conclusion, the Court of Justice has not condemned the real seat doctrine.

e) When interpreting the case law, it should however be kept in mind at all times that the Court of Justice can only deal with the factual situations that are submitted to it.

25. *Incorporation or real seat?* It is remarkable how much importance the Court of Justice attaches to the home state or the state of incorporation. In view of this, some authors[98] have argued that the Court of Justice has expressed

[98] E. WYMEERSCH, "Centros: a landmark decision in European Company Law", in TH. BAUMS, K.J. HOPT and N. HORN (eds.), *Corporations, Capital Markets and Business in the Law*, Kluwer Law

a preference for the incorporation doctrine over the real seat doctrine, and that the real seat doctrine can no longer hold out.

Although in the Centros, Inspire Art and Überseering cases the Court of Justice did indeed explicitly recognize the freedom to decide where to incorporate a company regardless of where its real seat is located, we believe that it is not correct to state that the real seat doctrine is destined to disappear.

On the contrary, in the Cartesio and (to a lesser extent) Daily Mail cases, the Court of Justice continues to scrupulously respect Article 48 of the EC Treaty which, as set out above (under 1), puts all existing connecting factors (registered seat, central administration or principal place of business) on an equal footing. Indeed, in the Cartesio case the Court of Justice has decided that, on the basis of the freedom of establishment, it is permissible for a real seat state to require of newly incorporated companies that they have a real seat located within its territory.

The consequences of the consistent case law of the Court of Justice must come as a shock for "real seat" adepts. Indeed, as soon as a company is incorporated in full accordance with the law of any Member State adhering to the incorporation doctrine, it can conduct its business anywhere in the EU, without having to change the corporate law applicable to it. Thus understood, the EU system in many ways approaches the system applicable in the US[99] – but with a lesser degree of harmonization applying to many of the legal forms involved.

One can fairly confirm that, in this respect, the Court accepts the incorporation doctrine (in its theoretical form) to its fullest extent: if a company, under its home state law, can continue to be governed by that home state law regardless of where it conducts its business, all other Member States should recognize the legal capacity of that company. They cannot – except in highly exceptional circumstances, none of which the Court has so far admitted – impose additional conditions on the company for operating in their territory[100], and they certainly cannot require a reincorporation.

As a result, the scope of the real seat theory has been limited. Member States cannot, on the basis of their own conflict of law rules, object to the existence of a company validly incorporated in another Member State. This means that real seat state A has to recognize a company which is validly incorporated in incorporation state B although its principal place of business is located in state

International, 2000, 629-654 and the references in M. SIEMS, "Convergence, Competition, Centros and Conflicts of Law: European Company Law in the 21st Century", http://papers.ssrn.com/sol3/papers.cfm?abstract_id=853865, 6 and in S. GRUNDMANN, *European Company Law*, Intersentia, Antwerp – Oxford, 2007, 499.

[99] C. TIMMERMANS, "Chapter Three, Methods and Tools for Integration" in R.M. BUXBAUM, G. HERTIG, A. HURSCH, K.J. HOPT (eds.), *European Business Law*, W. De Gruyter & Co, Berlin, 1991,135, (6).

[100] Such additional requirements are in any event not permitted if the sanction for non-compliance is the loss of legal capacity of the company. The Court has never dealt with a situation where additional conditions (which are not discriminatory compared with conditions applicable to national companies), are imposed by a real seat state in the host state and where the violation of these conditions does not result in the loss of legal capacity, but in, e.g. founders' or directors' liability.

A. This is indeed a restriction on the real seat theory: the connecting factor for valid corporate existence under the conflict of law rules seems to be, according to the Court of Justice, the place of incorporation. In other words, the relationship between the home state of incorporation and the company seems to be final.

Nevertheless, referring to the freedom of choice between a branch and a subsidiary is challengeable, as the concept of a "branch" seems to imply dependence on and subordination to a main office. If a company only has a letterbox in its "home country", and conducts all its activities in another Member State, one could argue that there is no "branch" in the host state[101]. This is however, as set out below (under 26) not an argument that may be easily accepted by the Court of Justice (see also below, under 26)[102].

In general, there will be disappointment among legal scholars about the outcome of Cartesio, because it is a step back from unlimited corporate mobility throughout Europe. While such disappointment can be understood, we strongly believe that before taking the step of unlimited corporate mobility throughout Europe – either by adopting new legislation or by a fundamental revision of the case law – the concept and the foundations of such unfettered corporate mobility should be looked into in more detail.

26. *Light vehicle competition.* Of the cases so far decided by the Court of Justice in the field of corporate mobility, only some lead to a certain degree of uneasiness[103]. Segers[104], Centros and Inspire Art[105] each concerned companies whose founders (or acquirers) opted for an ultra-light limited company under the law of England and Wales for exercising all or at least the major part of their economic activities in another Member State where the choice of any vehicle governed by the law of such other Member State granting limited liability to its members would have imposed stricter standards on its members. The Court of Justice clearly ruled that the mere fact that the right of free establishment is used in order that "*a national of a Member State who wishes to set up a company chooses to form it in the Member State whose rules of company law seem to him the least restrictive and to set up branches in other Member States*"[106] cannot as such be

---

[101] H. GILLIAMS, Y. VAN GERVEN, J. WOUTERS and P. WYTINCK, "Kroniek van rechtspraak: Europees ondernemingsrecht", *Tijdschrift voor Belgisch Handelsrecht* (B), 1999, 762.

[102] V. SIMONART, "L'application du droit belge aux sociétés constituées dans un autre état de la communauté, et, en particulier, aux *Limited*", *Revue Pratique des Sociétés* 2008, referring also to Segers, § 16.

[103] Compare with the remark, registered in Annex 3 of the Winter Report summarizing the responses to the consultation launched by the High Level Group of Company Law Experts (Winter Report, Annex 3, 153), that these cases are "smelly".

[104] For very critical comments, see C. TIMMERMANS, "Chapter Three, Methods and Tools for Integration" in R.M. BUXBAUM, G. HERTIG, A. HURSCH, K.J. HOPT (eds.), *European Business Law*, W. De Gruyter & Co, Berlin, 1991, 136, (7).

[105] For comments, see H.-J. DE KLUIVER, "Inspiring a New European Company Law? – Observations on the ECJ's decision in *Inspire Art* from a Dutch perspective and the Imminent Competition for Corporate Charters between EC Member States", *ECFR* 1/2004, 121 et seq.; H. DE WULF, *Tijdschrift voor Belgisch Handelsrecht* 2004, 89.

[106] Centros, §27.

qualified as an abuse of that right, while remaining deaf to all pleas made by the (actual and potential) host states concerning the grounds on which they should be allowed to fight abuses of the freedom of establishment[107].

The result is known: in order to avoid a proliferation of "Limiteds" governed by the law of England and Wales[108] or similar light vehicles[109], other Member States are considering introducing a light vehicle of their own[110].

One feels less uncomfortable with Überseering (see also above, under 19): it does indeed seem that refusing court standing in Germany to a Dutch BV whose shares were sold to two German residents and whose real seat had allegedly been moved to Germany was disproportionate[111]. Nevertheless, Überseering seems to go beyond the proportionality principle, as the Court of Justice requires full recognition of legal capacity.

27. *Need for a Fourteenth Directive and for harmonization.* As pointed out under 20, the case law of the Court of Justice does not provide a clear solution in all scenarios. In this respect, we do not understand why the Commission, in its working document issued at the end of 2007 (see above, under 8), decided against proposing a Fourteenth Directive, preferring instead to await the case law of the Court of Justice. This means that the development of European law in the field of corporate mobility would to a large extent be dependent upon the "accidental" factual situations the national courts decide to submit to the Court of Justice (which by nature will tend to be more orientated to the incorporation doctrine than the real seat doctrine – see above, under 4). For this reason, we support the recent initiative taken by the European Parliament (see also above, under 8) to put the Fourteenth Directive back on the agenda.

---

[107] For an analysis, see V. SIMONART, "L'application du droit belge aux sociétés constituées dans un autre état de la communauté, et, en particulier, aux *Limited*", *Revue Pratique des Sociétés* 2008, 164-1167, no. 59-61. In his opinion on the Cartesio case, Advocate General Maduro attached strong importance to the possibility for the Member States to reject a purely artificial connection factor (n° 29), but it must be admitted that neither the Centros nor the Inspire Art case were very encouraging in this regard.

[108] See e.g. in Belgium the services advertised by BellBrooks Europe (http://www.bellbrooks.eu/officebelgium).

[109] On this issue in a Belgian context, see V. SIMONART, "L'application du droit belge aux sociétés constituées dans un autre état de la communauté, et, en particulier, aux *Limited*", *Revue Pratique des Sociétés* 2008, 111-206; E. NAVEZ and C. GUYOT, "La *Private Limited Company* de droit anglais: une alternative à la SPRL?", *Revue du notariat belge* 2008, 130 et seq. While one may challenge the bad reputation in this regard of these Limiteds at a general level, those advertising their use on the Continent do use this as a selling argument and may in any event be encouraging as light a vehicle as possible.

[110] See, for Belgium, *De Tijd*, 24 June 2008. France, the Netherlands and other countries are considering comparable initiatives, or have already lowered their minimum capital requirements (see the paper by J.-M. NELISSEN GRADE and M. WAUTERS on the concept of capital – see also M. BECHT, C. MAYER and H.F. WAGNER, "Where do firms incorporate? Deregulation and the cost of entry", http://papers.ssrn.com/sol3/papers.cfm?abstract_id=953820, 4).

[111] See in this regard paragraphs 48 and 63 of the judgment, confirming that Überseering by no means intended to move its corporate seat.

Just to give a few examples:
It is not entirely clear how the Court of Justice would react if a company moved its activities to a real seat state: to what extent can the host state impose its own national corporate law requirements on the imported company? We suspect that in this case a Member State should respect the requirement of equal treatment, set out in Article 48 of the EC Treaty, and thus not impose more stringent conditions on foreign companies than on its own national companies (non-discrimination).

As set out above (under 6) the Winter Report suggests that the host state should be allowed to do so provided (i) that such national corporate law rules support a requirement of legitimate general interest, are not disproportionate, require only what is necessary and appropriate to secure the interest concerned, are non-discriminatory and are sufficiently transparent; and (ii) where the company has originally been incorporated in a real seat state, that such national rules be limited by the principle of reciprocity, i.e. that the home state must accept that the host state imposes the rules it would itself impose in the converse situation[112]. It is not entirely certain that the Court of Justice would follow this approach, when one considers the Überseering case. Moreover, this approach could possibly have a considerable influence on the state competition debate: states opting for the incorporation doctrine would give their resident companies far more freedom of establishment elsewhere in the European Union than real seat states, unless the latter, because of a higher degree of harmonization, would not feel the urge to impose additional rules on top of what the imported company is already subject to.

Likewise, the position the Court of Justice would take in the light of the freedom of establishment with regard to a move from a real seat state to an incorporation state, leading to statelessness, is difficult to predict.

We therefore believe that there is room for a legislative initiative on the impact of a transfer of real seat (and the measures the Member States involved could take to avoid abuses of light vehicle competition), as well as on the change of corporate law.

For the change of applicable law, the European legislator could look for inspiration to the rules on the transfer of seat of a European Company and the rules on cross-border mergers. If such a change is admissible in that context, it should also be admissible in the context of a cross-border transfer of seat, provided that European law, as it has done for the cross-border merger and even more pertinently for a transfer of seat by a European Company, ensures an acceptable set of protective rules for all stakeholders. It is doubtful whether, in putting such a directive in place, a choice will have to be made between incorporation and real seat: as is the case for a cross-border merger (see above, under 16), a transfer of seat according to the rules of the Fourteenth Directive could simply function as a means for a company to change its applicable law.

[112] Winter Report, 103-106.

The question then arises whether the Member States are ready to take this additional step. This may require, as set out below, an intensification of the level of harmonization as it exists today.

28. ***What kind of competition do we want?*** When considering the case law of the Court of Justice, one thing is certain; the Court of Justice promotes a very liberal interpretation of the freedom of establishment[113]: once validly incorporated in an incorporation state, a company can develop activities anywhere in the European Union. We are not certain that we can see what exactly is driving the Court of Justice in taking this attitude: is this an open invitation to the Commission and the Council to speed up the harmonization process, which would neutralize the effects of a free choice of governing law[114]?

As the Commission itself has pointed out, "*the twin objectives of any initiative [on the matter of cross-border transfer of seat] should be to improve the efficiency and competitive position of European companies by providing them with the possibility of transferring their registered office more easily and, hence, [choosing] a legal environment that best suits their business needs, while at the same time guaranteeing the effective protection of the interests of the main stakeholders in respect of the transfer*"[115].

The Court of Justice has on different occasions held that "*a company exists by virtue of the national law which determines its incorporation and functioning*"[116] (see above, under 1). If all national laws concerned offer a comparable or at least equivalent minimum framework for the functioning of the company, freedom of establishment would no longer be "*a means to escape the law of origin*"[117], but a true choice to opt for the location that best fits the company's status, activities and needs. Everything that is not covered by this minimum standard could continue to be governed by national law, and thus be subject to healthy state law competition.

Or is it a truly liberal choice for a system of state law competition[118] as it already exists in the US? In the latter case one should keep in mind that, whereas regional differences in corporate law may still be important in the

---

[113] This is also the perception in US doctrine: see e.g. R. DAINES, "Does Delaware Law Improve Firm Value?", http://papers.ssrn.com/paper.taf?abstract_Id=195109, 6 (published in *Journal of Financial Economics* 40 (2001 a), 525-558); L. BEBCHUK and A. COHEN, "Firms' decisions where to incorporate", http://papers.ssrn.com/abstract_id=304386, 1; O. BAGILL, M. BARZUZA and L. BEBCHUK, "The market for corporate law", http://papers.ssrn.com/abstract_id=275452, 1 (also published in 162 *Journal of Institutional and Theoretical Economics* 134-171 (2006)).

[114] Centros, §28.

[115] Commission Staff Working Document – Impact assessment on the Directive on the cross-border transfer of registered office, SEC(2007)1707, http://ec.europa.eu/internal_market/company/docs/shareholders/ia_transfer_122007_part1_en.pdf, 5.

[116] Überseering, §81; Daily Mail, §19.

[117] Winter Report, 106.

[118] For a (theoretical) analysis of the efficiency of such state law competition, see T. DELVAUX, "La concurrence entre ordres juridiques est-elle efficace ? – Quelques réflexions à propos de la liberté d'établissement des sociétés", *Revue Pratique des Sociétés* 2004, 207 et seq.

US[119], "*U.S. firms incorporated in any given state may transact on equal footing in any state. Consequently,* ***being incorporated in any other state is not supposed to affect how a firm's operations are going to be taxed or regulated****. Similarly, the corporate law of any given state, which largely affects the relationship between shareholders and managers, applies equally to all the firms incorporated in that state regardless of where they are located*"[120] (emphasis ours). To put it differently, regardless of the rationale behind the position of the Court of Justice, in both cases it remains a fact that the average protective cushion offered for all stakeholders concerned (shareholders, management, creditors, financiers, suppliers, employees, tax authorities, regulators) is better developed in the US than it is in Europe. One may thus validly assert that state competition works in a satisfactory manner in the US: there may be different reasons for that, but one thing is certain: the starting points for such competition seem, generally speaking, to be of a higher quality: the cushion can take more blows. One may have a different view regarding what the cushion should look like[121], but one must admit the usefulness of the existence of such a cushion in order to develop an internal market. In matters of employee participation and taxation this is already widely acknowledged, but it may have to stretch beyond that.

Moreover, to what extent regulatory competition functions well has been a hotly debated question, in particular in the US. As indicated by L. Bebchuk and A. Cohen, the dominant trend in legal doctrine seems to be that regulatory competition creates a "*race-toward-the-top*" that benefits shareholders, as the desire to attract incorporation would induce states to develop and provide corporate arrangements that enhance shareholder value. However, a more sceptical approach holds that state competition would encourage states to provide rules that are too favourable to corporate managers and controllers with respect to corporate issues that have a major effect on the private benefits of managers and controllers.

We will not spend too much time on the argument that the market itself may offer adequate protection against abuses of light vehicles. Market auto-regulation has it limits, as has been all too harshly demonstrated by the recent financial crisis, and it often comes too late, certainly for those who were already the victim of practices triggering the market's expulsive reaction.

[119] Winter Report, 31. See however L. BEBCHUK and A. COHEN, "Firms' decisions where to incorporate", http://papers.ssrn.com/abstract_id=304386, 14: adopting the Revised Model of the Business Corporation Act (or its predecessor, the MBCA) did not seem to have a statistically significant impact on a state's ability to retain firms.

[120] L. BEBCHUK and A. COHEN, "Firms' decisions where to incorporate", http://papers.ssrn.com/abstract_id=304386, 1.

[121] Very interesting in this regard is the (only very partially successful) approach of the Takeover Bids Directive (2004/25/EC) vs. the situation in the US as described by L. BEBCHUK and A. COHEN, "Firms' decisions where to incorporate", http://papers.ssrn.com/abstract_id=304386, demonstrating that the state differences in takeover bid law and case law may play a much more important role in the choice of the incorporation state than has been generally admitted.

While this is certainly crucial in assessing the consequences of the incorporation doctrine as interpreted by the Court of Justice, we believe these questions are also fundamental in making it easier for real seat states to accept the import of foreign companies.

What is the model the Court of Justice and the Commission want to achieve? Which elements do they have in mind when they put themselves in the place of a company faced with deciding which Member State's law it wants to be governed by? On several occasions the Commission has continued to stress that the effective and proportionate protection of shareholders and third parties (i.e. the main stakeholders, including employees) must be "*at the core of any company law policy*"[122]. We can agree with that statement as such, and it would therefore be good to have at least a clear view of the protective measures the Commission has in mind when considering the issues of corporate mobility. The Court of Justice seems to accept a form of state law competition where the market for applicable corporate law acts as a regulator protecting the interests at stake.

Opening the European market for all companies requires a sufficient degree of trust in each corporate form that is "exported" to other Member States under the cover of freedom of establishment. While harmonization is far advanced as regards the legal regime in respect of public limited liability companies thanks to the Second Directive (including its latest amendments and the constant concern to improve its scope and efficiency[123]) and continuously improving with regard to listed public limited liability companies[124], this is not the case for private limited liability companies, and even less so for other forms of companies having legal personality. The proposal for a Council Regulation on the Statute for a European private company[125] invokes *inter alia* the risk of lack of trust for the cross-border use of certain corporate forms as a reason for introducing an SPE.

It is worth noting that, already as of the Second Directive, the European harmonization model in the field of company law had let go of the private company[126]. Such limitation of its scope is justified in the 5th preamble: coordination "*is especially important in relation to public limited liability companies,*

[122] See the Action Plan, 2.1, 8; see also the Impact Assessment on the Directive on cross-border transfer of registered office, SEC(2007) 1707 (http://ec.europa.eu/internal_market/company/docs/shareholders/ia_transfer_122007_part1_en.pdf).

[123] See e.g. the paper by J.-M. NELISSEN GRADE and M. WAUTERS on the concept of capital.

[124] See e.g. the paper by H. LAGA and F. PARREIN with regard to corporate governance. In general, it cannot be denied that the focus of the Commission over the past decade has clearly been on the listed public company (see already C. TIMMERMANS, "Chapter Three, Methods and Tools for Integration" in R.M. BUXBAUM, G. HERTIG, A. HURSCH, K.J. HOPT (eds.), *European Business Law*, W. De Gruyter & Co, Berlin, 1991, 130, (1). As he rightfully points out, company law has to be considered independently from capital market law, because of the difference in aim and scope).

[125] Com (2008) 396/3, http://ec.europa.eu/internal_market/company/epc/index_en.htm.

[126] C. TIMMERMANS, "Chapter Three, Methods and Tools for Integration" in R.M. BUXBAUM, G. HERTIG, A. HURSCH, K.J. HOPT (eds.), *European Business Law*, W. De Gruyter & Co, Berlin, 1991, 131, (2).

because their activities predominate in the economy of the Member States and frequently extend beyond their national boundaries". Whether even back then that was entirely correct may be doubted: at least in the United Kingdom, Germany and the Netherlands, the private company is often used for larger businesses that may have cross-border interests[127]. Today, in the words of the Commission itself, "*small and medium-sized enterprises (SMEs) account for more than 99% of companies in the European Union but only 8% of them engage in cross-border trade and 5% have subsidiaries or joint ventures abroad. While it has become easier in recent years to set up businesses across the EU, more needs to be done to improve the access of SMEs to the Single Market, facilitate their growth and unlock their business potential*"[128]. If the concept underlying this support for the conquest of the Internal Market by SMEs solely consisted of allowing each SME to freely choose where it could operate within the Market while benefiting from the lightest legal structure and regime conceivable, that would be a disappointing result.

In making this point, we are not necessarily pleading for a stringent regime for such companies, or at least not to the same degree for all of the larger and smaller private companies[129]. We also believe enhanced disclosure obligations and the resultant increased transparency to be a useful tool in establishing trust and confidence[130], both in a national and a cross-border environment. Therefore the Commission's recent plans to simplify the business environment for SMEs[131] may come a little bit as a surprise in this respect since we believe one should make a choice: either one prefers rather stringent rules as regards the content, or one leaves a large degree of freedom but provides for sufficient information. Moreover, it should be kept in mind that while disclosure may indeed to a certain extent protect those who become creditors of a company by free choice, it does not help those who either involuntarily (e.g. tort creditors) or by virtue of their public function (e.g. tax authorities) find themselves in

---

[127] Ibid.

[128] Proposal for a Statute for a European private company, Explanatory memorandum, 2, no. 1.

[129] For example, the proposal for an SCE sets the minimum capital requirement at €1, but complements this by setting out uniform rules on distributions, based on a balance sheet test and possibly, if the Member States so wish, an additional solvency test. It must moreover be noted that this new "harmonized" corporate form will exist as a mere option alongside the national form available for private companies. It will thus only lead to more harmonization if it turns out to be (more) successful (than the SE). Once again, the rules on employee participation may turn out to be a complicating factor in this respect.

[130] See in this respect the Winter Report, 123.

[131] See the Proposal for a Directive amending Council Directives 78/660/EEC and 83/349/EEC as regards certain disclosure requirements for medium-sized companies and obligation to draw up consolidated accounts, COM(2008) 195 final (http://eur-lex.europa.eu/LexUriServ/LexUriServ.do?uri=COM:2008:0195:FIN:EN:PDF; see also the announcement by Charlie McCreevy *(Commissioner for the Internal Market and Services)* of major initiatives on accounting rules for small businesses, MEMO/08/589 (http://europa.eu/rapid/pressReleasesAction.do?reference=MEMO/08/589&format=HTML&aged=0&language=EN&guiLanguage=en).

that position[132]. This also means that the Commission will inevitably have to consider tax harmonization as part of the exercise, because the ease of mind of tax authorities that they will recover taxes reasonably due to them is a legitimate concern of an interested stakeholder. But the question of what is reasonably due to each national tax authority will become considerably easier to answer as harmonization in this field progresses.

We do believe that the European legislator should be aware of the issue and should investigate exactly what common ground is needed to avoid reciprocal mistrust when "exporting" certain corporate forms.

[132] H. DE WULF, annotation of ECJ 30 September 2003 (Inspire Art), *Tijdschrift voor Belgisch Handelsrecht*, 2004, 90.

Bibliography

Case law

European Court of Justice
ECJ 21 June 1974, 2-74 (Reyners).
ECJ 3 December 1974, 33/74 (Van Binsbergen).
ECJ 10 January 1985, 229/83 (Leclerc).
ECJ, 28 January 1986, 270/83 (Avoir fiscal).
ECJ, 10 July 1986, 79/85 (D.H.M. Segers).
ECJ, 7 July 1988, 143/87 (Stanton).
ECJ, 27 September 1988, 81/87 (Daily Mail and General Trust Plc).
ECJ, 13 July 1993, 330/91 (Commerzbank).
ECJ, 17 July 1997, 43/00 (Andersen og Jensen).
ECJ 17 July 1997, 28/95 (Leur-Bloem).
ECJ, 16 July 1998, 264/96 (ICI).
ECJ, 19 February 1998, 8/97 (Commission/Greece).
ECJ, 9 March 1999, 212/97 (Centros Ltd vs. Erhvervs- og Selskabsstyrelsen).
ECJ, 5 November 2002, 208/00 (Überseering BV vs. Nordic Construction Company Baumanagement GmbH (NCC)).
ECJ, 30 September 2003, 167/01 (Inspire Art).
ECJ, 13 December 2005, 411/03 (Sevic Systems AG).
ECJ, 16 December 2008, 210/06 (Cartesio Oktató és Szolgáltató bt).

Selected Legal Doctrine

J. ARMOUR, "Who should make corporate law? EC Legislation versus Regulatory Competition", http://ssrn.com/abstract=860444, 52 p.

T. BALLARINO, "La mort annoncée de la réglementation allemande des fusions internationales", *Rev. trim. dr. eur.* (Fr.) 2006, 721-726.

O. BAGILL, M. BARZUZA and L. BEBCHUK, "The market for corporate law", http://papers.ssrn.com/abstract_id=275452, (also published in 162 *Journal of Institutional and Theoretical Economics* 134-171 (2006)).

C. BARNARD, "Social dumping and the race to the bottom", *E.L.Rev.* 2000, 71.

L. BEBCHUCK and A. COHEN, "Firms' decisions where to incorporate", http://papers.ssrn.com/abstract_id=304386, 1 (also published in 46 *Journal of Law and Economics* 383-425 (2003)).

M. BECHT, C. MAYER and H.F. WAGNER, "Where do firms incorporate? Deregulation and the cost of entry", http://papers.ssrn.com/sol3/papers.cfm?abstract_id=953820, 38 p.

P. BEHRENS, annotation of ECJ, 13 December 2005, 411/03, *CML Rev.* 2006, 1669-1688.

J. BELLINGWOUT, "Company Migration in Motion: the KPMG Report 1993", in J. WOUTERS and H. SCHNEIDER (eds.), *Current issues of cross-border establishment in the European Union, Maklu-Nomos-Bruylant, Ius Commune Europaeum Series No 14*, Antwerp, 1995, p. 75-88.

J. BLUMBERG, "Over het grensoverschrijdende associatieconcern, zetelverplaatsing en internationale fusie", *Tijdschrift voor Privaat Recht* (B)1992, 802-843.

F. BOUCKAERT, "Kan een bedrijfstak door een buitenlandse vennootschap in een Belgische vennootschap worden ingebracht of aan een Belgische vennootschap worden verkocht volgens de bepalingen van artikel 174/54 e.v. Venn.W.?", *Tijdschrift voor Rechtspersoon en Vennootschap* (B) 1997, 398-301.

P. CABRAL and P. CUNHA, "'Presumed innocent': companies and the exercise of the right of establishment under Community law", *E.L.Rev.* 2000, 157-166.

J. CH CASCANTE, "Niederlassungsfreiheit contra Sitztheorie - Goodbye 'Daily Mail'?", *Recht der internationalen Wirtschaft*, 1999, 450.

C. CLOTTENS, "Vrijheid van vestiging en zetelverplaatsing na het arrest Inspire Art: is the sky the limit?", *Tijdschrift voor Rechtspersoon en Vennootschap* (B) 2006, 686-689.

M. CRUYSMANS, annotation of ECJ 9 March 1999 (Centros), *Tijdschrift voor Belgisch Handelsrecht* (B) 1999, 364-366.

R. DAINES, "Does Delaware Law Improve Firm Value?", http://papers.ssrn.com/paper.taf?abstract_id=195109.

J. DEGUEE, "'Forum shopping' usage ou abus de la liberté d'établissement", *Revue Pratique des Sociétés* (B) 2000, 51-83.

H.-J DE KLUIVER, "Inspiring a New European Company Law?", *E.C.F.R.* 2004, 121-134.

T. DELVAUX, "La concurrence entre ordres juridiques est-elle efficace ? - Quelques Réflexions à propos de la liberté d'établissement des sociétés", *Revue Pratique des Sociétés* (B) 2004, 207-273.

T. DELVAUX, "Fusion internationale et libertés de circulation", *Journal des Tribunaux* (B) 2006, 146-148.

PH. DE PAGE en B. VAN DE WALLE DE GHELCKE, "Les personnes morales étrangères et l'ordre public international belge", *Revue Pratique des Sociétés* (B) 1979, 6 - 7.

H. DE WULF, annotation of ECJ 30 September 2003 (Inspire Art), *Tijdschrift voor Belgisch Handelsrecht* (B) 2004, 89-90.

H. DE WULF, "Grensoverschrijdende fusie na Sevic en de tiende Richtlijn", http://www.law.ugent.be/fli/WP/WP2006-pdf, 18 p.

B. DRIJBER, annotation of ECJ 30 September 2003, *S.E.W.* 2004, 229-232.

B. DRIJBER, annotation of ECJ 13 December 2005 (Sevic), *S.E.W.* 2006, 292-293.

J. ERAUW, *Handboek Belgisch internationaal privaatrecht*, Mechelen, Kluwer, 2006, 615 p.

K. GEENS, "Over internationale zetelverplaatsing", in *Facetten van ondernemingsrecht: Liber amicorum Frans Bouckaert*, Leuven, Universitaire Pers, 2000, 563-577.

K. GEENS, "Overpeinzingen bij bijna een halve eeuw vennootschapsrecht", *Tijdschrift voor Privaat Recht* (B) 2001, 69-84.

K. GEENS, "Zetelverplaatsing van de Europese vennootschap", in *Liber Amicorum Lucien Simont*, Brussels, Bruylant, 2002, 1033-1039.

K. GEENS, "De nieuwe harmonisatiedynamiek van het vennootschapsrecht: een 'eerste klas' begrafenis van het Europees vennootschapsrecht na vijftig jaar?", *Tijdschrift voor Rechtspersoon en Vennootschap* (B) 2006, 75-89.

K. GEENS and M. WYCKAERT, "Cross Border Merger and Minority Protection: an Open-Ended Harmonisation", *Utrecht Law Review*, volume 4, issue 1, March 2008, also published in *European Company Law* volume 5, issue 6, December 2008, 288-296.

S. GILCART, "Liberté d'établissement des sociétés. L'affaire 'Inspire Art': un nouvel arrêt 'inspiré' de la Cour de justice européenne", *J.D.S.C.* 2004, 102-104.

S. GRUNDMANN, "Regulatory Competition in European Company Law – Some Different Genius?", in G. FERRARINI, K.J. HOPT and E. WYMEERSCH (eds.), *Capital Markets in the Age of the Euro. Cross-Border Transactions, Listed Companies and Regulation*, The Hague, Kluwer Law International, 2002, 561-595.

S. GRUNDMANN, *European Company Law*, Intersentia, Antwerp – Oxford, 2007, 807 p.

L.L. HANSEN, "Merger, Moving and Division Across National Borders – When Case Law Breaks through Barriers and Overtakes Directives", *European Business Law Review*, 2007, 181-204.

J. HEYMANN, "Les fusions intracommunautaires", *Rev. crit. dr. intern. privé* (Fr.) 2006, 667-678.

M. HOFTÖTTER, "Niederlassungsfreiheit für Gesellschaften: Welcome to Delaware", *European Law Reporter*, 1999, 156.

K.J. HOPT, „Comparative Company Law" in *The Oxford Handbook of Comparative Law*, Oxford, 2006, p. 1161-1191.

J.-G. HUGLO, "Liberté d'établissement et libre prestation de services, Chronique", *Rev. trim. Dr. europ.*, 1999, 738.

C. KIRCHNER, R. PAINTER and W. KAAL, "Regulatory competition in EU Corporate Law after Inspire Art: Unbundling Delaware's Product for Europe", http://ssrn.com/abstract=617681, 49 p.

U. KLINKE, "European Company Law and the ECJ: The Court's Judgments in the Years 2001-2004", *E.C.F.R. (European Company and Financial Law Review)* 2005, 270-321.

V. KOROM and P. METZINGER, "Freedom of Establishment for Companies: the European Court of Justice confirms and refines its Daily Mail Decision in the Cartesio Case C-210/06", *European Company and Financial Law Review* 2009/6, 125-160.

P. LAGARDE, "Liberté d'établissement et rattachement des sociétés", *Rev. crit. dr. intern. privé* (Fr.) 2003, 524-536.

P. LAMBRECHT, annotation of ECJ 9 March 1999 (Centros), *Journal des Tribunaux* (B) 1999, 341-343.

S. LEIBLE and J. HOFMANN, "Uberseering und das (vermeintliche) Ende der Sitztheorie", *Recht der Internationale Wirtschaft* 2002, 925-936.

S. LEIBLE and J. HOFFMANN, „Wie inspiriert ist ‚Inspire Art'?", *EuZW* 2003, 677-683.

K. LENAERTS, "Het personeel statuut van een Belgische vennootschap bij overbrenging van de werkelijke zetel naar het buitenland", annotation of R.v.St. 29 June 1987, *Tijdschrift voor Rechtspersoon en Vennootschap* (B) 1988, 112-115.

K. LENAERTS and P. VAN NUFFEL, *Europees Recht in Hoofdlijnen*, Maklu, Antwerp, 1999, 911 p.

Y. LOUSSOUARN, "Le droit d'établissement des sociétés", *Rev. trim. Dr. europ.*, 1990, p. 236-246.

K. MARESCEAU, «Het vrij vestigingsrecht, de problematiek van de zetelverplaatsing en zijn impact op het internationaal privaatrecht: een stand van zaken na de zaak Cartesio», *Tijdschrift voor Belgisch Handelsrecht* 2009/6, 581-609.

J. MCCAHERY and E. VERMEULEN, "Does the European Company Prevent the 'Delaware Effect'?", http://papers.ssrn.com/sol3/papers.cfm?abstract_id=693421, 785-801.

J. MEEUSEN, "De werkelijke zetel-leer en de communautaire vestigingsvrijheid van vennootschappen. Analyse van het arrest Überseering van het Hof van Justitie", *Tijdschrift voor Rechtspersoon en Vennootschap* (B) 2003, 95-127.

H. MUIR WATT, "La liberté d'établissement des sociétés commerciales exerçant une activité intracommunautaire", *Rev. crit. dr. intern. privé* (Fr.) 2004, 173-184.

M. RAAIJMAKERS, "Uberseering: vestigingsvrijheid en erkenning van rechtspersonen en vennootschappen binnen de EU", *Ars Aequi* (Ndl.) 2003, 380-385.

M. RAAIJMAKERS, "Sevic: grensoverschrijdende fusie binnen de EU", *Ars Aequi* (Ndl.) 2006, 629-634.

S. RAMMELOO, "At Long Last: Freedom of Establishment for Legal Persons in Europe Accomplished", *Maastricht Journal of European and Comparative Law*, 2004, 379-413.

J. RONSE, "Overzicht van rechtspraak (1964-1967) – Vennootschappen", *Tijdschrift voor Privaat Recht* (B) 1967, 652-654.

P. RYAN, "Will there ever be a "Delaware of Europe?" http://papers.ssrn.com/sol3/papers.cfm?abstract_id=763164, 187-200.

W. SCHON, "The mobility of Companies in Europe and the Organizational Freedom of Company Founders", *E.C.F.R.* 2006, 122-146.

M. SIEMS, "Convergence, Competition, Centros and conflicts of law: European company law in the 21st century", *E.L. Rev.* 2002, 47-59.

V. SIMONART, "L'application du droit belge aux sociétés constituées dans un autre état de la communauté, et, en particulier, aux *Limited*», *Revue Pratique des Sociétés* 2008, 111-206.

J. STUYCK, "Zetelverplaatsing en vrije vestiging van vennootschappen in de EEG", annotation of ECJ, 27 September 1988, *Tijdschrift voor Rechtspersoon en Vennootschap* (B) 1989, 198-203.

T. TILQUIN, "Le transfert d'une universalité ou d'une branche d'activité", *Journal des Tribunaux* (B) 1996, 493-509.

C. TIMMERMANS, annotation of ECJ 27 September 1988, (Daily Mail), *S.E.W.* 1991, 69-73.

C. TIMMERMANS, "Chapter Three, Methods and Tools for Integration" in R.M. BUXBAUM, G. HERTIG, A. HURSCH, K.J. HOPT (eds.), *European Business Law*, W. De Gruyter & Co, Berlin, 1991, 129-148.

C. TIMMERMANS, *Company Law as Ius Commune*, Antwerp, Intersentia, 2002, 23 p.

A. UGLIANO, "The New Cross-Border Merger Directive: Harmonisation of European Company Law and Free Movement", *European Business Law Review*, 2007, 585-617.

D. VAN GERVEN, "De Europese Vennootschap en het Europees Economisch Samenwerkingsverband", *Tijdschrift voor Rechtspersoon en Vennootschap* (B) 2006, 129-149.

G. VAN HECKE and K. LENAERTS, *International privaatrecht*, Ghent, Story-Scientia, 1989, 435 p.

J. VAN RYN, "Conséquences juridiques du transfert en Belgique du siège social d'une société étrangère et du transfert à l'étranger du siège social d'une société belge", annotation of Cass. 12 November 1965, *Revue Critique de Jurisprudence Belge* (B) 1966, 399-410.

G.-J. VOSSESTEIN, Modernisation of European Company Law and Corporate Governance – Some considerations on its legal limits, Ph.D. thesis, University of Leiden (The Netherlands), 2008, 237 p.

J. WOUTERS, "Het Europese vestigingsrecht voor ondernemingen herbekeken : een onderzoek naar de grondslagen, draagwijdte en begrenzingen van de vrijheid van vestiging van ondernemingen in de Europese Unie", thesis, KULeuven, 1996-1997, 725 p.

J. WOUTERS, "Grensoverschrijdende fusie en vrijheid van vestiging van vennootschappen in de Europese Unie", annotation of ECJ 13 December 2005 (Sevic), *Tijdschrift voor Belgisch Handelsrecht* (B) 2006, 407-417.

M. WYCKAERT, "De toepasselijkheid van de artikelen 759 e.v. W.Venn. bij grensoverschrijdende herstructureringen: het water mag niet langer te diep zijn voor Belgische juristen", *Tijdschrift voor Rechtspersoon en Vennootschap* (B) 2001, 214-218.
M. WYCKAERT, "Grensoverschrijdende fusies", *Tijdschrift voor Rechtspersoon en Vennootschap* (B) 2006, 90-103.
E. WYMEERSCH, "Centros: a landmark decision in European Company Law", in TH. BAUMS, K.J. HOPT and N. HORN (eds.), *Corporations, Capital Markets and Business in the Law*, The Hague, Kluwer Law International, 2000, 629-654.
E. WYMEERSCH, "Chapter 7. Cross-border transfer of the seat of a company – recent EU case law and the SE Regulation", in J. RICKFORD (ed.), *The European Company – developing a community law of corporations*, Antwerp, Intersentia, 2003, 83-94.
E. WYMEERSCH, "The transfer of the company's seat in European Company Law", *Common Market Law Review* 2003, 662-691.
E. WYMEERSCH, "De zetelverplaatsing in het vennootschapsrecht", in *Liber Amicorum J.P. de Bandt*, Brussels, Bruylant, 2004, 757-770.
E. WYMEERSCH, "Is a Directive on Corporate Mobility Needed?", *European Business Organization Law Review,* 2007, 161-169.

Transcripts of Corporate Mobility Session

Paper: *Marieke Wyckaert and Filip Jenné*
Respondent: *Levinus Timmerman (Hoge Raad der Nederlanden, University of Rotterdam)*
Chair: *Jan Meyers (Cleary Gottlieb Steen & Hamilton, K.U.Leuven)*
Rapporteur: *Dominique Maes (K.U.Leuven)*

A. Abstract

When discussing the topic amongst ourselves in the workgroup, we discovered that we were as divided as a "real seat" adept and an "incorporation seat" adept can possibly be.
The reason for this is that company law can be approached in a twofold manner:

1. one can consider it as a technique or as a facility for organising a business; or
2. one can defend a notion of company law that should incorporate social responsibility and accountability.

In the second approach, company law also encompasses means to protect minority shareholders, creditors, employees and possible other stakeholders.
For a scholar or a practitioner adhering to the first – narrower – approach, the present state of the case law of the European Court of Justice appears to be completely satisfactory. The liberal approach followed by the European Court of Justice leads to a situation comparable to the USA situation, whereby state law competition can fully play its role and where it has not led to insurmountable problems, albeit in a context of further advanced harmonisation of company law. On top of that, US company law is not built around a concept of creditor protection; such creditor protection is governed by insolvency law.

When adhering to the second – wider – notion of company law, the same case law of the European Court of Justice raises the following issues:

1. it does not offer any stakeholders' protection;
2. the European Court of Justice seems inclined to follow the rule of reason very, if not too, narrowly;
3. it invites parties concerned to use other cross-border mobility techniques without legislative basis than those that are regulated, such as the European Company and the cross-border mergers, which creates legal uncertainty as to what is allowed and not.

The majority of the members of the workshop keeps thinking that there is hence a case for a Fourteenth Company Law Directive.

B. Response to paper by Levinus Timmerman

1. Marieke WYCKAERT and Filip JENNÉ wrote an excellent report on corporate mobility within the European Community. Especially their analysis of the judgments of the European Court of Justice is clarifying. I fully agree with their finding that the European Court of Justice does not have the discretion to repeal the real seat doctrine. Article 48 of the EC Treaty places the registered office, the central administration and the principal place of business on the same footing as connecting factor for enjoying the right of establishment. The Cartesio judgment confirms this way of reasoning. The European Court of Justice allows a real seat state to prevent a company incorporated under its law from transferring its seat to another Member State, if the company wishes to retain its status as a company governed by the law of the Member State of incorporation. In this judgment, the European Court of Justice upholds the real seat doctrine.

2. This does not mean that the European Court of Justice leaves the real seat doctrine unaffected. I have the impression that the European Court of Justice seizes the opportunity in every appropriate judgment to undermine the real seat doctrine. This phenomenon can be seen in the Cartesio judgment. The European Court of Justice gives the real seat state the opportunity to prevent a transfer of the seat. At the same time, the European Court of Justice warns that a company can convert itself into a company governed by the law of another Member State, if this Member State permits it to do so. In my opinion, this *obiter dictum* of the European Court of Justice is a targeted attack on the real seat doctrine to the same extent as this was the case in the Überseering decision. A company can circumvent complications with the real seat doctrine by choosing a cross-border conversion, provided that the host state allows such a transfer. It is crystal clear that the European Court of Justice makes it more difficult for real seat states to apply the real seat doctrine effectively. The real seat doctrine is becoming a dull knife. The *obiter dictum* is also an open invitation to Member States that have the ambition to attract the incorporation of foreign businesses, such as the United Kingdom, to introduce in their legislation facilities for cross-border conversion.

3. I am an admirer of the Tenth Company Law Directive. The reason is that the Tenth Company Law Directive facilitates cross-border mergers, while it at the same time aims at protecting interests of the minority shareholders, the interests of the creditors and those of the employees. One of my cherished ideas on company law is that it is two faced, it has two dimensions: company law should offer facilities to businesses, for instance, for doing business, for merging and splitting and for transformation, etc. Company law is a facility. But there is also the other side of the coin, the other face: company law has also the purpose

of guaranteeing the interests of minority shareholders, creditors and employees. Between those two dimensions there arises a permanent tension. This tension, to which practitioners of company law are exposed every day, is one of the most fascinating aspects of company law. In my opinion, the main problem of the national company laws of the Member States is that Member States still disagree on the scope and the depth of this protective side of company law. For instance, the UK is traditionally rather lenient in the protective aspects of company law. Here, one may find the explanation why the United Kingdom is so satisfied with the incorporation theory to which it adheres wholeheartedly. On the other hand, the German tradition is rather stringent in guaranteeing the interests of creditors and employees. Other Member States, such as Belgium and the Netherlands, take up a middle position. In many Member States, there seems to be a trend towards the reinforcement of the facilitating aspect of company law. But in my opinion the exact scope of this tendency is rather unclear at the moment.

4. As I already indicated, I admire the Tenth Company Law Directive, as it takes both dimensions of company law I underlined into consideration: it facilitates cross-border mergers, but it also protects the interests of minority shareholders, creditors and employees. In my opinion, the problem with the case law of the European Court of Justice in the field of freedom of establishment is that it allows all kinds of cross-border movements and cross-border transactions without protecting the interests of minority shareholders, creditors, etc. The only protection the European Court of Justice offers is the rule of reason, and this is a very weak protection which is restricted to extreme cases of abuse of the freedom of establishment. Here you find the deficit of the jurisprudence of the European Court of Justice, the "*verdriet*", the sorrow of the case law of the European Court of Justice in this field. This deficit makes this jurisprudence, to my taste, unsatisfactory. This jurisprudence thwarts the way in which company law should be arranged and practised, in my opinion. Probably it is not justified to blame the European Court of Justice for this deficit. The European Court of Justice has the task to interpret and apply the provisions of the European Treaty and there might be little room for other judgments and interpretations than the European Court of Justice has given. And it is the European legislator that fails to promulgate directives which deal with the mobility of companies within the European Union and which respect both dimensions of company law. It may not come as a surprise that I support the plea by Marieke WYCKAERT and Filip JENNÉ for the issue of the Fourteenth Company Law Directive.

C. Discussion

Jan MEYERS

It seems to me, in the abstract, that it is useful for a complex subject as "corporate mobility" not to wander off in all possible directions. This subject seems to be eminently fit for a very confused discussion. Hence, I would propose a little bit of structure in the discussion and to distinguish perhaps two broad topics:

1. The first topic would be the case law of the European Court of Justice in the field of corporate mobility.
2. The second topic would be the more specific topic of cross-border mergers. Is everyone happy with the Tenth Company Law Directive? I am not totally, but I understand that many people are very happy with it. Is there any need for further legislative action or can we just rely on the Sevic case? What is the residual value added of the European Company?

I propose to start with the broader topic of the case law of the European Court of Justice in the field of corporate mobility. In this respect, I would like to list a couple of questions as a guide for the discussion:

1. Should, in the abstract, a choice be made between real seat and incorporation as a connecting factor? If so, who should make such choice? The European Court of Justice or the European legislator?
2. Is the European Court of Justice too liberal or too soft on companies from incorporation jurisdictions?
3. Is there, in this connection, a risk for a "race to the bottom" or legislative competition between Member States in the wrong direction?
4. Should certain minimum standards apply, and who should define them? Should it be the European Court of Justice on the basis of a more liberal interpretation of the rule of reason or should it be the European legislator?
5. Is there, as has also been suggested earlier during this session, real value added in having a Fourteenth Company Law Directive, or can we live happily without it by just relying on the Tenth Company Law Directive?

Let us start with addressing the first couple of questions.
As to whether a choice should be made between real seat and incorporation as a connecting factor and, if so, whether the European Court of Justice or the European legislator should make such choice, I propose not to spend too much time. I do not think that the European Court of Justice will change its mind. I do not think that the European legislator will take an initiative either. Except for certain recent European legislation (such as the Takeover Bids Directive), where the European legislator has opted for the registered seat as the connecting

factor, I do not believe it to be realistic to expect that the European legislator will take an overall initiative to choose between the two factors.

I would propose to focus more on the second subject: is the European Court of Justice too liberal or too soft on companies from incorporation jurisdictions? After all, corporate form means limitation of liability, and for limitation of liability to be recognised across borders, should certain minimum standards apply? Is the European Court of Justice wrong in being relatively liberal and being market oriented? Are certain forms of abuse to be regulated through limitations on the corporate form, or is more targeted legislation needed and more effective?

A couple of statistics exist in this respect. I generally do not believe in "race to the bottom" or legislative competition. It has not really happened in the United States. Indeed, in the United States, which is by and large a sort of an incorporation universe, the State of Delaware is obviously market leader. Depending on the statistics and from year to year, 60%-70% of all new US incorporations are effected in the State of Delaware. There is not really any competition, as the next States in line (i.e. the States of California and New York) have "market shares" of 4% or 3%. That is not regulatory competition. It should also be noted that, at least with regard to stock corporations, Delaware law is not a "bad" law. It is reasonably sophisticated and has very good jurisprudence, which could even be a benchmark for many countries in Europe. The question of the "race to the bottom" is hence not quite visible. On the other hand, in Europe, there is indeed the phenomenon of the UK private limited companies. The Becht, Mayer, Wagner study of 2006, one of the few studies made in this respect, has suggested that in the period between 1997 and 2005, 70,000 new foreign private limited companies were incorporated in the UK and 26,000 of them have their main place of business in Germany.

Jules STUYCK, K.U.Leuven

I am utterly surprised to hear the statement of Marieke WYCKAERT that the European Court of Justice was wiping away possible grounds of justification under the rule of reason. Marieke WYCKAERT and Filip JENNÉ seemed to be happy with at least the Überseering case, but not so much with the Centros and Inspire Art cases. I also heard Levinus TIMMERMAN being very critical about the judgments of the European Court of Justice for more or less the same reasons. I felt that someone should take the floor to defend the European Court of Justice.

I am not a company lawyer and, hence, I look at the case law of the European Court of Justice from a specific angle, namely the angle of the freedoms of the Treaty. I also try to see the coherence with the other case law of the European Court of Justice. When considering such case law, it strikes me, for example in the Inspire Art case, that it has been described as a discrimination case. It is indeed about discrimination, and discrimination is something which the

European Court of Justice will never accept. It also concerns a limitation on the freedom of choice of a company between the subsidiary and the branch, which is a fundamental freedom pursuant to Article 43 of the EC Treaty. Considering the Centros case, people knew that the company was a company incorporated in England. This is information which people had and which is relevant information (at least if one has creditor protection). Also this case relates to the freedom of choice of a company between the subsidiary and the branch. Finally, looking at it from the perspective of the rule of reason, it is true that, especially in the Überseering case, there seem to be various grounds of justification and subsequently the European Court of Justice condemns the position of the relevant Member State. Is it right under corporate law to invoke grounds of justification, or should one be more specific? This is also a question of proportionality and methodology. The abuse theory is "lip service". The Court has accepted the abuse theory in many cases, on the so-called "U-turn". It accepted the theory, but never accepted there was such a case, as Member States then invoke a very general legislation, which is not very specific about the abuse one wants to combat. So, under a "rule of reason" reasoning, it all depends on what the Member States are arguing. It is certainly not the fault of the Court of Justice. The question arises as to whether the legislator should deal with the problem. Probably it should. But I do not believe that the case law of the European Court of Justice is wrong from a rule of reason point of view.

Henri SWENNEN, University of Antwerp

In company law, the European Court of Justice did not have a clear "U-turn" case yet. What people who are not fully aware of European law think is that the Centros case was about an abuse. It was not. Centros was not a "U-turn". A real "U-turn" would have been that Danish traders would have found a structure whereby a company in Denmark which is losing money would, due to capital requirements, transfer its seat to the United Kingdom in order to avoid the capital requirement, and subsequently return to Denmark (not as a company with a registered seat in Denmark of course, because that would lead to Danish law being applicable again, but establishing a branch in Denmark while the sole business of the company is Danish business). That would have been a "U-turn", like a "U-turn" in goods which are exported to another country just to re-import them as intra-community goods coming from a different Member State. But that was not the case in the Centros case.

What is allowed under the freedom of the EC Treaty, is, for instance, that if one would like to sell product A in Belgium, but such sale is not permitted with the specifications as it is manufactured in Belgium, one searches in Germany whether one can buy this product there with other specifications and subsequently imports the German product into Belgium, meeting the rule of reason. This does not work with company law, and that is the reason why the European Court of Justice held that corporations are legal entities created by the law of the Member State. This product originated from the Member State. The second problem with the rule of reason, as mentioned by Jules STUYCK, is that none of the Member States has a kind of "product regulation" of companies. There is no law saying that, if one establishes a company, one should have a minimum capital or a minimum guarantee. The product is not regulated by way of a general regulation, but every Member State has what is called "*Typenzwang*" (there are certain types of companies; types are limited and are regulated type-by-type). That is the issue. That is the difference between general rules that are invoked when a product is imported from another Member State and the situation in corporations.

Hans DE WULF, University of Ghent

Marieke WYCKAERT and Filip JENNÉ ended their presentation with a rather ardent plea in favour of more harmonisation. They defend that, with more harmonisation, the whole debate of the "clash" between real seat and incorporation doctrines will disappear. This conclusion is certainly correct, but is this realistic? This seems to me like going back to the 60s, when the idea was "we first have to harmonise most aspects of company law before we can allow companies to establish themselves freely all over Europe". So, would this not turn back the clock 30 years?

My second, totally different, remark is that – as Becht and others have shown – indeed more than 50,000 incorporations of Limiteds in the UK by continental Europeans have been seen. But is this something one should worry about? Ultimately, what one can achieve by incorporating a Limited, or by using the Centros case technique, is avoiding minimum capital requirements. If one keeps all its activities in Belgium, Belgian law and other laws of continental Europe will largely still be applicable to European activities. I do not know whether this really poses a problem. In addition, there are some – albeit inconclusive – statistics gathered by German scholars, which indicate that in Germany there is already a decline in the use of Limiteds. I wonder whether the recent surge in the use of Limiteds is not mainly due to certain intermediaries who are good salesmen and that, in five years' time or some time after that, people will realise that the Limiteds do not really have that many benefits for them.

Marieke WYCKAERT

We are not defending that more harmonisation is needed before companies can move around. Companies will move; that is a "fact of life". Companies will continue to conduct business all over Europe. The question which we are raising is rather whether, acknowledging this "fact of life", the European Commission should at least not consider continuing harmonisation? We are of course not defending that activities should stop moving within Europe until further harmonisation is achieved, as that would indeed turn back the clock.

As to your last remark, I believe that we should ask Jonathan RICKFORD's opinion. He already indicated that we give these UK Limiteds a very bad reputation which maybe they do not deserve. Maybe the protection linked to UK Limiteds is a lot bigger than we believe. But it is certainly true that intermediaries are selling UK Limiteds as light vehicles which are easy in use and easy in abuse.

Jonathan RICKFORD, British Institute of International and Comparative Law

I have heard on a number of occasions today people say that the UK Limited provides no protection to creditors. On the face of it, that is an inherently absurd statement.

The UK economy is not doing particularly well in the last few months, but we do somehow manage to find an adequately secure regime for the creditors of the over two million private companies operating in the United Kingdom. I would invite the people who say that the UK Limited does not provide adequate protection to creditors to read the law. If ordinary courtesy does not require that, then academic discipline does. The conclusion that will be reached is this: there is no minimum capital. Now, if it is a sin not to have minimum capital, I plead guilty. But the view in the UK (and we have considered it in law reform projects on numerous occasions in the last half of the last century and the beginning of this century) is that minimum capital is not a substantial benefit but a disadvantage. As for other creditor protections, I am not aware of any respect in which the UK Limited provides less protection for creditors than do continental limited liability companies. To the contrary, I am aware of a number of respects in which it provides more protection. For example, the UK system for accounting transparency and enforcement is far and away the most effective in the European Community. The levels of compliance are fantastically high, due to the system of automatic and computerised enforcement. I confidently expect a very large proportion of the UK Limiteds operating in continental Europe to be caught by our system of accounting transparency and reporting. They will be automatically dissolved and their directors and shareholders will be personally liable on the grounds of absence of a corporate personality, if they do not properly file their accounts. I could list other bases on which UK law protects creditors. I would also say that it is also untrue that the United Kingdom adopts a rigid incorporation doctrine approach. We apply the law on wrongful trading, we apply the law on disqualification of directors and we apply the law on public interest winding-up to foreign companies which are operating in the United Kingdom, whether they have their real seat there or not, in appropriate cases. So, it is not the case that we are single-mindedly incorporation doctrinaire.

The second point which I would like to make is in relation to the Centros and Inspire Art cases, which are the two cases that you object to. In the Centros case, the Danish regulator was seeking to enforce a rule which had exactly the same effect as the effect of the German rule in Überseering. It insisted on registration, which it denied, before the company could carry on any business at all. As a result, the company was completely disabled. The European Court of Justice did not say that the creditor protections were outlawed in Denmark. It actually said that certain kinds of additional creditor protections were legitimate to meet the concerns of the Danish government. In the case of Inspire Art, some of the restrictions were discriminatory. Some of the restrictions were additional labelling for the UK company, which was already disclosing itself as a Limited and as a foreign company. Some of the restrictions were additional and, in my view, disproportionate in that they apply special rules to a foreign company which did not apply to a Danish company. So, I believe this case law is open to defence.

As to regulatory competition and the race to the bottom, I would like to state the following. I was responsible for leading the Law Reform Project in the UK which led to the new complete re-enactment of the UK Companies Act in 2006. We looked at these issues. At no time did it occur to us that any possible public policy objective was the promotion of the incorporation of UK companies abroad. It simply did not enter into the calculation. What we were seeking to do (as all large Member States conducting a responsible company law reform policy would do) is to seek to provide an optimal commercial environment for companies operating within the jurisdiction. So, the problem arises only if those people who criticised the UK Limited as not providing an adequate creditor protection can point to a defect in the regime put in place. It is true that we are proposing to change it and we are proposing to change it by requiring, as a replacement for the old-fashioned capital maintenance (which we invented in the early 19th century), solvency certification. There is a question whether the replacement is equivalent. I think it probably is. It is, however, extremely uncertain whether it will be adopted in the UK, as there is a significant resistance to it just as there is in continental Europe.

Levinus TIMMERMAN

We all know that the United Kingdom has this famous wrongful trading rule. This rule is, however, very difficult to apply effectively outside the United Kingdom. For instance, in respect of a UK Limited with all of its activities in the Netherlands, it is very difficult for the judiciary in the Netherlands to apply the wrongful trading rule. Is that not the real problem?

Jonathan RICKFORD

The wrongful trading rule operates in a winding-up. The wrongful trading rule says (in a winding-up) that, if the directors have conducted themselves in circumstances where insolvency was imminent, without giving priority to the protection of creditors, they are personally liable. In the case of a UK

Limited with its centre of main interest (more or less the same as its real seat) in the Netherlands, the Dutch Court will have jurisdiction. If there is a public policy in the Netherlands that directors in vicinity of an insolvency should take particular care of creditors (and I would encourage it, as it seems to me as thoroughly desirable), the Dutch Court is fully entitled to impose a personal liability on the directors and to lift the corporate veil in that way. And if it did, I would applaud it. In the workshop on capital and creditor protection we were also discussing this, and colleagues from the Catholic University of Louvain proposed a harmonised rule to that effect, which of course equally the Winter Group (of which I was a member) also proposed. So I support it.

Levinus TIMMERMAN

In the Netherlands, we are not certain as to whether we are allowed to apply our liability rules on, for instance, Limiteds incorporated in the United Kingdom. That is one of the problems which we have with the case law of the European Court of Justice.

Jacques MALHERBE, University of Louvain

How to reconcile the Daily Mail and Cartesio cases? One may consider that the transfer of seat is an abuse to the detriment of the country of origin, at least tax-wise. That was what the Daily Mail case was about. So, would it be a possible, under those two cases, for a country to decide that, although the real seat is transferred from the country of origin to the host country, the company retains its original nationality? In other words, would one be able to switch in the country of origin from the real seat doctrine to the incorporation doctrine? One would, of course, create a potential for double taxation, but that is another issue.

This reminds me of a Belgian legislation in 1940. At that time, the legislature had decided that a Belgian company could move its seat to a Belgian colony (or to any other country where the government would reside) without losing its legal personality. Unilever did that and moved to Congo. During the war, Unilever extended its duration and had to pay registration taxes (which it did; it paid registration taxes due by foreign companies, as Unilever considered that it had ceased to be Belgian and, because of the real seat doctrine, it had become colonial). After the war, the Belgian registrar of taxes assessed an additional tax on Unilever, alleging that Unilever had remained Belgian, thereby applying a sort of incorporation doctrine (as Unilever's real seat was in Congo). This case was argued and lost. So, Belgium had in fact moved from the real seat doctrine to the incorporation doctrine. Could this be done today in a European setting? I do not know.

Marieke WYCKAERT

I think that Jacques MALHERBE is right in saying that it is difficult to reconcile Daily Mail and Cartesio. This is due to the simple reason that, as is often the case in company law, Daily Mail is coloured by tax law (which makes it different). This also touches upon one of the questions which our Chairman has raised: what about the tax implications of all the matters which we discussed? Nobody expected Cartesio to be what it was. Now that it has been rendered, one sees the logic, but one also sees that Daily Mail remains special because of the taxation aspect and one may also wonder whether, if Daily Mail would be submitted to the Court today, the judgment would be the same. It is doubtful.

Jan MEYERS

When reading literature on the case law of the European Court of Justice about corporate mobility, I am struck by the fact that the tax reasoning and tax concerns often pollute the legal reasoning. The corporate and tax reasoning should be separated.

Corporate form and exportability of corporate form is one aspect. In this respect, I would follow a "free establishment" logic and basically use the same approach *mutatis mutandis* as in the United States of America. This was a market based approach.

Tax, but also employee participation and a number of other things, are quite different matters. In tax, particularly at the corporate level, the main connecting factors are the seat of effective management and the source of revenue. One cannot simply transpose the entire corporate reasoning as to corporate mobility to the tax level, as this would raise really big concerns. For example, the European Court of Justice decision rendered in the de Lasteyrie du Saillant case in 2004 cannot be transposed to the corporate area. Said case dealt with exit taxes, in the case of a French individual who left the country. That cannot be transposed to the corporate area. I cannot see the European Court of Justice ever calling into question the jurisdiction of a state to be able, in case of a true migration, to tax latent gains. The correct approach there should be (and is also the approach finally taken in the EU Directive of 23 July 1990) that, if one moves across borders as a result of a corporate reorganisation, one can get a tax free treatment and escape exit tax, provided that the relevant assets are kept in the jurisdiction connected to a permanent establishment of the foreign corporation. This is, I believe, the only approach that can politically function in a European context.

Marieke WYCKAERT

What Jan MEYERS says is correct. This, however, brings us back to the beginning of the debate and to the response of Levinus TIMMERMAN. We all agree that tax is a separate issue. But what about director's liability: is that part of corporate law, or not? What about employee participation? These are main questions today, and I do not have a clear answer to them.

Loes LENNARTS, Universities of Utrecht and Groningen

One brief addition to what Marieke WYCKAERT and Levinus TIMMERMAN have already said. We have seen a tendency of certain Member States being afraid that they can no longer apply their own law to foreign companies, because they will not succeed to convince that the rule of reason applies by re-characterising some rules of company law as rules of insolvency law. We also have this tendency in the Netherlands, as Inspire Art shows. A simple solution would be to re-characterise some rules of company law as rules of insolvency law. This solution may however not be easy, as the European Court of Justice might see it as a mere trick. This is also what Levinus TIMMERMAN was trying to get at. It is a matter of qualification in private international law, of course: how do you qualify a rule like the wrongful trading rule or the "*action en comblement du passif*"? It is, however, also a matter of the case law of the European Court of Justice, which should decide whether this is, or is not, a way of evading the rule of reason by simply relabelling.

Robbie TAS, K.U.Brussels and K.U.Leuven

I would like to raise another issue. Do you believe that the case law of the European Court of Justice does at all say that one cannot apply the company law rules of the country where the company has its real seat to that company? In my opinion, one could say that this case law is about free establishment. Hence, one cannot prevent, for instance, the case of a company with registered seat in an incorporation country moving its real seat to a real seat country (or having its real seat there as from its incorporation), i.e. the typical "light vehicle" problem. Could one not defend that, while under the case law of the European Court of Justice it is not allowed to raise an issue of re-establishment or registration, a company could in fact have double nationality, whereby the legal personality under the incorporation country would be respected but, in addition, all the normal company law rules of the company where the company has its real seat would also be complied with? Would that not be a solution and solve the problem of the "light vehicle", wherever the "light vehicle" comes from? Überseering might give the impression that this is prevented or prohibited by the European Court of Justice, but I am not sure that this has been finally decided.

Filip JENNÉ

In such situations, you could indeed in principle apply both company laws. Issues will, however, arise when the relevant company does not comply with one of both company law regimes. For instance, if one of the company law regimes requires a minimum share capital and the relevant company does not have such minimum capital. How will you sanction that? Überseering clearly indicates that, in such case, the host state cannot sanction this by not recognising the legal capacity of the company.

Marieke WYCKAERT

I understand that what is being proposed by Robbie TAS is that if, for instance, a company incorporated in (incorporation) country A moves its seat to country B, one would simply apply the law of country B without any requirement of registration. I believe that the example given by Filip JENNÉ is valid in this respect. For example, if in country A there is a minimum capital requirement of X, and in country B a minimum capital requirement of amount X + Y exists, what happens if the company does not have that latter (higher) minimum capital? Probably the European Court of Justice will rule that you cannot impose the higher capital requirement, as would be a logical position in line with the current case law of the European Court of Justice. So, I am not certain the proposal would work. We will, however, read the case law again with that in mind and see whether we can find an argument for that position, but I am afraid so.

Jan MEYERS

I heard big satisfaction and enthusiasm from my panel members about the Tenth Company Law Directive. I do not know whether this is widely shared in the room. I do personally not fully share it. It is probably a useful piece of legislation, but there are a couple of "snags" in it and some of them are really too horrible to contemplate. One being, for instance, Article 10.3 (which caters for the option that Member States have to provide for a cash exit right for dissenting shareholders). This, I believe, is a potential impediment. It sometimes makes me feel nostalgic for going back to the days of Sevic. Sevic was, and is, quite doable. Large cross-border mergers were done under Sevic without any specific framework. The ArcelorMittal merger was done under Sevic. Also the BNP Paribas Banca Nazionale del Lavoro merger in 2007 was done under Sevic. These mergers were effected without the Tenth Company Law Directive and no real major issues have arisen. So what is the opinion on the Tenth Company Law Directive and its value added, the question whether it should even be expanded to other legal forms and to other corporate reorganisations like demergers?

Jonathan RICKFORD

I am a supporter of the Tenth Company Law Directive. Its great advantage, compared to the European Company, is that it avoids all those appalling problems of characterisation of which parts of the European Company constitution are subject to European directly applicable law and which parts are subject to the law of registration. On the whole, the Tenth Company Law Directive produces a single legal system to which the resulting company is subject, and that system will have the benefit of the legal certainty that applies to the national legal system in question. So, it seems to me that the result is a hugely superior vehicle to the European Company for cross-border mergers.

On the particular point raised by Jan MEYERS, I believe it is worth considering the extent to which the case law on freedom of movement restricts the authority of the Member States in the way in which they implement the Tenth Directive on cross-border mergers, or indeed for that matter the European Company. For example, Germany has an implementation for the European Company which requires appraisal rights for creditors and shareholders if the European Company involving a merger of a German company is to be registered outside Germany, but not if the European Company is to be registered within Germany. I believe that raises issues about the level playing field in freedom of establishment terms and whether the establishment of the European Company (which is clearly an exercise of freedom of establishment) is not to be subjected to stringent rules on the equality of treatment of one transaction as compared with another. But it seems to me that similar issues arise on the matter which Jan MEYERS has raised, i.e. creditor protection in the cross-border merger area. If the Member State in question does not provide the same creditor protection for a domestic merger, then is it legitimate to use the excuse of the fact that freedom of establishment is being exercised to impose a more stringent creditor protection requirement? I think that is debatable.

Transcript of Panel Debate

Klaus J. HOPT, Max Planck Institute, Chair
I propose to focus on matters the Commission could take action on or, to the contrary, should not do, as to produce conlusions the future EU Commission could look at. In this manner we are preparing the ground.

I have a question for Gerard Hertig on financial reporting: I would like to broaden the question from technical financial reporting to disclosure in general and the role of disclosure in this particular financial crisis. Is disclosure a real panacea, should we leave it to the enlightened self-interest of market participants or do we need mandatory disclosure?

Gerard HERTIG, ETH Zürich
To answer your first question, which is whether we should make disclosure mandatory, I am rather hesitant since there are costs and benefits with disclosure anyway. Coming back to the discussion in the workshop on financial reporting, we have some data on the costs of financial reporting, no data on the costs of non-mandatory financial reporting. One general point before going into this in more detail: we talk a lot about the fact that we do not have empirical data. That has not stopped lawyers from doing anything and it is not totally serious. In addition, what is hidden behind it is another major issue I would like to throw in, namely the interest group discussion: you never know who exactly is pushing for what at the EU level. For instance, it is always puzzling to hear accountants say that financial accounting is overly complex: they cannot be serious because otherwise they would be out of business. Their reason for saying that is that they want it to become even more complex. So on the disclosure side, in some areas people want to make it simpler, in other areas more complex; we do not know what the end result might be. From the financial crisis point of view, it is really hard because nobody knows. One thing is 100% certain: the whole business about fair value and mark to market being wrong, I cannot even begin to understand. Was hiding the current value of your product or financial situation helping you? It cannot be true, it cannot work. So here the issue is not about disclosure and transparency but the issue is about capital adequacy and capital requirements, which is totally different. And here, probably more transparency will help to build investor confidence as long as they trust the models and you enforce the models.

Klaus J. HOPT
How about convergence between US GAAP and IFRS? Probably we need it but it is a difficult process. Some people told me that there is a danger that it will be taken too much towards the American side. Is that so, and what are the chances that we could come to a really good compromise?

Gerard HERTIG

Well, I used to think that convergence was a great thing, that we should have more of it. I have, I think, radically changed my mind. First of all, nothing guarantees that if we have convergence towards IAS/IFRS we will have uniformity; we will have differences as much as before, because we can implement converging rules in different ways; so that does not help you too much. And secondly, despite the current situation which is market oriented, if you have just one system, it does hamper innovation. I have seen some academic papers recently that have taken the reverse position: we need more diversity. It is not accounting that is important, especially for large firms, but analyst coverage in the market. That is what we should look at; it is analysts rather than just the convergence of systems, because you can have software that I believe can make things much more comparable.

Philippe PELLE, European Commission

Regarding the initial comments on the exemption for micro-entities, i.e. the carve-out from the Accounting Directive, I should stress that whenever the Commission proposes legislation, there has to be an impact assessment, so also for the costs of the proposed exemptions this will have to be performed.
is a question from the floor. It is Karel Van Hulle, of course.

Karel VAN HULLE, K.U.Leuven and European Commission

As to convergence between IAS/IFRS and US GAAP, it seems like after having come a long way, we are now having second thoughts because there would still remain differences in interpretation or implementation, but the question is whether that uniformity is really necessary; what is the difference between comparability and uniformity?

Klaus J. HOPT

We have to move on to capital. The European Private Company (SPE) has already been mentioned, and my first question would be whether it is compatible to have a specific regime for the SPE on the one hand while not moving on the other side, i.e. the S.E. My second question: we are discussing EU company law, but insolvency law is also important, of course – wrongful trading, the group dimension, shadow directors; but these are related to issues pertaining to the board. If one looks at the shareholders, perhaps a solution could be interesting along the lines we just reformed our German GmbH law: credits of shareholders to their company are no longer regulated in company law, but in insolvency law. Do you want to respond to that?

Harm-Jan DE KLUIVER, University of Amsterdam

That is an interesting question. Well, questions are always easier than answers and this is no exception. I must confess that when I think of legal capital I always see the picture of the famous Belgian painter René Magritte ("*Ceci n'est pas une pipe*"). That is what we see in legal capital. In itself, it is not what it is about. All of us who teach students know that when we talk about legal capital, students think it is about money, but it is basically about a legal construct. Having said that, the question is: what are we going to do about that? Legal capital in itself is not an interesting subject, I think; the interesting subject is what the objective is that we want to achieve. It seems to me that over the past 10 or 15 years we have been thinking more about creditor protection than about shareholders. What about the relationship between legal capital as a part of company law and insolvency law? The interesting thing in the paper by Nelissen Grade and Wauters and the discussion this morning is that the fundamental question whether we are still talking about company law or insolvency law becomes increasingly important because of EU company law and the mobility of companies. The matter is not so important if you have a company in a certain jurisdiction and the applicable company law is supplemented by insolvency law. But if these two bodies of law are drifting apart, then it becomes much more complicated, and that is what we see in Europe due to corporate mobility, due to the SPE. We will see mismatches between company law and insolvency law. And that is a good reason, as Jonathan Rickford has already indicated, to think really hard about what should be done about harmonisation of insolvency law. I myself am convinced, as the Winter Report already indicated some years ago, that we should strive for a certain level of harmonisation of insolvency law, specifically the wrongful trading.

Klaus J. HOPT
That is a clear message to the Commission. Personally, I would not care so much where the rule is, whether it is in company law or insolvency law – it's a functional thing – but simply to leave it out would be a wrong idea.

Philippe PELLE
Wrongful trading was discussed in the High Level Group and action was envisaged for the medium term in the Action Plan of 2003. As you know, we re-consulted on the future priorities for the Action Plan in 2006 and, at the time, the response of stakeholders was to say: wrongful trading, well, no real interest; on the borderline of insolvency law but rather more insolvency law than company law. After 30 years of negotiation on the SE statute, some of my colleagues are, let us say, reluctant to engage in another 30 years of negotiation on harmonisation of insolvency law. This being said, this does not mean that for some specific items there may not be good reasons for re-examination. It may be an item to keep in mind for the future; and this is my personal opinion, since for the time being there is nothing in the pipeline.

Jaap WINTER, University of Amsterdam
Just a short recommendation to Philippe Pellé and his friends at the Commission. The thrust of the comments is that it does not matter where you regulate it; it is a functional problem of how to protect creditors in case of looming insolvency. The argument of some to say that it is a matter of insolvency law, and that therefore we should not do anything in respect of company law, is a nonsensical argument. The problem is real, and that is what you need to solve. And hopefully this crisis will get us more sensitive again to what insolvency means. And, as a second argument, if it takes another 30 years to have any solution on harmonised insolvency law in Europe, we'd better start today.

Paul DAVIES, University of Oxford
Just one point on this functional issue of wrongful trading between company law and insolvency law. There may be a functional issue as to the enforcement of the rule. If one takes the view that this rule is to be enforced only when the company is in liquidation or in an insolvency procedure, then there is a good reason for treating this as part of insolvency law rather than part of company law; but I agree with Jaap Winter that this is only secondary: it is not a reason for not acting, but it may be a reason for placing it in one slot rather than the other.

Klaus J. HOPT
We now shift the discussion towards 1S1V, and Eddy Wymeersch who wants to say a few words about pyramids.

Eddy WYMEERSCH, University of Ghent
The intention was to give you some ideas about 1S1V and more specifically as applied in groups and pyramids. The first question I would like to deal with is: why is 1S1V a problem? I think not having 1S1V means a greater cost of capital, it allows controlling shareholders to pocket for themselves and to benefit unduly, it clearly creates conflicts of interest with the company, it leads to controlling shareholders appropriating the control premium which you see in takeover bids, and the concentrated ownership model leads to weaker monitoring. And, finally, some people say it just is not right – but that is of course a value statement which is not scientifically justified. We should broaden the issue of 1S1V to all cases of disproportionality, because there are many cases in which shareholders have voting rights which are disproportionate to their financial stake, and among the CEMs that were identified in the ISS study of 2007 there are what colleague Garrido calls "true" and "false" exceptions. We see a whole range of new exceptions coming in, such as empty voting, breaking the link between voting rights and financial interest.

The arguments can be analysed as follows: the increase in the cost of capital is clear: that is the famous Dutch discount which we saw a couple of years ago when companies had quite strong protections against takeovers – and I do not know whether we still see it, since things have changed in the Netherlands, as we know. This point is not of concern to a controlling shareholder. On conflicts of interest we have a real issue, which is called tunnelling, and we see quite a lot of cases in which controlling shareholders make very aggressive use of their power. Then the issue is: should we mandate 1S1V or should we combat abuses? In my view, it is better to combat abuses than to introduce a principle of which we do not know where it will lead us and which is foreign to most of our continental legal traditions. And, by the way, I am not certain that it is that different in the US –in that respect too, US law is not the same as UK law. The control premium was dealt with at least in one case: Article 5 of the Takeover Directive, and in most jurisdictions we go for the highest price as the bid price. So the real issue is not 1S1V in my view, but the (correct) use of control. We have some data about that from another study by our colleague Ronald Gilson and to which he referred at a conference on corporate governance in Stockholm in 2004. He said that the effect of CEMs is very different according to the jurisdiction in which it is used: it leads to 1% of tunneling by the controlling shareholders in Swedish companies but 28% in Italian companies and even 36% in Mexican companies. So CEMs do not have the same effect everywhere. If we want to deal with the issue, I think we have to deal with the way control is being exercised and used, and we have to do away with private benefits of control, and this mainly through conflict rules rather than 1S1V. Other people have somewhat different feelings but we have discussed this before.

Now, as for group law, company groups constitute a clear example of possible abuse by a controlling shareholder. But we have several rules: accounting rules on related party transactions, very strict rules on supervision in banking, including in conglomerates which are very important these days and should not be forgotten, we have corporate governance codes in which arms' length transactions are recommended (but not imposed), and finally the tax rules on transfer pricing are extremely important. So we already have quite a lot of rules dealing with intra-group transactions. Apart from that we do not have any specific company law systems except for the German group law, but I would not necessarily recommend this for the rest of Europe – I think it is even no longer recommended in Germany.

In Europe, intra-group dealings are dealt with – and I am referring to a report we worked on with Klaus J. Hopt and others – on the basis of the famous French Rozenblum case. Its rationale is simple. If you have intra-group transactions you have to respect two basic rules: first, if one company gives an advantage to another, there should be something coming in return – this is what I call *quid pro quo*, which is nothing more than common sense; and second, if you give credit to another company you have to make sure that that other company is able to repay you, so no credit if the debtor company is likely to fail – which is also a rule of good sense and nothing more.

In terms of action, as a recommendation to the Commission, it would be useful that the Commission develops – probably in conjunction with the EU Corporate Governance Forum where these items are also on the agenda – a regime for minority protection. And that would include rules on disclosure, rules on conflicts of interest, rules on control acquisition outside takeover bids – a very delicate subject – and approval by non-conflicted shareholders of some very important transactions that affect the companies within the group or pyramid.

Klaus J. HOPT
I always wondered why Italy has so many pyramids and Sweden seems not to have that. Can one give a reason for that? Is there any evidence why that is so?

Eddy WYMEERSCH
A probable explanation that it is probably cheaper to use pyramids in Italy, whereas in Sweden you can achieve the same result through multiple voting rights – which do not cost so much; don't forget that pyramids are expensive in terms of administration and taxes.

Klaus J. HOPT
The topic of corporate governance is so broad that one could ask a hundred questions. I therefore ask a very specific question. You have these two different shareholder constituencies: the public companies with the board and the controlled company. If you were forced just to mention one single action as the most promising to take on each of the problems, which would it be? For the board and for the controlling shareholders. It would be interesting for the Commission to hear Paul Davies' thoughts on that.

Paul DAVIES
The single most important thing to do for the board is reforming it. Gerard Hertig suggests we eliminate it. I do not think I really have an answer. The reason it is difficult to pick one thing out is that almost everything you might try has been tried, and we don't know that any of it works any better than any other bit. I think that is for a very good reason, namely that we are talking about a system here. So it is probably the wrong question to ask. In fact, I am sure it is the wrong question to ask. It is certainly the wrong question, because what you are talking about is a system of corporate governance and therefore it is the wrong thing to pick one bit and change it. Now, controlling shareholders. What do you want to do? You want to get rid of them or want to keep them? You want to deal with the tunnelling problem. I think we could pursue stronger enforcement of the rules that already exist.

Jonathan RICKFORD,
British Institute of International and Comparative Law
What Paul Davies might have suggested, but on the other hand he might not have believed in it, is exporting the UK listing rule, the general meeting approving related party transactions. Of course, many people might not like that suggestion.

Eddy WYMEERSCH
Then by a qualified majority, not the controlling shareholder.

Klaus J. HOPT
Let us move forward to corporate mobility and I have two difficult questions for Levinus Timmerman. What is the future of Cartesio in relation to what we are discussing? And secondly, if the Commission does not move on the Fourteenth Directive – suppose that the new Commission takes the same route: to what degree would the European Court of Justice be able to step in and repair that to a certain degree?.

Levinus TIMMERMAN,
Hoge Raad der Nederlanden and University of Rotterdam
These are very difficult questions indeed. I think that the problem with Cartesio is that it contains two messages. One message is to uphold the real seat doctrine and the other message is that you can circumvent this doctrine by using the cross-border conversion if the host country permits such a conversion. That is a problem with the interpretation of this Cartesio decision.

Klaus J. HOPT
We then turn to Philippe Pellé and the general question is, asking him without committing the Commission, how to move forward. Is better regulation the real answer? What about confining oneself to cross-border things, and in particular – and that in a way is the topic of all our workshops today – how does the financial crisis influence the agenda of the Commission if you consider that for the coming years?

Philippe PELLE
What can I say in my personal capacity as well as as the Commission's representative? I can only repeat that any proposal that the Commission could make has to be accompanied by an impact assessment, so I am not really in a position to assess the impact of any of the proposals that have been heard today, nor their proportionality, subsidiarity and necessity. So it is pretty difficult. Perhaps what I can do is to give you an indication as to where we stand in the Commission for the time being in the field of company law and corporate governance.

Basically, the first priority is simplification, perhaps to a larger extent than you might like. I refer to financial reporting, and the exemption for micro-entities, for instance, a subject which we are examining.

There are a number of amendments to the existing Directives that are in the pipeline, in negotiation in the Council and the Parliament for the time being. This is in particular the case of the First Company Law Directive where we propose to abolish the obligation to publish in the National Gazette data which have already been made accessible through electronic platforms. However, we are encountering some difficulties in some Member States because of resistance by the regional press. The regional press in some Member States is for part financed by those publication obligations ("announces légales"). So that is an issue. But the estimated economies for reduction of the administrative burden are hovering around €600 million. Actually, it is the major measure for simplification in company law, setting aside financial reporting.

The envisaged simplification of the Directives on domestic mergers or domestic divisions pertains to simplifying disclosure requirements when there is duplication of information. As is the case for the Eleventh Company Law Directive, the aim is to ensure some mutual recognition of certified information where it is provided in one Member State. Simplification is an overarching objective of the Commission, not only in the field of company law.

The second project is the European Private Company. We have invested a lot of time and resources over the last year in this project, and I will come back to it in a minute. The financial crisis obviously raises a number of interrogations. There is a lot of activity, particularly in the field of financial services which is being revisited. You have the De Larosière Working Group focussing on the European financial architecture and supervision. This, of course, is not company law. There are also a number of groups, at the Commission level but also international groups, working on financial regulation and the need to revisit it. Now, there is some overlap. When we met with the G20 on 15 November, the Commission pinpointed compensation schemes and remuneration as one issue that has to be revisited, particularly for the financial services sector. It is also an issue that the President of the European Commission, Manuel Barroso, mentioned at the last European Council. The Commission will revisit its Recommendation on executive remuneration that was published in 2004. So that is something that will come. As to the calendar, it is difficult to say yet what it will be because we are waiting for the green light from our Commissioner.

Now, if I am allowed to come back to the proposals that were put forward to the Commission, in the course of the day, on the European Private Company, we had comments in relation to capital, basically. I know that Jonathan Rickford talked to the Commission about the proposals we had with regard to the European Private Company. We are making some movements even if we did not follow up yet on the KPMG study on the alternative to the capital maintenance regime that was mentioned earlier today. Nevertheless, through the European Private Company Statute, we are testing the water, seeing whether there would be an appetite in Member States not to substitute the current balance sheet test but to allow for directors to issue a solvency certificate. Actually, in the compromise that has been reached under the French presidency on the European Private Company Regulation, the proposal now reads like – and I apologize towards Jonathan Rickford– a copy-paste of the rules on the balance sheet test plus a Member State option for requiring directors to issue a solvency certificate. We do not say anything about what the nature of the insolvency test should be. We only mention the certificate. Member States do not want us to "freeze" an insolvency test in this Regulation because it is still very much at the level of experimentation in some of them. Actually, I was a provocative proponent, when we started working on the reduction of administrative burdens, of abolishing the Second Company Law Directive. As we put it forward at a meeting of the Company Law Experts Group which is composed of Member States, "that would be one way forward to enhance competition between Member States". Surprisingly enough, only one Member State was in a position to support that; one out of twenty-seven. So you see, there is not a lot of appetite to revisit the *acquis communautaire*, only at the margin. Member States are actually conservative in this field.

So much for the European Private Company. When we discussed capital, I took good note of the many proposals to continue work and reconsider the rules on wrongful trading. We are familiar with this in France, so, personally I have no problem with that. This principle already exists in a few Member States. It is a matter of persuading Member States of the necessity to move forward in this area. Perhaps now, the financial crisis being here, there will be more openness to that idea.

1S1V – I do not want to say anything. There is a lot of debate.

As regards group law, I am not saying that this is something we have to look at but, against the background of the financial crisis, there is work going on on what are called "ailing banks" and there is a White Paper that might see the light towards the middle or end of the year, and that has clear interactions with company law. This is something we are currently examining, but I can't say much more at this stage.

Cross border mobility. The Fourteenth Directive on the transfer of the registered office: We produced an impact assessment, and that impact assessment is public. It is on the website of the Commission. And the conclusion was that there was not enough evidence in support of coming forward with the Directive. We had to wait to see whether the Tenth (Cross-border Merger) Directive was producing an effect. It could be used as a vehicle for companies to transfer their seat, their registered office. At the time, we also linked that to the Cartesio case. We did not mention Cartesio explicitly, but we were hopeful that the Court of Justice would go along the same trail as the one it had opened with Centros, Sevic and the rest. Obviously, now that the Cartesio judgment has been rendered, we have to analyse the effect of it. We are not as enthusiastic as we were expecting to be, so it is something we will have to reconsider at some point in time. It is a politically sensitive issue in the EU.

I noted from Eddy Wymeersch the issue of empty voting. It is one which is on the table, certainly on the table of the European Parliament. Mr Lehne will report on the transparency for institutional investors. Special inquiry rights are also something we might reconsider. Also, the monitoring of the application of the codes of corporate governance is something that is taking place. We have mandated a study to this effect. So that is where we are, and again I am very grateful for the ideas today.

Klaus J. HOPT

Thank you very much for this kind and frank information on what the Commission is doing. I may have one question for Eddy (Wymeersch), because he was heading the SLIM group at that time. Are you satisfied with what has happened with the simplification or would you think one needs more?

Eddy WYMEERSCH

I think there is still a lot of work to be done, both on those changes that have been adopted in this Amending Directive but also on many other things. I still remember that, with regard to the branches of companies in other states, publication, translation, filing and so on still have to take place, and that is a field in which you could simplify considerably. But I see many other fields.

Philippe PELLE

In this respect, there is also the issue of the architecture of the business registries. What we would look for is an interconnection of the national business registries. It is very optimistic, because sometimes they are "local". But that would be a way forward to simplify the issues.

Gerard HERTIG

In view of the crisis, what I miss in the programme is how to deal with failures in risk management in many companies, banks as well as others. If you look at it, it is not that easy to do, but I could figure out at least two things. One is improved information flows within the firm and a second is to improve the liquidity of firms.

If you push it a bit further, you quickly come back to the old system that they had in Germany where they had employee participation to improve information flows and hidden reserves to improve the financial liquidity of firms, and maybe one way to go ahead would be to stop looking too much at the Anglo-Saxon way and go back to the old German way of doing things.

Klaus J. HOPT

As a conclusion, I think the basic general questions remain, of course: what role for the market and what role for law and, in between, self regulation? This is the perennial question, together with the general discussion between the lawyers and economists and also between Europeans and Americans on the role for the federal law. Personally, I do not share the opinion of Roberta Romano, but I am also not of the opinion of my colleagues at the Max Planck Institute who tend to be very much in favour of inclusion in a civil code. I think we do not need this in our areas.

The European Union's Involvement in Company Law and Corporate Governance

Jaap Winter[1]

Introduction

It was an honour to speak at the special commemoration of Professor Jan Ronse on the occasion of the conference on the European Company Action Plan of 2003 organised by the Jan Ronse Institute, chaired by Professor Walter van Gerven and in the presence of former Minister of Justice Van Deurzen and of the Ronse family. This contribution is a reflection of my presentation. Part I addresses the EU's involvement in company law and its evolution. Part II deals with its more recent involvement in corporate governance.

Part I. The EU and Company Law

1. Treaty and harmonisation

The basis of the EU's involvement in company law is the freedom of establishment, an element of the free movement of persons. This freedom includes "the right to take up and pursue activities as self-employed persons and to set up and manage undertakings, in particular companies or firms..., under the conditions laid down for its own nationals by the law of the country where such establishment is effected, subject to the provisions of the Chapter on capital" (Article 43 Treaty of Rome). In order to attain freedom of establishment, the Council and the Commission are required to "co-ordinate to the necessary extent the safeguards which, for the protection of the interests of members and others, are required by Member States of companies or firms ..., with a view to making such safeguards equivalent throughout the Community" (Article 44(2)(g)). This Treaty provision is the basis for the harmonisation of company law in the European Union. It is a rather peculiar basis. It takes a specific angle to the harmonisation process: the protection of shareholders and

[1] Professor of Company Law at the University of Amsterdam, Acting Dean of the Duisenberg School of Finance, former Chairman of the High Level Group of Company Law Experts of the European Commission. The first part of this contribution is derived from my article in the Liber Amicorum for Eddy Wymeersch, Perspectives in Company Law and Financial Regulation, published in 2009 after the Leuven Conference was held, see pp. 43-60.

others which is required by Member States' company laws. The protection of shareholders and others, in particular creditors, was very much in the minds of the original authors of the Treaty. There was a concern among Member States in those days, we speak of 1957, that shareholders and creditors would not invest in companies from other Member States or do business with them, as they would not be familiar with the company laws to which such companies would be subject and particularly with the protections afforded to them under these company laws. In addition, Member States feared that without a rigorous harmonisation programme, Member States would race to the bottom by creating company laws with ever reducing protection for shareholders and creditors in order to compete with other Member States for the incorporation or registration of companies in their jurisdictions. The Netherlands was seen as Europe's bottom in those days, not only geographically but also in terms of company law. Dutch company law was very flexible, with a minimum of mandatory rules. Regulatory arbitrage that would lead other Member States to race to that same bottom was to be avoided. I will not go into the question whether such a race to the bottom would have ever occurred without Article 44(2)(g) and the harmonisation programme. For now I just note that approaching company law legislation with the primary objective of making protections for shareholders and creditors equivalent across the EU is indeed a peculiar approach to company law.

On the basis of Article 44(2)(g), eleven Directives have been adopted in the meantime. They primarily deal with formalities of company law such as incorporation, publicity, capital formation and protection, (cross-border) legal mergers and split-ups, accounting, branches, etc. Some call the resulting EU company law trivial.[2] Member States have discovered fundamental differences of opinion on such core issues as the organisation of the board, the role and rights of shareholders, group relationships, employee co-determination and corporate control. In these areas, nothing of substance has been agreed by Member States; projects were either abandoned (the Fifth Directive on the structure of the company dealing with board structures and the rights of shareholders, and the Ninth Directive on group law) or Member States have agreed to disagree and to leave it to Member States individually (e.g. the Statute for the Societas Europaea on board structures and the Thirteenth Directive on takeover bids).

2. Political process

In light of the political decision-making in the EU process we should perhaps be surprised that so many Directives have actually made it to their adoption. The right of initiative lies with the Commission which has a primarily, but

---

[2] L. Enriques, 'EC Company Law Directives and Regulations: How Trivial Are They?', in J. Armour and J. McCahery (eds.), *After Enron, Improving Corporate Law and Modernising Securities Regulation in Europe and the US* (Oxford: Hart Publishing, 2006), pp. 641-700.

maybe not exclusively, European agenda. But the key decisions are made by the Council of Ministers. The Council consists of representatives of the current 27 Member States' governments. Decisions in the Council are often, perhaps more often than not, driven by each Member State's government negotiating to preserve and further national Member State interests. They are doing this on a number of dossiers which are discussed simultaneously and which should all lead to some form of regulation or action at EU level. Member States find it difficult to suppress the inclination to make deals across dossiers, to agree to certain other Member States' wishes, say on an agricultural issue, in order to get their agreement on a company law issue. The compromises that follow often have little to do with the merits of the issues dealt with. Directives then require approval from the European Parliament. The Parliament functions mainly along party lines, but MEPs sometimes are sensitive to national issues and particular concerns of the Member States they are representing. In some cases all MEPs from a particular Member State vote in a certain direction to protect perceived national interests, as it is said the German MEPs from left to right did when voting down the Takeover Bids Directive in June 2001.

A complicating factor in this political process is that in many dossiers the question is raised whether it is really for the EU to regulate or whether regulation should be left to Member States. Member States over time have become sensitive to this question: after some decades, they witnessed that many of their powers had effectively been transferred to the EU and would need to be shared with other Member States. In the Maastricht Treaty of 1992, Article 5 was introduced, providing that in areas which do not fall within its exclusive competence, the Community shall take action, in accordance with the principle of *subsidiarity*, only if and insofar as the objectives of the proposed action cannot be sufficiently achieved by the Member States and can therefore, by reason of the scale or effects of the proposed action, be better achieved by the Community. The words "cannot be sufficiently achieved" and "be better achieved" leave ample opportunity to challenge EU interference in almost any area. Subsidiarity is an argument often heard and used when Member States do not like the possible outcome of an EU regulatory process.

Linked to these factors troubling the political decision-making process is the fact that Member State governments also make up the key decision maker at EU level, the Council of Ministers. This has the effect that these governments, but also everybody else who has a role or an interest in the subject matter to be regulated, can and often need to play chess on two chess boards: national level and EU level. If, for example, a certain national legislative development is not desired by a Member State government, or by those who lobby that government, it or they can argue that this is a matter for the EU to regulate and not for any single Member State. This often serves as an efficient delaying tactic, as agreement at EU level is difficult to achieve. Or, vice versa, a deadlock at national level can sometimes be broken by forging an agreement with other

Member States at EU level. Playing simultaneous chess on two boards is what the vast lobbying industry in Brussels is all about.

All these factors contribute to the political decision-making process in the EU being highly complex and its outcomes highly unpredictable. The focus and efforts of the EU to improve its legislative process through the Better Regulation initiatives[3] are not suited to dealing with these fundamental complicating factors, which lie at the root of the political structure of the EU. They have caused three somewhat overlapping trends in EU legislation of company law in this century.

3. Three trends

The first trend is a strong emphasis on *subsidiarity*. This trend can be seen from abandoning the Fifth and Ninth Directives on the structure of the company and on group law, which are now no longer issues where the EU seeks a legislative role for itself. This trend is also clear from the efforts to simplify current Directives, in particular the Second Directive on capital maintenance. The thrust is to remove from the Directives anything which is not really necessary or clearly helpful.[4] Finally, we see this trend from the development of not imposing certain elements of legislation on Member States but either giving them options to apply or not apply certain EU rules (see the Thirteenth Directive on takeover bids and the opt-outs that Member States have been given from the rules on defence against takeovers, provided they give opt-in rights to companies)[5] or leaving out of an EU legislative instrument core elements of regulation (see the SE Statute, leaving anything contentious for Member States to regulate themselves in their legislation implementing the SE Statute).[6]

The second trend is the *privatisation of company law*. This trend is visible at national and at EU level. The SE Statute, for example, leaves the choice for a one-tier board structure or a two-tier board structure to those incorporating the SE themselves, see Articles 39 and 42 SE Statute. Similarly, companies have the right to opt in to application of Articles 9 (board passivity) and 11 (breakthrough) of the Thirteenth Directive on takeover bids, if the Member

[3] See http://ec.europa.eu/governance/better_regulation/index_en.htm.

[4] See Directive of the European Parliament and of the Council of 6 September 2006 amending Council Directive 77/91/EEC as regards the formation of public limited liability companies and the maintenance and alteration of their capital 2006/68/EC [2006] OJ L 264/32. See, for the general thrust to simplify company law, the report on the public consultation on the future priorities of the company law action plan, http://ec.europa.eu/internal_market/company/consultation/index_en.htm.

[5] G. Hertig and J. McCahery, 'An Agenda for Reform: Company and Takeover Law in Europe', in G. Ferrarini, K.J. Hopt, J. Winter and E. Wymeersch (eds.), *Reforming Company and Takeover Law in Europe* (Oxford University Press, 2004), pp. 21-49, who advocate the option approach for EU company legislation. My concern with this approach is that the design and effects of the options to be given to Member States will be subject to the same political factors I have described above and are likely to be used particularly to protect national interests.

[6] See L. Enriques, 'Silence is Golden: The European Company as a Catalyst for Company Law Arbitrage', *Journal of Corporate Law Studies* (2004), p. 77.

State does not impose application of these rules, see Article 12. Finally, and perhaps most importantly, the regulation of corporate governance to a large extent is left to companies and their shareholders. Codes of corporate governance are to be adopted at Member State level, and in most if not all Member States these codes have been drafted by committees consisting of representatives of companies, shareholders and other private entities. Furthermore, these codes are not binding upon companies, but companies must explain to what extent and for what reasons they do not comply with the code to which they are subject, see Article 46a(1)(a) and (b) of the Fourth Directive on annual accounts, as amended by Directive 2006/46/EC, L 224/1. The enforcement is primarily in the hands of shareholders.[7]

The third trend is that where Member States do reach agreement in spite of conflicts between national interests and perceptions, the outcome is typically an *ugly compromise* creating problems for companies that have to apply the resulting rules. The Directive accompanying the SE Statute on the involvement of employees, in particular the rules on participation of employees in a board of the company, are a fine example. The Directive is replete with provisions whose only purpose is to prevent a German company subject to German co-determination rules from escaping those rules by merging into an SE. The rules create a complex set of provisions detailing which majorities of employees of participating companies can in different circumstances outvote German employees in order to not apply the German co-determination rules to the SE. If no agreement is reached, a set of standard rules apply, the interpretation of which would be a tough challenge for the European Court of Justice and some of which actually are mutually conflicting.[8] Another example is offered by the opt-out and opt-in rules combined with the reciprocity rule of Article 12 of the Thirteenth Directive on takeover bids. These rules result in preserving the existing situations in Member States with respect to takeovers and defence instead of creating a level playing field for takeover bids which is the stated objective of the Directive. They also create rules which are either easy to circumvent and manipulate or incredibly difficult to apply and which are possibly in breach of the Treaty itself and of the EU's obligations under the WTO as they by definition exclude non-listed and non-EU companies from obtaining as good a position as a bidder as EU listed companies can obtain.[9]

[7] See the Statement of the European Corporate Governance Forum on the comply-or-explain principle of 22.02.2006, see http://ec.europa.eu/internal_market/company/ecgforum/index_en.htm.

[8] See Jaap Winter, 'De Europese Vennootschap als sluis voor in- en uitvoer van vennootschapsrecht', *Nederlands Juristenblad* (2002), p. 2034-2040.

[9] Jaap Winter, 'You must be joking', *Ondernemingsrecht* (2004), p. 367.

4. The EU's legislative remit in company law

In light of all this, I believe the remit of the EU's involvement in company law should be modest, at best. In line with the principle of subsidiarity, it should focus on those issues where individual Member States cannot provide solutions, and, in addition, on those issues where the evidence of a benefit of a solution at EU level over a solution by individual Member States is clear. These issues are most likely to arise with companies whose shares are listed on a regulated market. The securities laws to which these listed companies have become subject in Europe are to a very large extent harmonised, if not uniform, across the EU following the many far reaching directives and secondary regulations that have been adopted under the Financial Services Action Plan. A key aspect of the new rules is to ensure that companies in Europe have efficient access to capital markets across Europe and that their investors are offered equivalent protections on these markets. As a result, a key feature of listed companies, i.e. their relation to the capital markets, is regulated practically uniformly across the EU. There are more likely to be company law issues for these companies that require EU solutions or where EU solutions are clearly preferable to Member State solutions than for non-listed companies.

Finally, the subject of corporate governance warrants EU attention, particularly so for listed companies for the reason I have just set out. Regardless of how narrowly or broadly one defines corporate governance, at its core lie the functioning of the board or boards and the relationship with shareholders, which typically find their legal basis in company law. In the harmonisation history of EU company law these were precisely the areas where Member States failed to agree on any form of harmonisation, the keystone of which was the abandoned Fifth EU Directive. The EU has re-entered the field, now under the heading of corporate governance, *inter alia* through EU Commission recommendations on the role of non-executive directors and remuneration of directors[10] and the Shareholders' Rights Directive.[11] I will come back to this renewed EU approach in the second part.

5. A new avenue for progress: the free movement of capital

The legislative remit for the EU in company law may be limited, but this does not mean to say that the EU will not have an important impact on the company

---

[10] European Commission Recommendation of 15 February 2005 on the role of non-executive or supervisory directors of listed companies and on the committees of the (supervisory) board, European Commission Recommendation of 14 December 2004 fostering an appropriate regime for the remuneration of directors of listed companies, European Commission recommendation on directors' remuneration and European Commission Recommendation of 29 April 2009 – further guidance on structure and determination of directors' remuneration.

[11] Directive 2007/36/EL of 11 July 2007 on the exercise of certain rights of shareholders in listed companies.

laws of Member States in different ways. The European Court of Justice has proven to be a particular driving force, with its judgments on the freedom of establishment. The *Centros*, *Überseering* and *Inspire Art* judgments[12] have established that, where Member States have not agreed on harmonisation of certain aspects of company law, a Member State may not impose barriers to the freedom of establishment merely because a company with an establishment in that Member State is incorporated in another Member State in which it does not perform any real business activities. Restrictions imposed on such a company, such as not allowing registration of the establishment in the Member State, denying legal standing in court and imposition of additional administrative and substantive legal burdens, are not justified by the fact that the company does not adhere to the same capital maintenance rules as companies incorporated in the Member State itself. This case law has had at least three effects: (i) an increased trend towards using English limited liability companies instead of the national form of limited company for doing business in other Member States, in particular Germany,[13] (ii) a fundamental discussion on whether the real seat theory is still a viable theory on the basis of which to apply company law of one Member State to a company incorporated in another Member State,[14] and (iii) some Member States have initiated proposals to deregulate their laws on limited companies, like the Netherlands and Germany.[15] This may lead to a convergence of company law from the bottom up, through incorporation choices of companies and legislative action by Member States without any EU legislation.

The case law on freedom of establishment is now well understood and its effects are becoming clear. The question is whether the other freedom relevant to company law will have similar effects. This is the free movement of capital. The ECJ by now has established important case law based on the free movement of capital in the area of so-called golden shares. "Golden shares" refers to arrangements, either in law or in the company's constitution, made by Member States with respect to companies in their jurisdiction, typically companies that have been privatised, and which confer on a Member State

[12] Case C-212/97, *Centros Ltd v. Erhvervs- og Selskabsstyrelsen*, [1999] ECR I-1459; Case C-208/00, *Überseering BV v. Nordic Construction Company Baumanagement GmbH*, [2002] ECR I-9919; Case C-167/01, *Kamer van Koophandel en Fabrieken voor Amsterdam v. Inspire Art Ltd*, [2003] ECR I-10155.

[13] M. Becht, Colin Mayer and Hannes Wagner, 'Where do firms incorporate? Deregulation and the cost of entry', *ECGI Law/Working Paper 70* (2006), http://papers.ssrn.com/sol3/papers.cfm?abstract_id=906066.

[14] E. Wymeersch, 'The transfer of the company's seat in EU company law', *ECGI Law/Working paper 08* (2003), http://papers.ssrn.com/sol3/papers.cfm?abstract_id=384802.

[15] In the Netherlands a proposal to simplify and make more flexible the law applicable to the *besloten vennootschap* (limited company) has been submitted to the Parliament. According to this proposal the minimum capital requirement, currently EUR 18,000, will be abolished. For the German proposal to change the law applicable to the Gesellschaft mit beschränkter Haftung, see http://www.jura.uni-augsburg.de/prof/moellers/materialien/materialdateien/040_deutsche_gesetzgebungsgeschichte/momig/. The German proposal does not abolish minimum capital altogether but reduces it from EUR 25,000 to EUR 10,000.

certain powers of control over those companies, or the ability to prevent certain shareholders from acquiring control over those companies. This is a crucial issue in the development of the EU. It is about striking the right balance between the EU's objective of creating a single market without artificial barriers imposed by Member States and the Member States' concerns about losing control over businesses that are crucial to their economy and national infrastructure. The case law shows that the ECJ leaves Member States only very little scope to fence off companies with golden share structures, which are quickly considered to hinder the free movement of capital as they are liable to dissuade investors (either direct investors interested in participating in control or portfolio investors not interested in participating in control)[16] from investing in the company. As with the freedom of establishment, the ECJ accepts only limited justifications of any impediment to the free movement of capital.[17]

So far, the case law on the free movement of capital relates to Member States and state actions, rather than to companies and citizens. However, the recent *Volkswagen* case may open up new avenues for development of EU company law on the basis of the free movement of capital.

6. *Volkswagen*

The *Volkswagen* case[18] deals with the "Volkswagen Act", a special Act of the German legislator dealing with certain governance arrangements for Volkswagen AG. After World War II the trade unions had started up the car-making business of Volkswagen, without it being clear who actually owned the business. In 1959/1960 the Federal German government and the government of the state of Lower Saxony discussed and agreed with the trade unions on the ownership of the business. It was decided that Volkswagen was to be a publicly held company, an Aktiengesellschaft, in which the Federal State and Lower Saxony would each hold 20 per cent of the company's share capital and the rest would be offered to the public. To date, Lower Saxony has maintained a stake of approximately 20 per cent in Volkswagen, by subscribing for and investing in new shares whenever they were issued by the company. The Federal State has sold its shares. Part of the deal struck in 1959-1960 was that minority shareholders would be protected against a party trying to take control of the company without acquiring the full share capital. At the same time this would protect employees against a possible hostile bid that could lead to lay-offs in

[16] The ECJ has repeatedly ruled that both types of investors, distinguished in the Commission's statement of 19 July 1997 relating to certain legal aspects of intra-Community investments, Pub. no C 220, are protected by the free movement of capital.

[17] Case C-367/98, *Commission v. Portugal* [2002] ECR I-04731; Case C-483/99, *Commission v. France* [2002] ECR I-04781; Case C-503/99, *Commission v. Belgium* [2002] ECR I-04809; Case C-463/00, *Commission v. Spain* [2003] ECR I-4581; Case C-98/01, *Commission v. United Kingdom* [2003] ECR I-4641; Case C-174/04, *Commission v. Italy* [2005] ECR I-4933; and Cases C-282/04 and 283/04, *Commission v. Netherlands* [2006] ECR I-9141.

[18] Case C-112/05, *Commission v. Germany* [2007] ECR I-8995.

Germany. The parties agreed to the adoption of three key governance provisions:

- the voting rights of each Volkswagen shareholder are limited to a maximum of 20 per cent of the total votes that can be cast, even if the shareholder holds more than 20 per cent of the share capital;
- special resolutions of the general meeting of shareholders of Volkswagen which would require a 75 per cent majority under standard German law require a majority of 80 per cent;
- Germany and Lower Saxony may each, as long as they are Volkswagen shareholders, appoint two members to the Volkswagen supervisory board.

These provisions were not only incorporated in the articles of association of Volkswagen AG, but were also imposed on the company and its shareholders by the Volkswagen Act. As a practical result, Lower Saxony, by maintaining its 20 per cent in Volkswagen, could veto important resolutions in the general meeting and no other shareholder could acquire more voting rights than Lower Saxony.

Germany had argued that all of this was nothing more than a private agreement between parties who had disputed the ownership of the company, a private agreement which had merely been confirmed by the Volkswagen Act. The Court rejected this argument. The Volkswagen Act, a state measure, imposed these arrangements on the company and its shareholders and did not allow for the shareholders being able to decide to change them.[19]

Germany then argued that the voting cap and the super majority requirement did not restrict the free movement of capital, because they applied without distinction to all shareholders, including Lower Saxony, and worked both to the benefit (reduced chance of a third party acquiring cheap control with a relatively low percentage) and detriment (reduced ability to exercise control oneself with a relatively low percentage) of all shareholders, including Lower Saxony. The Court rejected this argument as well. But in doing so, and by arguing that the Act does restrict the free movement of capital, the Court took a new turn. The Court basically argued that the 80 per cent super majority requirement created an instrument for Lower Saxony, as an approximately 20 per cent shareholder, to procure for itself a blocking minority allowing it to oppose special resolutions on the basis of a lower level of investment than would be required under general company law. The 20 per cent voting cap supplements this legal framework and enables Lower Saxony to exercise considerable influence on the basis of such lower investment. The combination of the 80 per cent super majority

[19] In the cases against the Netherlands, the Court considered introducing certain clauses into the articles of association granting special rights in companies the Netherlands was privatising as taking a state measure. In *Volkswagen* the 20% voting cap and the 80% majority requirement did not create special rights, but there was a clear state act in the form of the Volkswagen Act. It would be interesting to see how the Court would rule if the state acted as a shareholder to include certain restrictive clauses in the articles of association of a company which do not grant special rights to the state. See on this J. van Bekkum, J. Kloosterman and J. Winter, 'Golden Shares and European Company Law: the Implications of Volkswagen', *European Company Law* (2008), p. 9.

requirement and the 20 per cent voting cap, the Court ruled, diminishes the interest in acquiring a stake in the capital of Volkswagen as it is liable to limit the possibility for other shareholders to effectively participate in the management and control of Volkswagen. By arguing in this way, the Court made instrumental to its reasoning the investment Lower Saxony held in Volkswagen and continued to maintain at around 20 per cent by subscribing for newly issued shares. The Court uses vague words in this respect. It does not rule that the provisions of the Act as such are liable to deter investors, but states: this "situation", i.e. rules combined with a private investment by Lower Saxony, is liable to deter investors from other Member States. This raises at least two interesting questions: How would the Court have ruled if Lower Saxony had not maintained its investment at around 20 per cent and its investment had dropped significantly as a result of share issues to others? Could the Volkswagen Act still be saved if Lower Saxony was to sell a significant part or all of its shares in Volkswagen?[20]

By drawing Lower Saxony's investment decisions into its reasoning, the Court at least conceptually opens the door to applying the free movement of capital to the private sphere. In *Volkswagen* the Court did not have to dwell on this, as the Volkswagen Act itself is clearly a state act. But broadening the scope of the free movement of capital by bringing it into the private sphere would not be surprising, in light of the trends in the case law of the Court on the other Community freedoms. The free movement of capital case law has traditionally trailed the case law on the other freedoms but has picked up quite a bit over the last decade. And recent case law shows only few differences between the doctrinal features of this freedom compared with the others.[21]

7. Free movement and the private sphere

For the other freedoms, the Court has already addressed the question whether and to what extent they could be applied to private persons. In particular the free movement of workers has triggered Court rulings that apply the freedom into the private realm. In cases such as *Walrave*[22] and *Bosman*[23] the Court held that provisions limiting the free movement of workers were adopted in a collective manner (e.g. by international cyclist and football organisations), these

[20] Interestingly, at the Volkswagen annual general meeting held on 24 April 2008, Porsche, which in the meantime had acquired a 30% stake in Volkswagen, sought to get shareholder approval for removing from Volkswagen's Articles of Association the provision copying the Volkswagen Act. The resolution was rejected as "it did not obtain the required majority" (i.e. still 80% under the Articles of Association), according to the Volkswagen website, see http://www.volkswagenag.com/vwag/vwcorp/info_center/en/news/2008/04/AGM.html. The Volkswagen saga has since continued, with the final stage of Volkswagen taking over Porsche in a rare turn of events.

[21] L. Flynn, 'Coming of Age: the free movement of capital case law', *Common Market Law Review* (2002), pp. 773-805.

[22] Case C-36/74, *Walrave and Koch* [1974] ECR 1405.

[23] Case C-415/93, *Bosman* [1995] ECR I-4921.

provisions should be caught by Articles 39 and 49 EC and should be subjected to the same standards applicable to state measures. In *Ferlini*[24] the Court went a little further by arguing that the discrimination prohibition of Article 12 EC also applies to a case where an organisation (in this case an organisation of Luxembourg hospitals) exercises a certain power over individuals and is able to impose conditions upon them as a result of which the exercise of fundamental freedoms guaranteed under the Treaty is made more difficult. And in *Angonese*[25] the Court ruled that the requirement imposed by a private bank in Northern Italy for candidates applying for a job at the bank to prove their bilingual capabilities (Italian-German) by means of a diploma that can only be obtained in one province of Italy constitutes prohibited discrimination on the basis of nationality. The precise extent of this case law is not yet clear. One interpretation is that the prohibition against discrimination may be applied against any person (as shown in *Angonese*), while the prohibition against restrictions on the free movement of workers only applies to measures of a collective character with semi-public implications (*Walrave, Bosman, Ferlini*).[26]

For the free movement of goods, the Court traditionally takes the view that Articles 28 and 29 only apply to measures taken by Member States and not by private persons.[27] There is a back door, however, through which even this freedom may have its effects on the actions of private persons. In *Commission v. France*[28] French farmers repeatedly and violently obstructed Spanish farmers from selling their strawberries in France. The Court ruled that the actions undertaken by the French government were manifestly inadequate to ensure freedom of intra-Community trade in agricultural products on its territory by preventing and effectively dissuading the perpetrators of the offences in question from committing and repeating them. It is for the Member State concerned to adopt all appropriate measures to guarantee the full scope and effect of Community law so as to ensure its proper implementation in the interests of all economic operators. The actions of the French farmers were extreme, but the case may provide the basis for a more general rule that if private persons repeatedly and consistently obstruct the exercise of the Treaty freedoms by others, Member States may have to take measures to guarantee that these freedoms can be exercised.

There is no reason why the extension of the Treaty freedoms to the private sphere as follows from the case law referred to above could or should not also

---

24 Case C-411/98, *Ferlini* [2000] ECR I-8081.

25 Case C-281/98, *Angonese* [2000] ECR I-4139.

26 P. Oliver and W.-H. Roth, 'The Internal Market and the Four Freedoms', *Common Market Law Review* (2004), p. 423.

27 Oliver and Roth, 'The Internal Market' (note 29, above), p. 422, with references to relevant case law.

28 Case C-265/95, *Commision v. France* [1977] ECR I-6959.

apply to the free movement of capital.[29] Speculating about the application of the free movement of capital into the private realm, the example of the role of securities intermediaries refusing to facilitate the exercise of cross-border voting rights comes to mind. I will come back to this thorny issue below, but for now it suffices to say that banks and brokers, as a result of the widespread ownership of traded securities through book-entry trading accounts, have become indispensable for the exercise of voting rights by the investors. In the words of the Court in *Ferlini*, the banks and brokers exercise a certain power over individuals and are able to impose conditions upon them as a result of which the exercise of fundamental freedoms guaranteed under the Treaty is made more difficult. This is precisely what banks and brokers do by not facilitating the exercise of voting rights by their clients through the chains of intermediaries across borders. The resulting inability to exercise voting rights across borders is liable to dissuade investors from investing in companies in other Member States and is therefore a restriction on the free movement of capital. A different approach, based on the *Commission v. France* ruling, could be that Member States, allowing banks and brokers in their jurisdiction to facilitate the exercise of their clients' voting rights in their own jurisdiction but consistently refuse to facilitate (i) the exercise of voting rights by their clients on shares held in companies in another Member State and (ii) the exercise of voting rights by investors from other Member States on shares in companies within the jurisdiction of the banks and brokers, fail to adopt all appropriate measures to guarantee the full scope and effect of the free movement of capital so as to ensure its proper implementation in the interests of all economic operators. The first, *Ferlini*-based reasoning would allow for a case against the banks and brokers being brought directly by investors, with the possibility for the national court to request a ruling from the European Court on the interpretation of Article 56 EC on the basis of Article 234 EC. The second, *Commission v. France*-based reasoning would allow for the Commission

[29] Oliver and Roth refer to the complication that the justifications which may be available for Member States under the Treaty may not be available for private persons. In particular, private autonomy, protected by national constitutions and the very essence of the European market economy, does not show up as a justification, see note 28, above, p. 423. The justification for private persons to restrict the Treaty freedoms is indeed problematic. But in this respect the free movement of capital is no different than the other freedoms where the Court has brought them into the private sphere. For a different view, see B.J. Drijber, 'De Dertiende Richtlijn tussen Europese politiek en Europees recht', *Ondernemingsrecht* (2004), p. 140, holding that Art. 56 EC does not have any horizontal effect. See for further speculation into the possible horizontal effect of the free movement of capital I. van der Steen, 'Horizontale werking van de vier vrijheden en van het discriminatieverbod van artikel 12 EG', *Nederlands tijdschrift voor Europees recht* (2001), p. 8, relating to the effect of the free movement of capital on the ability of companies to defend themselves against hostile takeover bids. See also the report of the European Corporate Governance Forum working group on proportionality, referring to cases in which foundations hold control over listed companies through mechanisms that allow for control rights disproportionate to the investment made by the foundation to further different stakeholder and societal interests. The report suggests that the free movement of capital may offer a fruitful avenue that can be explored to restrict the use of disproportionate mechanisms by such foundations to situations which are acceptable and justified under the Treaty, see p. 19 of the report of June 2007, see the posting on the website dated 12.09.2007 http://ec.europa.eu/internal_market/company/ecgforum/index_en.htm.

to adopt a policy not unlike its policy on golden shares, directed at ensuring that Member States require their banks and brokers to facilitate cross-border voting by their own clients and by investors from other Member States. Where a Member State fails to do so, the Commission could bring an action against that Member State before the European Court. Both avenues would allow for creating solutions to the problem of cross-border voting without legislation at EU level.

8. Ius Audacibus: company law and EU law

Capitalism is not for the faint hearted, it is said. It is based on people who are willing to take risks in order to reap the fruits if they succeed. This is what produces wealth, and wealth allows us to prosper as a society.

Both company law and EU law are instrumental to this objective. Company law first of all facilitates entrepreneurship, the risk-taking by business in order to generate profits. But it also seeks to protect those who are affected by companies against careless exploitation.

EU law creates a European space for entrepreneurship, where people and capital can move freely to create optimal results without artificial restrictions. Company law and EU law therefore have a common characteristic: they are both law for the brave, *ius audacibus*. It is only natural that they meet, for example in the free movement of capital.

Part II. The EU and Corporate Governance

1. The EU approach?

Following the High Level Group's report on Modernisation of Company Law of November 2002,[30] the EU has re-entered the terrain it had previously abandoned with the Fifth EU Directive. Not in the traditional way of trying to regulate the substance of corporate governance at EU level, as was intended with the Fifth Directive, but in a more distanced way. The substance of corporate governance is linked directly to the core of company law: the structure and operation of boards of companies and the relationship with their shareholders. As this core of company law is designed differently across Member States, based on different legal, social, financial and cultural traditions, it is unlikely that Member States at EU level will reach agreement on a single model to be applied across the EU. It is also very doubtful whether creating and imposing such a model would really be efficient. But the EU can co-ordinate the efforts of Member States to protect and where necessary improve the integrity of their

[30] See the report A Modern Regulatory Framework for Company Law in Europe of November 2002, http://ec.europa.eu/internal_market/company/modern/index_en.htm#background.

corporate governance models. This is particularly so because of the warm reception the so-called "comply-or-explain" model has received in Member States. This model avoids mandatory legislation on the substance of corporate governance by implementing corporate governance codes, compliance with which or proper explanations for non-compliance are to be enforced primarily by shareholders. The High Level Group and the European Corporate Governance Forum recommend this model as a means to create and improve corporate governance in the EU.[31] It has now been formalised in an amendment of the Fourth and Seventh Directives on annual accounts and consolidated accounts. Article 46a of the Fourth Directive requires companies whose shares are listed on a regulated market to include in their annual report a corporate governance statement. Such a statement must refer to the corporate governance code the company is subject to or voluntarily applies, including an explanation of any deviations from that code. Corporate governance codes at Member State level and "comply or explain" have become the cornerstone of the EU's approach to corporate governance.

I have always been slightly surprised by the warm reception of this model. Across the EU it has been widely welcomed as a superior approach to governance compared to the mandatory legislation in the US through the Sarbanes-Oxley Act. But if we are honest, we should admit this is one big experiment. There is little or no experience with corporate governance codes or with "comply or explain" in most Member States. There are several reasons to doubt whether we have an infrastructure which is sufficiently conducive to making the code and comply-or-explain model successful.

2. *The proper regulatory regime*

There is little understanding of what type of regulatory environment is required for a system of corporate governance codes and "comply or explain" to function properly. Article 46a of the Fourth Directive, the legal basis for this system across the EU, does not require Member States to designate a corporate governance code with which listed companies should comply or in relation to which they should explain deviations. Most Member States now have designated such a corporate governance code, but not all. And where they have done so, the way the requirement to comply or explain has been embedded in law is often different. Some Member States have included this requirement in their company law, applying to companies in their jurisdiction whose shares are listed (either in that jurisdiction or elsewhere). Others have included this requirement in the listing rules, applying to those companies who have a primary share listing in that jurisdiction. The result is that some companies, incorporated for example in Germany or the Netherlands and with a share listing in the UK,

[31] See the previous note for the report of the High Level Group. See also the Statement of the Forum on "comply or explain" (note 8, above).

need to comply with two corporate governance codes, whose provisions will not always be compatible. In the reverse case, a UK company listed in Germany or the Netherlands, no code applies at all. This may lead to *code arbitration*, a prime example of which we see with AirBerlin Plc, incorporated in the UK and listed in Germany and not required to comply with either the UK Combined Code or the German Corporate Governance Code. The European Corporate Governance Forum has recommended that this be solved by introducing a rule that a listed company is required to at least comply or explain in relation to one code and in case of double application can choose which code to apply.[32]

In addition, there is no consistent and well-tested model working across the EU for monitoring compliance with codes. In some Member States monitoring has been formally arranged by publicly appointed committees who publish annual monitoring reports. In other Member States private organisations provide some monitoring, in others securities regulators are involved in monitoring of the application of codes. There is also no general understanding of what makes a relevant and good explanation for deviation from the code and what are just boiler plate explanations.

Because of these issues, the European Corporate Governance Forum asked the Commission to launch a study on the infrastructure in Member States for codes and "comply or explain". The study was conducted in 2009 and the results have recently been published.[33] I will not go into the results at length, but the study confirms that there are wide differences between Member States in terms of code infrastructure, monitoring and level of explanations for deviations from the code. One finding of the study is that where securities regulators are engaged in monitoring the application of the code, in Spain and Portugal for example, this leads to a higher level of disclosure of deviations as they require explanation on a provision-by-provision basis, but such disclosure appears to be of a more box-ticking nature. The study is a first step in understanding the functioning of corporate governance codes in the EU, as a necessary point of departure for strengthening the infrastructure supporting it.

3. Cross-border voting by shareholders

What can or should be done to ensure compliance with the code or at least sufficient explanation for non-compliance? The system assumes that shareholders should enforce the application of the code rather than securities regulators, for example.[34] This in turn assumes that shareholders can exercise certain rights effectively in order to enforce proper compliance or explanation, but it is not

---

32 See the statement of the Forum of 24 March 2009 on cross-border issues of corporate governance codes, see http://ec.europa.eu/internal_market/company/ecgforum/index_en.htm#statements.

33 See http://ec.europa.eu/internal_market/company/ecgforum/studies_en.htm.

34 Expressly supporting this: the European Corporate Governance Forum in its statement of 6 March 2006 on "comply or explain", see http://ec.europa.eu/internal_market/company/ecgforum/index_en.htm#statements.

clear that shareholders actually have these rights in all Member States and it is certainly clear that most shareholders cannot exercise their rights efficiently across borders. The Directive on Shareholders' Rights, which has been adopted to solve problems of cross-border voting in the EU, is precisely not doing that.[35] Europe is struggling with the exercise of voting rights by shareholders in companies located in another Member State. Today, shareholders typically hold their shares through securities accounts with intermediaries such as banks and brokers. When holding shares in a company in another Member State, usually a chain of intermediaries in various jurisdictions exists between the shareholder and the company, each holding shares for the next intermediary until the ultimate shareholder is reached. It is often not clear legally and practically whether the ultimate shareholder, as the person who has invested in the shares and, in principle, holds the economic risks attached to the shares, is entitled and able to vote the shares. The chain of intermediaries leads to multiple contractual and ownership claims in various jurisdictions and there is no EU or other rule clarifying that the entitlement of the ultimate shareholder at the end of the chain allows him to control the exercise of the voting rights. And practically, the securities intermediaries do not have systems in place allowing for the swift identification of ultimate shareholders, or the passing on of voting instructions or powers of attorney along the chain. For the intermediaries, facilitating the exercise of voting rights by their clients is a burdensome service to their clients and most intermediaries simply do not provide the service, or at least will not ensure that the next intermediary down the chain will also provide the service.[36]

A typical cross-border problem that cannot be solved by Member States individually and therefore calls for an EU solution. The problem has been identified as such and the EU has sought to address it. The Shareholders' Rights Directive[37] is aimed at solving problems of cross-border voting. Recital 11 states:

"Where financial intermediaries are involved, the effectiveness of voting upon instructions relies, to a great extent, on the efficiency of the chain of intermediaries, given that investors are frequently unable to exercise the voting rights attached to their shares without the cooperation of every intermediary in the chain, who may not have an economic stake in the shares. In order to enable the investor to exercise his voting rights in cross-border situations, it is therefore important that intermediaries facilitate the exercise of voting rights."

---

[35] Directive of the European Parliament and of the Council of 11 July 2007 on the exercise of certain rights of shareholders in listed companies 2007/36/EC [2007] OJ L 184/17; see also the recommendations made by the European Corporate Governance Forum on solutions for cross-border voting – see statement of 24 July 2006, http://ec.europa.eu/internal_market/company/ecgforum/index_en.htm.

[36] For a description of the problems underlying cross-border voting, see Jaap Winter, 'Cross-border voting in Europe', in K.J. Hopt and E. Wymeersch (eds.), *Capital Markets and Company Law* (Oxford University Press, 2003), pp. 387-426.

[37] Directive of the European Parliament and of the Council of 11 July 2007 on the exercise of certain rights of shareholders in listed companies 2007/36/EC [2007] OJ L 184/17.

But then, typical of the EU process of lack of agreement and then agreeing on a Directive which does not make sense, the Directive completely fails to provide any useful content that would allow shareholders to effectively exercise their voting rights along a chain of intermediaries. Securities intermediaries are not required to exercise voting rights according to the instructions of their clients or to pass on such voting instructions to the next intermediary in the chain or to provide powers of attorney to their clients to vote directly.[38] Instead, the real issue is moved to a possible recommendation from the Commission to Member States, which in itself, by definition, will not be able to solve the problem as Member States can choose to ignore it and not impose any obligation on securities intermediaries. A solution to the problem of cross-border voting requires a mandatory solution through a Directive or a Regulation. Without it, many and an increasing number of shareholders will not be able to participate effectively in the enforcement of the application of corporate governance codes.

4. Controlling shareholders and disproportionality

There are also questions in cases where the company is controlled by a major shareholder and (non)compliance with the code fulfils the major shareholder's wishes (possibly to the detriment of minority shareholders). The instrument of a corporate governance code and "comply or explain" have been developed in the UK in an environment with relatively few controlling shareholders and predominantly dispersed share ownership. In such a situation the code provides a useful instrument to start a dialogue between, often, institutional investors and the company on the quality of its governance. But this is completely different where a controlling shareholder dominates the shareholders meeting and has control over the board. In such a situation, the controlling shareholder through its control over the board determines to what extent the company complies with the code or wishes to deviate and then explains primarily to itself in the shareholders meeting what choices have been made. As a shareholder, it then welcomes those choices and leaves the minority shareholders with little or no say in the application of the code. Does the code and "comply or explain" have any meaningful enforcement effect under these circumstances? This situation is aggravated when the controlling shareholder has been able to enhance its controlling position through instruments that allow it a disproportionate level of control, such as multiple voting rights shares, voting rights restrictions, pyramid structures. Such instruments may provide an incentive to the controlling shareholder to abuse its control to the detriment of the company, as the effects of the abuse will be borne disproportionally by the other shareholders. After having called for substantial research into whether there is

[38] The European Corporate Governance Forum had recommended the inclusion of such obligations for intermediaries in the Directive, see its recommendation of 24 July 2006, see http://ec.europa.eu/internal_market/company/ecgforum/index_en.htm.

a need to regulate structures which create disproportionate control rights, EU Commissioner McCreevy abandoned this in October 2007.[39] This creates a continuing weakness in the code infrastructure in many Member States.

5. Convergence and evolution

When the European Corporate Governance Forum was set up by EU Commissioner Bolkestein, its purpose was to be *inter alia* to further the convergence of corporate governance systems in the EU. The members of the Forum resisted this objective, as they believed convergence could not be an objective in itself. Convergence may happen, but only to the extent the circumstances driving the development of corporate governance systems in Member States point in similar directions. In essence this is an evolutionary perspective on the development of corporate governance systems. This development is triggered by a wide variety of determinants, such as share ownership, finance and investment, board structure, traditions of enforcement and punishment, politics and culture, which may mutually influence each other and are influenced by other factors and developments. Well known evolutionary mechanisms such as path dependency, adaptation and exaptation and variation play a role in the evolution of corporate governance systems.[40] Evolution teaches us also that a crisis is a moment to watch, as temporary balances and tendencies are disturbed and organisms and systems need to adapt to a new reality. In that sense, we are blessed with the financial crisis that we currently have on our hands. I would like to pick one element of the multitude of possible causes and factors determining this crisis, an element which is of particular relevance to corporate governance. Of the many parties who have been held responsible for the crisis, shareholders have been reproached for their overly short term orientation which has led them to push companies to provide continuous, immediate financial performance, to the detriment of long term sustainable development of companies. For financial institutions in particular, this continuous capital market pressure to increase profits has contributed to an environment in which risks were systematically ignored and subordinated to overall profit goals. The financial crisis, in a sense, has been the excessive result of what Peer Zumbansen calls *financial capitalism.*[41] It is one thing to establish this, quite another to come up with a solution that solves or at least mitigates this problem. Simply legislating in order to restrict the rights of shareholders, which seems to be the route that

---

[39] For the reports on disproportionality, see http://ec.europa.eu/internal_market/company/shareholders/indexb_en.htm. The European Corporate Governance Forum did recommend that several measures should be taken, including a higher level of disclosure of disproportionate control structures, see the statement of the Forum and the paper of the Forum's working group on proportionality of 12 September 2007, http://ec.europa.eu/internal_market/company/ecgforum/index_en.htm#statements. See also the contribution of Klaus J. Hopt in this book *supra* p. 10.

[40] See further my paper The Evolution of Corporate Governance Systems, to be published in 2010.

[41] Peer Zumbansen, The Evolution of the Corporation: Organization, Finance, Knowledge and Corporate Social Responsibility, CLPE Research Paper 06/2009, see www.ssrna.com/abstract=1346971.

the Netherlands and Germany propose to take, is unlikely to have much of an impact on the short term focus of shareholders, in particular when they are the only states who take such measures. On the other hand, just suggesting to institutional investors that they should become more engaged shareholders, as the UK is doing,[42] is not going to have any real effect either if the underlying reasons for the short term behaviour of institutional investors are not addressed.

An important cause for the overriding focus of shareholders on short terms gains is that even shareholders with long term exposures, such as pension funds, have in fact become short term oriented as a result of the extreme diversification of their equtiy investments. It is said that large pension funds such as Calpers and APG invest in over 7,000 and 4,000 companies respectively. This necessarily reduces most of these investments to short term investments as it is impossible for such funds to understand the ins and outs of each of the companies in which they invest. The investments and their expected returns are continuously compared to other companies in which they could invest. If they expect better results going forward from such other investments then the current investment is sold and replaced by such other investments. Hence the need for continuous liquidity, so that investments can be switched quickly. There is much more to be said about the investment behaviour of pension funds, but here I just hold that as a result even pension funds no longer invest for the long term. At best they are long only investors, in the sense that they do not also short certain companies in order to gain from a stock price drop.

Here the crisis may change matters. APG and PGGM, the two largest Dutch pension fund managers, have announced that they wish to reduce the number of their equity investments to a few hundred instead of over 4,000, and they may wish to keep that smaller number of investments for longer periods of time. Such an investment policy may be more resilient and less vulnerable to the turmoil on volatile financial markets which has cost these funds huge sums of money that will take years to recover. If pension funds such as these should indeed change their investment policies in this direction, this could have a major impact on the governance of companies in which they invest. Investing in bigger holdings held for a longer period of time increases the exposure to every individual investment. In exchange, the pension funds are likely to ask for more information relating to the strategy and performance of the company. They may also ask to be represented on the board of the company, in order to more directly share in the control of the company. This type of engaged investment would probably also call for specific arrangements on exit, in order to prevent a sudden drop in share price when a block of shares is put to the market or a third party acquiring control over the company. Such elements trigger all sorts of company law and securities law questions (equality of shareholders in

[42] See for example the Walker Review, looking into the governance of banks, whose final recommendations include recommendations on the engagement of institutional investors, see http://www.hm-treasury.gov.uk/walker_review_information.htm.

respect of providing information, sharing price-sensitive information with such long term engaged investors, acting in concert, independence of non-executive board members). An evolutionary approach to corporate governance suggests that a jurisdiction that is better able to deal with these questions and to facilitate such engaged long term share ownership by institutional investors is likely to attract more such investors, which would help companies in those jurisdictions to foster long term and more stable relations with key shareholders. In this way, financial capitalism may be mitigated to allow more sustainable development of such companies. Institutional investors may thus become engaged principals and bridge the gap between the two core governance models of dispersed ownership and concentrated ownership.

Such an evolution will not be a panacea for all corporate governance problems and will probably raise new questions that need to be addressed, for example relating to the protection of minority shareholders who may be prejudiced by institutional investors, alone or acting in concert, taking part in the control of the company. But, for sure, it will be an interesting evolution with promising features, requiring a better understanding of the nature of investment and asset management and their impact on corporate governance. I believe this is an important area for future research and possibly facilitating regulation with the goal of strengthening corporate governance. The EU, with its traditional predominant model of concentrated ownership, is well placed to lead here.